THE LIBER CELESTIS OF
ST BRIDGET OF SWEDEN

VOLUME I · TEXT

———

EARLY ENGLISH TEXT SOCIETY
No. 291
1987

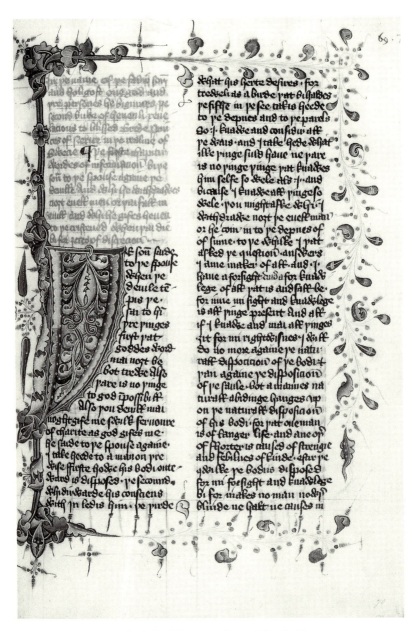

F. 69ʳ   The opening of Book II

THE LIBER CELESTIS OF ST BRIDGET OF SWEDEN

The Middle English Version in British Library MS Claudius B i,
together with a life of the saint from the same manuscript

EDITED BY

ROGER ELLIS

VOLUME I · TEXT

Published for
THE EARLY ENGLISH TEXT SOCIETY
by the
OXFORD UNIVERSITY PRESS
1987

Oxford University Press, Walton Street, Oxford OX2 6DP

Oxford New York Toronto
Delhi Bombay Calcutta Madras Karachi
Petaling Jaya Singapore Hong Kong Tokyo
Nairobi Dar es Salaam Cape Town
Melbourne Auckland

Associated companies in Beirut Berlin Ibadan Nicosia

Oxford is a trade mark of Oxford University Press

British Library Cataloguing in Publication Data

Bridget, of Sweden, Saint
The liber celestis of St. Bridget of
Sweden.—(Early English Text Society).
Vol. 1
1. Mysticism
I. Title   II. Ellis, Roger   III. Series
248.2'2   BV5080
ISBN 0–19–722293–5

Set by Joshua Associates Limited, Oxford
Printed in Great Britain at the
University Printing House
by David Stanford
Printer to the University

CONTENTS

LIST OF PLATES

ACKNOWLEDGEMENTS

Books I, II, V, and VII of this text began life as a doctoral thesis completed thirteen years ago under the scholarly, rigorous, and very patient, eye of my supervisor Dr Anne Hudson. It is a pleasure once again to thank her for her part in it. I am grateful to the trustees of the British Library for permission to reproduce the facsimiles in this volume.

FOR MY PARENTS

INTRODUCTION

This work is a critical edition of the sole surviving copy, in MS British Library Claudius B I, hereafter Cl, of an anonymous ME translation of the *Liber Celestis* of St Birgitta (or, as the English commonly call her, Bridget) of Sweden (1303–73). Also edited here, from the same MS, is a life of the Saint translated from the relevant portions of the Office prepared in the Saint's honour in 1376 by the Archbishop of Uppsala, Birger Gregersson. The length of the work has dictated its appearance in two volumes. Volume I consists of the basic text and this Preface, which describes the editorial methods here followed and briefly introduces the *Liber*. Volume II will contain an introduction, explanatory notes, bibliography and glossary. The introduction will include a description of the manuscript and its language (both manuscript and translation will be dated *c.* 1410–20), and will consider the relation of the translation to its Latin sources, and to the other ME translations of the *Liber*, from which it will be shown to be independent.

St Bridget's story is fairly well known, especially in its later years, from the mass of evidence presented in support of her canonization, a process which began formally in 1377 and was brought to a successful outcome when Pope Benedict IX canonized her in 1391.[1] Born into one of the most powerful families in Sweden, Bridget's life was characterized from its beginnings, according to her biographers, by an attentiveness to the spiritual realm which resulted, even in her childhood, in visions and revelations. In or about 1344, the newly widowed Bridget underwent a climactic spiritual experience. A lasting consequence of this 'conversion experience' was her decision to found a new religious Order (the first professions took place at the mother house, Vadstena, in 1384). For our purposes, though, a more important effect of the Saint's conversion was her receiving of the revelations, some 700 in all, which eventually became the *Liber Celestis*. Moves for an edition of the revelations were made on at least two occasions during her lifetime.[2] The first such edition, it is thought, was produced to accompany a mission of Bishop Hemming of Åbo to Pope Clement

---

[1] For the canonization process, see *Acta et Processus Canonizacionis Beate Birgitte*, ed. by I. Collijn, hereafter *A et P*, *Samlingar utgivna av Svenska Fornskriftsällskapet*, hereafter SFSS, Ser. 2, Latinska Skrifter, I, Uppsala, 1924–31.

[2] For fuller comment about the early editions of the *Liber*, see *Sancta Birgitta Revelaciones Book I*, ed. by C.-G. Undhagen, SFSS Ser. 2, Lat. Skrift., VII: 1, Uppsala, 1978, pp. 1–50.

VI in 1346–7, within a very few years, that is to say, of the Saint's conversion to the spiritual life: its precise extent and contents are
unknown. It was probably the work of Mathias of Linköping, the fore-
most Swedish theologian of his day and the Saint's chief confessor at
the time.

Between this first 'edition' and the next, twenty and more years
intervened. Most of this time the Saint spent in Italy in the company
of a small group of family, friends and spiritual advisers. (She had
left Sweden to take part in the Papal Jubilee of 1350 at Rome, and
she never returned to her homeland.) The growing body of revelations was translated into Latin and preserved by the Saint's two
confessors, Peter of Alvastra and Peter of Skänninge. Not until
c. 1370 were positive moves made to have the revelations authori-
tatively edited and widely circulated. Then the task was given to a
relatively new member of the group, a Spaniard, Alphonse. Formerly
Bishop of Jaen and a man with a wide circle of friends in high places,
Alphonse had quitted his see and come to Italy to enter a semi-
eremitical order, and there, some time after 1368, he had met St
Bridget and attached himself to her entourage. His intense spiritu-
ality, great learning, and range of social contacts made him the obvious choice to edit the *Liber*.

The *Liber* was ready in time for the canonization process set up in
1377 by Pope Gregory XI, and resubmitted to the new commission
appointed by his successor, Urban VI, in 1378. The earliest references
to it occur in a *Vita* of the Saint prepared in anticipation of the canonization process by the two Peters and submitted to the Bishop of
Spoleto on December 17, 1373.[1] Alphonse revised this work between
May and autumn 1377,[2] and, as part of his revision, added cross-
references to the text of the *Liber*. Comparison of these with references to the *Liber* by both Alphonse and Peter of Alvastra in their
testimonies to the resumed canonization process (16th Sept. 1379 and
30th January 1380 respectively),[3] throws light on the development of
the text during this period. Judging from Alphonse's additions to the
Vita, we find the *Liber*, by the autumn of 1377, subdivided into Books
and chapters (thus *A et P* p. 95: 'Vide in libro questionum [*sc.* Book V]

---

[1] For this *Vita*, see *A et P* pp. 73–101.
[2] On this point, see *Sancta Birgitta Revelaciones Book V*, ed. by B. Bergh, SFSS Ser. 2,
Lat. Skrift., VII: 5, Uppsala, 1971, p. 15, and S. Ekwall, *Vår äldsta Birgitta-vita och dennas
viktigaste varianter, Kungl. Vitterhets Historie och Antikvitets Akademiens Handlingar*, Hist.
Ser. 12, Stockholm, 1965.
[3] *A et P* pp. 363–414, 472–562.

in ultimo et penultimo capitulo').[1] The subdivisions are still rudimen-
tary at best: chapters are not numbered; commonly, indeed, the *Vita*
refers to the *Liber* simply by numbered Book (p. 79: 'in fine quarti
libri'); sometimes it does not even give the number of the Book (p. 91:
'que . . . reuelacio . . . in libro reuelacionum plenius continetur'). By
September 1379, on the other hand, the *Liber* has been much more
thoroughly prepared for publication: Alphonse and Peter are referring
to it very precisely, by numbered Book and chapter, and Alphonse, in
addition, by subsection and catchphrase (e.g. p. 369: 'vt clarius hoc
videri poterit in secundo libro . . . xv capitulo et in vi° libro lii capitulo
§ Et tunc ego'). In the two years separating the revision of the *Vita* and
the testimony of the two disciples, then, we may see the text of the
Alphonsine edition acquiring something like its final form. The references to the *Liber* in the testimonies of 1379–80 have a further sig-
nificance for us: so far as they go, they match almost exactly the
subdivisions by Book and chapter of all manuscript and printed copies
of the *Liber*. We can therefore see the Alphonsine edition as crucial for
the development of the text of the *Liber*.

The two later witnesses have something further to tell us about the
Alphonsine edition, too. Both refer consistently to Book VII as
'ultimus' (e.g. p. 373 'in ultimo libro . . . xix capitulo'): they also
acknowledge the existence of an eighth Book (e.g. p. 375: 'super libro
. . . viii° . . . qui intitulatur liber celestis imperatoris ad reges'). This
new Book, as Alphonse tells us in his preface, ch. 8 of the *Epistola
Solitarii ad Reges*, was partly created out of material already edited in
the preceding seven Books of the *Liber*. Logically, therefore, references to Book VII as 'ultimus' point to a stage in the production of the
Liber before Alphonse added his *Epistola* and newly-edited Book VIII
to it. This earlier stage we may call an earlier edition of the *Liber*, as
Undhagen does: it contained Books I–VII, but not Book VIII.
Whether we should identify this earlier edition with the version of the
Liber submitted to the canonization proceedings in 1377, and with the
version Alphonse had beside him when he revised the *Vita*, probably
in that same year, is an open question.

The precise extent of the two editions is also matter for debate.
Both may also have included other Books of revelations. Widely preserved in manuscripts, and accorded the *imprimatur* of the *editio princeps* in 1492, these other Books include texts which would have been of

---

[1] As preserved in all MSS copies of the Latin, Book V has no chapter divisions, but
only a sequence of numbered *interrogaciones* and *revelaciones*.

especial relevance to the newly-established Order, i.e. the lessons of the Brigittine Office (*Sermo Angelicus*) and the Rule of the Order (*Regula Salvatoris*); another Book, largely composed for revelations left behind in Sweden when the Saint went to Rome, and so unavailable to Alphonse when he was editing the *Liber* (*Reuelaciones Extrauagantes*); and four prayers by the Saint to Christ and the Virgin (*Quatuor oraciones*).

No manuscript copy of the *Liber* has survived which can be clearly identified with either Alphonsine edition. Nevertheless, there is widespread and longstanding scholarly agreement that important traces remain of the later edition in one major manuscript grouping, called β by editors, which approximates most closely to it in shape and content.[1] The β group is of particular interest for the present enquiry. A subgroup, ε, includes all but two of the English manuscripts of the Latin text, and may therefore fairly claim to constitute a distinctive English tradition of the text (it also provided the immediate source of Cl's translation). This tradition was distinguished, *inter alia*, by the omission of Book VIII.[2] ε thus (and Cl after it) inadvertently restored the text of the *Liber*, in this respect at least, to the form of the first Alphonsine version. The *Liber* came to England within at most 35 years of the Saint's death: as Colledge has shown, the anonymous *Chastising of God's Children*, dated, according to him, some time between 1382 and 1408, uses Alphonse's *Epistola* in a way that suggests great familiarity with the text on the part of the anonymous writer, and so, since the *Epistola* circulated from the beginning as an element of the *Liber*, of the *Liber*.[3]

---

[1] Note, in particular, the agreement between the Alphonsine editions and β in respect of the number of chapters in Books IV (130), VI (109), and VII (32) (so R. Ellis, '"Flores ad fabricandam . . . coronam": an investigation into the uses of the Revelations of St. Bridget of Sweden in 15th century England', *Medium Ævum* 51, 1982, 183 n. 7, and Undhagen, *Book I*, pp. 17, 21–2, the latter in error in claiming, p. 17, that Book VII had '31 or 32' chapters in the Alphonsine edition).

[2] On this point, see further Ellis, '"Flores ad . . . coronam"', 165–6. ε also has a distinctive form of Alphonse's *Epistola*. It uses the *Epistola* as a sort of epilogue to the *Liber*, one of the two purposes for which Alphonse had intended it. Wanting Book VIII, it also cut the true prologue to that work, ch. 8 of the *Epistola*.

[3] See *The Chastising of God's Children*, ed. by J. Bazire and E. Colledge, Oxford, 1957, pp. 34–7. In fact, the *terminus a quo* for its composition can be narrowed to a date after 1391, because it refers (p. 178) to Bridget as 'þat hooli ladi . . . seint bride', and must thus have been composed after her canonization. The earlier dates of *c.* 1370 and 1373 given for its arrival by W. P. Cumming (*The Revelations of Saint Birgitta*, ed. by W. P. Cumming, EETS os 178, London, 1929, p. xxix and nn. 1, 2) are not to be relied upon. They depend on the witness of Bale in 1557 and Pits in 1616 concerning ownership of copies of the *Liber* by Thomas Stubbs and Richard Lavenham. According to Pits, the former died in 1373; according to Bale, both were preaching on the *Liber c.* 1370. Stubbs, how-

The earliest surviving manuscript copy of ε has been dated 'saec. XIV ex.'[1]

In so far, then, as Cl is a faithful translation of its Latin original (a proposition which remains crucially to prove in Volume II), the Alphonsine editions represent a point both of departure and of ultimate appeal. The force of this comment will be the more readily appreciated even from a cursory examination of the text before us. In principle, the Alphonsine edition witnesses to the collaboration of three parties, and allows us to distinguish at least three hands, three voices, in the production of the *Liber*: those of the saint, of her translators the two Peters, and of Alphonse her editor-in-chief. The distinguishing of these voices from one another, however, proves as difficult as the distinguishing of the fictional levels of *The Canterbury Tales* from one another (or, to take a parallel nearer home, of Margery Kempe's part in the creation of her *Book* from that of her two scribes). In their *Vita* the two Peters deny themselves any greater role in the production of the *Liber* than that of faithful translators, whose translation was later checked by the Saint 'ne vnum verbum ibi plus adderetur uel deficeret, nisi que ipsa in visione diuinitus audierat et viderat' (*A et P* p. 84). At the same time, the few fragments of the saint's original Swedish to have survived show that, on two occasions at least, the translator acted not only as scribe, but also, in some measure, as editor, of the revelations.[2] The same is true in yet greater degree of the labours of Alphonse. Divinely commissioned to edit the *Liber*, he is given greater powers than the scribes: 'conscribat et obscura elucidet et catholicum sensum spiritus mei teneat' (*Rev. Extrav.* ch. xlix). Nevertheless, he is almost as shadowy a figure as the translator-scribes. We see him clearly at work in Book VIII, and yet more clearly in *Celeste Viridarium*, a compilation of revelations on the life of Christ and the Virgin which he produced for the nuns at Vadstena. Within the *Liber*, however, he reveals himself clearly only in prologues to Books V, *Sermo Angelicus*, and the earliest published version of the

ever, was still alive in 1381 (see *Dictionary of National Biography*, LV, 121). Lavenham may have died 1381–3, or may have lived until 1410 (*DNB* XXXII, 211–2); the two manuscript copies of the *Liber* ascribed to him, viz. BL Royal 7 c ix and Bodley 169 (so Cumming, p. xxix n. 1, and *DNB* ibid.) are both dated 15th century, and, if indeed his, would point to a date much later than '*c.* 1370'.

[1] In support of this date, see *Den heliga Birgittas Reuelaciones Bok VII*, ed. by B. Bergh, SFSS Ser. 2, Lat. Skrift., VII: 7, Uppsala, 1967, p. 43; Undhagen, *Book I*, p. 193, argues for a later date.

[2] For an edition of these fragments, see B. Högman, *Heliga Birgitta originaltexter*, SFSS 205, Uppsala, 1951.

Regula: also, since by then he was accompanying the Saint, in the revelations received during the last year of her life, and published as the later chapters of Book VII (the rubrics to those later chapters contrast strikingly in respect of circumstantial detail with the practice elsewhere in the *Liber*). How much of the wording of the *Liber* is his, in the absence of detailed comments like that provided by Love for his version of the ps.-Bonaventuran *Meditationes*, we cannot tell. It is equally difficult to tell how far the *Liber* owes its distinctive shape, or shapes, to him. In common with other medieval narrative collections, and even with Margery Kempe's *Book*, whose individual episodes can often be read similarly as elements in a narrative collection, the *Liber* attempts more than one narrative shape. At beginning and end it attempts a spiritual autobiography (the early chapters of Book I, the later chapters of Book VII); Book IV appears to have attempted something similar, on a smaller scale, with its opening and closing revelations (chs. ii, cxxix). Books II–III shape their material differently, according to subject matter, revelations about the knightly and episcopal orders (we might compare the way in which Margery collects into one place her revelations on the life of Christ). Another Book, given early in the Saint's career as a single revelation made up, like Julian's showings, of several separate items, is published as a free-standing item (Book V). Even chapter divisions are open to debate: sometimes separate revelation events are lodged in the one chapter (e.g. II. xxvi, VI. lii), at other times a single revelation is spread over several chapters (e.g. II. xxv–xxvii).

The difficulties thus created for the modern reader would matter less if individual revelations gave a clearer picture of the contexts in which they were received. Unfortunately, the reticence of translators and editors in the face of the divine message is compounded by the way in which the *Liber* presents its human protagonists, especially the Saint herself. Present mostly in the humble role of third person, like Margery after her, she is carefully painted out of the picture as a distinct and separate figure, so as to oblige the reader to attend not to the human medium but to the divine message transmitted through that medium. Most of what we know of the Saint in the *Liber* we learn from the words addressed to her by the divine speakers: and their messages apply only in the most general terms to her personal situation. This avoidance of a narrowly limiting frame of reference accords very well with the need for the *Liber* to address, and reach, as wide an audience as possible, and to embody unambiguously what Alphonse was appointed to safeguard in it, the 'catholicum sensum spiritus [Dei]': it is also of a piece with the medieval predilection for a literature of instruction, revealed, for example, in the prose contributions to *The Canterbury Tales*. It does not accord so well with the scholar's need for dates and names and places, nor with the desire of the religious reader to meet with, and receive support from sharing the experiences of, a fellow-pilgrim. The reader will find in the following pages hardly anything to match the circumstantial detail of Margery's *Book*. One such detail, it will be remembered, concerns her meeting in Rome in 1414 with a surviving member of the Saint's household. Speaking to Margery through an interpreter, 'Seynt Brydys mayden' told her how her mistress 'was goodly and meke to euery creatur and þat sche had a lawhyng cher'. The landlord of the house where Margery was then staying confirmed the picture; though he had known the Saint herself, 'he wend lityl þat sche had ben so holy a woman as sche was, for sche was euyr homly and goodly to all creaturys þat woldyn speken wyth hir'.[1] The warmth and spontaneity of those reminiscences find almost no echo in the *Liber*.

Editorial Principles

In the present work, punctuation has been modernized in accordance with the intentions of the scribe or, where this was unclear, the phrasing of the Latin. Paragraphing is modern. Capitalization is modern, and conservatively applied. Word division has been modernized. Contractions are expanded silently in accordance with the scribe's general practice. Latin quotations are italicized. The usual signs indicate emendation: ⟨ ⟩, the restoration of the text where letters or words are illegible; [ ], the addition of letters or words to the original. Letters or words suppressed or transposed in the present text appear in the apparatus after the corrected form.

The scribe uses both cursive and formal scripts for his corrections, and occasional corrections are entered in the hand of another scribe. Such corrections are incorporated into the body of the text without comment, except that (i) the original of a corrected form will be duly noted in the apparatus when it is still visible, (ii) marginal and interlinear additions to the text of a word or more will be indicated in the body of the text by ` ´ around the added material.

[1] *The Book of Margery Kempe*, ed. by S. B. Meech and H. E. Allen, EETS 212, London, 1940, p. 95.

The attitude to emendation is generally conservative. Except for obvious nonsense readings, the text is emended consistently only when reference to the text of the Latin indicates probable error in Cl's copy of the translation (and occasionally when Cl faithfully follows ε in error and produces a nonsense reading). The readings of the Latin originals are sometimes quoted in the apparatus (as *Lat.*) in support of such emendations. A word of caution is, however, necessary concerning the status of these Latin readings. Emendations to Books I, V, and VII are made on the authority of the critical editions of these works; emendations to the *Life*, on the authority of the critical edition of Gregersson's Office.[1] Emendations to Books II, III, IV, and VI are made on the authority of the *editio princeps* of the *Liber*,[2] and may need to be modified when critical editions of these Books appear.

The use of the Latin as a check against the English is further complicated by the following divergences of the translation from its source: Book I, ch. xv of the *Liber* appears as ch. 18, and chs. xvi–xviii of the *Liber* are displaced to become chs. 15–17, of Cl; Book VI, ch. lxv of the *Liber* is not translated, and ch. lxvi is translated, with ch. lxiv, as Cl's ch. 64, so that its numbering of the remaining chapters of Book VI is two short of what it should be; and Book VII, ch. xiii of the *Liber* is divided into two in Cl, so that its numbering of the remaining chapters of Book VII is one more than it should be.[3]

Lastly, major gaps in Cl's text, occasioned by the loss of one leaf or more of the MS, are made good by the use of material from the other major ME translation of the *Liber*, in MS British Library Julius F II, hereafter *Ju*. Such passages are edited in accordance with the principles enunciated above, except that the textual apparatus is kept to a minimum.

---

[1] For full details about the editions of Books I, V, and VII, see above p. ix n. 2, p. x n. 2, p. xiii n. 1. For the critical edition of Gregersson's Office, see *Birger Gregerssons Birgitta-Officium*, ed. by C.-G. Undhagen, SFSS Ser. 2, Lat. Skrift., VI, Uppsala, 1960.

[2] For the *editio princeps*, see *Revelationes Sanctae Birgittae*, imp. B. Ghotan, Lubeck, 1492, hereafter *Gh*.

[3] In the first two cases, we have probably to reckon with simple error in Cl or its exemplar. In the third, we have to reckon with error in the archetype of the β_2 subgroup: see further p. xii n. 1 above.

A LIFE OF ST BRIDGET

Translated from Archbishop Gregersson's *Officium Sanctae Birgittae*

[Sho had] ⟨eu⟩ir in hir compan⟨i⟩ oneste ⟨w⟩omen þat serued hi⟨r⟩ . . .   f. 1ʳᵃ
⟨a⟩lso oneste men þat might bere hir euir testemone of oneste; and sho
was noȝt idill, no with no personnes wald sho trete bot þat were
honest. Sho gladli wroght þinges þat ware to Goddes wirshipe, and
profite vnto hir euen cristen. Sho chesed hir one confessoure þat was a   5
maistir of diuinite, a gude clerke and a gude man in lifinge, and to him
was sho oft times shryuen, and noght wald sho leue vndiscussid in hir
conciens: and hir confessoure wald sometime say þat Bride had one
token of grete grace, for sho charged als mikill a litill þinge als oþir
comon men charged one grete þinge. When hir husband was fro hir,   10
sho wald wake þe maste parti of þe night in praiere, and sho spared
noght hir bodi in [k]nelinges and bettinges.

Fell one a time þat sho praied hertli vnto God þat sho might be
taght some maner of prayinge, and þare was sente to hir fro heuen a
praiere of þe passion, and of Cristes lifynge, | þat sho saide euerilka   f. 1ʳᵇ
dai. In tokeninge of it, oure ladi apered vnto hir sonne eftir and saide   16
vnto hir, 'I haue getin þe þat praiere throwe þe whilke þou sall haue
comforthe in mi son.' Sho fasted oft and keped hir fro delicious metes
als mikill as sho might for persaiuinge of hir husbande and oþir: sho
did grete almos, and had one house for þe pore, in þe whilke þare was   20
one certain þat weshed þaire fete and cled and serued þaime oft time.
Sho had grete will to comone with gude men and wise, and of holi
menes liuinge, and of þe Bibill, þat sho does translete vnto hir modir
tonge.

Fell in one tyme þat scho was in dispaire of hir life in trauellinge of   25
childe, and sodanli þare entirde one woman, þe faireste þat euir sho
sawe, clothed in white silke, and laide hir hand on all þe partise of hir
bodi, and als sone as þat woman was wente furth againe sho was
deliuered withouten any perell: and sho wiste wele it was oure ladi, als
sho schewed vnto Bride | eftirward.   f. 1ᵛᵃ

Sho laide mikill besines in techinge of hir childir, and ordayned   31
þaime a maistir to teche in faithe and in gude condicions; and if þai

---

1 sho had] *om., Lat.* secum habuit   1-3 *first four lines of column rubbed in margins:*
oneste (*l. 2*), might, ne (*of* testemone) *just legible*   12 knelinges] netlinges, *Lat.*
genuflexionibus   29 als] also

did ani syn, sho wepid for þaime full sore, so þat Saint John þe
Baptiste aperid vnto hir and saide, 'For þou wepid þat þi son hase
greued me and wald noȝt faste mine euen (for þou had leuir þat he
serued God and me þan þat he ware a kinge), þarefore sall I helpe him
5 and arme him with mine armes.'

   Also hir husband, þat 'was' one worthi man of armes, sho cherest to
þe drede of God and his reuerence, so þat sho made him to cune sai þe
oures of oure ladi (and sai þaime euirilkea dai) and sterrid hyme
to þe werkes of merci and gude dedis, and made him in will to seke
10 Sainte Jame, and scho with him, in grete trauell. Fell þat when þai had
bene at Saint Jame and oþir holi places in þe ȝere, comminge againe,
hir husbande toke seknes in Fraunce, in one cite [þ]a[t] hate Attra-
batum. þan come Saint Dines vnto Bride, þat was full desolate for hir |
f. 1ᵛᵇ husband sekenes, and comforted hir, saiand vnto hir on þis manere, 'I
15 ame Dines þat come fro Rome to þis cuntre to preche Goddes worde,
and, for þou hase lufid me, I sall helpe þe: and þis þe token, þat þi husband sall noȝt die of þis sekenes.' And in þat cite sho saw mani
meruails: howe þat sho suld wende to Rome and to Jerusalem, and
how þat sho suld passe oute of þis werld. When hir husband had lange
20 bene seke and couerd, þai come home againe vnto Swethen, and
avowed bitwene þaime chastite, and for to entire religiouse lifinge
terme of þaire liue, and þus þai ordained of þaire þinges: and þe
husband in þis gude purpose died in þe Abbai of Olvastre.

   In þe þirde ȝere bifore þe dede of hir husband aperid oure ladi vnto
25 hir and saide, 'I am whene of all men. I sall shewe þe howe it was with
mi son in his manhede, and howe he suffird on þe crosse: and þis to
f. 2ʳᵃ token, | þou sall com vnto holi places where I was conuersant, and þou
sall se with þi gosteli ee mi son.' In þe ferde ȝere bifore þe dede of hir
husbande, oure halowe in þe kingedome of Swethen, þat is called
30 Saint Bot[ui]d, aperid vnto Bride in hir contemplacion, and saide þat
he and oþir has getin grace of God, þat sho suld here and see mani
spirituall þinges, and þat sho suld fele þe spirit of God in hir soule.

   Eftir þe dede of hir husband apperid Criste vnto hir in one white
cloude, and saide þat he was hir God, and bad þat sho suld noȝt be
35 ferde, for it was none illusion, for he aperid vnto hir noȝt allonli for hir,
bot for þe hele of mani one mo. xxviii ȝere fro sho bigan to haue þe
spirit of God, sho neuir dwelled, no went, bot als þe spirit of God

---

8 sai] *marg.*, saide   12 þat] hase   19 werld] werld cite werlde
20 come] *twice*   22 of þaire¹] of þaire of, *second* of *subpuncted*   30 Botuid]
Botrad, *Lat.* Botuidus

stirrid hir. In þe biginninge of þe reuelacions þat ware shewed vnto hir, it was biddin hir þat sho suld obei to one maistir of diuinite, and shewe him hir reuelacions þat were shewed vnto hir; and þat sho did with all hir besines.

Eftir | þe dede of hir husband, sho departed hir gude amange hir childir and pore folke, and also sho changed hir clethinge and hir lifinge, and þat sho had done grettir þinges had sho noȝt bene bodin to go to Rome. Diuers folk saide þat sho was wode for þat sho went in febill cleþinge, and þai reproued hir þarefore, and sho answerd and saide þus: 'Nother for ȝou I began, no for ȝou I will leue. I haue besoght in mi hert þat I might laste in þis purpose.' Thretti ȝere werid sho no linun clothe bot kerchefes on hir heued; bot ofte time sho wered þe haire. Before hir bed laye þare one tapet, and þareon wald sho li: sho had vndir hir one quessing, and apon, one singill clothe or elles one mantill. And when sho was asked wheþir sho might reste for colde, þat warn so grete in þat cuntre, sho wald sai sho had within hir so grete one hete þat þe colde þat was withoute suld noght make hir to li on ani softir bedde. Sho knelede so oft and wakid so mikill þat it was woundir þat euir so | tendir a bodi might suffir so grete penance and bodeli disese.

Euirilke Friday was sho wonte to take of one birninge taper v hote dropes and drope vpon hir bare fleshe, so þat of þase v dropes lefte þare v woundes: and if þai helid bi þe next Fridai, sho wald take hir nailes and riue vp þe skin, so þat hir bodi suld neuir be withoute wounde, so þat sho might continuli hafe minde of þe passion of Criste. Sho had hard knottes aboute hir bodi, þat ware continuli with hir, night and dai. Euirilke Fridai wald sho hald þe rote of gencian in hir mouthe, in minde of þe bittir gall þat was put vnto his mouthe, and þus sho did als oft, euirilke dai, als sho saide ani idill worde.

Fell on a time when Bride had bene at þe Kinge of Swethen of þe bedinge of God, when sho come againe sho fande him at þe dede. þan bigan sho to wepe, þat he was so lange time ponished in sekenes, dredand hir at it had bene for hir sin. þe fende aperid vnto hir and saide, 'Whi febils þou so þi sight? Wethir þat þi teres sall wende vp to heuen?' Sone þan aperid Criste | in forme of man vnto hir and saide, 'This sekenes of þis childe is noȝt for þi sin, bot it is of febilnes of kinde and for his mede. Before time he was called Benet, bot fro nowe furthe sall he be blissed, and he sall be called þe son of teres and of

f. 2rb
6

10

15

f. 2va
20

25

30

f. 2vb
36

7 bodin] bondin, *medial* n *subpuncted and ruled through*   11 besoght] bene soght
34-5 whi febils þou so . . . hir and saide] *twice* (*second,* þane), *marg.* va-cat *to second*

praiere, and I sall make ende of his disese.' Eftir þis, vpon þe fifte dai,
was þare herde þe sweteste sange betwene þe childes bed and þe wall
þat ani had herd, and þan passed þe saule of þat child, and þe spirit
saide, 'Se what teres þan d[o]se nowe: þe son of teres wendes vnto
5 riste and blisse (for teres are odious vnto þe fende).'
　　Eftir þis two ʒere Criste bad Bride ordaine hir to go to Rome in pilgrimage, for 'þare arn þe stretis streued with gold and made rede with
þe blode of saintes: þare is a gude wai vnto heuen for þe perdon þat
f. 3ʳᵃ saintes desereued þare in þaire life. þou sall | dwelle in Rome while þe
10 time þat þou see bothe þe Pope and þe Emperoure': and þat felle in þe
ʒere of oure lorde anno mccclxvii, and to þaime bothe was sente bi hir
reuelacions of reforminge of hali kirke. Fell þat when sho was went
oute of hir awne cuntre sho was comforted with mani reuelacions, and
was biden hir þat sho suld lere grammere, whare Saint Agnes oft time
15 teched her, and within a litill time sho profeted so greteli þat sho
couthe vndirstand and speke wele Latin. Sho viset ofte times with
grete trauell holi places in Rome, and sho thoght right wele þat time
þat sho wald speke no worde to none bot if sho ware asked, and þan als
shortli as sho couthe with honeste. Sho keped so wele hir een þat sho
20 sawe bot right fewe in þe visage, and if þare ware ani likinge in hir
seinge, sho wrote it vp to shriue hir þareof. If sho spake ani worde þat
were greuinge to God, also sone sho felde a grete bittirnes in hir
f. 3ʳᵇ mouthe als it | had bene of bronston, and þan wald sho right sone
shriue hir þareof. Also, if ani spake vnto hir ani idill wordes þat greued
25 God, alsone sho felde in hir nese a stinke, als it were of bronstone. Sho
wald euirmore haue with hir one þat sho suld obei vnto. Sho loued so
greteli wilfull pouert þat all þat sho hade, sho put it into oþir mennes
handes, and when sho wald haue oght to hirselfe or to ani oþir, sho
suld aske it mekeli in þe name of Iesu Criste, als it had neuir bene hir
30 awen. Oft times when sho had full gret nede, sho wald aske for oþir þat
had noght so grete nede as sho had hirselfe. Fell, eftir, þat sho was
bedin wende to Cecille and Napils for to visit holi bodis þat in þaire
liue loued Criste, 'and þare is moste principall Saint Thomas þe
apostill, and þare sall I shewe þe preuatees': and þan sho was somwhat
35 disesed þat sho suld noʒt haue wharewith to ga. Criste saide vnto hir,
f. 3ᵛᵃ 'He þat hase a medowe, he spares it noʒt to a horse þat | trauels for
himselfe. So will I sustene all mi seruandes þat trauels for me. I ame
lorde mighti enogh.' And, treweli, so it was, for, als lange als sho was in
Naples, þe whene and oþir gentils sende hir þaire sandes sufficient to

4 dose] dise　　　22 sone] sone as　　　31 noght] *twice, second subpuncted*

hir lifelode, and in þat cuntre broght sho mani to þe right wai with hir
gude wordes and gode ensampils. þare was made vnto hir a heuenli
reuelacion, þe whilke sho shewede vnto þe bishope, a maistir of
diuinite, and oþir clerkes and lewed men, tellinge opinli withouten
drede þe sinnes þat were vsid in þe cite. þan turned sho againe to þe 5
cite of Rome, right as one be to þe hiue, vsinge hir pilgrimage with
grete ioi and likinge of saule. One wirshipfull man and a trewe saide in
þe presens of þe Abbot of Peruse and oþir mani þat he mete Sainte
Bride betwix Saint Jones and Campum Florum with hir compani, and
sho was lifted vp so hee þat þe feet was hegher þan þe hedes of þaim 10
þat went with her, and hir visage shane so bright þat þe bemes þareof
tou|ched to heuen: so þat God shewed in hir als he dide sometime in f. 3ᵛᵇ
þe prophete Ezechielle, þat was lifted vp in þe spirit bitwene þe heuen
and þe erthe. Fell eftir þis þat Christ aperid vnto hir, and bad hir
wende vnto Jerusalem, and sho bigan to excuse hir bi sekenes and 15
elde. þan saide Criste, 'I made þe in þi kinde: I sall strenth þe. I sall
puruai for þe bi þe wai: I sall lede and bringe þe againe to þis place.'
Whan sho com to Jerusalem, þare had scho mani reuelacions of þe
birth and of þe passion of Criste, of þe state of two kingedomes and of
þe turninge of þe panims, and Criste saide vnto hir, 'Mi wordes gone 20
bifore, and mi techinge sall cum eftir. þare are mani ʒit vnborn, þat
sall take mi wordes wel likingeli. Eftir þi dede sall mi wordes dwell, for
þay are noght als one floure þat sone will fade, bot als a fruite þat euir
sall laste.'

Fell when sho come againe to Rome, twelue monethes sho was 25
trauelled with [sekenes.]

[Loss of one leaf, containing end of *Life* and beginning
of *Liber Celestis*]

---

26 sekenes] *om., Lat.* graui infirmitate

THE LIBER CELESTIS OF
ST BRIDGET OF SWEDEN

[The beginning is lost from Claudius and supplied here from Ju]

f. 4ʳ Here begynnys þe ferst booke of þe hevenly reuelacyons of God to blissid Bregith schewyd, pryncesse of Neryce of the kyngdom of Swecye. These be the wordys of oure Lord Iesu Cryst onto his electe spouse, of the sertificacion of his excellent incarnacyon and þe
5 repreffe of brekynge of oure feyth and baptyme, and how he byddys his forseyd spouse to love hym.

'I am the makere of heuen and erde, oone in the godhyd with the fadyr and the holy gost. I am he þe which spac to þe prophetis and patriarkys, hom þei alle abood. For the whech desir[e], accordyng to myn
10 promys, I haue takyn manhed withowte ony synne or concupissens, entrynge the wombe of a virgine as þe sunne schynes throw a cristal ston. Like as the sunne in scynnyng perishis the glas and hurtys it nat, likewyse the virginyte of myn modir is not corrupt nen defylid in, through the assumpcion of myn manhed. I haue takyn manhed on
15 swech wyse as I forsoke nat myn godhed, nen I was no lesse in þe godhed with the fadyr and the holy gost gouernyng alle thingis, allthough I was in þe mayden wombe with myn manhed. For, like as bryghtnesse is neuer separat fro the fyre, so myn godhed is neuer separat from myn manhed. In myn deyinge, ferderemore, I haue
20 suffred myn body, withoute ony spot of synne, to be torne fro the soole of myn foote onto the crowne of myn hed for the synnes of all pepyl, and to be crucyfied. And þat same body dayli is offred now in the awter, þat mankynde the more feruently shuld loue me and remembre me þe oftynere, and myn gret benefetis.

25 'But now holly I am forget, dispised and contempned, and expulsed as a kynge is fro his kyngdom. In qwos sted the cursed theff the fende is electe and honoured. I wold haue had myn kyngdom to haue been in mankynde, and of ryght I owgth to haue ben as kynge and lord, for I made man, and I bought hym with myn precious blood. But now he has brokyn
30 þat feyth the whech he promysid me in his bapteme, he has defilyd and disspised myn lawes þe whech I gaf to hym. He has lovyd his owne will and wyll nat here me. Also he has exalted the dewle above me and gevyn hym his feyth, the whech is a verry theff, for he robbys þe soule

9 desire] desirid   12 scynnyng] scynmyng

[CI continues]

of man þat I haue boght with mine awen blode. Bot he dose noght þat   f. 4ʳᵃ
as mightier þan I, for I ame so miȝti þat I mai all þinges with a worde:
so right þat for þe praier of all saintes I wald noȝt do one point againe
þe right. Bot man, for he hase fredome of will, wilfulli dispices mi biddinges and consentes to þe deuell; þarefore it is right þat he haue   5
knawinge bi experiens of his tirantri. For þat deuell was made of me
gude, fro þe whilke he fell bi his awen euill will. þarefore he is mi
seruand to vengeaunce of þe wirker of euell.

   'Neuirþeles, all if I be þus dispiced, ȝit I ame so merciable þat whosomeuir askes mi merci and mekis him, I forgife þat he hase trespaste,   10
and I sall deliuer him fro þe wikked theefe. And treuli, he þat abides in
contempt of me, I sall visit vpon him mi righttwisnes, þat all þat heres
þareof sall tremell and whake, and þai þat I punishe sall sai, "Allas,
þat euir we ware conceyued or born! Allas, þat euir we stirred to
wrethe þe lord of þe hie mageste!"   15

   'þarefore, mi doghtir, whome I haue chosen, and with whome I speke   f. 4ʳᵇ
in mi spirit, lufe me with all þi herte: more þan fadir, modir, son or doghtir, or ani oþir þinge in þe werld, for I made þe of noght and I offird all þe
partis and þe membres of mi bodi to be torment for þi lufe. And ȝit with
swilke a charite I lufe þi saule, þat, or I suld want it, if it were possibill, I   20
wald be festened againe to þe cros. Folowe þou þarefore mi mekenes, for
I, kinge of blis and of aungels, was cled with simpill cleþinge; I stode
naked at þe piller, and herd with mi eres all þe scornes and reproues. Sett
mi will bifore þine, and take ensampill at mi modir, þe whilke, fro þe
biginninge of hir life to þe ende, wald noþinge bot þat I walde.   25

   'And if þou will do þus, mi hert sall be with þi hert and it sall be
enflammed with mi lufe, as þou sees a dri tre enflammed with fire. þi
saull sall þan be fulfilled with me, and I sall be within þe, and make all
temporall þinges bittir to þe, and þe luste of þi fleshe als it were
venim. þou sall | riste in þe armes of mi godhede, where no fleshli luste   f. 4ᵛᵃ
of syn is, bot swilke ioi and delite of þe spirit at fulfilles þe saule with   31
swilke gladnes þat it can nowþir thinke ne couet bot þe blisse þat it
hase. Tharefore lufe me allone, and þou sall haue in plente all þat þou
will desire. Is it noȝt wretin þat þe oile of þe widowe failed noght to
God had gifen rain to þe erthe, eftir þe worde of þe prophete? I am a   35
trewe profite. þarefore, if þou trowe to mi wordes and fulfill þaime, ioi
and gladnes sall noȝt faile to þe withouten ende.'

Secundum capitulum. Wordes of Jesu Criste whi he
chese hir to his spouse.

'I am maker of heuen and erthe, of þe see and of all þat is in þaime, one
verrai God in substaunce with fadir and holi goste, makinge all þat is
5 bot noȝt made, almighti, stedfaste in beinge, withoute chaunginge,
withoute biginning and withoute ende. I, kepeand mi godhede, and
makinge feliship bitwene it and manhede, was born of a maiden, þat in
f. 4ᵛᵇ one persone suld be þe verrai son | of God and son of þe maiden. I
hinge on þe cros, and was dede and berid, bot þe godhede was
10 noþinge hurt: for, all if I were dede in manhede and flesh þat I tuke, I
leued neuirþeles in þe godhede, in þe whilke I was one God with þe
fadir and þe holi goste. I ame þe same þat rase fra dede to life, and eftir
stied vp to heuen, þe whilke nowe spekes with þe.

'I haue chosen þe and taken þe to mi spouse, for it pleses me and
15 likes me to do so, and for I will shewe to þe mi preuai secretis. For þou
arte mine be a manere of [r]ight, foralsmikill as þou assigned thi will
into mi handes at þe time of diinge of þi husband, eftir whose bereinge
þou had grete þoght and made praiere how þou might be pore for me:
and þou had in will and desire to forsake all þinge for me. And þan
20 when þou had bi right made þe þus mine, it langed to me to puruai
f. 5ᵣᵃ and ordeine for þe; wharefore I take þe | to me as mi spouse vnto mi
awen propir delite, eftir it is acordinge and seminge þat God haue his
delite with a chaste saule. As þou knawes, it langes to a spouse to be
honestli and semingli araied and to be redi when þe husband will
25 make þe weddinge. þan arte þou made clene when, with forþinkinge
þat þou hase sinned, þou calles to minde howe, in baptime, I clensid
þe fra Adam sin, and howe oft eftirwarde, fro þou was fallen in sin, I
suffird þe and supported. Also, þe spouse awe to haue tokens of þe
husband vpon hir breste. So sall þou euir bere freshe in knawlage of
30 minde þe benefice and þe werkes þe whilke I haue done for þe: howe
nobilli I made þe, howe largeli I gafe mi giftes to þe, howe sweteli I
boght þe, and howe gudeli I restored þe to þine eritage, if þou will
haue it. þe spouse awe to do also þe husbandes will. Mi will is þat þou
loue me aboue all oþir and at þou will desire noþinge bot mi
35 plesaunce.

f. 5ʳᵇ 'Bot I make compleininge of man, for I made all þinges | for him and

---

11 leued] leued it, it *subpuncted*   16 right] hight, *Lat.* iure   19 and¹] and
þan when þou had be right made þe þus mine it langed me to puruai, *exc.* and, *marginal*
va-cat

subiected þaime to him, and he lufes all þinges bot me and hates noþinge bot me. I boght againe to him þe eritage þe whilke he had lost—and he is so fere and straunge fro reson þat he hase leuir þe sonefailinge wirshipe of þis werld, þe whilke is noȝt bot as þe fame of þe see, þan þe wirshipe of God of heuen, þat is euir abidinge and a 5 perpetuall gude.

'þarefore, if þou, mi spouse, desire noþinge bot me, and if þou leue and forsake noȝt alloneli childir and kinrede, bot also wirshipes and riches of þe werld, for mi loue, I sall gife þe most preciouse and sweteste rewarde, and þat is nouþir gold ne siluir, bot it is mine awen 10 selfe, þat ame kinge of blis. I will be þi rewarde. And if þou be ashamed to be pore and dispised, take hede to me þi God, howe pore and reproued I was for þe. I seke heuenli frendes and noght erthli. Thinke þat, if all I lufe of all mi herte, I sall neuir do one point againe rightwisnes, and þarefore, as þou hase trespaste be all þe membirs of 15 þi bodi, þe behoues make | asethe bi all þe same partis. And take f. 5ᵛᵃ comforth of þis, þat for a gude will and purpos of amendinge bi a litill wilfull penance I chaunge right into merci, and forgifes right greuous punishinges for amendinge bi a litill wilfull penaunce. Wharefore, take vpon þe gladli a litill trauale, þat þou mai þe sonner come to grete 20 rewarde. It is acordinge þe wife to be in trauaile with þe husband, þat þai mai þe more traistli eftirwarde riste togidir.'

Capitulum tercium. Wordes of Iesu Criste to enforme
þe spouse to loue.

'I am þi God, þe lorde, whome þou wirshipes. I am he þat vphaldes 25 heuen and erthe with mi might. þai are noȝt vphalden with non oþir þinges, ne pilers. I ame he þe whilke is ilke dai in þe auter offerde vndir liknes of brede, verrai God and man. I haue chosen þe to wirshipe mi fadir and loue me. Obei to mi spirite. Gife wirshipe to mi modir as to þi ladi. Wirshipe all mi saintes. Kepe right bileue | and f. 5ᵛᵇ faithe, þe whilke he sall teche þe, þat throwe mi helpe ouercome þe 31 conflict of two spirites, one of falshede, þe oþir of treuthe. Kepe verrai mekenes, þe whilke is—gife God louinge for his giftes.

'Bot now mani hates me and mi werkes, and haldes mi wordes bot vanite. þe deuell, þat is a foule avowterer, þai haue and loues. If þai do 35 oght for me it is done with gruchinge and bittirnes of saule, ne þai wald noȝt knawlege mi name bot for drede of man and of confusion

17 comforth] *marg.*, nota bene   gude] gude dede, dede *subpuncted and deleted*

befor man. þe werld is loued so dereli þat niȝt and dai þai sese noȝt of
trauaile for þe loue of it, and ai mare and mare kindles in þe lufe of þe
werlde. þe serues of whilke men pleses me as if a man gafe monee to
his enemi to þat ende þat his son be slaine. So doo þai. þai gife to me a
5   litill almouse and wirshipes me with þaire lippes, for þe prosperite of
þe werld suld encrese to þaime, and þai mai abide in þe werldes wir-

f. 6ʳᵃ shipe, and sin, throw whilk þe | gude saule of þaime is slaine, þat it mai
noght profite in gode.

'Wharefore if þou will loue me of all þi herte and noþinge desire bot
10 me, I sall drawe þe to me bi charite, as þe precious stone called
magnes drawes iren, and I sall set þe within mi arme, þe whilke is so
strannge þat none mai strech it oute, so starke þat none mai bowe it, so
swete þat it passes all þinges of sauoure, so þat it mai haue no likenes
to worldli delites.'

15   Capitulum quartum. Wordes of Iesu Criste to knawe a
            gude spirit fro þe euell.

'I ame þi maker and þi againebier. Whi was þou ferde of mi wordes,
and whi thoght þou doute wheþir þai ware of a gude spirit or euell?
What haues þou funden in mi wordes þat þou suld not haue done eftir
20 þi consciens? Bad I þe euir þinge againe reson?' þe spouse answerde,
'Neuir, bot all at þou hase saide are trewe, and I haue erred euell.'

þan answerde þe lorde, 'I haue bidin þe do thre þinges bi þe whilke

f. 6ʳᵇ þou mai knawe | a gude spirit. I bad þe wirshipe þi God þat made þe
and haues gifen þe all þat þou haues. þis techis þe þi reson, for to
25 wirshipe God abouen all oþir. I bad þe kepe right faithe–þat is, to
trowe þat noþinge is made, ne mai be made, withoute me. I bad þe
kepe resonable continence and mesur of all þinges, for þe werld is
made þat man suld vse it eftir nede and to asethinge of nede and noȝt
of luste.

30 'Right as bi þeere þou mai knawe a gude spirit, right so be thre,
contrari to þere, þou mai knawe ane euell spirit. He stirres þe to seke
in þi werkes þine awen glorie and þanke, and to be proude of þinges
þat are gifen þe; he stirres þe to mistrouthe and misbeleue; he stirris
þe to vse all þinges eftir þi luste; and ofte times he deseiues þe vndir
35 liknes of gude. þarefore I haue bidin þe þat euir þou discuse þi
consciens and oppenli shewe it to som spirituall wise men. And haue
neuir doute bot þe gude spirit is with þe, when þou desires noþinge

  · 7 þe] *Quire catchphrase,* whilk þe good, *below*   12 it²] *twice*

bot God, and art enflawmed all with his lufe, | for alloneli I stire   f. 6ᵛᵃ
þareto, and it is impossibill þat þe deuell negh þe when þou art so disposed, for þe deuell is mi creature, as all oþir are, and I made him
gude, bot throwe his awn malice he is euell. Neuirþeles, I am his lorde,
and þarefore he mai cum nere to no man, euell ne gude, bot he be suf-   5
fird of me, outher for his awen sinnes or elles for oþir cause knawen to
mi preuai dome.

    'And þarefore þare is som þat falsli and vntrewli sais of me þat þai,
þe whilke are mi seruantes, of oure grete deuocion gase oute of þaire
minde and are traueld with euell spirites. þai make me like to a man   10
þat had a chaste wife þat loues and traistis hir husband, and ȝit he
takes hir vnto þe avowtrere. Swilke one were I if I betuke vnto þe
fendes pouere þe rightwis man þat haues to me deuocion of charite.
Bot, for I ame trewe, þare sall no fende haue lord[s]hipe of my deuote
seruand. And þarefore if somtime mi frendes seme oute of minde, þat   15
is noȝt for þai suffir passion be pouere of þe fende, ne for þai serue | me   f. 6ᵛᵇ
of birnand deuocion, bot owþir for defaute of brain or for mekinge of
þaime or for som oþir cause knawen to me. It mai be somtime þat þe
deuell takes powere of me to noie þe fleshe of gude men for encrese of
þaire blisse in time comminge, and sometime þai perplex thaire con-   20
ciens. Bot in þaire saules þat haues in me verrai faith and delite he mai
neuir haue lordschipe.'

        Capitulum quintum. Of loue `and´ of liknes of hali
        kirke to a castell.

'I ame maker of all, kinge of blis and lorde of aungels. I made to me a   25
nobill castell, in þe whilke I put mi chosen derlinges. Bot mi enemis
has vndirmined þe ground, and þai haue noied mi frendes so mikill
þat þai haue so streited þere [fete] in þaire stokkes þat þe merke is
gone oute. þai hafe stopped þair mouthes with stanes and hili
punished þaim with hunger and thirste. Thai persewe also þe lorde of   30
mi frendes, and nowe mi frendes cries eftir helpe. Right cries vengeance and merci cries to spare.'

    þan spekes | þe lorde to his oste of heuen þat standes beside. 'What   f. 7ʳᵃ
sai ȝe of þaime þat þus haues entird and occupied mi castell?' And all
þai answere as it were one voice, 'Lorde, in þe is all right, and in þe we   35
se clereli all þinges; þou arte þe son of God withoute biginninge and
withoute ende, to whame is gifen all dome. Deme þou, for þou arte

    14 lordshipe] lordhipe   19 me] men, *Lat.* a me   28 fete] *om., Lat.* pedes

jugge.' To whame þe lorde answers and sais, 'All if ȝe se and knawe all
þinges in me, ȝit, for mi spouse þat standes nere, sai ȝe a rightfull
dome.' þai saide, 'þis is riȝt, þat þai þe whilke vndirmined þe wall be
punished as theues, and þai þat abides in malice be punished as intru-
5 sores, and þai þat are thrall be deliuerde to fredome, and þe hungri be
fulfilled with mete.'

þan spake Mari þe modir of God. 'Mi lorde and derrest beloued
son, þou was in mi wombe verrai God and man, and þou halowed me
þat was ane erdeli vessell bi þi awen fre gudenes. I beseke þe hafe
f. 7ʳᵇ merci ȝit ones vpon þaime.' þan answerde þe lorde to | þe modir, 'The
11 worde of þi mouthe, þat is blissed, as a sauer of souerain swetenes
ascendes into þe godhede. þou art þe ioi of aungels and of all saintes,
and whene, of whame þe godhede hase gladenes and all saintes hase
comforth; and for þi will euir fro þi ȝonge age was mi will, þarefor I
15 will do as þou desires.' And þan he saide to þe oste of saintes, 'For þe
praieres of mi modir and for ȝoure charite I will bige againe þe wall,
and I sall hele þaime þat are oppressed within, and I sall wirshipe
þaime an houndrethfolde for þe wronnge at þai suffir. þai þat dose þe
wronnge, if þai aske merci I sall gife þaime both merci and pese, and if
20 þai set noȝt bi me, þai sall fele mi rightwisnes.'

þan spake þe lorde to þe spouse, 'Mi spouse, I haue chosen þe, and
I haue broght þe into mi awen spirit. þou heres þe worde of me and of
mi saintes, þe whilke, all if þai see in me clereli all þinges, ȝit þai speke
f. 7ᵛᵃ þus for þe, þat | þou suld vndirstande, and for þou, beinge in dedeli
25 fleshe, mai noȝt se me clereli as þai do þat are hali spirites.

'Nowe I sall shewe þe what all þis bitakens. þe castell biforesaide is
hali kirke, þe whilke I bigged of mi blode and of þe blode of mi saintes,
and ioined it togidir with ciment of charite, in þe whilk I hafe put mi
chosen frendes. þe grounde of þis is trewe faith: þat is, to trow me
30 riȝtfull iugge and mercifull. Bot nowe þis grounde is vndirmined, for
all troues me oneli mercifull. And, forsoth, he is a wikked jugge, þe
whilke of merci leues euell sinners vnponished, throwe þe whilke þai
take boldnes þe more to oppresse rightfull liuers. Bot I am bothe
rightfull jugge and mercifull, for I sall noȝt leue þe leste sin vn-
35 ponishede, ne þe leste gude dede vnrewardede.

'Be þis mine are þai enterd into hali kirke þe whilke sinnes con-
tinualli withouten drede and denies þat I ame rightwis, and distrubles
mi frendes as þai are into stokkes. To mi frendes is proferde nawþir ioi

22 haue] haue boght, boght *subpuncted*   23 þe] to þe   24 þat] *twice*
dedeli] dedeli sin, sin *subpuncted*   32 whilke²] whilke of

ne comfurthe, bot sorowe | and all reproue, as men þat were vexed with   f. 7ᵛᵇ
euell spirites. If þai sai treuthe of me, it is saide þat þai make lesinges:
þere is no liste to here þaime speke right or treuthe. I, þaire God, and
maker of all, am blasphemede. þai sai þai wote neuir if þare be ani
God. "And if þare be ani," þai sai, "we charge it noȝt." Thai caste   5
doun mi baner and defoiles it vndir fete, and þai sa þus: "Whi suffird
he, and what profete does his passion for vs? If he will gife vs oure will
it is enogh to vs. Late he vs haue oure will, and kepe he to himselfe his
kingedome of heuen." I wald entir vnto þaim, bot þai sai, "Late vs sonner die or we leue and forsake oure awen will."   10

    'Se nowe, mi spouse, what kine puple there are. I made þaime, and
with a worde I miȝt destruy þaime, and ȝit se howe þai are proude
again me. Neuirþelesse nowe, what for þe praiers of mi modir and of
all saintes, I ame ȝet so mercifull and pacient in suffiringe, þat I wald
sende mi wordes | to þaime, and I will offir to þaime mi merci. If þai   f. 8ʳᵃ
will ressaiue it, I sall be plesed. If þai will noght, þai sall so fele mi   16
rightwisnes þat riȝt as opin theues þai sall be confunded byfor aungels
and men, and of all þai sall be foriugged. And as men þat are hanged
on galows are deuoured with fowles of rauaine, right so þai sall be
deuoured of fendes and all wastid awai. And as þai þat are punished in   20
stokkes of trees findes no riste, so þese men sall on euirilkea side finde
bittirnes and sorowe. A birnand flode sall flowe into þaire mouthe, ne
þaire wombe sall neuir be fulfilled, bot þai sall ilke dai be renewed to
torment. Mi frendes, forsothe, sall be saued and þai sall be comforted
in þe wordes þat passes fro mi mouthe. þai sall se mi right with mi   25
merci. I sall cleþe þaime in þe armoure of mi charite, and I sall make
þaime so mighti and so strannge þat all þe aduersaries of þe faithe sall
fall bakwarde as clai, and withouten ende sall be ashamed, when þai
sall se mi rightwisnes and | how þai haue misvsed mi paciens.'   f. 8ʳᵇ

Here biginnes þe sext chapitir, in þe whilke he liknes   30
his enemis.

'I likken mine enemis to þe ferest bestis þat neuir is filled, ne neuir can
haue reste, whose hert is so void fro mi charite þat þare entres into it
neuir o thoght of mi passion. þare passed neuir ȝit oute of þe inward
partis of þaire herte swilke o worde: "Lorde, þou boght vs. Thanke   35
and louinge be to þe for þi passion." How mai mi spirit be with þaim
þat hase no charite to me? þaire hert is full of vileste wormes, þat are
worldli affeccions. þe fende hase put his stinke in þaire mouthe, and

þarefor mi wordes pleses þaime noȝt. Wherefore with mi sawe I haue
departed þaim fro mi frendes: and right as þare is no bitterere dede
þan þat at is caused be sawe, right so þai sall be put fro me to þe moste
bitter tormentes, and þe deuell sall sawe þaime in soundir and departe
5   þaime fro me. þai are so odius and hatefull to me, þat all þat consentis
f. 8ᵛᵃ | and cleues to þaim sall be departed fro me. Herefor, I sende mi
frendes for to departe þe deuels fro mi membris, for þai are mi verrai
enemis.

'Mi frendes are in þis case sente as knightes, for he þat chastises his
10 fleshe and abstenes fro vnlawfull werkes, he is verraili mi knight. þai
sall haue mi wordes þat I spake in þe stede of a spere, faithe for a
swerde in þe hande. In þe breste of þaime sall be þe habirgeon of
charite, þat whateuir fall þai lufe me neuirþeles. þai sall haue þe
shelde of paciens bi þaire side, þat all þinges be suffird pacientli: for,
15 eftir right þat I had ordained, I might noȝt entre into þe ioi of maieste
withoute sufferance of tribulacions in mi manhede. How will þai þan
entir? If þe lorde suffird, it is no woundir if þai buse suffir. If þe lorde
suffir betinge, it is no woundir if þai buse suffir wordes. Bot drede þai
noȝt, for I sall neuir forsake þaime. Right as it is impossibil þat þe
f. 8ᵛᵇ deuell touche þe her[t]e of God and departe it, so it is | inpossibill þat
21 þe deuell part þaime fro me. And for þai are als it were þe clennest
gold in mi sight, þarefore, all if I proue þaim sometime be fire, ȝit will I
noȝt forsake þaim, for I do it for encrese of þaire rewarde.'

viim capitulum. Wordes of oure ladi techinge þe
25   manere of lifinge.

'I am Mari þat broght furth verrai God and man, þe whene of aungels.
Mi son lufes [þ]e of all his herte, and þarefore lufe þou him. þou buse
be araied with clothes of grete honeste, and I sall shewe þe what þai
sall be. þe bose haue a shirt, a cote, a mantill, a nowche in þi breste, a
30 crown, and shone on þi fete.

'To spirituall meninge, þe serke is contricion, for riȝt as þe serke is
next þe fleshe, so contricion and confession is þe first wai of turninge
vnto God, throw þe whilke þe saule is clensed þat was bifore glad to
sin, and so þe foule fleshe is refreined fro his lustes. þe two shone are
f. 9ʳᵃ two willis. One is will to amend sinnes þat are done; | þe toþir is will to
36 do gude dedis and for to abstene fro euell. Thi cote is hope to God.

16 withoute] *twice, first subpuncted*   20 herte] herde, *Lat.* cor   27 þe] me,
Lat. te

This cote haues two sleues: þat þou hope merci and right. Traiste so
in merci þat þou reklesli forgete noght rightwisnes, and so þinke on
rightwisnes and dome þat þou forgete noȝt merci, for God dose neuir
rightwisnes withoute merci, ne merci withoute rightwisnes.

'þe mantill is faith, for, right as þe mantill couers all oþir clothis 5
and all are enclosed within þat, right so with faith a man mai comprehend and come to knawlege of all oþir. þis mantill sall be melled
with þe takenes of þi husbandes lufe and his charite: for to þinke
howe he mad þe, howe he broght þe within his awen spirit, and
howe he hase oppened þi gasteli een to behald him. þe nowche vpon 10
þi breste is minde of his passion, þe whilke sall euir be stedfasteli
festened in þi breste: howe he was skorned and scorged: howe he
was, in all partis, bathed in his awen blode and depe doluin in
veynes and senews, and ȝit he | hange on life in þe cros: how for f. 9ʳᵇ
sharpe suffiringe of grete paine in þe oure of deinge all his bodi 15
tremelled and whoke: howe at þe laste he commendid his saule into
þe handes of þe fadir. Late þis broche be euer in þi breste. þe
crowne on þi hede is chastite in þi will, and late þat be so stedfastli
set þat þou haue leuer suffir all paine þan be defoiled againe. And
with þat, be honeste and shamefull, and þinke noȝt, ne desire noȝt, 20
bot þi God þi maker, whame when þou hase, þou hase all þinge.
And, þus araide, abide þi husbande.'

Capitulum octauum. Wordes of our ladi, techinge howe
sho sall loue and wirshipe hir son.

'I am wheene of heuen. þou art right besi howe þou mai lufe me. Wit 25
þou for certain þat whoso lufes and wirshipes mi son loues and
wirshipes me, for I lufed him with swilke feruour þat we ware bothe as
we had bene one: and he so wirshiped me þat was a vessell of erthe þat
he enhawnsed me abouen all aungels. And þarefor þou sall me þus
wirshipe: "Blessed be þou God, maker of all þinges, | þe whilke f. 9ᵛᵃ
vouche[d] saufe to com down into þe wombe of þe maiden Mari. 31
Blessed be þu God, þat comforthet and gladded maiden Mari þi
modir eftir þi ascencion, and in þat comforthe þou visit hir. Blissed be
þou God, þat tuke vp into heuen þe bodi of þi modir, maiden Mari,
and beside þi godhede set hir in wirshipe abouen all aungels. Haue 35
merci of me for þe praier of her." '

6 mai] mai be   8 charite] charite and howe he has oppened þi gastli eyn, *margi-*
nal va-cat   17 euer] eueir   23 our] ourur   31 vouched] vouche

Capitulum ixm. Wordes of oure ladi, in þe whilke sho
teches of hir.

'I ame wheene of heuen. Loue mi son, for he is moste honeste, and
when þou hase him, þou hase all honeste. He is moste to be desired,
5 and when þou hase him, þou hase all þat mai be desired. Lufe him, for
he is moste vertuous, and when þou hase him, þou hase all vertuse.

'I will tell þe howe sweteli he lufed mi fleshe and mi saule, and howe
he hase wirshiped mi name. Mi son lufed me or I luffed him, for he
was mi maker. He knit þe weddinge of mi fadir and mi modir with
10 swilke chastite þat a[t] þat time þere was no weddinge more chaste, for
f. 9ᵛᵇ þai commoned bot eftir þe | lawe be cause to bringe furth childe. And
when it was tald þaime bi þe aungell þat þai suld bringe furth a
maiden, of whome suld springe þe hele of þe werld, luste was dede in
þaime, þat þai had leuir haue died þan hafe commoned togidir bi
15 fleshli lufe. 'Neuir'þeles I sai to þe for siker þat þai commoned in
fleshe bi Goddes charite, and for þe worde of þe aungell þat broght þe
message, and for none desire of ani luste bot againe þaire will, moued
bi þe lufe of God. And so of þe sede of þaim mi fleshe was broght
furthe bi Goddes charite, and fro mi bodi was made, God sent fro his
20 godhede mi saule, made of noght, to þe bodi. And onone mi saule with
bodi was halowed, þe whilke aungels keped both night and dai. Fro þe
time þe saule was halowed and knit with bodi, it is inpossible to sai
with worde þe ioi þat come to mi modir.

'And eftir þe curs of mi life, he tuke and lift mi saule firste to his
25 godhede, for it was principall and ladi of þe bodi: eftirwarde he tuke
f. 10ʳᵃ mi bodi, | so þat þare is no creatures bodi so nere God als mine. Take
now tent and se howe mikill mi sone loued mi saule and mi bodi. Bot
ȝit þare is some led with ane euell spirit þat denies þat I was
assumpted in bodi and saule; and som sais þai wote neuir. And
30 þarefore I do þe to wit þat þis is þe treuthe in sikirnes, þat I am
assumpted vnto þe godhede bothe in bodi and in saule.

'Here also howe mi son hase wirshipe[d] mi name. Mi name, as it is
redde in þe gospell, is Maria. What time þat aungels heres it, þai are
glade in consciens and þai þanke God þat hase done to me swilke
35 grace, and þat þai se þe manhede of mi son glorified in godhede. Also
þai þat are in purgatori ar passingli glad of it, as þe seke þat ligges in
bed, þat herres þe worde of comforthe þat pleses in his saule. Also

10 at] as　　　15 Neuirþeles] neurþeles　　　24 of] *twice*　　　32 wirshiped]
wirshipe

aungels, þat are gifen of God to kepe rightwise men, when þai here þis
worde Maria, þai drawe nere to þaim whame þai kepe, and is singlerli
glad of þe profete (for it is sothe þat God hase set aungels to all men
for to kepe þaim, and all if þai take hede | to mannes saule, nowþir for   f. 10ʳᵇ
þat are þai departed fro God, ne þai leue noȝt God, bot ai are in his   5
sight and enflawmes and excites þe saule to god, to Goddes plesaunce;
and euel aungels ar gifen to men for to proue þaime).

'Also all euell fendes are ferde for þis name and dredes it, and,
where þai here it, þai fle awai and leues þe saule at þai desesed. Bot
right as a bird of rauaine, if he here a sounde or a noise, he leues his   10
prai, right so fendes, when þai here mi name þai are so ferde þai leue
and forsake þe saule þat þai noied. Bot som amendinge of life folowe,
as a maste swifte arowe þai fle againe and takes it into þaire daungere.
Ne þare is no man so cold or drie in þe loue of God, bot if he be finallie
dampned, þat calles on þis nam with will and entent at forsake sin and   15
turn no more againe, but þe deuell onone leues him and gose awai fro
him and turnes neuir againe to him, bot if it be so þat he take | againe   f. 10ᵛᵃ
full will for to syn dedeli. Neuirþeles he is somtime suffird to trowble a
gude man for his bettir and fore his more rewarde, bot he sall noȝt
haue him in lordshipe of possession.'   20

Capitulum decimum. Wordes of oure ladi, shewinge
hir entent in ȝonge age, and þe maner of conceiuinge
hir son, and of his passion.

'I am wheene of heuen, þe modir of God. I saide to þe þat þou awe to
haue a nouche vpon þi breste. I will now shewe to þe more oppenli   25
howe I, fro biginninge þat I herde and vndirstode at þare was a God, I
was ai besi for mi gosteli hele, and full ferde howe I suld kepe me. And
fro I herde more plainli þat God was mi maker and iuge of all mi
werkes, I lufed him als entereli als I might, and euirilke oure I was
ferde and þoght I suld noȝt offende him in worde ne dede. Forthir-   30
mare, when I herd þat he had gifen þe lawe and þe preceptes to his
pepill, and what miracles and meruails he had shewed vnto þaime, I
purpossed stedfastli in mi saule to loue | none bot him. And so all   f. 10ᵛᵇ
werldli þinges ware to me woundir bittir.

'Eftir þis, when I herde þat he, þe same God, suld bi againe þe   35
werld, and suld be born þareto of a maiden, I had so grete a charite to
him þat I thoght of noþinge, ne desired noþinge, bot him. I drowe me

6 þe saule] þe saule þe, *second* þe *subpuncted*   17 againe²] a againe

awai and wex straunge, eftir þat I might, fro comon speche and presens of fadir and modir and frendes, and all þat I might gete I delte to þe nedi, kepinge to miselfe þinge necessari–mete and drinke and cleþinge. Noþinge might plese me bot alloneli God, and þarefore I
5 desired euir in mi herte þat I might leue and se þe time of his birth, if I might happeli be a worthi handmaiden to seruis of his modir. Also, I vowed in mi herte euir to kepe maidenhede if it plesed and suld be acceptabill to God, and neuir to haue possession in þe werld. And, if God wald it were oþerwise, I desired fulfillinge of his will and noȝt of
f. 11ʳᵃ mine, for I trowed þat he might all þinge and þat he wald not | bot þat
11 at was prophetabill to me. þarefore I committed all mi will into his gouernance.

'When þe time come, eftir þe lawe, þat virgins and maidens suld be presented in þe tempill of God, I was amange þaime for þe obediens
15 of mi fadir and modir, and I thoghet þare was noþinge inpossibile to God; and for he knewe þat I desired noþinge bot him, he might kepe me in mi virginite if it plesed and liked to him: if he walde oþirwise, his will be fulfilled. Fro þe time I had herd all þat was commaunded in þe tempill, and turned home againe, I brint in more lufe of God þan I did
20 before, and euirilkea dai I was enflawmed with newe hetis of lufe. Wharefore I withdrowe me fro all folke more þan I was wonnt, and abode nightes and daies passinge dredeand þat mi mouthe suld noght speke, ne mine eres suld noȝt here, aniþinge contrari to mi Goddes plesaunce, or þat mine een suld see aniþinge þat were delitable. I was
25 ferde also in kepinge of cilens þat I suld happeli noght speke swilke þinges as suld be spoken.

f. 11ʳᵇ   'When I was þus | allon miselfe turbled in mi herte and committed all mi hope vnto God, it come sodainli to mi herte to þinke on þe grete might of God: howe aungels and all creatures þat are made serues him:
30 howe his ioy is vnspekeable and mai noȝt haue ende; and as I was wounderinge þareof, I sawe thre grete meruails. I sawe a stern, bot noȝt swilke one as shinnes in heuen. I sawe a light, bot noȝt swilke as is in þe werlde. I felid a swete sauour and odoure (þare is non swilke of erbes ne of na oþir þinge, for it mai noȝt be discriued with tonge) with
35 þe whilke I was fulfilled, and þan in ioi I made grete gladnes. Anone eftir þis I herd a voice, bot noȝt of mannes mouthe. And þan I was ferde, dredand for illusion.

'Bot onone þare aperid ane aungell of God, as a man of soueraine

bewte, noght clethed, and he said to me, "*Aue gracia plena et cetera*:
haile, full of grace, þe lorde is with þe. þou art more blissed þan all
oþir women." When I had herd þis, I was astoned, merueilinge what |
þis suld betaken, or whi he profird to me swilke a salutacion. I wist   f. 11ᵛᵃ
wele and trowed miselfe vnworthi ani swilke, for I held me noȝt worthi   5
ani gude; bot I wiste wele it was noȝt vnpossibill to God for to do what
him liked. þan saide þe aungell againe, "þat sall be born of þe is hali,
and it sall be called þe son of God; and as it hase plesed him, so it sall
be." Neuirþeles I held me noȝt worthi, ne I asked noȝt of þe aungell,
"Whi or when sall it be?", bot I asked þe maner, "How it sall be þat I,   10
vnworthi, be þe modir of God, þe whilke fleshli knawes no man." And
þe aungell answerd to me as I saide, "To God is noþinge vnpossibill,
but what he will be done, sall be done."

'Eftir þe whilke worde of þe aungell, I had þe moste feruent will þat
might be had to be þe modir of God. And þan spake mi saule þus for   15
lufe: "Lo, I here redi: þi will be done in me." At þe whilke worde anone
was mi son conceiued in mi wombe with vnspekeabill gladnes of mi
saule and of all mi partis. When I had hym þus in mi wombe, and bare
him withoute ani sorowe, paine, heuenes or desese, | I meked miselfe   f. 11ᵛᵇ
in all wise, knawinge wele þat he was almighti whame I bare, and when   20
I childed him withoute paine or ani sin, as I conceiued him, I childed
with so grete gladnes, both of bodi and saule, þat mi fete feled noȝt þe
erthe where þai stode. And as with a grete gladnes of mi saule and mi
partes he entered into me, right so with vnspekeabill ioi and gladnes of
þe same saule and oþir partees, and withoute hurtinge or harminge of   25
mi virginite in his birthe, he passed fro me. þan, when I sawe and toke
hede to his grete fairnes and bewte, mi saule droped dewe of deuocion
for ioi, knawinge miselfe vnworthi swilke a son.

'When I tuke hede to þe places in þe handes and fete þat nailes suld
go throwe, þe whilke I had herd bi prophecies suld be festened to þe   30
cros, þen mi een were full of teres and wepinge, and mi hert ferde
[s]ore as it had departed asoundir for sorowe. And þan mi son biheld
mi een wepinge, and wex heui and sori as to þe dede. When I con-
sidered þe might of | his godhede, I tuke comforthe to me againe,   f. 12ʳᵃ
knawinge wele þat so he walde it sulde be, and so to be was most   35
profete to man, and þan all mi will I conformed to his will. And so mi
ioi was euir mengid with sorowe.

'When þe time come of þe passion of mi son, his enemis rauished
him, and buffeted him in þe cheke and nek, and spittinge in his visage

32 sore] fore

þai scorned him. þan he was lede to þe piler, where he did of his awene clothes and put his awene handes to þe piler, þe whilke his enemis band withoute merci. þus bounden he had no maner of helinge no clothinge, bot right as he was born, naked, so he stode
5 and suffird shame of nakedhede. þan fled his frendes: bot enemis stode aboute togedire and scourged his bodi þat was innocent fro sin and clene fro filthe. When I herd þe firste stroke, standinge nere, I fell downe as dede, bot takinge againe mi spirit I sawe his bodi betine and scourged vnto þe ribbes þat all men might se: and, þat to

f. 12rb sai is more bittir, þe scourges made furris in þe fleshe. When | mi
11 son so blodi and so ragged and reuin in his fleshe stode þat in him might be founden no place hole for to scourge, þan a man with a grete spirit saide, "What suld ȝe sla him þus vndemide?" And onone he cutt his bandes in two, and mi son did on his clothes. þan sawe I
15 þe place full of blude where mi sonnes fete stode, and ilke man might knawe where he wente bi his stepes þat made þe erth all blody, ne thay wald noȝt gife hime space fulli to clethe him, bot, for to haste him, þai constreined and drewe him furth as a thefe. And þan mi son whiped þe blode fro his awen een.

20   'Whan he was demed, þai put vpon him þe cros to bere, and, fro he had borne it a litill space, þan one come and tuke it to bere furth. In þe mene time þat mi son whent to þe place of þe passion, some smote him in þe nekke, some in þe face, and þat so mightili þat all if I sawe noȝt þe smiter, ȝit I herde þe sounde of þe strokes. When I had comen

f. 12va with | him to þe place of þe passion, I sawe all þinges redeli araied to
26 his dede. And þan mi son did of his awen clothes, þe whilke þe ministirs saide were þaires, for he was dampned to þe dede. Mi son þan standinge naked as he was born, one persone broght him ane helinge, with þe whilke he couerd his preuai partis.

30   'þan þe wode turmenturs raueshed him and streined him in þe cros, festenand firste þe right hand to þe stoke, þe whilke was redi bored, and so þai bored throw þe hand where þe bone was moste sade. þan þai drowe þe toþir hand with a rope vnto þe stokke and festened to on þe same wise. Forthirmare, þai festened to þe cros þe
35 right fote abouen þe left with two nailes, þat all þe vaines and senows

---

2 and ... handes] *twice, first* (and put in his awen in his handes, *first in subpuncted*)
ruled through   4 helinge] helpinge, *Lat.* operimenti   7 fro] for   9 betine]
subpuncted   10 þe^1] þen, n *subpuncted*   in] into, to *subpuncted*   fleshe] fleshe
þou, þou *subpuncted*   12 might] *twice, first subpuncted*   scourge] scourges, *final* s
subpuncted   with] *twice, first subpuncted*   14 cutt] cuttes, es *subpuncted*

were streined and braste. þan þai happed a crown of thornes vnto his
heued, þe whilke prikked so sharpli þe reuerent hede of mi son þat his
eene were filled of þe blode þat flowed oute, his eres were stopped,
and all his berde was besene þarewith.

'When mi son | stode so blodi and bledd, haueinge compassion of   f. 12ᵛᵇ
me þat stode biside, he beheld me with blodi een and me to Jon mi   6
sistir son, and him to me, he commended. In þat time I herd som sai
þat mi son was a theefe, som þat he was a lier, som þat none was so
worthi dede as mi son: of þe whilke heringe mi sorowe ai renewede.
Bot, as it was saide, when þe first naile was festened, I fell as dede at þe 10
first stroke, mi een beand mirke, mi handes tremelland, and mi fete
whakinge, þat I loked noȝt vp for bittirnes of sorowe till he was
festened all to; and þan I, seinge mi son so wrechedli hange, most
heueli and consternat, I might noght wele stande.

'þan mi son, seinge me and his frendes wepand withoute com-   15
forthe, with one wepinge voice and one hie, he cried to þe fadir and
saide, "Fadir, whi hase þou forsaken me?": as if he saide, "þare is none
to haue merci on me bot þou, fadir." þan aperid his een halfe dede, his
chekes fallen, his semblant heui, his mouth open, his tounge blodi, his
wombe cleueand to his bake, and all his hu|murs wasted awai as if he f. 13ʳᵃ
had no entrals, and so all þe bodi left pale in langoure for fluxe, in   21
passinge of blod. His handes and his fete were streined eftir þe forme
of þe cros and conformed þareto. þe berde and þe hare were all
tosprenkeld with blode.

'And when mi son þus reuen and bla blodi stode, alloneli þe herte 25
was freshe, for it was of þe beste and stronngeste kinde; for he toke of
mi fleshe þe clenneste bodi and beste complexiond. His skin was so
tendir þat, were he neuir so softli scourged, anone þe blode wente
furth, and þe blode was so freshe þat it might be sene in þe clene
skyne. And for he was of þe beste kinde, þarefore was þare a stronnge 30
fight in his bodi bitwene life and dede, for when þe paine fro þe vaines
or sinows or oþir partes went to þe herte þat was freshe and vncorrupt,
it vexid it and trauailed it with an vntrowabill sorowe and passion. And
sometime þe sorowe went fro þe hert vnto oþir partees and so
proloined | þe dede with grete bittirnes.   f. 13ʳᵇ

'When mi son, þus vmbiset with painnes and sorowes, had take   36
hede and behalden his frendes wepinge, þe whilke had leuir with his
helpe haue suffird þe same paine or for to haue bene in hell soner þan

27 mi] mi bodi, bodi *subpuncted*   37-8 his helpe haue suffird] *twice,* haue suffird
his helpe *subpuncted*

haue sene him suffir so painefulli, he loued so wele his frendes þat þe
sorowe of compassion he had for þaire sorowe passed all þe bittirnes
of tribulacion þat he suffird in his awn bodi or hert. þan, for
ouremikill angwis of pine in þe bodi of his manhede, he cried to þe
5 fadir and saide, "O fadir, into þi handes I commend mi spirit." And
when I, heuieste modir, herd þat, all membres of mi bodi trembled
and whaked with grete bitternes of hertli sorowe: and as ofte eftir as I
thoght on þis voice, it was to me as it had bene freshe and present.

'When he drowe nere to dede, þat þe herte for violens of paine suld
10 breke, þan tremeld all his membres, and þe hede somwhat bowed
done. þe mouth was sone opin, and þe tonge all blodi. þe handes
withdrewe þaim somwhat fro þe places of þe holes þat were bored,
f. 13ᵛᵃ and þe fete bore more vpe þe | weght of þe heued and of þe bodi. þe
fingers and þe armes in maner streched þaimselfe, and þe bake
15 strongeli was streined to þe stoke. þan saide som to me, "Mari, þi son
is dede." Som saide, "He is dede, bot he sall rise againe." And when all
oþir were goinge awai, þan come one and festened a spere so mightili
into his side þat it went and passed almoste bi þe toþir side, and when
it was drawen oute, þe hede aperid rede of blode. þan me thoght þat
20 mi herte was persed throwe, when I sawe þe herte of mi son so bored
throwe.

'Eftirwarde, he was takine doun of þe cros, whome I tuke vpon mi
knees, as he had semed leprous and bloo, for his een were dede and
full of blude, his mouthe was cold as snowe, his face drawen togidir
25 and contractid. His handes were so starke, þai might noȝt be put
forthir þan aboute þe nauill. And I had him on mi knees, as a man contracted in all membres. Eftirwarde þai put him in linnen clothe, and
with a linnen I wiped his woundes and spered and closed his een and
his mouthe, þe whilke were opin in his dede. þan þai put him in þe
f. 13ᵛᵇ graue. O howe | gladli I wald haue bene put þarein with him if it had
31 bene þe will of mi son! Eftir þat þere were done, com Jon and led me
into an hows. Se now, mi doghtir, what mi son haues suffird for þe.'

Capitulum xi. Wordes of þe son to þe spouse, techinge
þe maner of liuinge and continens of all mannis
35   membris bi ensampill of his swete passion.

The son of God spake to þe spouse and saide, 'I ame þe maker of heuen
and erthe, and it is mi verrai bodi þe whilke is sacrid on þe awter. Lufe
me of all þi herte, for I haue lufed þe, and tuke miselfe wilfulli to mi

enemis for þe, when mi modir and oþir frendes left in þe bittereste
sorowe and heuenes for me. When I sawe þe spere, þe nailes, þe
scourges, and oþur kindes of passion araied and made redi, I letted
noȝt to go furth gladli to þe paines of mi passion. When mi heued was
on ilkea side bledinge bi þe crown of thorn, þan on ilke parte þe blode 5
flowed oute, and | if mi enemis had touched mi herte, I suld soner haue   f. 14ʳᵃ
suffird it to be departed in soundir and wounded, or I wald haue
wannted þe. And þarefore, treuli, þou arte vnkinde and þou loue me
noght for so mikill charite as I haue shewed to þe.

'Sen mi heued was prikked and enclined to þe crosse for þe, þi 10
heued suld be enclined and bowed to mekenes. Sin mi een were full of
blode and of wepinge for þe, thin een suld abstene and forbere all
delitabill sightes. Sin mi eres were full fullfilled all of blode and herd
wordes of detraccion, þarefor þou suld kepe þine erres fro all
vnhoneste, vnprofetabill and vnacordinge speche. And sithen I dranke 15
with mi mouthe þe moste bittir drinke, þi mouthe suld be spered to all
euell and opin to gode. And syn mi handes were streined oute with
nailes, þi handes suld be streched oute to þe pore and to fulfillinge of
mi commandementes. And luke at þi fete, þat is, þine affeccions, with
þe whilke þou suld com to me warde, be crucified fro lustes, þat right 20
as I suffird for þe in all mi membres, so all þi membres suld be redi to
do me seruise and plesaunce, | for I aske of þe more seruise þan of oþir   f. 14ʳᵇ
bicause þat I haue done to þe more grace þan to oþir.'

Capitulum 12. Howe þe gude aungell of þe spouse
praies for hir, askinge for hir allaneli þat was propheta-   25
bill to hir.

The gude aungell, kepare of þe spouse, was sene prai to Criste for þe
same spouse: to whome þe lorde answerde þus: 'He þat will prai for
aneoþir awe to prai for þat at is helefull for him. þou arte as fire þat is
neuir slokened, euir birninge in mi charite. þou sese and knawes all 30
þinges when þou sese me. þou will noþinge bot at I will. þarefore sai
me what is profetabill and spedefull to þis spouse.' þe aungell saide,
'Lorde, þou knawes.' þe lorde answerde, 'All þinges þat are and sall
be were withoute begininge in me, and I knawe all þat is in heuen and
erthe, ne in me is no chaunginge. Neuirþelesse, þat þis spouse mai þe 35
bettir vndirstand and knawe mi will, sai þou nowe what is to hir

2 nailes] mailes   6 flowed] flowted, t *subpuncted*   24 spouse] spouse for,
for *subpuncted*

f. 14va prophetabill.' þe aungell | saide, 'Sho has a proude herte and a grete,
and þarefore hir nedis a wande to be tamed and chastised.' þe lorde
saide, 'Mi frende, what will þou þan aske for hir?' þe aungell
answerde, 'Lorde, I aske to hir merci with þe wande.' þe lorde saide,
5 'For þe I sall do so to hir, for I do neuir right withoute merci, and þarefore þis spouse awe to lufe me of all hir herte.'

Capitulum 13. Howe Goddes enemi hase thre deuels within him, and þe dome of him.

'My enemi hase within him thre deuels. One sittes in his preuei
10 membres, þe second in þe hert, and þe þird in þe mouth. þe first is
like to a shipman þat makes þe watir to entir be [þe ke]ll, till throw
waxinge it filles þe shipe, and þan ouirflowes þe watir and þe shipe
drownes. Bi þe ship is vndirstanden his bodi, þe whilke was waueringe
þrowe temptacion of þe deuell and his coueitise. Into þe whilke, watir
15 of luste entird first bi likinge þat he had and delited him in thoghtes.
f. 14vb And for he withstode þaime | noght bi penaunce, ne stopped noȝt his
freelte with nailes of abstinence, þarefore þe watir of luste grewe and
wex in him into consent. þus þan þe shipe of his bodi att þe laste filled
with þere watirs of lustes, þai passed oute to dede and so drowned þe
20 shipe in luste þat it might noȝt com to þe hauen of gosteli hele.

'þe second deuell, þat sittes in his hert, is like a worme in a appill,
þe whilke etes firste þe kirnels of þe appell and leues þare his filth, and
þan passes furth bi all þe appill till he had made all þe appell corrupe
and unprofetabill. þus dose þe deuell. Firste he files his will (and
25 makes it vicious) and his oþir gude desires, þe whilke are, as it were,
þe kirnell in þe appill, of whome procedes þe strengþe of þe saule and
all meritori gude. And when he has voided þe herte of þese godes, he
leues, in stede of þare, þoghtes and affeccions of þe werld, þe whilke
þat he hase loued, and he moues þe bodi to what him likes, bi þe
f. 15ra whilke his strengþe | and gosteli knawlege is febild, and bygins to be
31 irke of his life. He for sekirnes is a appill withoute kirnell, þat is to say,
a man withoute herte, þe whilke withoute hertli lufe entirs mi kirke
and hase no godeli charite.

'þe þird deuell is like to ane archar þe whilke shotes in bi windous
35 to men þat are unware and noȝt wele avised. Hopis þou noȝt þe deuell

---

11 þe kell] litill, *Lat.* per carinam   25 and] and makes, makes *ruled through and*
subpuncted   30 strengþe] *Quire catchphrase*, and gostly, *below*

sittis in him þat spekes no time bot of him? þat þinge he loues beste he
names ofteste. His bittir wordes, with þe whilke he hurtes oþir persones, are as þai ware sharpe arrous, þe whilke he shotes in at as mani
windous as he sclaundirs simpill persones bi his vndiscrete wordes.
þarefore I, þat ame sothfaste, swerris in mi treuthe, þat I sall deme   5
him as a comon woman to fire of brunston, and as a traitur to be dis-
membird in all his parties, and as a dispiser of his lorde vnto perpetuall confusion.

'Neuirþeles, as lange as þe bodi and saule is togidir, my merci is
redi to hym. þis is þe þinge þat I re`quire´ and aske of him, þat | he be   f. 15rb
oft times in place where God is wirshiped and luffed, þat he dred no   11
re`proue´, ne desire [no] wirshipe, and at no euell þinge be named ani
time bi his mouthe.'

Capitulum 14. Wordes of Criste to þe spouse, techinge
hir þe maner of praiing, and of thre maner of men þat   15
serues God in erthe.

'I ame þi God, verrai God and man in one persone, þat was crucified
and is euirilke dai in þe handes of þe preste. When þou sall prai to me,
end þus þi praier: "I prai lorde to þe þat þi will be fulfilled, and noȝt
mine"; for when þou praies for þaime þat are dampned, I here þe   20
noght. Also sometime þou desires somwhate againe þine awen gosteli
hele, and, þerefore, it is nede to þe for to commit all to mi will, for I
knawe all þinges and I will graunt ne puruei to þe noþinge bot þat is
profetabill. Forsothe, þare is mani þat praies, bot noȝt with right
entent, and þarefore þai are noght worthi to be herde.   25

'þare are thre kyndes of men þat serues me in þis werld. | The firste   f. 15va
are þai þat trowes me God, gifer of all and mighti abouen all oþir. þai
serue me of þis entent, þat þai mai haue temporall gudes and
wirschipe: bot þai set noȝt bi heuenli gudes, and þai leue and lose
þaime gladli for to haue þe gudes þat is in þe werlde present. I late   30
þaim haue temporall prosperite eftir þaire will, and so heuenli gudes
are loste fro þaime. I reward þaime with temporall for þe gude dedis
þai do for me vnto þe laste point: þare leues noȝt vnrewarde. þe
secound maner of men trowes me God allmighti, and a rightfull and a
strait jugge, and þai serue me for drede of paine and noȝt for loue, ne   35

10 to] to mi mer, mi mer *subpuncted*   require] reqnre   12 reproue] repoue
no wirshipe] of wirshpipe   · 19 praier] *marg., nota*   32 with temporall] with
temporall with, *second* with *subpuncted*

desire of heuens blisse; for if þai were noȝt ferde and drede me, þai
walde noȝt serue me.

'þe þirde troues me maker of all and verrai God, both rightfull and
mercifull, and þai serue me noght for drede of ani payne bot with a
5 gudeli lufe and charite, and þai had leuer suffir all maner of paine
f. 15ᵛᵇ þene þai wald ones greue me or stire me to wrethe. | þese maner of
men are worthi to be herde in þaire praiere, for þaire will is [e]ft[ir] mi
will. þe firste maner of man sall neuir go oute of paine, ne neuir se mi
face. þe second sall noȝt haue grete turment, ne he sall noȝt se mi face,
10 bot if he amend and correcte þat drede with penaunce.'

> Capitulum 15. Howe þe spouse sawe a saint aske
> question of God, whi þe deuell trauelled so a woman
> saule, and of hir del[i]ueraunce fro þe deuells pouer bi
> oure ladi.

15 It was sene to þe spouse þat a saint of blisse spake to God of a saule þat
in a liffand woman was gretli tempted bi þe deuell, and saide, 'Whi is
þe saule of þis woman, þat þou boght with þi preciouse blode, þus
disessed and troden vndir fote with þe deuell?' To þe whilke question
þe deuell answerde and saide, 'For bi right hir saule is mine.' þan
20 saide þe lorde, 'Bi what lawe makes þou chalange to it?' þe deuell
f. 16ʳᵃ answerde, 'þou wote þat þere is two | wais: þat one ledis to heuen and
þe toþir to hell. When sho had knawen and taken avisement of bothe
þe wais, hir consciens and hir reson taght hir þat sho suld take mi wai,
and for sho had fre chose and will to turn into what wai hir had leueste,
25 sho chase freli to go with hir wil into þe wai of syne and so for to walke
in mi wai. Eftirwarde I deceiued hir with thre vices–with glotoni,
coueitise of monee, and licheri. And þarefore I sitt now in hir wombe
and I hald hir with fiue handes. With one hande I held hir een, þat sho
see noght spirutall þinges. With þe second I hald hir handes, þat sho
30 do no gude werkes. With þe þird I hald hir fete, þat sho go noȝt to
gude places. With þe firth I hald hir vndirstandinge of þe hert, þat sho
be noȝt ashamed for to sin. And with þe fifte I hald þe will of þe herte,
þat sho turn noȝt to contricion.'

þen þe blissed maiden Mari saide to hir son, 'Son, compell þe
35 deuell to answere treweli to a question I sall aske of him.' þe son |
f. 16ʳᵇ saide, 'þou art mi modir, þe qwene of heuen, modir of merci,

---

7 eftir] ofte, *Lat.* secundum   13 deliueraunce] delueraunce   28 held]
twice, second subpuncted

comforth of þaime þat are in purgatori, gladnes of þaim þat are pil-
grims in þe world, ladi of angels, moste excellent with God, and
princes of þe deuell. Wharefore bid and command þou him what þou
will, and he sall answere.'

þen þe blissed maiden asked of þe deuell, 'Fende, what entent had 5
þis woman or sho entird into þe kirke?' þe deuell answerde, 'Sho had
will for to abstene fro sin.' þen saide þe maiden Mari, 'Syn þe firste
will þat sho had lede vnto hell, wheder ledis þe will of abstinence fro
sin, þe whilke sho nowe hase?' þe deuell answerde, 'It ledis to heuen.'
þan saide maiden Mari, 'þan mai þou make no claime, for, be þe same 10
sho suld haue gone to hell for þe firste will, sho sall now go to heuen
for þe second will. Bot answere, deuell, and sai what will sho haue
nowe in hir consciens in þis point and time þat sho is nowe in þe
kirke.' þe deuell answerde, 'Sho hase | now contricion in hir saule for f. 16ᵛᵃ
þat sho hase done, and sho wepis sore, and sho purposese neuir to do 15
þe sinnes more, bot for to amend hir als mikill as sho mai.'

þen asked þe maiden of þe deuell if þere thre synnes–gluttri,
couetise of mone, and lichere–might be togidir in þe same hert and
saule with þere thre vertuse: contricion, wepinge, and purpose of
amendinge. þe deuell answerde, 'Nai.' þen saide þe blissed maiden, 20
'Telle me þan whilke exille and putt oþir oute of þe saule.' þe deuell
answerde, 'þe vertuse sall put oute þe sinnes.' 'þan,' quod þe blissed
maiden, 'is þe wai spered to hir þat ledis to hell. Bot answere me to a
question. And [one ad]vowtrer lige in waite of þe spouse for to defoile
hir, what sall þe husband do þan?' þe deuell answerde, 'If he be a gude 25
husband and gentill of hert he sall defende his spouse and put his life
in iuperde for his honeste.' þan saide þe maiden, 'þou arte werst
avowtrere, and þe saule of a man is þe spouse of | mi son, whome he f. 16ᵛᵇ
boght with his awen blude. þou hase falsli ofte times corrupted and
with violens raueshed þis spouse. And þarefore to mi son, þat is hus- 30
band beste and moste gentill of herte, and lorde vpon þe, it langes to
defende hir, and þe bothe fro hir and fro him for to flee.'

Capitulum xui.

'I am Jesus þat spekes with þe, þe whilke [was] in þe maidens wombe
verrai God and verrai man, euen in worthinis with þe fadir, gouerning 35

---

13 in³] *twice, second subpuncted*   24 And one ad] and   33 xui] xui howe
Goddes enemi hase thre deuels within him and þe dome of him (*erroneous rep. ch. title*
I.13)   34 was] *om.*

all þinges, all if I were with þe maiden. I likken ane enemi of myn to thre þinges: firste, to ane egill þat flies in þe aire, vndir whome oþir fowles takes and hase flight. þe secound, I likken him to a fouler, þat syngges in a whistill anointed with haldinge glewe, and when þe birdes
5 heres þe swetenes of þe voice, þai flie to þe whistill and are taken and
f. 17ᵃ caght with þe glewe. þe þirde, he is like to a champion þat | is firste in all debate.

'First, he is like to ane egill for pride, throw þe whilke he suffir[s] 'to haue no soueraine, bot he raisses all þat he mai with þe clese of his
10 malice. And þarefore I sall cutt of þe winges of his pouere and his pride, and I sall take fro þe erthe his malice, puttinge him in a pot of fire þat mai noȝt be slokkend, where he sall be turment withoute ende bot he amend him.

'Also, he is like to a foweler saide before, for he drawes to him bi
15 swetenes of wordes and faire heghtes all þaim þat he mai, bot he þat euir commes to him he endaungers þaime to confusion and þai mai neuir eftir rise to fredome. þarefore þe fowles of hell sall pike oute þaire een, þat þai sall neuir se mi ioi, bot euirlastinge derkenes; þai sall cut of þaire eris, þat þai sall noȝt here þe wordes of mi mouthe.
20 For þe swetenes þat þai haue vsed, þai sall fele bittirnes fro þe crown
f. 17ʳᵇ of þe heued to þe sole of þe fote, for it is riȝt | at þai suffir as mani pains as þai broght men to perdicion.

'He is also like to a campion, þat is firste in all malice. He will gife stede to none, bot he purposes to depres all. þare he sall be as cham-
25 pion, firste in all paine, and his paine sall euir be renewed and neuir faile. Neuirþeles, as lange as þe saule is in þe bodi, mi merci is redi.'

Capitulum xuii. Howe in þe howse of God awe to be all mekenes.

'In mi howse awe to be all mekenes, þe whilke nowe is sett at noȝt.
30 þare awe to be a strange walle bitwene men and wemen, for all if I might defende þaime all and hald þaime withouten walle, ȝit for þe cautell and fals sotelte of þe deuell, I will þat a wall departe þe dwellinge places of bothe, þe whilke I will be stronnge and noȝt full hie, bot of a gude mesure. I will þe windous be bright and moste
f. 17ᵛᵃ simpill. I will þe couerynge be mesu|rabili hie, so þat noþinge shewe
36 þare bot þat sweteli sauour mekenes.

2 vndir whome] vndir whome vndir, *second* vndir *subpuncted*   8 suffirs] suffir
9 þat he] *twice, first subpuncted*   mai] mai outher   10 sall] noȝt, noȝt *subpuncted*

'For þai þat nowe bigges howses to me, þai are like to maistir biggers, to whome, when þe lorde of þe bigginge comes, thai take bi þe here and drawes him vndirfete. Thai put clai abouen, and gold vndirfete. So do þere biggers to me. þai set vp clai: þat menes, þai set vp temporall howses þat sall sone faile vnto heuen; bot of þe saule, þat is 5 more precious þen ani golde, þai charge noȝt. If I will entir to þaime be mi prechours, or bi gude thoghtes, þai take me bi þe [h]ere and castes me and tredes me vndirfete: þat menes, þai blaspheme me and mi werkes. And bi mi wordes þai sett no more bi þan bi clai, bot, for-sothe, þai held þaimeselfe full wisere þan me. If þai wald bige to mi 10 wirshipe, þai suld firste bige þaire saules.

'þarefore, whosoeuir biggis mi house, of all wise charge he souerainli þat þare be noȝt one peni spended þere, þe whilke is falsli getin, for, treweli, þere is mani þe whilke knawes | wele þat þai haue f. 17ᵛᵇ gude falsli getin, and ȝit nowþir þai are heui þerof, ne þai haue no will 15 to restore ne make satisfaccion to þaime þat are robbid and spoiled, all if þai might make asethe if þai walde. Bot for þai trowe þat þai sall noȝt haue þaime in posession withouten ende, þarefore þai gife to kirkes parte of swilke gude wronnge getin, weninge þat I ware reconsiled and plesed bi swilke giftes, and oþir gudes wele and treuli getin 20 þai resereue to þaire aires. Forsothe, þis plesses me noȝt, for who þat euir wald plese me in his gifetes, he suld firste haue will to amend him of all ill, and þan to do all þe gude he might. He suld also sorowe and waiment þe sin þat he hase done, and restore, if he miȝt, and if he mai noȝt in dede, restore in will all fals bigettin gudes with full purpos and 25 will neuir to trespas so more. If he were noȝt of life to whome he suld make restorans of swilke gudes, þan mai he gife þaime to me, for | I mai f. 18ʳᵃ gife ilke man his awen. And if he mai noght ȝeld againe, if he þan with purpose to amende and with a contrite herte meke him to me, I ame riche enoghe to ȝeld for him, and I mai restore to all þat are spoiled 30 and robbid thaire gudes, other in þis werld or in þe werld þat is to com.

'I will shewe vnto þe what þe house bitakens þat I will haue bigged. In þat house is religion, of whome I ame fundament and grownd, bi whome all þinges are made and are vpstandinge. In þis house are 35 foure walles. þe firste is mi rightwisnes, bi þe whilke I sall deme þe aduersaris of þis house. þe seconde is mi paciens, bi þe whilke I sall lightin with knawlege and vndirstandinge þe dwellers in þat house. þe þird walle is mi pouer, bi þe whilke I sall comforthe þe dwellers

5 temporall] temporall gudes, gudes *subpuncted*   7 here] ere, *Lat.* crines

againe all þe fals engynes and kastes of þe deuell. þe ferth walle is mi
merci, þe whilke reisaiues all þat askes it.

'In þis walle is þe ȝate of mi grace, bi þe whilke is comon entre of all.

f. 18rb þe | helynge of þe house is charite, throw þe whilke I couer and hide
5 all þe sinnes of þaim þat loues me, þat þai be noȝt fordemed for þe
sinnes. þe louere [o]r window of þe rofe bi þe whilk þe son sall entyre
is consideracion of my grace, bi þe whilk þe hete of mi goddhede
enters to þe dwellers. þat þe wall sall be grete and strange bitokens þat
þare mai none distrue mi wordes in þat place. þat it sall be mesurabili
10 hye betokens þat mi wisdome in parti mai be comprehend of mi
creatures, bot noȝt fulli. þe simpill windous and bright bitokens þat
all if mi wordes bene plaine and sympill, ȝete bi þaime þe light of
knawlege of God sall entire into þe werld. þe roofe þat is mesurabili
hie bitokens þat þai ware shewed abill to be vndirstanden and knawen
15 what þai mene.'

Capitulum xviii. þe lorde likkens himselfe to a mighti
kinge þat hase foure þinges, and of þe tresoure houses.

'I ame as a grete kinge and mighti, to whome langes foure þinges.
f. 18va Firste, he awe to be ri[che]. þe se|cond, him awe to be milde. þe þird,
20 him awe to be wise. þe firth, him awe to be charitefull. I ame verrai
kinge of aungels and of all men. Firste I ame richeste, for I gife to all
þat þaime nedis, nor I haue neuir þe les eftir mi giftes. I ame mildeste,
for I am redi to gife [to] all þat askes, and to forgife. I ame wisest, for I
knawe what is profitabill to ilkea man. And I ame moste charetefull,
25 for I ame more redi to gife þan ani for to aske.

'I haue two howeses to kepe in tresoure. In þe tone are put þinges
þat are heui and of grete weght, as lede and oþir, and þe place where
þese are is set aboute with sharpe prikkinge pikes. Bot he þat biginnes
firste to turn þese and to bere þaime vpon him, þai are to him eftir-
30 ward als light as ani plum, þe whilke bifore were heui, and, fro he has
born þaime vpon him, þai wax right swete þat were bifore full sharpli
prikkinge. In þe secound tresori semis bright gold and precious stanes
f. 18vb and mani swete drinkes and of | gude reflaire. Bot treuli þat gold is clai,
and þo drinkes is poison.

35 'To þese two tresoure houses is two wais, þere sometim þare was
bot one. In þe entre of þe wais stode sometime a man and cried vnto

---

thre men, þe whilke went bi þe toþir wai, saynge, "Here mi wordes:
here mi wordes. And if ȝe will not abide and here, behald with ȝour
een, and see þat þe wordes are treue þe whilke I spake. If ȝe will
nouþir here nor see, handill and proue with ȝoure handes þat þare is
no falshede in mi wordes." þan saide þe firste of þo men, "Here we   5
and see we if his wordes be trewe." þe seconde saide, "It is fals all þat
euir he sais." þe þirde saide, "I wote wele his wordes are trewe, bot I
set noȝt bi þaime."

'What menes þese two tresoure houses bot mi loue and þe loue of
þe world, to þe whilke are two waies? Abieccion and perfite forsakinge   10
of a mannes propir will ledis to mi lufe, and luste of fleshe ledes to þe
lufe of þe werlde. It semis to som | þat mi lufe is grete charge and   f. 19ʳᵃ
heuenes as it were heui lede, for when þai suld faste, wake, and
refreine þe fleshe lustes, it is seminge to þaime herd and heui as it
were lede. If þai here wordes of shame or reproue, and þai dwell in   15
religion or in praiere, it semis to þaime as þai were amang prikkand
thornes, and so þai are angwisht ilke oure.

'Bot he þat will be in mi loue, late him gete him a gude will and a
continuall desire for to turn his charge to bere it, and to do it, and late
begine at lifte it soburli, and so kindeli þinkeynge þus, "þis mai I wele   20
do if God helpe me": þan, if he haue perseuerance in þat at he hase
bigon, he sall sone eftir bere with swilke a gladnes þo þinges þat
semed bifore heui and chargeous þat all maner of labour, in fastinge,
in wakinge and oþir braunches of penaunce, sall be to him as light as a
fedir of a plume. And in þat place sittes and restes mi frendes, þe   25
whilke to euell men and | slawe is, as it were, set aboute with sharpe   f. 19ʳᵇ
prikkinge prikkes: bot to mi frendes it is soueraine reste and as light as
a rose.

'þe right wai to þis place is forsakinge and forþinkinge and dispisinge of his awen will, what time þat a man hase consideringe of mi   30
passion and mi charite, settis noȝt bi his awen will bot withstandes it
with all his miȝtes, and enforses himselfe aie to hiere dedis of perfeccion. And, all if þis wai in þe biginninge be heui, ȝete eftirwarde it is
woundir delitabill, so forsothe þat þo þinges, þe whilke semed in þe
bigininge impossibill to suffir, be vse are made moste esi and light, and   35
so he sall fele wele in himselfe þat it is þus wretin: "*Iugum' domini suaue
est*: þe ȝokke of þe lorde is swete."

'þe seconde tresori is þe werld, in þe whilke is gold, precious

20 at] at þe, þe *ruled through and subpuncted*   21 if God] *twice, second subpuncted*
35 bigininge] bigiminge   36 wretin] wretin þe second tresori   Iugum] inicium

stones, and drinkes of swete sauoure. Neuerþeles, when þai are tasted
þai are bittir and venomus. Whosomeuir beris gold, it sall fall þat
f. 19ᵛᵃ when his bodi is | febill and his membris waxis waike, þe margh is oute
of þe bones and his bodi dies, þan sall he leue þe gold and precious
5 stones, and he sall finde þaime no bettir þan clai. Also, þe swete
drinkes are þe delites of þe world, þe whilke semis delitabill, bot when
þai com into þe wombe, þei febill þe hede, þai greue þe herte, and
turnes vpsodoun all þe gude hele, and so a man eftirward waxis dri
and fadis as hai dose. And when þe oure of dede comis, all swilke
10 delites waxis bittir as venom. þe propur will of a man ledis vnto þis
house, and he gase þaretowarde when he is rekles, and gifes no fors to
withstand euell affeccions þat he hase, ne he þinkes noght what I haue
made, commanded and bedin, bot what at euir commis in his thoght,
be it lawfull or vnlawfull, onone he fulfilles it and dose it.

15 'Be þis wai gose thre maner of men, bi whome I vndirstande all
þaim þat are reproued fro blisse, þe whilke loues þe werld and þaire
f. 19ᵛᵇ awen propir will. To | þere men I cried when I stode in þe entre of þese
wais, for when I bicome man in mannes fleshe I shewed to men, as two
wais, what þai suld flee and what þai suld do, whilke was þe wai to life
20 and whilke to dede (for bifor mi comminge into fleshe þare was bot
one wai, bi þe whilke all men, both gude and euell, went to hell). I was
he þat cried þus: "O ȝe men, here mi wordes, þe whilke ledis to euirlastinge life, for þai [are] trowe and bi ȝour wittis ȝe mai knawe þat
[þai] are trewe. And if ȝe here not or mai noght here, see and take hede
25 bi ȝoure sight þat þai are trewe." Right as with bodeli een ilke bodeli
þinge mai be sene, with þe een of faithe and treuth [mai be sene and
trowed þinges vnvisibill]. þare is mani simpill men in hali kirke, þe
whilke wirkes bot litill gude and ȝit þai are saued bi faithe, for [þai]
knewe me þair maker and þair againbier. þare is no man bot he mai
f. 20ᵛᵃ knawe þat I ame God, if he take hede howe þe erthe bringes furthe | his
31 fruyt, howe þe heuen sendes down raines, howe tres waxes grene,
howe ilke beste in his kinde vpstandes, how sternes in þe firmament
serues to men, howe mani þinges falles contrari to mannes will. Be þis
mai be seene þat man is mortale, and God disposes all þinges, for were
35 God ne were, in þaire þinges suld none ordir be kepid. þarefore it is
to be concluded þat all þinges are of God, resonabli disposed for
edificacion of man, ne þere is noþinge in þe werld þat is withoute

16 fro] for   18 I²] and I, and *subpuncted*   23 are] *om.*   24 þai] ȝe
here¹] he here, he *subpuncted*   26-7 mai ... vnvisibill] *om., Lat.* cerni possunt
inuisibilia et credi   28 þai²] he

reson ne vpstandes. And þarefore all [if] m[a]n, for þe febilnes of his kinde, mai noȝt vndirstand ne knawe mi vertue, ȝit he mai se it bi faith and trowe it.

'A, ȝe men, if ȝe will not knawe mi pouer and vndirstande it, ȝe mai fele with ȝour awen handes þe werkes þat I and mi saintes hase done, 5 for þai are so openli shewed þat þare mai no man dout bot þai are mi werkes. Who raised þe dede and gafe sight to þe blinde, bot God? Who put fendes out fro men, bot God? And I taght | neuir þinge bot f. 20ᵣᵇ holesom and profetabill bothe to bodi and saule, and esi for to do.

'Bot som sais, "Late vs here and proue if his wordes b[e] trewe." 10 þere are þose men þat standes in mi seruise noȝt for loue of me, ne for to l[e]ue þaire awen will, bot for to do þaire awen will with mine. þase men are in perilus case, for þai wald serue two men and ȝit þai can noȝt sereue wele þe tone. And when þai are called to rekeninge, he þat þai haue serued more sall rewarde þaime.   15

'þe second man sais, "It is fals all þat he spekes, and þe scripture vntrewe." I ame God, maker of all, and withouten me noþinge is made. I made bothe þe newe lawe and þe ald, and þai passed fro mi mouth, no in þaime is no falshede, for I ame sothefastenes and treuthe. Wharefore þai þat sais þat I ame fals, and holi scripture is vntrewe, þai 20 sall neuir see mi face, for þaire awen conciens tels þaime þat I ame God, and all þinges are eftir disposicion of mi | wille. Heuen gifes f. 20ᵛᵃ þaime light and þai can noȝt gife light to þaimeselfe; þe erthe bringes furth fruite; þe aire mostes þe erthe and makes it fruitefull; all bestis hase a certaine disposicion. Dyue[l]s knawelege me; rightwis men 25 suffirs woundirfull þinges for mi loue. All þese ȝe see, and bihald me in mi rightwisnes, and ȝe wald take hede howe þe erthe opind and resaiued wikked men, þe fire brent þe proude. So þai might also se me in mi merci, if þai tuke hede howe þe stone gafe watir to þe gude men and þe watir of þe see gaue þaim leue and stede to pas bi it, þe fire 30 brent þaime noght, heuen as it had bene þe erthe fed þaime and norished þaim. And þarefore, for þai sawe þese þinges and ȝete sais I lie, þai sall neuir se mi face.

'þe þird man sais, "We knawe wele þat he is God, bot we charge it noght." þese men sall euir be torment in painnes, for þai dispise me 35 þaire Gode and þaire lorde. Is it noght a grete contempt þat þai sall vse mi gifetes and ȝet dispise to do me seruis? And þai had of þaire

f. 20vb awen | wisdome swilke þinges as þai vse for þaire awen profite, þan
ware it bot a litill contempt.

'Forthirmare, þai þat will bigin with a birnand desire to do mi will,
to þaime I wil doo mi grace, and þai þat profetis in mi charges fro dai
5 to dai, with þaim sall I laboure, and I sall be þaire strenthe, and I sall
enflawm þaime and make þaime to desire more þen þai do. þai þat
sittes in þe sete at semis to prike, and ȝit is moste restfull, þai are in
tribulacions and paines bothe dai and niȝt and are neuir wery, bot þe
more þai suffir, þe more þai are redi to suffir, and it semis to þaime-
10 selfe right litill all þat þai do. þese are mi derrest frendes, bot þare is
woundir fewe of þaime, for þe drinkes of þe seconde tresore hows
plesi[s] oþir mikill.'

Capitulum 19. Wordes of reprouinge of certaine
sinners, and howe God sall d[e]me eftir paciens.

15 'I ame maker of heuen and of erthe. I haue thre with miselfe. I ame
f. 21ra most miȝti, | wiseste, and moste vertuous. I ame so mighti þat aungels
of heuen wirshipes me; fendes of helle dare noȝt luke on me; all
elementes standes at mi liste. I ame so wise þat þare mai none comprehend ne take mi wisdome, for I knawe all þat is, was, and sall be. I ame
20 so resonabill þat þare is noȝt þe leste worm ne none oþir beste, be it
neuir so foule, þat is made withoute resonabill cause. I ame so full of
vertu þat of me, as a gude welle, springes all gode and vertue and all
swetenes. And þarefore þare mai none be miȝti withoute me, ne wise,
no vertuouse. And þarefore þe men þat hase grete pouere in þe werld,
25 þai sine agains me, for I gaue þaim strengh and powere at þai suld wirshipe me, bot þai take þe wirshipe to þaimeselfe, as if it were of þaimeselfe, no þe wreches takes no hede to þaire awen febilnes. If I sent to
f. 21rb þaime þe lest sekenes, onone þai sulde faile, and all þinges suld | irke
þaime. Bot howe þan sall þai be stronnge to suffir mi pouer and þe
30 paines of helle?

'And ȝit sinnes more againes me þai þat are callede wise men. I haue
gifen þaim witt, vndirstanding and wisdome, þat þai suld loue me, bot
þai knawe no take no hede to noþinge bot to temporall profete. þai loke
all bakwarde to þairc delitabill desires, bot þai gife me no thanke, þat
35 gafe þaime all, for, be þai gude, be þai ill, þere mai none fele ne vndir-

12 plesis] plesi   14 deme] dome   26 þaimeselfe] þaimeselfe ne þe
wreches takes no hede to þaire awen febilnes if I sent to, *exc.* þaimeselfe, *ruled through*
35 ne] none, no *subpuncted*

stande withoute me, all if it be so þat I gife to ill men fredome to do
what þaim liste: and so þare mai no man haue vertue bot of me. And
þarefore I mai sai þe comon prouerbe þat is amange pepill, "He þat is
pacient and sufferand, he is dispised of all." So I, for my paciens, þai
hald me bot a fole, and all men dispises me. Bot full wo sall þai be   5
when I sall shewe mi dome to þaime eftir swilk paciens. þai sall be as
it were clai before me, þat falles done and hase none vphaldinge or it
come into þe depnes of hell.'

Capitulum xx. Godeli | wordes betwene þe modir and   f. 21ᵛᵃ
þe son, and also to þe spouse, how sho sall arai hir to   10
weddinge.

The modir saide vnto þe son, 'Mi son, þou art kinge of blis, lorde
abouen all lordes. þou made heuen and erthe of noght and all þat is: in
whome, þarefore, be all þi desire and all þi will done.' þe son saide, 'It
is an ald prouerbe, "þat is lerid in ȝouth is kepid in age." Right so, for   15
þou, modir, lerid in þi ȝonge age to folowe mi will, and to leue þine;
þarefore þou hase saide wele, "Be þi will done." þou art as it were
preciouse gold, þe whilke is betin oute of brode on an hard stethi, for
þou was smete with all tribulacions bifore oþir persons in mi passion.
When mi hert brake in mi passion, for mi ouirpassinge paine, þi hert   20
was wounded þarethrow as it had bene with a maste sharpe thorn, and
þou wald gladli at þat time it had be cut in sonder, if it hade plesed me.
Neuerþelesse, and þou had might haue with|stand mi passion and hafe   f. 21ᵛᵇ
hade mi life, ȝit wald þou it not bot eftir mi will. And þarefor þou saide
wele, "*Fiat voluntas tua*," þat is, "Be þi will done." '   25
þan spake Mari to þe spouse, 'þou spouse of mi son, luf mi son, for he
loues þe. Wirshipe his saintes þat are assistent to him. þai are as it were
sternes innumerabill, whose brightnes mai noȝt be likned to no temporall light, for right as þe light of þe werlde hase deference in brightnes
fro derkenes, right so, and mikill more, þe light of saintes passes þe light   30
of þis werld. I sai þe treuli þat if saintes were sene in þaire clernes þat þai
haue, þere might no mannes een bihald þaime, for þe febilnes of þe sight
mai noȝt suffir so excellent brightnes.'
þan spake þe son of þe maiden vnto þe spouse, saiand, 'Mi spouse,
þou awe to haue foure þinges: first, þou buse be redi to þe weddinge of   35
mi godhede, in þe whilke is no fleshli luste, bot þare is alþirswetteste

19 mi] mi person, person *subpuncted*   36 alþirswetteste] alþirswetteste delite,
delite *subpuncted*

f. 22ra gasteli delite, þe whilke | it semis and is acordinge God for to haue in a
chaste saule. And þarefore lat nowþir loue of childir, ne of fadir, ne of
modir, ne of oþir gudes, draue þe awai fro mi loue, for if þou do, þou
sall be like to foli virgins, þe whilke were noght redi when þai ware
5 called to þe weddinges, and þarefore þai ware excludid and entird
noght.

    'þe second, þat þou buse trowe to mi wordes, for I ame sothfaste
and oute at mi mouthe com neuir bot treuthe, ne þere neuir might be
fundene in none of mi wordes bot treuthe. Somtime I vndirstand mi
10 wordes on gosteli maner, somtime as þe lettir soundes, and þan I will
mi wordes be vndirstandin nakedli as þai are spokine, for þare mai
neuere man reproue me of lie.

    'þe þird, þe behoues be obedient, þat þare be no membre in þe
whilke þou hase trespassed, bot þou make it to do dewe penance and
15 amend it, for all if I be mercifull, I forsake noȝt rightwisnes: and
f. 22rb þarefore obei gladli and mekeli to þaime at þou art halden [to]. | And
all if þare seme to þe sometime a þinge resonabill and profitabill, ȝit
do it noȝt againe obediens, for it is bettir be obedience to forsake
and leue þine awen will, all if it be gude, and folowe þe will when it
20 is noght againe þe hele of þi saule no vnresonabill, þan þe to do þine
awen will.

    'þe ferthe, þe behoues be meke, for þou arte coupled in gosteli
mariage, and þarefor þou awe to be meke and shamefull in þe cominge
of þi husbande. Luke þi seruant be refreined and sett in gude mesure:
25 þat menes, chasti þi bodi bi discrete abstinence. þan sall þou be frute-
full with gosteli seed, þat sall profete to moni one. Luke þu florishe
and bringe furth froite in mi grace, þat all þe saintes of mi blisse, of
þe wine of swetenes þat I sall gife þe, mai haue gladnes. Mistraiste
noght for noþinge mi gudenes. I sai þe for certaine þat, right as
30 Zacari and Elizabeth had vnspekeabill gladnes and ioi of saule for þe
f. 22va child þat I had hight to þaime, right so þou sall | haue gladnes of mi
grace þat I sall do to þe, and oþir sall haue ioi of þe same bi þe. To
Zacari and Elizabeth spake bot mi aungell. Bot þi God, and makere
of aungels, spekes with þe. þai two broght furthe Jon mi beste and
35 derreste frende. Bot I will haue bi þe moni gosteli sonnis and none
fleshli. I sai þe treuli þat John was like to a rede full of swetenes of
honi, for þere entird neuir none vnclene þinge into his mouthe, ne
he ressaiued neuir bot in mesure his necessaris, ne þare passed neuir

oute of his bodi moisture of kindeli sede, and þarefore he might wele
be called aungell and maiden.'

Capitulum xxi. How Iesus þe husband-spouse spake to
his spouse in figure and liknes.

The husband Iesu spake to his spouse in figure and likenes, saiand, 'A   5
wise man in one lawefull wisdome had þe beste gold and briȝt gletir-
inge; to whome a simpill milde man com to [b]ie it. þe man þat had þe
gold | saide, "þou sall noȝt hafe þe gold bot þou gife me againe bettir   f. 22ᵛᵇ
gold and of more quantite." To whom þe toþir answerde, "I desire so
greteli þi gold þat, or I want it, I will gife what þou desires," and so he   10
gaue bettir gold and of more quantite for þe toþir bright gold, and put
it vp, purpossinge to make of it a ringe to his fingir. When a litill time
was passed, com þe firste man þat had þe bright gold firste vnto þe
meke milde man and saide, "þe golde þat þou hase boght and putt vp
is no gold, as þou trowes, bot it is a vileste froske þe whilke is broght   15
vp and norished in mi breste, and fede with mi mete, and þat þou
profe and se þat I sai trewe, opin þe place where þou hase put þe gold,
and þou sall see howe þe froske sall skipe vnto mi breste, wheþir it was
broght furth and norished."

'When he wald and opend þe deske of þe cophin where he put þe   20
gold, onone | þe froske aperid, and þe coueringe vpon iiii hingels like   f. 23ʳᵃ
sone for to fall. And when þe frende[s] of þe simpill milde man sawe
þe froske skipe vnto þe breste of þe tothir man, þai saide, "Sir, þi gold
þat þou boght is within þe froske, and if þou will þou mai þus com
þarto. Whoso will take a sharpe spere, and festened in þe bake of þe   25
froske, where is holnes, he sall sone haue þe gold. If þare be none
holnes, take þen þe spere and festin in þe froske with grete might, and
so þou sall com to þat þou boght."

'Who is þis þat hase firste þe golde bot þe deuell, þat offirs to men
riches and wirshipe, þe whilke is bot a vanite! He sais þat þo þinges   30
þat are fals are trewe, and he makes trewe þinges to seme vntrewe. He
hase in his possession þat nobill precious gold, þe resonabill saule, þe
whilke bi might of mi godhede I made more vndedeli, stabill, more
precious þan oþir sternes or planetes, and more delitabill to miselfe   34
þan ani oþir creature, | to þe whilke I ordained þat it suld haue rested   f. 23ʳᵇ

---

7 bie] lie   17 sai] saide, de *subpuncted*   21 onone] *Quire catchphrase,* þe
froske, *below*   þe¹] *twice*   coueringe] coueringe of þe coueringe   22 frendes]
frende   31 seme] seme fals, fals *subpuncted*

and dwellet withouten ende with miselfe. I boght þis saule fro þe pouere of þe deuell with bettir gold, and of more hei prise, when I gafe þarefore mi fleshe innocent and clene fro all maner of sin, and suffird so bittir a passion þat þare was no parte of mi bodi withoute wounde.
5 When I had þus boght it, I putt it in þe bodi, to þe time I wald take it to þe place where is mine awen worthi godhede.

'þis saule of man, of þis wise boght, is made and turned nowe into þe moste foule and vilest froske, skipinge aboute bi pride and dwelland in þe flowand mire of licheri, and þarefore þe deuell mai
10 wele sai to me, "þe gold þat þou boght is no gold, bot it is a froske broght furthe and in þe breste of mi luste: þarefore departe þe bodi fro þe saule, and þou sall se onone howe he sall fle to þe breste of me." To whom I answere þus, "þou knawes þat a froske is horribill to þe sight
f. 23ᵛᵃ and in voice, and venomose to þe touche, | and þarefore to me it is
15 nowþir delite no comforthe; þarefore it is norished and broght vp in þi breste. Be he þine withouten ende to dwell with þe."

'Swilke was þe saule of him of whome I speke to þe. þat saule is [as] it wer[e] þe werste froske, full of all vnclennes and luste, fede and norished in þe breste of þe deuell. To whose bodi I drowe nere be
20 dede, þe whilke bodi hanges on foure hingels, þat will sone faile: þat are strenthe, fairnes, wisdom and sight, þe whilke begins all to faile. And when þe saule sall be departed fro þe bodi, it sall onone flie to þe deuell, of whose milke it was broght vpe. And for sho hase forgetin þe loue þat I shewed in t[a]keinge o[n] me þe tormentis þat sho was
25 worthi, sho ʒeldes noght again lufe for mi lufe, bot sho reues fro me mi right, for sho serues me [noʒt] þat boght hir, bot sho hase delite to serue þe deuell. þe voice of hir praier is to me as þe voice of a froske;
f. 23ᵛᵇ þe sight of hir is to me abho|minabill. Her heringe sall neuir here mi ioy ne mi gladnes, ne hir venomouse touche sall neuir fele mi
30 godehede.

'Neuirþelesse, for I ame mercifull, and it were perseiued þat ani contricion were in þe saule, or gude will, all if þe saule be noʒt clene, if a sharpe spere prikked it, þat is to me[ne], if it be in minde, þe drede of mi straite dome, ʒit sho suld finde grace and sho wald
35 consente. And if þare ware funden no contricion no charite in hir, whoso wald prike hir with a sharpe blaminge and hard reprouinge, ʒit might þare be some hope, for as lange as þe saule leues in þe bodi, mi merci is redi.

17-18 as it were] it weri   24 takeinge on] tokeninge of   26 noʒt] om.
hase] hase no   33 mene] me

'þarefore take hede þat I was dede for charite, bot þare is none þat
ȝeldes me charite againe, bot reues me mi right. For it were right þat
men leuid so mikell þe bettir þat þai are dereli boght with grete pains
and passions. Bot nowe þe bitterere þat I suffird for þaime, þe wers
þai leue; | þe more þat I haue shewed sin abhominabill, þe more   f. 24ʳᵃ
bo[l]deli þai sin, and þarefore take gude hede þat I ame [noȝt] worthe   6
withoute cause, for þai turn mi grace to þaime into wreth. þarfore,
þou mi spouse, ȝelde to me þat þou awes to me, þat is, kepe to me þi
saule clene, for I died þarefore to þat ende.'

Capitulum xxii. Wordes of profetabill co[n]ninge   10
bitwene þe modir and þe spouse, and howe þe spouse
answerde þat sho drede two þinges.

The modir spake to þe sonnes spouse and saide, 'þou arte þe spouse
of mi son. Wharefore tell me what desire þou hase in þi saule, and
what þou askes.' þe spouse answerde, 'Ladi, þou knawes all, and   15
þarefore þou wote mi desire.' þe blissed maiden saide, 'All if I knawe
all þinges, ȝit, þat þai mai here þat standes beside, I will here þe
speke.' þe spouse answerde, 'Ladi, þare is two þinges þat I drede. þe
firste is, þat I drede for mi sinnes, þe whilke I | wepe noȝt fore no   f. 24ʳᵇ
amend as I wald. þe seconde, I ame sori þat þi son hase so mani   20
enemis.' þan þe maiden Mari saide, 'Againe þe firste I gife þe iii
remedis. Thinke firste þat all þinges þat hase life, as froskes and oþir
bestis, þai f[e]le moni times vnprofete and disese, and ȝit þare life is
noght ai, for þaire spirit dies with þe bodi. Bot þi saule and all menes
saules lifes ai. þe second: thinke þe merci of God, þat no man is so   25
grete a sinner bot, if he prai forgifenes with contricion and purpose of
amendment, his sin sall be forgifen him. þe þirde: þinke what ioi þe
saule hase þat leues withouten ende with God.

'Againe þe seconde (þat is, mi son hase so mani enemis) I gife oþir
thre remedis. Firste, þinke þat þi God and þi maker is þaire jugge, and   30
þai sall neuir deme him more, all if it be so þat he support pacientli for
a time þaire malice. þe second: þinke þat þai are þe sonnes of damp-
nacion, and | howe greuous and intollerabill it sall be to þaime for to   f. 24ᵛᵃ
brin withouten ende. þai are þe werste seruantes, for þai sall wannt þe
eretage. Bot, forsothe, þe childir sall haue þe eritage.   35

6 boldeli] bodeli, *Lat.* fiducialius   þarefore] þarefore for to   noȝt] *om.*
10 conninge] cominge   23 fele] fole   33 and¹] and þai are, þai are *ruled
through*

'Happin þou will sai, "þan it is noȝt nedefull to preche to þaime." I
sai, "Ȝis, forsothe," for amange euill men is ofte times gude men, and
þe childir of Goddes chose, þe whilke leues þe gude and dose euell, as
did a mannis son was called Waster, þe whilke wastid his fadirs gudes,
5 goinge into fer contrese fro home where he liued in sin. And so ofte
times dose moni, þe whilke eftirwarde throwe prechinge are stirred
and compunt and turnes againe to þaire fadir: þe whilke so mikill þe
more welcom home, þat þai haue before [bene] greuous sinners. And
þarefore it suld soner be prechede to þaime þan to oþir, and all if it be
10 so þat þe prechoure se þat allmoste þai are all euell, ȝit sall he þinke in
his saule þus: "Happeli þare is som amange þis compani þe whilke in
f. 24ᵛᵇ time comminge sall be mi souerance and lordes, | and þarefore I will
preche to þaime." Forsothe, þis prechoure sall haue þe beste rewarde.
'þe þird: thinke þat euell men are suffird to life for þe proue of gude
15 men, at, when þe gude men are assaied with þe euell condecions of
þaime, þai mai deserue reward for þaire paciens, as þou mai vndirstande bi ensampill. A rose is swete to þe sauour, faire to þe sight, softe
to þe touche, and it groues noȝt bot amange thornes, þe whilke are
sharpe to þe touche, foule to þe sight, and of no gude sauoure. Right so
20 gude and rightwis men, all if þai be softe in paciens, faire of maners,
swete of ensampill, ȝit mai þai noght profete, ne be proued what þai
are, bot amange euell men. Somtime þou sese þe thorn defendes and
kepes þe rose, þat it be noght taken awai before it be ripe. So is euell
men occasion to gude men (and þai be noȝt ouerpassinge sinners)
25 when be þaire malice þai are refreined, þat þai be noȝt ouir glade, or
f. 25ʳᵃ elles do outrage in ani oþir | sin. Wine is neuir wele kepid bot in
drestes of lies, ne gude men mai noght stand stabilli in vertue, and
profit, bot if þai be assaied in tribulacions and persecucions of euell
men; and þarefore support þou gladli þe enemis of mi son, and þinke
30 þat he is þaire jugge, and þat he might distruie þaim all in a moment of
time if þat it were his rightwisenes þat þai were distroied. And þarefore, as lange as he suffirs, suffir þou þaime.'

Capitulum 23. Wordes teches þe propirtes of a feined
man and of him þat is þe enemi of God.

35 'Swilke a man semis to oþir as he were semeli araied, stronge and faire
and wele sittand in þe bataile of his lorde. Bot take þe helme fro his

8 bene] *om.*   25 when] and when, *Lat.* quandoque   31 if þat] *trsp.*

heued, and he is abhominabill to behalde and vnprofitabill to all
werkes. His braine semes naked. He hase eres in his fronte, een in þe
hindir parte of his heued. His nose is cut awai; his chekes are con-
tracted, as it were a dede man. þe cheke bone | on þe right parte, with   f. 25rb
þe middis of þe lippe, is fallen awai, þat þare is noght lefte on þat parte   5
bot a naked neke. His breste is full of crepinge wormis, and his armis
are as þai ware two serpentes. His herte is fulfilled with þe werste
scorpion. þe bake is as it were a brint cole. His entrels are stinkand
and corrupt, as it were fleshe full of filth. His fete are dede and
[vn]abill for to go. And what þere bitakens, I sall tell þe.   10

'Swilke a man semis vnto men, [o]w[t]ewarde, araied in gude condicions and wisdome, and manli in mi wirshipe. Bot it is noʒt so, for,
and þe helme were taken fro his heued, and he ware shewed to men as
he is, he ware vileste of all oþir. His braine is all naked, for his vnwis-
dome and þe lightenes of his condicions be moste opin takens   15
discurres him to gude men þat he is vnworthi swilke wirship. If mi
wisdome sauerd to him, he suld wele witt þat þe more wirship he is set
in, he suld be cled in þe herder conuersacion and of more penaunce.
He hase eres in his forhede, for he desires noʒt | bot lofinge and   f. 25va
praissinge of man, for to haue wirshipe, and so he takes to him pride,   20
þare he suld be a mirrour of mekenes in dignite and wirshipe vnto
oþir, for he wald of all be called grete and gude.

'He haues his een bihinde his heued, for his thoght is euir on þaire
present þinges and noʒt of mi blis, and how he mai plese men and noʒt
me, and what þe fleshe desires and noght þe saule. His nose is cutt   25
awai, for all discrecion is taken fro him, bi þe whilke he suld deme
bitwene sin and vertue, bitwene þe wirshipe in heuen and in erthe,
bitwene þe riches [of] þe werld and of blis, bitwene þe delites of þis
shorte life and of þe life þat neuir sall ende. His chekis are contracted,
for þe shame þat he suld haue to me, and þe bewte of vertuse, throw þe   30
whilke he suld plese, are all dede. For þe shame of man þai leue sinninge, bot not for þe shame of me. þe tone parte of þe cheke bone with
þe halfe right lipe is fallen done, þat þare leues noʒt bot a naked |
throte, for þe folowinge of mi werkes and þe prechinge of mi wordis   f. 25vb
with feruent praiere and deuocion is fallen down, so þat þare leues   35
noʒt bot þe naked throte of his glutteri. þe folowinge of euell werkes
and sin—seculer besines—semes to þaime holesom and faire.

10 vnabill] abill, *Lat.* inutiles   11 owtewarde] awkewarde, *Lat.* exterius
12 manli] namli, *Lat.* strennuus   28 of¹] and   35 praiere] *twice, first sub-*
puncted

'þe breste is full of wormes, for in þe breste, where suld be minde of mi passion and of mi werkes, and of mi preceptis and lawe, þare is nowe besines of temporall þinges–coueitise of þe world–þe whilke, as wormes, bites þe consciens, þat it mai noght þinke on þe gosteli gude.
5 In his hert, where I wald dwell and mi charite suld haue his sete, þare sittis þe werste scorpione, þe whilke stangis with his taile and flaters with his face, for his speche is woundir plesaunt and resonabill, bot þe hert is full of vnright and fallas, so forsothe þat he gaue no fors all if his kirke ware distrued or he wald want his will. His armes is as þai ware
f. 26ʳᵃ two serpentes, for he strikes out [bi] his malice | to þe simpill, callinge
11 þaim with simpilnes to him, and gettis occasion for to dissese þaime wrechedeli, and, as it were a serpent, he windes himselfe in þe fourme of a cerkill, for he hides so his malis and his schrewdnes þat vnnethes mai any deprehend his sotell purpos for to disese. He is vileste serpent
15 in mi sight, for right as þe serpent is more hated þan oþir bestis, so he þis is more foule to me þan ani oþir. He bringes to noght mi riȝtwisnes, and he haldes me as a man þat wald noght venge him.

'His bake is as it were a brint cole, for his werkes, þat suld be strange and clene and honeste for ensampill to oþir, þai are nowe so febill þat
20 he mai noght suffir a worde for mi loue bot if it be for his awen profit: bot he is stronnge enoghe to þe werld. And þarefore when he wenis to stande he sall fall, for he is as dede and as blake in mi sight, and mi saintes, as it were brint blake cole. His entrols are stinkand, for his |
f. 26ʳᵇ thoght and his affeccion stinkes in mi sight, þat none of mi saintes mai
25 suffir it, bot all turnes þaire sembland fro him and askes dome vpon him. His fete are dede. His fete is two affeccions þat he hase to me: þe tone is will to amend wrannge þat is done, þe second is will to do wele. Bot þaire fete are all dede, for all þe merewe of charite in þaim is wastid awai, and þare leues noþinge bot harde bones. And so he
30 standes bifore me. Neuirþeles, as lange as þe saule is in þe bodi, he mai finde mi merci.'

Capitulum 24. Howe þe fadir spake in presence of
heuenli oste on pleininge wise, and þe answere of þe
modir and þe son.

35 The fadir spake, heringe all þe saintes of heuen. 'Befor ȝou I make mi complainte. I take mi doghtir to a man þat diseses hir ouirmikill, for he streines hir fete in stokkes of tre, þat all þe mergh gose oute.' þe son

8 fallas] *marg.* lace   10 bi] *om., Lat.* per   28 þe] *twice, first subpuncted*

answerde to þe fadir, 'Fadir, sho is | þe doghtir þe whilke I boght with   f. 26ᵛᵃ
mine awen blude, and I weddid hir to miselfe: bot sho is nowe
rauished fro me.' þan spake þe modir þus to þe fadir: 'þou arte mi
lorde and mi God, and þe membris and all partis of þi son were in mi
bodi. He is verrai þi son and mi son. I denied noþinge to þe in erthe.   5
Haue merci þarefore on þi doghtir for mi praiers.'

þan spake þe aungels and saide, 'þou art oure God, and all þat we
hafe we haue in þe, ne we nede no þinge bot þe. When þi spouse went
fro þe, we all had ioi and gladnes, bot nowe we are heui and sori, and
no woundir: for sho is taken into þe handes of þe werste terant, þe   10
whilke confoundis hir with all maner of shame and reproue. Wharefore, haue merci vpon hir for þi grete merci, for hir nede and
wrechedenes is woundir grete, and þare is to hir no comforthe no
helpe bot þou, God almighti.'

þan answerde þe fadir to þe son and saide, 'Mi son, þi plaint is mi   15
plaint; þi worde is mi worde; þi werke is mi werke. þou | arte vn-   f. 26ᵛᵇ
departeabill in me and I in þe. þi will fullfilled be.' þan saide he to þe
aungels, '3e are mi frendes, and þe flawm of 3oure charite brinnes hote
in mi herte. I sall do merci to mi doghtir for 3oure praiers.'

Capitulum 25. Wordes of Criste to þe spouse, howe his   20
ri3t suffirs euell men on thre wise and his merci spares
þaime on þre wise.

'I ame makere of heuen and of erthe. Mi spouse, þou had meruaile
whi þat I suffir euell men so pacientli. þat is for I ame mercifull. Mi
rightwisnes suffirs þaime on thre wise, and mi merci spares þaime on   25
thre wise. First, mi right suffirs þaim þat þai haue all þaire tim, and
all þaire time be fulfilled: right as a rightwis kinge þat hase prisoners,
if it be asked of him whi he slaes þaime noght, he answers, "For 3it is
no3t þe time of generall courte commin where þai sall stand to þaire
answere." 3it I support euell men vnto þaire | time come, þat þaire   f. 27ʳᵃ
malice opinli mai be shewed to oþir. Tolde I noght lange before of   31
reprouinge of Saule or it was knawen to þe pupill, þe whilke, for I
wald haue his malice shewed to þe pupill, I suffird and lange supported? þe seconde cause is, for euell men hase done some gude
werkes, for þe whilke vnto þe laste point I will rewarde þaim, and for
þai sall no3t come to mi blise I wald rewarde þaim here. þe þird   35

7-8 we hafe] we hafe in þe, in þe *subpuncted*   16 worde . . . worde] wordes . . .
wordes, *final* s *of both subpuncted*

cause: þat þe wirshipe of God and his paciens be shewed, for þe
whilke cause I supported Pilate, Herode and Judas, þat are dampned.
þarefore, if ani aske whi I support and suffir him and him, late him
take hede to Pilate and Judas.

5   'Also, mi merci spares euell men, firste, for mi grete charite: þe
paine of hell is full longe. þarefore, for mi moste charite, I support
þaime into þe laste point, þat þaire paine, þe whilke sall be so longe,
or þe latter paine begin. Also, at þaire kinde be wasted in vices, for sin

f. 27rb consumis and wastis kinde, and | þarefore, at þai suld noght finde þe
10 dede more bittir, þe kinde of þaime is febilled and wasted before, for
þe more febill þe kinde is, þe more esi is sufferaunce of dede. The
þirde cause whi mi merci spares þaime is for þe profete of gude men
and conuersione of euell: for whane gude men and rightwis are
disesed and turbled with euell men, oþir it refreines þaime fro euell,
15 or elles it encresses þair mede.

'Also, euell men somtime lifes for profete of euell men, for when
euell men se þe fall of oþir euell men and þaire wikkednes, þan
þ[i]nke þai þus: "What profete is to vs for to go folowe þaime? And
sin God is so pacient, it is bettir to turn vs to him." And so sometime
20 þai are conuerted and leues ill, for þe consciens telles þaime þat it
suld noȝt be done. þarefore it is saide þat if one be betin of a scorpion, if he eftirward anoint it with þe oile in þe whilke anoþir is
slaine, he is helid. So, ofte times, it falles þat one euell man takes hede

f. 27va to infortune of an | oþir and rese[i]ues compunccion, and throwe con-
25 sideracion of ane oþir wikkednes and vanite he is helid.'

Capitulum 26. Howe þe oste of aungels loued God, and
howe generacion suld haue bene in Paradise.

The oste of aungels come to God, and þai all saide, 'Louinge and
honour be to þe, lorde God, þe whilke is and was withouten ende. We
30 are þi seruauntes, and for þre causes we loue and wirshipe þe. Firste,
for þou made us of noȝt, þat we suld be blissed with þe, and þou gafe
vs so passinge a light þat it mai noght be discried with tonge, in þe
whilke we suld euir more be glad. þe second cause: for all þinges are
made of noght and vphalden in þi gudenes and in þi stabilnes, and all
35 þinges standes in þi will and abides in þi worde. þe þird cause: for

10 for] *marg.*, nota   13 whane] whame   16 of] of gude men, gude men
ruled through   18 þinke] þanke   24 -fortune of an] *twice*   reseiues]
reserues   31 be blissed] *twice*

þou made man of noght, and for him þou tuke manhede | (for þe   f. 27ᵛᵇ
whilke is oure moste ioi) of chasteste modir þat bare þe, þat heuens
might noght hald, comprehende, ne conclude.

'þarefore be to þe louinge and blissinge abouen all þinges for
aungels dignite, þe whilke þou hase sett vp in so grete wirshipe. Be 5
þine abidinge withouten ende, and stabilnes, abouen all stabill þinges
þat are or mai be. Be þis charite vpon man whome þou hase made of
noght. Alloneli þou, lorde, þou suld be drede for þi might and grete
pouere. Allonli þou, lorde, suld be desired for all þi grete charite.
Alloneli þou suld be loued for þi stabilnes. And þarefore be louinge to 10
þe withoute cesinge into þe worldes of worldes. Amen.'

þan answerde þe lorde, 'ȝe wirshipe me worthili for all mi
creatures. Bot tell me whi ȝe wirshipe me so for man, syn he hase
sterred me more to wreth þen ani oþir creature. I made him more
excellent þen all | oþir bodeli creatures, and I suffird neuir so mikill f. 28ʳᵃ
hard paines for all mi creatures as for him, ne I boght none so dere, 16
and ȝit all oþir creatures kepes þaire ordir bot man, þe whilke greues
me ȝit moste of oþir. As I made ȝou to gife me louinge and wirshipe, I
made man for þe same. I gaue to him a bodi as a spirituall tempill, in
þe whilke I put a saule, as ane aungell of grete bewte (for þe saule of 20
man is of aungels vertu and strenthe), in þe whilke tempill I, God and
his maker, was þe [th]er[d]e in whome he suld haue delite and lufe.
Eftir, I made anoþir tempill like to him of his awen rib.

'Bot now, þou spouse [mai aske] howe, of þese, childir suld haue
bene born if þai had noȝt sinned. To þat I answere, forsothe, of 25
Goddes charite and loue (þat ilkeane of þaim suld haue loued oþir)
and menginge togidir of kindes (throw þe whilke þai suld bothe haue
bene enflawmed togidir), þe blode of charite suld haue bene | fruc- f. 28ʳᵇ
tuose and growen in þe womens wombe withoute ani foule luste; and
so when þe child hade bene conceiued withoute sin and withoute 30
delectacion of luste, I be mi godhede suld haue sente a resonabill
saule þareto. And so, withouten sorowe or paine, sho suld haue born
hir childe and broght it furthe, þe whilke born infaunt suld onone
haue bene perfite as Adam.

'Bot man set noght bi þis wirshipe, when he consented to þe deuell 35
and desired more wirshipe þen I had giffen him. And so he fell inobedient, for þe whilke mi aungell come vpon þaime, and þan þai were

2 ioi] ioi and   9 all] *twice*   13 syn] *twice, second* (sin) *subpuncted*
22 therde] erthe, *Lat.* tercius   24 mai aske] *om., Lat.* potes querere   25 To]
twice   29 foule luste] *marg.,* nota

ashamed of þaire naked, and onone þai felid mouinge of luste in fleshe and suffird hunger and thirste. þan wanted þai me, for when þai had me þai felt no h[o]unger, ne no fleshli luste, ne sham, bot I was to þaime all gude, all swetenes, and all delite. And when þe
5 deuell was glad of þaire forfete and losse, I was moued bi pite vpon
f. 28ᵛᵃ þaim, | ne I forsoke þaime noght, bot thre maner of merci I shewed to þaime. When þai were naked I cled þaime, and I gaue þaime brede of þe erthe, and, for licheri þat þe deuell throwe þaire inobediens had raised amange þaime, I gaue in þaire sede disposicion to
10 ressaiue resonabill saule, þe whilke I suld gife þareto bi mi godhede. And all þat þe deuell stirrid þaim to for euell, I turn it into gude to þaime.

'Forthirmare, I haue shewed to þaime how þai suld life and wirsh[i]pe me, and I haue suffird þaime to comon fleshli togidir lawe-
15 fulli, noghtwithstandinge þat bifore I had gifen leue þai ware ferde to comon on þat wise. Also, eftir þat Abell was slaine, when þai had mourned and abstened fro swilke comoninge lange time, I had compassion and comforde þaime. And þan when þai knewe mi will, þai fell againe to swilke comoninge and broght furth childir, of whose
20 kinde I, þaire maker, [hight] þaim to be [b]orn.

f. 28ᵛᵇ 'Eftirwarde, when þe malice of Adam [sons] was greteli growen, | I shewed þan mi rightwisnes vnto þe siners, and mi merci to þaime þat were mi chosen, whome I was plesid with and kept fro perdicion and losse: and I wirshiped þaim, for þai kepid mi biddinges and trowed
25 stedfastli to mi bihestis. When þe time was comin for to haue merci, I shewed þaime mi meruailes bi Moises, for I saued mi pupill as I had hight. I fed þaime with aungell fode. I went bifore þaime in þe liknes of a piler of a clowde and fire. I gaue þaime mi lawe, and I shewed þaime mi preuei secretes, and þinges þat were for to come, be mi
30 prophetis.

'Eftir all þis, I, þe maker of all, chase vnto [me] a maiden born of a man and woman, of whame I tuke mankinde, and it liked me to be born of hir withouten fleshli comoninge with man, or sin; þat right as þe firste childir in Paradise suld haue bene born throwe misteri of
35 diuine charite, and þorowe charite and loue þat was bitwene man and woman withoute all maner of foule luste, right so mi godhede
f. 29ʳᵃ withoutin lusti comoninge of fleshe, and | withoute hurtinge of þe

---

3 hounger] haunger   14 wirshipe] wirshped   15 ferde] ferde on, on *ruled through*   20 hight þaim to be born] þaim to beforn, *Lat.* promisi me nasciturum
21 sons] *om., Lat.* filiorum Adam   31 me] *om., Lat.* elegi michi

clennes of þe maidenhede, tuke mankinde of a maiden. þus, þan, verrai God and man, cominge into fleshe, fulfill[ed] þe lawe and all scriptures, þe whilke were prophesied of me bifore.

'And I began a newe lawe, for þe olde was right harde to bere, ne it was none oþir bot figure of þe þinges þat I wald suld be done in þe 5 newe lawe. For in þat ald lawe it was lefull to a man for to haue mani wifes, þat þai suld [noȝt] pas to dede barein or þat þai suld [noȝt] menge with þe pupull þat ressaiued noght þe lawe bot lifed eftir will. Bot in mi newe lawe it is biddin to one husband for to haue one wife allone, and it is forbedin while sho liues for to hafe ani oþir. 10

'Whilke þat euir þan þai be þat in Goddes drede, and of gudeli charite, weddis þaime togidir for to bringe furth childir, þai are a spirituall tempill of God, in whome I will be þe þirde for to dwell.

'Bot men and wemen are weddid now in þese dais for seuen causes: þe firste, | for fairnes and bewte of þe visage. þe second cause is for f. 29rb riches. þe þird, for to knawe and haue experiens of þe vnsemli gladnes 16 and luste þat is in flesheli comoninge. þe ferthe, for þare is gediringe of mi frendes and outrage of g[l]uttiri. þe fift, for þare is pride in cleþinge, in mete and drinke, in jugelinge and oþir vanitese. þe sexte cause is þis, to bringe furthe childir, bot noght to þat ende þat þai suld 20 be norishet and taght to loue God and drede him and for to be a gude lifer, bot for to haue wirshipes and riches in þe werld. þe seuent cause is alloneli lust of licheri, as it were bestis.

'þese come togidir with one assent and acorde before þe dores of þe kirke, bot þe affeccion of þese men and þaire inwarde thoght of hert is 25 all contrari to me, and þaire will, þat is all to plesance of þe werlde, is sett before mi will. If þaire thoght of herte were to plese me, þai suld comitt þaire will into mi handes, and þai suld make þair weddinges with drede of me; and þan suld I consent vnto þaime, | and I wald be f. 29va thirde with þaime. But nowe mi consent, [þat] suld be þaire heued, bi 30 þe whilke þai suld b[e] gouerned, is awai, because þat lichori is in þaire minde and in þaire thoght, and noght mi lufe.

'Fro þens þai go to mi awter, where þai here þat þai suld be on hert and on saule, bot þan flees mi herte awai fro þaime, for þai will take no he[t]e of mi herte, ne þai will noȝt sauour in mi fleshe. þai seke hete 35 þat sall sone faile and perishe, and þai seke gladnes in fleshe, þat wormes sall sone ete. þarefore swilke weddinges are made withoute

2 fulfilled] fulfill   7 noȝt^{1,2}] om.   14 seuen] twice, first ruled through
18 gluttiri] guttiri   30 þat] om.   31 be] go bi, marginal mark   35 hete^1]
hede, Lat. calorem

þe bond of þe fadir of heuen and his anhede, and withoute charite of
þe son, and withoute comforth of þe holi goste.

'Eftirward, when þai þat are þus weddid commes to bed, onone mi
spirit gose fro þaime, and a spirit of vnclenenes comes to, for þai
5 comon noght bot fore luste of licheri, ne þaire is non oþir þinge thoght
ne spoken of bitwene þaime. Neuirþelesse, if þai will amend and turn
f. 29ᵛᵇ þaime, mi merci is redy | to tak þaime and be with þaim, for of mi
mikill merci I sende into þaire sede a lifand saule, þe whilke I made of
noght bi mi might, and I graunt somtime þat fadirs and modirs þat are
10 euell bringes furth gude childir. Neuirþeles, þai bringe furthe oft
times euell childir, for childir oft times folous, as fer as þai mai, þe
condicions of þaire bringers furthe, and ȝit þai wald folowe þaime
more if mi paciens wald suffir it. Swilke maner of weddinge sall neuir
se mi face bot if þai forþinke and amend þaime (for þare is no sin so
15 greuous bot it mai be done awai with penaunce).

'And þarefore, I sall turn me to spirituall weddinges, swilke as is
acordinge þat God haue with a chaste bodi and a chaste saule, where
sall be oþir seuen gudes contrari to þe forsaide seuen euels. Firste,
þare is desired no bodeli bewte ne shape, ne þe sight of noþinge þat is
f. 30ʳᵃ bodeli delectacion, bot alloneli | þe faithe and þe lufe of God. þe
21 second is þat þai desire noght to haue in possession bot necessaris to
lifinge, and noþinge to waste. þe þirde, þat þai fle all idell wordes and
foule of vnhoneste. þe ferde, þat þai gife no fors if þai se noght bodeli
frendes, ne fadir ne modir, bot þat I be þe lufe [and] desire of þaim. þe
25 fift, þat þai couete to kepe meknes inward in saule and outewarde in
shewinge. þe sext, þat þaire will be neuir to do licheri. þe seuent, þat
þe childir, bothe doghtirs and sonnes þe whilke þai gete, thai norishe
bi gode conuersasion to God and be gude ensampill, and bi prechinge
of spirituall wordis.

30 'þan stand þai furthe at þe dores of mi kirke, and, if þai kepe to me
þaire faithe vndefoiled and vnbroken, þai assent in me and I in þaime.
þai go furth to mi auter, and with mi bodi and mi blode þai are fede
and haues þaire spirituall delite, in þe whilke delite þai purpose and
will be one herte, one fleshe, and of one will, and I, verrai God and
f. 30ʳᵇ man, mighti in | heuen and in erthe, sall be þe þirde to þaime, and I sall
36 fulfill þaire herte.

'þe toþir temporall weddinges [begins] in þe luste of licheri, as þai

---

5-6 thoght ne spoken] spoken ne thoght ne spoken, *first three words subpuncted and ruled
through*   10 bringes] bringers   24 and] of   28 and¹] and to
37 begins] *om., Lat.* incipiunt

ware bestes, and wers þan bestes. Bot þere spirituall weddinges begins
in Goddes charite and þe loue of Gode, noght settinge to plese ani bot
me. þe euell spirit stirres and fulfilles þe firste maner of weddinges
and counceiles fleshli delites, in þe whilke is noght bot stinke and
euell sauoure. And þere men of gosteli weddinge are filled with mi 5
spirit, and þai brin in þe fire of mi charite, þe whilke sall neuir faile. I
ame o God, thre persones and one in substance. As it is impossibill to
departe hete fro fire, so it is impossibill swilke spirituall mariage to be
departed fro me or let me to be thred with þaime. Onnys was mi bodi
riuen and dede in passion, bot it sall neuir be dede no riuen more. So 10
þai sall neuir die fro me þat are incorperate to me bi a right faithe and
a perfite will; for, whereeuir þai stande, | sittis or walkis, I ame þe þirde f. 30ᵛᵃ
with þaime.'

Capitulum 27. Wordes of þe modir to þe spouse, howe
þare is thre þinges in a dawns, and of her tribulacion of 15
þe dede et cetera.

The modir spake to þe spouse and saide, 'Mi doghtir, I will þou knawe
þat where is a dawns, þare is thre þinges: vaine gladnes, mikill speche,
and void trauaile. When ani bodi sorowfull or heui entres þe dawnsing
howse þat his frende is in þe gladnes of þe dawns, þe whilke sees him 20
com in, heui and sorowe[inge], he leues þe dawns, and in compassion
makes sorowe with his frend. This dawns is þe werlde, þe whilke
turnes aboute in mani besines (and to foles it semes gladnes!) in þe
whilk are þre þinges: vaine gladnes, vnhonest speche, and mikill vaine
trauaile, for all þat a man trauailes for he sall leue bihinde him. He þat 25
is in þe dawns of þis werlde, þat takes hede to mi trauaile and to mi
sowrowe and with compassion sorows with me, as I was departed | fro f. 30ᵛᵇ
þe werld, [late him] departe him fro it for compassion of me.

'In þe dede of mi son I was as a woman þat haues fiue speres festind
in mi herte: þe firste, nakidnes shamefull and full of reproue, for I saw 30
mi moste chaste and mightieste son stand naked at þe pilere, haueinge
no maner of helinge. þe second was his accusacion, for þai accused
and called him traitur and lier, þe whilke I knewe wele was rightwis
and trewe, ne he wald greue none. þe þird spere þat was to me was þe
crown of thorn, þe whilke prikked so sharpli his heued þat þe blode 35

14 þe¹] þe spouse, spouse *subpuncted*   20 frende] frende þat   21 sorowe-
inge] sorowe   25-6 þat is] *trsp.*   27 as] and as   28 late him departe]
departes   30 saw] was

flowed oute into þe mouthe, into þe eres, and into þe berde. þe ferthe
was his lamentabill vois in þe cros when he cried to þe fadir and saide,
"O þou fadir, wharefor has þou forsaken me?" as if he wald sai, "Fadir,
þare is none to haue merci on me bot þou." þe fi[f]te spere þat went
5 throw and periste mi hert was þe bittireste dede of mi son, for of as
f. 31ʳᵃ mani vaines as I sawe þe precious | blode come oute, so moni speres of
sorowe went throwe mi herte.

'þe vains of his handis and of his fete were bored throwe, whose
paine wente withoute comforthe vnto his herte, and fro þe herte
10 againe to þe synows. And for cause his herte was frescheste and beste
of kynde, þarefore þere was a gret strife in him betwene life and dede,
and þe more bittirli þe life langwiste furth amange þe paines and
sa[r]es, and when he drewe nere to dede, for vntollerabill paine, þe
herte was nere bristinge: þan tremelid and whaked all his membres,
15 and þe heued þat was before bowed to þe breste lifte himselfe a litill
vpwarde. þe een bifore closed halfe opened, and þe mouthe opynde,
þat þe tonge might be sene full of blode. þe fingers and þe armes þat
were before in maner contracted streched oute, and in gifinge of þe
saule þe heued bowed againe to þe breste. þe handes a litill drowe
f. 31ʳᵇ awai fro | place of þe woundes, and þe fete b[or]e þe more char[g]e.
21 'þe handes wex dry, þe een blinde, and þe visage pale as dede. þe
eres herde noȝt; þe mouthe might noȝt speke. þan failed mi fete, þat
all mi bodi fell to þe erthe. Risinge vp eftirwarde fro þe erthe, I sawe
mi son more dispised þan þe leprose, and þan I committed to him all
25 mi will, for I wiste wele þat all þinge was done bi his will, for withoute
his sufferance it miȝt noght haue bene done. And þane I thanked him,
if all I had sorowe menged with gladnes, when I sawe him, þat neuir
synned ne dide euell, with swilke loue and charite suffer grete paines
for synners. And þarefore, ylke one þat is in þe werld, take hede in
30 what plite I was in þe dede of mi son, and kepe he it euer in his
mynde.'

Capitulum 28. Wordes of God as he hade bene wrothe, and þe hard sentens in dome of one.

34 The spouse sawe God as he had bene wrothe saiande, 'I ame withoute
f. 31ᵛᵃ | biginninge and withoute ende: þare is nowþir ȝers ne daies ne

---

4 fifte] firste   6 precious] *Quire catchphrase*, blude, *below*   13 sares] sawes
20 bore ... charge] be ... chare, *Lat.* sustentabant maius pondus   25 all] all mi,
mi *subpuncted*   26 his] his wele and, wele *subpuncted*

chaungeing at me, bot all time es anentes me as an oure or a moment.
Whosomeuir sese me, sese all þinge þat is in me and vndirstandes it at
a pointe. For þou mi spouse art bodeli, þou mai noȝt knawe ne
persaiue as a spirit. þarefore I sall shewe to þe what is done.

'I sat as it were in dome (for all dome is giuen to me), and þare come   5
one for to be demed at þe barre, to whom þe fadirs voice soundid þus:
"Wo is to þe þat euer þou was born"; and þus he saide noȝt for him for
[w]o þat he had made him, bot for to se[me] eftir þe custome of þem
þat are wonnt to sorowe in compassion of oþir. þan saide þe voice of
þe son: "I bled mi blode for þe, and I suffird þe bittirest pain for þe,   10
bot þou hase no parte of, no profite of, mi paine, for þou art made
str[a]unge þarefro." þe voice of þe spirite saide, "I haue soght all þe
corners of þi herte if I might finde ani softnes of charite in þi herte. Bot
| þou arte caldeste and harddest as a stone. [I] haue not at do with þe."   f. 31ᵛᵇ
þese thre voices ar noȝt herde as i[f] þai were thre goddes bot be cause   15
þat þou mai noȝt oþirwise vndirstand þis mistere. Anone eftir, þase
thre voices of þe fadir and son and holi goste were turned intill one
voice alloneli, þe whilke voice saide þus: "þe kyngdome of God is noȝt
þine ne aght to þe be ani wai."

'þe modir of merci held hir silence and opind noȝt hir merci, for he   20
þat suld be demede was vnworthi hir merci. And all saintes cried with
one voice and saide, "þis is Goddes right, þat he þis be exiled foreuir
fro his realm and his blisse." And þan saide all þai þat were in purgatori, "þare is no paine so bittir with vs þat is sufficent to ponishe þe
sinnes of him þis. þou arte worthi to haue grettir tormentes þan we   25
haue. And þarefore þou sall noȝt be with vs." þan cried he þat suld be
dampned with ane horribill voice, "Wo; wo be to þe kindes þat

[Loss of leaf containing rest of I. 28, and beginning of
I. 29. Missing material supplied from Ju.]

| entrid myn modyr wombe, of þe wheche I am made." The secunde   f. 27ʳ
tyme he cried, "Cursid be þat owr in þe wheche I procedyd on lyve fro
my modir wombe." The iiide he cryed, "Cursid be that owr þat myn   30
sowle was joyned to myn body, and cursid be he þat gaff me body and
sowle." ' Than ageyne hym come iii horribyl voyces fro helle seynge,
"þu cursed sowle, come to vs to euirlastynge deth." The secunde they
cried, "Come, cursid sowle, to owr malyce. There is non of vs þe

8 wo] þof, *Lat.* penituit   seme] se   12 straunge] stronnge   14 I] *om.*
15 if] it   25 sinnes] sinners

wheche shal not let to felle the with peyne." The iiide tyme þei cried,
"Come, cursid sowle, heuy as ston, þe whech is euir drownnyng and
neuir towchis bottom to rest. So thow shal descende into þe depe pet
depper than we, þat þu shal not stynte tyl þu come to þe deppest place
of the pit." '

Than seys our lord, 'Like as a man hauyng many wyffis, seynge the
falle of oon, turnes to anodyr þat stondys, and he is joyefull with them,
so I haue turnyd awey myn face and mercy fro hym, and turne me to
myn seruant, and I shall joye with them. þerfore whan þu has herd
thus his fall and mysery, fle the word and his concupiscens. Whedyr I
suffred nat as bittir passion for þe word þat I myght nat a kept this
soule as lytly? Forsoth I myth, but ritwosnesse askyd so, þat, as a man
offendys in all his membris, so he must make mendis in all his
membris. þerfore þe godhed, petyenge man, was in so gret cherite þat
he wold take manhed of a vyrgyne, in the whech manhed God suffred
all peyne, the wheche man owt to haue had. þerfore yf I of myn cherite
had takyn thyn peyne vpon me, stonde in verry humylite as myn
seruant doos. Schame no thinge, drede no thinge but me. Kepe þin
mouth þat, and it wer myn wyl, þu shuld neuir be in wyl to speke. Be
nat hevy of temporall thingis, | for they be transitory and I may make
riche and poer hom þat I wyl. þerfore, myn spowse, put þin trust holly
in me.'

[I. 29] These are the wordys of þe virgyne Mary to here doughtir of
ii ladyis. On was called pride and the odyr mekenesse: be þe wheche
mekeness þat blissid Mary is signyfied, and of the meetyng of þe seyd
blissid Mary to here seruantis in tyme of there deth.

The modyr of God spekys to þe spouse of her sone, seynge, 'þer
be ii ladyes. Oon is the whech has noon spiritual name, for she is not
worthi. Anodyr is humylite, wheche is called Mary. Vpon the ferst
lady þe dewle is lord. To þis lady her knyght seyde, "þu lady, I am
redy to doo for the þat I may. Onys lete me vse thin cowche, for I am
mygthy and stronge, gret hertyd. I drede noo thinge. I am redy to go
to deth for the." To hom sche answerid, "Myn seruaunt, þin cherite
is gret, but I sytte in a hy sete, nene I haue but oon sete. And þer be
iii yatis betwen vs. The first yate is so streyght þat if ony man go
þrow yt he shal be all torevyn. The iide is so sharpe þat it prykys to
the senews. The iiide is so hoote þat þer is non refreshinge but
anoon he meltis as bras. I sitte hy, and he þat wyl sitte with me,
hauyng but oon seete, schal falle vndir me into a gret myst." To

14 man] man and

whom þe dewle answeryd, "I shal geve myn lyff for the, for I set
nought be þe fall." This lady is pride. He þat woll goo to her must
go yn at iii yatis. He goos in to þe ferst yate the whech gevys all þat
he has to þe lawde of þe pepyl and for pride. And yf he have nought,
he puttys to all his good wyl how he may be prowde and praysed. He 5
gos in the secunde

[Cl continues]

| ʒate, þat trauails and dose all his werkes and spendes all his time, f. 32ʳᵃ
his thoghtes and his strengþes to mantene his pride; and if he might
win wirshipe and riches with ryuinge of his awen fleshe, he will
gladli spend his fleshe in trauaile. He entirs þe þirde ʒate þat hase 10
neuir riste, ne neuir ceses, bot brins as fire in desire to come to
wirshipe and pride of þe world, and when he haues þat lange
traualed fore and desired, he mai noght lange abide in stabilnes, bot
he sall fall downe all wrechedli. And ʒit sall þe pride abide still in þe
werld.'   15
þan saide mekest Mary, 'I sitt in a sete þat is wide and brode. And
abouen me is nowthir son ne mone, sterne ne cloudes, bot þare is a
merueilous and vnsupposeabill bright clernes, þe whilke passes fro
þe beute and fairnes of Goddes mageste. Within me is nowþir
precious stonnes no erthe, bot þare is a passinge riste in þe vertu of
God. Beside me is nowþir wall no closoure, bot þare is a glor[i]ous 21
oste | of aungels and holi saules. And, all if I sit abouen in grete f. 32ʳᵇ
hight, I here neuirþeles mi frendes þat are in erthe, þe whilke sendes
to me euirilke dai þaire sighynges and þaire wepynges. I se þaire
trauale and þaire besines, more þan is þe trauails of þaime þat 25
striues and feghtes for þaire ladi pride. þarefore I sall visit þaim, and
I sall sett þaim with miselfe in mine awen sete, for it is brode and
wide ynowe, and it mai take all.
'Bot ʒit þai mai noʒt com and sit with me, for þare is two walles
betwene vs, bi þe whilke I sall lede þaim sekirli þat þai mai come to mi 30
sete. þe firste walle is streit werld: bot mi seruantes sall be in þe werld
comforthed bi me. þe seconde wall is dede; and for comforthe of
þaim, I, þaire derrest modir and ladi, sall mete þaime in þe time of
dede, þat þai mai in þe time and oure of dede haue consolacion and
comforth. And I [sall sett] þaim in þe sete of heuens blis and ioi, and 35

19 þe] þe bright clerenes, bright clerenes *ruled through and subpuncted*   21 glori-
ous] glorous   31 firste] firste sete, sete *subpuncted*   35 sall sett] *om., Lat.*
collocabo

in þe arme of euerlastinge loue, þat þai mai reste in passinge grete |
f. 32ᵛᵃ gladnes withoute ende.'

Capitulum xxx. Wordes of oure lorde Iesu Criste till his
spouse of þe moste charite.

5 'I ame God þat made all þinge of noght for to serue man and to edefie
him. Bot man misvses into his harme all þat I made for his profite.
Forthirmare, he settes ouir litill bi God and lufes him lesse þan his
creature. The Iewes did me thre kindes of pains in mi passion. þe first
was þe tre [on] þe whilke I was festened, scourged and crouned. þe
10 second was þe irren with þe whilke þai festened mi handes and mi
fete. The þirde was þe bittir drinke of gall þe whilke þai gaue me. Also,
þai blasphemed me and saide I was a fole, for I suffird gladli þe dede,
and þai called me a lier for mi doctrine and techinge. Swilke maner of
men are nowe greteli multiplied in þe werld, and fewe dose me nowe
15 comforthe, for þai festin me to þe tre be þaire will þat is redi to sin. þai
f. 32ᵛᵇ scourge me be þair impaciens, for þare will | none suffir a worde for mi
loue; and þai crone me with þe crown of thorn of pride, willinge to be
hier þen I, and more to be made of. þai prike mi handes and mi fete
with þe iren of hardenes of herte, for þai haue grete gladnes of sin, and
20 þai harden þaimeselfe so þat þai drede me noght. For þe gall I tasted,
þai offerd to me tribulacion; for þe passion, to þe whilke I went gladli,
þai call me here a fole.

'I ame mighti to drown þaim and all þe werld for þar sinnes and I
wald. And if I wald drown þame, þan suld þai þat were lefte serue for
25 dred vnto me. Bot þat were no right, for man suld serue me for loue
and charite. If I come visibleli in persone amange þaime, þer eyne suld
noȝt suffis to se me, ne þair eres to here me. Howe suld a dedli man se
him þat is immortale, vndedeli? And ȝit for lufe and charite I haue to
f. 33ʳᵃ man I wald dye for him againe | if it were possibill.'

30 þan apered maiden Mari, to whome hir son saide þus: 'What wilt
þou, mi modir, mi chosen?' Sho saide, 'Mi son, for þi charite, haue
merci on þi creature.' He answerde, 'I sall do mi merci for þi sake.'
þan spake þe lorde to his spouse and saide, 'I ame þi God and lorde of
aungels. I ame lorde of dede and life. I will dwell in þi herte. Se whate
35 charite I hafe to þe. Heuen and erthe and all þinges þat [are] in þaim

9 on] *om.*   festened] fes festened, fes *subpuncted*   15 festin me] festind me
nowe, nowe *subpuncted*   34 herte] herte þat is bot a litill gobett, *exc.* herte, *sub-*
puncted and ruled through   35 are] *om.*

F. 33rb Book I ch. 31: St John the Baptist interprets a vision of
the Virgin Mary to St Bridget

mai noȝt comprehend me. And ȝit I dwell in þi hert, þat is bot a litill
gobet of fleshe. Whome mai þou þan drede, or whom mai þou nede,
when þou has in þe mightieste God, in whome is all gude?

'þarefore, in þi herte, þe whilke is mi tabernakyll, awe to be thre
þinges: a bed to vs at rest in, a sete to sitt in, and a light to be lightened 5
and comforthed in. Be þan (in þi herte) oure bed to rist in, abstinens
fro euell thoghtes and fro werld|li desires, and euir haue in minde þe   f. 33ʳᵇ
endeles blis. þe sete sall [be] will to abide with me. And if þou haue
som time will for to stand, ȝit it is a[gaine] kinde ai to stand. He is euir
standinge þat hafes euir will to be with þe werld and neuir to sit with 10
me. þe light sall be faith, bi þe whilke þou sall trowe þat I mai all
þinges, and I am all mighti abouen all þinges.'

Capitulum xxxi. Howe þe spouse sawe oure ladi
coroned and araied and howe Saint John declare[s] hir
vision.   15

The spouse sawe þe whene of heuen, modir of God, haue a precious
croune and passingli worthi on hir heued and hir [here] in a | woundir-   f. 33ᵛᵃ
full semillines sheweynge furth vpon þe shuldirs. Sho sawe hir haue a
cote of gold more brightli shynynge þan it mai be tald, and a mantill of
gold of þe bright coloure of heuen. When þe spouse stode all in 20
suspens, for þe grete meruaile þat sho was of so faire a vision, and was
all astoned inward in saule, anone aperid to hir Saint John Baptiste
and saide, 'Here besili what þis bitokens: þat sho is clennest maiden
and vndefoiled. þe mantil of heuenli coloure bitokens þat all
temporall þinges and werldli þinges were dede to hir. þe golden cote 25
bitokens þat sho was euir, inward and outewarde, brinnynge in godeli
charite.

'Hir sone put in hir crowne seuen lillis, and amange þaime he putt
seuen stones. þe first lilli was hir meknes; þe secounde was hir drede;
þe þirde, obediens; þe ferth, paciens; þe fifte, stabilnes; þe sext, 30
mildnes, for of mildnes sho gifes to all at askes. þe seuent is merci to
helpe in nede. In what nede þat euir a | man be, if he call vpon hir with f. 33ᵛᵇ
all his herte he sall be saued. Amanges þase bright shynnynge lillis, þe
son hase seuen stonnes moste precious.

4 in] *subpuncted*   5 lightened] light likened, light *subpuncted*   8 be] *om.*
9 stand . . . againe] stand he is euir standinge þat haues will euir ȝit it is a, *subpuncted and,*
exc. stande, *ruled through* (againe *on authority Lat.* contra)   14 declares] declare
17 here] *om., Lat.* capillos   32 in nede] *marg.,* nota   a man be] a be a man,
superior b *and* a *to reverse order* be, a man

'þe first stone is singuler vertuoste, for þare is no vertu in no spirit, ne in no bodi, bot sho hase þat vertu on more excellent wise. þe second stone is þe moste perfite clennes, for þis qwene of heuen was so clene þat one spot of sin miȝt neuir be founden in hir fro sho was
5 born into þe werld vnto þe last dai of hir dede, ne all þe fendes might noȝt finde als mikill vnclennes in hir where þai might sete þe point of a nedill. And it was no woundir if sho was clennest: for where was it semeli þat þe kinge of blis suld ligge bot in þe clennest vessell and moste worthi to be chosin befor both aungels and men? þe þirde stone
10 was hir fairnes and bewte, for hir bewte is praissed and loued of
f. 34ʳᵃ aungels and men and þe ioi of all | aungels and holi saules is filled and encressed be it.

'þe ferthe precious stone of hir crown is hir wisdome, for sho is ful- filled with God and with godli wisdome, and of hir is filled and moste
15 perfite all wisdom. þe fift is hir strengþe, for sho is so stronnge with God þat all þat is made of noght and oþirwise made, sho mai thirst all downe. þe sext stone is hir clerenes, for sho is so clere þat aungels, þe whilke hase eyn brighter þan light, are illumined of hir, and þe deuell dar noght luke ne behold hir clerenes. þe seuent stone is fulnes of all
20 delite and of gosteli swetenes, þat in hir is in þat plente þat þare is no ioi bot it is encresid be it, þare is no delite bot it is þe fuller and made perfite be it and be hir blisfull sight, for sho is fulfilled and replete of all grace more þan all oþir saintes. Forsothe, sho is þe vessell of clennes in þe wh[i]lke lai þe brede of aungels, and in þe whilke 'is' all |
f. 34ʳᵇ swetenes and bewte.
26   'Hir son put þere seuen stones amange þe seuen lillis þat were in hir crowne. Wherefor, o þou spouse of þe son of hir, honoure and wir- shipe hir with all þi herte, for, trewli, sho is worthi all maner of louynge and wirshipe.'

30   Capitulum xxxii. Howe Criste teches þe spouse þat sho sall both forsake and gadir.

'Thow awe to be as a man þat forsakes, and as he þat gedirs togedir. þou awe to forsake riches and to gedir togedir vertuse: forsake þose þinges þat sall faile and gedir togedir þo þinges þat sall euir abide;
35 forsake visibill þinges þat mai be sene and gedir togedir þinges

---

5 fendes] frendes, *Lat.* diaboli   11 aungels²] aungels and men, and men *sub- puncted*   13 wisdome] wisdome and, and *subpuncted*   24 whilke] whlke is] lai

vnvisibill. Forsoth, I sall gife þe gladnes of þe saule for fleshli luste, and þe ioi of heuen for þe ioy of þe world; þe wirship of aungels for worldes wirshipe; þe sight of God for þe siȝt of fleshli frendes, as fadir or modir, and miselfe, gifer and maker of all þinges, for þe possession left of worldli gudes.

'Tell me thre þinges | þat I sall aske. þe firste: wheþir will þou be riche in þe werld or pore?' Sho answerde, 'Lorde, I will rather be pore, for riches dose me no gude, bot bringes me into besines and drawes me fro þi seruis.' 'Tell me þe seconde. Fand þou euir in mi wordes þat come oute at mi mouthe anyþinge worthi reproue of fals eftir þi herte?' Sho answerde, 'Trewli nai, bot all is spoken eftir reson.' 'Tell me þe þirde, wheþir pleses þe bettir, þe luste of þe fleshe þat þou had before, or þe spirituall likinge þat þou hase nowe.' Sho answerde, 'I am ashamed in mi hert to þinke on þe firste fleshly luste, and it is nowe to me as it were venom, and so mikill it is nowe þe more bittir to me þat before I lufed it in grete feruoure of loste. I had leuir die þan go againe þareto, for þis spirituall likinge hafes no comparison ne likenes þereto.'

'Þan,' quod he, 'þou proues in þiselfe þat all þinges are trewe þat I haue saide. Whi dredes þou þan? Whi art þou besi in þi thoght for I drowe olonge þo þinges þat I saide I wald suld | be done? Behald þe prophetes, þe apostells and holi doctures, if euir þai fand in me aniþinge bot treuthe, and þarefore þai set noght bi þe werld nor be his coueitise ne lustes. Or elles whi hopes þou þat prophetes prophecied so lange bifore þinges þat suld come eftirwarde, bot for God wald þat þinges suld first be knawen be worde and eftirward suld folowe þe werkes, þat þe simpill might be taght to þe faithe? All þe misteris of mine incarnacion were told longe before to þe prophetis. And þe stern þat went before þe kynges, þe whilke þai ware worthi to see þat trowed to þe wordes of þe prophete, was first spoken of before, and eftirward, when it was sene, þai were þe more certified. So mi wordes sall be told before, and eftirwarde, when þe werkes come, þan are þai more euidentli trowed.

'I haue shewed þe thre þinges: firste, þe consciens of one whose syn, when I had shewed | it and made it opin knawen, I proued it with allþeremaste euidenses. Bot whi? Hopes þou noȝt þat I might, if I wald, sla him and drown him at a point? Bot for leringe of oþir and euidens of mine awen wordes, for to shewe to oþir howe rightwis,

3 þe²] þe of   10 fals] *twice, second subpuncted and ruled through*   23 noght] noght noþinge, noþinge *subpuncted and ruled through*   31 when] whent

howe pacient I am, and howe wreched in whome þe deuell hase lordshipe, þarefor, I suffir him as ȝit. For, what for þe will þat he haues to
be in sin, and what for þe luste þareof, þe deuell haues þat powere
growen in him, þat nowþir softnes of wordes, ne sharpnes of thretinge,
5   ne for no drede of hell, mai remowe ne call him fro it. And he þat haues
euir will to syn, all if he do it noght in dede, ȝit it is worthi þat he be
taken withouten ende to þe deuell, for þe lest sinne in þe whilke ani
hase likinge, ne amendes him noght, it is to him enogh perdicion.

'I shewed þe oþir two. þe deuell traueld and wexid þe bodi of þe
f. 35ʳᵇ tone, | bot he was noght in þe saule; bot þe saule of þe toþir was be-
11   shadowed with his malice. Neuirþeles, he was noȝt in þe saule, ne he
had no power of it. Bot happeli þou mai aske yf þe consciens and þe
saule be noght both one: "How þan is he in þe consciens and noght in
þe saule?" I sai þai are noȝt bothe one. Bot right as þe bodi hase two
15   eene, with þe whilke he sees, and all if þe sight be taken awai, ȝit mai
þe bodi abide hole, right so is it in þe saule, for all if þe knawlege of þe
saule and þe consciens be sometime distrubbled anentes consideracion of paine, ȝet for all þat, þe saule is noght hurte with sin ai. And
þarefore þe deuell had pouer in þe consciens of swilke a man, and not
20   in þe saule.

'For þe þride, I sall shewe þe, in wose bodi and saule þe deuell hase
all lorshipe, þe whilke, bot if he be constreined be mi power and mi
speciall grace, he sall neuir be put oute ne go oute of him. Fro some
f. 35ᵛᵃ men he gose | oute gladli and sone, and some he leues noȝt bot if he be
25   constreined agains his will. Into some þe deuell entirs, outhir for
trespas of þaire bringers furthe, as fadir and modir, or for some preue
dome of God, as in childir ʼandʼ folis: into some for misbeleue, or els
som oþir syn. þe deuell gose oute of þase sone if he be caste oute bi ani
persone þat can coniurisons or craft of castinge oute of fendis. And if
30   he cast oute ani so for vainglori or for ani temporall lucre, þan hase þe
fende pouere to entire bothe in him þat hase caste him oute and into
him oute whome he is caste, fore in nowþir was Goddes charite. Bot
fro þaim whose bodi and saule þe fende hase all in possession he went
neuir oute bot be mi pouere.

35   'Right as sharpe azelle, if it be mengid with þe moste ducet wyne,
it infectes all þe swetnes of þe wine, and is neuir departed þarefro,
right so þe de[uell] gose neuir oute of þat it hase in possession bot
be mi pouer. What menes þe wine bot þe saule, þe whilke to me was
f. 35ᵛᵇ sweteste of all creʼatures, for sho was so dere to me, þat I made mi

27 childir and] þe childir of, of *with superior mark*   37 deuell] de

synows be kut, and mi fleshe be rent into þe ribbes, for hir, and, or I
suld want hir, ȝet wald I suffir dede againe for hir. þis wine is keped in
lies and drestes, for I haue put þe saule in a bodi, in þe whilke as in a
closed vessell it was keped vnto mi will. But vnto þis swete wine þare
is mengid full euell azell, þat is, þe deuell, whose malice is to me more   5
bittir, sharpe, and more abhominabill þan ani azell. þis azell sall be
departed fro þis man be mi pouer, and in þis man whose name I tell þe
I sall shewe mi merci and mi wisdome, and in þe firste man mi dome
and mi rightwisnes.'

Capitulum xxxiii. Howe Criste likenes his frendes to   10
scolers þat hase þre þinges.

'Mi frendes are as þai were scolers þat hase thre þinges: first, a conninge
consciens abouen þe kinde of brayne; þe second, wisdome | withoute   f. 36ra
man, for I in persone teches þaime inward in saule. þe þirde, þai are full
of swetenes and of Goddes lufe, for þai sall ouircome þe deuell.   15
   'Bot men noweodaies leres on contrari wise. First, þai will be conninge, for b[o]st, at þai mai be called gude clerkes. þe second, þai will
be konninge for to haue þerebi riches. þe thirde, þai will be conninge
for to haue wirshipes and dignites, and þarefore, when þai go to þaire
scole and entirs, I go fro þaime. For þai lere for pride, and I teche 20
mekenes: þai entir for coueitise, and I had noght where I might lene to
mi heued. þai entir for to haue dignites, and þai haue envi þat oþir
suld be to þaime souerains. Bot I was demed of Pilate, and scorned of
Herode. And þarefore I go fro þaime, for þai lere noȝt mi lore.
   'Bot for I ame mild and gude, I gife to ilkane þat he askes. He þat 25
askes me a l[o]fe he sall haue it: he þat askes a strawe, it sall be gifen to
him. Mi | frendes askes a lofe–þat is, gudeli wisdome, in þe whilke is f. 36rb
mi charite; þat is þaire askinge and þaire desire, and þat [þai] lere. Bot
oþir askes a strawe (þat is, werldli wisdom): for right as þare is no
profite in a strawe bot þat it is þe mete of vnresonabill bestis, so in þe 30
wisdome of þe world, þe whilke þai seke, is no profit no none
refeccion of saule, bot allonli a nam and a vaine trauaile. For when a
man dise, all swilke wisdome gose to noght and he mai no langer be
sene of þaime þat he desired to be praised of.

---

3 a²] a bodi, bodi *subpuncted*   8 dome] *twice, second subpuncted*   12 a] as
13 wisdome] wisdome with, with *subpuncted*   17 bost] best   21 where]
where to, to *subpuncted*   26 lofe] lufe, *Lat.* panem   28 þai] ȝe   31 no
profit no] no profit no profite

'Wharefore I ame as a grete lorde þat hase mani seruauntes, þe whilke dispenses, to all, þinges þat are necessarri on þe lordes behalue. So bothe gude aungels and euell are at mi commandment. And þarefor, þai at will lere mi wisdome, þat is, þai at will serue me, mi
5 gude aungels serues þaime and refreshes þaime with comforthe and trauell of grete delite, and euell angells are assistent vnto þe wisemen
f. 36ᵛᵃ of þe world, þe whilk en|spires and teches þaime eftir þaire awen will, and þai stire grete thoght and grete trauale. Neuirþelesse, and þai wald loke to me, I suld suffice to gife þaime brede withouten trauele,
10 a[nd] to fill þaim with þe werld, þe whilke þai haue neuir ynogh of, for þai turn to þaim swetenes into bittirnes.

'þarefore, þou mi spouse, þou awe to be as a chese, and þi bodi as a chesefat, in þe whilke þe chese is clensed fro all vnholesomnes. Right so þi saule, þat is to me swete and delitabill as a chese, awe to be
15 purged and proued in þe bodi till a bodi and saule accorde in ane, and till bothe hold one fourme of continens, and to þe fleshe obei to þe spirit and þe spirit gouern þe fleshe to all manere of vertu.'

  Capitulum xxxiiii. Wordes of Criste to þe spouse, howe
  hir buse haue foure þinges.

20 'I ame maker of heuen and erthe, þe whilke was verrai God and man in þe wombe of þe maiden, þe whilke was dede, rose and stied to heuen.
f. 36ᵛᵇ þou art a newe spouse þat art comen vnto an vncothe | place, and þarefore þe buse haue foure þinges: first, þe spech of þe place; þe second, for to haue clothes seminge and acordinge; þe þird, þat þou
25 can dispose daies and times eftir þe ordinance þat is in þe place; þe fourte, þe moste be vsed to newe maner of metis.

'For þou art commyn fro þe chaungeabill world into stabilnes, þe buse haue a newe spech, þat is, abstinens fro vain wordes and vnprophetabill, and sometime fro lawefull wordes, fro commendacion of
30 þe sadnes of silens and stilnes. Thi clethis sall be inwarde meknes and outeward, þat þou hald noȝt þiselfe inwarde holier þan oþir, ne þat þou be noȝt ashamed to shewe þe meke outewarde befor oþir. Gouernaunce of þi time is–þat as þou hase time to gete þe temporall ese, so take þe nowe time to þi saule and ordein it so þat þou will neuir sin
35 agains me. Thi newe mete is abstinens fro glotoni and fro delectas-
f. 37ʳᵃ sions with discresion os | kinde mai bere and suffir, for þat abstinens

10 and] þat 15 accorde] *twice* 22 art¹] aret, e *subpuncted* 35 Thi]
af all p thi, *Lat.* quarto (af all p, *error for* ferþ?)

þat is oure possibilite of kinde pleses me noght, for I aske resonabill þinges, and þat lust be chastised.'

þan sone aperid þe deuell, to whome þe lord saide, 'I made þe of noght, and þou sawe all mi rightwisnes in me. Tell me if þis newe spouse be lawfulli mine. And for to proue þe right, I suffir þe to se hir 5 hert, þat þou mai þe bettir knawe what þou sall answere. Loues sho aniþinge so wele as me, or wald sho chaunge me for ani oþir?' þe deuell aunswert, 'Sho lufes noþinge so wele as þe, and, or sho wald want þe, sho wald suffir all maner of torment, if þou wald gife hir þe vertu of paciens. I se as it were a breninge braunde descend fro þe into 10 hire, þe whilke bindes hir hert so fast to þe þat sho þinkes noght bot þe.' þan saide þe lorde to þe deuell, 'Sai me how sho sittis in þi herte, or howe þat þe grete loue þat I haue to hir plese þe.'

þe deuell answerde, 'I haue two een: þe tone is a bodeli eye, all if I be noght bo|deli, with þe whilke I se and behald þinges so clereli þat f. 37rb þare is noþinge so preue ne so derke þat mai be hid fro me. þe second 16 is a spirituall eye, with þe whilke I se ilke paine, be it neuir so litill, and I knaw for what sin it is paine, ne þare is no sin so litill þat is not purget with penance bot I knawe it. And all if it be so þat þare are no membres more p[a]ssible þan þe eyn, ȝit wald I full gladli suffir two 20 brenninge brandes to perishe mi eyn withoute cesinge, so sho had no spirituall eyn to luke.

'Also, I haue two eris: one bodeli ere, with þe whilke I here and knawe whateuir be spoken, be it neuir of so preue wise. þe second is spirituall, with þe whilke I se ilke thoght and effeccion þat is to sin, be 25 it neuir so preue, bot it be done awai with penance. þare is a pain of hell þat boiles vp as maste hate birninge brase, þe whilke I wald suffir to flowe into mine eres withoute cesinge, so þat sho suld here noþinge with spirituall eres. I haue | also a spirituall herte, þe whilke I wald f. 37va withoute cesinge to be kutt into smale gobettes and ai to be renwed to 30 þat torment, so þat hir hert wer cold in þi loue.

'Bot sin þou art rightwise, tell me one word þat I sall aske: whi loues þou hir so wele, or whi hase þou noȝt chosen to þe one holier, one richer and a fairrer?' þe lorde answerde, 'For right wald so, and asked at it suld be so. þou was made of me, and þou sawe all rightwisnes in 35 me. Tell þou me, þat sho mai here, what right was it, þat þu, euell, suld fall, or what was þi thoght when þou fell?' þe deuell answerde,

17-18 and I knaw ... so litill] *twice, first* (knawe) *subpuncted and ruled through* 20 passible] possible, *Lat.* passibiliora 22 luke] luke to 25 and] *twice, first subpuncted* 28 flowe] folowe, *first* o *subpuncted*

'I sawe thre þinges in þe: I sawe þi blis, and þi honoure aboue all þinges, and I thoght it mi blisse. And þarefor, beinge proude, I thoght noght allonli to be þi pere bot also to be abouen þe. þe second, I sawe þe more mighti þan ani oþir þinge; þarefore ȝete I coueted to be more mighti þan þou. þe þird, I sawe þinges þat were to come, and for þi blis and wirshipe was withoute begininge and suld be withoute ende, |

I had envi to þe, and I thoght þat I wald euir be turmentid with þe bitterest paine, at þou might distroied be and di, and in þat thoght I fell; and þarefore was helle made.'

þe lord saide, 'þou asked of me whi I loue so wele þis woman. Forsothe, for I chaunge all þine malice into gode. For þou was proude, and wald haue me þi maker to be þi pere, þarefore I meke me in all þinges, and I gedir sinners to me, and makes me like to þaim and gifes þaime mi blis. Also, for þou had so sh[r]ewed a desire þat þou wald be more of pouer þan I, þarefor I make sinners to hafe powere on þe, and for to be mighti with me. þe þird, for þou had enui to me, I ame so charitefull þat I wald offir miselfe for all oþir. Sai þou þan, deuell, þat þis woman mai here, syn þi derke hert is illumined, what maner of lufe and charge I haue to hir.'

þe deuell answerd, 'If it were possibill, þou wald moste gladli suffir

in ilke of þi membres | swilke one paine spiritually as þu suffird ones in all þe membris vpon þe crose, or þou wald forgo hir or wannt hir.'

þan saide þe lorde, 'Syn þan I am so mercifull þat I deny no merci to him þat askes, aske þou mekeli mi merci and þou sall hafe it and [I sall] gife it to þe.' þe deuell answerde, 'I sall noght do þat; for when I fell, to sin, to euell thoght and euell speche, paine was made a statut, and ilkea spirit þat fell sall haue his awn paine. And þarefore, or I suld ones bowe mi kne bifor þe, I had leuer swolowe all painnes within me, as lange as þe mouthe miȝt opin or spere to paine.'

þan saide þe lorde to his spouse, 'Lo, howe indurat is þe prince of þe world, and howe mighti he is agains me, suffird of mi preue rightwisnes. I miȝt forsothe, and I wald, distroye him bi mi might in a point, bot I do him no more wrange þan to mi gude aungell in heuen. When

time commis þat nowe drawes nere, I sall | deme him with all his folowers. And þarefore, mi spouse, go furth ai in gode werkes, and lufe me of all þi hert, and drede noþinge bot me. I ame lorde aboue þe deuell and aboue all þinges þat is.'

---

6 begininge] begiminge   11 gode] gode þou, þou *subpuncted*   14 shrewed]
shewed, *Lat.* prauam   21 membres] *Quire catchphrase,* swilk one, *below*   23 I
am] *trsp., superior marks*   24–5 I sall] *om.*   35 go] gose

Capitulum xxxv. Howe Mari teches þe spouse howe
sho sall take hede to þe passion of hir son.

Mari spake: 'Doghtir, take hede to þe passion of mi son, whose
membres were to me as mine awen membres, and as mine awen hert,
for as oþir childir were wonnt to be in þair modirs wombe so was he in 5
mine. Bot he was conceiued of a brinnande charite of Goddes lufe:
oþir are conceiued be luste of fleshe; and þarefore John his awntis son
sais wele, "*Verbum caro factum est.*" þat menis: "God þus is becomen
man." For bi charite he come and was in me. A worde, and lufe, made
him to be within me. Forsothe, he was to me as mine awne hert. þare- 10
fore methoght, when he was born of me, as halfe mi hert was born and
passed oute of me, and when he suffird, me thoght | þat halfe mi hert f. 38ᵛᵃ
suffird. Right as þat þinge þat is halfe within and halfe withoute, if þe
part withoute be prikked, als mikill paine felis þe parte þat is within,
right so when mi son was scourged and prikked, it was to me as mine 15
awen hert had bene scourged and prikked.

'Also I was nerere in þe passion and I went noȝt awai. I stode
nerrere to his crosse, and right as þat prikkes sarer and sharplier þat is
nerest to þe hert, so was mi sorowe more greuouse þan was ani oþir
þat stode beside. When he loked fro þe crosse to me and I to him, þan 20
went þe teres oute of mi eyn as blode oute of vainnes; and when he
sawe me in þat sorowe, it encresid so his sorowe þat þe sorowe of his
awen woundes were noght allmoste felid, for þe paine he had of þe
sorowe he saw in me. And þarefore I sai to þe plainli, þat his sorowe
was mi sorowe, for his hert was mi hert. 25

'Right as Adam and Eue sald þe werld for ane appill, so mi son and I
boght againe þe werld as with one hert; and þarefore, mi doghtir,
þinke howe it | stode with me in þe dede of mi son, and it sall noght f. 38ᵛᵇ
þan be greuouse to þe, ne heuy, to forsake þe werld.'

Capitulum xxxvi. Howe þe lorde answerd to þe aungell 30
þat praide for þe spouse, and of thre maner of merci

The lorde answerde to þe aungell þat praide for his spouse, 'þou art as
it were þe knight of a lorde, þat put neuir awai his helme for irksomnes, ne for drede turnes neuir awai his eyn fro þe bataile. þou arte
stabill as ane hill, breninge as a flawme of fire. þou arte so clene þat in 35

7 John] *twice, first ruled through*   24 to] *twice, first subpuncted*   34 his] *twice, first subpuncted*

þe is no filth. þou askes merci to mi spouse, and, if þou knawe and se all þinges in me, ȝit, þat mi spouse mai here, sai what merci þou askes to hir.

'For þare is thre maner of merci. One merci is, bi þe whilke þe bodi
5 is ponished and þe saule is spared, þat was gifen to mi seruant Job, whose fleshe was ponished, bot þe saule was kepit. þe second merci |
f. 39ʳᵃ is, bi þe whilke nouthir þe bodi ne þe saule feles no haues paine, as þare was a kinge, þat was in all maner of lustes, and neuir felt whils he leued sorowe ne paine to bodi ne to saule. þe þird merci is, throw þe
10 whilke bothe þe bodi and þe saule are ponished while þai are togidir, þat þare be tribulacion in bodi and sorowe in hert, as Petir had, and Paule, and oþir saintes.

'For þare is thre maner of men in þe world. þe firste falles into syn and rises againe. I suffir swilke men sometime to be turbled and
15 disesed in body, þat þe saule be saue. þe second wald euirmore life þat þai might euirmore sin. þai haue all þaire will and hert in þe werld, and if þai ani time do gude for me, þai do it in þat entent þat þe temporall gudes suld growe to þaime and encrese. To þese men I gife nowþir paine of bodi ne gret sorowe of herte, bot þai are left to þaire
20 awen power and to þaire awen will, for þai sall haue here reward for þe
f. 39ʳᵇ lest | gude þat euir þai did for me, þat þai be turmentid and punished withoute ende; for, sine þaire will is withoute ende to sin, þair paine sall haue none ende.

'þe þirde is þe state of [þa]me þe whilke hase more drede to sin
25 agains me and to offende mi will þan of ani paine, and þai had leuir be ponished withoute [en]de with intollerabill paine, or þai wald of purpose, and wittingli, stire me to wrethe. To þese maner of men is gifen tribulacion of bodi and of hert, as to Petir and Paule, þat þai amend all þat þai haue trespassed in þis werld; or for encrese of þaire
30 blis and for ensampill of oþir þai are purged a time.

'This thre maner of merci I haue done in þis kyngdome with thre persones whose names are knawen to þe. þarefore, þou aungell mi seruant, what merci askes þou to mi spouse?' þe aungell saide, 'Merci of bodi and saule, þat sho amend all þat sho hase sinned in þe werld,
35 þat no sin of hir come into þi dome.' þe lorde saide, 'Be it eftir þi will.'
f. 39ᵛᵃ þan spake þe lorde to þe spouse, 'þou art mine: | þarefore, as it likes and pleses me, I sall do to þe. Loue noþinge as me. Clens þou þe

---

14 men] *twice, second ruled through*   15 þe saule] *twice, first ruled through*
21 turmentid] turmendtid   24 þame] whome   26 ende] aide, *Lat.* in eternum   33 spouse] spo spouse

euirilke oure beseli fro syne with þe counsell of þaime to whome I
haue committed þe. Hide no syn, no leue none vndiscussed. Hald no
syn light syn, ne rekles none, for all þat ar reklest of þe, I sall bringe
þaim again to minde and to dome. Ne þare sall no sin þat þou hase
done come to my dome, þe whilke is ponyshed in þi life with penance. 5
And þe synnes þat pennance is noght done fore, outhir þai sall be punished in purgatori or bi mi oþir preuei dome but if þai be amended
here be satisfaccion.'

Capitulum xxxvii. Howe þe modir comend[s] hir son of
thre godes.   10

The modir spake. 'My son had thre godes. Firste, þare had none so
delicate a bodi as he, for it was of þe two beste kyndes, godhede and
manhede, and so clene þat, right as þare is no spot in þe fairest eye,
right so þare might no deformite be funden in his bodi. þe seconde
gude was þat he | synned neuir, for oþir childir sometime hase þaire   f. 39ᵛᵇ
fadirs syn and þaire awen bothe. Bot, forsothe, þis son synned noght: 16
and ȝit he bare þe charge for þe sin of all oþir. þe þird gude was þat
some dies for Goddes lufe for þe more rewarde: he dies as wele for his
enemis as for me, and oþir frendes of him.

'Bot when his enemis crucified hym, þai did foure þinges to him.   20
First, þai crouned him with thornes. þe second, þai persed his handes
and his fete with nailes. þe þird, þai gafe him gall to drinke. þe fird,
þai thirled his side.

'Bot I make nowe mi plaint þat mi son is mikill more bittirli festined
to þe crosse of his enemis þat nowe leues in þe werld þan þat tim be þe 25
Jewes. For all if þou sai þat it mai noȝt be so (for it is impossibill to him
nowe to die), neuirþeles, þai crucified him with þaire awen synnes and
vices. As, if a man wald do reproue and hurt þe [i]mage of aneoþir, all
if it might fele no | hurt, ȝit is he worthi blam, as if he hurt, for his euell f. 40ʳᵃ
will, right so þe vices and þe synnes throwe þe wilke þai crucifi mi son 30
gosteli are to him more greuouse and more abhominabill þan þe
synnes of þaime þat crucified hym in bodi.

'Bot happeli þou will aske howe þat þai haue crucified him. Forsothe, þai put him firste on þe crosse, þe whilke þai haue ordeyned for
him, when þai set noȝt be þe precepts ne commandmentes of þaire   35

6 fore] fore bot, bot *subpuncted*   9 comends] comend   24 is] is now, now
subpuncted   26 so] so þat, þat *subpuncted*   28 image] þamage
32 synnes] synners

maker and lorde. And þai vnhonest hym, as it were with spittinge, when he warnes [þa]im be his seruantes þat þai suld serue him. Bot þai set noȝt bi þaime, bot dose what þaime likes.

ʿþan þai crucified þe right hand when þai hald right fore wrange,
5 and sais, "Syn is noȝt so greuouse ne so odiouse to God as it is saide, ne God punishes no man withouten ende, bot he hase maneshet him for to make him at drede. Whareto boght he man if he wald [h]e
f. 40ʳᵇ pereshed?" Thai take no hede þat þe leste syn, if a man | haue delite þarein, is ynowe to euirlastinge turment, and þat God sall noght leue
10 þe lest syne vnponished, ne þe leste gude dede vnrewarded. þarefore sall þe paine be euirlastinge, for þai hade will euir to syn, þe whilke will mi son, þat behaldes all hertes, alowes for dede: for right as þai haue þe will þai wald haue þe dede, if mi son suffird it.

ʿþan þai crucifie þe left hand, þat turnes vertu into vice, and in pur-
15 pose for to sin to þe ende of þaire life, saiand, "We sai anes at oure ende, 'God haue merci of me' (id est, miserere mei deus): þe merci of God is so mikill þat we sall haue forgifnes." Forsothe, it is no vertu for to hafe will at syn and noght to amende, for to will and desire rewarde and noght for to trauaile, bot if þare were contricion in hert and þat he
20 wald gladli amend if he might, for sekenes or for oþir impediment.

ʿEftir þis þai crucified his fete in doynge of syn, ne þai þinke noȝt ones on þe bittir paines of mi son, ne þai thanke him noght ones of þe
f. 40ᵛᵃ inwarde partis | of þaire hert and sais, "O full bittir was þi passion, God. Louinge and thanke be to þe for þi dede." þus sai þai neuir. þai
25 crown him with þe crown of thornes and of scorn, when þai skorn his seruauntes, and when þai hald vanite to serue God þai gife him galle to drinke (and when þai are glad and reioise þaime in syn, ne þai will noȝt enes þinke howe greuous syn is). þai thirll his side, when þair will is to haue perseuerans in syn.

30 ʿI sai þe treuli, and þou mai tell þat to mi frendes, þat þis maner of pupill bifore mi son is more vnriȝtwis þen þai þat demed him, more vnmercifull þen þai þat demed him or crucified him, more vnwise þan þai þat solde him, and more peine is ordeined for þese men þen for þaime.

35 ʿForsoth, Pilate knewe wele þat mi son had noȝt trespassed, ne was worthi no dede, and ȝete for he drede to lose temporall pouer, and sedi-cion of þe Jewes, he demed as agains his will in maner mi son to þe dede. What suld þere men drede and þai serued him, or what suld þai lose of

þair awen wirshipe and dignite if þai wirshiped him? And þarefore |
þai sall be demed more greuosli þan Pilate, for þai ar wers þan he in   f. 40ᵛᵇ
þe sight of mi son. For Pilate demid at þe askinge and will of oþir with
a maner of drede, bot þere pepill demes him be þaire awen will withoute ani drede when þa [vn]wirship him [bi] syn, fro þe whilke, and   5
þai wald, þai might abstene, bot þai abstene not fra sin, ne þai are not
shamed for `syne´ þat is done, for þai considir not, ne takes no hede,
þat þai ar vnworþi Goddes benefice þat serues him not.

   'þai are wers þen Judas, for when Judas had betraised him, he wiste
wele þat he was God, and he wist wele þat he had synned grettli agains   10
him, bot he dispaired and hasted his daies to hell, trowynge himselfe
vnworthi to life. Forsothe, þase men knawes wele þaire synnes, and þai
take perseuerauns in þaime. And þai will haue no contricion in hert, bot
þai wald, with violence and might, gete heuen, and do no gude þarefore:
bot for a vaine hope þai wene to haue it, taken no hid þat it sall be giuen   15
to none | bot to þe werker and to him þat suffirs somwhat for God.   f. 41ʳᵃ

   'Also, þai are wers þen þai þat festened him vnto þe crosse, for
when þai saw þe werkes of mi son (þai were gude)–howe he raised þe
dede, clensed þe leprows–þai thoght þat he did swilke þinges as þai
herd noȝt done before, and vncustomabill meruails: "He smites   20
downe when he will, with a worde. He knawes oure thoghtes. He dose
what he will. If he go furth on þis wise, we sall all be soiet to him and to
his pouere." And þarefore, at þai suld noȝt be soiets to him, tha crucified him for envye. Forsothe, if þai had knawen þat he had bene þe
kynge of blis, þai wald neuir haue put him on þe crosse.   25

   'Bot þese men sese his werkes euirilk dai, bothe grete and mereuei-
lous. þai vse his benefice, and þai here how þai suld serue him and
come to him, bot þai þinke þus in þaire hertes: "If all temporall gudes
suld be forsaken, if his will and noght oures suld be done, it suld be
heui and intollerabill." And þarefore, dispisynge | his will, [þ]a[t] it   f. 41ʳᵇ
suld noght be abouen þaire will, þai crucified mi son be þaire indurat   31
and hard hert, ekynge, againe þaire awen consciens, syn vnto syn. And
þarefore þai are weres þen þai þat festenid him vpon þe crosse, for þe
Jewes did it for envye, and for þai wist noȝt þat he was God, and þese
men dose it of a malice and of presumpcion for cause of þaire awen   35
luste, þe whilke þai will noght wannt. And þarefor þai do more paine

---

  1 þarefore] *twice, second subpuncted*   5 vnwirship ... bi] wirship ... for, *Lat.*
inhonorant per   fro] for   12 knawes] *twice, second subpuncted*   13 per-
seuerauns] perseuerauins   30 þat] and   31 noght] *marg.,* þei vse hys beny-
fice   32 againe] agaaine   36 do] do no

to him spiritualli þan þai did bodeli, for þese men are abowt againe, and so ware þai noȝt þat time. þarefore, spouse, be obeisant to mi son and drede him, for he, right as he is mercifull, so is he rightfull.'

Capitulum xxxviii. Wordes of þe fadir to þe son how he
5   assignes him to þe newe spouse.

The fadir spake to þe son: 'I come with charite to þe maiden, and I take þi verrai bodi. þarefore þou arte in me and I in þe. Right as fire and hete is neuir disseiuerde, [so it is impossibill to disseiuer þe
f. 41ᵛᵃ godhede] fro manhede.' þe son answerde, | 'All blisse and wirshipe be
10   to þe, fadir. Be mi will in þe and þine in me.' þe fadir saide againe, 'Son, I assigne to þe þis newe spouse as a shepe to be gouerned and norishet, of whame, as þe lorde of þe shepe, þou sall haue chese to þi fode, milke to drinke and wole to þi cleþinge. And þou, spouse, sall obei to him, and haue thre þinges: þe moste be pacient, obedient, and
15   gladli redi.' þan saide þe son to þe fadir, 'þi will is with pouere, power with mekenes, mekenes with wisdome, wisdome with merci. þi will, þat is and sall be withoute bigynninge and withoute ende, be made and fulfilled in me. I take hir to me into mi charite, into [þ]i pouere, into þe gouernance of þe holi goste, for we are noȝt thre goddes bot
20   one.'

þan saide þe son to his spouse, 'þou hase herd howe þe fadir hase assigned þe to me as a shepe. þarefore þe buse be sympill and pacient as a shepe, fructuouse to norishynge and to clethinge.

'þare is thre men in þe werld. þe firste is naked. þe second is thirsti.
f. 41ᵛᵇ þe þird is houngry. þe first | betakens þe faith of mi kirke, þe whilke is
26   naked, for all men are ashamed to speke mi faithe and mi command- mentes, and, if ani speke it, þai are scorned and dispised, and reproued as liers. þarefore, mi wordes þat commes oute of mi mouthe, as it were woll, sall clethe þis faithe, for right as woll groues bi hete in
30   þe wombe of þe shipe, so, be þe hete of mi godhede and manhede, mi wordes passes furthe into þi herte, þe whilke sall clethe mi holi faithe bi witnes of treuthe and of wisdome, þe whilke sall proue mi faithe suthfaste, þat nowe is halden bot vaine. And so þai þat before hase bene slawe to cleth mi faithe with þe werkes of charite, throwe þe
35   charite of mi wordes be þai turned and kindeled againe to speke trais- teli and to wirke strangeli.

6 spake] *twice*   8-9 so . . . godhede] *om., Lat.* sic deitatem . . . impossibile erit
separari   10 me] mine, in *subpuncted*   18 þi] mi, *Lat.* tuam

'þe second betakens mi frendes, þe whilke, as þe thirsti, desires þat mi wirshipe were perfite, and þai are greteli distrubled of vnwirshipe done to me. þai, when þai [here],

[Loss of two leaves containing rest of I. 38, 39, 40, 41 (beg.) Missing material for chs. 38, 41, supplied from Ju.]

| are refreshid with þe swetness of myn wordis and with gret cherite to   f. 34ᵛ
her whatkenes grace I geve to synneris. þe iiide betokenys them þat   5
thinkes in þer herte thus: "Yf we knew the wil of God and hou we
might leve and wel be infoormyd of good weye, we wold gladly do þ[o]
þingis þat we might." These are hungry to knowe myn weye, and noo
man can fylle them, for no man shewys perfitly þo þingis þat are to be
doone. And yf they telle, yit noo man levys aftir them. þerfore I myn-   10
self shal shewe them what þei shal do. þerfore þu myn spouse, whech
art myn shepe, kepe pacyens and obediens. þu art myn and þerfore þu
must folow myn will. And he þat wil folow þe wil of anodir man owys
to haue iii thingis. þe first, he must [b]e of on concent. þe iide, he
must do like werkis, and þe iiide, he must withdrawe him fro his   15
enemyes. Whech ar myn enemyes but pride and all synnes? þerfore
fro þese | þu must withdrawe þe and þu coueyte to folowe myn will.'   f. 35ʳ
  [I. 41] | These were the wordis of oure creatore, the heuenly com-   f. 35ᵛ
pany and his spowse beynge present, and hou þe seide oure makere
compleyned of fyue kenys men, þat is the Pope with his clergye, and of   20
ylle laymen, and of Juys and paynemys, and of helpe sent to his frendis,
be þe whech all men are vndirstondyn, and of the most cruel sentens
gevyn ageyns his enemyis.
  'I am makere of all thingis. I was begotyn of myn fadyr before
Lucyfer, schinynge and inseparatly in my fadir, and myn fadir in me,   25
and oon spirit in vs bothe. þerfore is oon God the fadir, the sone and
the holi gost, and nat iii goddis. I am he þat promysid Habram euir-
lasteinge heritage and brought myn pepill forth fro Egipte by Moyses.
I am þe same the whech spac in prophetis. Myn fadir send me into þe
wombe of a maydin, not departinge him fro me but abidynge insepara-   30
billy with me, þat man goinge awey fro God shuld turne ageyne | be
myn cherite onto God. Now ye myn company of seyntis beinge   f. 36ʳ
present, the whech sees and knowys all thinge in me, neuirtheles, for
the cogniscioun and instruccioun of this present spowse, þe whech

3 here] *om.*   7 þo] þat   14 be] he

may not vndirstonde spiritual thingis but be bodyli exsamplis, þerfore
I compleyne befor you of these fyve men stondyng here present, þat
thei hath offendyd manyfold weyis. Likewise as be Israel name was
vndyrstondyn myn pepil of Israel, so now be þese fyue men I vndir-
5 stonde all the men of this word. The first is the gouernor of the chirch
and all clergie. The iide is ylle lay men. þe iiide the Jewys. þe iiiite is
the paynemis. The vte is myn frendis. But of the Jury I outtake [and
make]

[Cl continues]

f. 42ʳᵃ | excepcion of all þe Jewes þat are preueli cristened, and þai serue me
10 with a clene charite, and with a right faith and a perfite werke in
preueite. And for þe painym, I make excepcion of all þo þat wald
gladli walke in þe wai of mi commandmentes, if þai wist howe, or if þai
were taght, þe whilk also dose gude werkes as wele as þai can and mai.
þese sall noȝt be iuged with ȝou. Bot nowe I pleine on þe heued of mi
15 kirke, þat sittis nowe in mi sete, þe whilke I toke to Petir and to his
successours to sit in a threfolde dignite and auctorite: first, for to haue
auctorite to bind saules and vnbinde þaime fro sin; þe seconde, to
opin heuen to þaime þat dose penaunce; þe þird, for to spere and
close heuen to þaim þat are cursed. Bot þu þat suld vnbind saules and
20 bringe þaime to me, þ[ou] ar[t] trewli þe slaer of saules. For I ordaind
Petir for to be sheperd and keper togidir of mi shepe, bot þou dis-
f. 42ʳᵇ parpels þaim | and all tohurtes þaime.

'þou art wers þan Lucifere. He had envi to me, and desired to slee
none bot me, þat he might be lord in mi stede. Bot þou art so mikell
25 wers þen he, þat noght alloneli þou slaes me be þine euell, throwe þe
whilke þou puttes me fro þe, bot also þou slaes oþir saules be þin euell
ensamepill. I boght saules with mi blode, and I committed þaime to þe
as to mi trewe frende; and þou betakes þaime againe vnto þe enemi fro
whame I boght þaime.

30 'þou art more vnrightwis þan Pilate, for he demed noȝt to dede bot
me: þou demes noȝt allonli me as no lorde, no worthi ne gude, bot also
þou dampnes þe innocent saules and leues þe gilti vnponished. þou
art more enemi to me þen Iudas, þat solde me allone: bot þou selles
both me and innocent saules for a [fo]ule wynynge of a vaine name.
35 þou art more abhominabill to me þan þe Iewes, for þai crucified

7-8 and make] *om.*   17 seconde] seconde to haue, to haue *subpuncted and ruled*
through   20 þou art ... slaer] þai are ... slaers   26 slaes] slaees
34 foule] saule

alloneli mi bodi. þou crucifies and punishes mi chosen saules, to whame
þi malice is wers and sharper|þan ani swerde. And þarefore, for þou arte   f. 42ᵛᵃ
like to Lucifere, more vnrightwis þan Pilate, more enemi þan Iudas,
more abhominabill þen þe Ieues, I mai bi right compleine vpon þe.'

þe lorde said to þe lewed pepill, 'For þi profit I made all þinges.   5
þou sometime consentid in me and I in þe. þou gafe me þi faithe, and
þou hight me with othe and swerynge þat þou suld serue me. þou hase
nowe left and gone fro me, as a man þat knawes noght his God. þou
takes mi wordes as lies, mi werkes for vanite. þou sais mi will and mi
biddynge are ouir heui to bere, and greuouse. þou hase broken þi   10
faithe þat þou hight, and þe athe þat þou made. þou hase left and forsaken mi name, and þe felishipe of mi saintes, and þou hase chosen
felishipe with fendes. þou thoght þare was nothinge worthe to be
made of bot þiselfe. All þinges þat are mine and þat I haue biddin do,
þou haldis hard to do, and what likes þe, þat is esi. And þarefore, I   15
make plaint worthily vpon þe, for þou hase broken all þine [faithe] þat
þou gafe me in baptime and eftirward. Forthir|mare, for þe charite þat   f. 42ᵛᵇ
I shewed þe in worde and dede, þou reproues me as I ware a lier, and
for mi passion þou calles me foole.'

þe lorde sais to þe Iewes, 'I began with 30u mi charite. I chese 30u   20
to mine awen pepill. I deliuerd 30u of thraldome and gafe to 30u mi
lawe, and entird 30u into þe land þat I had hight vnto 30ur fadirs. I
sent mi prophetis to comforth 30u, and of 30u I chese a maiden as it
liked to me to take ma[n]kinde. Bot nowe I pleine vpon 30u, for 3it 3e
will noght trowe. "Criste come no3t 3it, bot he is for to come." '   25

þe lorde sais vnto þe panim, 'I made þe of noght, and boght þe as I
did þe cristen, and all gude dedis I did for þe. Bot þu, as a man were
oute of minde (for þou wote noght what þou dose), and as it were a
blind man (for þou wote neuir whidir þou walkes), þou wirshipes a
creature for God, falshede for treuthe, and bowes [bifor] þi vndir-   30
lowte; and þus for I pleine on þe.'

þe lorde saide to þe fifte: | 'Come vp nere to me, frende.' And onone   f. 43ʳᵃ
he saide to þe oste of heuen, 'Mi wele lufed frendes, I haue one frende,
bi þe whilke I vndirstand mani. He is as a man enclosed amange
enemis, and put in hard thraldome. If he speke oght, þai stone his   35
mouthe. If he do ani gude, þa put a spere in his breste. Say nowe, mi
frendes and all mi saintes, how lange sall I suffir þese men and swilke
contempte?'

Sainte John Baptist answerde, 'þou art as it wer þe clennest mirroure, for all þinges are sene and knawen in þe as in a mirroure. þou art þe soueraine swetnes, in whome all godes sauoures to vs. þou art as it were a sharpest swerde, for þou demes all þinges in
5 euenhede.'

þan answerde þe lorde, 'Treuli, mi frende, þou sais sothe. Mi chosen derlinges ses in me all gode as right, and so dose euell spirites, if all þai knawe noght in light, bot in þaire awen consciens. Right as a man þat is in prisson and somtime lered lettirs, all if he be in derknes,
f. 43rb he can þat he lered, and ȝit he sese it noght– | so fendes, all if þai see
11 noght mi rightwisnes in þe light of mi clernes, ȝit þai se it and knawes it in þaire awen consciens. I ame as a swerde þat departes two þinges, so þat I giue to ilkone as are worthi.'

þan saide þe lorde to Saint Petir, 'þou art þe foundir of faithe and
15 of mi kirke. Tell me, þat myne oste mai here, right vpon þis fife maner of men.' Petir answerde, 'Honour and louynge be to þe, lorde, for þi charite þat þou makes with worde. Blissed be þou of all þine oste, for þou makes vs to see and knawe in þe all þinges þat are made. Forsothe, þis is trewe rightwisnes: þat þe firste, þe whilke sittes in þi sete
20 and hase Lucifers werkes, þat he lost with schame þe sete þat he presumes to sit in, and he be partefere of Lucifers paine. Of þe seconde þis is right: þat syne he went fro þi faithe, he go down to hell, þe heued donwarde and þe fete vpwarde, because he dispised þe þat
f. 43va suld haue bene his heued. Of þe þird þis is right, þat he se noȝt | þi
25 face eftir his malice, for fals beleuors sall noȝt se þi face. Of þe fourte þis is right, þat as a man out of minde he [be] bunden and closed in dirke places. Of þe fift is right: þat he haue helpe.'

þan saide ʿþeʾ lorde, 'I swere bi God þe fadir, whose voice Iohn Baptist herde in Iordane flode; I swere bi þe bodi þat Iohn sawe,
30 touched and baptized in Iordane; I swere bi þe spirit þat aperid in liknes of a doufe in Iordane, þat I sall do riȝtwisnes vpon þase fife maner of men.'

And þa[n] saide þe lorde, ekynge þe paine to þe first of þe fife, 'þe swerde of mi felnes sall entir into þi bodi, þe whilke sall entir in þe
35 hier part of þe heued, and it sall go so depe and with so grete violence þat it sall neuir be drawen oute. þi sete sall be drowned as it were a heui stone, þe whilke stintis noght or it come to þe grounde of þe

6 sothe] sothe my frendes in me, *exc.* sothe, *subpuncted and ruled through*   17 of] of þine, þine *subpuncted*   22 go] gon, n *subpuncted*   23 þat] þat þou, þou *subpuncted*   26 of] of his, his *subpuncted*   he be] he (*orig.* be)   33 þan] þat

depnes. þi fingers, þat is þi accessoures, sall brine in fire of brunstone
þat mai neuir be slokned. þi armes, þat is þi vicaris, þat suld be
streched oute to profite of saules, for þai er streched to wyn gude of þe
| werld and wirshipe, þai sall be demed in þat paine þat Dauid spekis   f. 43ᵛᵇ
of þus: "*Fiant filii eius orphani*" (and be þe childir of him faderles and 5
his wife as a widowe, and straungers sall take awai his substance).

'Who is his wife bot þe saule, þe whilke is forsaken fro heuen and is
wedowe fro Godd? His sons are vertuse, þe whilke it was supposed þat
he had, or elles gude simpill men þat were his suggets. And þaire dignite and oþir gudes sall be deuolued to straungers fro þaim. And þai, 10
for misvse of þaire dignite, sall enherit confusion endeles, and þe arai
of þaire heued sall be drowned in þe clai of hell, fro whens þai sall
neuir rise vpe, þat right as þai were here abouen oþir bi wirshipe and
pride, right so þai sall be drouned lawer in helle, þat it sall be inpossibill to come oute. 15

'þaire membres, þat is all clerkes (þat is, þaire folowers and
fawtours) sall be departed and kut awai fro þaime as it were a | walle   f. 44ʳᵃ
þat suld be distrued, in þe whilke a stone suld noght leue on a stone,
ne þe cyment suld noȝt leue to þe stones. So þare sall no merci come
vpon þaime, for mi charite sall neuir make þaime warme, ne þai sall 20
neuir be bigged in þe endles mansion of þe blis of heuen: bot þai sall
with þaire heuedes be departed fro all gude, be turmentid and
punished.

'To þe second I sai, forsothe, for þou will noȝt hald þe faith þat þou
hase hight me, ne haue to me charite, I sall send to þe a beste, þat 25
passes furth fro one inpetuose beke, þat right as þe bekke flowes into
þe inward partis of þe beste, right so þe best sall seke þe vpe and lede
þe into þe inwarde partis of hell, fro whens þou sall neuir mowe ryse.

'To þe þird, I sai þat for þou, Iewe, will noght trowe þat I am
comen, þarefore when I com to þe second dome, þou sall se me noght 30
in mi blis, bot in þi awen consciens, and þou sall proue þat all þinges
ar trewe þat I haue saide, | and þere leues noþinge bot paynes to þe   f. 44ʳᵇ
eftir þi deserte. Vnto þe fourt I sai þat, for þou charges noght nowe to
trowe, ne will noght knawe me, þi derkenes sall gife þat light, and þi
hert sall haue swilke brightnes as þou mai knawe with mi domes, þat 35
þai are trewe: bot þou sall come to oþir light.

---

10 sall] *twice, first subpuncted*   And] *and* dignite, dignite *ruled through*
12 fro] *for*   17 a] *Quire catchphrase,* walle, *below*   20 neuir] *neuiir*
32 trewe] *trewee*   35 swilke] *swilke* dirkenes, dirkenes *subpuncted* þat] *twice,
first subpuncted*

'I sai to þe fifte, I sall do to þe þre þinges: firste, I sall fill þe within with mi hete; þe second, I sall make þi mouth more stabill and harde þan ani stone, þat stones rebounde fro þe into þe casters; þe þird, I sall arme þe with mi armoures, þat no spere sall noye þe, bot, as dose
5 þe wax at þe fire, al þinges sall melt and wax soft before þe. þarefore be þou of gude comforthe and stand manli, for right as a knight in bataile hopis þe helpe of his lorde and so lange he feghtes as ani moistur is in him, so stand þou strangli and feght, for þi lorde God sall gife þe swilke helpe as no man mai vndirstand. And for þou hase bot a
f. 44ᵛᵃ litill nowmbir, I sall wirshipe and multiplie þe. | Mi frendes þat sese
11 and knaws þere þinges in me standes on þat wise before me. þe wordes þat are nowe saide sall be fulfilled, for þe oþir sall neuir entir into mi realm as lange as I ame kinge, bot if þai amend þaim. Heuen sall be giuen to ˈnone bot to þaim þat mekesˈ þaim and dose penence.'
15 þan answerde all þe oste, 'Lord God, be louinge and wirshipe to þe, þat is withoute bigininge and ende.'

Capitulum 42. Wordes of þe modir, bi þe whilke sho
tellis howe sho plesed God bi meknes, obediens and
speciall charite.

20 The modir spake: 'I had thre þinges bi þe whilke I plesed my son. Firste, I had mekenes, þat no creature, nowþir aungell na man, was meker þan I. þe secounde, I had obediens, bi þe whilke I studeed howe I suld be obedient to mi son in all þinges. þe þird, I had speciall charite. And for þese I was on þre wise wirshiped of mi son.

25 'Firste, I ame made more honorabill þan aungels or men, for þare is no vertu in God bot in shynnes in me, all if he be welle and maker of all. I ame, forsothe, his creature, to whome before oþir he hase
f. 44ᵛᵇ grauntet speciall grace. Also | for obediens I gat so mikill grace þat þare is no sinner so fowle, and he turne to me with purpose to amend
30 him and with a gude herte, he sall haue forgifenes.

'Also, for mi charite, God is so ner to me þat he þat sese him sese me: and whoso sese me sese þe godhede and manhede in me as in a mirowe, for he þat sese God sese thre personnes, and he [þat] sese me sese as thre personns, for whi, þe godhed enclosed me in him with bodi and saule,
35 and he filled me in all vertu, so þat þare is no vertu in God bot it shewis in me, all if he be God, fadir and gifere of all vertuyse. Right as, if

10 þe] þei   29-30 amend him] *marg.*, nota bene   33 þat²] *om.*
35 vertu¹] vertu and   36 of all vertuyse] *twice* (*second*, vertuse)

þare were two bodis knitt togidir, all at þe tone resaiued þe toþir
resaiuede, so hase God done to me, for whi, þare is no swetenes bot it is
in me, as if a man had a kirnell of a not and wald comine part with
aneoþir. Mi saule and mi bodi were clenner þan þe son or þan a miror,
and as in a miror [þre persones] might [be sene], and þai stode nere, so   5
þai, þe fadir, son and holi gaste, mai in mi clennes. Forsothe, | I had a son   f. 45ra
in mi bodi with godhede and manhede as in a miroure, for þat I ame
glor[i]fied. Wharefor, þou spouse of mi son, stodi to folowe mekenes,
and loue noþinge bot mi son.'

Capitulum 43. Wordes of þe son of gode informacion bi   10
liknes of þe date, and of one heui birden.

The son spake: 'Somtime of litill gude sprynges grete rewarde. Amange
froites þe dactile is of merueilouse sauore, whose stone, if it be taken and
put into þe fate erthe, it waxis fructuose and fate, and growes into a grete
tre. Bot and it be put in hungri erthe and drye, it dwines awai. þat erthe is   15
ouer dri þat hase delite in sin, in þe whilke erthe, if þe sede of vertu be
sawen, it rises ne waxis noȝt set. Bot þe erthe of þat saule is fat, þe whilke
knawes sin and forþinkes þat it hase sinned: in þe whilke erthe, if þe
stone of þe dactill be sawen, þat is þe felnes of mi dome and of mi
powere, it settis thre rotes in þe saule. First, it þinkes þat it mai do right | 20
noght withoute mi helpe, and þarefore it opins þe mouthe at prai me. þe   f. 45rb
second, it biginnes to gife some almus for mi lufe. þe þird, it forberis
oþir occupacions for to serue me.

'And þan sho bigins to abstene in fastinge and forsakinge of hir awene
propir will: and þat is þe bodi of þe tre. Eftir þat, þe braunches of charite   25
waxis when he drawes and stirres all þat he mai to gude. þan waxis þe
froite, when he teches oþir als mikill as he can, and he purposses with all
his entent to encrese mine awen wirshipe. Swilke froite pleses me
souerainli. And so fro a litill gude he gose vpwarde vnto a perfite gude,
for first þe bodi is roted bi a litill deuocion; þan it waxes bi abstinens; þe   30
braunches are multiplied bi charite; and þe froite waxis fat bi preching
of Goddes worde. On like maner wise, a man fro a small euell gose
downward to Goddes curse and to werse turment.

'Bot wote þou euir whilke is þe heueest charge and birthinge to bere
of all þinges þat growes? Forsothe, it is þe birdyn of a childe when it   35

---

5 þre persones, be sene] *om., corr. agst. Lat.*   5-6 might . . . clennes] þe fadir son
and holi gaste might and þai stode nere, so þai mai in mi clennes   8 glorified] glorr-
fied   33 downward] donwward

f. 45ᵛᵃ comis to þe time of birth and mai | noght be born, bot it dies within þe
wombe of þe modir, and of þe charge þe modir bristes and dies; whome
þe fadir beris with roten filth and with þe child to þe graue for to beri. So
dose þe deuell to þe saule, for trewli, a viciouse saule is as sho were wife
5   to þe deuell, whose will sho folowes in all þinges.

'First sho conceiues a childe of þe deuell, when sin pleses hir, in þe
whilke sho hase gladnes, for right as þe modir conceiues þe child of a
litill sede, þat is bot foule filth, and so bringes furth fruyte, on þe same
wise þe saule, when it hase delite in sin, sho bringes furth fruyte vnto þe
10   deuell. þe membres ar formed and þe bodi hase strenthe, when syn is
ekyd vnto syn and encresid fro dai to dai. þus, when sinnes are encresid,
þe modir biginneth to bol[n]e.

'Bot when þe time commis of childinge, sho mai noȝt child, for when
þe kinde is wastid in syn, þe life is irksome, and he wald gladli sin more
15   bot he mai noght, ne God will noght suffir it. þan is strenth and com-
forthe all awai, and on ilke parti commis to sorowe besines, and for |
f. 45ᵛᵇ cause he mai noght fulfill his will. þan at þe laste brestis þe wombe,
when he hase dispaire of himselfe to do ani gude dede. þan dies sho,
when he blasphemis Goddes dome and reproues it. And so he is led of
20   fadir þe deuell to be berid in þe graue of helle, where, with þe foule filth
of sin and þe child of foule luste, sho is berid withouten ende. þus þou
mai se howe, of litill, sinnes encreses and waxes and growes to dampnacion.'

Capitulum 44. þe lorde spekis bi liknes of a grete bee,
25   and telles þe condicions of þe werld.

'I, lorde and maker of all, made þe werld, and it spices me. I here a voice
in þe world, as it were of a grete bee, þat gedirs honi in þe erthe, for riȝt as
þe more be, when he flies, he fallis onone to þe erthe with ane hase voice,
so I here in þe werld ane hase voice þat sais, "I charge riȝt not what com
30   eftir þis." Forsothe, all cries nowe, "We charges noȝt ne settes noght bi."
For treuli, men charges noght ne settes not bi what I haue done of mi
f. 46ʳᵃ charite, monishand and warninge þaim bi ani | prophete, prechinge bi
miselfe, and suffirynge for þaim passion.

'þai charge right noght what I haue done in mi wreth, amendinge and
35   blaminge þaime þat were euell and inobedient. þai se þaime dedeli and

2 and²] and beris, beris *subpuncted*   3 child] childir, ir *subpuncted*
5 folowes] fowlowes   12 bolne] bolme   22 howe of] *trsp.*   26 I¹] I ame,
ame *subpuncted*

vncertaine of þe time, and þat, þai charge it noght. þai her and se mi
rightwisnes, þe whilke I did for sin in Pharao and Sodomites, to mani
kynges and oþir princes, þe whilke also I hight euirilke dai to do be
swerde and tribulacions. And ȝit are þa[i] as blinde to þaime.

'þarefore as þe grete bee flies furth to what þinge þaime likes, so þai 5
flie sometime, skippinge be pride; for pride liftes þaime vp, bot þai fall
downe againe when þai retorne to þaire lichery and gluttery þat þai
vsed befor. þai gedir swetenes in þe erthe, bot it is to þaimeselfe, for
nowe man laboures and gedirs for þe profite of þe bodi and noght of
þe saule, for worldli wirshipe and noght for heuenli. þai turn 10
temporall gude to þaime into euirlastinge paine.

'þarefore, for þe | praiers of mi modir, I sall sende to þir bees, fro f. 46ʳᵇ
whom mi frendes ar exempet, þe whilke are alloneli in bodi in erthe,
mi clere voice, þe whilke sall preche þaime merci: and, if þai will here
it, þai sall be saued.'

15

Capitulum 45. Wordes of þe fadir to þe spouse, howe
sho sall clethe hir for comminge of his son, and certain
questions and answers.

The fadir spake. 'þou spouse of mi son, do on þi cloþinge, and stand
stabill, for mi son comis nere to þe. His fleshe was pressed as in a wine 20
pressure. Right as man trespast in all his membris, so mi son made
asethe in all his membris. Mi sones here was standinge; his sinows
drawen inwarde; þe iunctures were drawen oute fro þare kindeli
knottes; þe handes and fete were festynd; þe saule was trubbled and þe
hert all in sa[r]e; þe bowels were drawen to þe bake—for man had 25
sinned in all his membris.'

þan spake þe son to þe heuenli oste þat stode to, and saide, 'All if ȝe
knawe all þinges in me, ȝit, for mi spouse þat | is here, sai ȝe to me, f. 46ᵛᵃ
aungels, what is þat þat was withoute begininge and sall be withoute
ende, and what is þat at made all þinges of noght, and noþinge hase 30
made him?' þe aungels answerde as with ane voice, 'Lorde, þou arte
he. We bere to þe wittnes of thre þinges: first, at þou art maker of
noght of vs and of all þinges þat are in heuen and erthe; þe second, þat
þi lordshipe and pouer are as þou is, withoute biginninge and withoute ende.'

35

þan saide he to þe prophetes and patriarches, 'I aske of ȝou what he
was þat b[r]oght you fro seruage vnto fredome. Who departed þe watir

4 þai] þare   25 sare] sawe   37 broght] boght, *Lat.* adduxit

of þe see befor ȝou? Who gaue to ȝou þe lawe? Who gaue to ȝour
prophetes þe spirit of tonge and of speche?' þai answerde, 'þou, lorde.
þou broght vs fro seruage; þou gafe þe lawe; þou gaue vs spirit to
speke.' þan saide he to þe modir, 'Sai, modir, sothfast witnes, what
5   þou knawes of me.' þe modir answerde, 'Before þe time þe aungell
f. 46ᵛᵇ come fro þe to me I was hole with bodi | and saule. When þe aungell
had saide his worde, þi bodi was in me with godhede and manhede,
and I felt þi bodi in mi bodi. I bare þe withouten sorowe; I childid
withouten disese. I wand and wappid þe in clothis. I fede þe with mi
10 milke. I was with þe fro þi birth to þi dede.'
    þan saide þe lorde to þe apostils, 'Tell me what he is whame ȝe
sawe, herde and felte.' þai answerde, 'We herde þi wordes and wrate
þaim. We herd þi grete þinges wha[n]e þou gafe þe lawe, when þou
commanded fendes with þi worde, and þai went oute fro men, when
15 þou raised þe dede with þi word, and helid þe seke. We sawe þe in
manis bodi. We sawe þi grete þinges in a godli blisse with manhede.
We sawe þe taken to þi enemis and hange on þe crose. We sawe in þe
þe bitterest dede and þe laid in þe sepulcre. We felt þe eftir þou was
risen fro dede, and we handild [þi] here, þi visage, þe places of þi
20 woundes and of oþir partis. þou ete and spake with vs. þou art sotheli
f. 47ʳᵃ þe | son of God and of þe maiden. We felid also when þou stied vp to
þe right hand of þi fadir, where þou arte sittinge withoute ende.'
    þan saide þe lorde vnto þe vnclene spirites, 'All if ȝe hide þe treuth
in ȝour consciens, I bid ȝou sai who hase febled ȝoure powere.' þai
25 annswerde, 'Right as theues, bot if þaire fete be stressed in hard tree,
þai will noght sai þe treuth, so, bot we be constreined be þi ferdfull
gudli pouere, we suld noght sai sothe. þou art he þat come done to
helle with þi might and þi strengh and tuke possession of þi right.'
    þan said þe lorde, 'Lo, all þat are spirites, and are noȝt cled in bodi,
30 bers trewe witnes to me, and þai þat hase spirit and bodi, as men, sais
agains me. Som knawes treuthe and charges it noght; som knawes it
noght and þarefore þai charge it not.'
    þan saide he againe to þe aungels, 'þai sai þat ȝoure witnes is fals,
f. 47ʳᵇ þat I ame noght maker of all, ne all þinges are noght knawen | in me,
35 and þarefore þai loue more mi creature þan me.' He saide to þe
prophetes, 'þai sai againe ȝou þat mi lawe is bot vanite, þat ȝe ware
deliuerd fro seruage bi ȝoure awen strengþe and wit, þat ȝe had a fals
spirit, and ȝe spake eftir ȝour awen propir will.' þan saide he to þe

---

13 whane] whame   19 þi¹] om.   30 men] men bers witnes agains me and,
exc. men, *subpuncted and ruled through*

modir, 'Som sais also þat þou was noght a maiden. Oþer sais þat I tuke
no bodi of þe. Oþir knewe wele I did, bot þai gif no fors.' þan said he
to þe apostils, 'Also, þai sai againe ȝou, for þai sai þat ȝe are liers, and
þat þe newe lawe is withoute prophete and reson. Oþir þare is þat
trowes it trewe, bot þai set noȝt bi it. Nowe I aske of ȝou who sall be 5
jugge of þir?'

þai all answerde, 'þou, God, þat arte withoute biginninge and
ende, þou Iesu Crist, þat arte with þi fadir: to þe is giffen dome of þi
fadir. þou sall be þaire iugge.' þe lorde saide, 'I þat before pleined of
þaime am nowe þaire iugge. Neuirþeles, all if I mai all and knawe all, 10
ȝit gife ȝe ȝoure dome vpon þaime.' þai answerde, 'As all þe werld in |
þe bigininge perished in watir of flode, so nowe it is worthi þat all þis f. 47ᵛᵃ
werld perishe, for malice and wikkednes is nowe more þan was þan.'
þe lorde saide, 'For I ame rightfull and mercifull, ne I do no dome
withoute merci, ne merci withoute rightwisnes, þarefore ȝit ainis, for 15
þe praiers of mi modir and of mi saintes, I sall sende vnto þe werld mi
merci. If þai will noȝt here it, so mikill more sharpe sall þe right be þat
sall shewe eftir.'

Capitulum 46. Wordes bitwene þe modir and þe son,
and howe 'he' discries himselfe, and opynions of him. 20

Mari spake to þe son and saide, 'Blissed be þou þat art withouten
biginning and ende. þou had þe moste honeste and most semli bodi:
þou was moste manli and moste vertuouse: þou was þe worthiest
creature.' þe son answerde, 'þe wordes þat commis fro þi mouthe are
to me full swete, and, as it were þe moste swete drinke, þai delite þe 25
inward partis of mi herte. þou arte to me sweteste of all oþir creatures.
Right as when ma|ni visages are sene in a miroure, þere pleses none so f. 47ᵛᵇ
mikill as þi awen visage, so I, all if I lufe of speciall wise all mi saintes,
ȝit loue I none so wele as þe, of whom I tuke fleshe and ame man
broght furth. þou arte as it were mirre, whose reflaire passes vp to þe 30
godhed and broght it doune into þi bodi. And þat same reflaire drowe
þi saule and bodi into þe godhede, where þou arte nowe with bodi and
saule. Blissed be þou, for aungels are glad of þi bewte, and all þat
calles vpon þe with trewe and gude herte are deliuerd in þi vertu. All
fendes are ferde in þi light, ne þai dare noght com nere to þi brightnes, 35
bot will euir be in dirkenes.

'þou gafe me thre maner of louinges, for þou saide þat I hade þe
    5 trewe, bot] bot trewe bot   36 bot] bot ȝe

moste honeste bodi, þat I was moste manli and vertuouse, and
worthieste of all creatures. And to þese thre is none agains[a]is bot þai
allonli at hase bodi and saule. þai sai þat I haue one [vn]honeste bodi,
moste outecast of men, and vileste creature.

f. 48ʳᵃ   'What is more vn|honest þan for to prouoke and stire oþir to syn?
6   Bot þai sai þat mi bodi stirs and drawes to sin. þai sai, forsothe, þat
sin is noght so foule as it is saide, ne displeses noȝt so mikill God.
þai sai þare suld noþing be bot God wald, ne þere mai noþing be
made withoute him. Whi suld not þa vse þo þinges at are made "eftir
10   oure awen will? þe freelte of oure kinde askes þat, and so þai lifed
þat were befor vs." þus spekes nowe men to me. þai sai mi manhede
is vnhoneste, in þe whilke I aperid amange men verrai God, for I
stird þaime to hate sin, and shewed howe greuouse it is. þai sai of
me as if I stire þaime to þat at both is vnhoneste and vnprophetabill,
15   for trewli þai sai þat þare is noþinge honeste bot sin, and þat at is
plesand to þaire willes.

'Also þai sai þat I ame most vnmanli. What is more vnmanli þan
he þat, when he spekes þe trewth, oþir stoppes his mouthe with
stones and smites him in þe visage, and sais to him wordes of
f. 48ʳᵇ   reproue, and he venges him noght, all if he might? So do þai | to me.
21   I speke to þaim treuthe bi docturs and holi scripture, and þai sai þat
I spake lesinges. þai stop mi mouth with stones of obstinasie when,
for all þat I mai sai, þai lett noȝt to do furth þaire sinnes, as avowtry,
manslaghter and oþir. þai gife me wordes of reproue, and sais, "If he
25   were God moste mighti, he wald venge swilke tran[s]gressions." All
þis suffir I with mi paciens. And I here þaime sai ilke dai þat þe
paine of helle is noght endeles, ne sharpe, ne bittir, as it is saide, and
þai deme mi wordes as lesinges.

'þe þirde, þai deme [me] vilest creature. What is more outecaste in
30   a howse þan an hounde and a kate? For þe whilke he [þat] might
chaunge wald gladli take a gude hors. Bot men haldes me wers þen a
hounde. He wald noght want his hound for to haue me, and or he wald
want þe skine he wald caste me awai and forswere me. What þinge is
þat at is plesant, þe whilke is not more feruentli thoght and desired
35   þan I? And þai hald me bettir þan oþir creatures, þai wald loue me
before oþir. þe lest þinge þai haue, þai loue more þan me, and þai
f. 48ᵛᵃ   make | sorowe for all þinge, sauand for me. þai sorowe for þaire awen

---

    2 againsais] agains oþirs   3 vnhoneste] honeste, *Lat.* inhonestam   18 his
mouthe] his mouthe his, *second* his *subpuncted*   25 transgressions] trangressions
29 me] *om.*   30 þat] *om.*

harmes and þaire neghburs; þai are heuy at displesant worde; þai
sorowe þat þai offend oþir men þat are more worthi þen þai. Bot þai
sorowe noght þat þai offend me, maker of all. What man þan is so
outecaste and noght set bi, þat asked and suld noght be answerde, and
gafe and suld noght be rewarded aniþinge? Forsothe, I am moste oute- 5
caste and vileste in þaire sight, for þai hald me worth no gude,
notwithstandinge þat I ame giffere of all gudes.

'þarefore, modir, for þou haste tastid more of mi wisdome þan
oþir, and þare passed neuir fro þi mouthe bot treuthe (as fro [m]i
mouthe), I sall excuse me in þe presens and sight of all mi saintes. 10
And befor þe firste, þat saide I had þe moste vnsemli bodi, I sall
proue þat I haue bodi moste honeste and semeli withoute deformite
and sin, and all men sall see þat he for his speche sall fall into
endeles reproue. He þat saide þat mi wordes were lesinges, and þat
he knewe noght wheþir I ame God or | noght, I sall proue me verraili f. 48ᵛᵇ
God, and he, as it were clai, sall flete into helle. þe þirde, þat demed 16
me vilest, I sall deme him to euirlastinge dampnacion, þat he se
neuir mi gladnes ne mi blisse.'

þan spake he to þe spouse. 'Stand stedfastli in mi seruise, for þou
art commin as into a stronge walle, in whame, when þou art closed, 20
þou mai noȝt slipe ne mine þe grounde. þarefor, suffir a litill tribulacion, and þou sall fele reste endeles in mine arme. þou knawes þe
fadirs will; þou hase herde þe wordes of þe son, and þou felis mi spirit;
þou hase delit and comforthe in spekinge with mi modir and mi
saintes. þarefore stand stedfastli, or eles þou sall fele mi rightwisnes, 25
be þe whilke þou sall be compelled to do þo þinges þe whilke I
monish nowe godeli, and of gud will.'

Capitulum 47. Wordes of God in liknes of clethinge,
spekinge of þe olde lawe.

'I ame þat God þat somtime was called God of Abraham, God of 30
Ysaac, God of Iacob. I ame God þat gafe þe lawe to Moises. þis lawe
was | as it had bene a clothe, for, right as a modir þat hase a child in hir f. 49ʳᵃ
wombe ordeins clethinge þareto, so God ordained lawe, þe whilke is
noght bot a clothing, a shadowe and figure of þinges þat suld [be]
done in time comminge. I cled miselfe in þis clothinge of þe lawe. 35
Forþirmare, as þe child, when he waxis, þe olde clothinge is chaunged
and new taken, so I did of þe clothinge of þe olde lawe, and toke þe

9 mi] ani   21 mine] minde   34 be] *om.*

clethinge of þe new lawe, and gaue it as [b]leue þare to all þat wald be
cled þarein with me.

'This clothe is noght straite ne harde, bot of a gude mesure in ilke
parti. þis lawe biddis noght faste ouirmikill, or trauell ouirmikill, or
5 sla þiselfe, or to do aniþing ouir possibilite of miȝt; bot it is prophetabill to þe saule, and discrete and mesurabill to þe bodis chastisynge;
for þe bodi, when it cleues ouirmikill to sin, sin wastis it and consumes
it. þarefore, in þe newe lawe is funden two þinges. þe firste is discrete
f. 49ʳᵇ temperans, and sobir vse and rightfull, | of all þinges þat langes to bodi
10 and saule. þe seconde is esines to kepe þe lawe, for he þat mai noght
stand in o þinge, he mai abide in aneoþir, þare it is fonden þat he þat
mai noght be a maiden, he mai lawefulli be in weddinge, and he þat
falles mai rise againe.

'Bot þis lawe is nowe reproued and disspised of þe werld. þai sai
15 nowe þat þe lawe is straite, foule and greuouse. þai sai it is straite, for
it biddis a man hald him content with þinges necessary and flee outrage and waste. þai wald haue all þinges oute of reson, as it were
bestis, aboue might of bodi. And þarefore it is strait to þaime. þai sai
also þat [it] is greuouse, for þe lawe biddis þat luste suld be hade bi
20 reson and in couenabill times. Bot þai wald haue þaire luste more þan
nedis and oþir times þan is ordeined. þai sai also þat it is vnresonabill,
for it biddes þat a man suld loue mekenes and gife to God thanke of all
gode. Bot þai wald be proude of gudes þat God haues gifen, and haue
to þaimeseluen þe thanke. |

f. 49ᵛᵃ 'And so is mi clothe set at noght and despised. I fulfilled all þe olde
26 and ordeyned þe newe, for þe ald were full harde, and þai suld haue
le[s]tit till I had comen to dome. Bot þai haue fowlli cast awai þe
clothe with þe whilke þe saule is heled, þat is right faith, and þai put
sin to sin, throwe þe whilke þai will betraise me. Sais noght Dauid in
30 þe sawter buke, "He þat ete mi brede thoght in me perdicion"? In þe
whilke wordes I will þu take hede to two þinges: first, þat he sais
noght, "He þinkes", bot he sais, "He thoght," as `if' i[t] were nowe
paste. þe second, he notes þare bot a man þat betraises. Bot I sai þe,
forsothe, þai are mi traitures þat are now, noȝt þai at were or sall be,
35 bot þai þat nowe liues. Also I sai þat noght allonli o man, bot þare is
mani.

---

1 as bleue] a sleue   5 ouir] ouir and, and *subpuncted*   19 it] *om.*
27 lestit] lefte it, *Lat.* durarent   29 sin²] sin with, with *subpuncted*   32 as if it
were] as I swere, *pointed, Lat.* quasi preteritum est

'Happeli þou mai aske of me, "Is þare not to l[o]fe[s], one spirituall and inuisibill, bi þe whilke aungels lifes, and saintes? þe second is of þe erthe, þe whilke men etis. Bot aungels and saintes will noþinge bot eftir þi will, and men mai non oþir wise bot as | it pleses þe. Howe mai þai þan betraise þe?"

'I answere before mi heuenli oste, þe whilke knawes and sees all þinge in me: "Forsothe, þare is thwo maner of bredes, one brede þat aungels etes in mi rewme, þat þai be fillid with mine vnspekabill blisse. þai betraise me noght, for þai will noþing bot as I will. Bot þai betraise me þat etis mi brede on þe aweter.

'I ame verraili þat brede. In þat brede is trewli sene thre þinges, figure, sauoure and roundnes. I ame verraili þat brede, for whi, I haue, as þat hase, thre: þat is, figure, sauoure and roundenes. Sauour, for riȝt as, withoute brede, all mete is vnsauery and, as it were, of no comforthe ne gladnes, so withouten me, all þinge þat is is vnsauery, and bothe vnstedfaste, seke and veyn. I haue also figure of brede, for I ame of þe erthe: I ame of a modir maiden, þe modir of Adam, Adam of þe erthe. I haue also roundenes, for I ame withoute biginninge and withoute endinge. þare mai no man se or finde ende or biginning in mi wisdome, in mi power, | or in mi charite. I ame within all þinges and abouen all þinges so fer, þat if a man wald flee withoute as swift as a bolt, ȝit suld he neuir finde ende ne depnes in mi wisdom, powere and might.

'For þese thre, sauour, figure and rondenes, I ame þat brede þat in þe awter is sene as brede, felte as brede, bot it is turned into mi bodi, þat was festind on þe crosse. Right as dri þinge þat will sone brine, if it be put to þe fire, it is sone wasted and consumed, and þare leues noþinge of figure of trees, bot all is fire, right so when þo wordes are saide, "Hoc est corpus meum," þat at was before brede is onone made mi bodi, ne it is noght wasted ne brint as trees bi fire, bot þe su[b]stance of brede is turned into mi bodi bi þe might of mi godhede. þarefore, "þai þat etes mi brede betraises me."

'What manslaghter mai be more abhominabill þan þat where a man slaes himselfe? Or where is wers prodicion and treson þan at þe man and þe wife, þe whilke are knit togidir bi a band þat mai noght be | lowsed, þe tone betraies þe toþir? What sais þe man when he will betraise þe wife? Forsothe, he sais to hir vndir simulacion, "Go we to þat place, þat I mai fulfill mi will with þe." And sho, in simpilnes,

f. 49vb 5

10

15

21

25

30

35 f. 50rb

---

1 lofes] lufe, *Lat.* panes   14 is] is saueri, saueri *subpuncted*   19 man] man finde, finde *subpuncted*   30 substance] sustinance

as redi to fulfill þe husbandes will, gose with him. Bot he, when he
findes time conabill and place, bringes furthe agains hir thre instrumentes of perdicion. Owthir he hase o þinge so heui in his hand þat
with one stroke he slaes hir, or so sharpe þat onone it persis hir bodi,
5 or els he strangils hir, and when sho is dede, þe traitur thinkes in himselfe, "Nowe hafe I done wrannge and euell. If mi trespas be opinli
knawen, I sall be dampned to dede." And þarefore he gose and puttes
and hides þe dede bodi of his wife in a priue place, þat his sin be noght
discured.

10 'Thus dose nowe prestes to me, þe whilke is mi traitures. Thai and I
are knit togidir with a band when þai take brede in þaire handes, and,
rehersinge mi wordes, þai make þereof mi verrai bodi þat I tuke of þe
maiden (and all aungels mai noght do þat, for I gafe þat dignite
f. 50ᵛᵃ alloneli to prestes, and I haue | chosin þaime to þe soueraine ordirs).
15 Bot þai do to me as traiturs, for þai shewe to me a glade visage and a
plesant, and ledis me into a preue place for to betraise me. þen shewes
þo þrestes a glad face, when þai seme gude and simpill. Thai lede me
to a preue place, when þai procede and gose vnto þe awter. þan am I
redi, as a spouse or a wife, for to do and fulfill all þaire will.

20 'Bot þai betraises me. First, þai smite me with one heui þinge, when
diuine office þat þai sai to me is so greuouse to þaime and so chargeouse. Forsothe, þai haue leuir speke an hundreth wordes for þe
world þan one for mi wirshipe. þai had leuer gife one hundreth marke
of gold for þe world þan one for mi lufe. þai had leuer trauale ane hun-
25 drethfalde for þaire awen profite þan onis for m[i]ne. Throw þis
charge þai thirste me downe, as I were a dede man, fro þaire hertis.

'þe second, þai prike me with a sharpe iren þat enters into mi
bowels, when þe preste gose to þe auter and þinkes and forþinkes þat
f. 50ᵛᵇ he hase sinned, haue|inge a stedfast will to sin againe when þe sacrifice
30 is made, and þus he þinkes: "Me fo[r]þinkes þat I haue sinned, but I
sall noght put hir fro me þat I haue sinned with, þat I sin no more."
þare men prikkes me with a full sharpe iren. And in þe þird wise þe
spirit is choked, when þai þinke þus: "It is gude and likand to be with
þe werld. It is gude to do licheri. I mai noght forbere. I sall do mi will
35 in mi [y]o[u]th, and when I wax ald þan sall I abstene, and þan will I
amend me": so þat þe spirit is chokked of þis thoght.

'Bot it mai be asked and meruailed whi þaire herte is so calde and

1 as redi] *twice, first subpuncted*   2 conabill] *marg.*, hoc est corpus meum
5 hir] hir bodi, bodi *subpuncted*   25 mine] mne   30 forþinkes] foþinkes
35 youth] thoght, *Lat.* iuventute

þaire lufe irkes with vertu and gude, þat þai mai neuir be made warme,
ne rise vnto mi charite. Right as fro þe ise rises no flawme, all if þare be
fire put to, for it alloneli meltis and relentes, right so þese men, all if I
gafe þaime mi grace, þan þai here þe wordes of mi warninge, ȝit rise
þai noght to þe wai of life, bot þai dri and fail fro all gudenes; and so   5
þai betraise me, shewinge | þaimeselfe as þai ware simpill, and are   f. 51ra
noght, and for þai are distrubbeld and greued of mi wirshipe, in þe
whilke þai suld haue delite, þarefor, þai abide so in will for to sin þat
þai make þaim to sin into þe ende.

    'Also, þai hide me and puttes me into a preuei place, when þai þinke   10
þus in þaire herte: "I wote þat I haue sinned. Neuirþeles, and I withdrawe me fro þe auter, all men sall be sclandird of me, and I sall be
demed euell of þaime." And so þai go vnwisli to mine auter, and þai
put me before þaime, and þai trete me with þaire handes, verrai God
and man, and so I ame with þaim in a preua place, for þare is none þat   15
takes hede how foule and vnclene þai are, before whame I lige, verrai
God, as in a preuai place.

    'For all if þe werste prest, þat is preste, sai þese wordes, "*Hoc est
corpus meum,*" he sacres mi verrai bodi, and I lige bifor him, verrai God
and man. Bot when [he] applies me and puttes me to his mouthe, þan I   20
ame absent fro him bi grace with mi godhede and manhede, and þe
forme of brede | and sauour abides with him. Bot I mene noght þat I   f. 51rb
ame noght þare verrai God and man, bot þat þe euell preste hase me
noght present to him bi þe same effect of grace as haues þe gude
preste, all if I be before both in verrai godehede and manhede.   25

    'Se nowe þat þo prestes are noght mi prestis, bot verrai traiturs. þai
sell me and betraisses me as did Judas. þare is nowþir Jewes ne
panims wers þen þai, for þo prestes are in þe same sin throwe þe
whilke Lucifer fell. þe dom of þaime is Goddes curs, as Dauid cursed
þaime þat obeis noght to God. For right as Dauid, when he was right-   30
full prophet and kinge, cursed noȝt of euell will, ne be malice, or wreth
of impaciens, bot be þe rightwisnes of God, so I, þat am bettir þen
Dauid, curses not swilke prestes bi wreth or euell will, but bi þe right
of God.

    'And þarefore, cursed be all þat þai take and receiues in þe erthe to   35
þaire profit, for þai loue noght God, and þe maker þat gafe swilke
þinges to þaime. Cursed be þe mete and drinke þat þai put in þaire
mouthe. Turn it into | þe mete of wormes and þe saule into helle.   f. 51va

---

5 fail] failand   20 he] *om.*   32 þat am] *trsp., with superior marks to reverse*
34 of] *marg.,* hoc est corpus meum

Cursed be þe bodi of þaime þat sall rise into helle for to brine þare
withoute ende. Cursed be þo ȝers þat þai liued viciousli. Cursed be
þat oure in þe whilke þai sall begin painnes in helle and neuir ende.
Cursed be þaire eyn, with þe whilke þai sawe þe light of heuen.
5 Cursed be þaire eres, with þe whilke þai herd mi wordes and charged
þaim noght. Cursed be þaire taste, with þe whilke þai tasted mi giftes.
Cursed be þaire touche, with þe whilke þai tretid and handilled me.
Cursed be þaire smell, with þe whilke þai smelled erthli delites, bot
noȝt me, þat ame moste delitabill of all oþir.

10   'Bot it is asked howe þai are cursed. To þe whilke I answere, þaire
ein are so cursed þat þai sall not se God in himselfe, bot þe derknes
and paines of helle. þaire eres are cursed, for þai sall noȝt here mi
wordes of comforthe, bot þe crie and noyse of þe fendes of helle. þaire
f. 51ᵛᵇ tast is cursed, for þai sall not taste þe swetenes of mi | endeles gudes
15 and blisse bot endelesse bittirnes. þaire touche is cursed, for þai sall
noȝt trete ne handell me, bot endeles paines of hote fire. þaire smelle
is cursed, for þai sall noȝt smell þe swetest odure of mi kingdome þat
passes all þinges of reflaire, bot þai sall haue stinke in hell, bittirrere
þen gall and wers þan brunstone.

20   'þai are cursed of heuen and erthe, and of all creatures þat hase no
saule, þe whilke obeis Goddes will þat þai set at noght and dispised.
And þarefore I, þat ame sothfaste and trewe, sweres in mi godhede þat
if þai dye in þat life and disposicion at þai are nowe set inne, mi
charite ne mi vertu sall neuir be with þaim, bot þai sall be dampned
25 withouten ende.'

> Capitulum 48. Wordes of þe godhede to þe manhede in
> presens of þe oste of heuen and o[f] þe spouse againe
> certein cristen: and þarefore take gude tent.

f. 52ʳᵃ The spouse sawe in heuen þe grete oste and Gode spe|kinge to þaime
30 þus: 'In þe presens of ȝou, mi frendes, þat knawes and sese all þinges in
me, mi godhede spekis to mi manhede, as if a man spake to himself.
Moises was with þe lorde in þe hill fourti daies and fourti nightes, for
whose absens so lange time fro þe pupill, þai keste gold into þe fire and
þareof made liknes of a calf, þe whilke þai called þaire God. And þan
35 saide þe lorde to Moises, "þi pupill hase sinned, and I sall distruye
þaime as it were a þinge first wretin and eftirwarde raised oute of buke."

11 in] in his face, his face *subpuncted*   18 all] *twice, second subpuncted*   27 of⁵]
howe   29 spe-] *Quire catchphrase,* kinge to, *below*

'þan saide Moises, "Mi lorde, do noght so. Haue minde howe þou
broght þaime throwe þe Rede See and shewed to þaime þi meruailes.
If þou distroie þaime, where is þe treuth of þi beheste? I prai þe do
noght þat, for þi enemis will sai, if þou do, þat God of Israel is euell,
þe whilke broght þe pupill throw þe Rede See and slowe þaime in   5
disserte." þer wordes plesed God mikill.

'I ame þe same Moises in figure. Mi godhede spekes to þe man|hede   f. 52ʳᵇ
as to Moises and sais, "Lo, howe þi pupill settes me at noȝt and dispises me. All þe cristen sall be slaine and þaire faith sall be distroied."
Mi manhede answers, "Lorde, nai. Haue minde þat I broght throwe   10
þe see þi pupill in mi blode, when I was all torent fro þe hight of þe
heued to þe sole of þe fete. I hight to þaime þan endeles life. þarefore
haue merci on þaim for mi passion." With þese wordes is þe godhede
gretli plesit and sais, "Be þi will done, for to þe is gifen all dome." Lo,
frendes, howe mikill mi charite is.   15

'Bot nowe before ȝou þat is mi frendes (aungels and saintes, and
oþir þat are in þe werld in bodi), I make pleininge þat mi pupill hase
gedred trees and made fire, and cast in gold, of þe whilke is risen vp a
calfe þat standes on iiii feet, and hase both hede, throte, and taile, and
him þai wirshipe as God. When Moises had tarid in þe hill, þan saide   20
þe pupill, "Whe wote noȝt what is bifallen to him", and þan were þai
displeised þat he had broght þaime oute of thralldome, and saide,
"Seke | we anoþir god to go befor vs."   f. 52ᵛᵃ

'So dose now þese cursed prestes to me, for þai sai, "Whi life we
more straiteli þan oþir? What sall be oure rewarde? It is bettir to vs to 25
be in oure pesse and luste. þarefor, we sall lufe þe werld, of þe whilke
we are sikir, for of his behest we are vnsekir." þan gedir þai stikkes
when þai set all þaire wittes vnto lufe of þe worlde. þai make fire when
þai hafe a perfite will to þe werld. þai bren, when þe luste brinnes in
þe saule and passes oute to dede. Eftirwarde, þai caste gold into þe   30
fire; þat is, all charite and wirshipe þat þai suld do to me, þai shewe it
for þe world.

'þan rises vp a calfe, þat is a foule loue of þe worlde, þe whilke hase
foure fete: sleuth, impaciens, vaine gladnes, and auarice. For treuli, þo
prestes þat suld be mine are full slawe to mi wirshipe, ouer impacient   35
to suffir, ouir glade to werldli blisse, and þai hald þaim neuir paied of
þat þai haue. þis calfe hase one heued and one throte: þat is, so hie
desire to gluttri þat it haues neuir ynough, all if þe see flowed into it.

11 when I was all torent] *twice, second subpuncted*

f. 52ᵛᵇ   þe tale of þis calfe is malice | of þaime, for þai wald no man suld haue
gudes and [þai] `miȝt leet´.

'Bot þai subuert all þaime þat wald be mi seruantes throwe þaire
euell ensampill. Swilke a calfe is in þaire hert, and in þat þai haue
5 þaire delite, and þai þinke and sai of me as þai did of Moises: "He
hase bene lange awai. His wordes semes to vs bot vanite, and his
werkes are chargeouse. We will hafe oure luste. Oure might and oure
luste sall be oure God." Ne þai hald þaime noght paied of all þis, ne it
is noght enough to þaime for to forgete me all, bot if þai haue me as
10 þaire mawmet and ydole.

'Painems wirshiped trees and stones and dede men, emange
wh[am]e one ydole was called Belzebub, and his prestes offird to him
frankensens, and made to him knelinges and sanges of louinge and
wirshipe. Also, all þat was of þaire sacrifice vnprophetabill, it fell to þe
15 erth, and it was etin and dewowred with birdes and flies, and þe
f. 53ʳᵃ prestes keped to þaimeselfe alloneli þat at was pro|phetabill and gud.
þai sperid a dore vpon þe ydole and keped þe keye, þat none oþir suld
entir.

'And þus dose prestes to me in þis time. þai offird to me encense,
20 þat is, þai speke and preche faire wordes for to gett glorie and þanke to
þaimeselfe, and noght for mi lufe bot for temporall profite. And þarefore, as þe odoure of encens is not handild bot sene and sauerd, so
þere wordes commis to no profite of saule, for þai are noght handild
be wirkinge eftir þaime ne rutid in þe herte; bot alloneli wordes are
25 herd delitabill for a time.

'þai offir praiers, bot noȝt at is plesant to me, as it were þai þat cries
faste with mouth, and in þe herte kepis silence. þai stand beside me
criand faste with mouth, bot þe herte is wauering in þe werld: and if
þai suld speke with ani man of wirshipe, þai þinke what þai speke of,
30 þat þai faile noght, for drede þai be notid and blamid. Bot prestes
praies to me as men rauished, þat wote noȝt what þai sai, for þai speke
one with þe mouth, and þai haue aneoþir in herte: of wose wordes þe
f. 53ʳᵇ herer mai haue no sikir|nes.

'þai bowe þaire kneis to me: þat menes, þai hight me meknes and
35 obediens, bot forsothe it is Lucifer meknes, for þai are obedient to
þaire awen desires and noght to me. þai haue a keye to spere þe dore
vpon me, bot þai open [it] when þai sai, "Be þi will done in heuen and
in erthe." And þan þai spere it when þai fulfill þaire awen will, and

2 þai] *om.* miȝt leet] m (*rest erased*)   12 whame] when   37 open it] opend

kepis þat mi will no more þan it ware a mans in prisson þat mai noȝt be sene no herde.

'Also þai kepe þaimselfe þe keye, when þai lete þaime at wald do mi will, and, if þai miȝt, þai wald forbid þat mi will suld noȝt be fulfilled bot eftir þaire awen will and desire. þai appropir to þaimselfe in mi 5 sacrifice þo þinges þat þai call prophetabill, and þai will chalaunge straitli all þaire dette and wirshipe, bot þe bodi of man þat falles to ded, for þe whilke þai were principalli halden to offir þe sacrifice, for þai hald it to þaim of no wauntage, þai late it be taken to flies (þat is, to wormes), and of þe dede of þe bodi or of þe hele of þe saule þai gife no 10 fors.

'Bot what was saide to Moises? | "Sla þaime þat hase made þis   f. 53ᵛᵃ ydole." And so þai were, bot noght all. So sall nowe mi wordes come and sle þaime, some both bodi and saule bi endeles dampnacion. Som sall be smiten to forþinkinge and repentance and so sall life, som to 15 more hasti dede. For swilke prestes are to me right odious and hate-full, and to what sall I liken þaim?

'Forsothe, þai are like to þe froite of a thorn, þat is faire withoute, and rodi, and inward full of prikkes and vnclenes. So com þai to me as men rudi in charite and seminge to men honest and clene. Bot þai 20 are within full of all filth. þe froite of þe thorn, and it be put in þe erthe, þare springes vp oþir þore. So þai hide þaire sinnes in þaire hert, as it were, in þe erthe, and þaire malice is so roted in euell þat þai ar noȝt asshamed to make þaire bost opinli of þair sin, of þe whilk oþir persones takes ofte ensampill to do euell, and to þinke 25 þus: "If prestes do þus, mikill more it is lawfull to vs for to do so." And noȝt allonli þai are like to þe froite, bot also to þe thorn, for þai haue dedein for to be touched with ani blaminges or correccions or | f. 53ᵛᵇ monishinges to gode, and þe cause is, for þai hald no man wiser þan þaimeselfe. þarefore þai wene þat þai mai lawfulli do what þaim 30 likes.

'þarefore I swere in mi godhede and manhede to all aungels þat her [m]e þat I sall breke þe dore þat þai spere vpon mi will, and mi will sall be fulfilled, and þaire will sall be distroied to noght, and it sall be closid withouten ende in paine. þarefore, as it was saide somtime, I 35 sall bigin mi dome in þe clergye and at þe auter.'

Capitulum 49. Wordes of Criste to þe spouse þat he is
likened to Moises.

þe son spake: 'I likened miselfe firste to Moises in figure, fore, when
he suld lede oute þe pupill, þe watir stode as a walle on þe riȝt side and
5 lift. Sikirli I ame þat Moises in figure, for I hafe br[ogh]t oute þe cristen pepill, and opyne heuen to þaim, and I haue shewed þaime þe wai.
Bot nowe haue I chosen me oþir frendes more speciall and secrete to
f. 54ʳᵃ me þan þe prophetis. þo are prestes, þe whilke noȝt allonli | heres mi
wordes, bot also þai trete me euirilke daye with þaire handes, þat no
10 prophet ne aungell might neuir do. þe same prestes, þe whilke I chese
frendes to me in place of prophetis, þai crye noght to me with swilke
desire and charite as þe prophetis did. Bot þai crye with two contrary
voices. þai cri noght as þe prophetis did, þat said, "Com, lorde, for
þou art full swete," bot þai cri, "Go fro vs, lorde, for þi wordes are
15 bitter and þi werkes are greuouse, and dose to vs grete sclaundir." Lo,
what þese cursed prestes sais.

'I stand before þaime as it were þe mildeste shepe, of whame þai
take wolle to þaire clethinge and milke to þaire refreshinge. And ȝet,
for all mi lufe, þai haue abhominacion of me. I stand before þaime, as
20 it were a geste, þat sais, "Frend, gife me necessaris to mi lifinge, and
take of God þe beste reward." þarefore, þai put me awai as if I ware a
wolfe þat lai in a spie vpon þe husbandes shepe, and for þe herber þat
f. 54ʳᵇ I aske, þai confound me as | a traitur, and þai put me awai as vnworthi
for to hafe gesteninge.

25 'Bot ˋhowˊ sall a gest þat is so congid do? Sall he oght bringe furth
armoure againe him þat so congis him? No forsoth, þat is no right, for
he þat is a lorde and hase possession, he mai graunt it and deny it as he
will. What sall þe geste do þane? Forsothe, he sall sai þus to him þat
puttes him awai, "Frend, for þou will noȝt herbere ˋmeˊ more, I will go
30 to anoþir þat sall do to me þe dede of merci." þan he commis to
aneoþir þat sais to him, "Sir, þou arte welcom. All þat I haue is þine.
Be þou lorde of it and take þi ese. I will be to þe seruaunt and geste."
In þat herbere where I here þat worde I ame greteli plesid to abide and
dwelle.

35 'Bot, forsoth, I am nowe as a geste þat is congid and put awai in ilke
place; and all if I might entir be mi powere where I wald, ȝit mi right-

5 broght] brint *or* bruit   17 þe] þe midill, midill *subpuncted*   21 þarefore]
þarefore for   25 how] *also marg.* what, *subpuncted*   31 welcom] welcom and,
and *subpuncted*

wisnes sais þus, "I sall noght entir bot to þaim þat ressaiues and takes
me as þaire God, and noȝt as a gest, with gode will, and vnto þaime þat
puttes þaire | will fulli into mi handes." '   f. 54ᵛᵃ

Capitulum 5[o]. Wordes of þe modir to þe son of blis-
singe and lowinge here mai ȝe rede.   5

Mari spake to þe son. 'Mi son, blissed be thi name withouten ende
with þi godhede, þat is withoutin begininge and ende. In þi godhede
are thre meruails, might, wisdom and vertu. þi pouer and might is as
it were a stre in a fire. þi wisdome is as it were þe see, þe whilke for
gretenes mai noght be ladin vp, þe whilke waxes also þat sometime it   10
couers þe hye hilles. So þi wisdom mai not be comprehended, bi þe
whilke þou made man abouen all þi werkes, and bi þe whilke þou
hase dissposed fowels in þe aire, bestes in þe erthe, fishes in þe see
(and to ilke of þaime þou hase gifen þaire time and þaire ordir), and
bi þe whilke þou giffes and takes mannes life at þi likinge, and bi þe   15
whilke þou giffes wisdome to þe meke and kepis it fro þe proude.
Thi vertu is as þe light of þe son, þat is bright in heuen and fulfilles
erthe with his light. So | dose þi vertu. It fulfilles all þat is,bothe hie   f. 54ᵛᵇ
and lawe, and þarefore þou, mi son, þat art mi God and mi lorde, be
þou blissed.'   20
þe son answerde, 'Mi derrest loued modir, þi wordes are to me full
swete, for þai com fro þi saule. þou art as it were a bright morninge þat
shinnes abouen all heuenes. Thi light and þi clerenes passes all aungels. þou hase drowyn to þe throwe þi brightnes þe verrai son þat is
mi godhede, so, forsothe, þat þe son of mi godhede, when it com into   25
þe, it festned so in þe þat it made þe warme in mi charite abouen all
oþir, and of þe brightnes of it þou art made more clere in mi wisdome
þen ani oþir.
'All þe derkenes of þe erthe is flemed, and heuenes, be þe, aire set in
clerenes. I sai in mi treuthe þat þi clennes, þat plesed me abouen aun-   30
gells, drowe mi godehede into þe, throwe whose warmnes þou were so
enflawmed þat þou closed within þe both God and man, þe whilke
haues | giuen light to man and gladded aungells. þarefore blissed be   f. 55ʳᵃ
þou of me, þi son, and þare sall noþinge be asked of þe bot it sall be
graunted. And wosoeuir askes merci with will to amend, bi þe þai sall   35
haue grace. For right as hete passes fro þe son, so bi þe sall be

gifen all merci. þou art as it were a large flowand welle, þat flowes
merci to þaime þat hase nede.'

þe modir saide againe to þe son, 'All vertu and blis be to þe, mi son,
for þou art God mi merci. Of þe is all gude þat I hafe. þou art as a sede
5 þat is noght sawen and gifes, neuirþeles, so plenteuousli froite þat
passes þe hundreth and þe thousand fruite. Of þe commis all merci,
þe whilke for gretenes mai nowþir be nowmbird ne spoken, and it mai
wele be betakend in þe hundreth nowmbir, þe whilke is nombir of
perfeccion, for of þe, Gode, is ilke perfeccion.'

10 þe son answerde to þe modir, 'Forsothe, modir, þou liknes me wele
to a sede þat hase multiplied and greteli waxen and was neuir sawen,
f. 55ʳᵇ for with mi godhede I come in|to þe, and mi manhede was neuir sawen
in þe throwe midlinge of kindes, and ȝit is it so growen in þe þat of it
flowes all merci. And sin þi wordes of soueraine swetnes drawes to þe
15 merci fro me, aske what þou will, and I sall graunt.'

þe modir saide, 'Mi son, sen I haue getin of þe graunt of merci, I
aske merci and helpe to þe gilti and to þe nedi. Forsothe, þare is iiii
places: þe firste is heuen, in þe whilke are aungels and holi saintes
saules, þat nedis noþinge bot þe, whome þai haue, and in þe all maner
20 of gude. þe second place is helle, whose dwellers are fulfilled with
malice, and þai are excluded fro all merci. þere mai no gude com to
þaime more.

'þe þird place is purgatori. And þai þat are þare nedis thre maner of
merci, for þai ar on thre wise punished. þai are desesed in þaire
25 heringe, for þai here noþinge bot sorowes of paine. þai are turmented
in þaire sight, for þai se noþinge bot þaire awen wrechedenes and
disese. þai are turmentid in þaire touche, for þai fele þe hete of fire
f. 55ᵛᵃ and of paine þat is | intollerabill. þarefor mi son, mi lorde, gife þaime
þi merci for mi praiere.'

30 þe son answerd, 'I sall gife þaime gladli, for þi lufe, thre maner of
merci: for þai sall haue ese in þaire heringe, comforth in þaire sight, and
þaire paine sall be lesse and more milde. Also, fro þis oure forward, all
þat are in þe moste paine of purgatori sall be esid and com to þe middis
paine, and all þat are in þe middes pain sall com to, and be esid in, þe
35 hiest paine. And þai þat are in þe esiest paine sall com to reste.'

þe modir saide, 'Louinge and honour be to þe, mi lorde. Bot, son,
þe fourt place is þe werld, where þe dwellers nedis thre þinges. þe
firste is contricion for sin. þe second is satisfaccion. þe þirde is gosteli
strengþe for to do gude dedes.'

40 þe sone answerde, 'Whateuir he be þat calles on þi name and hopis

in þe, with purpose to amend þat at he hase trespaste, these thre
þinges sall be giuen to him, and, moreouir, he sall haue þe kingdome
of blisse. I haue so mikill swetenes in þi wordes þat I mai deni noþinge
þat | þou askes, for þou will noþinge bot þat I will. þu art as it were a   f. 55ᵛᵇ
flawme þat brinnes in clerenes of light, of whome all oþir takes light   5
and encreses in brightnes. [S]o þ[ai], of þat grete charite þat stied vp
into mi herte and drowe me downe to þe, þai all sall be whikned and
kindled to life þat were dede and slaine in sin. And þai þat are dull and
slawe, as þe smoke of þe fire, þai sall be kindled and encrese in mi
charite.'   10

      Capitulum li. Wordes of þe modir blissinge þe son, and
      howe þe son liknes þe modir to a floure.

þe modir spake to þe son, 'Blissed be þi name, mi son, Iesu Criste,
and honor be to þi manhede abouen all þinges þat ar made of noght.
Blis be to þi godhede abouen all þinges þat are gode, þe wilke with þi   15
manhede is one God.' þe son answerde, 'Mi modir, þou art like to a
floure þat growes in a valei, aboute þe whilke were fife hie hilles. þe
floure grewe | of thre rotes, and þe stalke had no knottes. þis floure had   f. 56ʳᵃ
v fine leuis, full of all swetenes, and þe vale grewe w[i]th þe floure
aboue þe hilles, and þe leues spred þaime obrode aboue þe hight of   20
heuen, and abouen þe ordirs of heuenli angels.

  'Mi wele-beloued modir, þou art þe vale, for þe mekenes þat þou
had befor oþir. þis mekenes grewe ouir fife hilles. þe firste was
Moises for pouere. He had power on þe pupill as if it had been closed
in his [f]i[s]t. Bot þou hase closed þe lorde of all lawe in þi wombe,   25
wherfore þou art hiere þan þat hill. þe second hill was Heli, þe
whilke, for halines, was with bodi and saule taken into holi place. Bot
þou, mi derrest modir, hase a saule þat is taken vp abouen all þe ordirs
of aungels vnto þe trone of God, and þi clennest bodi is þarewith;
wharefore þou art hier þan Hely.   30

  'þe þird hill was þe strengþe of | Samson þat was more þan þe   f. 56ʳᵇ
strengh of oþir men, and ʒit þe deuel ouircom him with sotell
falshede. Bot þou, modir, ouircom þe deuell with þi strengh, wharefore þou art hiere þan Sampson. þe fourt hill was Dauid, þat was a
man eftir mi hert and eftir mi will; and ʒit he fell vnto sin. Bot þowe, mi   35
modir, folowed all mi will and neuir sinned. þe fift hill was

Salamon, þat was full of wisdome; and ȝit he was made a foole. Bot
forsothe, þou, mi modir, was full of wisdome, and þou was neuir
vnwise ne begilled: wharefore þou arte hiere þan Salomon.

'þe floure wex and grewe of thre rotis, for þou had thre þingis fro þi
5   [y]o[u]th, obediens, charite, and gudeli knawleche and vndirstandinge; oute of þe whilke rotes grewe a right stalke þat had no knottes,
þat is, þi will þat wald neuir bot þat I wald.

'Also, þis floure had fife leuis þat wex obrede obouen þe ordirs of
aungels. Forsoth, mi modir, þou art þe flour of þese fife leuis. þe first |
f. 56ᵛᵃ lefe is þi honeste, þat is so mikill þat aungels persaiues and sese þat
11   þou passes þaime bothe in holines and honeste. þe seconde lefe is þi
merci, þat was so mikill þat it sawe nede of all wreches and had compassion of þaime. And þou had þe bittirest and moste paine in time of
mi passion. Aungells are full of merci, bot ȝet þai suffird neuir sorowe.
15   Bot þou, mi mildest modir, had merci on wreches when þou felt þe
sorowe of mi dede, and for merci þou wald soner suffir sorowe and
paine þan to be excusid of it. And þarefore, þi merci ouirspredis þe
merci of aungels.

'þe þird leefe is þi mildnes. Forsothe, aungels are mild and coueites
20   gode to all. Bot þou, mi modir derrest, had in bodi and saule a will as
aungell, and þou did gude to all men, and þou denys ȝit noþinge to
none þat askes of his profite; wharefore þi mildnes is more excellent
þan aungell. þe fourt leef is þi fairnes and bewte. Aungels takes hede
ilke of þaim to oþirs bewte, and of þe farnes of saules and of bodis,
f. 56ᵛᵇ with meruaile. Bot | þai see þe bewete of þi saule, more excellent þan
26   all [þat] is made of noght, and þai see þi honeste of þi bodi, þat it is
more excellent þan is of all þinges þat are made. And so þi bewte
passes þe bewte of all creatures.

'þe fift leefe was þi gudeli lufe, throw þe whilke þare was noþing
30   likinge to þe bot God (and so is to aungels God allonli þaire delite).
Bot when þai sawe þi delite in God, þaime thoght þan in þaire consciens þat þaire delite brint þan as light in gudeli charite, for þai sawe
þi delite as þe moste hote and brinninge fire sendinge vp a flawme to
mi godhede. And þarefore, mi swetteste modir, I saide treuli þat þi
35   gudeli lufe ouirpassed aungels.

'þis floure þat hade there fife leues, honeste, merci, mildnes,

---

4 fro] for   5 youth] thoght, *Lat.* iuventute   obediens] obediens and gudeli,
and gudeli *subpuncted*   7 neuir] neuir be, be *subpuncted*   10 aungels] aungels
sese and, sese and *subpuncted*   12 sawe] sawe no, no *subpuncted*   20 a] a
devise, devise *subpuncted*   21 denys] deniys, i *subpuncted*   26 þat¹] *om.*

fairnes, and souerain delite was full of all swetnes, and who þat will
taste it, him most drawe ner and resaiue it in himselfe, for so did þou,
mi gude modir. þou was so swete to mi fadir þat he ressaiued þe all-
togidir into his spirit, and þi swetenes plesed | him moste.   f. 57ra

'A floure also bers sede bi hete and vertu of þe son, of þe whilke   5
commis froite. Bot blissed be þe son of mi godhede, þat tuke manhede
of þi maidenli wombe. For right as sede, whereeuir it be sawen,
bringes furth swilke frute as þe sede is, so mi membris were like to thi
membres in forme and face. Neuirþelesse, I was man, and þou woman
and maiden. þis vale is con[u]aied abouen all hilles with his floure,   10
when þi bodi was taken vp abouen all ordirs of aungels with þi holieste
saule.'

Capitulum lii. Wordes of þe modir to þe son, prainge
þat his wordes be festined in þe hertis of hir frendes.

þe blissed maiden spake to hir son. 'þou art blissed, mi son, mi Gode,   15
lorde of aungels, and kinge of blis. I prai þe þat þi wordes, þe whilke
þou spekis, take rote and be feste in þe hertes of þi frendes, and so
stedfastli abide in þaire saules als glewe cleued to Noe shipe, þe |
whilke might noght be weshin awai be no tempest ne veddir. Also, I   f. 57rb
prai þat þai be sprede of brod in þe werld, as braunches and floures of   20
swetenes þat sendes wide þare swete reflaire. Also I pray þat þai
bringe fruite furth and wax swete, as it were a date, whose swetenes
delites greteli þe saule.'

þe son answerde, 'Blissed be þou, mi derrest modir, as mine aungell Gabriel saide: "Be þou, Mari, blissed before all wemen"; and I   25
bere wittnes þat þou art holiest and blissed abouen all aungels. þou
art as it were a floure in þe gardin, þe whilke is more excellent in
sauoure of swetenes, vertu and fairnes þan all þe floures þat standes.
þese flowres are mi chosen derlinges, fro Adam into þe ende of þe
world, þe whilke I planted and set in þe gardin of þe world to burion   30
and to bringe furth froite of vertuse. Bot amange all þat were and sall
be, þou art passinge and moste excellent in sauoure of gode life and
meknes, in fairnes of maidenhede and clennes, and in vertu of
abstinens.

'I bere þe | witnes þat in mi passion þou was more þen a martir. In   f. 57va
abstinens þou was more þan a confessoure. In merci and gude will   36

8 frute] frute whereuir it be sawen, *exc.* frute, *subpuncted*   10 conuaied] consaiued   11 vp] vp all, all *subpuncted*

þou was more þen ane aungell. Wharefore, for þi sake, I sall rote and
festen mi wordes in þe hertes of mi frendes as glewe þat is strangeste,
and þai sall be del[a]ted as flourres of swete sauour: þai sall bringe
furth froite as þe date of soueraine swetenes.'

5   þan saide þe lorde to þe spouse, 'Sai to þi frende þat he expone
þese wordes þat are wretin vnto his fadir, whose herte acordes to mi
hert, and he sall shewe þaime to þe archebisshope, and he to anoþir
bishope, and fro þe time þat þai be wele enformed, thai sall sende
þaime to þe third bishop.

10   'Sai to him þus on mi behalfe: "I am þi God, whome þou loues
before all oþir thynges. Take hede and see-þe saules þat I haue boght
with mi preciouse blod are as þai were saules þat knawes noght God,
whom þe deuell hase in thralldom so horribili þat he punish[es] þaime
greuouseli in all þair partise. And þarefor, if mi woundes sauers

f. 57ᵛᵇ aniþinge in þi | saule, if þou set oght be mi scourginges and paines þat
16   I suffird, shewe in þi dedis howe mikill þou lufes me, and make mi
wordes þat I haue spoken with min awen mouthe for to be oppinli
knawen, and bere þaime in þine awen persone to þe hede of þe kirke.
And I sall gife þe so mi spirit þat where þou findes two in discension

20   and discorde, bi þe vertu þat I sall gife þe, þou sall acorde þaime, if þai
will trowe. Forthirmore, and for more euidens of mi wordes, þou sall
bere, with þe, witnes to þe bishope of þaim to whame mi wordes has
sauerde and gifen delite.

   ' "Mi wordes are, as it were, a þing, þe whilke, þe more hete it hase,
25   þe sonner it relentes and meltis. So mi wordes, þe more a man etis
þaime and chewes þaime small in þe feruoure of mi charite, þe more
he waxis fat in heuenli swetenes, and in desire of inwarde gladnes in
mi loue. Bot þai are dispised of some, for gosteli swetnes sauours
þaime noght. þe prince of þe erthe, whome I haue chosen to be |

f. 58ʳᵃ treweli with me, he sall help and haue godes treweli getin; he sall finde
31   to þe necessares be þe wai." '

    Capitulum liii. Wordes of beneson and louing betwene
    þe modir and þe son.

Mari spake to þe son. 'Blessed be þou, mi son, God and lord of
35   aungels. þou art he wose vois þe prophetis herde, whose bodi þe
apostils sawe, and whome þe Jewes and þe enemis felt. þou art one

---

3 delated] delited, *Lat.* dilatabuntur   13 punishes] punish   29 be] be
with, with *subpuncted*   34 God] mi God, mi *subpuncted and ruled through*

God with godhed and manhede, and þe holi goste. For treuli þe prophetes sawe þe blisse of godhede; þe appostils sawe þi manhede, whome þe Iewes festined to þe crosse. And, þare[fore], be þou blissed withoute bigining and withoute ende.'

þe son answerde, 'Blissed be þou, for þou art maiden and modir. 5 þou art þe arche þat was in þe lawe, in þe whilke was þre þinges: a ʒerde, aungelfude and tabils. With þe wande was þre þinges done: first, it was chaunged into a serpent þat was withoute venom. þe second, þe se was departed þarewith. þe þird, watir was broght oute of þe stone. 10

'I am þat ʒerde in figure, þe whilke lai in þi wombe and tuke of þe man|hede. As þe serpent was fertfull to Moises, so am I to mine f. 58ʳᵇ enemis, fro whome þai flee and dredes me, and hase me in abhomi- nacion as a serpent, notwithstandinge þat I ame withoute venom of malice, and full of grace and merci. I suffir miselfe to be taken and 15 halden of þaime if þai will; if þai seke me, I com againe to þaime. I rin to þaime as þe modir to þe son þat was loste and is funden, if þai call vpon me. I giffe þaime mi merci, and I forgife þaime synnes, if þai crie to haue forgifnes. All þis do I to þaime, and ʒit þai hafe abhominacion of me as of a serpent. 20

'Also, be þis ʒerde þe se was departed, when þe wai to heuen, þat was before closed and speret bi sin, was made patent and opin be mi blode and mi paine. For treuli, þan braste þe see and þat might noght be gone before. þan was made a wai, when þe paines of all mi membres com nere to þe herte, and þe hert braste for violence of þo 25 pains. Eftir, when þe pupill was passed þe see, Moises lede þaim noght onone into þe land of beheste, bot into desert, wher þai suld be taght and proued. | So nowe, when þe pupill takis faith and knawinge f. 58ᵛᵃ of mi commandmentes, þai entre noght onone to heuen, bot it is nedfull at þai be proued in þe wildirnes of þis werld howe þai lufe 30 God.

'And it is to knawe þat þe pupill greued God in wildirnes bi thre þinges. First, for þai made an ydole and wirshiped it. þe second, for þai couetid fleshe as þai had before in Egipt. þe þird, for pride, for þai wald haue gone and foghten with þe enemis withoute Goddes will. On 35 þe same wise feghtes men nowe againe me in þe werld. First, he wirshipes an ydole, for he wirshippes more þe world, an[d] þinges þat

3 þarefore] þare   4 bigining] begiining   9 departed] departed þere parted, *exc.* departed, *subpuncted*   17 modir to þe] *twice*, to þe modir *subpuncted* 18 synnes] synmes   37 and] þan

ar in þe werld, þan me, þat ame maker of all þat þare is; and so þe werld is þaire Gode and noght I. For I saide in mi gospell, "Where þe tresoure of man is, þare is his herte." Bot þe tresour of man is þe werld. þarefore to it and noght to me is all his lufe and his herte, and þarefore, as þe

5 pupull did, so sall þese fall be swerde of endles dampnacion as anentes þe saule.

f. 58vb 'Also, þai sin be desire of fleshe, for I haue gifen all þinge to man | for to vse to his nede and in mesure, bot he will haue it eftir luste to outrage, if kinde might suffice. He wald withoute cesinge do licheri, ete, drinke

10 and haue oþir desires, and neuir cese of sinning if he might. And þarefore it sall fall as it did to oþir in disserte; þai sall die sodaine dede. What is þis present life bot as a pointe to eternite and euirlastingnes? þarefore þai sall die in bodi, as it were a sodaine dede for shortnes of þis present life, and þai sall be in paine anentes þe saule withoute ende.

15 'þai also sinned in desert be pride. So wald men now be þaire pride stie vpe into heuen, and þai triste in þaimeselfe and noght in me, doynge þaire awen will and forsakinge mine. þarefore, as þat pupill was enemise, so sall þese be slaine in þe saule of fendes, and þaire paine sall euir abide. þus þai hate me as a serpent, and wirshipes one

20 fals ydole for me, wald haue þaire awen desires and noght mine, and luffes þaire awen pride befor mi mekenes. Neuirþelese, I am merci-

f. 59ra full, þat if þai turn to me with contricion of hert, | as a mercifull fadir, I turn me to þaime, and resaiues þaime to grace.

'Also bi þis wand watir was broght oute of þe stone. þis stone is þe

25 harde hert of man, þe whilke, if it be smetin with mi drede and lufe, þare flowes oute teres of contricion and penance, for þar es none so vnworthi ne so euell, if he turn him to me, if he inwardeli take hede to mi passion, if he drede mi power and lufe mi gudenes, and take consideracion howe trees bringes furth fruite, and þe erth also, bot he sall

30 breste on wepinge and all his partis sall be moued and stirrid to deuocion in me.

'Also (for þe secound) in þe arche was manna. Right so, mi modir and maiden, in þe lai þe fode of aungels and of holi saules, and of rightwis lifers in erthe, to whome noþinge pleses bot mi swetnes: to

35 whome þe world is all dede, þe whilke, if it were mi will, wald haue no bodeli fode. Also in þe arke were þe tables of þe lawe. So in þe was þe lorde of all lawes. And, þarefore, be þou blissed before all þinges þat are made of noght in heuen or erthe.

7 for²] twice, first subpuncted   12 þarefore] twice, first subpuncted   26 flowes] folowes, Lat. effluunt

Eftir þis he spake to | þe spouse and saide, 'Say thre þinges to mi f. 59rb
frendes. When I was bodeli in þe werld I tempird so mi wordes þat
gude men were þe bettir be þaime, and euell were made gude bi
þaime, as be ensampill in Mawdelein, Mathewe, and oþir mo. Also, I
mesured so mi wordes þat mine enemis miȝt noght febill þaime. And, 5
þarefore, lat þaime þat mi wordes ar sent to trauaile with feruo[u]re of
spirit, þat gude be þe bettir and euell forsake sin. And be þai war þat
mine enemis lete not mi wordes.

'Forsoth, I do no more wrange to þe deuell þan to aungels in heuen.
And I wald, I cuth speke wordes þat all þe werld suld her. I might also, 10
and I wald, opin hell, þat all men suld se þe paines. Bot þat were noght
right, for man suld serue me þan for drede, þe whilke is halden to
serue me for loue and charite: for þare sall none entir heuen bot he
haue charite. For þan did I wronge to þe deuell, if I suld take him þat
is bicommen his man fro him withoute gude meritori werkes. Also I 15
suld þan do wronge to | aungels þat is in heuen if I suld euen him þat is f. 59va
a clene spirit, and moste birnand in charite, v[n]to þe spirit of most
vnclene man. þarefore þare sall none entir heuen [bot] if he be purged
in þe fire of purgatori as gold in þe fourneis, or elles þat he be so longe
time exercide in gude werkes in erthe þat þare be funden in him no 20
filth ne foule spot for to spurge.

'If þou knawe noght to whome mi wordes sall be sent, I sall tell þe.
He is worthi to haue mi wordes þat wele desereues þaime throwe his
werkes, þat he com to heuen, or elles þat he hase deserued þaim
throwe gude werkes þat ar passed. To þaime sall mi wordes be made 25
opin, and into þaime þai sall entir, for þai þat sauers mi wordes, and
þai þat hopes mekeli þat "Mi name is wretine in þe boke of life," þai
holden mi wordes. þai þat sauers þaime noght, þai considir mi wordes
and onone þai kaste þaime awai.'

Capitulum liiii. Wordes to þe spouse of þe spirit of hir 30
thoghtes. *Require hic inferius*.

þe aungell spake þus to þe spouse: 'þare is two spirites; one | is made f. 59vb
of noght, an[o]þir vnmade. þe spirit þat is noȝt made hase thre þinges.
First, he is hote; he is swete and clene. Firste, he is warme of himselfe
and of none oþir þinge þat is made, for he, with þe fadir and holi goste, 35
is maker of all and allmighti. þan warmes he, when a saule

6 feruoure] feruoire   17 vnto] vto   18 bot] *om.*   22 whome]
wohome   33 anoþir] anvnþir

is all birnand in þe lufe of Gode. Also, he is swete, when þare is noþinge plesand to þe saule, ne waxis swete to it, bot God, and minde of Goddes werkes. Also, he is so clene þat no sin mai be funden in him: noþinge foule, corruptibill ne changeabill.

5 'He makes [hote], bot noght as materiall fire, ne as þe visibill son: bot his hete is þe inwarde lufe of þe saule, and þe desire þat rauishes vp þe saule into God. He waxis also swete to þe saule, bot noght as delitabill wine or luste of ani werldli þinge; bot þe swetenes of þat spirit is vncomparabill to all temporall swetnes. And he þat sauers it 10 noȝt mai noȝt knawe it be thoght. Also, þat spirit is so clene as it ware þe beme of þe son, in þe whilke mai be funden none vnclennes.

'þe second spirit þat is made of noght hase oþir thre þinges: he is f. 60ʳᵃ birnand, | bittir, and vnclene. He is brinynge and consuminge as fire, for he kyndles þe saule þat he has in possession with þe fire of lichere 15 and of coueitise, þat þe saule þinkes not, ne desires noght ellis, bot fulfilling of swilke likynges: in so mikill þat somtime, for to haue swilke lustis, þai lose þe temporall life, all erthli wirshipe and com-forth. Also, he is bittir as galle, for he enflawmes so þe saule with his delite, þat he settes noght bi þe ioyes of heuen, bot he calles endles 20 gudes foli. All þat euir is of God, and þat he is halden to do, semis to him bittir and noght swete, bot as abhominabill as a vomet or gall.·

'Also, he is vnclene, for he makes þe saule so vile, and redi to sin, þat sho is ashamed of no sin, ne sho wald forsake no sin, were it no more for shame of man þan of God. And þarefore he is cald a 25 brinninge spirit, for he brinnes euir to wickednes and settis oþir on fire with him. He is bittir, for all gud þinge is bittir to him and he f. 60ʳᵇ makes it bittir also to oþir. Also, he is vnclene, | for he hase his delite in vnclennes, and sekis þe felishipe of swilke.

'Bot now mai þou aske and sai to me, "Art þou noȝt a spirit made as 30 he is? Whi þan art þou noght swilke ane as he?" I answer[e], I ame made of þe same God þat he is made of, for þare is bot one God, fadir, son and holi goste (noght thre goddes bot one God), and we are both wele made and to gude, for God made noþinge bot wele and gude. Bot I ame as a sterne, for cause I stode and abode in þe gudnes and charite 35 of God. And, þarefore, as a stern is noght withouten clerenes and brightnes, ne swilke a cole is noght withoute blaknes, right so a gude aungell, þe whilke is a stern, is noght withoute brightnes of holi goste,

---

5 hote] *om., Lat.* calefacit   8 of þat] of þat þinge, of þinge *ruled through,* þinge *subpuncted*   13 birnand] *Quire catchphrase,* bittir, *twice below*   27 to] to him delite] delite also, also *subpuncted*   30 he²] he is, is *subpuncted*   answere] answerd

and all þat euir he hase he has of þe fadir, son and holi goste, be whose lufe he is warme, be whose brightnes he shinnes, and ay cleues to him and conformes him to his will, ne he will neuir þinge bot þat God will: þarefor he brinnes in lufe and is clene.

'Bot þe deuell is as it were a foule blake cole, latheste of all creatures, for, as he was made fairer þan oþir, so he fell laither þen | oþir. Right as an aungell of God shinnes in Goddes light, and withoute cesinge brinnes in his charite, so þe deuell is euirmore kyndelinge in malice, þe whilke is insaciabill as þe gudenes of þe holi goste (and his grace is vnspekeabill).

'Also, þare is none in þe werld so rotid with þe deuell bot somtime þe gude spirit stirris and moues his hert to godenes, ne þare is none so gude bot þe deuell touches him somtime with temptacion. Bot, forsothe, it is for encrese of grete blis of gude men, and noght for þaire euell, þat God suffirs mani of þaime be tempted of þe deuell. For treuli þe son of Gode, one in godhede with þe fadir and holi goste, was tempted in his manhede. Mikill more his chosen suld be tempted for þaire grete rewarde. Also, mani gude men falles oft times in sin, and þaire consciens is perplex throwe fallace of þe fende, bot throwe þe vertu of þe holi gost, þai rise more mighti and standis þe more strange.

'Neuirþeles, þere is none bot he knawes in his consciens wheþir þe suggestion of þe deuell ledis to sin | or to gude, if he will beseli examin it and þinke wele of it. And þarefore, þou spouse of mi lorde, þou hase noȝt to doute of þe spirit of þi thoghtes, wheþir it be gude or euell, for þi consciens shewes to þe what þou sall do and what þou sall leue.

'Bot what sall he do with whame þe deuell is full? Forsoth, þe gude spirit mai noȝt entre into him þat is full of þe euell spirit. Him buse do thre þinges. Firste, pure and hole confession of sinnes, for, all if his hert may noȝt full be contrite sone because it is so harded in sin, ȝit confession dose þat gode, þat it makes þe deuell to gife a cesinge of sin, for it ceses at tempt, and suffirs þe saule to make a skipe towarde þe holi goste. þe second, him most hafe mekenes, þat he purpos fulli to amend sinnes þat he hase done, and for to do þe gude dedis he mai. þan beginnes þe deuell for to go fro him. þe þird, if he will optene againe þe gude spirit, him moste prai and biseke God with a meke spirit, and be con|trite of sinnes þat ar don with verrai charite, for charite to God slaes þe deuell. He had leuer ane hondreth times die þan a man shewed þe lest gude point of charite to God, he is so full of envy and malice.'

Eftirward spake þe blissed maiden to þe spouse and saide, 'Nowe, þou spouse of mi son, do vpon þi clothes and take to þe thi nouche, þat menis þ[e] passion of mi son.' þe spouse answerde, 'Set þou it on me, mi ladi.'

5 þe maiden saide, 'Forsothe, I shall. I will tell þe howe mi son was disposed, and whie he was so feruentli desired of þe fadirs. He stode as a man emiddes, bitwene two cites, and a voice of þe tone cite cried þus to him, "þou man þat standes in þe middes wai betwene þe cites, þou art a wise man, for þou can eschewe perels þat are like to falle, and 10 þou art stronnge and mighti to suffir diseses. þou hase so stronge on herte þat þou dredis right noght. þarefore we desire þe and we haue

f. 61rb abedin þe. Opin oure dore" (for þe enemis | vmbiseged it þat it suld noȝt be opynd).

'þe voice of þe second cite saide þus, "þow man, here oure plaint 15 and oure seynge, þat art moste strange and moste manli. We sit in dirknes; we suffir hungir and intollerabill thirste. Take hede þan to oure wreched nede. We are smiten down as it were hai with a sithe. We are walowed and dry fro all gode. All oure strenghe is failed. Comm to vs and saue vs, for we haue abiden þe alloneli, and we haue 20 hopid in þe, oure deliuerere. Come and releue oure nede: turn oure sorowe into gladnes. Be þou oure helpe and oure hele. Com, o þou worthieste and blissed bodi, þat passid fro þe clene virgin."

'Mi son herd þese two voices fro two citees, heuen and hell, and þarefore he had merci, and, with his bittirest passion and shedinge of 25 his blode, he opind þe ȝates of hell, and deliuerd and tuke oute his frendess. He opind also heuen, and, gladynge aungels, he entird into it þaime at he deliuerd fro hell. Mi doghtir, þinke on þis and haue þaim euir befor þine een.' |

f. 61va Capitulum lv. Wordes of þe lorde, howe he liknes him-
30 selfe to a mighti bigger, et [c]etera.

'I am like to a mighti lorde þat bigged a citee and called it eftir his awen name, in þe wilke he made a palais, and in þe pailais diuers chambirs to put in his necessaris. When he had bigged his palais and ordained for his þinges, he dispoised and partid his pupill into thre 35 partis, and saide þus: "I mon wende into fere cuntrees. Abide ȝe and trauaile manli for mi wirshipe. I haue puruaid and ordained for ȝou all þat is nedefull to ȝou. Ȝe haue defenders of citee fro enemis. I haue

ordeynde laborers to fede 30u, and I haue bidyn þat þai sall gife me þe
tent part of þarre laboure, þe whilke þai sall reserue and pai to mi
profit and wirshipe."

'Bot when a litill time was passed, þe name of þe cite was forgetin.
And þan said þe domesmen, "Oure lorde is gone into fer contrese. 5
Gife we right dome, and do we rightwisnes, þat we be noght reproued
when oure lorde comes againe, bot þat | we resaiue of him wirship and f. 61ᵛᵇ
blissinge." þan saide þe defenders of þat citee, "Oure lorde tristis in
vs, and he hase ordained þat we sall kepe his house. þarefore, do we
abstinens fro outrage of mete and drinke, þat we be noght vnabill to 10
fight. Abstene we also fro ouirmikill slepe, þat we be noght dissaiued,
as men þat are vnware. Be we wele armed and ai wakinge, þat if þe
enemis com we be noght vnredi, for vpon vs hanges moste þe wirshipe
of þe lorde and þe hele of þe pepill."

'þan saide þe laborers, "þe wirship of oure lorde is mikill and his 15
reward is glorius. þarefore, trauaile we mightili and gife we him noght
allonli þe tent parte of oure labour, bot also offir we to him all þat is
lefte ouir oure nedfull sustinance, for so mikill þe more glorius sall þe
thanke and þe rewarde be as he sees in vs plente of charite."

'Bot eftir þis, when a litill time was passed, þe lorde of þe cite and of 20
þe palais was forgetin. And þan þai spake þus | to þaimeselfe: "Oure f. 62ʳᵃ
lorde taris lange and we wote neuir if he sall com againe. þarefore
deme we eftir oure awen will, and do we whateuir vs likes." þan saide
þe defendoures, "We are folis, for we trauaile and we wate noght for
what rewarde. Late vs þarefore acorde for [e]ure with oure enemis, 25
and slepe we, and drinke we with þaime, and charge we noght whose
enemis þai were." þan saide þe laborers, "Whi kepe we oure gold to
anoþir, and who sall haue it eftir vs? We wote neuir. þarefore it is
bettir þat we vse it and dispose it to oure profite. Wharefore, gife we þe
tent parte to þe jugges and domesmen, for when þai are plesid we mai 30
do what vs likes."

'Forsothe, I ame like to þat mighti lorde, for I haue bigged me a
citee þat is in þe werld, and in þat a palais–þat is, holi kirke. þe name
of þe werld was Goddes wisdome. In þe biginninge, in þe whilke it
was made, þis name was wirshiped of all, and God was loued of his 35
creature in his wisdome, and was prechid | meruolous. Bot nowe þe f. 62ʳᵇ
nam of þis citee is withoute wirshipe and chaunged and called mannis
wisdome.

9 and he hase ordained] *twice, second subpuncted*   25 eure] oure

'þe domesm[e]n, þat demed firste in rightwisnes and in þe drede of
God, are nowe turned into pride and for to begile and supplant þe
pore and þe simpill man. þai desire to be faire of speche for to haue
prassinge of man. þai speke þinges of plesaunce for to gete fauoure.
5 þai shewe þaire wordes smotheli, for þai wald be called gude and
mild. þai ressaiue giftes, and so peruertis dome. þai are wise for þaire
temporall auantage and for to haue þaire awen will. Bot þai are dome
in mi will and wirshipe. þai trede simpill men vndirfote, and makes
þaime to be still. þai strech oute þaire coueitise to all, and treuthe þai
10 turn into fals, and right to wrannge. þis is þe wisdome þat nowe is
loued, and mine is forgetin.
'þe defenders of þe kirke, þat suld be curteis knightes, þai se mine
enemis impugne mi kirke and þai make dissimulacion. Thai here
f. 62ᵛᵃ howe þai reproued it, and þai charge it noght. þai knewe, and | felis, þe
15 werkes of mine enemis contrarious to mi commandmentes, and þai
suffir it pacientli. þai se þaime euerilk dai, howe at þaire awen likinge
þai do þe dedeli sinnes and are noght rep[e]ntant, bot sleps in sin. And
þai bind þaim bi othe and swerynge to be of þaire felishipe.
'þe laborers is all comunt[e], þe whilke refusis mi comandmentes,
20 and haldes mi giftes and mi tendes. þai offir giftes to þaire domesmen
and jugges beforesaide, and dose þaime reuerence, þat þai mai finde
þaime wele willinge and plesed. Trewli, I mai sai boldeli þat þe
swerde of mi drede and of mi kirke in þe werld is cast awai and in þe
stede of it is ressaiued a bage full of siluer and monee.'

25 Capitulum lvi. Wordes how God declares þat is saide
before.

'I said to þe before þat þe swerd of mi kirke was caste awai, and in
stede of it þare is taken a seke full of siluir, whilke is opin on þe tone
p[ar]te and depe on þe toþir, for whateuere entres findes neuir
30 bothom ne grounde, ne it is neuir filled. þis is þe sekke and purs of
f. 62ᵛᵇ coueitise, | þat passes all maner and mesure, and it is so fer gon þat
God is dispised, and noþinge is desired bot monee and þaire awen
propir will.
'Neuirþeles, I ame as a lorde þat ame both fadir and jugge, to
35 whame, when he gase to juggement, þai speke þat standes beside,
"Lorde, go sone furth and gife þe dome": to whome þe lord sais,

1 domesmen] domesman   17 repentant] repntant   19 comunte] committ
23 mi²] mi drede kirke, mi drede *subpuncted*   29 parte] pte

"Abide a while till tomorn; for happeli mi son mai in þe mene time
amend him." When þe next dai is commen, þe pupill sais to him,
"Lord, go furth and gife dome. Whi taris þou so and will noght deme
þe gilti?" þe lord answerde, "3it abides a while if mi son will amend
him, and if he will no3t þan sall I do right." On þe same wise I suffir a 5
man vnto þe laste pointe, for whi, I ame both fadir and jugge.
Neuirþelesse, for mi right is vnchaungeabill, all if I tari lange, 3it I sall,
forsothe, ponis þe sinners þat will no3t amend þaime, or elles I sall do
merci to þaime þat turnes fro syn.

'I saide þe also before þat I departed þe pepull into thre partis, 10
domes|men, defenders and laborers. Clerkes betakens þe domesmen   f. 63ʳᵃ
þat hase chaunged Goddes wisdome into mannis vaine wisdome. So
clerkes is wont to do, þe whilke hase resaiued mi ten commandments,
and þai haue put þaim all into one werd. þis is þe werd: "Put furth þi
hand and gife me monee." þe wisdome of þaime is to speke faire and 15
do euell, to shewe [ou]t[e]ward as þa wer mine, and to wirke contrari
to me. þaire sininge for giftes suffirs gladli men in sin, and with þaire
euell ensampill þai hindir þe hele of þe simpill man.

'Also, þe defenders of þe kirke, þat suld be, are vntrewe, for þai hafe
broken þaire othe and þaire beheste þai made when þai ware made 20
knightes. þai sin ofte againe þe faithe of mi kirke, and againe it þai suffir gladli statute and constitucion to be made. Also laborers, þat is þe
commune, are [as] þai ware wilde bulles, þat hase thre þinges. þai
skrape vp þe erthe with þaire fete: þai ete to þai be full: and þai haue
þaire luste eftir þaire desire. So | dose nowe þe commune. With all   f. 63ʳᵇ
þaire effeccions þai scrape to þaime temporall gudes. þai fill þaime-   26
selfe with outrage of gluttrie and vanite of þe werld, and þai fulfill
withoute reson þe lustes of þe fleshe.

'3it, all if I haue mani enemis, þare is amange þaime mani preue
frendes, as it was saide to Heli þat troued I hade no frende of life bot 30
himselfe. "I haue," quod God, "seuen thousand men, þe whilke bowed
neuer þaire knees before Balle." So I haue nowe amanges mani
enemis mani preuei frendes, þat wepis ilke dai for mi mani enemis
hase so grete powere, and for mi nam is so dispised.

'And þarefore, for þe praiers of þaim, as a gude charitefull kinge þat 35
knawes þe euell of þe cite, suffirs paciently þe dwellers, and sendes
lettirs to his frendes, biddinge þaim to beware on þe parell, so I send
wordes to mi frendes, þe whilke ar no3t so derke to vndirstand as

---

14 werd¹·²] werld   15 and²] and to, to *subpuncted*   16 outeward] eftirward,
Lat. simulare   23 as] *om.*   37 send] send mi, mi *ruled through*

is þe Apocalips þat I shewed to Jon, for I wald in mi time, of mi spirit,
it suld be plainli expounde; ne þai ar noȝt so derke as þe þinges | þat
Paule sawe when he was rauishet, þe whilke were not lefull to be
spoken; bot þai are so opin þat all, both small and grete, mai knawe
5　þaim and vndirstand þaime. And þai ar so light þat ilke man mai take
þaime þat will. þerefore, I will þat mi frendes make mi wordes to com
to mine enemis, as in hape þai be turned. And be þaire dome and
perill shewed to þaime þat forþinke þaire sinnes and euell dedis, for
elles juggement sall com to þe cite, and as þat wall is all tobroken
10　where no stone cleues to, or þare is noght two stones in þe ground, so
it sall be done to þe cite of þe werld.

　　'þe domesmen sall brin in þe moste hote brininge fire. þare is no
fire hatter þen þat at is norishet with fattnes. Bot þese domesmen were
right fatt, for þai had more fredome to fulfill þaire luste of will; þai
15　passed oþir in wirshipe and habundance of temporall gudes, and þai
were more habundant in malice and wikkednes. And þarefore þai sall
brin in þe moste h[o]te caldron.

　　'þai þat suld | haue defended þe kirke sall be hanged in þe hiest
gibet or galowes. Galows ar of two trees standinge vpright, and þe þird
20　ligynge ouirtwarte. þis is þe cruell paine þat þai haues þe whilk hase
two trees: firste, for þai trowed noght mine endeles reward, ne þai
laburd noȝt þareto with wirkynge. þe second is, þat þai mistraisted of
mi powere and of mi gudenes, þat I wald noght ne might gife þaime
enoghe. þe ouirthwart tree is þair shrewed consciens, for þai vndir-
25　stode wele and did euell, ne þai ware noȝt ashamed to wirke againe
þaire consciens. þe helter is endeles fire, þat may neuir be slokinde
with watir ne kut with sheris, ne it sall neuir ende ne briste with age.

　　'On þis galowe, where is þe most paine and fire þat mai noȝt be
slokend, þai sall hange, and þai sall haue confusion of traiturs, for þai
30　were vntrewe. þai sall here reproues, for mi wordes displesed þaime.
þar sall euir be cursinge and werieing in þaire mouth, | for it was swete
to þaime befor to be luffed of man and praissed. And liuand kro[w]is
sall all toriue þaime in þis gibet, þat is, deuels þat are neuir filled, and
þai sall neuir be all consumed, bot þai sall euir life in turment, for
35　withoute ende sall þare liue þaire turmentoures. þare sall be wo þat
neuirmare sall haue ende, and wrechednes þat sall neuir be lesse. Wo
is to þaime þat þai were born and wo at þaire life was proloyned.

　　'Also, þe right of laborers sall be as it were of bullis. Bothe þe flesh

---

and þe skyn of bole is tugh and hard. þarefore þe dom sall be euir moste harde; þat is, dede of hell þat sall turment þaim þat hase dispised me, and hase loued þaire awen will for mi commandment.

'þarefore mi lettir and mi wordes is þis: "Trauaile mi frendes ai sadli, þat mi wordes com to mine enemis discreteli and wiseli, þat þai mai here if þai will and leue sin." Yf it so be þat ani men sai when þai haue herd mi wordes, "Abide we ȝit a litill while; he sall | not come so sone; it is noght ȝit his time," I swere in mi godhede þat put Adame oute of Paradise, þat gose to Pharao ponishinge be ten plages, þat I sall com to þaim sonner þan þai wene. I swere in mi manhede, þat I tuke of þe maiden withouten sin for þe hele of men, in þe whilke I had tribulacion in herte (and suffird pain in fleshe and dede) for þe lufe of men, in þe whilke I rose and stied vp to heuen and sittis on þe right hand of mi fadir, verrai God and man in one persone, þat I sall fulfill mi wordes. I swere in mi spirit, þe whilke was sente on þe apostels on þe Pentecoste dai, and enflawmed þaime þat þai suld speke tounges of all folkes, þat, bot þai turn þaim to [me] with repentance as freil seruandes, I sall be venged in mi wreth vpon þaim.

'þan sall þaim be wo in bodi and saule: wo þat þai come lifynge into þe werld and leued vnclene: wo for þaire luste was bot litill and vaine, and þe turment sall be withouten end. þan sall þai fele þat nowe þai will noght trowe, for mi speche was | wordes of charite. þan sall þai knawe þat I warned þaime as a fadir, and þai wald noght here me. And þarefore, sin þai wald noght trowe to mi wordes, þai sall trowe to mi dedes.'

f. 64rb

f. 64va

Capitulum lvii. Wordes of likenes þat þe cristen dose to God þe son as did þe Jewes.

þe son spake to þe spouse. 'þe cristen dose nowe to me as sometime dide þe Jewes. þai caste me oute of þe tempill, and had gud will to haue slaine me, bot, for mi oure was noght ȝit commin, I passed oute of þaire handis. So dose cristen men nowe to me. þai caste me oute of þaire saule, þat suld be mi tempill, and þai wald gladli sla me if þai might. I ame in þaire mouthe as it were rotin fleshe and stinkand, and þai deme me as a man þat spake lesinges, and þai set right noght bi me. þai turn þe bake to me, and I sall turn þe hindir parte of mi heued to þaime, for in þare mouthe is noþinge bot coueitise, and in þaire bodi is licheri as in a beste. þere is noþinge plesinge to þaire

17 me] *om.*   freil] freli

f. 64vb heringe bot pride, ne to þare | sightis bot delites of þe world. Mi
passion and mi charite is to þaime abhominabill, and mi life greuouse.
'þarefore, I sall do as a beste þat hase mani denys. If he be huntid,
he flees fro one to anoþir. So sall I bicause þat þe cristen pursuis me
5 with ill werkes, and þai hunt me fro þe den of þe hert. þarefore, I
will entir into þe painnems, in whose mouth I ame noȝt bittir ne
vnsauere. I sall be in þair mouth swete as honi. Neuirþelesse, I ame
so mercifull þat whosoeuir askes forgifenes, and will sai, "Lorde, I
knawe me þat I haue sinned greuousli, and I will gladli amend me be
10 þi grace. Haue merci on me for þi bittir passion," I will take and
ressaiue him gladli. And forsothe, I sall com a geant to þaime þat
abides in euell, se ferdfull þat þai sall noȝt dare moue a finger agains
me. I sall come so strannge þat þai sall be [be]for me as a migge, and
I sall com to so sharpe þat þai sall fele wo in þis life, and wo
15 withoute ende.'

f. 65ra   Capitulum lviii. Wordes of þe modir to þe | spouse, and
        of þe modir and son togidir.

Mari spake to þe spouse: 'Spouse, take hede and behald þe passion of
mi son, þe whilke passed in bittirnes þe passions of all saintes. Right
20 as a modir, and sho sawe hir oneli son kit gobetmele, suld be turbled
on þe moste bittir wise, so I was turbled in bittirnes when I sawe þe
passion of mi son.' þan þe modir spake to þe son: 'Blissed be þou, mi
son, þat art holi, as it is þus sungen: "Holi, holi, holi, God lorde of
hostis." Blissed be þou, for þou art swete, swetter and allþerswetteste.
25 þou was swete befor þe makeynge of þe werld, swetter þan aungels,
and allþerswettest to me in þi takynge of fleshe.'
    þe son answerde, 'Blissed be þou, mi modir, before all aungells.
Right as I to þe was swetest, so I ame to euell men bittir and allþir-
bittireste. I ame bittir to þaime þat sais I made mani þinges withoute
30 resonabill cause, þe whilke blasphemis me as I had made man to dede
f. 65rb and noȝt to life. O wreched and wode | thoght! Wheþir I þat am moste
rightwise and moste vertuouse made aungels withoute resson? Nai
forsothe, for I made all þinges wele, and of mi lufe and charite I gafe
all gude þinges to man, and he turnes all mi gudes into euell to him-
35 selfe. (Noght þat I haue made oght euill, bot because þat man

---

4 bicause] *twice, second subpuncted*   13 þai] þai þat   befor] for   24 þou¹]
þou mi son, mi son *subpuncted*   31 I þat] *trsp.*   34 þinges to] *twice*, to þinges
subpuncted

oþirwise þan he is halden moues his awen will agains Goddes ordinance, and þis is euell).

'Bot to þaim I am bitter þat sais I gaue man a fredom for to sin and
noght to do welle. þai sai þat I ame vnrightwise for þat I dampne som
men and som men I saue, and þai gife me þe cause of þaire euell, 5
sainge þat I withdrawe fro þaime mi grace. Bot I ame to oþir alþer-
moste bittir, þat sais mi lawes and mi biddinges are moste hard and of
moste difficulte, and þat no man mai fulfill þaime, and þat mi passion
auailes noght; and þarefore þai set noght þarebi.

'I swere in mi life, as I sware some time to þe prophetes, þat I sall 10
excuse me before all mi aungels and saintes, and þai sall wele se and
proue, to whame I am bittir, | þat I haue resonabeli and wele made all f. 65va
þinges to profete and techinge of man, and þat þare is no wyr[m]e þat
mai vpstand withoute cause. þo men þat haues me more bittir sall
proue þat I gaue to man fredom of will for his gude, and þai sall knawe 15
þat I ame rightwise, þat gifes to a gude man þe blisse of heuen, and, to
þe euell, paine and turment. It were not seminge þat þe deuell, whilke
was made of me gude, and be his awen malice is euell, þat he suld haue
felishipe with þe gude liuers.

'Also, euell men sall knawe and proue þat þere is none euell in mi 20
defaute, bot for his awen, for treweli I wald gladli, if it were possibill,
take and suffir swilke paine for euirilke man as I suffird onis in þe
crosse for all men, so I might bringe þaime againe to þe heretage þat I
haue hight þaime. Bot man hase euir his will contrari to mine, to
whome I gafe fredom of will for þis cause, þat he miȝt serue me if he 25
wald, and he suld haue for his rewarde blis endeles, and if he wald
noght he suld hafe | paine with þe deuell, for whose malice, and his f. 65vb
folowers, hell is rightwiseli made. Bot I, for I ame full of charite, I will
noȝt þat man serue me constreined be drede as an vnresonabill beste,
bot of gudeli charite, for þare mai none see mi face þat serues me 30
agains his will or for drede of paine. þo men to whome I am most
bittir sall knawe in þaire consciens þat mi lawe was lightest and mi
ȝoke swettest, and þai sall sorowe withoute comforth þat þai dispised
mi lawe, and þat þai loued more þe werld, whose ȝoke is more
greuouse and harder, þen m[i]ne. 35

þan saide þe modir, 'Blissed be þou, mi son, mi God. I prai þe þat,
syn þou was to me moste swete, þat oþir be partifers of mi swetnes.'

4 do] do euell, euell *subpuncted*   6 sainge] sainge and   13 wyrme] wyrne
(*also marg.*)   14 sall] sall knawe þat I a rightwise sall, *subpuncted*   35 mine]
mne

To whome þe son answerde, 'Blissed be þo[u], mi derrest modir, for
þi wordes ar full swete and full of charite. And þarfore, whosoeuir
resaiues into his mouthe of þi swetenes and haldes it perfiteli, it sall do
him profite. Who þat ressaiues it and castes it oute, so mikill sall he
f. 66ʳᵃ haue þe more bittir paine.' | þan saide þe maiden, 'Blissed be þou, mi
6 son, for all [þ]i lufe.'

> Capitulum lix. Wordes of Criste, in presens of þe
> spouse, of a liknes.

'I ame he þat neuir saide fals. I am halden in þe werld as a carll whose
10 name is in reproue. Mi wordes ar halden foli, and mi house is halden a
foule cote. þis carlle had a wife, þat wald noþinge bot eftir his will. She
had all þinges in possession with hir husband, to whome sho was
obedient as to hir lorde, for sho had him euir as hir lorde. þis churll
had mani shepe, for whose kepinge he hired a shepherd for fife
15 shillinges, þat he suld puruay þaime ofe þat was necessari to þaire life.
þis shepehird, for he was gude, he vsed þere þe gold to profit of þe
shepe. When a litill time was passed, þare com anoþir shepherd wers
þen þe firste, þe whilke boght him with þe gold a wife, to whome he
bare his mete, and risted with hir, and gaue no fors of þe shepe, and
20 þarefore wreched bestis deuoured and disparpild þaime.
f. 66ʳᵇ   'þe churll, seand þe disparpilling | of þe shepe, cried and saide, "My
shepeherde is to me vntrewe. Mi shepe ar loste, and som ar deuoured
of fers bestis, both bodi and fleshe, and som ar dede and þe bodis
[noȝt] etin." þan saide þe churles wife to þe husband, "Mi lorde, þe
25 bodis þat ar etin we sall neuir haue again, and þerefore take þe bodis
þat ar dede and not ete, and ber we þaim to oure house and vse we
þaim. If we want altogidir, it will be till vs intollerabill." þe husband
answerd, "Howe sall we do þan? For þe bestis þat slewe þaim had teth
enwenomed, and þarefo[re] þe fleshe of þe shepe are infected with
30 venom. þe skyn is all totore and þe wolle is gone togidere." þe wife
answerd, "If þai be so fullid and enfected, and þarefore we wannt
þaim, whereof sall we life þane?"
    'þe husband saide, "I se in thre places shepe liueand. Som of þaime
ar like to dede shepe, þe whilke for fer dar noȝt breth. Som liggis in þe

---

1 þou] þo   3-4 do him] *twice, second subpuncted*   6 þi] mi, *Lat.* tua
16 shepehird] shephehird   24 noȝt] *om., Lat.* incomesta   etin] etin we and
þarefore take we þe bodis þat ar etin, *subpuncted and (exc.* etin we) *ruled through*
29 þarefore] þarefo   33 þe husband saide] *twice, first subpuncted and ruled through*

depe clai, ne þai mai noȝt helpe þaimselfe. Som hides þaim and dar
not com furthe." "þan," quod þe wife, "com furth and late vs lifte |
þaime vpe þat wald rise, and mai noght rise withouten help, and vse f. 66ᵛᵃ
we þaim."

'Behalde,' sais þe lorde, 'I ame as þe churll, for I ame halden in þe 5
werld bot as one asse þat is broght vp in his den eftir his maner and his
condiscions. Mi name is þe disposicion of holi kirke. This name is had
in reproue, for þe sacramentes of hali kirke, þat is baptim, creme,
vnement, penance and weddinge, are taken in scorn and gifen in
coueitise. Mi wordes ar demed foli, for mi wordes, þat I spake with 10
min awen mouthe with liknes, are turned fro gosteli perdon to bodeli
comforth. Mi house is noght sett bi, for erthli þinges are loued for
heuenli.

'Be þe first shepeherd þat I hade I vndirstode mi frendes, þat is mi
prestes, þe whilke I had som[time] in holi kirke. To þaime I com- 15
mitted mi shepe, and power to sakire mi worthiest bodi, and to gouern
and defende þe saules of mine chosen, to whome also I gaue fife gudes
more preciouse þan ani gold: þe whilke a[re] consciens knawinge
abouen all vnresonabill bestes, þat suld haue discresion betwene gude
and euell, treuthe | and falshede; also, vndirstandinge and wisdome of f. 66ᵛᵇ
spirituall þinges, þe whilke is nowe forgetin, and mannes wisdom 21
alloneli lufed; also, chastite; also, temperance of all þinges and abstinens to þe mesurabill demeninge of þe bodi; and also stabillnes in
gude vertuse, wordes and werkes.

'Eftir þis firste shephird, þat is, mi frendes þat somtime were in mi 25
kirke, þare is nowe entirde oþir euell and wikked shephirdes, þe
whilke hase boght þaime a wife for gold: þat menis, þai haue taken in
stede of chastite and clennes a womanli bodi, þat is incontinens, for þe
whilke mi spirit is gone fro þaime, when þai haue a full will to sin and
to fulfill þaire will and þaire lust. þan mi spirit is absent fra þaim, for 30
þai gife no fors of no euell so þai mai haue all þare will and lust. þo
shepe þat ar all deuoured is þo whose saules are in hell, and þe bodis
berid in graues þe time of generall risinge to endles dampnacion.

'þe shep whose fleshe leuis, and þe spirit is awai, menis þaim þat
noþir lufes ne dredes me, ne þai hafe nowþir deuocion ne affeccion 35
to me. Forsothe mi spirit is fer fro þame, for þaire fleshe [is] poy-
sond with þe venommouse | teth of fers bestes: þat menes, þe saule f. 67ʳᵃ
of þaime and þaire thohtes, þat are betakend be þe fleshe of þe shepe,
and þe entrels are as bittir to me and abhominabill as fleshe þat wer

15 somtime] som, *Lat.* olim   18 are] a   36 is²] *om.*

enpoysonde. þe skin, þat menes þaire bodi, is drie fro all gude and charite, and noght apt to profit in blis bot for to be take to perpetuall fire eftir þe laste dome. þe wolle, þat is þaire werkes, are so vnprofetabill in all wise þat þare is noþinge funden in þaime for þe whilke þai
5 were worþi for to haue mi charite and mi grace. O þerefore mi wife, bi whome I vndirstand þe gude cristen, what sall we do?

'I se liueand shepe in þre places. Som ar like to dede shepe, þat dar noght breth for drede. þai ar þe panems, þat wald gladli haue þe right faith and bileue and þai wiste howe, bot þai dar noght brethe: þat
10 menes, þai dar noght leue þe faith þat þai haue and ressaiue anoþir. þe second shepe are in hilles and dar noght com furthe; þai ar þe
f. 67rb Jewes, þat standes vndir couiringe and | wald faine com furth and þai wist þat I were born. þai kepe þaime vndir couiringe; þat is, in þe figures and takens þat signified me in þe lawe, and are nowe verrali
15 fulfilled in me, þai hope to haue hele. And for þat vaine hope þai drede to com to þe riȝt bileue.

'þe þird shepe þat cleues and standes in clai are þe cristen þat are in dedeli sin. þai wald, for drede of paine, gladli rise, bot þai mai noȝt for þaire greuouse and heui sinnis, for þai want all charite. þarefore, o
20 þou mi wife, þat is, ȝe gude cristen, helpe ȝe me, for right as þe man and þe wife awe to be one fleshe and one membir, so þe cristen is mi membir, and I his, for I ame in him and he in me.

'þarefore, o þou mi wife, þat is, ȝe cristen, ren ȝe with me to þe shepe þat hase ȝet spirit, and help we þaime and fede þaime. Haue
25 ȝe compassion of me þat boght þo shepe full dere, and ressaiue it with me, and I with þe: take þou þe bake and I will gladli lede þe heued bitwene mi handes. I bare sometime all þe shepe on mi bake,
f. 67va when I was sore wonded and fest | to a stake. O ȝe mi frendes, I lufe þose shepe so tendirli þat, if it were possibill, I wald suffir þe same
30 dede for ilke shepe in speciall þat I suffird onis on þe crosse for all togidir; and I had leuer, if I might die againe, bye þaim againe þan I wald want þaim.

'I crie to mi frendes, with hole and all hert, þat þai spare nouthir trauaile ne gudes for me, and sin þai spared me not fro wordes of
35 reproue when I was in þe werld, spare ȝe noȝt nowe to speke þe treuthe for me. I was noȝt asshamed to suffir þat spitefull dede for þaime, bot, right as I was born, naked I stode in þe sight of mine enemis. I was smiten with þaire fiste on þe tethe. Mi her was drawen with þair fingers. I was scourged with þaire scourges. I was festned to a
40 stake with þair instrumentes, and I hinge with two theues on þe crosse.

'þarefore, ȝe mi frendes, spare ȝe noȝt to trauaile for me þat suffird, for lufe and charite, swilke paines for ȝou. Trauale ȝe manli and
hertli, and gife helpe to þe nedi shepe, for I swere in mi manhede,
þat is in [þe] fadir and þe fadir in me, and be mi godhede | þat is in   f. 67ᵛᵇ
mi spirit, and mi spirit in it and in me, and I in it, and we thre one   5
God in thre persones, þat whosoeuir trauails and bers mi shepe with
me, I sall mete with him in þe middis wai for to help him, and I sall
gife him, for þe moste preciouse sowde and rewarde, miselfe, to be
his endeles blis.'

Capitulum lx. Wordes of þe son to þe spouse of thre   10
maner of cristen folke.

þe son spake to þe spouse and saide, 'I am God of Israell, þe same þat
spake with Moises. When he suld haue ben sent to þe pepill, he asked
a taken and saide, "þe pupill trowes me noght." Sin þat it was þe
pupill of God þat he was sent to, whi mistraisted þai God? Bot þou sall   15
knawe þat in þe pupill was thre maner of men. Som trowed to God and
to Moises. Som troued to God and not to Moises, thinkynge þat he
spake of his awen hede and his awen presumpscion and wroght also.
Som troued nouþir God ne Moises.

'Right so þare is now thre maner of folke amange þe cristen, þe   20
whilke | are bitokened in þe Ebrwes. Som þare are þat troues wele to   f. 68ʳᵃ
God and to mi wordes. Som troues to God and noght to mi wordes, for
þai can noȝt haue discrecion bitwene þe gude spirit and þe euell. Som
troues nouþir God ne mi wordes, ne to þe with whome I haue spoken
mi wordes. Bot, as I saide, if som of þe Ebrwes mistraisted Moises, ȝit   25
all passed þe Rede See into wildirnes with him, where þai [þat] troued
noght wirshiped ydols and stirrid God to wreth, and died a wreched
dede, and þai ware þo allonli þat had mistraiste.

'And þarefor, for mannes hert is tareyng to trowe, þarefor mi frendes
sall bere mi wordes to þaime þat sall trowe him, and þai sall eftirward   30
teche oþir þat can not ȝit haue discrecion bitwene one gude spirit and
one euell. If þe herrers aske a taken, I sall shewe þaime a wande, as
Moises did: þat menes, þe plaine trewthe of mi wordes. For, as Moises
ȝerd was right and ferdfull, for it chaunged into a serpent, so mi wordes
are right, þat þare mai no falshed be funden in þaime, and ferdfull, for   35
þai sonden right[fu]ll dome. Lat þaime purpose and wit|nes þat þe   f. 68ʳᵇ

4 þe¹] om.   5 mi¹] mi manh, manh *subpuncted*   21 whilke] *Quire catchphrase,*
are, *below*   26 þat] om.   29 tareyng] trareyng   36 rightfull] right sall

deuell went oute and left Goddes creature for þe sound of one worde
of mi mouth, and, bot he [be] refreined be mi pouer, he might `moue
and´ stir hilles. What pouere þan is he ofe, þe whilke þrow Goddes
pouer flems þe deuell with þe sounde of a worde?

5   'Also, right as þe Ebrewes þat nowþir troued God ne Moises went
oute of Egipt into þe land of beheste amange oþir againe þaire will, so
mani cristen againes þaire will gose with mi chosen derlinges, and
traistes not in mi pouer þat I miȝt saue þaim. þai haue no faith to me,
ne to mi wordes, bot þai haue a vaine hope to mi vertu. Neuirþelesse,
10   mi wordes withoute þair will sall be fulfilled and þai sall be constreined to perfeccion to þai com to þe place of mi plesaunce.'

Here endes þe firste boke of heuenli reuelacions shewed bi God and
oure ladi on forsaide wise to Saint Bride, pryncesse of Nerice in þe
realme of Swecye.

---

2 be¹] *om.*   pouer] pouer and, and *subpuncted*   14 realme] reaalme. *Rest of f.*
68ʳᵇ, 68ᵛ blank exc. catchword 68ᵛ: in þe name

[BOOK TWO]

In þe name of þe fadir, son and holi gost, one God and þre persones,
he[re] biginnes þe second buke of heuenli reuelacions to blissed
Bride, princes of Nerice in þe realme of Swecie.

þe firste chapitir. Wordes of informacion bi þe son to
þe spouse againe þe deuille, and whi he withdrawes   5
noȝt euell men or þai fall in euill, and whi he gifes
heuen to þe cristened when þai die bifor ȝeres of
discrecion.

þe son saide to þe spouse, 'When þe deuile tempis þe, sai to him þre
þinges: "First, þat Goddes word mai noȝt be bot trewe; also, þare is   10
noþinge to God impossibill; also, þou, deuill, mai noght gife me swilk
feruoure of charite as God gifes me." '

He saide to þe spouse againe, 'I take heede to a man on þre wise:
firste, howe his bodi outeward is disposed; þe secound, whidirwarde
his consciens within ledis him; þe þirde, | what his herte desires. For
treweli, as a birde þat bihaldes þe fishe in þe see takis heede to þe   16
depnes and to þe parels, so I knawe and considir all þe wais, and I take
hede what ilke þinge suld haue, ne þare is no þinge þat knawes himselfe so wele als I. And bicause I knawe all þinge so wele, þou might
aske whi I withdrawe noȝt þe euell man or he com into þe depnes of   20
sinne: to þe whilke I þat asked þe question answers.

'I ame maker of all, and I haue a forsight and a forknawlege of all þat
is and sall be, for inne mi sight and knawlege is all þinge present, and
all if I knawe and mai all þinges, ȝit for mi rightwisnes I will do no
more againe þe naturall dispocicion of þe bodi þan againe þe dis-   25
posicion of þe saule. Bot a mannes naturall abidinge hanges vpon þe
naturall disposicion of his bodi: for þat one man is of langer life, and
aneoþir of shorter, is caused of streng[þ]e and febilnes of kinde, eftir
þe qwilke þe bodi is disposed. For mi forsight and knawlege bifor
makes no man nowþir blinde ne halt, ne causes in | him no seknes ne
noies him noȝt, bot it is of preue cause hid in kinde, for sinne and   31
indisposicion of kinde makis mishap in membris. Ne it is noȝt so
bicause I will haue it so, as if mi will made it to be so. And all if I mai all

---

2 here] he   18 þinge²] *twice, second subpuncted*   20 of] *twice, first subpuncted*
25 bodi] bodi and, and *subpuncted*   28 strengþe] strengie   30 in] *twice*

þinge, ȝit will I noȝt contrari mi right. And þerfore þat one man liues
langere þan anoþir is bi þe strengþe of his nature, þe wilk I knewe
bifore.

'I make to þe a liknes. And þare ware two wais full of pittes, to þe
5 whilke were bot one passage, and one wai went doneward and þe
toþir vpwarde; if it were þus wretin in þe entrees of þe wais: "Whosoeuir bigins þis wai sall entir it with grete lust and likinge of fleshe,
bot he sall ende it in grete confusion and wrechednes. And who will
go bi þe toþir wai, he sall bigin it with litill trauaile and ende it in
10 grete gladnes and comforthe"—one went first þat was [b]lind, till he
come to þe entre of þe two waies: and þan þaire sight was gifen
þame, þat þai sawe wele and rede whidir þe wais led. þan aperid
two men, kepers of þe same wais, takinge hede to þe forsaide men
f. 69ᵛᵇ and | þus spekinge togidir: "Abide and take whe hede whilke of þese
15 wais he wald chese to go." þe waifarynge man avised him and tuke
heede to þe wais, and whidir þai lede, and vsinge gude counsaile he
chese þe wai whose biginninge was a litill trauaile and þe ende
gladnes and ioy, and left þe toþir þat bigane in gladnes and endid in
sorow, for him þoght it was more siker and tollerabill begin with
20 trauaile and ende in riste þan þe contrari.

'What supposis þou þis bitokens? I sall tell þe. þese two wais are
gude and euell þat are bifore man, of þe whilke, bi fredome of his will,
he mai chese whedir he will. To þaire two wais ledis one wai, þat is
barnede, in þe whilke he is blinde, and knawis noȝt what is bitwene
25 gude and euell till he com to ȝeres of discrecion and resonabill opin
knawlege: for þan biginnes he to knawe wheþir is bettir, to haue a litill
sorowe and endeles blis þan a shorte gladnes and endeles sorow. And
wheþir he chese þe tone or þe toþir, he sall finde þame þat sall
f. 70ᵣᵃ nowm|bir his steppes.

30 'In þese wais are mani þat fals, for some dies on o wise, som of
anoþir, som in ȝouth, some in age, and all eftir þaire naturall disposicion (þe whilke I will noȝt contrari: for if I contraried it, I gaue þe
deuell occasion agains me, þe whilke I will noȝt haue cause to
punich againe mi right). And þarefore I sall do no more againe þe
35 naturall disposicion of bodi þan of saule. Neuirþelesse, considir þou
mi gudnes and merci: I gife þe kingdom of heuen to all þat are
baptized and dies bifore ȝeres of discrecion. For þus it is wretin:
"*Complacuit patri meo talibus dare regnum celorum.*" þat menis: "It liked

---

10 blind] likand, *Lat.* cecus   22 whilke] whilke he mai   24 in þe whilke]
twice, second subpuncted   38 talibus] *twice, second subpuncted*

mi fadir to gife to swilke þe realme of heuen." Also, of mi pite I do merci to enfauntes and barnes of þe panems, for all þaire barnes þat dies bifore ʒers of discrecion, for cause þai mai noʒt com to clere sight of mi visage, þai sall com to a place noght lefull to þe to knawe, where þai sall abid withoute torment. Whosoeuir com bi þat one wai of barn- 5 heede and innocent age vnto þo two wais, þat is ʒeres of| discrecion of f. 70ʳᵇ gode and euill, þan is it in his power to chese whilke of þase wais are more plesand. And eftir his chose sall folow his rewarde, when þai sall knaw and wele vndirstande þe writinge and scripture sett in þe entre of þe waise, þat "It is bettir and more auantage to bigin with litill 10 dissese, and ende in grete gladnes, þan to bigin with ioy and end with sorow."

'Neuirþeles, somtime dede commis to þe bodi or þe time þat þe condicion of naturall disposicion askes it, as bi manslaghtir or owterage of drinke and swilke, for þe malice of þe deuell combris him 15 so þat, if he lifed langer in þe worlde, he sulde be dettur to ouirmikill paine. And also þe gude men somtime are withdrawen be dede before þe time of þaire naturall disposicion, for of þe hie charite þat I haue to þame, and for þe feruent lufe and labor in refreininge of bodeli lustes þat þai haue to me, I take þaim awai in þe beste time, as withoute 20 bigininge it was in mi forknawelege. And so sometime þe euell dies bifore time of naturall disposicion for to | excuse him fro þe grettir f. 70ᵛᵃ pains, and somtime þe gude dais bifor þe time of his naturall dispo- sicion for to haue sikirnes of blis.'

Capitulum secundum. How God pleined of a saule in   25
þe presens of þe spouse, and þe answere of Criste to þe
deuill, whi he suffird þis saule and oþir euill take and
touche his verrai bodi.

God was sene wroth and saide, 'þe werke of mi hande þat I haue done moste for and wirshipt moste, þat moste dispises me. þis saule, to 30 whome I haue shewed besili mi charite, hase done to me þre þinges. He hase turned fro me his sight, and loked to mine enemi. He hase festened his will to þe werld, and he hase geuen to it his troste, þat he might gladli sin agains me, and tuke to him a faillinge traste. I haue refte fro him his desire.'   35

5 com bi] bi com bi   5-6 barnheede] barnheede of, of *subpuncted*   21 bigi-
ninge] bigiminge   26 presens] presens in þe, in þe *subpuncted*   32 his] *twice,*
second subpuncted

þan made a deuell a grete cri and saide, 'Juge, þis saule is mine.' þe
juge asked, 'Bi what cause?' þe deuell answerde, 'þe same þat þou

f. 70vb pleined of: þat is, for he dispised þe his maker. þarefor | he is made mi
seruant, and sin he was sodanli taken awai, how mai he sodanli plese

5 þe? When he liued in hale bodi he serued þe not in hert, for he lufed
more þi creature þan þe. He tuke his ponisheinge with inpaciens, and
for he tuke no heede to þi werkes as he suld haue done, he had no
charite into þe ende of his life. And þarefor, sin þou tuke him sodanli
awai, bi right he is mine.' þe juge answerde, 'Sodaine dede dampnes

10 not, bot þarwith, bifore, werkes þat are discordinge fro mi will; ne will
withouten deliberacion dampnes not.'

þan com þe modir of God and saide, 'Son, and a rekles seruande
haue a right dere and familiar frende, sall noȝt þis frende helpe þe
seruant? Or if þe frende aske for him, sall he noȝt be saued?' þe juge

15 answerde, 'All right sall be menged with merci and wisdome: with
merci, þat sharpnes be made smothe; and with wisdom, þat equite be
keped. For if it be swilke a forfet þat is noȝt worthi to be forgeuen, for

f. 71ra familiarite of þe frende ȝit, right | sauide, it mai haue mitigacion.' þan
saide þe modir, 'Mi moste blissed son, þis saule had me euermore in

20 minde, and did me swilke reuerence þat for me it made soueraine
solempnite, all if it were colde and indeuote to þe. þarefor, haue merci
of it.'

þe son saide, 'Mi blissed modir, þou sees and knawes all þinge in
me. þou knawes þat þis saule, all if it had þe in minde, ȝit þat was

25 more for þis temporall profit þan spirituall. For whi, he tretted noȝt
mi clennest bodi as he suld. þe stinke of his mouthe wald noȝt lat him
fele þe swetenes of mi lufe and charite. þe lufe of þe worlde hid fro
him mi passion. Hope of forgeuenes and reklesnes to take heede of
his ende shortide his life. And all if he resaiued me ilke dai, he was

30 noȝt þarefor mikill þe bettir, for he disposid him noȝt as he suld haue
done. For he þat will resaiue a worþi lorde to his herber, he awe noȝt
alloneli to arai himselfe, bot also all þat langes to houshald. And so

f. 71rb did he noȝt. For all ife he ordainde his house, ȝit he swepid it | noȝt
besili with reuerens, ne he strewed it noȝt with floures of vertuse, ne

35 he fulfilled noȝt with dewe abstinens þat at langed to þe howsehald of
his membres. And þarefore what he hase deserued, þou knawes. All if
I be incomprehensibill and vnabill to take defoule (I ame in ilkea
place with mi godhede), neuirþelesse, mi delite is not bot with a clene
man, all if I entire both into þe clenne and into þe sinner. Gode men

15 sall] *twice*

resaiues þe same bodi þat was fest to þe cros and stied vp into heuen, þe whilke was figurd and bitakned in manna and in þe widows mele, and euell resaiues þe same: þe gude to more comforth, þe euell to more rightwise jugement, for cause þai are noȝt ferde, so vnworthi, to ressaiue so grete worþines.'

þan saide þe deuell, 'Sin he ressaiued þe so vnworþili, and for þat his dome was þe more harde, whi suffird þou him so vnworþi to touche þe so worþi?' þe juge answerde, 'þou art noȝt moued bi charite to aske þis question, for þou hase none, bot mi suthfastenes stires þe to aske it for mi spouse þat | is present and heris. Right as both gude and euell touches me in mi manhede and þe mekenes of mi paciens, so both þe gude and þe euell etes me on þe awter, þe gude for þaire more auauntage, þe euell þat þai fall noȝt in dispaire, bot þat þai trowe þat, if þai will, þai mai chaunge þaire will and conuert þame to gude, sin I suffir þame to take mi verrai bodi. And how might I shewe a more charite þan þat I, clennest, entirs into a vessell of moste vnclennes? And ȝit, bi insampill of þe materiall s[o]nne, I mai noȝt take ani defoule. Bot þou and þi frendes settis noȝt bi þis charite.'

þan saide þe modir againe, 'O þou Goddes son, how oft times turned he to þe and he drede þe, all if not as he suld haue done! Also he forthoght þat he greued þe, all if it were no perfite repentance. I prai þe, mi son, lat þis profit him for mi sake.' þe son answerd againe, 'I am, as þe profete saide, verrai son, bot fer bettir þan þe materiall son. For þe materiall son entirs nawþir within hilles ne saules; bot I pers and entirs bothe. And right as an hill lettis þe materiall [son], þat it | touches noȝt þe erthe, so is sin obstakill to me, þat mi charite mai noȝt entir þe saule. And what comforth were it to me if I entird one parte of þe saule and fand it clene, and aneoþir parte were stinkeand? þarefor put firste awai all þat is foule: þan sall it be faire, of þe whilke sall springe swetenes.' þe modir answerde, 'Be þi will done with merci.'

Capitulum tercium. Wordes of þe modir of God spoken
in meruaile to þe spouse, how in þe werld is fiue maner
of howses and fiue maners of dwellers in þame.

The modir spake: 'It is woundir þinge þat þe lorde and kinge of blis is dispised and sett at noght. He was in þe erthe as a pilgrime goinge fro

5

f. 71ᵛᵃ

11

15

20

25

f. 71ᵛᵇ

30

35

---

17 sonne] sinne, *Lat.* sol   21 þat] þat if, if *subpuncted*   23 fer] *twice, second*
subpuncted   25 son] *om.*   33 in²] *twice*

place to place, and knokkid on mani mennes dores to haue commin in. þe werld was a parceíl of grounde in þe whilke was bigged fiue maner of houses.

'When mi son com to þe firste dore in pilgrime wede, he knokked
5 and saide, "Frende, opin and take me in to þi riste, and for to dwell with þe, þat wilde bestis noie me not, þat weders ne tempestes com
f. 72ʳᵃ noȝt vpon me. Gife me | of þi cleþinge, throw þe whilke mi colde mai be warmed and I mai hele mi naked. Gife me of þi mete, bi þe whilke I mai be comforted and fede, and take þi þanke and þi reward of þi
10 God." þan answerde he þat was within, "þou art ouir inpacient, and þerefore þou mai noȝt accorde ne dwell with [vs]. þow art ouir lange, and þarefor we haue no cleþinge for þe. þou art ouir couetouse and gluterows, and þarefor we mai noȝt fille þe, for couetise has no grownde na ende."

15 'Criste þe pilgrime, þat was withoute, saide againe, "Frende, take me in gladli and wilfulli, for I [am] closed in full litill place. Gife me cloþes, for þare is none so litill clathe in þi house bot it is enoghe to make me warme. Gife me mete, for a crome of brede mai fill me, and a drope of watir mai refreshe me and gife me strenthe." þan answerde
20 againe he þat was within, "We knawe þe wele; þou art meke in wordes and i[m]portune in askinge. þe semis as þou held þe paide with litill, bot ȝete þare mai noþinge fill þe. þou arte moste colde and werst for
f. 72ʳᵇ to clethe. þarefor go þi wai, for I sall | gife þe right noȝt."

'þan commis he to þe second hous and sais, "Opin þi dure and se
25 me. I sall gife þe what þe nedis. I sall defende þe fro þine enemis." He þat was within answerde, "Mine een are febill. It wald do þame harme to luke on þe. I haue enoghe. Me nedis noȝt of þine. I ame miȝti and stronge: who mai noie me?" þan commes he to þe þirde house and sais, "Frende, opin þine eres and here me; strech oute þi handes and
30 fele me; opin þi moute and tast me." He þat dwellis þare answerde, "Crie hiere, for whi, I sall wele here þe. If þou be light, I sall drawe þe to me. And if þou be swete, I sall ressaiue þe and tast þe."

'þan com he to þe fourte hows, whose ȝate was as if it had bene halfe opin, and saide, "Frende, and þou knewe and toke heede howe
35 vnprofitabill þi time is spendid, þou wald take me in to herber. If þou knewe and herde what I haue done for þe, þou wald haue compassion on me. And þou were avised what þou hase greued me, þou wald forþinke and aske forgeuenes." He answerde, "We are as it were dede

---

6 bestis] bestis þat, þat *subpuncted*   11 vs] wa, *Lat.* nobiscum   16 am] *om.*
21 importune] inoportune, *Lat.* importunus   29 þine] þiene

men in abidinge | and desire of þe, and þarefor haue compassion on f. 72ᵛᵃ
oure wrechedenes, for we gife oureselfe to þe on þe moste gladli wise.
Se and bihald oure mischefe, and þe wrechedenes of oure bodi, and
we are redi to what at likis þe."

'þan com he to þe fifte house, þe whilke was all opin, and saide, 5
"Frende, here will I gladli entir. Bot wit þou wele þat I seke softer
reste þan on pelows of plume, more feruent hete þan wolle is wonte to
gife, fresher mete þan bestis fleshe." þai answerde þat were within,
"þare ligges hamers at our fete, with þe whilke we sall gladli breke
oure fete and oure thees, and we sall gladli gife merwe and mergh to 10
reste on þat sall flowe oute. We sall opin to þe with gude will oure
bowels and entrels of oure bodi: entere þare. For right as þare is
noþinge softer to þe at riste on þan our merwe, so þare is noþinge
bettir for warmnes þan oure bowels. Oure hert is fresher mete þen
bestes fleshe: we sall gladli ordeine it to þi mete. Come in: þou arte 15
wondir swete to þe taste and desirows to lufe."

'þese forsaide fiue howshalders bitokens | fiue states of men in f. 72ᵛᵇ
erthe. þe firste is þe vntrew cristen, þat sais þe domes of mi son are
vnrightwis, his promisses fals and his biddinges vntollerabill. þai sai
in þaire þoght, and blasphemis, to þe prechours of mi son, "If þare 20
were one allmighti, he suld be so hie þat none suld reche him; so
brode and so hie þat none might clethe him. He mai not be filled with
mete, and he is moste vnpacient: þare mai none dwell with him." þai
sai he is langest, for þere coueitise hase nowþir mesure ne ende. þai
plaine ai of defaute, and supposes euell or ani com. þai sai he mai noȝt 25
be filled, for heuen and erthe sufficis noȝt bot he haue oþir giftes of
man. þai hald þe moste foli þat a man gife gudes for his saule. And þai
sai he is vnpacient for he hates sin and vices, and sendes to þame con-
traries of þaire desire, weninge and supposinge þat noþinge is faire ne
profetabill bot þat at þaire will desires. 30

'And ȝit, forsoth, mi son is almiȝti in heuen and erthe, maker of noȝt
of all þat is, and | noȝt made of aneoþir, hafinge stabill beinge befor all f. 73ʳᵃ
oþir, and eftir him sall noþinge be. He is langest, hiest, bradeste,
with[in] all þinges, withoute, and abouen. And all if he be so miȝti, ȝit
of his grete charite he desires to be clede be þe seruis of man: and ȝit 35
nedis he no cleþinge þat clepis all oþir, for withowten ende and
begininge he is clede vnchaungeabilli with perpetuell ioi, honoure and
blis. He desires to be fede with þe charite of man, and ȝit is he þe fode

of aungels and men, þat suffi[ci]s all þinges and nedis none oþir. He
askes pees of man þat is þe reformoure and maker of pees.

   'And þarfore, whosoeuir will resaiue him, he mai sonn fill him with
a blith saule, and with a crome of brede, if he haue gude will. On þrede
5 will clethe him if it be giuen of a birnand charite. One drope will slokin
his thirst, and þe will be gude. He mai resaiue him into his herte and
speke with him þat hase a stedefaste and a birnand deuocion; for Gode
is a spirit, and he will þat flesheli þinges and bodeli be chaunged into
f. 73rb spirituall, and | sone failinge þinges into abiddinge, and he takes and
10 haldes as done to himselfe all þat is done to ani of his; and he charges
noȝt so mekill þe outewarde gude as he dose þe will, of what entent it
is done.

   'Bot þe more mi son cries to þame bi priuei inspiracions, þe more
he moneshes þame be his prechoures, so mekill þai are þe more con-
15 trari to him in saule, ne þai here him noȝt, ne turnes noȝt þaire will to
him, ne entirs him noȝt with werkes of charite. þarefore, when time
commes, þaire falshede þat þai vse sall be distrued, and trewthe sall be
trowed and made mikill of.

   ' þe second are Jewes harded in sin. þai hald þaimeselfe resonabill,
20 and þaire wisdome þai take for laue. þai preche þaire awen dedis, and
haldis more commendabill þan oþir. If þai here þe werkes of mi son,
þai hald þame worþi reproue and settis noȝt bi þame: and þai haue in
dedeine his biddinges and his wordes, insomikill þat þai hald þame
mikill fouler and þe wers when þai haue herde what langes to mi son,
f. 73va and þe more vnhappi and wreched if þai | folowed his dedis. As longe
26 as þe world lokis blithli on þame, þai hald þameselfe moste blissed.
While þai hafe þaire strenghis, þai hald þaimselfe moste stronge.
þarefor þaire vaine hope sall fall to noȝt, and þaire blisse sall turne to
confusion.

30   'þe þirde state of men is painims, of whome som ilke dai cries in
scorn and sais, "What is he þat Criste? If he be gudeli to gife þere present gudes, we will resaiue þame gladli. If he be mild to forgife sinnes,
with a gude will we sall wirshipe him." Bot þese pepill hase closed þe
eyn of knawlege, for þai vndirstand nawþir þe rightwisenes ne þe
35 merci of God. þai stope þaire eres, and herres noȝt what mi son dide
for þame and for all oþir. þai spere þaire mouthe, and enqueres noȝt
what sall come to þame, or what were þaire profite. þai falde

1 sufficis] suffirs   23 his^1] *twice, first subpuncted*   insomikill] insomikill fouler,
fouler *subpuncted*   24 wers] *also marg.*   33 closed] closed merci of God þai
stope þair eres and heres, *anticipating l. 35*

þaire handes, and will noȝt trauall to seke þe right wai how þai might fle lesinge and finde trewthe. þarefor, for þai will noȝt knaw and beware when þai might, and hase time, þai sall fall | and be ouircaste f. 73ᵛᵇ with þaire housynge, and þai sall be combred in þaire awen tempeste.

'þe fourte manere of men are þe Jewes and painems þat wald faine 5 be cristen if þai wiste how, and wald do þat might plese mi son. þai here ilke dai of þame þat is aboute þame, and þai vndirstand, throw þe voice of inward lufe, what mi son hase don and sufferd for all men: and for þat þai crie to mi son in þaire consciens, and sais, "O þou lorde, we haue herd þat þou hight to be giuen to vs. þarefore we abide þe. Come 10 and fulfill þi biheste. We se and knawe þat þai þat are wirshiped as goddes haue no vertu of godhede, ne charite of saules, ne commendinge of chastite; bot we haue funden in þaim lufe of bodi and of worldli welefare and wirschipe. We vndirstand of þi lawe, and we here þi grete meruailus werkes in all merci and rightwisnes. We here of þi 15 prophecies of þi prophetis þat abode þe. Wherefor, moste mercifull lorde, we prai þat þou come. We sall gife oureselfe to þe | gladli, for we f. 74ᵃ knawe þat þe charite of saules is in þe, and all discrete and wise vse of þinges is in þe, and all clennes and endeles life. þarefor com to vs sone and gife vs light, for we die langueshinge in abidinge." þere folke cries 20 þus to mi son, and þarefore þaire dore is halfe opin, for þai haue gude will to þe gude life, bot þai com not ȝit þereto in effect. þese are worthi to haue grace of mi son, and comfort.

'In þe fifte hous ar mi frendes and mi sonnes, þe dore of whose saule is full opind to mi son. þai here mi son gladli and with gude wille when 25 he calles, and noȝt alloneli þai opin þe dore blitheli when he knokkes, bot þai com redeli to mete with his comminge. þai breke all þat is wronge in þame with þe hamers [of] Goddes commandmentes, and araies riste to mi son: bot noȝt in þe plumes of foules, bot in acorde of vertuse and in refreininge and chastissinge of euell affeccions, þe 30 whilke is þe merewe of all vertuse. Also, þai make warmnes to mi son, bot noȝt swilke as is be w[o]ll bot in birninge | and feruent charite, f. 74ʳᵇ for cause þai gife noȝt alloneli þaire gudes to mi son bot þaimselfe. Also, þai araies fode to mi son fresher þan ani fleshe: þat is, þare awen hert moste perfite, for þai desire noȝt ne luffes noȝt bot þair 35 God. þe househalder of heuen and lord is in þaire hert, and he þat gifes fode to all oþir is sweteli fede of þaire charite. þai haue euir þaire een to þe dore, þaire eres to þe lorde, and þaire handes to fight, þat þare entir no enemis. þou doghtir, folow þe condiciouns of

18 discrete] discreste   28 of] and   32 woll] will, *Lat.* lana   34 Also]
twice, first subpuncted

þere folke as mikill as þou mai. For þai haue sett þaire gronde in a
stone of soueraine sekirnes, and forsothe oþir howses hase taken þaire
grounde in clai: wherefor, when þe winde commis, þai are onone
blawen done.'

5   Capitulum 4m. Wordes of Goddes modir to þe son for
       þe spouse, and how Crist is figured by Salamon, and of
       a fell sentennce againe þe fals cristen.

Mari þe modir of Gode spake to þe son and saide, 'Mi son, take
hede. þi spouse wepis, for þou hase fewe frendes and mani enemis.'
f. 74va þe son answerde, | 'It is wretin þat þe childir of þe kingdome sall be
11 caste oute, and straunge childir sall haue þe heretage. Also it is
wretine þat a qwene com fra fer cuntre to se and behalde þe riches of
Salamon, and to her his wisdom; and when sho had sene and herde
þat sho desired, for meruale sho loste allmoste hir spirit. Bot þai þat
15 were in his awen realme nowþir toke hede of his wisdome ne
meruaile of his riches.

'I ame þe same Salamon in figure, mekill more riche and wiser þan
he, for whosoeuir is wise he is wise of me, of whome commes all
wisdome. And mi riches is endeles life and blisse, þe whilke I haue
20 both hight and gifen to þe cristen, as to mi childir, for to haue
inp[a]ssibill posession withouten ende, if þai wald folow me and trowe
mi wordes. Bot þai take no fors of mi wisdome: þai dispise both mi
werkes and mi bihestes, and settis at noȝt mi riches. What sall I do þan
to þame?

25 'Forsothe, bicause mi childir will noȝt haue þe heretage, straungers,
þat is, [panems], sall haue it, for þai, as þe straunge qwene, bi whome |
f. 74vb I vndirstonde trewe saules, sall come and greteli meruale þe riches of
mi blis and mi charite, insomekill þat þai sall leue þe spirit of þaire
mistrowthe and þai sall be fulfilled with mi spirit. What sall I do þan to
30 childir of þe kingedome? I sall do as a wise potter þat bihaldes þe
mater þat he made first of clai; and if he persaiue it noȝt honest ne
abill, he castes againe to þe erthe and brekes it. So sall I do to swilke
cristen, þe whilke suld be mine, for I made þame to mine awen ymage
and likenes, and boght þame with mi blode. For þai are made foule,
35 and deformes þameselfe so contemptibill, þai sall be troden vndirfote
as erthe, and be broken and thirste downe to helle.'

Capitulum 5m. Wordes of þe lorde, in presens of þe
spouse, of his grete magnificens, and a woundirfull
figure, and how Criste is bitokened be Dauid and þe
euell cristen and þere painems bi his thre sonnes, and
how holi kirke is vphalden in þe seuen sacramentes. | 5

'I ame nowþir stone ne tree, ne made of none oþir, bot maker of all þat   f. 75ʳᵃ
þat is, stabli abidinge, withoute biginninge and ende. I come into þe
maiden and dwelled with hir, noȝt leuing ne losinge mi godhede, for I
þat was be mi manhede in þe maiden and with stedfaste abidinge of mi
godhede, I, þe same, was regninge in heuen with þe fadir and holi   10
goste, and kinge in erthe, be mi godhede. Also I enflammed þe maiden
with mi spirit, bot not so þat þe spirit was twinned and departed fro
me, for þe same spirit þat enflawmed hir was in þe fadir and me, son,
and mi fadir and I in þe same spirit, one God and noȝt thre.
   'I ame like to Kinge Dauid, þe whilke had þre sonnes. One was   15
called Absolon, þat soght þe life of his fadir. þe second was called
Adonias, þat soght to an had his fadirs realme. þe þird was Salamon,
and he gat it and had it. þe first son bitokens þe Jewes, for þai soght mi
life and mi dede and dispised mi consaile. And þarefor, knawinge
þaire rewarde, I mai sai, as Da|uid saide of Absolon, "Mi son Absolon"   f. 75ʳᵇ
(þat menes þe Jewes) "where is now ȝour son?" I hade compassion of   21
ȝow whome ȝe desired suld com, and I haue proued be mani tokens
þat I haue comin. And now I haue more compassion, sainge againe þe
same word, "Fili mi, Absolon," fore cause I se ȝoure ende in wrechednes of dede. þarefor, of þe hiest and moste charite, I sai þe þird
time, as Dauid, "Fili mi, Absolon: who sall graunt me to die for þe?"   25
Dauid wist wele þat he might noȝt with his dede call againe his son fro
dede to life, and ȝit for to shewe þe loue of his fadirli charite, and þe
redines of his gude will, he spake as he walde, if it had bene possibill,
haue taken dede for his sonnes safinge in life.
   'So sai I, o ȝe mi sonnes, Jewes, þat all if ȝe haue euell will to me,   30
and, inasmikill as ȝe might, ȝe haue done contrari and againes me, ȝet
wald I, and it were possibill and plesinge to mi fadir, die ones for ȝou: I
haue so mikell compassion of ȝoure wrechedenes, þat | throw þe   f. 75ᵛᵃ
sentens of rightwisnes ȝe haue procured to ȝoureselfe. I saide ȝou bi
worde what ȝe suld do, and I shewed bi ensampill of dede. I went bifor 35
ȝou as þe hen bifor þe birdis, þat ȝe suld rest ondir þe wenges of mi
charite. Bot ȝe dispised all þat I dide, and þarfore, all þat ȝe desired is

---

10 I] I se, se *subpuncted*   17 an] and   20 sai] *twice, second subpuncted*

now fled and passed awai fro ȝou. Ȝour ende is wrechednes, and all
ȝoure trauaile is waine.

'In þe secound son of Dauid ar bitakened þe euell and þe fals
cristen, for þat son trespassed agains his fadir in his age, and þoght
5 þus: "Mi fadir is ane old man and is febill, for his strenth failes fast. If I
speke aniþinge wrange he answers noȝt. If I do aniþinge contrari to
him, he sall noȝt venge him, bot, whateuir I do againe him, he sall
suffir it pacientli. And þarefor I will do what me likes." And so he went
furth with so[m] of his fadir seruantes into þe wode in porpose for to
10 regne: in þe whilke wode were sertaine trees. Bot, throwe wisdome
and will of þe fadir, his counsaile was chaunged, and þai þat were with
f. 75ᵛᵇ him ware shamed and reproꞁued.

'þus dose þe cristen now to me, and þus þai þinke: "þe tokens of
God, and his domes, are noght now shewed so openli as þai were
15 wont. We mai speke what we will, for he is mercifull and takes no
hede. Do we þarefor what vs likes, for he will sone forgife." Also þai
mistraiste of mi powere, as if I were now febler to do what me likes þan
I was sometime. þai wene þat I hafe lesse charite, as if I walde noȝt
nowe haue merci on þam as I had on þaire fadirs befor þame. þai
20 wene and haldis mi dome vnstabill and slidand, and mi rightwisnes
bot vanite. And þarefor þai go vp to þe wode with som of þe seruauntes of Dauid, þat þai might trestli regne.

'What menis þis wode, in þe whilke is bot a fewe trees growand, bot
hali kirke, þat vpstandis bi seuen sacramentes as bi a fewe trees? þis
25 wode þai go to with a few seruauntes of Dauid: þat menis, with a fewe
gude werkes, in þe whilke þai trest so mikill þat, what sin þat þai be in
or dose, þai wene to haue forgifnes and heuen as bi right of heretage. |
f. 76ʳᵃ Bot as þe son of Dauid þe whilke, againe þe fadirs will, wald haue
optened þe realm, was put of with shame and reproue, for he desired it
30 vnrightfulli, and it was gifen to a bettir and to a wisser, so þai sall be
expelled and put fro mi kingdome, and it sall be gifen to þame þat dose
mi will, for þere mai none optene [it] bot if he haue charite, and be
clen and gouern him eftir mi herte: elles mai he noȝt com nere me.

'þe þird son of Dauid was Salamon, þe whilke bitokens þe
35 paine[m]s. When Bersabe herd þat oneoþir þan Salamon suld regne,
sho entird to Dauid and saide, "Mi lorde, þou swore to me þat
Salamon suld regne eftir þe, and now þare is anoþir chosen. Ife he go
furth and hafe prosperite, I sall be demed to þe fire as a vowtres and mi

---

5 failes] failest   6 aniþinge²] ani aniþinge, ani *subpuncted*   9 som] son,
Lat. quibusdam   32 optene it] optened   35 painems] painens

son sall be bastarde." When Dauid herd þis, he satt vpward and saide,
"I swere bi God þat Salamon sall sitt in mi sete, and he sall regne eftir
me." And þan he commandid to his seruauntes þat þai sull enhauns
Salamon in his sete, and þat þai suld preche him kinge whome Dauid
had cho|sen. þai did þe commaundment of þaire lorde, and with grete   f. 76rb
powere þai set him in his trone, and flemed all þe toþir and broght   6
þame into seruage þat consentid vnto his broþir.

'This womman Barsabe, þat held hirselfe as a vowtres if þare hade
bene ani oþir kinge chosen, menes þe faithe of þe paine[m]s, for þare
is no wers avowtre þan to trowe anoþir god þan him þat made all   10
þinges of noght. And as Barsabe did to Dauid, so þare is some of þe
painems þat commis to me with a meke hert and contrite, sainge þus:
"Lorde, þou hight to vs þat we suld in time comminge be cristen. Fulfille now in vs þi biheste. If a oþir kinge, þat is of a oþir faithe þan þi
faith, rise vpe on vs, we sall as wreches be brint, and as a vowtrees þat   15
had taken f[o]r þe lawfull husband þe avowtrer, we sall die, and all if
þou life withoute ende in þiselfe, ȝet þou sall be dede fro vs, and we fro
þe, when þou sall be put fro oure hertes be þi grace, and we are agains
þe bi oure mistraiste. þarefor fulfill þi bihest, and comforthe oure
febilnes, and gife light to oure derkenes, | for, and þou make delai and   f. 76va
kepe þiselfe fer fro vs, we sall perishe."   21

'When I here þis, as Dauid, I dresse me vpwarde be mi grace and
merci, and I swere be mi godhede, þat is with mi manhede, and be mi
manhede þat is in mi spirit, and be mi spirit þat is bothe in godhede
and manhede, þat I sall fulfill mi biheste, for I sall sende mi frendes,   25
þe whilke sall lede in mi son Salamon, þat is þe painems, into þe
wode, þat is into þe kirke, in þe whilke are seuen sacramentes as seuen
trees: þat is, baptime, penance, confirmacion, þe sacrament of þe
awtir, ordir, weddinge, and oyntinge. And þai sall reste in mi sete, þat
is, in mi right faithe and beleue of þe kirke, and euell cristen sall be   30
þaire seruantes. Bot þai sall euer ioi and be glade of mi endeles
heretage and perpetuell swetenes, þe whilke I sall ordeine for þame.
þese (þat is, þe euell cristen) sall sorow and morne in wrechednes þat
sall bigin in þis present life and laste withouten ende. And þarefore mi
frendes, for now is time to wake, slombir þai noȝt ne slepe, ne | be þai   f. 76vb
noȝt irke, for þai sall hafe a gloriouse rewarde eftir þaire trauaile.'   36

9 painems] painens   16 for] fra, *Lat.* pro   23 manhede] manhede þat is in
mi spirit, *exc.* manhede, *ruled through*   26 þe²] *twice, also marg.*   27 in] in to,
to *subpuncted*

Capitulum 6m. Wordes of þe son, in presens of þe spouse, of a kinge þat was in þe felde with his frendes on þe right hand, and enemis, and how Criste is bitokened bi þis king.

5 The son spake: 'I ame as a kinge þat stode in þe felde, on whose right hande were his frendes, and his enemis on þe left. And as þai stode, þare come a voice criand to þame on þe right hand, where all stode wele armed, for þai hade þaire helmes wel bonden, and þaire visage turned to þe lord. þe voice cried þus: "Turne ȝou to me, and trowe ȝe
10 me. I haue gold to gife ȝou." When þai herd, þai turned þame to him. And þe voice saide againe, "If ȝe will se þe gold, vnbinde ȝoure helmes againe eftir ȝoure awen will." When þai had done as he bade, he band againe þe helmes, bot all on contrari wise þat þai were bifore, for þe holes bi þe whilke þai suld haue sene and luked furth, þai were sett in
f. 77ʳᵃ þe bakeside of þe heued, and þe bakeside of þe | helme shadowed
16 byfor þe ein, þat þai might noȝt se ne loke. And he lede þame as blind eftir him.

'When þis was done, frendes of þe kinge tolde to þaire lorde þat his men were dissaiued and begiled of þaire enemis. To whome þe lorde
20 saide, "Go ȝe furth emange þame and cry þus: 'Vnbynd ȝoure helmes and sai þat ȝe are begilled and dissaiued. Turn ȝou to me and I sall resaiue ȝou in pese.' " þat wald þai noȝt here bot toke it for skorn, as þe seruandes þat herd it tolde to þe lorde. þan saide þe lorde, "Sen þai haue dispised and set me at noȝt, go ȝe to þame on þe left syde,
25 and sai þus thre þinges: 'þe wai is redi to ȝou and þe ȝat is opyn. þe lord will in his awen persone mete with ȝou in pese. And þarefor trowe ȝe stedfastli þat þe wai is redi. Hope ȝe stabilli þat þe ȝate is opyn and þat þese wordes are trewe. Meet ȝe in charite with þe lord, and he sall with pese and charite resaiue ȝou, and he sall lede ȝou into perpetuall
30 pese.' " When þai had herd þe wordes of þair messagers, þai trowed þame and þarefore þai were resaiued in pese.

f. 77ʳᵇ 'I am þis kinge, for I haue þe cristen on þe | right hand (to whome I ordain þe gude of endeles blis), whose helmes were bunden, and þaire visage turned toward me, when þai had a perfite will to fulfill mi
35 plesance and to obei to mi biddinges. þan was all þaire desire vnto heuen. Bot eftirward þe voice of þe deuell, þat is pride, come into þe werlde, and shewed werldli riches and fleshli lustes, toward þe whilke

---

10 to²] to þame, þame *subpuncted*   15 þe⁴] *Quire catchphrase,* helme, *below*
17 eftir] eftir þaime, þaime *subpuncted*   23 þe³] þe s.

þai turne[d] fro me when þai gaue þaire lufe and þaire consente to pride. And for it þai did downe þaire helmes, when þai fulfilled þe luste of will in dede, and set temporall þinges bifor spirituall. When þe helmes of Goddes will was þus putt down, and þe armoure of vertu also, þan bigan pride to be swilke a maistir in þaim þat, if þai might, 5 þai wald euer syn withoute ende.

'And þair een are so blinded þat þe holes of þe helmes, bi þe whilke þai suld loke furthe beforn, standes bakwarde. þese holes menes consideracion bifore of þinges þat are to come, and auysi circumspeccion of þinges þat are present. þai suld throw þe firste hole see þe endlese 10 blisse and rewarde, | how likinge and delectabill þai are, and how hor-   f. 77ᵛᵃ ribill þe paine sall be, and how fertfull þe strait domes of God. Be þe second hoole þai suld se and behald whilke are commanded and whilke are forbed, in what þai haue trespaste agains Goddes biddinges, and how þai might þame amende. Bot þese holes standes 15 bihind, where noþinge mai be sene, for heuenli þinges are now forgetin, and þe loue of God is waxen colde. Bot þe lufe of þe world is so mikill made of and so sweteli halsed þat it ledis þaim, as it were a whele þat were welle anointed, to what at þai will.

'Neuerþelesse mi frendes, when þai see howe litelle I am taken hede 20 to, and how I am mispersoned, þe losse of saules and þe lordshipe of þe deuell, euerilke dai þai cri for þame to me in praiere, whose praiers hase thirled heuen, and þai haue entird into mine eres, and þai haue so enclined me þat I haue sent furth euirilk dai mi prechours, and I haue shewed þame tokens and multiplied to þame mi grace. Bot þai 25 dispise all, and continuli ekes | syn to sin.   f. 77ᵛᵇ

'þarefor I sall sai now to mi seruantes, and in suthfastenes I sall fulfill it, "Go ȝe furth to þame of þe left side" (þat is, to þe panems, þe whilke hase bene as ȝet on þe left side, þat is, noȝt set by). "Go ȝe furth and sai ȝe þus: 'þe lord of heuen, and maker of all, makes knawen to 30 ȝou þat þe wai of heuen is opind to ȝou. Haue ȝe will for to entir with siker faith. þe ȝate of heuen standes opin: traste ȝe treweli, and ȝe sall entir. þe kinge of heuen and þe lorde of aungels will mete with ȝou in his awen persone, and gife ȝou pees and endeles blissinge. Mete ȝe þan with him, and ressaiues him with þe same faith he 35 shewed to ȝou, for þe wai of heuen is made redi to ȝou. Ressaiue ȝe him now with hope þat he hase will now to gife ȝou heuen. Loue ȝe

---

1 turned] turne   13 are] are comandmentes, comandmentes *subpuncted*
21 how] how euerilke dai þai cri for þaime to me in praiere, *exc.* how, *ruled through*
27 sall²] *twice, second subpuncted*

him of all ȝour hert, and fulfill ȝour loue in werke, and entir ȝe þe ȝates
of God, fro þe whilke þo cristen sall be keped oute þat oþir will noȝt
entir, or elles makes þame vnworthi to entir.' I sai to ȝou in mi trewth

f. 78ra þat I sall fullfill mi wordes. I sall take ȝou for mi sonnes, and I | sall be
to ȝou a fadir, whome þe cristen hase disspised and noȝt set bi."

6   'Wharefor, ȝe mi frendes þat are in þe werlde, go ȝe furth sikirli and
cri ȝe, and shew to þame mi will, and helpe ȝe þat þai mai fulfill it. I
sall be in ȝoure hert and in ȝoure mouthe. I sall be ȝoure gide and
leder in ȝoure life and in ȝour dede. I sall noȝt forsake ȝou. Go ȝe furth

10 boldeli, for blis and ioi springes of trauaile. I might do all þinges in a
worde and in a pointe, bot I will þat ȝoure rewarde come to ȝou bi
trauaile and ȝoure honoure and wirshipe growe of manlines. Ne
meruell ȝe noȝt all if I speke þus, for if þe wisest man in þe werlde
wiste and considird how mani saules gose euirilke dai downe into hell,

15 he suld knawe þat þare is mo nomber þan is grauell stonnes in þe see
side or smale stonnes in þe bruikes. þarefor, þat þe nomber of þe
deuell were þe lesse, and so fewer were dampned, it is mi will þe perell
be knawen and mine oste be encressed. I speke þus þat happeli þai
mai here and amend thaime.'

20 Capitulum vii. Wordes of þe son to þe spouse howe his
f. 78rb godhede is likened to a | crowne, and howe þe states of
clerkes and lewed men are bitakenede bi Petir and
Paule, and what manere sall be keped againe ennemis,
and of condiscions anentes seculer kniȝtes.

25 The son spake to þe spouse: 'I ame a kinge of a crowne. Wot þu oght
whi I kall me kinge of a croune? Forsoþe, mi godhede was withoute
beginynge and sall be withoute ende. þarfor it is likned to a croune.
Right as in þe realme þe crowne sall be keped to him þat sall be kinge,
so mi godhed was kept to mi manhede as his crown.

30 'I had two seruantes, one a clerke, anoþir a lewed man. þe firste was
Petir, þat had office of a clerke. þe secound was Paule, as it had bene a
lewed man. Petir was knit in wedelake, bot he sawe þat weddinge
acorded noȝt with þe office of a clerke, bot his saule stode in perelle of
losse bi incontinens. þarefor he made diuorse of himselfe fro þe wed-

35 dinge, all if it were lefull, and with a perfite saule he kepet him all to
me. Paule kept his chastite and himselfe vndefoiled. Se now, þarefor,

6 mi] mai, a *subpuncted*   30 one a clerke] one clerke one a clerke, one clerke *subpuncted*   31 a¹] a lewed man, lewed man *subpuncted*

what charite I haue shewed | to þere two. First I gaue to Petir þe keis of ⟨f. 78ᵛᵃ⟩
heuen, þat what he band and lawsed suld be bonden and lawsed in
heuen. Also I gaue to Paule þat he suld be like to Petir in ioi and wirshipe, for as þai were in erthe ioined as felaws and peres, so þai are
now in heuen peres, glorified in endeles blis.   5

'Bot all if it be þat I haue þus ex[pres]sede þese two be nam, ȝit bi
þame and in þame I vndirstand mine oþir frendes, for, right as sometime in þe lawe I spake as i[t] had bene oneli to one man, meninge bi
him alle þe pupill of Israell, so now in þere two I vndirstand moni mo,
whome I haue fulfilled with mi blisse and mi charite.   10

'Eftir a certaine time was passed, sinnes and euel bigan to multi-
plie, and þe fleshe wax more freell and redi to sinne þan it was
wonte. þarefor, I gaue mercifull consaile bothe to clerkes and lewed
men, whome I vndirstode bi Petir and Paule, and I suffird clerkes to
haue gudes in hali kirke to profit of þair bodi, and for to vse þame in   15
mesure, þat þai might be þe more feruent and þe oftir occupied in
mi seruise. I suffird | also þe lewed to make weddinge eftir þe vse of ⟨f. 78ᵛᵇ⟩
holi kirke.

'Bot amange þe clerkes was one gude man and þoght þus: "þe
fleshe stirres and drawes me to euell luste, þe werld to euell sightes; þe 20
deuell puttes to me mani sotill begilinges and gildirs of sin. þarefore,
þat I be noȝt ouercommin of þe flesli luste, I will put to a mesure in all
þinges and werkes. I sall mesure me in etinge and restinge, and kepe to
me a resonabill dewe time to labor and praier, refreininge me and mi
fleshe with fastinge. Also, þat þe werld distracte me noght fro þe loue 25
of God, I will forsake all þe gudes of þe werld and folowe Criste in
pouert on þe sikerest wise. Also, þat þe deuell begille me noght, þat
makes falshede to seme treuthe, I sall sett miselfe to þe gouernans and
obediens of oneoþir, in whose gouernance I sall putt mi will and
schew me redi to fulfill whateuere he biddes." þis was he þat ordainde 30
firste religious place and liued perseuerantli þarein, liuinge com-
mendabill ensampill to be folowed of oþir. |

'þe state of þe lewed men was a while wele disposid. Som of þame ⟨f. 79ʳᵃ⟩
tillid þe erthe and gaue þame manli to bodeli trauaile. Some went in
shipes of þe see and led marchandise to oþir contres, þat þe plente of 35
one contre might releue þe nede of anoþir. Som trauailede with þair
handes in crafte. Amange whame þare was some þat defended þe
kirke, þe whilke are now called knightes, þat tuke vpon þame armour

---

6 expressede] excusede, *Lat.* expresse   8 it] I   25 fro] for, *Lat.* ab
37 Amange] amange was, was *subpuncted*

to venge þe wronge done to holi kirke and to discomfit þe enemis of it.
Amange þe whilke was one gude man, and mi frende, þat thoght þus:
"I till noȝt þe erthe as an husband. I passe noȝt þe flodes of þe se as
ane marchand. I trauaile noȝt with mi handes as ane man of craft.
5 What sall I þan do, and how sall I plese mi God? And namli, sin I ame
noȝt, as I suld be, manli in laboure of hali kirke (mi bodi is waike and
febill to suffir wowndes; mi hand is noȝt strange to smite þe enemis;
mi saule is irksome to þinke on heuenli þinges) what sall I do þane?
f. 79ʳᵇ Forsothe, | I wote what I sall do. I sall rise and binde miselfe with a
10 stedfaste othe vndir a temporall prince, þat I sall with all mi mightes
and mi blode defende þe right faith of holi kirke."

'þan commes þat frende of me to þe prinse and sais, "Lorde, I ame
one of þe defendoures of holi kirke, bot mi bodi is ouir softe to suffir
wowndes, mi handes waike to smite, mi saule vnstabill to þinke on
15 gosteli þinges. Mine awen will is plesand to me, and reste suffirs me
noȝt to stand strongli for þe howse of God. þare[fore] I bind miselfe
with one opin othe vndir þe obediens of holi kirke and þe, a, þou
prince, and þat I sall defende it all þe dais of mi life: and so, all if þe
will be dull for to trauaile, ȝet, for mi vow and swerringe, I mai be com-
20 pellid to trauaile." To whome þe prince answers, "I sall go with þe
vnto Goddes house, and I sall be wittnes of þi othe and of þine
biheste."

'When þai com togidir to þe awter, mi frende settis him on his knees
bifor mine awter and sais, "I ame ouir seke in mine fleshe to suffir
f. 79ᵛᵃ woundes; I make ouirmikill of mine awen | will. þarefore in þis present
26 tim I hight obediens to God and to þe þat art mi heued, bindinge miselfe
bi othe to defende holi kirke againe his enemis and to comforth þe
frendes of God, to helpe widows and fadirlesse childir, and neuir to do
aniþinge contrari to hali kirke or þe faithe. Also, if I happen for to erre, I
30 oblish me to þi correccion, and þis profession I make, þat þe more
straite I ame bunden to obediens, I mai so mikil þe more ethchew and
beware of sinne, and þe more feruentli soiet mi will to God and to þe,
and also þat I mai knawe þat þe more strait þat þe bond is of obediens,
þe more is þe perell to presume at contrari it."

35 'When he hase made þis profession at mine awter, þe prince wiseli
disposed to him an abit diuersed fro oþir seculers in tokninge of þe
forsakinge of his will. And þat he mai knawe þat he hase a soueraine to
whome he awe obediens, þe prince gaue him also a swerde in his

hande, and saide, "With þis swerde þou sall sla and distruy þe enemis
of God." He gaue on his arme a sheld and saide, "With þis sheld kepe
þe fro þe dartes and wharels | of Goddes enemis, and pacientli suffir if   f. 79ᵛᵇ
þou be hourt, and þe sheld be sonner broken þan þou flee."

'Mi clerke, þat was present, herd howe þat mi frende hight trewli to   5
kepe all þere þinges, eftir þe whilke profession mi clerke gaue him mi
bodi to be gastli strenghe to him, þat mi frennde so onnede to me be
neuir departed ne twinned fro me. Swilke one was mi frennde George
and mani oþir: and swilke one suld be knightes, þat suld haue þe nam
for worthines of þe abit and order, and for gude wirkinge and defense   10
of þe holi faithe.

'Bot here now what mine enmis dose now againe þat, and contrari
to þat, at mi frendis did bifore. Mi frendis entird monasteris of a discrete drede and þorowe a gudli charite. Bot þai at are now in monasteris, þai go into þe werlde fore pride and couetise, and hase thare   15
awen will, fulfillinge þe delites of þe bodi. Rightwisnes will at þai þat
dies in þat will fele neuir heuenli blis, bot þe pains of hell withouten
ende. Also wit þou welle þat cloistrers, þe whilke againe þaire awen
will, of a godeli charite, are made prelates, þai sall noȝt be reke|ned in   f. 80ʳᵃ
þe nombir of forsaid oþir.   20

'Also, knightes sometime þat bare mine armoure were redi to die for
right and for þe holi faithe. And þai ware besi to promote right, and
depresse and meke þe euell men. Bot here now how þai air changed. It
is more likinge now to die in batale for pride and couetise and envie,
eftir þe suggestions of þe deuell, þan to life eftir mi biddinges and   25
haue endeles blisse. þarefor all þat dies in swilke will, þe dome of
rightwisnes sall gife þame þaire sowde, and knit þaire saules withoute
ende with þe deuell. And þai þat seruise me sall haue rewarde and
sowde in heuens blisse withoute ende. I, Jesus Criste, verrai God and
man, and with fadir and holi goste euir God, spake þese wordes.'   30

Capitulum octauum. Wordes of Criste of a knight þat
left verrai knightehede, þat is, mekenes, paciens, obediens and faith, and howe dampnacion commes for
euell wille as for dede.

'I ame verrai lorde. þare is no lorde more excellent þan I, ne bifore   35
`me was ne´ | sall be eftir me, bot all lordshipe is of me and bi me.   f. 80ʳᵇ

3 þe¹] þe with, with *subpuncted*   7 frennde] frenndes, s *subpuncted*
12 mine] mine what mi

þarefore I ame a verrai lorde, ne þer mai none be called trewli a lorde
bot I, for of me is all power and might. I talde þe bifore þat I hade two
seruauntes. þe tone toke a perfite life vpon him and ended manli,
when innumerabil pepil folowed eftirward in þe same life. And nowe
5 sall I tell who was þe firste apostota fro þe life þat mi son profest him
to. Bot I tell þe noght his name, for þou knawes it noȝt, bot I sall tell þe
his entent and his loue.

'þare was one wald haue bene a knight, and come to þe tempill, and
when he entirde, he herd swilke a voice: "And þou will be a knight, þe
10 bihoues haue thre þinges. Firste, þe moste trowe þat at semis brede in
þe awter e[s] verra Goddes bodi and verrai God and man, and maker
of heuen and of erth. þe seconde, þe bihoues do more abstinens fro
þinne awen will þan þou hade bifore, fro þe time þou hase taken vpon
f. 80ᵛᵃ þe þis knighthede. þe þirde: þou sall noȝt sett bi þe wirshipe of | þe
15 worlde. And þan sall I gife þe gudeli delite and wirshipe euirlastinge."

'When he hade herde þare and auised him of þame, he herd anoþir
voice wonder ill, and contrari to þese þre voises, þus sainge: "If þou
will serue me, I sall gife þe oþir thre þinges. I sall make þe lorde of þat
þou sees, and to here þat is likinge, and to haue what þou desires."

20 'When he herd þis he þoght þus: "þe firste lorde bad þat I suld
trowe þat at I sawe noght, and he heghtes þinges þat at I knawe noȝt
of. He biddis abstene fro delites þat I desire and see, and for to hope
þinges þat are vncertaine to me. Bot þis lorde heghtes me wirshipe of
þe worlde to haue, and to here swilke delites as I desire. Forsothe, it is
25 bettir to me to folowe him, and haue þat I knawe and mai haue sikirnes
of, þan hope þinges þat are vncertaine." þis man þat þoght þus began
firste, on þis wise, to go bakwarde fro verrai knighthede, and forsoke
þe forsaide profession, and brake þe biheste. He keste down bifore his
fete þe shelde of paciens, and oute of his hand þe swerde of his defens,
f. 80ᵛᵇ and | so passed oute of mi tempill.

31 'þan said þat wikked voice to him: "If þou will be mine, as I haue
saide, go furth into þe stretis and f[e]lde on prowde and stoute wise,
þat þare be no spice no braunche of pride bot þou shewe againe þe
mekenes þat þe toþir lorde bade. And as he entird and made soiet
35 himselfe to be at all obediens, so sall þou suffir to haue no soueraine.
Bowe þou þi heued to no persone. Take a swerde in þine hand to shed
þe blode of þi broþir and neghboure for wirshipe of þe werld; lufe þou
þi bodi, and forbere no maner of fleshli luste þat is likinge to þe."

---

3 manli] nameli, *Lat.* viriliter   11 es] ev   32 felde] folde, *Lat.* campum
35 þou] þou sall, sall *subpuncted*

'When þis man had fulli assentid to his voice, his prince put his
hand in his nekke in place ordained þarefore (for, if þe will be gude,
þare is no place vnprofitabill for man; and, if þe will be euell, þare is
no place gude). Eftir he had þus taken knighthede, he went and vsed it
in all werldes pride, forgetinge as a wreche þe sharpe life þat he was   5
bunden to bifore. He had folowers withoute nowmbir, and, for his
wirshipe, he was þe depere | in dampnacion.   f. 81ra

'Bot þou mai aske and sai, "þare is mani wald be made mikill of,
and haue wirshipe, bot þai mai noȝt come þareto in dede. Wheþir sall
þai be ponished for þis euell will euen with þaime þat hase þaire   10
desire in dede?" To þe whilke I answere, he þat hase a full will and
dose all þat he mai for to be wirshipede in þe werlde, and for to be
called a vaine name, noȝtwithstandynge þat þe preue dome of God
suffirs him noȝt to haue þe effect of his will, ȝet I sai þe for certaine
þat, eftir þat will, he sall be ponished as he þat hase in dede, bot he   15
correct and amende þat will bi penance.

'I tell þe ensampill of two persones þat were knawen to mani. One
had prosperite eftir his awen will, and gat almoste whateuer he wald
desire. þe toþir had þe same will, bot he might noȝt get it. þe first gat
wirshipe of þe werlde, and loued þe tempill of his bodi, and, as he   20
desired, vsed in lordeshipe all luste. þe toþir was like in will, bot he
had lesse wirshipe, and he wald gladli ane hundreth times haue shede
þe blode of his neght|boure if he might haue fullfilled his couetise. And   f. 81rb
he did þareto at he might, bot he miȝt neuir fulfill his will fulli eftir his
desire. These two are peres and euen in þe horribill torment, þe   25
whilke, all if þai were noȝt dede one oure and one time, ȝit I speke on
þe tone saule as of bothe, for þare is one dampnacion of bothe. And, in
þe departinge of þe saule fro þe bodi, þere was one voice of bathe, þat
þus sounded of þe saule to þe bodi, sainge, "Tell me where is nowe þi
lusti sight of eine þou hight me, where þe luste is þou shewed me?   30
Where es þe delectabill speche þou bad me vse?" And onone þe
deuell answerde, "þe sight þat was bihight is nowe pouder, þe
wordes bot blast of winde and aire; þe luste is bot clai and rotin filth,
þe whilke sall noȝt awaile." þan cried þe saule, "Alas, alas! Howe
wrechedli ame I deceiued. I bihald thre þinges. Firste, I se him þat   35
in forme of brede was hight to me. He is kinge of kinges and lorde of
lordes, and þe abstinens þat he bad is moste profitabill." þan he
cried with hier voice and saide þus | þries, allas: "Allas, þat I was   f. 81va

16 amende] amended   29 sounded] souwnded

borne! Allas, þat mi life was so lange vpon erthe! Allas, þat I sall life in
perpetuall dede and neuir sall haue ende."

'Lo, what wrechedenes and sorowe wreches sall haue for contempt
of þaire God, and for a sone passinge temporall gladnes! þarefor, þou
5 mi spouse, þanke me þat hase called þe fro swilke sorowe and
wrechednes, and be obedient to mi spirit and to mi chosen derlinges.'

Capitulum ix. Wordes of Criste to ˋþeˊ spouse þat
declares þe forsaide chapitir, and of metinge of þe
deuell with þe forsaide knight, and of his rightfull and
10 ferdfull condempnacion.

'All þe time of þis life is bot as an oure anentes me. þarefore I sai to þe
þat þe instans þat is now was euir in mi presens. I saide þe bifore þat
þare was one þe whilke bigan verrai knighthed; oneoþir, þe whilke
wrechedeli forsoke and went fro it. And he keste downe his helme
15 bifor mi fete and his swerde to mi side, when he forsoke þe holi
f. 81ᵛᵇ pro|fession þat he made.

'His helme betakens his faiþe, with þe whilk he sulde haue defend
him againe þe enemis of his saule. Mi fete, with þe whilk I go towarde
man, is mi delite, þorow þe whilke I drawe man to me, and mi paciens,
20 þorow whome I suffir pacientli. þen keste he downe þe helme when
he entird into mi kirke and þoght þus: "I will folowe þat lorde þat consails me none abstinens, þat giffes me leue to do mi desires, þat suffirs
me to here þo þinges þat delites þe eres": and so he keste downe þe
helme of mi faith, when he preferred his awen will to mine, and lufed
25 bettir þe creature þan þe maker. For trewli, if he had kept trewe faith
and trowed me moste mighti, and rightwise demer and giffer of end-
lesse blis, he wald neuir haue desired ne dred þinge bot me. Bot he
keste mi faithe bifor mi fete when he sett noȝt bi mi faithe bot dispised
it, ne soght nowþir mi louinge, ne toke hede to mi paciens.

30 'Forthirmare, he keste his swerde to mi side. þe swerd bitokens þe
f. 82ʳᵃ drede of God, þe whilk Goddes kniȝt aw to haue | continuli in his
hand: þat menis, in his werkes. Mi side bitokens mi proteccion,
throwe þe whilke I norise and fostir mi sonnes as þe modir hir childir,
and I kepe þame and defend þame at þe deuell noie þame noȝt. Bot he

3 and sorowe] *twice, second subpuncted*   contempt] comtempt   12 þat³] *twice,*
second subpuncted   30-137/3 forthirmare . . . paciens] *twice,* va-cat *to second (var.*
readings l. 30 forþirmare, kest, þe swerde; l. 31 whilke, *om.* kniȝt, awe; l. 32 hande, mi
kepinge and mi protection; l. 33 throw, norishe; l. 34 *om.* þame¹, defende 137 l. 1 kest,
þinke; l. 2 *om.* mi²)   31 to haue] *twice*

keste awai þe swerde of mi drede when he wald noȝt þinge on mi
might, ne mi powere, ne set noȝt b[i] mi charite, ne toke no hede to mi
paciens. And forsothe he kest it to mi side when he þoght þus: "I
nowþir set bi his drede, his defens ne his | kepinge, for mi fortune com-   f. 82ʳᵇ
mis of mine awen wisdom and of þe nobelai þat I haue." And so, for-   5
sothe, he brake þe bihest he made to me. What is þe trewe promis þat
a man is halden to vowe to God? Forsothe, it is þe werke of charite,
þat, whateuir he do, he wirke for charite and lufe of God. Bot þis
promis hase he made voide, when he turned þe charite [of God] into
his awen lufe, and preferred his awen wille to þe delite and endles blis   10
þat is to com.

'Se how he was þus deseuerd and twinned fro me and fro þe
ensampill of mi mekenes, for, trewli, as þe bodis of cristen men, in
whome regnes meknes, are mi tempill, right so [in] whame regnes
pride are þe tempill of þe deuell, þe whilke gouerns þame eftir his   15
awen will and desire. When he was gone oute of þe tempill of mi
meknes, and had caste [a]wai þe helme of mi right faithe and þe
swerde of mi drede, he went into þe felde with all maner of pride, and
excercised himselfe in all maner of luste and fulfillinge | of his awen   f. 82ᵛᵃ
propir will, dispisinge mi drede and ai growinge and encressinge in his   20
awen lustes and sine.

'When he come to þe laste ende of his life and þe saule suld go oute
of þe bodi, þan deuels mete with it with grete fersnes, and þre voices
sounded oute of hell. Of þe whilke þe firste saide þus: "Is noȝt þis he
þat left and forsoke mekenes, and folowed vs in all maner of pride,   25
insomikill þat if he might hafe passed aboue vs two fete he wald haue
done it, so he might haue bene þe firste and had þe principalte in
pride?" To whome þe saule answerde, "Forsoþe, I am sho." þan saide
rightwisnes, "þis sall be þe rewarde of þi pride, þat þou sall fall fro
one deuell to onoþir to þou com to þe laste þat is in helle; and as ilke   30
deuell knewe and felt certeine paine and torment for ilke idill þoght
and vaine werke, so þou sall haue þe torment of ilke one, as þou was
partenere of þaire malice and wikkednes."

'þe secound vois cried and saide, "Is noȝt þis he þat hase made
apostasi fro þe knighthede þat he was professed in, and hase taken   35
vpon him | oure knighthede?" þe saule answerde, "Forsothe, it is I."   f. 82ᵛᵇ
þan saide rightwisnes, "þis is þi mede, þat whosoeuer folowes þe
ensampill of þi knighthede sall encrese þe tormentes throw his malice

---

2 bi] bu   9 of God] *om.*   13 as] as bo, bo *subpuncted*   14 in] *om.*
17 awai] wai, *caret mark*   28 whome] whowme, *second* w *subpuncted*

and his paines. And when he commes to þe, he sall smite þe as with a dedeli wounde. Right as he þat had a sore wounde, if he suffird wound vpon wound till þe bodi were full of woundes, he suld so intollerabili be tormentide þat he suld euir cri wo vpon wo, so sall paine vpon 5 paine come vnto þe, and þi sorowe sall be renewed abouen all oþir sorowe. þi paine sall neuir fall ne faile, ne þi wo sall neuir be lesse."

'The þird voice cried, "Is þis noȝt he þat solde his maker for a creature, and chaunged þe charite of his maker for þe lufe of him- selfe?" þe saule saide, "Ȝis, it is I." Rightwisnes answerde, "þarefore 10 sall þare be two oppeninges made to him. Bi one sall entir all maner of paine to him, þat is ordainde for þe lest sinne vnto þe moste, bicause þat he sold and cused his maker for his awen luste. Bi þe secound sall
f. 83ʳᵃ entir to him | all maner of sorowe and confusion withoute ani lufe or comforthe, for cause he loued himselfe instede of his God his maker. 15 þarefor his life sall laste withouten ende, and his paine also, for all saintes hase and sall turn fro him þaire visage." Lo, mi spouse, howe wreched þai sall be þat dispises me, and howe mikill paine þai sall purchese for a litill luste.'

20 Capitulum xm. Wordes of Criste to þe spouse as to Moisen of þe brenninge buske, and how þe deuell is vndirstand bi Pharaoo, and knightes þat are nowe bi þe pepull of Israel, and howe knightes and bishopes of þis present times ordains and araies dwellinge places to þe deuell.

25 'It is wretin in þe lawe þat when Moises kepede shepe in desert, and saw þe bushe enflammed and noȝt waste, he was dredinge and hid his visage. To whome a voice spake fro þe bushe and saide, "þe disese and þe aff[li]ccion of mi pupill sties vp into mine eres, and I haue merci on þame, for þai are oppressed in þe moste hard thraldo[m]e."
f. 83ʳᵇ 'I am þe voice | soundand fro þe bushe, þe whilke spekes now with 31 þe. Bi mi pupill, þat was Israel, I vndirstand knightes þat are in þe werlde, þe whilke hase made profession to mi knighthede and suld be mine. Bot þai are ouir hard oppressed of þe deuell. Forsothe, Pharao did thre euell þinges to mi folke in Egipt. Firste, in makinge of þe 35 walles, þe laborers had noȝt giuen to þame necessari mater with þe whilke þai suld make þaire tiles. þe seconde, for þe biggers had no

3 vpon] vup on   13 to him] twice   27 a voice] a voice a, second a subpuncted
28 affliccion] affeccion   29 thraldome] thraldone

thanke for all þaire trauaile, all if þai fulfilled þe charge of þe nombir
of tiles þat was assigned to þame. þe þirde, for þe ouirlokers of þaire
werke greuoseli tormentid þame if þai failed aniþinge of þaire
costommabill nombir of tile. þese pupill bigged to Pharao in þer grete
affliccion to allþairemoste citees.   5

'This Pharao bitokens þe deuell, þe whilke tormentes and diseses
mi knightes, þat aght to be mi pupill. I sai in trewthe, and mi knightes
had standen in þe firste institucion and ordinans þat was bigon of mi
frende, þai suld haue bene | to me as amange mi derer frendes. Right as   f. 83ᵛᵃ
Abraham, takinge firste þe commandment of circumcision throw his   10
obeisaunce to me, was made mi frende moste dere, and also all þat
folowed þe fathe of Abraham and his werkes, þai aire made partiners
of his lufe and of his blis, so, amange oþir ordirs, knightes plesed me
on speciall wise, bicause þai avowed to spende þaire blode for me. Bi
þat vowe þai plesid me souerainli, as Abraham dide in circumcision,   15
and þai were purged ilke dai in kepinge of þaire profession and
takinge on þame holi charite.

'Bot forsothe, þaire knightes are now oppressed in þe wreched
thraldome of þe deuell, þat he woundes þame with dedeli wounde,
and painefull haldes þame in torment and sorowe. Also, þe bishopes   20
of þe kirke, as þe childir of Israel, bigges to þame two citees. þe firste
is laboure of bodi, and vaine besines in getinge of worldeli gudes. þe
second is vnreste and turbill of saule. Labor is withoute and vnreste
within, þat makes spirituall þinges to seme heui and chargeous. Bot as
Pharao ministerd | noȝt þinges þat were necessari to making of tile, ne   f. 83ᵛᵇ
he gaue þame noȝt bernes full of whete ne wine, ne oþir þinges of   26
profet and comforthe, bot with mikill trauaile and sorowe þe pepull
gat to þame þe þinges þat were necessari, so dose now þe deuell to
þame. For, all if þai trauale with all besines at þai mai in þe werlde, ȝet
mai þai noȝt com to þat at þai desire, ne þai mai noȝt slokken þe þirste   30
of þaire coueitise. þarefor, within, þai are brent with sorowe, and,
withoute, with laboure and bodeli trauaile. And þat moues me to compassion of þair disese, seinge howe mi knightes now, and mi pupill,
bigges dwellinge places to þe deuell, and trauails withoute sesinge and
mai noȝt fulfill þaire desires, bot are euir more and more disesid in   35
vanites, in so fere þat þai report noȝt for þaire rewarde þe fruite of
benison bot þe reproue of confusion.

'Therefore, when Moises suld be sent to þe pupill, I gafe him a

29 trauale] trauale and

token for þre causes: firste, for euirilkea man in Egipt wirshiped one
God singulerli.

[Loss of leaf containing end of II. 10, beginning of II. 11:
missing material supplied from Ju]

f. 63ʳ And þer was called inn[u]merabil goddis, and þerfore it was worthi
f. 63ᵛ þat a signe | or tokin shuld be don, þat the ostencion and þe poere of
5 God þrou þe mervelous signe of oon God and oon makere of all thinge
shuld be beleuyd, and all ydollis and fals goddis repreuyd. The iide,
þat a signe was geven to Moyses in figure and representynge of myn
bodi to com. The brennynge buske and nat wastinge betokenys
nothinge but a virgine fecund and repleshid with the holy gost, child-
10 inge without ony corrupcioun. I serteynli procedid fro þat busk. I haue
takyn manhod of þe virgine flesch callid Mary. Also a serpent þat was
gevin to Moyses signified myn body. The iiide cause that a signe was
gevin to Moyses: for þe treuthe to be informyd of signes to be don and
fulfellid figuratifly, and þat þe treuthe of God shuld be preuyd the
15 more sewyr. Now I sende myn wordis to þe childre of Israel and to
myn knytis, to þe wheche it is not necessary now to shew no signe nen
toke[n] for iii causis. The first is on God and maker of all thingis by
scriptur is worschippid an knowyn by many signis. The iide is for þei
trowe nat me to be borne but þei knowe wel þat I am born and incarnat
20 withoute ony corrupcioun, for all scriptur is fulfellid, ne noon bettir
feith nen mor serteyn owys to be had or beleuyd than þe wheche is
prechid of me and myn holy prechoris. Thre thingis I haue don to þe
the wheche may be beleuyd. The first is þat myn wordis are trewe and
discorde nat fro þe trew feith. þe iide is þat the poure of þe dewle is
25 expulsid through vertu of myn word fro mankynde. The iiide is þat I
haue gevin to oon cherite to reforme froward hertis. þerfore dought
not in þese thingis, þe wheche are to be beleeued in me. Thei þat
beleuys in me belevis my wordis and conse[nt]s on me and I in them.
Therfore it is wretyn þat Moyses fro þe speche of God he coueryd his
30 face. But þu shal nat couere þin face. I haue openyd thin spirituall eyin
þat thou schuld see spiritual thingis. I haue oppenyd thin eren þat
thou schuld here tho thingis þat be of þe spirit of God. I shal shew the
likenes of myn body, how it was in þe passion and before, and how it
was aftir the resurreccioun, þe whech Mary Mawdeleyn and Peter

3 innumerabil] innimerabil   17 token] toke   28 consents] counsels

with many odir saw. þou shal here also myn voyce, þe wheche I spake
to Moyses in þe busch. The same thingis now is spokyn in thin sowle.'

[II.11] These were þe swete wordis of Crist of þe honor and joye of a
good and trewe knygth, and of þe manyfold metyngis of angel to hym
and hou þe glorious trinite has receyued him to euirlastinge reste for 5
his litil laboure.

'I haue told þe before of þe ende and peyne of a knight, þe whech
first went fro his cheualry or seruise professid. Now by a similitude I
telle þe (for odirwise þu may nat vndirstonde spiritual thingis) of the
joye and honowre of him þe whech has begunnyn a trewe seruise 10
manly and endid it more manly. þis myn frend whan he shuld dey, and
þe soule departe fro þe body, v legions of aungelis was send to mete
hym, amonge þe whech innumerabil dewlis com to cleyme | sum right f. 64ʳ
if þei might ony fynde, for thei are ful of malice. Than a voyce fro
heuen soundid clerly seyinge, "O lord and fadir, whedir is not this he 15
þe whech has boundyn himself to þin wil and perfitly has fulfellid it?"
Than he personally has answerid in his conciens, "Verily, I am he."
Ferderemore iii voyces was herd. On was of þe godhed seinge,
"Whedir nat I creat the and gaff the body and soule? þu art myn sone,
and þu has don the wil of thin fadir. þerfore come now to me þin 20
migthiest creator and swettest fadir. Euirlastinge eritage schal be
gevyn to þe, for þou art myn sone. þerfore þou must come to me and I
shal receyue the with honor and gladnesse." The iide voyce was herd,
of þe manhod, seyinge, "My brodir, come to þin brodir. I offred me for
the; I shed myn blood for the. Com þou to me, þe whech folwyd myn 25
will,

[Cl continues]

| [and gaue þi blode for mine] as I dide for þe: and fore þou was redi to f. 84ʳᵃ
ȝelde þi dede for mi dede and þi life for mine, þarefor, þou þat
folowed me in þi life, come nowe vnto mi life and to mi ioi þat sall
neuir ende, for trewli I knawlech þe mi broþir." þe þird voice was 30
herde on þe holi goste parti, þe whilke is with þe fadir and þe son, not
third god bot all þre persones is one God: "Come, mi knight, þat was
so desirows to me þat I chese to dwell within þe; þou was so manli
owteward þat þou was worthi to be defendid of me. þarefore, for þe
vnreste þou suffird in þi bodi, entir nowe into reste; and for þe 35

27 and gaue þi blode for mine] *om., cf. Lat.* quia rependisti sanguinem pro sanguine
as] a as, a *subpuncted*   29 vnto] vnto me in, me in *subpuncted*   35 nowe] *twice,*
second subpuncted

tribulacion of saule, entire into heuenli comforth; and for þi charite
entir into miselfe, and dwelle with me, and I with þe. Come, þarefor,
nobill knight vnto me, for þou desired noþinge bot me. þarefore com
with me, and þou sall be filled with a godli plesaunce and will."

5 'þan spake þe fife legions of aungels, as with þe sownde of fife
voices, and þus saide þe firste: "Go we bifore þis worþi knight, and
f. 84ʳᵇ bere we him in his wai, and present we his faithe | to oure God, þe
whilke he keped euir hole, and defendid it agains þe enemis of right."
þe seconde voice saide, "Bere we bifore him his helme: þat menis,
10 shewe we his paciens to oure God, þe whilke, if it be clereli knawen to
him, ȝit it sall be more gloriouse throw oure witnes, for he noȝt alloneli
with paciens suffird þinges þat were aduersari, bot also he gaue hertli
þankinge to God in times of aduersitees." þan saide þe þirde voice,
"Go we bifore him, and present we his swerde in þe sight of oure God:
15 þat menes, shewe we his obedience, throw þe whilke he was euir
verrai obedient, bothe in harde þinges and esi, eftir þe forme of
profession of his knighthede." þe fourt voice saide, "Go we and shewe
his hors to oure God: þat menes, bere we wittnes of his mekenes. Right
as þe hors beres þe bodi of þe man, so his mekenes þat went bifore and
20 folowed him also bare him to ilke gude werke, for, trewli, pride fande
noþinge in him þat he might chalange as his, and þarefore he rode
sikirli." þe fifte voice saide, "Come we and present we to God his |
f. 84ᵛᵃ basinet and his helme: þat menes, bere we testimoni of his gudeli
desires þat he had to God, and vertu, for he bare God in his minde
25 euirilke oure, and he hade him euir in speche and in his werkes, and
desired him abouen all oþir þinges, for he shewed himselfe euir as
dede to þe werld for þe lufe of his God. þarefore presente we þere
þinges to oure God, for þis knight is worthi to haue endeles reste for a
litill trauaile, and to be glad with his lorde, whom he hase desired with
30 so inward lufe." With swilke voices and merualows melodi of aungells
mi frende was born into endles riste.

'þan þe saule all in gladnes saide, "Blissed am I þat euer was I born
and made of noȝt! Blissed am I þat I serued God, þe whilke nowe I se!
Blissed am I, for nowe haue I ioi and blis!" Lo, þus come mi frende to
35 me, and þus was he rewardede. And all if it so be þat all shed noȝt
þaire blode for me, ȝit sall þai haue þe same mede for þaire gude will,
f. 84ᵛᵇ if whane time is oportune and nede to defende þe faithe | aske it, þai be
in will to gife þaire life for me: bi þe whilke þou mai se what a gude will
dose.'

7 to] *twice, first subpuncted*   20 him²] him bi, bi *subpuncted*   37 to] to þe

Capitulum xiim. Wordes of Criste to þe spouse of þe vnchangeabilnes of his right, and howe he shewes merci to þame þat are dampned, and of swete moni[ci]on to kinges forsaide.

'I ame verrai kinge, and þare is none worþi to be callede kinge bot I, 5 for of me is all honoure and power. I am he þat demed þe firste aungell, þe whilke fel be pride, coueitise, and envie. I ame he þat demid Caime and Adam and all þe werlde, sendinge a grete flode þat ouerflowed all for þe sinne of man. I ame he þat suffird þe pupill of Israell to be taken into thraldome, whame I deliuerd eftirwarde in 10 meruelows wounders and tokenes. In me is withoute bigininge, and sall be withoute ende, all rightwisnes, þe whilke in me sall neuer be lessed, bot it sall euer abide verrai and vnchangeabill.

'And all if it be so þat mi right seme in þe daies þat are | nowe f. 85ra somwhat milder, and God more pacient in deminge, ȝete is þat no 15 changeinge of mi rightwisnes, þe whilke chaunges neuir, bot it is a shewinge of more charite, for, treweli, I deme now þe werld with þe same rightwisnes and with þe same trewthe of dome þat I dit when I suffird mi pupill to serue þe Egipcians and ponishet þame in desert. Bot bifore þe incarnacion mi loue was hid within right, as light þat is 20 vmbishadowed with a cloude, and when mi manhede was taken, all if þe lawe þat was geuen were chaunged, mi rightwisnes was noȝt chaungede, bot it shewed more opinli and it was illumind more copiousli in charite bi þe same God.

'And þat on þre wise: firste, for þe lawe, þe whilke was hard for 25 þaime þat were inobedient and indurate, for to tame and chastise sharpli þe proude and rebelle, it was mitigate and made more esi. þe secounde, for þe son of God suffird passion and was dede. þe þirde, for bi merci he delais his jugementes more þan he was wont. And þarefore | he semis now mikill milder to sinners. For his rightwisnes f. 85rb semes wounder straite and fers in oure firste fadirs, in Noie flode, in 31 þame þat were slaine in wildirnes. And ȝet þe same rightwisnes is nowe with me, and euer hase bene. Bot nowe shewes merci more, þe whilke was þane hide in right: and þan I was mercifull, all if I shewed it preuali. For mi right is neuir withoute merci, ne I do neuir pite with- 35 oute rightwisnes.

---

3 monicion] monion   21 taken] taken and
it shewed more opinli, *exc.* chaunged, *ruled through*
puncted

22 chaunged] chaunged bot
32 ȝet] ȝet in, in *sub-*

'Bot nowe mai þou aske, if I be mercifull in all rightwis dome, howe shewe I merci to þame þat are finalli dampned? To þe whilke I answere bi ensampill. I sete as one sat in juggement, and his broþir come to be demed. To whome þe jugge sais þus: "þou arte mi broþir, and I `am´ jugge. And all if I lufe þe entereli, ȝet I mai noȝt, ne it semes me noȝt, to do againe right. þou sees all rightwisnes in þine awen consciens eftir þou hase deserued, eftir þe whilke þe bihoues be demed. If it were possibill þat I miȝt do againe rightwisnes, I wald gladeli bere juggement for þe."

f. 85va 'þus it fares of me, for I ame, | as it were, swilke a jugge, and man is mi broþir in manhede, þe whilke, when he comis to juggement, his consciens knawleges his trespas and his blame, and vndirstandes þat for sinne he is worthi to be blamed and scourged. Bot for cause I am rightwis, I answere to þe saule bi liknes, and I sai, "þou sees all rightwisnes in þine awen consciens. Sai me þan what þou art worþi." þan answers þe saule to me, "Mi consciens telles me mi dome, þat is worthi paine for trespas, because I haue noȝt bene obedient to þe."

'To whome I sai againe: "I, þi jugge, suffird all paine for þe, and shewed opinli to þe þi perell, and what wai þou suld go to eschewe paine, for treweli rightwisnes asked þat bifor satisfaccion were made for trespas, þou suld noȝt entir heuen. þis satisfaccion suffird I for þe, for þou was vnmighti to suffir it. I shewed þe be my prophetes what þinges were to come on me, and þare was noȝt one pointe vnfilled of all þat þe prophetes saide of me. I shewed þe all þe lofe I might, þat þou suld turn þe to me. And for þou wilfulli | turned þe fro me, þarefore arte þou worthi mi rightwisnes, for þou dispised mi merci. Neuerþelesse, I am so mercifull þat, if it were possibill I might die againe, I wald suffir sonner þe same paine againe for þe þat I suffird on þe crosse þan I wald se þe demed and forjugged be þat rightwisnes. Bot mi rightwisnes sais þat it is impossibill þat I dye againe. Mi merci sais, if it were possibill, I suld gladli die for þe.

'Now mai þou see how mercifull I ame, and how charitefull to þame þat are dampned, for, whateuir I do, I do it for to shewe mi charite: for, sotheli, I loued man in þe biginninge, and euir eftir, all if I semed wrothe. Bot þere charges no man ne settis be mi lufe. Bot neuirþelesse, nowe, for I ame rightwise and mercifull, I monesh þaime þat are saide knightes, þat þai seke mi merci, þat mi rightwisenes, þe whilke is stabill as ane hille, breninge as fire, horribill as þe þundir, sodaine as a bent bowe ordeyned to shot, finde þaim noȝt.

f. 85vb (marginal folio references at lines 11 and 26)

3 as] case   15 rightwisnes] rightwiswesnes

'I moneshe þaime on thre wise. Firste, I warn | þame, as a fadir his   f. 86ʳᵃ
sonnes, þat þai turn to me, for I am fadir and þaire maker of noȝt.
þarefore, and þai be turned to me, I sall gife þaim þe patrimoni, þe
whilke bi fadirli lawe and right is dewe to þame. And þai be turned
againe to me, all if I were dispised, ȝete sall I take þame againe with   5
gladnes, and I sall mete þame with mi charite. Also againe, I prai
þaime as a broþir. And þe þirde time I prai þame as a lorde, þat þai
turn againe to þaire lorde, to whome þai gafe þaire faithe and to
whome þai are halden to do seruys, and hase oblige[d] þame þareto bi
othe and swereinge.   10

   'þarefore, ȝe knightes, turn ȝou againe to me, ȝour fadir, and I with
charite sall bringe ȝou oute of disese. Knawe ȝe ȝour broþir, þat is
made for ȝou and like to ȝou. Turn ȝou againe to me, ȝour meke lorde.
For, treweli, it is right vnhoneste to ȝou to gife faithe to oneoþir lorde,
or ani seruise. Haue minde þat ȝe gaue me ȝour faithe þat ȝe suld   15
defende mi kirke, and þat ȝe suld helpe þe | pore and þe nedi. But se   f. 86ʳᵇ
nowe howe ȝe serue mine enemi; ȝe caste doune mi baner and ȝe raise
þe baner of mine enemi.

   'þarefor, ȝe knightes, come ȝe againe to me with verrai mekenes, þat
went firste fro me with pride. If it seme hard to ȝou at suffir aniþinge for   20
me, call to minde what I haue suffird for you. Into ȝour cause, I went with
blodi fete vnto þe crosse. I hade handes and fete persed and þirlled
throw for ȝou. I sparid no parte of mi bodi for ȝou. And ȝit ȝe dispise me,
and settis noȝt þarebi. þarefore, commis againe, and I sall gife ȝou þre
þinges to ȝour helpe. Firste, I sall gife ȝou strenthe againe ȝoure enemis,   25
bothe gosteli and bodeli. I sall also giue ȝou a manfull herte, þat ȝe sall
drede noþinge bot me, and all þinge sall be delitabill þat ȝe sall suffir for
me in trauaile. I sall also gife ȝou wisdome, throwe þe whilke ȝe sall
knawe verrai faithe and þe will of God.

   'þarefore, turnes againe to me and stand ȝe manli. I þat monishes   30
and warnes ȝou þus is he to whome | aungells seruis, þe whilke   f. 86ᵛᵃ
deliuerd ȝour fadirs þat were obedient to me, and þe inobedient I
punished and meked þe proude. I was firste in passion, and firste in
bataile. þarefore, folowe ȝe me, þat ȝe melt noȝt as dose wax againes
þe fire. Whi breke ȝe ȝoure coue[n]ant and ȝoure othe? Wene ȝe þat I   35
be lesse and vnworthiare þan ȝoure temporall frende, to whome, if ȝe
gife faithe, ȝe kepe it? Bot to me, þat ame kepare of hele and gifer

---

   9 þai] þaire, re *subpuncted*   obliged] oblige   17 enemi] enemi þarefore ȝe
knightes, *exc.* enemi, *subpuncted*   and ȝe] *twice, first subpuncted*   35 couenant]
coueant   36-7 ȝoure . . . me] *twice*

of life and honor, ȝe will kepe none hight, and if ȝe suffise noȝt to
breke it in dede, ȝit will ȝe gladli breke it in will. I am ȝet so mercifull,
and [haue] so [mikill] compassion of ȝour disese þat þe deuell hase
ȝou in, þat I will take ȝoure gude will for deede, if ȝe turn to me with
5 trewe charite.

'Trauaile ȝe þarefore for þe faithe of mi kirke, and I as a milde fadir
sall with all mine oste mete with ȝou, gifynge to ȝou fife godes. Firste,
ȝoure heringe sall be fulfilled withoute ende with endeles wirshipe. |
f. 86ᵛᵇ Also, ȝoure sight sall euer haue present þe visage and þe blis of God.
10 Also, þe loueynge of God sall euir be in ȝoure mouthe. Also, ȝoure
saule sall haue all þinges þat it sall desire, ne it sall desire noȝt
noþinge bot þat it hase. Also, ȝe sall neuir be departed fro ȝoure God,
bot ȝoure blisse sall laste withoute ende, in þe whilke blisse ȝoure
saule sall euir life.

15 'Ȝe knightes, herefore, takes heede what ȝoure reward is, if ȝe
defende mi faith for mi loue, and if ȝe preferre me to ȝoure awen liste.
Haue minde, if þare be resoun in ȝou, howe I suffir ȝou, and howe ȝe
do me swilke shame and reproue as ȝe wald noȝt suffir of ȝoure
seruantes. Bot all if I mai all þinges bi mi powere and might, and all if
20 mi rightwisnes cri vengeaunce on ȝou, ȝet mi merci, þat is inne mi
wisedome and gudenes, spares ȝou. And þarefor, seke ȝe merci, for of
charite I gife it, for þe whilke I aght to be mikill praide.'

Capitulum xiii. Wordes of þe miȝt of Criste to þe
spouse againe knightes of þese daies, and of þe forme
f. 87ʳᵃ   þat knightes | suld hald, and how God gifes þaime
26   might and strenthe in þaire iourenes.

'I am one God with þe fadir and þe holi goste. We are thre in
persones, none of vs disseuerd fro one oþir, bot þe fadir is in þe [s]on
and holi goste, þe son in þe fadir and holi goste, and þe holi goste
30 bothe in þe fadir and son. God sent his son to þe maiden Mari bi his
messagere, aungell Gabreell. Neuirþelesse, he þat sent and was sent
was one selfe God in Gabriel and bifore Gabriel. I þat spekes with þe
is þe same son, and God þe fadir sent me bi himselfe with þe holi
goste into þe wombe of þe maiden, whose clere bihaldinge and

---

1 of life] *twice, second subpuncted*   3 haue so mikill] so   7 godes] goddes
8 heringe] heryinge, y *subpuncted*   24 of²] *twice*   25 suld] *twice, first sub-*
puncted   gifes] *twice*   28 son] fon   33 same] same god, god *subpuncted*

presens aungels wantes neuir. For I þe son, þat was with mi fadir and
þe hali gast in þe maidens wombe, [was] with þe fadire and þe same
spirit in þe clere bihalding and sight of aungels, gouerninge and
vphaldinge all þinges þat are. And ȝet mi manhede, þat was taken of
me a[l]one, rested in þe wombe of Mari.   5

'þarefore, I, in godhede and manhede one Gode, for to shewe mi
charite and þe strenghe of mi holi faithe, dedeines noȝt to speke with
þe. And all if mi manhede be sene | beside þe, spekinge with þe, ȝet is   f. 87rb
þi saule and þi consciens verely with me and in me, for to me is
noþinge vnpossibill, ne hard to do, in heuen ne in þe erthe. I ame, as it   10
were, a mighti kinge, þe whilke, comminge with his oste towarde a
grete cite, fulfilles and occupies all places. So mi grace fullfilles and
strenghes all þi membris, for trewli I þat sustenes and vphaldes all
þinges, and disposes þaime with mi vertuousenes þat ouerpasses all, I
am withoute þe and withinne þe. I, þat ame with þe fadir and holi   15
goste, withoute biginninge and ende one verrai God, þat for mannes
hele suffird verrai passion, mi godhede ai keped vnhurt, þat rose, þat
stied vp to heuen, spekes now verely and trewli with þe.

'I tolde þe bifore of knighthede, þat was sometime to me full dere,
for it was knite to me with band of speciall charite, because þat in þaire   20
vowe þai obligede and band þaime to gife þaire bodi for mi bodi, and
þaire blode for mi blode. þerefore I consented in þaime, and I fes-
tened þaim to miselfe into one bande | and into one felishipe. Bot I   f. 87va
make mi plainte nowe of knightes þat suld be mine, and hase nowe
turned þameselfe fro me. I ame þaire maker, rawnsonner and helpar. I   25
made to þame bodi and membres, and all þinges þat are in þe werld,
to þaire prophet. I boght þame with mi awen blode; I purchased to
þame throw mi passion þe endles eretage. I kepe and defendes þame
in all perels. I gife þaim strenthe to wirke with.

'And ȝet þai turn þaimeselfe fro me, and settis nowþir bi mi passion   30
ne bi mi wordes, throw þe whilke þai suld delectabli fede þaire saule,
for now þai sett me at noȝt, and with all þaire hert and will þai gife
þaire bodi and blode to be rente and reuen and spilt for fame and
praisynge of man, and for fulfillinge of þaire awen lustes, chesinge wilfulli for to die for þe werld and þe fals promisses of þe deuell. And ȝet   35
bothe mi merci and mi rightw[i]snes is to þaim warde, for mi merci
kepis þaim þat þe deuell cumbir þaim noȝt with himselfe, and bi mi

2 was] and, *Lat.* eram   5 alone] aboue, *Lat.* solo   36 rightwisnes] right-
wsnes   37 þaim¹] þaim noȝt

f. 87ᵛᵇ rightwisnes I suffir þaim pacientli. þarefore, if þai | will turn to me
againe, I sall gladli ressaiue þaime againe, and I sall mete with þaime
with gude chere.

'And þarefor sai þou to him þat will turn his knighthede to me þat
5 on þis maner he mai plese me againe. Whosoeuer wald be made a
knight, he suld go furth with his hors and oþir apparell vnto þe kirke
ȝerde, and þere he suld leue it, for þe hors is noȝt made for mannes
pride bot for mannes profet, and for his defens and ouircomminge of
Goddes enemis. þan take he a mantill with a bande vpon þe front (as
10 þe deken takes þe stole) in signe of obediens and defens of mi crosse,
whome þe baner of seculer power sall go bifor, in taken þat he awe to
be obedient to seculer power in all þinges þat are noȝt contrari to
Goddes plesance.

'When he entirs þe kirke ȝerde, þe clerkes suld mete him with þe
15 baner of þe kirke, in þe whilke mi passion sall be painted and mi
woundes, in token þat he is bunden to defende holi kirke, and to be
f. 88ʳᵃ buxum and obedient to þe prelates of it. Bot when | he entirs into þe
kirke, þan sall þe baner of þe seculer power abide withoute, and þe
baner of God sall go bifor him into þe kirke, in token þat spirituall
20 power is more þan temporall, and þat men suld set more bi spirituall
þan temporall þinges.

'When mes is saide vnto Agnus dei, þe prelate, þat menes kinge or
som oþir, sall go to þe kniȝt toward þe awter, and sai þus: "Will þou be
made a knight?" If he answere, "ȝa," sai he þan, "Hight to God and me
25 þat þou sall defend þe faith of hali kirke, and þou sall obei to þe prelates of it in all þinges þat are noȝt agains God." If he answere, "I hight
þat," gife he to him þan a swerde in his hand, and sai þus: "Se, I take
þis swerde to þe into þi hand, þat þou spare noȝt þi life for þe kirke of
Gode, þat þou depresse þarewith Goddes enemis and defend his
30 frendes." Eftir þat, take he a shelde to him and sai þus: "Lo, I gife þe
þis sheld, þat þou kepe þe þarewith againes Goddes enemis, and þou
helpe widows and fadirles childir, and þat þou encrese on all wise þe |
f. 88ʳᵇ wirshipe of Gode."

'Eftir þis, lai he hise hande in þe neke of him þat sall be knight and
35 sai, "Lo, þou art now soiet to obediens and to pouste. And þarefore,
þat at þou hase bonden þe to bi profession, luke þou fulfill it in dede."
Eftir þis, happe he his mantill aboute him, and drawe it togidir bifore
with a band, þat he haue ilke dai in minde what he hase wowed to

32 þe] twice

God, and þat he hase bunden himselfe more straitli þan oþir are, in þe
visage of holi kirke, for to defend it.

'When þis is done, and Agnus dei is saide, þe prest þat singes þe
mes sall take him mi bodi, and þan sall I be within him and he in me. I
sall gife him strenght and helpe, and I sall kindill in him þe fire of mi   5
charite, þat he sall desire ne drede noþinge bot me his God. And
happeli, if he be no3t in þe kirke bot in þe felde for mi wirshipe and
defens of mi faith, and so þare take þe ordir of knight, it profetes him
neuir þe les, if he haue a gude meninge and right entent, for I ame in
ilk place be mi might, and, wharesoeuir | men be, þai mai plese me, if   f. 88ᵛᵃ
þai haue a gude will and a right meninge.   11

'I am þe selfe charite, ne þere mai none come to me bot bi charite.
And þarefore, I bid no man take vpon him þe forsaide knighthede, for
þan he suld serue for drede and no3t for lufe. Bot I sai þat whoso will
take it on his awen fredome vpon him, he mai plese me. And, forsothe,   15
it is acordinge þat, as apostasi is made fro trewe knighthede be pride,
so þe wai of returninge againe þareto is bi mekenes.'

Capitulum xiiii. Howe Criste is bitokenede bi a smith,
and his wordes bi golde, þe whilke sall be purpose[d] to
þaime þat hase godli charite, right consciens, and wele   20
ordeined wittes, and how prechours sall be besi and
no3t slawe for to sell go[l]d, þat menes for to preche
Goddes wordes.

'I ame a goldsmithe þat sendes his seruant aboute þe land to sell his
golde, and bidis do þre þinges. "First," he sais, "þu sall no3t take mi   25
gold bot to swilke men þat hase clere and bright shinninge ein. þe
secounde, bitake no3t mi gold to þame þat hase no consci|ens. þe þird,   f. 88ᵛᵇ
haue mi gold to sell for ten besantes of dubill weght, for he þat will
no3t wei mi gold twise, he sall no3t haue it. Bot beware of mine enemi,
for he wille noie þe on þre wise. Firste, he will make þe slawe in shew-   30
inge and profiringe mi gold to selle. Also, he will menge þinge þat is
euell with mi golde, to make þe seers and prouers to deme and wene
þat it be clai and filth, and no gold. þe þird, he will enforme his
frenndes how þai sall withstand þe, and sai plainli þat mi gold is no3t
gold."   35

10 plese me] *marg., nota bene*   15 on his] *twice, second subpuncted*   16 fro]
for   19 purposed] purpose   20 godli] goldli   22 gold] god, *Lat.*
aurum   27 gold] gold for   31 will] will no3t

'I am as I were swilke a goldsmith, for I made all þinges gude þat are in heuen and erthe, noȝt with hamers and bodeli instrumentes, bot with might and vertu of miselfe, and all þinges þat are, were, or euir sall be, are now freshe inne mi pr[e]sens, for þare is noȝt þe leste
5 worme ne þe leste corn withoute me, ne þare mai noþinge be hide fro mi forsight, ne vpstand withoute me, be it neuir so litill. Neuerþelesse,
f. 89ʳᵃ amange all þinges þat I haue made, þe wordes þat I spake mi‖selfe with mi propur mouthe are moste worthi, as it were gold amange oþir metals.

10   'þarefore I charge mi seruantes þat sall bere mi gold aboute þat þai beware of þre þinges. Firste, I charge þat þai take noȝt mi gold to þame þat haues noȝt clere ein and bright shinand. And if þou aske what þat menes, forsothe, I tell þe þat he sees clereli þat hase Goddes wisdome with a gudeli charite. And if þou aske how it mai be knawen
15 when a man hase þat, I sai bi þat at a man leuis as he knawes, and with-drawes him fro þe vanite and curiosite of þe werld. He þat sekes ne desires noþinge bot God, he hase clere-lokinge ein. To him sall mi gold be committed.

    'Bot he þat hase conninge and noȝt godli charite in wirkeinge, eftir
20 þat he hase conninge, he is like to þe blinde man, þe whilke semis as he hade ein, and ȝete he hase none, for he turnes him all toward þe werld and his bakside toward God. Also, mi gold sall noȝt be com-mitted to him þat haues no consciens. Who hase consciens, bot he þat
f. 89ʳᵇ cheses and chaunges sone failinge | and passinge þinges of þe worlde
25 for þe endles gudes of blis? He þat hase his saule in heuen and his bodi in erth, he þat þinkes ilke dai how he sall go oute of þe erthe and gife rekninge to God of all his dedis, to him sall mi gold be taken, þe whilke sall haue it to sell for ten besauntes twise weied.

    'Bi þe balans þat gold is weide in is bitokened consciens, and, bi þe
30 handes þat weies it, a gude will and a gude desire. One þe weghtes sall be put spirituall and bodeli dedis: þat menes, he þat will bie and haue mi gold, þat is mi wordes, him buse examen it in þe balans of his consciens, and him buse take gude hede þat þare bene giuen þarefor ten besantes þat are wele weied eftir mi will.

35   'þe firste talent is mannes sight, þat a man take hede what is bitwene þe bodeli sight and gosteli, what honeste is in bodeli bewte, and what in sight of spirituall creatures, as aungels and heuenli vertuse, þe whilke passes all sternes of heuen in þaire brightnes; what

---

4 presens] prsens   19 godli] goldli   24 failinge] faillinge, *first* l *subpuncted*

swetenes and what gladnes of saule is in kepinge of Goddes com-
mand|mentes. þis besant of bodeli sight and gosteli, þe whilke is in þe   f. 89ᵛᵃ
commandmentes of God, awes noȝt to be weied onlike in one balans,
ne peise onlike, for þe spirituall sight aw to wei more and pais doune
þe bodili, for þe spiruall sight suld euer be redi, and þe bodili awes to   5
[be] mesured eftir nede of bodi and profet of saul, so þat it be schit and
sperid vp fro all vanite and vnclennes.

    'þe seconde besant is gude heringe; þat a man take hede and con-
sidir þat foli wordes are noȝt worthi bot scorn, for þai [are] vanite and
a sone passinge aire. þarefore a man suld here gladli þe louinge of   10
God and songes of his wirshipe; also þe dedes and gude wordes of mi
saintes, and þinges þat are necessari and profetabill to bodi and saule,
and edificatori to bothe in gode. This manere of heringe suld weie
doune þe heringe of ribaudri, for þis heringe is of grete charite and
greteli paisinge, þare þe toþir is bothe light and voide.   15

    'þe þirde is þe besante of þe mouthe, so þat a mane weie and pais in
þe balans of his consciens howe profetabill and honeste wordes are of
edificacion and of sobirnes, and howe vnprofetabill and noiefull are
wordes vaine and idill, and so leue vaine wordes and loue gude. þe |
ferthe besant is þe taste. What is þe taste of þe werlde bot wreched; at   f. 89ᵛᵇ
þe biginninge trauaile, in continuanse sorowe, and bittirnes in þe   21
ende? Peise a man þan þe spirituall taste with þe temporall, and, if his
taste be noȝt ouir seke, þe spirituall sall weie and paise doune þe temporall, for þe spirituall hase neuir ende; it is neuir irke; it is neuir
lessed. þis taste bigins, in þis present life, in refreininge of lustes and   25
mesurabill disposicion of manis life in sobirnes, and it lastes withoute
ende, in heuen, in þe loue and swetenes of Gode.

    'þe fifte is þe talent of towchinge, þat a man take heede and pais
what wrechednes a man felis of his bodi, and what vnreste in þe
werlde, what contra[r]iouste of neghtbours, and how on ilkea side he   30
felis wrechedenes. Wei he and peis also what reste þe saule hase in þe
man of vertu, and what swetenes it is to be noȝt occupied ne besi in
werldli vanitese, and þan sall he fele consolacion and comforte. He
þan þat can wele vse his weghtes, putt he in þe balaunce þe spirituall
touche and bodeli, | and so he weie þat þe spirituall weie downe þe   f. 90ʳᵃ
bodeli, þe whilke spirituall touc[c]he biginnes with paciens of þinges   36
þat are contrariouse, it is continued in perseuerans of Goddes biddinges, and it lastes withoute ende in ioi and blis and moste quiete

pees. þarefor, treweli, he þat charges more bodeli riste and þe touche
of warldli gladnes þan of heuenli, is noȝt worþi to touche mi golde, ne
for to be blissed in mi gladnes.

'þe sext besant is þe werke of man, þat a man pees beseli in his con-
5 sciens both spirituall werke and bodeli. þe firste ledis to heuen, þe
secound to þe werlde; þe tone to endeles life withoute torment of
paine, þe secound to grete tribulacion with paine. Bot he þat desires
mi gold, charge he more in weinge þe spirituall werke, þat is grounded
in mi lufe and to mi wirshipe, þan þe bodeli werke. For þe spirituall
10 sall abide, and þe bodeli sall sone faile.

'þe seuent besant is disposicion of time, for man hase taken one
time to tent vnto spirituall þinges and a oþir to assethe þe bodeli nede,
f. 90rb | withoute þe whilke it mai noȝt abide and be. And, foralsmikill as he
sall gife rekeninge of his time as of his werke, þarefore þe time buse be
15 so spendid þat þare be more time to spirituall þinges þan to temporall,
and þat þe spirituall be more of reputacion þan temporall, and also
þat na time passe withoute resonabill discussion and euen weght of
rightwisnes.

'þe eghtend besaunt is rightfull disp[e]nssacion of temporall gudes
20 þat are graunted, so þat he þe whilke is riche, eftir þe faculte of his
gudes, gife gladli to þe pore in godli charite. Bot þou mai aske what he
sall gife to þe pore þat hase noȝt. I answere þat he hase a gude will, and
he þinkes þat if he had gude he wald gife gladli and freli. Swilke a wille
is alowed for dede. Bot if þe pore man haue swilke a will þat he wald
25 gladli haue worldli gudes as oþir hase, and he wald noȝt gife to þe pore
bot litill, and of þe werste, swilke will sall haue litill þanke, for it is
alowed for a smale dede. þarefore þe riche man þat hase gudes, gife he
f. 90va largeli with godeli charite, and he þat | haues noȝt, gife he a gude will,
and it sall profete him. And wit he wele–he þat paise and charges more
30 þe temporall gude þan þe spirituall, and gifes to me bot one peni and
ane hundrethe to þe werlde, kepinge to himselfe a thousand, he
nawþir weis ne mesures euenli. And þarefore, he is noȝt worthi to
haue mi gold, for I þat haues giuen all þinges and mai at mi liste take
all þinges awai, suld be reson haue þe bettir and þe more worþi parte.
35 For wit man wele þat temporall gudes were made and giuen to man for
profete and nede, and noȝt for outrage, waste, ne luste.

'þe nent besant is a besi consideracion of his time þat is passed and
gone bifore, þat he take heede what his life hase bene, and how he hase

19 dispenssacion] disponssacion, *Lat.* dispensatio   29 wele] wele þat, þat *sub-*
puncted   30 me] me a peni, a peni *ruled through*

amendid his werkes þat were noȝt gude. Also, þat he take hede wheþir he hase had fewer gude dedes or euell. And if he finde þat he hase done mo euell dedis þan gude, take he a perfite will for to amend þat is done amis, and gete he to him perfite contricion for his synnes, þe whilke, if it be sothefaste and stedefaste, it sall paise more before God 5 þan all | his sinnes.

'þe tent besant is a wise ordenance and disposicion of time to com, þat he purpose to lufe ne desire nothinge bot þat he knawes is to Goddes plesaunce, and þat he be redi to suffir gladli all tribulacion and disese for God, and also þe paines of helle, if it liked to 10 God and were his plesaunt will. þis talent passes all oþir, be whome all þinges þat mai fall are taken eseli, sobirli, and with gladnes of spirit. Whosoeuir offirs me and gifes me þere ten besantes, he sall haue mi golde.

'Bot, as I saide, be þai ware, for þe enemi will hinder and noie þame 15 (if he mai) þat hase mi golde, on þre maner. Firste, he will make þaime slawe and irkesome. þere is two maner of slewþes. One is bodeli, when it is irksome to þe bodi for to labour or rise or do swilke þinges. Oneoþir is gosteli sleuthe, when þe spirituall man, þat felis þe swetenes of mi spirit and mi grace, hase leuer to riste and haue com- 20 forthe allone in þat swetenes þan for to go oute to oþir, and helpe þame to haue sauour and parte with him in þe same | gosteli likinge.

'Hopes þou noȝt þat Petir and Paule had a plentewouse swetenes of mi spirit? And if it hade plesit me, þai wald haue derked and hid þameselfe in þe depest plase of þe erthe for to haue had comforthe of 25 þat swetenes bi þaimeselfe þan for to haue gone aboute in þe werlde. Bot sotheli, bicause þai walde oþir men had parte of þaire swetenes, and at þai might edifi oþir with þameselfe, þai chese soner, for þe profete of oþir, and of þe more mede and blisse of þaimeselfe, to comon vnto oþir parte of þaire swetenes, þan for [to] apropur and 30 kepe to þameselfe swilke spirituall grace. So þai þat are nowe mi frendes, all if þai wald gladli bi þameselfe haue comforte of mi graciouse swetenes, ȝet þai are halden to go furth and common to oþir parte of þe same gosteli gladnes. For, as he þat hase abundance of temporall gudes vses þaime noȝt alloneli to himselfe, bot also to helpe 35 of oþir, right so mi wordes and mi grace awe noȝt to be hide, bot to be shewed furth for edificacion of oþir.

'Mi frendes mai helpe, if þai will, thre | generacions of men. Firste, þai mai helpe þaime þat in mi forsight and forknawleche are to be

f. 90ᵛᵇ

f. 91ʳᵃ

f. 91ʳᵇ

dampned. And if þou aske how þat mai be, sen þai are vnworthi grace,
and fro þai be dampned it is vnpossibill to come againe to grace, I
answere bi ensampill. And þere were innumerabill pittes, bi þe whilke
he suld nedis fall þat were demed to be ponished in þe laweste place of
5 depenes; if ani wald stope, bifore execusion of jugement, ani of þees
pittes, he þat eftirward suld fall suld noȝt descend so depe as if þare
ware none stopped. So it is þat, all if mi rightwisnes haue ordened to
paines endeles certeine sinners for misvse of þaire awen fre will and
þaire indurate malice in time to com, knawen to mi preue dome, ȝit if
10 mi frendes refreine þaime fro some sines þat þai wald haue done, and
stere to do gode þat elles þai wald noȝt do, þai sall noȝt fall to so depe
dampnacion, ne so greuouse torment, as elles if þare were no
abstinens fro none euell, ne consent to no gude þai suld do. And so
f. 91ᵛᵃ þou mai se how mercifull I am to þaime þat | are to be dampned, of
15 whome, all if mi merci sai, "Spare," mi right, and þaire awen malice,
sais, "Punishe."

'þai mai also help þaim þat somtime falles to syn and be pennance
rises againe, when throw techinge þai wote howe þai sall rise, and are
wh[a]re bifore of þe perell of sinne, with hert at withstand eftirwarde
20 all vnresonabill lustes. Also, þai profite to þaime þat are perfite and
rightwis, þe whilke somtime es suffird to fall for increse of þaire awen
blisse and more confusion of þe deuell. For, right as a knight þat in
bataile hase one esi stroke is þe more witte and herte to fight, so mi
chosen derlinges, be persaiuinge of malicious temptacion of þe deuell,
25 are þe more hertid to spirituall labour and þe more sterid to fele
mekeli of þaime, and with besines to gete in feruour of spirit þe crown
of endeles rewarde. þarefore, I will noȝt þat mi wordes be hid fro mi
frendes, for when þai here of mi gracious gladnes þai mai þe more be
stirrede to deuocion.

30 'Also, mine enemi trauals þat mi gold suld seme no trewe golde bot
f. 91ᵛᵇ clai, stirringe men to mistriste | mi wordes. And þarefore, when mi
wordes are wretin, I will þat þe writer bringe to witnes men þat are
trewe, or one þat hase approued consciens, þe whilke sall examin þat
at is wretin, for happeli, and it be sent furth withoute testimoni and so
35 come into þe handes of þe enemis, þai will put to þe wordes of mi
trewthe wordes of þaire awen falsehede, and so mi wordes might be
enfamed anentes þe simpill men. Also, mine enemis stirres and puttes
in þe mouthe of som of mi frendes for to sai againe mi golde, and

7 to] two   19 whare] where   21 of þaire] *twice, second subpuncted*
32 writer] wirter

þarefore mi frendes sall answere þaime þus: "In þe gold of Goddes wordes is taght thre þinges and no mo: þe whilke is, to drede riteli, to loue gudeli, and to desire heuenli þinges wiseli. Proue þe wordes and se, and if ȝe finde oþirwise, sai þan agains þaime." '

Capitulum 15. Wordes of Criste vnto þe spouse of þe   5
wai of Paradise þat was opind in his comminge, and of
his hie charite he shewed to vs in suffiringe of grete
passions for vs fro time of his | birth to time of his dede,   f. 92ra
and howe þe wai of helle is nowe brode and þe wai of
Paridise straite and narrowe.   10

'þow mer[ua]les þat I speke and shewe þe swilke grete þinges. Hoppes þowe þat I do it for þiselfe allone? Nai forsothe, bot for þe edificacion of oþir and hele of oþir. For þe werld was sometime as it had bene a wildirnes solitari and forsakin, in þe whilke was bot one wai, þe whilke lede to þe moste depe pit, in þe whilke was two   15 receptakils, one of swilke depnes þat it had no grounde, into þe whilke whosoeuir were ressaiued, he might neuir come oute. þe second was noȝt so depe ne so horribill as þe firste, into þe whilke þai þat were ressaiued, þai had hope of deliuerance. Bot þai had delai and desire and experiens of derknes, bot no felinge of painnes.   20

'þai cried ilke dai with grete voice vnto a moste faire citee þat lai a litill beside, and was full of all gudes and fulfilled of delites. þai cried mightili, for þai knew þe wai bi | þe whilke þai suld go vnto þe cite. f. 92rb Bot þare was, bitwix, a wildirnes, and a wode so straite and so thike þat þare might none passe it. þus þan þai cried and said: "O þou 25 God, com and gife vs helpe. Shewe vs þe wai and gife light to vs þat abides þe. þere is nowþir helpe ne hele to vs bot in þe." þis crie com vp to heuen into mine eres, and drowe me for to hafe merci. I þan, mitigate fro offens throwe þat cri, come personalli into þe wildirnes as a pilgrime.   30

'Bot or I wald biginne to make mi journe and mi trauaile, a voice of Saint John Baptist sounded bifore, and saide, "þe ax is put vnto þe rote of þe tree": þat menes, "Be a man now redi, for þe ax is redi, and he is commin þat can ordein þe wai to þe cite and put awai all lettinges and obstakils." And, forsothe, fro I was commin, I traueld fra 35 risinge of þe son to goinge down of it: þat menes, fro mi birth to þe

---

8 his¹] *Quire catchphrase,* birth, *below*   11 meruales] merciles   13 edifica-
cion] edififficacion   23 mightili] mightilii

time I suffirde dede on þe crosse, I wroght þe hele of man, for in mi

biginninge I flowe into wildirnes fro þe persecusion of He|rode and oþir
enemis. I was tempted of þe deuell, and oþir persecucions I suffird of
men, and mani trauails I had. I ete and dranke and fulfilled oþire neces-
5 saris of kinde withoute sin, for instruccion of trewe faithe, and clere
shewinge and prouinge of þe verrai kinde of man þat I had takin.

'When I was ordeininge þe wai to heuen and remoued þe obstakils,
þornes and sharpe prikkis prikked mi side, and bittir nailes and sharpe
wounded bothe mi handes and fete. Mi tethe, mi chekes were all to-
10 rent. þis I suffird pacientli and went noȝt bakward, bot with more fer-
uore I passed furthe þan dose a beste to mete for ani hungir. þou sees
þat when a man profirs to som rauinouse beste a spere, þe beste, for
desire to haue þe man, rinnes wilfulli on þe spere and woundes him
inward in his bowels. So I brente with swilke lufe and charite vnto
15 mannes saule þat, when I sawe all þe sharpe paines and bittir
tormentes ordeined for me, I was as mikill þe more redi to suffir þame

for desire of mannes saule as I sawe | man with þaime wilfull for to sla
me, and so passed I furth throwe þe wildirnes of þe werlde in trauaile
and disese, and ordeined þe wai to blis in mi blodi swete.

20 'Forsothe, þis werld mai wele be called a wildirnes, for all vertu is
failed and forsakin in it, noȝt leuinge bot wilde vices and sinnes, in þe
whilke, as I saide, was bot one wai þat lede to helle. In þe whilke þe
right euell went to endeles dampnacion, and þe gude to þe derknes
forsaide: whose lange desire of saluacion I herd mercifulli and come as
25 a pilgrime to trauaile, and vncouthe, redeinge þe wai be þe power of
mi godhede þat ledis vnto heuen, þe whilke mani of mi frendes sawe,
and þe hardenes, with difficultees of þe passage. And ȝit with gladnes
of saule mani of þaime folowed me lange time.

'Bot now þe w[o]is is chaunged þat somtime bad be redi, and þere
30 growes now againe so mani buskes and thornes in þe wai þat men

cesis and leuis to go þarebi: and nowe | is þe wai of hell so oppin and
brode þat mani gose þarein. Neuirþelesse, mi wai is noȝt ȝit alltogidir
reklest, forȝetin, for I haue ȝet a fewe frendes þat for desire of þe
heuenli countre walkes þareinne, and þat on preue manere, as þe
35 birde þat flies fro buske to buske, for þe wai of þe werld is nowe
seminge allmoste to all men soueraine ioi and blis. þat makes mi wai
so straite, and þe wai of þe werld so opin and wide.

13 þe²] þe cro, cro *ruled out*   17 wilfull] wilfulli   18 werlde] werlde a, a
subpuncted   23 derknes] derknesnes   29 wois] wais, *Lat.* vox   30 and]
and þe, þe *subpuncted*   34 preue] preeue

'I cri nowe in þis wildirnes of þe werlde vnto mi frendes þat þai remoue oute of þe wai þat gose to heuen þe prikkinge thornes, and shewe it to þaime þat will go þarin, for, as it is wretin, þai are blissed þat trowes me and sawe me noȝt, and, þai are also blissed þat heres nowe mi wordes and fulfille þaime in dede. I ame, forsothe, as a modir 5 þat metes with hir son when he erres in his wai, and haldis him light, þat he mai see for to go right. Scho metes him for loue in þe wai and shortes his wai, drawes to him and halsis him with gladnes.

'So sall I mete with mi charite | to all mi frenndes þat turnes þaime f. 93ʳᵇ to me, and I sall gife light of godli wisdome bothe to þaire hert and to 10 þaire saule. I will embrase þaime to miselfe in þe heuenli courte, where is all blis, where no heuen is abouen, na erthe binethe, bot þe clere sight of God, where nowþir is bodeli mete ne drinke, bot þe delitabill swetenes of þe godhede. And to þe right euell men is opind þe wai of hell, into þe whilke whosoeuir entirs sall neuir come oute, 15 bot þai sall want ioi and gladnes and be fulfilled with endles shame, reproue and wrechednes. þarefor I speke þes wordes, and I shew þus mi charite, þat þai turn þaime againe to me þat hase turned þaim fro me, and þat þai knawleche me þair maker whome þai haue forȝetin.'

Capitulum 16. Wordes of Criste to þe spouse whi he 20 spekis more to hir þan to oþir þat are bettir þan sho, and of þ[r]e þinges he biddis hir, þre þat he forbedis, þre þat he suffirs, and þre þat he counsels.

'Mani meruails þat I speke with þe and noȝt | with oþir þat hase f. 93ᵛᵃ seruede me lange time and hase bettir life þan þou. To whome I 25 answere bi ensampill: þare is a lorde þat hase mani wines planted in mani diuers places, and þe wine of ilka vine sauers and hase þe tarage of þe erthe þe vine standes in. Eftir þat þe vine be pressed, þe lord will somtime drinke of þe lawer vine, and somtime of þe hier and þe bettir. If þe lorde be asked whi he dose so, he will answere, for þat wine 30 sauers him, and is likeynge to him for þat time, and ȝete he will noȝt þarefore caste oute and sett noȝt bi his bettir and hier vines; bot he reserues and kepes þaime for his wirshipe and profete to couenabill times þat þai are apt fore.

'Thus do I with the. I haue mani frenndes whose life is to me swetter 35

---

7 Scho] *over partially erased* help   him] he him, he *subpuncted*   14 delitabill]
delitabill of þe, of þe *subpuncted*   18 to] *twice*   22 þre¹] þe, *Lat.* tribus
27 tarage] trarage, r *subpuncted*   31 noȝt] noȝt taste, taste *subpuncted*

þan hony, more delitabill þan ani wine, and brighter þan þe son in mi
siȝt. Neuirþelesse, as I tolde þe in þe biginninge, I haue þe chosen
into mi spirit, for it plesit me to do so, and noȝt for þou art bettir and

f. 93vb holier þan oþir, or worthi to be in | comparison with merites of þaime,
5 bot allonli for I will do so, as, eftir mine awen will, I make of folis wise
men, and rightwis of sinners. And dem þou noȝt þat for I shewe þat
grace to þe, þarefore I sett noȝt bi oþir, for I do þe to witt þat I reserue
and kepe þaime in store to mi more worshipe, into þe time me likes to
hafe it. þarefor, meke þiselfe in all þinges and be noȝt distrubbild bot
10 of þi sinnes. Loue all folke, and þaime also þat semis to h[a]te and
speke euell of þe, for þai giue [þ]e grete occasion of encrese of mede.

'I bid þe do thre þinges, and I forbede þe thre. I suffir þe to do thre
þinges, and I counsell þe to do thre. First, I bid þe desire noþinge bot
þi God. þe secound, do awai all pride and boste. þe þird, þat þou hate
15 euer lichori of þe fleshe. I forbede þre þinges: first, all vain and foule
vnhoneste wordes; also, all exces and outrage of mete, and all super-

f. 94ra fluite of oþir þinges: also, þe ioi | and þe lightnes of þe werld. I suffir þe
to do þre þinges: firste, to haue mesurabill slepe for þe hele of bodi;
also, to haue resonabill wakinges for þe exersise of bodi; also, take
20 mesurabill mete to strenthe and vphaldinge of þi bodi.

'I counseill þe to do þre þinges. First, for to faste and to do oþer
gude dedis, for þe whilke þe kingdome of heuen is hight. Also, þat þou
dispose þo þinges at þou hase to þe wirshipe of God, and also þat þou
þinke continuli on two þinges in þi hert: firste, what I did for þe when
25 I suffird passion and died for þe. þe second, þinke on mi rightwisnes
and on þe dome þat sall be. þere two sall engendir drede and fere in þi
herte. Also, þare is one þinge þat bothe I bid, command, counseil and
suffirs: þat þou be obedient as þou arte holden. þat I bid and command, for I am þi God. þat I will suffir þe to do, for I am þi spouse and
30 husband. And þat I consell þe, fore I am þi frende.'

f. 94rb Capitulum 17m. Wordes of Criste to þe spouse, how þe
god|hede mai wele be called vertu, and howe þe deuell
supplauntes man in mani wise, and howe Criste haues
giffen to man mani remedies to his helpe.

35 The sone of God spake to þe spouse and saide, 'Trowes þou stedfastli

---

10 hate] hote, *Lat.* odire   11 þe^2] me, *Lat.* tibi   13 bid] bid do thre, do
thre *subpuncted*   14 awai] *twice, second subpuncted*   34 his] *twice, second sub-*
puncted

þat it is þe bodi of God, þe whilke prestes haldes in [þare] handes?'
Sho answerde, 'I trow stedfastli þat as þe worde of God sent to Mari
was made in hir wombe fleshe and blode, so I trowe þat it is verra God
and man þe whilke I se in þe preste hanndes.' To whome þe lord saide
againe, 'I ame þe sam þat spekes with the, dwellinge withoute ende in 5
godhede, and made man in þe wombe of þe maiden, kepinge mi godhede and noȝt leuing it. þe whilke godhede mai worþili be called
vertu, for in it are two þinges: þe moste mighti power, of þe whilke is
all power and might; and þe moste wise wissdome, of whome and in
wome is all oþir wisdome. All þinges, whateuir þai be, are resonabli 10
and wiseli ordained in mi godhede: | for þere is noȝt so litill a titill in   f. 94ᵛᵃ
heuen, ne mote in erthe, ne sparke in hell, bot is made, and resonabill,
and wisli ordained be mi godehede, fro whose presens þare mai
noþinge be hidde.

'þou meruails whi I saide, "a titill in heuen." Forsothe, as þe titill is 15
þe perfeccion of þe glosed word, so is þe word of God perfeccion and
ordeind for þe wirshipe of all. I saide, "a litill mote in þe erthe," for all
ertheli þinges are sone ouirpassinge and faillinge, and ȝet is þare
none, be it neuir so litill, þat ouirpasses þe disposicion and prouidens
of God. I saide, "a sperke in hell," for þare is noȝt in hell bot enuy, and 20
right as a sparke procedis fro fire, so fro vnclene spirites procedis all
malice and envie, so þat þaimeselfe with all þaire fauturs haue euir
envie and wantinge of charite. þarefor, because þat in God is perfit
conninge and paciens, all þinge is so ordeined þat noȝt mai escape
Goddes might, ne þare mai noȝt pleine þat [it] is vnresonabilli made. 25
For, trewli, all þinges are made on þe beste maner, and as it is most
accordinge to þaime.

'þarefore mai þe godhede wele be | called vertu. It shewed moste   f. 94ᵛᵇ
vertu in makinge of aungels, makinge þaime for his wirshipe, and for
to haue delite amange þaimeselfe, kepinge charite and obediens: 30
charite, throw þe whilke þai suld loue noþinge bot God; and obediens,
throw þe whilke þai suld obei to all his plesaunce. Again þar to, som of
þe aungels erred euell, and moued wrannge þaire awen will, for þai
turned thaire wille agains God, insomikill þat vertu was odious to
þaime, and þat was lefe and dere to þaime þat to God was contrarouse. 35
Of þe whilke inordinate mouinge and will, þai deserued to falle: bot
noght þat þe godhede made þat falle, ne ordened it to þaime,

---

1 þare] his   2 þat] þat it is þe bodi of God þat, exc. first þat, subpuncted
6 man] a of man over earlier e   15 titill¹] ti of titill over corr., marg. above, ti
25 it] om.

bot for þai, o misvse of þaire awen knawleche and fredome, procured
it to þaimeselfe.

'When God sawe þaime faillinge in þe heuenli oste, caused of þe
propir vice of þaimeselfe, þe trinite þan did vertu againe, for whi, he
5 made man with bodi and saule, and gaue to him [two] godes: fredome
f. 95ʳᵃ to do | gode, and fredome to leue euell. For, sinne it was so þat mo
aungels suld [noȝt] be made, it was rightfull þat a man suld haue
fredome to ascend and stie vp, if he wald, into þe worthines of aungels.
Also, God gafe þe saule of a man two þinges: þat are, resonabill
10 discresion, bi þe whilke he might deme bitwix two contraris, þe bettir
and þe wers; also, he gafe it strenghe to stand and abide in gode.

'Bot when þe deuell sawe þis charite of God vnto man, he thoght of
envie þus: "Lo, God hase made a newe creature þat mai com and stie
into oure place, and throw fight mai ouircome þat we reklesli forsake.
15 If we mai begile him and supplant him, he sall faile of þat purpose, and
þan sall he noȝt come to swilke dignite." And when he had avisede
him on what maner he might begile man, he assailed and begilled him
throw his malice, and throw rightfull suffiraunce þe deuell had þe
maistri.

20 'Bot when was man ouircommin? Forsothe, when he lost vertu, and
f. 95ʳᵇ did þat was forbed him, | when þe fals promisse of þe serpent liked
him more þan mine obediens; for þe whilke inobediens he suld noȝt
be in heuen, for he dispised God, ne in helle, for reson socoured þe
saule and made him to knawe his tresspasse with contricion for þat
25 he had done. þarefor vertuouse God, considirringe mannes
wrechednes, disposid to him a kepinge place of prisoninge, in þe
whilke he suld knawe bi experiens his sekenes, and paine of his inobediens, till he might deserue to come to þat dignite þat he loste. þis
same perseiued þe deuell, and wald sla þe saule of man for his
30 vnkindnes, and, puttinge in mannes saule his filthe, he hase dimmed
so and derked so þe knawleche þat nowþir he had þe charite ne þe
loue of God. þe rightwisnes of God was forgetin, and his dome was
noȝt thoght one, ne sett bi; his gudenes ne his giftes were noȝt lufed,
and so þe wreched consciens stode in erroure þat man had a foule
35 falle.

'Neuirþelesse, for all þis, ȝit lefte noȝt þe vertu of God man, bot he
f. 95ᵛᵃ shewed to him | bothe merci and right: merci, when he shewed to

5 two] *om., Lat.* duo　　7 noȝt] *om., Lat.* non deberent　　10 discresion] dis-
crecresion　　whilke] whhilke　　14 fight] fight ouir, ouir *subpuncted*　　32 his]
twice, first subpuncted　　37 him bothe] *twice,* bothe him *subpuncted*

Adam and to oþir gude men þat in time ordeinde þarefore þai suld be
holpin: and for þat þair feruoure and lufe was excited to God. He
shewed also his right into Noie flode, bi þe whilke þe drede of God
entird þe hertes of men. Bot for all þis ȝete lefte not þe deuell to
enquiete man againe, for he assailled him now with two malis. First, he 5
sent vnto him fals bileue, and eftir he sent dispaire: misbileue, þat men
suld noȝt trowe þe worde of Gode, and þat þai suld ascriue his
meruails vnto destani; despaire, þat þai suld noȝt hope to gete hele ne
blis againe þat þai had loste.

'Againe þe whilke two malices, oure vertuouse God gaue two 10
remedis. Againe dispaire, he gaue hope, naminge þe name of Abraham, of whose sede he hight to be born, þe whilke suld reduce and
bringe againe him and all þe folowers of his faithe vnto þe heretage þat
he had lost. Also he ordeined pro[p]hetis to whome he told and
shewed þe maner of redempcion, | and þe place and times of his   f. 95ᵛᵇ
passion. Againe þe secound, þat was mistrouthe, Gode spake to   16
Moises, and shewed him þe lawe and his wil, and fulfild all his worde
by tokens and werkes.

'Eftir þis ȝit cesid noȝt þe malice of þe deuell, bot, ai steringe man
fro euell to wers, he sent to his hert oþir two þinges: first, þat he suld 20
hald þe lawe vntollerabill and gruche in kepinge of it; þe second, þat it
be to him incredibill and hard to trowe þat God wald suffir tribulacion
or die for charite and loue of man. Bot agains þere two euels, þe vertuouse God gafe two remedis. Firste, þat man suld noght be vnquieted
and pleine of þe hardnes of þe lawe, God sent his awen son into 25
þe maidens wombe, þe whilke toke þare mankinde and fulfilled all þe
hardenes of þe lawe, and eftirward made it more esi. Againe þe
secound, God shewed allþeremoste vertu, for whi, þe maker was dede
for his creature, and þe rightwis man had mikill tribulacion for þe gilti,
and þe innocent | suffird wronge for þaime þat had done amis vnto þe   f. 96ʳᵃ
laste pointe, as it was bifor saide bi prophetes.   31

'And for all þat, ȝit cesid noȝt wikkednes of þe deuell, bot he raised
newe vp againe man with oþir two malices. First, he sent into þe hert
of man þat he suld scorn mi wordes; and, þe secound, he suld forget
mi werkes. Againe þe whilke, þe vertu of God hase shewed two 35
remedis. First, þat mi wordes suld be in wirshipe, and mi werkes suld
be taken in exsampill, þarefore hase God led þe into his awen spirit,
and bi þe he will shewe his will in erthe to his frenndes, specialli for

two causes. First, for þat þe merci of God be knawen, throwe þe whilke men, called againe fro erroure, mai lere to kepe in minde þe charite of Goddes passion. þe second cause, þat þe rightwisenes of God be knawen and taken hede to, and so þat his straite and sharpe
5 dome be drede.

'þarefor sai þou to þis persone, þat, sin mi merci is commin, he
f. 96ʳᵇ shew it opinli and profere it plaineli, þat men lere for to seke | it and beware of mi dome. Also sai to him þat all if mi wordes be wretin, ȝit þai sall first be preched and tolde and so be fulfilled in dede, as þou
10 mai knawe bi ensampill. When Moises suld take þe lawe, þe ȝerde was made redi bifore, and þe tabills planed, and ȝet he did no mirakill with þe ȝerde till it was nede and time asked: and þan he did mirakills and declared þe trewthe of mi wordes be dede. Also, when þe newe lawe was comin, mi bodi wex firste vnto þe dewe age, and þan were mi
15 wordes herde. Neuirþelesse, all if mi wordes were herde, þai had noȝt might nor strenthe till þere come werkes, ne þai were noȝt fulfilled or I fulfilled all þinges þat were prophecied of me in mi passion. So it is now. All if þe wordes of mi charite be wretin, and awes to be born and shewed to þe werld, ȝit mai þai not haue full strenthe, to þai come to
20 plaine light of wirkinge.'

Capitulum 1[8]. Of þ[r]e meruails þat Crist dide to þe
spouse, and how þe sight of aungels, for bewte, and þe
sight of fendes, are intollerabill. |

f. 96ᵛᵃ 'I haue done to þe þre merueilous þinges. þou sees with spirituall ein,
25 and þou heres with spirituall eris, and þou felis with þi bodeli hand mi spirit moue in þi liuand breste. þe sight þat þou hase is noȝt sene to þe as it is, for if þou sawe þe bewte of angels and of holi saules, þi bodi might noȝt abide þe sight, for it wald briste in sounder as a vessell corrupt and roten, for ioi þat þe saule suld haue of þe sight. And, forsothe,
30 if þu saw deuels as þai are, other þou suld liue with ouirmikill sorowe, or þou suld die sodanli for þe fertfull sight of þaime. And for þis cause, spirituall þinges are sene to þe and shewed in bodeli liknes: as aungels, in liknes of men þat hase life and saule (for aungels lifes with þaire spirit). Deuels are shewed to þe in forme þat liknes dede and is
35 dedeli, as in forme of bestis or of oþir creatures þat hase a dedeli spirit. (For when þe fleshe dies, þe spirit dies: bot, forsothe, deuels with-

outen ende dies and withouten ende liues.) Spirituall wordes are saide
to þe with likenes, for þi spirit | mai noȝt oþirwise take þaim: and ȝit
amange all oþir þinges þis is more meruaile, þat mi spirit is felt moue
in þi hert.' f. 96ᵛᵇ

þan answerde sho, 'O þou, mi lorde, son of þe maiden, what menes 5
it þat þou wouches safe to herber swilke a pore widow as I am? For I
am pore in all gude werkes, and hase litill vndirstandinge of consciens,
and I am consumpt and wastid in sin in langnes of time.' To whome he
answerde, 'I haue thre þinges. First, I mai make þe pore riche, and þe
fole þat hase litill wit to be sufficientli vndirstandinge and konninge. 10
Also, I mai make þe olde man ȝonge, as þe bird called fenix bringes
into þe valei dri stikkes, amange whame he bringes stikkes of a tre þat
is drie withoute and hote within of kinde and nature: into whome
comes firste þe hete of þe son beme, and is set on fire, and of þat all
oþir stikkes are brinninge. So bose þe gedir togidir vertuse, throw þe 15
whilke þou mai be renewed fro sin; amange þe whilk, þou moste haue
one tree | hote within and dri withoute. þat menis one hert þat is clene f. 97ʳᵃ
and dried withoute fro all delite of þe werld, and within full of charite,
þat þou will desire noþinge bot me. þan sall þe fire of mi charite entir
first into þat tre, and so þou sall be kindled in all vertuse, in þe whilke, 20
when þou art brint and purged fro sin, þou sall rise as a bird renewed,
doande awai þe skin of all viciouse and shrewed delectacion.'

19 capitulum. Wordes of Criste to þe spouse, how God
spekes to his frendes bi his prechours and bi tribulacions, and howe Criste is bitakened bi him þat awe 25
þe bees and holi kirke bi þe beehife, and þe cristen bi
þe bees, and whi euell cristen is suffird to liue amange
þe gode.

'I am þi God. Mi spirit broght þe in to here mi wordes, to see liknes,
and to fele mi spirit with ioi and deuocion of saule. In me is all merci 30
with right, and right with merci. I am as he þat sees his frenndes fall fro
him into a wai where is a depe pit and horribill, | oute of þe whilke þere f. 97ʳᵇ
mai no man rise, and to whome I speke bi þaime þat hase knawleche of
scripture. And also bi scouringe of scourges, I warne þaime bifor of
þaire perell. Bot þai charge it not, for þai falle into þe depnes, giffinge 35
no fors of mi wordes.

'All mi wordes are as þai were þis on worde: "Sinner, be þou turned

8 of] oft   29 liknes] liknes merci with right, *exc.* liknes, *subpuncted*

to me. þou walkes perrilousli, for þare is trappes set for þe in þe wai, þe whilke þou sees noȝt, for þi hert is in derkenes." Bot þis worde is noȝt sett bi. þis is mi merci þat is reklest. And ȝit, all if I be so mercifull þat I warne þaime þus when þai sinne, neuirþelesse I am so

5 righ[t]full, þat if all aungels wald drawe þaime, þai miȝt noȝt be conuerted bot if þaimeselfe in desire wald stir and moue þare will to me þe gode. And, forsothe, if þai turne þaire will to me and consent in me with þaire affeccion, all þe fendes mai noȝt hald þaime fro me.

'I tell a likenes. þere is a worme called a bee, in possession of his

10 lorde, þe whilke dose to his kinge thre maner of reuerens, and haues of

f. 97va him thre maner of | vertu. First, þe bees bringes to þaire kinge all swetenes at þai mai gete. Also, þai stand at his liste, and whereeuir þai flie or be, þaire charite and loue is euir to þair kinge. Also, þa folowe him and serues him stabilli for rewarde, for þe wilke þai resaiue of

15 þaire kinge thre maner of gude. First, þai haue bi his voice certaine time when þai sall go furth to laboure. þe seconde, þai haue of him þaire gouernance, and ilkeane of þaime charite to oþir, for, of his presens and prinshede, and of þe charite þat he hase to þaime and þai to him, ilkeane of þaime is knitt with oþir in charite, and haues

20 gladnes of oþirs profete. þe þirde, throw charite þat ilkeane hase to oþir and comforthe of his hede, ilkone bringes furth froite. Right as fishes plaies togidir in þe see, and so sendes and castes oute þaire frie þat is froitfull in þe see, right so bees of charite ilkane to othir and loue of þ[a]ir hede, and gladnes, þai bringe furth froite, of whose charite

25 throw mi merueilous vertu passes furth a maner of sede as it were

f. 97vb dede, þe whilke sall haue life throwe | mi gudenes.

'þe lorde of þe bees, þat is besi aboute þaime, sais þus to his seruant, "Mi seruand, it semis to me þat som of mi bees are seke and mai noȝt flie." To whome þe seruand sais, "I vndirstand noȝt what þe

30 sekenes is, bot, if it be so, I wald wit howe I might knawe it." þe lorde answers, "þou mai com to knaulech of þe sekenes bi thre tokens: first, for þai are vnmighti and slawe in fleiinge, and þat is for þai haue loste þaire kinge, of whame þai suld haue had stedfast solace and comforthe. þe secound, for þai flie oute in oures vncertaine and vn-

35 disposed to þaime, and þat is for þai bide noȝt to ressaiue þaire token of þe vois of þaire kinge, þare hede. þe þird is, for þai loue noȝt þaire [h]iue, and þarefore þai do noȝt bot filles þaimeselfe, and bringes no swetenes to þe hiue, of þe whilke þai miȝt leue eftirward. Bot,

5 rightfull] righfull   11 of] twice   24 þair] oþir, Lat. sue   37 hiue] liue, Lat. alueolo

forsothe, þe bees þat are hole and sounde and abill, þai are stabill in flight and stronge, and kepis a dewe time to | go furth and to turn again home, bringinge wax to big with þaire places and honi to þaire fode." f. 98ʳᵃ

'þan answert þe seruant to þe lorde, "Sin þai are vnprofetabill and seke, whi suffirs þou þaime langer, and whi are þai not slaine?" þe 5 lorde sais: "I suffir þaime to liue for thre causes, for þai do thre maner of prophet, bot noȝt in þaire awen vertu. First, þai occupie þe places þat are ordainde before, þat þe hombilbees com noȝt to occupie þaime and to distrubbill þe gude bees. þe seconde is, þat þe gude bees be þe more fructuouse and besi to trauaile, and gadir togidir froite, to 10 comforth and solace of þair kinge and þair awen profete, þat þai se vnfructuouse and euell bees so be besi to trauaile for fillinge allonli of þameselfe. þe þirde, þai helpe to defende þe gude bees.

'"þare is a maner of fleinge worm þat is wont to ete bees, whome þat all bees hates. þe euell bees hates him of envi, and of desire to holde 15 and kepe þaire awen life; and þe gude bees are moued to hate him of charite | and rightwisnes. And so, when þai knowe þat he is comminge, f. 98ʳᵇ þai gedir þaimeselfe all togidir to distroie þat worme, for if þe euell bees ware withdrawen, þe worme suld sonner noie þe gude bees, for cause þai are þan fewer. And for þis cause I suffir þe vnprofetabill 20 bees. Neuirþelesse, when heruest commis, I sall make purueans for mi gude bees, and depart þaime fro þe euell, þe whilke, if þai be oute of þe hife, þai sall die for colde, and if þai be within þe hife and gedir noȝt, þai sall die for hungir, for cause þai were slawe and rekles when þai might haue made purueans for þair fode." 25

'I am God, þe maker of all. I ame þe lorde þat hase þe bees in mi possession. I, throw mi inward charite, of mine awen blode, bigged ane hiue for bees–þat menis holi kirke, in þe whilke þe cristen bi onehede of faithe and comminge togidir of gude loue, suld be gedird and com togidir to dwelle. þe places of þaime are hertes, in þe whilke 30 swetnes of gude thoghtes and of holi affeccions suld abide | and dwelle, f. 98ᵛᵃ þe whilke suld com and springe of consideracion of mi charite in makinge of þe werlde and biynge of man, and of mi paciens in suffiringe and supportinge of sinners, and of mi merci in callinge againe of þaime to grace. 35

'In þis [h]ife of holi kirke is two kindes of men. þe first are þe euell cristen, þat gedirs noȝt to me bot to þaimeselfe, þat commes voide to þe kirke, and knawes noȝt þaire hede: þe whilke hase a stange for swetenes, and coueitise for charite. þe secound are þe gude cristen,

32 com and] com and com, *second* com *subpuncted*   36 hife] life, *Lat.* alueolo

þe whilke bringes to me thre maner of reuerens. Firste, þai take me for þaire hede and þaire lorde, and þai offir to me honi of swetenes and werkes of charite, þe whilke sauours to me right swete, and are to þaime right profitabill. Also, þai stand at mi will, for þaire will is eftir
5 mine. All þaire thoght is on mi passion, and all þaire werkes to mi wirshipe. Also, þai folowe me and are obedient to me where þat euir þai be, within or withoute, in tribulacion or in gladnes: þaire hert is euir withe mi hert, and þarefor þai hafe of me thre maner of vertu.

f. 98ᵛᵇ 'First, | þai haue of þe voice of mi vertu and inspiracion couenabill
10 time, bothe night and dai, and I stire þaime to chaunge night into light, and þe ioi of þe werld þat is sonne failinge into þe stabill ioi of blis þat sall neuir haue ende. þese men are resonabill in all þinges, for þai vse þaire present gudes eftir þe nede, and are stedfaste in all aduersitees, warre and wise in prosperite, mesurabill in bodeli delites,
15 besi and circumspect to do all þinge wele. Also, þai haue charite as þai were gude bees, so þat þai haue all one hert vnto me, and ilkeone luffes oþir as þaimeselfe, and me aboue þaimselfe and all oþir þinges. Also, þai are made bi me fructuose: þat menes, þai haue mine holi spirit and are filled with it, whose swetenes whoso wantes is vnfruc-
20 tuose and vnprofetabill: and þarefore he sall faile and bicome noght. Forsothe þe holi spirit kindils him whome he dwelles with in a gudeli charite, and opins þe felinge of his reson, and flemis awai pride and
f. 99ʳᵃ incontinens, and excites þe saule | to Goddes wirshipe and to set noȝt bi þe worlde.

25 'Bot bees þat are vnfroitefull knawes noȝt þis spirit, and þarefore þai sett noȝt bi þis gouernance, bot flees aned and þe felishipe of charite. þai are voide in all gude werkes, and changes light in derknes, comforth into heuines, and gladnes into sorowe. And ȝet for thre causes I suffir þaime to liue. First, þat vntrewe bileuers entir noȝt þe
30 places þat are bifor ordeined. If all euell men are withdrawen, þare suld leue bot fewe gude men, for whose paucite amange þaim suld enter þe fals trowers þat are mani, and dwell þare to ouirmikill disese of þaime.

'Also, þai are suffird for þe proue of þe gude men, for bi þe malice of
35 þe euell mai þe stabillnes of þe gude be knawen. And in time of aduersite it is wretin how pacient a man is; in time of prosperite howe sobir and stedfaste, for vices and sinnes þan somtime profirs þaime-selfe to þe gude men, and vertuse oft time enhawses a man in pride. þarefore euell are suffird to life with þe gude, þat þai be nowþir ouir

35 euell] eeuell, *first* e *subpuncted*

glad in vanite, ne ouir slawe and slepinge in | vertu, bot þat oft times f. 99ʳᵇ
þai hald vp þaire ein to God. Where þe lesse f[eg]hte is, þare is þe
lesse rewarde. Also, þai are suffird to liue for helpe of þe gude men,
þat þe painems, and oþire mistrowinge, drede þe more to noie þaime
þat semis gude, for þai are mani. And, right as þe gude withstande þe 5
euell of righttwisnes, with a gudeli charite, so dose þe euell cristen for
kepinge of þaire life, and eschewinge of Goddes offens, and so both þe
gude and euell helpis ilkone of þame oþir, þat þe euell for þe gude be
supported, and þe gude for malice of þe euell be þe hier rewarded in
blis.   10

'þe kepers of þees bees are prelates of þe kirke and ertheli princes,
be þaie gude or euell. But vnto þe gude kepars I, God and kepare of
all, spekes nowe, and warnes at þai kepe mi bees, and take gude hede
to þe goinge oute of þaime and þe comminge againe, and wheþir þai
be hole or seke. And in case þai can noȝt haue discrete knawleche 15
þareof, bi thre tokens þai sall persaiue it. First, þo bees are vnprofeta-
bill þat are slawe in fleinge and indis|posid, and when þai come home f. 99ᵛᵃ
bringes no swetenes. þai are slawe in flight þat settis more bi
temporall gudes þan bi heuenli, and dredes more þe dede of bodi þan
of saule, and spekes þus with himselfe: "Whi suld I haue vnriste when 20
I mai haue riste? Whi suld I profir miselfe to dede when I mai to life?"
þere wreches takes noȝt in minde how þat I, kinge of blis, moste
mighti, toke on me febilnes, and I þat ame verrai riste tuke on me
wilfulli vnreste for þaime whome I deliuerd and saued throwe mi
dede.   25

'þai are vndisposid whose loue and hert in ertheli þinges are set,
whose speche is gifen to vnhoneste, whose wirkinge is for þaire awen
propir auantage, whose time is þat at þe bodi desires. Forsothe, þai
haue no charite ne loue to þe hiue, ne gadirs to me na swetenes, þat
dose to me som werkes þat semis gude, for drede of torment and 30
paine, for all if þai haue som dedis of pite, ȝet þai forsake noȝt ne leues
noȝt þaire awne propir will and sinne. For þai wald so haue God þat
þai | left noȝt þe werld, ne suffird noȝt disese ne nede. þis men rinnes f. 99ᵛᵇ
with voide fete into þe hous, for þai flie noȝt with rightfull charite, and,
þarefor, when herueste commes, and þe time of repinge, þan sall þe 35
euell be departed fro þe gude men, and, for þai loued so þaimeselfe
more þan me, and couetise and lust, þai sall be tormentid with endles
hungir. And for þai set noȝt bi God, bot were irke to do gude, þai sall
be punishede with ouirmikill colde.

2 feghte] faithe, *Lat.* pugna

'And be my frendes warre of thre þinges: first, þat þe rotin filth of þe euell bees com not to þe eres of þaime, for þat is poison. Also, be þai warre of þe blake of þaire ein, for þe winges of þaime are als sharpe als a nedill, and kepe þai wele þaire bodis for þe tailes of þaime, in þe whilke are tonnges þat stonges full bittirli. Wise men þat takes hede to þe maners of þaime expown what þis bitokens, and drede þai perell þat can noȝt: flie both þaire felishipes, and | þaire euell ensampils, for ellis þai sall lere bi experiens þat þai wald noȝt lere bi heringe.'

þan spake þe modir, 'Blissed be þou, mi son, þat is, was, and sall be withoute ende. þi merci is swete, and þi right is mikill and grete. Mi son, spekinge bi likenes, meþinke it is with þe nowe as if a cloude stied vp into heuen, þe whilke a soft aire gose bifore, in þe whilke cloude aperid a þinge þat was somwhat derke. Bot he þat was withoute hous, felinge þe softnes of þe aire, lift vp his eine and, bihaldinge þe cloud derke, said þus: "þe derkenes of þe cloud bitokens to me rain to com," and þarefore, moued bi hole counsaile, he went hasteli and hid him in a preue place for þe raine. Oþir men þat were blind or elles þat set noȝt bi, or charged noȝt, þe softnes of þe raine aire, no drede noȝt þe derknes of þe cloud, þai fand in experiens þe [s]ame þat þe cloud bitokened. Eftirward, þe cloud wex and grew more, and went bi all þe heuen with swilke commocion, and impetuose fire so miȝti and strange, þat for þe com|mocion of it lif passed oute, and all þe inward partis of man and outeward bothe were so consumed and wastid at þat fire þat þare might noþinge leue.

'Mi sone, þis cloud bitokens þi wordes, þat semis to mani right dirke and incredibill, for þai are noȝt oft times herd ne declared bi tokens. Mi peticion, and þi merci, gose bifore þis cloud, for þou helpis and socours all ned[efu]ll wreches, and, as it wer a modir, þou cheris all to þiselfe. þis merci is as þe softeste aire þat blowes in þi paciens and suffrans. It is warme in charite, bi þe whilke þou calles to þi merci þam þat prouoked and sterid þe to wreth, and offirs pite to þi dispi[se]res. þarefor, all men þat heris þese wordes, lift þai vp þaire ein, and þai sall see in knawlech fro when þe wordes come. Inquire þai if þai [so]nd noȝt merci and mekenes. Take þai heede wheþir þai [so]nd þinges þat are present or þinges þat are to com, trewthe or

3 ein] ein and   þaime] þaime in þe whilke are tonges a þat, are tonges a *subpuncted*
7 and] *Quire catchphrase*, þaire euele, *below*   20 same] fame   23 passed]
passed it, it *subpuncted*   25 þat þare . . . leue] *twice*, (*second* miȝt), *second subpuncted*
29 nedefull] nedill   33 dispiseres] dispires   35, 36 sond] fand, *Lat.*
sonuerunt, sonant

falshede. And if þai find þaime trewe, it is gude consell þat þai fle
hasteli vnto a preue | place–þat menis, to verrai mekenes with gudeli   f. 100ᵛᵃ
charite. For when rightwisenes commes, þan for drede sall þe saule be
departed fro þe bodi, and fire sall close þe saule within himselfe, þat it
sall bren both within and withoute, and ȝit it sall noȝt be wasted ne   5
consumed.

'þarefore, I, qwene of merci, cries to þe dwellers of þe worlde þat
þai opin and lift vp þaire ein and se merci. I stere to þat and prais as a
modir, and I counseil þe same as a ladi. For when rightwisnes commis,
it sall be impossibill to againestand. þarefore, trowe ȝe stedfastli and   10
bihald, and proue in ȝour consciens þe trowthe, and so chaunge ȝour
will, and þan who þat shewes wordes of charite sall shew þe tokens
and dedis of þe same.'

Also eftir þis þe son spake to me and saide, 'I haue shewed þe bifore
þe liknes of bees, how þai resaiue thre gudes of þaire kinge. I sai þe   15
nowe þat þe knightes þat beris þe crose, whame I haue put in þe
landes endes of cristendome, suld be swilke bees. Bot nowe þai fight
agains me, for þai charge not saules, ne þai haue no compas|sion of þe   f. 100ᵛᵇ
bodis of þaime þat turnes to þe trewe faithe and to me fro errour; bot
þai oppres þaime and reues þaim liberte and fredome. þai teche   20
þaime noȝt þe faithe, bot þai priue þaime þe sacramentes, and so with
more sorowe þai sende þaime to helle þan if þai had stand still in þair
custumabile painemri; ne þai fight noȝt bot of entent to shewe þaire
pride, and for to encresse þaire couetise. þarefore, þare sall come a
time to þaime when þaire tethe sall be all frushed and broken. þaire   25
right hand sall be mained, and þe right fote, so þat, liuin[g], þai mai
eftir knawe þaimeselfe.'

20 capitulum. Wordes of God pleininge of thre þinges,
and howe he chase thre states fro þe bigininge, of
clerkes, knightes and laborars, and of paine ordainde to   30
vnkinde men and blis to þe kinde.

The gret oste of heuen was sene, to whame God spake and saide, 'All if
ȝe knawe and se all þinges in me, ȝet, for it likes me, I pleine in ȝour
presennce of thre þinges. First, | þat þo hifes of bees þat fro þe   f. 101ʳᵃ
bigininge were biggid in heuen, and oute of þe whilke þe vnprofetabill   35
bees went, are voide. þe secound, þat þe grete depnes þat mai noȝt be

26 liuing] liuins   29 and howe] *twice, second subpuncted*   35 bigininge]
bigiminge

filled, to whame nawþir trees ne stones mai gainstand, is euir opin, into þe whilke saules descendes as snawe fro heuen into erthe: and right as snawe for hete relentes into watirs, þe saules for þe grete tormentes of painnes are dissolued fro all gude and renewed into all
5 paine. Also, I pleine þat þare is fewe þat takes hede to þe voidenes of places fro þe whilke aungels fell, ne to þe falle of saules.

'I chese fro þe biginninge thre men, bi whame I vndirstande thre states þat are in þe werld. I chese first a clerke þat suld cri mi will bi voice and shewed it in dede. I chase also a defender as a knight, þat
10 suld defend mi frendes with his life, and suld be redi for me to all maner of labour and trauaile. Also, I chese a laborere, þat suld labour with his handes for to fede bodis with his trauaile. Bot þe clerke is now
f. 101ʳᵇ leprouse and | dome. For if a man walde se in a clerke fairnes and bewte of vertu, auise him wele, he sall haue horrour for to com nere
15 him for þe lepir of his pride and couetise. If he wald here him, he is made dome fro mi loueinge, and jangelinge inow for praisinge and name of himselfe. Howe sall þan [þe] wei be opind to þe grete swetenes of heuen, sin he is so febill þat suld preche it? And if he be dome þat suld cri, howe suld þe swetenes be herd of heuenli melodie?
20 'Þe second tremeles, þat whakes in his hert and hase noȝt in his handes. He tremeles and dredes for þe sclandir of þe werld, and los of his awen wirshipe. He is void in his handes, for he dose no gudeli werkes, for all þat he dose is for þe worlde. Who sall þan defende mi pupill, sen he þat suld be þe hede, and do it, is so dredinge? þe þirde
25 is a[n] asse, þat hase euir his hede enclined into þe erthe, and he standes with foure fete fold in togidir. Trewli, þe pepill is an asse, þe
f. 101ᵛᵃ whilke desires noþinge bot erthli, rekleses heuenli þinges, and | sekis werldli þat are sone passinge. He hase, as it were, foure fete, for he hase litill faithe and vaine hope, no gude werkes, bot a foule will aie
30 redi to sin. And þe mouth of glutteri and couetise is ai opin.

'Mi frendes, take ȝe hede howe þe forsaide depnes þat mai noȝt be filled might be lessed, hunger abated and asethed.'

þan answers þe modir of God, 'Blissed be þou, mi son. þi pleininge is rightwise. I and thi o[þi]r frennde has for mankinde none excusa-
35 cion bot one worde, in þe whilke it mai be saued; and þat is þis: "Iesu Criste, þe son of liuinge God, haue merci." þus I and þi frendes cries.'

þe son saide, 'þi wordes are right swete in mi eres. þ[a]i sauoure likingli in mi mouthe. Thai entir with charite into mi hert. I haue one

---

1 gainstand] gnaistand	3 for²] fro	17 þan þe] we þan	18 And]
twice, first subpuncted	25 an] as, *subpuncted*	34 oþir] ore	37 þai] þi

clerke, one knight, and one vilain. þe firste is delitabill as a wife, whome þe moste honeste husband desires in all his hert with gudeli charite. þe vois of þis sall be as a vois þat soundes in wodes. þi ii sall be redi to gife his life for me, ne he sall noȝt drede þe reproue of þe werlde, bot I | sall arme him with þe armoure of þe holi goste. þe þird f. 101ᵛᵇ sall haue so stedfaste faithe þat he sall sai þus: "I trow as stedfastli as if 6 I sawe þat I trowe. Also, I hope all þinges þat God hase hight." þis man sall haue will of profetinge in gode wirkinge and leuinge of euell.

'I sall putt thre wordes in þ[e] mouthe of þe first man, þe whilke he sall cri: firste, "He þat haues faith, wirke he as he trowes." þe secound 10 is, "[He] þat hopes sekirli, be he stedfaste in all gude." þe þirde is, "He þat lufes perfiteli, desire he in feruore of spirit to se þat he lufes." þe secound sall be stronge in trauaile as a lion, and ware of defaites, and stabill in perseuerans. þe þird sall be wise as a serpent, þat sall stande on his taile and helde vp his hede vnto heuen. þese men sall 15 fulfill mi will, and oþir sall folowe þaime, for, all if I name bot thre, I mene mani mo.' þan spake he to þe spouse and saide, 'Stande stabill. Be noȝt besi in þe werld, ne set noȝt bi reproue, | for I þat suffird all f. 102ʳᵃ reprofe am þi God and þi lorde.'

21 capitulum. Wordes of þe gloriouse maiden to þe   20
    doghtir of þe maner of takinge done of Criste fro þe
    crosse, and of bittirnes and swetenes in hir sonnes
    passion; and how þe saule is bitokened bi þe maiden,
    and þe lufe of God and of þe werld bi two ȝonge men.

Mari spake and saide, 'Mi doghtir, þou sall thinke fife þinges: first, þat 25 all þe membris of mi son in his dede wex colde, and þe blode, þe whilke in his passion flowed oute of his woundes and cleued to all his membris, ranne togidir. Also, þat he was prikked in hert so bittirli and vnmercifulli þat þe knight left noȝt till þe spere touched þe rib, and bothe partes of þe hert were vpon þe spere.   30

'Also, þinke how he was taken doune fro þe crosse. þai at tuke him doune set vp thre leddirs, one to his fete, anoþir to his shuldirs, and þe þirde to þe middis of his bodi. þe first went vp and held him bi þe middis. þe secounde | stied vp on oneoþir leddir and first drowe oute f. 102ʳᵇ one naile oute of one hand, and þan remoued þe leddir and draue oute 35 þe toþir, þe whilke nailes shewed ferrer withoute þe crosse. When he

3 wodes] wordes, *Lat.* siluis   9 þe¹] þi   whilke] whilke sall cri, sall cri *sub-*
puncted   11 He] *om.*

was comen doune þat bare vp þe bodi, anoþir went vp and draue oute
þe nailes of þe feet, and when he come nere þe erth, one held þe bodi
bi þe hede, oneoþir bi þe feet. I þat was þe modir held þe bodi bi þe
middill, and so we þre bare him to þe stone þat I had couerd with a
5 clene linen, in þe whilke we wand þe bodi. And I wald noȝt sewe þe
linnen clothe, for I wist in sekirnes þat he suld noȝt rote in þe graue.
Eftir þis come Mari Mawdelein and oþir holi wemen, and mani aungels, also moni as motes in þe son, for to profir and do seruise to þaire
maker.

10 'þere mai no man tell what sorowe I had þat time. I was as woman
childinge, þe whilke hase all hir membris tremelinge eftir þe birth of
hir barn, þat mai vnnethe brethe, and ȝet sho hase als mikill gladnes
within as sho mai, for cause þat sho knawes þat hir barn is born and
f. 102ᵛᵃ sall neuir tirn againe into swilke wre|chednes as it hase bene in. So it
15 was with me, for all if I were ouirpassingli heui for þe dede of mi son,
ȝet, bicause I knewe mi son suld neuir die againe, bot life withoute
ende, I was right glad in mi saule, and murninge was menged with
mirthe. I mai sai treuli þat wen mi son was berid, it was as two hertis
had bene in one graue. Is it noȝt wretin, "Where þi tresor is, þare is þi
20 hert"? So mi thoght and mi hert was euir in þe sepulcre of mi son.

'I sall tell þe,' sho saide, 'be ensampill of a certain man, in what
place he is now—as it were a maiden, to whome he ware weddid, bifore
whame standes two ȝonge men. Of þe whilke one saide to þe maiden,
"I conseill þat þou trowe noȝt him þat hase wedded þe. He is fell and
25 hard holddinge, and tareinge in rewardinge. And þarefore trowe to me
and to mi wordes, and I sall shewe þe anoþire þat is noȝt hard, bot esi
in all þinges. He will gife þe onone what þou desires, and plenteuosli
f. 102ᵛᵇ all þat mai delite and plese þe." When þe | maiden had herd þis, þe
maiden, þinkinge bi hirselfe, said þus, "þi wordes are swete to þe
30 heringe, þi persone is faire and gudeli. I trow þat I will folowe þi counsaile of þi wordes."

'And when she had drawen þe ringe of hir finger for to gife it to þe
ȝonge man, sho sawe aboue one writinge, in þe whilke were thre
wordes. þe first was, "When þou commis to þe top of þe tre, beware
35 þou take no drie braunch of þe tre in þi hand to hald þe bi, for þan
happeli þou mai fall." þe secound worde was, ["Take not consail fro
þine enemi." þe þird was,] "þut noȝt þi hert bitwene þ[e] tethe of þe

---

4 þe] þe a, a *subpuncted*   14 as] as if, if *subpuncted*   23 maiden] maiden I
trowe noȝt, *exc.* maiden, *subpuncted*   36-7 Take not . . . was] *om., cf. Lat.* caue ne
recipias consilium ab inimico; tercium erat   37 þe²] þi

lion." When þe maiden sawe þis, sho withdrewe hir hande, and held
still þe ringe, thinkinge on þis wise: "These thre wordes þat I se
wretine happeli bitokens þat he þis, þe whilke wald haue me to spouse
and wife, is noȝt trewe. It semis to me þat his wordes are vaine, þat he
is full of hate and shall sle me." 5

'And when sho thoght þus, sho luked vp againe and sawe aneoþir
writinge with oþir thre wordes. The first was, | "Gife to him þat gafe to   f. 103ra
þe." þe second was, "Take noȝt fro þe lord his awen propir gude." þe
þirde was, "Gife blod for blod." When sho had herd þis and sene þis,
sho thoght þus againe: "þe first thre wordes teches me and enformes 10
me howe I sall flee dede, and þe toþir þre howe I sall get and purches
life. And þarefore it is right þat I folowe þe wordes of life." þan þe
maiden vses gude counsaile, and called to hir þe seruande of him þat
first had wedded hir. And when he drewe nere, he þat wald first haue
begilled hir drowe himselfe ferr awai. 15

'Swilke one is þe saule of him þat was weddid to his God. þe two
ȝonge men þat stode bifore him are þe lufe of God and þe lufe of þe
world. Bot þe frenschip and lufe of þe werld drawes nere him þan þe
toþir, and spake to hym of þe werld. To whame, when he had almoste
proferd þe [r]inge of his loue, and consentid fulli to þaime, throwe þe 20
grace of mi son, he sawe a scripture: þat menes, he herd þe wordes of
merci, in þe whilke he vndirstode thre þinges. First, þat he suld
beware, for þe hier þat he went, and leuid fast to fail|linge þinges, þe   f. 103rb
more greuouse suld be his falle. He vndirstode in þe secound worde
þat þare is noþinge bot sorowe and besines in þe werld; and in þe 25
þirde worde, þat þe reward of þe deuell is ill. Eftir þis he sawe in
oneoþir writtinge wordes of comforthe: first, þat he suld gif all to God,
of whome he hase all; also, þat he suld rendir to God þe seruise of his
bodi, for God gaue his preciouse blode for him; þe þird, þat at he
aliene noȝt, ne make his saule strange to God, þe whilke made it of 30
noȝt and boght it dere. When he herd þis with gude auisment, þe
seruandes of God come nere to him and plesed him. Bot þe seruandes
of þe werld withdrowe þaime as straunge.

'Bot it is so þat now þe saule of hir is as þe maiden, þe whilke rase
newli fro þe arme of hir husband and awe to hafe thre þinges: faire 35
cloþis, þat sho be noȝt scorned of þe seruandes of þe kinge if ani
deformite were fonden in hir clothes. Also, hir buse be faire of con-
disciouns, and wele taght eftir þe will of þe husband, þat þe husband

---

7 was] *twice, second subpuncted*   19 of þe werld] *twice, first subpuncted*
20 ringe] kinge, *Lat.* annulum   34 hir] *twice*

f. 103va | fall noȝt in reproue for vnhoneste funden in hir werkes. Also, hir
moste be right clene, þat þe husband find in hir no spot of filth, for þe
whilke sho war worthi to be set at noȝt or to be repudiat.

'þan buse hir haue ledders vnto þe chambirs of þe spouse, þat sho
5   erre noȝt in þe preue wai þat gose þarto. And haue he þat sall lede hir
two þinges: first, þat he be sene of hir þat folowes. Also, þat what sho
teches be herd, and also whidir þat þe wai gose. He þat folous ani þat
gose bifore awe to haue thre þinges: first, þat he be noȝt tareinge ne
slawe in folowinge; þe secound, þat he be noȝt hid fro him þat gose
10   bifore; þe þird, þat he take heed with grete besines to þe steppes of
him þat gose bifore, and folowe him treuli. þat þe saule þan mai com
to þe bedchaumbir of þe spouse, it is nedfull þat sho be lede with a
gide, þe whilke lede and gide hir blisfulli vnto God, þe beste husband.'

15   Capitulum 22m. Wordes of þe glorious maiden
techinge þe doghtir spirituall and temporall wisdome
and howe þat spirituall wisdome eftir litill trauale
f. 103vb   bringes to mikill ioie and gladnes; | þe temporall
bringes to endeles dampnacion.

Mari spake: 'It is wretin, he þat will be wise, lere wisdome of þe wise
20   man. Wharefore I sai bi ensampill, as if þare ware one desiringe to
lere wisedome, seand two maistirs standand bifore him, saide þus: "I
wald gladli lere wisedome if I wist whidir it suld lede me, what
profete it suld do me, and what ende I suld haue þarebi." One of þe
maistres answerde, "And þou will folowe mi wisedome, it sall lede
25   þe into þe hiest hill, bot þare is hard stones in þe wai vndir þi fete.
þare is grete difficulte and hard passage vpward. If þou trauaile in
þis wisdome, þu sall hafe outeward derkenes and inward brightnes.
If þou hald it, þou sall hafe what þou will sekirli. Bot it is wonden
about as a serkill, and it sall drawe þe to hir more sweteli and more,
30   till þou haue gladnes in hir time on ilke parte."

'þe second maistir saide, "And þou will folowe mi wisedome, it sall
f. 104ra   lede þe vnto a flowri vale, | in þe whilke is mirth of all froites of þe
erthe. þare is softenes in þe wai vndirfete, and goinge doneward
þareto is litill trauaile. And þou abide in þat wisedome, þou sall se
35   outeward shininge clerenes, þe whilke, when þou wald vse it, it sall fle
fro þe; þu sall haue also þat þinge þat abides noght bot sone hase

---

14 þe] þe spouse, spouse *subpuncted*   16 howe þat] *twice,* þat how *subpuncted*
22 suld] suldbe, be *subpuncted*   35 shininge] shiminge

ende. And if þou come þarto in perfite fredom, þi fredome sall be refte
þe, and þou sall be left voide."

'When þis was saide, he thoght þus to himselfe, "I here þere two
meruailes. If I go vp into þe hill, mi fete will wax febill and mi bake will
werke. If I get þat þe whilke is outeward dime and dirke, what will it   5
profit me? If I walke in þat at neuir sall haue ende, when sall þare be
comforth or riste to me? þe toþir maistir hightes me þinge þat hase
shinninge clernes withoute, bot it sall noȝt dwell, for it is wisdome
with litterature þat sone sall haue ende. What profit is þan to me in þat
at hase no stabillnes?"   10

'While he was þus þinkinge in his saule, þare aperid sodanli a man
bitwene þe two maistirs þat saide: "All | if `þe´ hill be hie and haue dif-   f. 104rb
ficulte in steinge vp, ȝet `is´ þare abouen þe hill a clere clowde, of þe
whilke þou sall haue refreshinge. þat at outwarde semis derke mai be
broken, and so þou mai haue gold þat is withinne hid, and kepe in   15
posession withouten ende in gladnes."

'þere two maistres are two maner of wisdome, spirituall and flesli.
þe spirituall wisdome is to gife God a mannes propur wille, and with
all hert and werke for to desire heuenli þinges. It mai noght trewli be
called wisdome bot wordes and werkes acorde. þis wisdome ledis vnto   20
þe blissed life, bot it is stoni and harde to come þareto. It is hard to
withstand a mannes flesli affeccions. It is hard to sett noȝt bi olde
custummabill lustes, and to forsake and not lufe worldli wirshipe. And
ȝet, all if it be hard, when a man þinkes þat þe time is short and þe
werld sall haue ende, and þarefore he stedefastes his saule fulli to   25
God, þare sall apere to him aboue þe hill a clere cloude, þat is consolacion and comforthe of þe holi gost, whos comforthe he sall be
worþi þat sekis none oþir gladnes bot God.

'How suld | þe chosin derlinges of God haue bigon so hard þinges   f. 104va
and so bittir, bot þe spirit of God had wroght with þe gude will of man   30
as with his awen instrument? A gude will broght þe spirit to [þame],
and þe gudli charite þat þai had vnto God, for þai labord in gude will
and desire to þai were made stronge in werke. When þe comforthe of
þe spirit was getin, þe gold was getin oneone of godeli delite and
charite, throw þe whilke þai suffird noȝt alloneli contrarious þinges,   35
bot also, in suffiringe for God, throwe consideracion of þe reward þai
had grete gladnes.

'This delite semis derke and dim to þe f[le]ssi luffers of þis werld,

31 þame] om.   34 oneone] onenone   godeli] godeli charite, charite subpuncted   38 flessi] ffussi, ruled through

bot, to þe luffers of God, it is more clere shinand þan þe son and brighter þan gold, for þai breke þe derkenes of vices and sties vp vnto þe mount of paciens, haueinge in contemplacion þe cloude of comforthe þat neuir hase ende. Bot it biginnes in þis present life, and as a
5 serkill it is wounded about, till it com to endles perfeccion. Bot þe
f. 104vb wisdome | of þis werld ledis into þis vale of þis present wrechednes, þe whilke semis full of floures in abundaunce of gudes, and meri in worshipes, and soft in luste. þis wisedome sall sone haue ende, ne it haues no more of profite bot oneli sight and heringe.

10 'þarefore, mi gude doghtir, seke and enquire wisdome of þe wise man, þat menes, of mi son, for treweli he is wisedome, of whame is all wisdome. He is þat serkill þat neuir hase ende. I crie as modir to þe doghtir, "Lufe wisedome, þat within is as gold, and withoute is in despite (bot, within, it brennis in charite): outwarde laboriouse, and
15 inward full of froite of gude werkes. And if þou be turbled of þe charge, þe spirit of God sall be þi comforthe. Take to and vse þe till þou be fallen in custome. Luke þou turn noȝt again to þou com to þe hight of þe hill and of þe montane.

'þare is noþinge so hard bot in stabill and resonabill contin[u]anse
20 of vse it sall be esi and light, ne þare is noþinge so honest at þe begin-
f. 105ra ninge bot it | waxis wane and ill-hewed bi disconten[u]ans. þarefore stie þou vp into spirituall wisdom, þat sall bringe þe to laboure of bodi, to contempte of þe werld, to a litill tribulacion, and endeles blis. þe wisedome of þe werld is fals, disseiuinge and prikkinge, þe whilke
25 will lede þe to gediringe of temporall gudes and to þis present worldes wirshipe. Bot it sall lede in þe ende to þe moste vnblis, bot it be besili sene bifore and eschewede.'

Capitulum 23m. Wordes of þe glorious maiden to þe
    doghtir for declaracion of hir meknes, and howe þat
30   mekenes is bitokened bi a mantill, sheweinge þe con-
    dicion of mekenes, and of þe froite.

'Mani meruailes þat I speke with þe. Sikir, I do it þat mi mekenes be knawen and shewed. As þe hert is not glad of no parte of þe bodi while it is seke, vnto þe time it hase getine hele againe, and þan it is more
35 glade þan it was bifore, right so howe mikill þat euir man sinnes, if he
f. 105rb turn him to me with all his hert and verrai men|dinge of his euell,

1 þan] *twice, first subpuncted*   19 continuanse] continanse   20 at] þat
21 discontenuans] discontenans

onone I ame redi to resaiue his conuersion, ne I charge not howe
mikill he hase sinned, bot with what entent and will he turnes and
commis againe fro sin. I am called of men þe modir of merci. And
trewli, doghtir, þe merci of mi son made me mercifull, and his
sufferans made me haue compassion. And þarefore he sall be a wreche 5
þat drawes noȝt nere to merci when he mai.

'Com þou, þarefore, and hide þe vndir mi mantill, þe whilke semis
outewarde litill worth, and ȝet it is within profitabill on thre wise.
First, it kepis fro tempestuose aire. Also it defendes fro colde and fro
raine of cloudes. þis mantill is mi meknes, þe whilke of luffers of þe 10
worlde is dispised and compleined as foli, and foli for to folowe. What
is more in reproue þan for to be called foole, and nowþir be wrothe ne
answere againe? What is more in reproue þan for to forsake and leue
all, and leue in nede? What is more painefull to werldli men þan for to
make dissimulacion of his iniuri and comitt himselfe to gouernance of 15
anoþir | for mekenes, bicause he haldis himselfe moste vnworthi?   f. 105ᵛᵃ

'O mi doghtir, this was mi meknes, mi ioi and all mi wille; for I
thoght to plese none bot mi son. Doghtir, þis mekenes, to þaim þat
will folowe it, vailes to thre þinges: first, for it kepis fro tempestuose
aire and corrupe–þat menes, fro reproue and dispite of man. Right as 20
a stronge impetuose aire on ilke parte makes a man colde, so reproues
will sone caste down þe inpacient man þat takes no forsight of þinges
þat are to com, and þai exempt his saule fro charite.

'Bot whosoeuir takes hede besili to mi mekenes, bere he in minde
what reproues I, [la]de of all þinges, herd, and seke he mi plesaunce 25
and louinge and noght his awen. Considir he wele þat wordes are bot
winde and aire, and he sall sone for sufferans be refreshed. For what
skill are worldli men so vnpacient for wordes of reproue, bot for þai
seke more þaire awen louinge þan Goddes, and mekenes is none in
þaime, for þaire ein are stopped with sinnes? þarefore, all if mi right- 30
wisnes | wretin sai þat wordes of reproue awe noȝt to be herd or suffird f. 105ᵛᵇ
withoute cause, ȝete eftir þai be said, it is vertu and mede to here
þaime and suffir þaim pacientli for God.

'þarefore, mi mekenes defendes fro colde: þat menes, fro flesle
frenshipe. þare is on[e] maner of frenshipe, in þe whilke a man is 35
loued for þare present gudes, as þai þat spekis þus: "Fede þou me and
I þe while whe life, for I sall gife no fors who sall fede þe eftir dede.
Worship þou me and I sall wirship þe, for I charge noȝt þe wirship þat

9 fro colde] *twice, first subpuncted*   25 lade] bode, *Lat.* domina   34 menes]
menens   35 one] no, *Lat.* quedam

sall be in time to come." Forsothe, þis is a colde frenshipe, for it hase no warmnes of God, and it is as snawe congeled in þe lufe and compassion of þe nedi neghbour, vnfroitefull to ani rewarde. In time to come, when þe felishipe is departid and þe burd taken down, with frenshipe is endid perpetuell profit or fruite. þarefor, whosoeuir folowes mi meknes, he dose gude to all bodis, bothe frendes and enemis, for þe lufe of God: to frendes, | bicause þai are stedfaste and stabill in þe loue of God; to enemis, for þai are þe creatures of God, and happeli sall turne to gudenes eftirwarde.

'Also, consideracion of mi meknes defendes fro þe vnclennes of raines and watirs þat commis downe fro clowdes. A clowd commis of mostur and of vapores. þai are lift fro þe erthe with hete and aire condensed in þe aire, of þe whilke commis thre þinges: raine, haile, and snawe. þis clowd bitokens mannis bodi, þe whilke commis of vnclennes, and it hase thre þinges, as a cloude: seinge, heringe, and felinge.

'Bi seinge it desires and couetes þo þinges þat it sese, as gudes of þe werlde, faire visages, and grete lordshipes and large possessions, þe whilke are noȝt bot as þai were a maner of raine þat commis fro þe cloudes, and f[ou]les þe saule in desire of gediringe togedir of gudes, makinge mikill vnreste throwe grete besines, and descendes bi vnprofetabill thoghtes, and eftirward distrubles greteli bi þaire | sonn failinge.

'For þe bodi hase heringe, þarefore it heres gladli his awen praisinge and honour, wirshipe of þe werlde and swilke þinges þat are delitabill to þe bodi and noies þe saule: þe whilk are noȝt bot as a snawe þat will sone relent, and makes þe saule colde to God and euell-willi to mekenes. Also, for þe bodi hase felinge, þarefore it gropis and felis gladli his lustes and bodeli reste, þe whilke is bot haile congelid of watirs of vnclennes, þat makes vnfroitefull to spirituall gudes, and stronge to worldli, and soft to all maner of delites of bodi.

'Herefore, who þat will be defended fro þis cloude, flee to mi mekenes and folowe it, and he sall be kepid fro lust of sight, þat he couet not þo þinges þat are vnlawefull, and fro delite of heringe, þat he here noȝt againe treuthe, and fro lust of fleshe, þat he fall noȝt to none vnclene mouinges. I sai þe treweli þat consideracion of mi mekenes is, as it were, a gude mantill þat kepis þaime warme þat | bers it: þat menys, þat are meke in þoght, worde and werke. A bodeli mantill warmes noȝt bot þaime þat vses it on þaime. Ne mi mekenes

f. 106ra

f. 106rb

f. 106va

4 taken] takend   5 endid] endid with   20 foules] failes, *Lat.* maculans

profites noȝt to þaime þat þinkes on it bot if þai folowe it in dede. And þarefore, mi doghtir, with all þi mightes clethe þe with þis mantill, and flee þe mantels þat wemen of þe werld weres and vses, for þai haue pride withoute and no warmnes within.

'Wit þou wele, bot þe loue of þe werld wax first vile to þe, and þat 5 þou þinke euir on þe merci of God and how vnkinde þou hase bene to him, and also þat þou þinke what þou hase done and what þou dose, and what sentence of dome þou art worthi for þi dedis, þou mai not haue ne vse þe mantill of mi meknes. Wherefor hopis þou þat I meked me so lawli, and howe deserued I so speciall grace, bot þat I thoght 10 and knewe wele þat I was noght, ne had noght of miselfe? þarefor I desired noȝt, ne wald, mi louinge, bot oneli þe louinge of þe maker and gifer of all.

'Flee þan, mi doghtir, to þe mantill of mi mekenes, and þinke | þat f. 106ᵛᵇ þou art more sinner þan oþir. Also, if it seme to þe þat ani are euell, 15 þou wote noȝt if þai sall tomorn be conuertede to gudenes and vertu, ne þou wote noȝt of what entent or what cause þai do euell: þat menes, þou wote noȝt wheþir þai do it of sad purpose or freelte. And þarefore prefere not þiselfe to any swilke, ne deme þou no men in thi hert.'

Capitulum 24. Wordes exhortatori of þe maiden Mari 20
vnto þe doghtir, meninge and compleining for þe
paucite of hi[r] frendes, and howe þe wordes of Criste
are vndirstandin bi floures, and inne whome þai sall
bringe furth froite.

Mari spake and saide, 'I was as a persone þat went beside one hoste 25 with weri bakke for þe grete birthin I bare, haueinge sore armes and ein full of wepinge teres, lukinge if ani wald of compassion helpe to bere mi birthin. þis menes, þat I was full of tribulacion and heuines fro þe | birth of mi son till his dede. I bare a grete charge of mi bake, for f. 107ʳᵃ I stode stedfastli in þe seruis of mi God, and, whateuir come to me, I 30 bare it and tuke it pacientli. Also, I bare a grete and a heui charge bitwene mine armes, when I suffird more tribulacion and sorowe of hert þen ani oþir creature. I had mine ein full of wepinge teres, when I biheld in þe membres of mi son þe places of þe nailes and þe passion þat he suld suffir, and all þinges to be fulfilled in him þat prophetis 35 had spoken of bifore.

'Bot nowe I take hede to all þat are in þe werlde, if þare be ani þat

20 wordes] wordes of   22 hir] his

haues compassion of me and calles mi sorow to his minde, and, treuli,
I finde right fewe þat þinkes on mi tribulacion. þarefore, mi doghtir,
all if oþir haues rekleste and forgetin me, ȝet forget þou me noȝt.
Behald mi trauaile, and folowe it as mikill as þou mai. Se mi sorowes
5 and mi wepinges, and sorowe þou for I haue so fewe frendes. Stand
stabill, for mi son comis to þe.'

f. 107rb   þe son com onone and saide, 'I am þi God and lord | þat spekis with
þe. Mi wordes are as if þai were floures of a gude tre. And if all floures
of one tre come of one rote, ȝet of all þo floures comes noȝt froite. So
10 mi wordes are as flowres þat commis oute of þe rote of gudeli charite,
and mani takes and resaiues þaime, bot ȝet þai com noght to ripe froite
in all þaime, for som haldis þaime bot a certaine time and eftirward
castes þaime awai, and so þai are vnkinde to mi spirit. Som, bicause
þai are full of charite, takes þaime and kepis þaime still, and of þaime
15 bringes furthe froite of deuocion and of hali wirking.

'þarefore þou mi spouse, for cause þou art mine, bi Goddes lawe vs
bose haue thre howeses. In þe firste sall be þinges necessari to þe
bodi: firste, brede and drinke, and þan oþir fode. In þe second sall be
thre—first, clothinge of linen, þan cloþinge of wolle, and clothinge of
20 silke, þat commes of þe werke of wormes. In þe þird house awe to be
oþir thre: first, instrumentes, and vessels þat sall be fillid full of
f. 107va   liquore. Also liuand instrumentes, throw þe whilke bodeli | þinges are
holpin, as is hors and asses and oþir swilke; also instrumentes þat are
moued and stirred bi þaim to.'

25   Capitulum 25. Wordes of admonicion spoken of Criste
            to þe spouse of prouision to be made in thre houses,
            and how a gude will is vndirstonden be brede, premedi-
            tacion of God bi drinke, and gud wisdome bi oþir fode,
            þe whilke wisdome standes noȝt in letturere bot in saule
30   and in gude liuinge.

'I, þe same þat spekis with þe, am maker of all þinge of noght, and
noght made. Bifor me was noþinge, ne mai be eftir me, for I was euir
and euir sall be. I ame also lorde, whose power mai noȝt be withstonden, and of whome is all power and lordeshipe. I speke to þe as a
35 man to his wife. Mi wife, vs moste haue thre houses. In one sall be
brede, drinke and oþir fode. (Bot þou mai aske, what is bitokened be
brede, wheþir þe brede on þe awter or noght? Forsothe, þat brede,

8 a] a tre, tre *subpuncted*   24 þaim to] *trsp.*

bifor þis worde be saide, "*Hoc est corpus meum*", is werrai brede, bot, fro
| þe wordes be saide, it is no brede, bot mi verrai bodi þat I tuke of þe   f. 107ᵛᵇ
maiden, and verali was crucified on þe crosse, and þarefore I speke
noȝt þareof.)

'Bot þe brede þat we suld gedir into oure house is a gude will and   5
clere. Bodeli brede hase two gude þinges if it be pure and clene. First,
it comforthes and it gifes vaines and sinnows strengþe. Also, it
ressaiues to þe selfe all þe filth þat is within, and gose þarewith vnto
þe purgacion of man in þe last digestion. Right so, a pure and a gude
will first comfortes, for if a man will noþinge bot þat God will, ne   10
labores noȝt bot to Goddes wirshipe, and with all his desire wald passe
oute of þe world and be with God, þat will gladdes and comfortes a
man in gudenes, and encreses in him þe loue of God, and makes þe
werld to him vile and not to be sett bi, st[r]enghes his paciens and his
hope to come to blisse in time comminge, so ferforthe þat it makes him   15
to take gladli | whateuir fall or come.   f. 108ʳᵃ

'And also a gude will puttes oute of man all filthe. What filthe noies
more þe saule þan dose pride, coueitise and licheri? Bot when þe
filth of pride or of ani oþir vice commis in þe saule, it gose awai if a
man þinke þus: "Pride is vaine. It is noght accordinge ne seminge þat   20
he be praised þat resaiues gudes, bot he þat gifes it. Coueitise is vaine,
for all erthli þinges are left at þe laste, and forsakin. Licheri is foule
stinke, and þarefore I will noȝt of it. Bot I will folowe þe will of mi
God, whose rewarde sall euir last, and whose gudes sall neuir wax
olde." þan sall all temptacion of pride and coueitise go awai if þe gude   25
will haue perseuerans in gude.

'þe drinke þat we sall haue in oure house is premeditacion and
forþoght of Goddes plesance in all þinges þat sall be done. Bodeli
drinke hase two profetabill þinges. First, it makes gude digestion. So
whosomeuir, when he purposes to do a þinge, considirs and besili   30
þinkes, or he do it, what is þe wirshipe of God and | howe it mai be   f. 108ʳᵇ
done, what is profetabill to þe neghboure and to his awen saule, and
will do noþinge bot at he mai plese God with–þan sall þat werke haue
a gude proces, as a gude digestion. þan is it deprehendid and takine
onone if þare be ani vndiscrete circumstance in þe werke profirde.   35
þan sall noþinge be wrange in þe werke, bot right and resonabill. And
he þat hase noȝt forthoghtes and premeditacion in his werke of
Goddes wirshipe, ne sekis noȝt þe profete of saule, all if þe werke

---

7 it³] *twice*   14 strenghes] stenghes   16 gladli] *Quire catchphrase,* whateuir
fall, *below*

seme in prosperite a while, it sall go and turn to no valewe at þe last,
bot if it be amendid and correctid. Also, drinke slokkens thirste.
Where is a wers thirste þan is þe sin of coueitise and wreth? And if a
man wald þinke bifore what profit commis þareof, howe sone it sall
5 ende, what reward he sall haue if he withstonde it, onone bi grace of
God þat shrewed thirste is slokind, and þe hete of gudeli charite and
desire of god commis toward. He is glad þat he did noght þo þinges
f. 108ᵛᵃ þat come firste to | minde, and he sekis occasion howe he mai ethchewe
þaim eftir þis, with þe whilke he had bene begiled if forthoght of
10 premeditacion had noȝt holpin him to be ware in eschewinge. Mi
spouse, þis is [þe] drinke þat awe to be gedird into oure hous.

'Also, þare bose be oþir fode, and soule, to þe brede, for thre causes.
First, for with brede it makes bettir sauor, and is more accordinge to
þe bodi þan is brede allone. So dose þe spirituall fode and soule (þat
15 is, godli wisdome). To him þat hase a gude will (and will noght bot
Goddes plesaunce) and gude premeditacion of forvisement (þat he do
noȝt bot þat at is to Goddes wirshipe) sauours right wele Godes wisdome.

'Bot þou mai aske whilke is þe devine wisdome, for þare is som so
20 simpill þat þai can noȝt on right maner sai one Pater noster, and
anoþir hase grete conninge and mikill litterature. Is þis Goddes wisdome? Forsothe nai! For devine wisdome is noght alloneli in litterature, bot it is in a clene hert and gude life. Whosoeuir þinkes besili, on
f. 108ᵛᵇ his wai to dede, of þe maner of his dede, and of þe dome | eftir dede, he
25 is a wise man. He þat castes fro him worldli vanite, and oþir waste and
outrage, and haldes himselfe content with þinges þat are necessari to
him, and trauailes as beseli as he mai in þe lufe of God, this man hase
þe s[o]ule of wisdome to his brede and drinke, throwe þe whilke bothe
þe gude will and forthoght of God sauours him mikill þe more.

30 'When a man þinkes of his dede, and of his nakednes in his dede,
and avises him of þe ferdefull dome of God, where nothinge is hide,
nothinge is left vnponished, and þinkes also of þe vnstabillenes and
vanite of þe werld, hopes þou noght þan þat it is both saueri, swete
and gladsom to him þat he left his awen will before, and soietted him-
35 selfe to God in abstinens fro sinne? Is noght þan þe fleshe more
comforted, and þe blode þe bettir? þat menes, all seknes of saule, as
slawthe and lightnes of condiscions, is helid and putt awai; þe blode of

---

1 sall] sall and, and *subpuncted*   5 withstonde] withstonden   8 to] *twice*
11 þe] *om.*   þat] þat we   19 so] so spirituall, spirituall *subpuncted*
25 and¹] and of, of *subpuncted*   28 soule] saule

Goddes charite is þe more freshe, for he demes þat þe þinges suld be
bettir luffed þat lastis euir þan þo þat sonn | failes. And for þat it is þat   f. 109ʳᵃ
þis wisdome is noght allonli in knawinge of lettirs bot in gude
wirkinge.

'We se wele þat þare is mani wise man to pleasaunce of þe worlde   5
and fulfillinge of þair desires. Bot þaie are vnwise and fooles to fulfill
Goddes commandmentes and his will, in refreininge of þaimeselfe fro
vicious likinges and lustes. Forsothe, þai are no wise men, bot folis
and blinde, takinge no hede to þinges euirlastinge, bot preferringe
þaime þat sone endes. þare is som oþir men þat are foles vnto þe   10
likinge and wirshipes of þe werld, and are ware and wise inoghe in þo
þinges þat langes to Goddes biddinges and will, and þai are verraili
lightned and hase opin ein, for þai enfors þaimeselfe euir to come to
verrai life and light. þe firste forsaide men walkes in derkenes and
hase leuer, as more delitabill to þaime, for to be in derknes þan in   15
light, or for to trauaile and seke þe wai þat gose to light.

'þarefore, þou mi spouse, gadir and puruai we into oure houses
þese thre þinges: þat is, a gude will, a forthoght of | Goddes wirshipe,   f. 109ʳᵇ
and godli wisdome. Of þere, we aw to be glad. All if I speke to þe, ȝet I
moneshe all mi chosin derlinges in þe werld, þe whilke I vndirstonde   20
bi þe, for þe saule of ilke rightfull man is mi spouse. I ame maker and
gainebier of it.'

Capitulum 26. Wordes of maiden Mari to þe doghtir
and of Criste to þe spouse, what clothes sall be had in
þe second howse, and howe bi þo clothes is bitokend þe   25
pees of God and of þe neghboure, werkes of merci and
pure abstinens.

Mari spake to þe doghtir. 'Set and emprint þe nowche of mi sonnes
passion, as Saint Laurence printed [it] into himselfe, thinkinge þus in
his saule ilke dai: "Mi God, he is mi lord and I his seruant. þe lorde   30
Iesu Crist was naked and scorned. Howe semis it me þan to were
precious and delicate clothinge? He was scourged and festined to a
tre. It is noght semli þan þat, if I be his seruant, I be withoute sorowe
and tribulacion." þarefore, when he was streched vpon þe coles, þat
his grese melti[d]e and ran into þe | fire, and all his limmes were   f. 109ᵛᵃ
enflawmed in fire, he beheld into þe heuen with his een and saide,   36

13 þaimeselfe] þaimeselfe ti, ti *subpuncted*   16 trauaile] trauaile or, or *subpuncted*
29 it] *om.*   35 meltide] meltile

"Blissed be þu mi God, mi maker, Criste Iesu. I knawe me gilti, þat I haue noȝt in mi dais lifed wele as I suld haue done. Also, I knawe þat I haue don litill to þi wirshipe. þarefore, bicause þi merci is althermoste, I prai þe þat þou do to me eftir þi merci." And with þis worde
5 þe saule was departed fro þe bodi.

'Lo, mi doghtir, he þat loued mi son so w[e]lle, he þat suffird so mikill for his wirshipe, ȝet he held himselfe vnworthi to optene and come to heuen. Howe are þai þan worthi þat liues all eftir þaire awen will? þarefore, haue þou euir in minde þe passions of mi son and of his
10 saintes, for wit þou wele, þai suffird noȝt withoute grete cause, bot for to gife oþir exampill of lifinge, and for to shewe howe straite dome mi son askes for, sen he will noght þat þe lest sin passe withoute amendinge.'

þan com þe son and spake to þe spouse thus. 'I saide þe bifore what
15 þinges awes to be in oure houses. Amang oþir þinges þare bose be
f. 109ᵛᵇ clo|thes in thre maner of kindes: first, linen clothe þat growes on þe erthe; þe second, a pilche þat is of bestis; þe þirde is cloth of silke, þat commis of wormes. First, þe linen clothe hase two gudes, for it is softe
20 and loses noght þe coloure, bot þe more it is weshen, þe clenner it is. Also, þe pilch hase two gudes, for it couers þe bodi and warmes it. Also, þe silke hase two gudes, for it semis right faire and delicate, and it is dere to bie.

'þe firste clothe of linen, þat is softe, bitokens pees and riste, þe
25 whilke a deuote saule suld haue to God: þat he will nothinge bot þat God will, and so þat he stere noȝt God to wreth bi sinne, for þare mai be no pees bitwene God and a saule bot if þe saule sese of sinninge and lustes be refreined. Also þou awe to haue pees vnto þi neghboure, doinge him no wronge, helpinge him in nede, in pacient suffiringe of
30 him when he sinnes againes þe. What mai fall vnto þe saule more
f. 110ᵃ vnblissedli þan for to desire euirmore to sin and neuir | haue ynoghe, and for to be in wreth euir agains his broþir of Criste and neuir to riste? Herefor þe saule suld haue reste bitwene it and God, bitwene it
35 and neghtbour, ne þare mai be nothinge more restfull and quiete þan for to sese of sinne and noȝt be besi with þe werld: noþinge esier þan to be glad of þe neghboures welefare, and for to desire þe same to him and to himselfe.

'þis linen clethinge awe to be next þe naked of þe fleshe, for, amange all vertuse, pees and riste fro sin suld be next þe hert, in þe

6 wele] wole   12 for] for mi son, mi son *subpuncted*   19 it is] is it is, *first* is *subpuncted*

whilke is specialli Goddes abiddinge, and into þe whilke he is drawen
bi pees and þere kept still: þe whilke pees, as it were linen, growes of
þe erthe, for verrai pees and paciens springes oute of consideracion of
manis seke freelte. A man, þat is of þe erthe, suld euir take hede to þe
infirmite of his awene kinde, howe he waxis wrothe onone if he be 5
greued; onone he hase sorowe if he be hurt.

'And if he þinke hertli of his freell condicion of himselfe he sall
noght gladli do to an|oþir þat he wald no3t suffir himselfe. þan kepis f. 110ʳᵇ
pees his colour, þat menes, his stabill abidinge, and [i]f pees somtime
chaunges colour and wexis blake bi impaciens, so mikill it sall be eftir- 10
warde þe whitter anentes God þat it is oft time weshin with penance.
Also it is þe more glad and ware to suffir, þe ofter it is so woshen eftir
oft distrublance, and gladnes in hope of þe reward þat he abides, for
pees suld make him þe more ware þat he [f]all noght bi impaciens.

'þe secound, þat is of skinnes, bitokens þe werkes of merci. þis 15
cloþinge is of skinnes of dede bestes; þat bitokens mi saintes, for þai
are as simpill bestis. þe saule suld be cled in þis clothinge; þat
menis, it suld folowe and do dedis of merci, eftir þat mi saintes did,
for þai hid þe filthe of a sinfull saule, and clenses it, þat it apere
noght foule ne spotti in mi sight. Also, þai kepe þe saule fro cold. 20
What is þe cold of a saule bot at þe saule is indurate to mi lufe?
Againe whilke colde availes þe werkes of merci, þat clethis þe saule
þat it periche | noght for colde, and be thaime God visites þe saule, f. 110ᵛᵃ
and it drawes nere to God.

'þe þird clothinge is silke, þat commis of wormes, and it semis right 25
dere in biinge, þe whilke bitokens vertuose abstinens, þe whilke is full
of fairnes and bewte in þe sight of Gode, aungels and gude men. It is
dere to bie, for it semis to man right harde for to reistreine his mouthe
fro mikill and vaine speche, to refreine þe lustes of his flesche fro
lichori and outrage of glutri, and fro oþir likinges. It semis him right 30
hard to go agains his will, bot, be it neuir so hard, 3it it is right profitabill, and in all wise it is right faire.

'þarefore mi spouse, bi wome I vndirstonde all trewe and gude men,
puruei we into oure second house pees to God and oure neghtboure,
þe werkes of merci, in compassion haueinge and helpinge of þaime at 35
are nedi, and abstinens fro lustes. All if þis be more dere þan þe oþir,
so it is fairrer þan þe oþir, in so fere þat withoute it, þare is none oþir
vertu faire. þis abstinens buse springe and come fro wormes. þat
menes, fro | thoght of his excesses þat he hase done agains God, and of f. 110ᵛᵇ

9 if] of   14 fall] sall, *Lat.* cadat

ensampill of mi meknes and abstinens, þe whilke for man was made like
to a worme. Lat man take in minde how, and howe oft, he hase sinned
agains me, and howe he hase amendid him, and he sall finde þat no
abstinens ne no trauaile is sufficient to amend þat he hase sinned agains
5 me. Thinke he also of þe paine of me and of mi saintes, whi we suffird,
and he sall knawe suthfastli þat if I suffird so grete paine, and mi saintes,
þat were to me obedient, I sall aske grete paine of þaime and punisment
þat will noȝt obeie. þarefore þe gude saule do he abstinens gladli, and
thinke he howe euell his sinnes are besili, þe whilke gnawes þe saule as
10 wormes: of whilke consideracion he sall engendir abstinens, as silke
comis of wormes, with þe whilke he sall be cled in all his membris, þat
God and all holi oste of saintes haue ioi of him and he endles blis.'

Capitulum 27. Wordes of Criste to þe spouse of þe
instrumen[tes] | þat sall be in þe þird house, and bi þo
15   instrumentes are bitokend gude thohtes, chastissed
wittes, and trewe confession, and of a generall clausure
of þaire houses.

The son spake to þe spouse of þe þird, in þe whilke he saide gose thre
maner of instrumentes: 'Firste, swilke instrumentes as men putt
20 liquore in; þe second suld be instrumentes for þe erthe, as billes and
axes; and þe þird suld be swilke instrumentes as horses and asses.

'In þe firste hows, where is instrumentes of liquore, som instrumentes suld be for liquide liquores, as are watir, oile and wine, and
som for bittir and thike standinge liquors, as is mustard and mele and
25 swilke oþir. Forsothe, þere liquors bitokens thoghtes of þe saule,
bothe gude and euill. A gude þoȝt is, as it were, oile þat is swete, and
delitabill wine. One euell thoght is, as it were, mustarde þat is bittir,
for it makes þe saule bittir. And right os a man hase somtime nede of
thike liquors, þe whilke, all if þai profit noȝt | mikill to þe sustinance of
30 þe bodi, ȝete þai help to purge þe bodi and þe braine and hele þaime,
so it fares of euell thoghtes. þai make noȝt þe saule fatt, as dose oile of
gude thoghtes, ȝet, bot somtime ane man had þame, he suld wene he
ware bettir þan he is, and þat he had þinges of himselfe, þe whilke he
knawes now þat he hase of God. And so þai are necessari to a man, þat
35 he knawe þe freelte and febilnes he haues of himselfe, and þat his
strenghe is of me.

14 instrumentes] instrumen   18 gose] gose bi   34 he] *twice*   35 and¹] of
man and, of man *subpuncted*

'þarefor it is þat I suffir, of mi grete merci, man somtime to be temped with euell þoghtes, to whome if a man consent noȝt, þai are a purgacion of þe saule, as mustard is for þe braine, and þai are occacionli kepers of his vertuse. And, all if þai be bittir to suffir, as is mustard sede, ȝete þai hele greteli þe saule, and þai lede it to þe 5 endles life and hele, þat mai noȝt be gettin withoute grete bittirnes. þarefore be þai neuir consentid to, bot vessels of þe saules in þe whilke gude thoghtes mai be put, be þai | ordainde besili and clensid f. 111ᵛᵃ continuli, for it is spedefull þat euell thoghtes com for oure prouinge and encressinge of mede. Bot be þe saule ware þat sho consent noght 10 to þaime, ne haue in þaime no delite, for elles will all swetenes be put oute, and allonli bittirnes dwell and abide.

'In þe second house also sall be two maner of instrumentes: first, a plowghe to ere þe lande, and a bill for destruccion of thornes and wedis: also, an axe, and swilke instrumentes as are necessari bot 15 within and withoute. Instrumentes with þe whilke þe erthe suld be tilled, as þe ploughe, bitokens menes wittes, þat suld be helpli to a mannes neghboure as þe ploughe is to þe erthe, for euell men are as þe erthe, bicause þaire thoght is all one erthli þinges. þai are drie withoute compunccion for sin, bicause þai hald þaire sin noȝt of charge. 20 þai are cold fro godli charite, for þai seke noȝt bot þaire awen will. þai are heui to do gude, bot oneli for wirshipe of þe werld.

'þarefore a gude man | suld tell þaime bi his wittes, as þe ploughe f. 111ᵛᵇ dose þe erthe; firste, informinge þaime bi his mouthe to þe wai of liue, and to do all þe gude werkes thai miȝt. Also, he suld tell þaime 25 with his ein bi ensampill of simpill lokinge, þat he gafe no mater to þaime of wanton lokinges ne lichourous, bot ensampill to be sobir in all partis of his bodi, and þat he here no vanite, bot go gladli with his fete to all gudenes and Goddes seruise. If þe saule be þus telid, I sall send þe raine of mi grace, and þan sall þe gude man haue grete 30 likinge, when he sees þe euell man bringe furthe fruite, and gude lifinge, throwe þe grace of God, and his besines, þat bifore was barein as a drie erthe.

'Also, þere are instrumentes nedefull for to arrai with swilke þinges þat are necessari inward, as an ax, þe whilke bitokens a discrete entent 35 and avisment of his wirkinge, þat all þat he dose be done for þe wirshipe of God, and noght for mannes prassinge. And if he | finde ani f. 112ʳᵃ wede, thorn, or oþir point of pride, kut it awai with þe axe of discrecion, for, right as he is haldin to profite to his neghboure þat is

8 þai] *twice*   21 þai²] þair

withoute him, so is he holden to bringe furthe froites, gude werkes
within himselfe, for a man suld noght oneli trauaile withoute bot
within also, euir avisinge himselfe of þe entent whi he trauailes.

'In þe third house suld be whike and liuand bestis, instrumentes as
5 hors, asses, and oþir bestis, bi whome is vndirstanden verrai and trewe
confession, þat forthirs bothe þe whike and dede. þe life of þe best
bitokens þe saule þat I made to liue euir. Sho bi confession is ilke dai
more nere and more nere vnto God, for right as a beste, þe ofter and
þe bettir he is fede, þe strongere he is to bere a charge, and þe fairrer
10 to þe sight, right so confession, þe oftir þat it is made and þe more
beseli, bothe of þe smallest sinnes and gretest, þe more it helpis and
forthirs þe saule and makes it clerer in þe siȝt of God: ȝa, it entirs riȝt
into þe hert of God.

f. 112ʳᵇ   'Also, confession | helpis þe dede; þat menes, þo dedis þat ware
15 whike or a man sinned dedli, and eftir are slaine bi sinninge dedli,
whikken againe throw confession and perfite will of amendinge; ne þai
mai noght be togidir in one vessell, swete smellinge þinges and stinkinge þinges. For if ani man sla his gude dedis with dedeli sinne, and he
shriue him with will to amend and purpose to kepe him fro sin, onone
20 bi vertu of shrift and meknes þe gude werkes whikkens againe þat
bifore were dede, and þai profit a man and are helpli to blis endeles.
Bot if he die withoute shrifte, þo dedes þat were wroght bifore þe
dedeli synnes whikkens noght againe, ne helpis him noȝt to blis, all if
þai alege somwhat þe pains þat he suld elles suffir on more greuouse
25 wise; or elles, þai turn to profite of oþir if þai were done for Goddes
wirshipe and of gude entent, and noght for praisinge of þe werlde (for
þan þai die with him þat did þame, for cause he tuke his mede in þe
werld, for whome he did þaim). |

f. 112ᵛᵃ   'þarefor, mi spouse, bi whome I vndirstonde all mi frendes, gete we
30 to oure house two þinges, in þe whilke God is speciali plesid. Bringe
we vnto þe firste house brede of gude will, þat we desire ne will
noþinge bot þat God will. Bringe we drinke of gude forthoght, þat we
do noȝt bot for Goddes wirshipe. And bringe also oþir mete: þat
menes, gostli wisdom, thinkinge besili what is now and what sall be
35 hereeftir. Into þe second house we sall gett pees fro sine bitwene God
and vs and pes fro strife to our euen cristen; also, þe werkes of merci to
þame þat hase nede, and perfite abstinence fro all þat at wald distrubill pees. Vnto þe þird house we sall drawe gud clene thoghtes. We

34 thinkinge] thinkinge now, now *subpuncted*

sall kepe wele and chasti oure wittes, and we sall make clene shrift of
all þat we can bringe to minde.

'Bot all if þair houses be hade, ȝet mai þai noght be kepet withoute
dores and oþir þinges nedefull. þe dore sall be hope, þat sall haue two
chekes. One sall be þat he fall noȝt into dispaire; þe second, þat he be 5
noght presumptuose: bot againe dispaire, traiste euir in þe gudenes | of f. 112ᵛᵇ
God of blis; and again presumpcion, drede paine eftir he deserues, ne
be not broken ani time for aduersite or tribulacion. þe loke of þis dore
sall be perfite charite, þat kepis þe dore fast spered so þat þare entir no
enemi, for, right as a dore þat is withoute loke geues opin and fre entre 10
to a manes enemi, so hope hase no sekirnes withoute charite, for, all if
a man traiste neuir so wele, and he haue no charite, ne lufe not God,
his enemi þe fende entirs vpon him, and þarfor vertuose hope buse be
shewed throw gude wirkinge in þe loue of God als mikill as he mai:
and if he mai not com to in dede, þan haue a gude will, traistinge fulli 15
in God and louinge him, and þat sall helpe him to kepe him fro sine
and to bringe him to blis.

'Right as a loke hase mani wardes within, þat it be noȝt sone
vndone, so in charite bose be grete besines þat God be noȝt greued,
drede þat God go noght awai fro him, a breninge feruour in þe loue of 20
God, a besi thoght how he mai | folowe him, and a sorowe þat he can f. 113ʳᵃ
noȝt do as he suld and wald. þare buse be mekenes, þat he hald all
litill or noȝt þat he dose in þe reward of his sinne and trespase. If þis
loke of charite haue þer wardes, þe enemi, þat is þe fende, mai noȝt
entire. 25

'Also, þis loke buse hafe a kei to vndo it with, þe whilke sall be one
hertli desire to be with God, acordinge on swilke wise with gudeli
charite and gudeli werke, þat he will noþinge bot þat God will, and
noght bot God himselfe. þe kei of swilke a desire closes God in þe
saule and þe saule in God. þe husband and þe wife–þat menes God 30
and þe saule–alloneli sall haue þis kei, þat God mai haue fre entre to
delite himselfe in þe vertuse of þe saule, and þe saule to com to God
when it likes. þis kei muste be kepit bi mekness of saule and wakinge
fro sin, thankinge God for all his gudenes, for þare is not þat gude is
bot of him. And also God muste kepe it on his parti bi his might, and 35
his charite, þat þe fende begile not þe saule. Se nowe, spouse, what þe
| charite of God is to þe saule, and stand stabbilli in mi lufe and fulfill f. 113ʳᵇ
mi will.'

---

19 greued] greued and, and *subpuncted*   35 muste] muste be, be *subpuncted*

Capitulum 28. Wordes of Criste to þe spouse of þe
vnchaungeabilnes of himselfe and of þe perfitenes of
his wordes, all if werkes folowe noght onone, and howe
oure will suld be committed in all þinges to Goddes
5   wille.

The son spake to his spouse and saide, 'Whi art þou so turbild, for he
saide mi wordes were fals? Me nedis noȝt his preisinge, for I ame so
stabill þat I mai noght chaunge. And þarefore, þat men preisen me is
þaire awen profite and noȝt mine. Ne of mi mouthe come neuir fals
10 worde, for I ame euen verrai treuthe, and all þat I haue saide be
prophetes or oþir of mi frendes, it sall be treuli fulfilled, ne mi wordes
were noght fals for I saide one time one þinge and oneoþir time
aneoþir þinge, firste derkli, [þ]an opinli. Bot I shewed mani þinges to
stabilnes of þe bileue and besines of mi frendes, aftir diuers affectes in
f. 113ᵛᵃ diuers times, as it was li|kinge and plesinge vnto mi spirit. And þare-
16 fore, all if it semed to þaime þat wald noȝt or couthe noght vndirstonde mi wordes þat þai were fals, neuirþelesse þai are trewe and
might noght be fals; ne it was noght withoute skill þat I spake so derkli,
for right wald þat mi counseile suld be preua somwhat fro þaime þat
20 were euell, and mi gude frendes suld hertli abide mi grace, and
purchace þaime thanke and mede for abiddinge, for if þai had knawen
mi consaile þai suld haue thoght irke for longe time.

'Also I hight mani þinges, þe whilke for vnkindenes of men I haue
withdrawen for þaire malice. I had fulfilled mi hightes; and þarefor be
25 þou noȝt turbild in þiselfe þat vntrewe men reproues mi wordes, for
þat at semis to men inpossibill is possibill enoghe to me. Ne wondir
þou noght, all if deed folowe noght on[o]ne eftir mi wordes, for it is
noght withoute skill. For Moises was sent to Pharao with tokens, and
f. 113ᵛᵇ ȝit þai were noȝt shewed onone, for þan suld þe | obstinaci of Pharao
30 sone haue bene knawen, and Goddes meruals had noght bene shewed
on so mani wise. And neuirþelesse ȝete Pharao had bene dampned for
his malice, all if Moises had noght commin: bot his obstinaci had noȝt
bene so openli knawen. And so sall it be nowe.

'þarefore, stand stabili, for all if þe ploghe be drawen withe oxen,
35 ȝet it is eftir þe will of him þat ledis it. So all if ȝe here and knawe mi

---

3 onone] of none   10 þat] *twice, second subpuncted*   12 one time] *twice,*
second subpuncted   13 þan] and   20 abide] *twice, second subpuncted*
24 for] fro   27 onone] on me   30 and Goddes meruals] *twice (second,*
meruailes), second subpuncted

wordes, ʒet þai are noʒt fulfilled eftir ʒoure will bot eftir mine, for I
knawe howe þe land is disposed and how it sall be tilled. Commit ʒe
þarefor all ʒour will to me, and sai, "*Fiat uoluntas tua.*" '

Capitulum 29. Wordes of Saint John Baptiste, howe
þat God is bitokened be a birde, þe saule bi birdes, þe   5
bodi bi þe nest, and delites of þe werld bi fers bestis,
pride be [fo]ules of ravain, and þe ioi of þe werld bi
þe gildir.

John Baptist saide to þe spouse, '[þ]e lord Iesu hase | called þe fro   f. 114ʳᵃ
derkenes to light, fro filth to clennes, fro straitenes to largenes. And for 10
all þis þou art halden to thanke God full mekill. þare is a birde men
calles a pie, þat loues hir birddes, for þe egges went out fro hir awen
bodi. Sho makis hir a nest of olde þinges for thre causes: first, for rest;
also, to kepe fro rainnes, and to haue drines; and also for helpinge of
hir birdes and norishinge of þaime. When þe birds are clekked sho   15
cherises þaime to flie, first with mete, and eftirward with hir woice,
and þan bi ensampill of hir awen fleinge. þan þe birdis, for þai loue þe
modir, first þai flee eftir þe modir a litill aboue þe ne[s]t, and þan eftir
þaire might þai flee ferer, and at þe last, bi vse and crafte, þai are made
perfite in flight.   20

'þis bird bitokens God, of whame all saules are broght furthe as of a
modir. And to euirilke saule is ordainde a nest, for it is knit to a bodi of
þe erthe, in þe whilke God fedis þe saule | with gude affeccions and f. 114ʳᵇ
defendes it fro euell thoghtes, and giues it rist in drines fro þe raine of
euell wirkinges. Bot þe saule suld be rewler of þe bodi, to put it vnto 25
esi trauailes and puruei resonabli þarefore, and [God] as a gude
modir, to tech þe saule at profit in gude werkes; bot fleinge a litill
abouen his nest, him buse lere as touchinge gude heuenli thoghtes
howe vile his nest is (þat is, his bodi), how faire and howe bright are
heuenli þinges.   30

'þan cries God with voice þus: "Whoeuir folows me, he sall hafe
euirlastinge life, and he þat loues me sall noʒt die." þis voice ledis to
heuen. And, treuli, he þat heris noght þis voice, he is ouir vnkinde to
God or ouer defe. þe þird, God bringes furthe mannes saule to flight
bi ensampill of himselfe in his manhede, þe whilke had two [w]inges: 35

---

5 birdes] birdes of þat saule   7 foules] saules, *Lat.* aues   9 spouse]
sspouse   þeⁿ] ʒe   þe³] me þe, me *subpuncted*   11 halden to] halden to god,
god *subpuncted*   18 nest] next   26 God] *om.*   35 winges] þinges, *Lat.* alas

one was clennes of liuinge, anoþir gude wirkinge. Man suld folowe
þese eftir his might. Bot when þe birdes bigins to flie, þan most þe

f. 114va beware of bestis of rauaine, þat þai | com noght nere þaime on þe
erthe, for þe bird is noȝt so stalworth as þe beste. Also þaime buse
5 beware of fowles of rauein, for þese birdes are not so swifte as þai.
þarefore, it is moste sikir to dwell in priuate till þai be waxen. Also,
þaime buse beware of couatinge of þaire prai, for gildirs and snares.

'þe bestes þat are fell es werldli coueitise and delites, fro þe whilke
þe bird, manis saule, bose beware, for þai haue in vse to disseiue sone,
10 for cause þat when a man wenis best to hald þaime, þai slip awai, and
þan shewes þe likinge a full sharpe prikkinge in þe ende. Be also ware
of birdis of rauaine: þat menes, pride and coueitinge of wirshipes,
throw þe whilke a man coueites ai hier and hier, and wald flie before
all oþir, and hates þaime þat flies binethe. Be þe bird ware of these,
15 and desire he to dwell in preuei place of mekenes; and þinke þat oþir
are als gude as he. þe þirde is, þat he beware of þe snare, þat is,
worldli gladnes—for in þat is a snare. Vnskilfull gladnes and likinge

f. 114vb makis a man vnstabill of hert, | and þareof commis sorowe owthir in
dede o[r] elles bifor. And þarefore, mi doghtir, hie þe oute of þi nest bi
20 desire of blis, and beware of þe bestes of coueitise, and fro þe birdes of
pride, and fro vnskilfull gladnes.'

þan spake þe modir to þe spouse and saide, 'Ware þe fro þe birde
þat is smetin with pike, for sho will file and defoule all þat touches
hir—þat menes, þe vnstabill frenshipe of þis werld, as is þe aire, foule
25 and stinkinge in gettinge of fauoure and euell compani. Gife noght of
þis werldli wirshipes, ne take no hede to fauours, ne make no fors of
praisinge or laghinge, for of þese commes vnstabilnes of saule and
lessinge of gudeli charite. Stonde þarefore stabill, and God, þat broght
þe oute of þi nest, sall fede þe vnto þi dede, and bringe þe to riste,
30 where þou sall haue neuir no hungir, bot be in all blis and ioi.'

Capitulum 30. Wordes of praier of þe modir for þe
spouse, and for oneoþir saint, and how [Criste]
f. 115ra   accepted þe modir praer, | and of certificacion of trew
or fals holines in þis present life.

35 The modir spake vnto hir son and saide, 'Mi son, graunt to þi spouse
þat þi bodi mai be rotid in hir hert so þat sho mai be chaunged into þe

19 or elles] of erlles   27 commes] commes of, of *subpuncted*   32 Criste]
om., Lat. a Cristo   36 in] in þi, þi *subpuncted*

and fulfilled with þi lufe.' And þan þe modir spake of a sainte and
saide þat when he liued in þis werld he was as stabill in þe faithe as an
hille, for þare was no disese miȝt breke him, ne no likinge distracte ne
withdrawe him: 'He was redi at þi will as þe aire þat is blawen with þe
winde. He was breninge in þi loue as fire, þat warmes þaime þat are　5
cold, and wastis þaime þat are euill. þarefore his saule is now with þe
in blis. His bodi ligges lawer þan it suld. Graunt it a place of more
wirshipe, and lat him be wirschip[ed] in erthe þat wirshiped þe with
his trauaile.'

þan saide þe son, 'Modir, blissid be þou, þat leues noþinge　10
vntouched þat langes to mi frendes. It is noght seminge þat daint-
teuouse mete be giuen vnto wolues. It semis not þat þe saphir, þe
whilke kepis | þe bodi hole, be laide in clai. þis man, right as he was　f. 115ʳᵇ
stabill in þe faithe and brening in charite, so was he disposed in
chastite to mi will. þarefore, he sauerd to me as þe beste mete wele　15
sothin in paciens and tribulacion. Swete and gude in all gude will and
desire he was, and bettir in stalworthe wirkinge, bot he was beste in
gude endinge. þarefore, it is not seminge þat he be giuen to wolues,
þat menes coueitouse men, þat hase no mesure, ne no likinge of þe
herbes of vertu, bot of þe roten carion, and þaire speche is [n]oifull　20
vnto simpill men.

'Also, he was as a saphir bi clernes of fame of gude life, bi þe whilke
he shewed him trewe spouse of holi kirke and frende to God, a keper
of þe faith and a dispiser of þe werld. And þarefor, mi dere modir, it
semis noght þat a liuer of so grete gudenes, so clene a spouse, be　25
touched of euell liuers of þe worlde.

'Also, he was a light set on a candilstike bi fulfillinge of þe
commandmentes, and bi gude techinge of gude life, bi þe whilke he
strenghed | þaime þat stode and taght þaime to beware þat þai fell　f. 115ᵛᵃ
noght. He helpid þaime vp þat had fallen down, and þaim þat come　30
eftir him he stirrid to gude. Bot þai are noght worthi to se þis light þat
is blinded in þaire awen lufe. þai can noȝt knaw þis light þat hase þe
sekenes of pride in þaire ein. þai mai noght handill it þat hase scabbid
handes, and vnto couetouse men, and þaim þat loues þaire awen will,
þis lufe is hatefull and odious. þarefore, bifore þe time þat he be　35
raised vp, þai þat are foule moste be clensed, and þai þat are blind
most haue þaire sight.

---

8 wirschiped] wirschipe　　16 gude²] *twice, second subpuncted*　　20 noifull] ioi-
full, *Lat.* nociua　　23 him] him to þe, to þe *subpuncted*　　27 fulfillinge] fulfill-
linge

'Bot, forsothe, þe man þat þe worlde haldes a saint bi thre þinges is shewed no saint. First, for in his lifinge he folowed noght þe life of saintes. þe secound, for he had no glad will to be martird for Goddes sake. þe þird, for he had not charite discretli birninge, as saintes had.

5 Oþir thre þinges þare are for þe whilke þe pupill se[e]s som to be saintes, all if þai be none. þe first is lesinge of þaime þat is listi to plese

f. 115vb and disseiue. þe second is light and sone trowinge | of þaime þat are noght wise. þe third is couetise and slewthe of prelates and of examinours. Bot in trewthe, wheþir he is in hell or in purgatori, it is noȝt

10 ȝete lefull to þe to knawe. Neuirþeles, þou sall wit, when time commis of spekinge.'

Throwe þe godli grace of Alpha and O, here endes þe second buke of heuenli reuelacions, shewed bi þe fre gudenes of oure gloriouse God vnto blissed Bride, Princes of Nerice in þe realme of Sweci. *Deo*

15 *gracias.*

F. 116ra   Book III ch. 1: St Bridget presents a message from Christ
to a Bishop

[BOOK THREE]

In þe name of fadir and son and holi goste, well of all gracious biginninge, and in whame all gude endes, here biginnes þe þird buke of
heuenli reuelacions, þe whilke þe same one God hase graciouseli
shewed to blissed `Bride´, spouse to þe son of þe hie soueraine fadir,
Princes of Nerice in þe realme of Sweci. | 5

> Capitulum primum. Wordes of informacion and   f. 116ra
> monicion saide to a bishope of þe maner þat he suld
> hald in etinge, drinkinge, clethinge and praiinge, and
> howe he sall haue him bifore mete and eftir and in
> borde. And þe same he telles of slepinge. And howe in   10
> all he sall excercise a bishopes office.

Iesu Criste, God and man, þat come to take mankinde and to saue
saules with his awen blude, illumind and lightend þe verrai wai | and   f. 116rb
oppind þe ȝate of heuen, he sent me to ȝou: 'Here þou, to whome it is
giuen to here spirituall þinges. If þis bishope purposes for to go bi þe 15
straite wai, bi þe whilke few folke walkes, and to be one of þe fewe, þan
most him lai down þe birdin þat charges him–þat menes, þis werldli
coueitise–and take onli his nedefull findinge, eftir it falles to a bisho-
peli, meke and lawli sustinance. For so did gude Mathewe when he
was called of Criste: he lefte þe heui charges of þe worlde, and toke a   20
litill charge þarefore.

'Also, him bose be beltid for to go. For so sais þe scripture, þat
Tobi, `redi´ for to walke, fand a aungell standinge beltid. And þat bi-
tokens þat a bishope suld be girde and beltid with þe girdill of rightwisnes and of þe loue of God, redi to go þat wai þat he went, þe whilke 25
saide, "I ame a gude shepherd, and I put mi saule for mi shepe": redi
also with wordes to speke þe treuthe and do rightwisnes, both in himselfe and oþir, noght leuinge for manas, or reproues, or ani fals
fren|shipe, ne for no vain drede. Vnto eueri bishope þat is so arraide   f. 116va
sall Tobi com–þat menes, rightwis men sall folowe his lifinge.   30

'As for þe þirde: he muste ete brede and vatir or he passe furthe in

---

3 whilke] whilke in, in *subpuncted*   5 Sweci] *Quire catchphrase,* capitulum
primum, *below*   6 *at head of col., above illumination,* bryd and a bysheep
23 redi] *marg., after* standinge, *poss. meant as corr. subpuncted* beltide   aungell] aungell
beltide, beltide *subpuncted*

his wai, as it is wretin of Heli, þe whilke fand at his hede brede and watir. What menes þis brede giuen to þe prophete bot bodeli gude and gosteli? To him was ordainde in desert bodeli brede. For all if God might haue sustende him withoute bodeli fude, ȝete he wald þat he 5 suld be sustened with swilke brede, for ensampill þat it is Goddes will þat a man vse Goddes giftes sobirli to his bodeli comforthe. And ȝete, with þat, he had gosteli fode, when he was strenk[þ]ed þarewith fourti daies. For had þare noght bene giuen to him inward gosteli strenk[þ]e, and vnccion of grace, he suld haue failed and haue bene enentished 10 before he had endid his trauaile of fourti daies, for, of himselfe, he was seke and febill, and of God he had might to walke so lange a wai.

f. 116ᵛᵇ   'And þarefore, sin in ilke worde of God is | manes lifinge, we warn þe bishope þat he take a morsell of brede–þat menes, þat he loue God ouir all þinges. þis brede he sall finde at his hede–þat menes, his 15 reson sall shewe to him þat God suld be loued abouen all, for he is maker and gainebier, for he is langesufferande with paciens, and shewes endeles gudenes. We prai him also þat he drinke a litill watir– þat menes, þat he þinke inwardli of Cristes bitterest passion þat he suffirde. Who mai worthili þinke þe angwise þat he suffird when he 20 bisoght þe fadir þat, if it were possibill, þe paine might passe fro him, and when þe dropes of blode rane into þe erthe? Bid þe bishope þat he drinke his watir with brede of charite, and þan sall he haue comforthe to walke in þe wai of Iesu Criste.

'And when he hase bigone to go on his wai, þan sall he, fro prime of 25 þe dai, þanke God with all his herte and þinke besili on þat what he hase done, and aske helpe of God to wirke his will. |

f. 117ʳᵃ   'And when he dose on his clothis, he sall prai on þis manere: "Powdir of askes awe to be with askes, and erth with erthe. Neuirþeles, sin bi Goddes ordinance I ame ordainde a bishope, I clethe mi bodi with 30 clothes, þat commes of þe erthe, not for pride ne fairenes, bot for couiringe, þat þe nakednes be noght sene. Ne I reke noght wheþir þis cleþinge be preciouse or vnpreciouse, bot þat it be acordinge to þe bishopes astate and reuerence of bishophede, so þat he mai be þe clethinge be knawen a bishope, to amendinge and enforminge of oþir. 35 And þarefor I prai þe, moste mild God, þat þou gife to me stabilnes in hert, þat I wax noght proude of þe prise of askes and erthe, ne þat I haue no vainglori of coloure; bot gife me strenthe þat, right as mi clethinge is wirshipfull bifore oþir men for mine estate, so þe clethinge

---

7 strenkþed] strenkied   8 strenkþe] strenkie

of mi saule be plesinge vnto þe, þat hereeftirward I be noght spoiled
for mi vainglori, ne put to dampnacion."

'And | þan, eftir `þis´ praier, sall he sai his seruise and singe his   f. 117rb
oures. Neuirþeles, a clene hert plesses God als mikill in soft saiinge as
in singeinge, if it so be þat man be occupied oþirwise in gude werkes.   5
When he hase saide his mes, do he in execucion þe office of bishophede, takeinge gude hede þat he be noght more besi aboute temporall
þinges þan spirituall.

'When he sall go to þe borde to ete, sai he on þis maner in his
hert: "O þou lorde Iesu, þat fedis þe bodi, þat sall rote, with bodeli   10
fode, þou helpe me so to take þat is nedefull to mi bodi, þat throwe
none owtrage þe fleshe wax rebell agains þe saule, ne slawe in þi
seruise, ne throwe ouir grete scarsnes wax noȝt to faint, þat it mai
noght serue þe. Bot þou gife me grace so to take mesurabli þat þe
erthe be so sustened with ertheli þinges þat þe lorde of þe hert[h] be   15
not greued." And when he is at þe borde he mai haue wordes of
comforthe, so þat þai be noght vnhoneste, ne vaine, ne þat þai gife
no mater of sin to | þaime at heres. For right as, in a bodeli borde, all   f. 117va
metis are vnsaueri bot if þare be gude lessons and leringe, þarefore,
at a bishopes burde suld owþir be gude lessons and gude redinge, or   20
gude comoninge, þat þai mai be edefied þe whilke sittes aboute. And
in þe endinge, be þare thankinge made to God. And þan sall þe
bishope go to se and luke bukes of perfite liuinge, to comforth with
his saule.

'Eftir his super, he mai haue his consolacion with þaime þat are   25
homeli with him. Neuirþeles, right as a modir, when sho will wene hir
childe and make it to leue sokinge, sho anointes hir pape with som
bittir þinge, at make þe childe to withdrawe him fro þe milke and to
vse him in som sadder mete, so suld a bishope draw his menȝe to gude
wordes and to drede God. For, if he knawe one `of´ his meine sin   30
dedeli, he suld stir him to amendment. And, if he will noght amend
him, he suld put him awai fro him; for, if he hald him still for his bodeli
comfort or profite, he sall not be blameles of his sin.

'And | [when] he sall go to his bede, he sall examin besili his dedis   f. 117vb
and his thoghtes of þe dai þat is passed, þinkinge þus: "O þou God,   35
maker of mi bodi and saule, þou se me with þi merci and gife me þi
grace, þat I wax noght slawe in þi seruise for ouirmikill `slepe´ or

---

3 þis] þebe(?), *exc.* þ, *erased*   7 hede] he hede, he *subpuncted*   10 hert]
marg., nota bene   15 herth] hert, *Lat.* terre   19 þarefore] and þarefore
34 when] *om.*;   go] god, d *subpuncted*

ouirmikill vnriste in mi slepe. Bot mesur so mi slepe to þi wirshipe, and so streng[þ]e me againe þe fende, þat I be noght lettid in þi seruis, ne of na thinge þat is nedefull to recreacion of mi saule or bodi." And when he rises, if þare [be] aniþinge þat hase bene þat night of mis-
5 gouuernance, clens it with shrift, þat þe slepe of þe night foloweinge be noght charged with it.'

Capitulum 2m. Wordes of þe maiden to `þe´ doghtir shewing oportune remedi of þe difficulte þat commis in þe wai, and how paciens is bitokend bi þe clothinge, þe
10 ten commaundmentes bi ten fingers, heuenli desire and irksomnes of þe world bi two fete, and of thre ennemis þat he hase in his wai. |

f. 118ra The modir of merci spake vnto þe spouse. 'Sai vnto þe bishope þat, if he will wende in þe wai þat is shewed to him, he sall finde thre hard
15 difficultes þarein to him. For, firste, þe wai is strait. Also, þare is þarein prikkinge thornes. And, þe þirde, þe wai is full of stones and not euen. Againe þe whilke I giue thre counsails. þe first: þat þe bishope clethe him in stronge clothe, suteli sewed, againe þe straitnes of þe wai. þe second: þat he haue his fingirs aie bifore his visage, and
20 loke throwe þaime as þai were holes, and so kepe himselfe fro prik-kinge of thornes. þe þird: þat he sett his fete warli, and asai, at euere stepe, wheþir he mai set sikirli þe toþir or noght, and set noȝt bothe his fete downe togidir bot he be sekir of þe sewrete of þe wai.

'þe sharpe wai bitokens malice of euell men agains him and gude
25 liuers, þat scornes and reproues þaire werkes and all þat þai do of
f. 118rb mekenes. Againe | þe whilke manere of pupill, þe bishope sall clethe him with paciens and stabilnes, for þai will make swilke as oþir haldes chargeouse for to bere at þe right esi to bere to him, and sufferabill. þe thornes bitokens aduersitees of þe worlde: againe whilke he sall hald
30 þe ten commaundmentes and þe counsails of God, þat, when þe þorne of aduersite, oþir of pouert, prikes, he take hede to þe prikkinge passion and pouert of Crist. If þe þorn of wreth or invie prike, take hede to þe loue of God þat he bad kepe for God, to God, and euen cristen.

35 'þe þird, þat he suld beware of settinge of his fete, bitokens resona-bill and skilfull drede. For a gude man suld haue two fete. þe first suld be as a ȝerninge and desire of endles gudenes: and þarein suld be

2 strengþe] strengie.   4 be] om.

discrecion, for he suld not desire þaime for his awen worthines, bot eftir þe will of God, as he will bi his grace reward him. þe seconde fote suld be forsakinge of þe world, and þat buse be also with discrecion, þat is, to be noght [irke] for aduersite þat is in þe werld, ne for disese in lifinge, ne for more restfull lifinge, ne fore | ne excludinge of werldli trauaile, bot oneli fore fleinge of sin and sinfull occasions, and desire of heuenli life and gladnes.

'And, forthirmare, him moste beware of thre enemis þat are in þe wai. þe first will whistill in his ere to stope his heringe. þe seconde standes bifor him to prike him in þe ein. þe þirde is bifor his fete, criand loude, and hase a snare in his hand to bind þaime with when he liftes þaime fro þe erthe.

'þe first is þo men, or elles þi thoghtes, þat sais þus to þe: "Whi dose þou so grete penance, and liues so straiteli? It is bettir to go bi þe more esi wai þat þe multitude gose bi. What hase þou to do howe anoþir liues? Whi suld þou blame oþir if þai wirship þe and þine? What fors is it to þe howe þat þai liue? If þou be gude, it is enogh to þe, and so mai þou haue frenshipe of oþir and be commendid of þaime". þe secound enemi, þat will put oute þine eine, as þe Philistens did to Sampson, is fairnes of bodeli sightes, worldeli possessions, wide|nes of clothes, diuers araies, worshipe and fauour of men. þese blindes resone, and makes þe lofe of God slawe in a mannes thoght; þai stir a man lightli to sinne, and makes him to set þe lesse bi sin. Wharefor a bishop suld hald him paide with þo þinges þat are necessari and nede-full to his astate. Bot þare be mani had leuir stand at þe mile of coueitise with Sampson þan loue hali kirke eftir þe chargeis þat þai haue taken.

'þe þird enemi þat cries so hie, and hase þe snare, and sais, "Whi haldes þou downe þi heued, and gose so mekeli furthe, and leues wirshipes? It is bettir þat þou be a preste and a bishope, þat þou mai be wirshiped of mikill folke, and come to grete dignite, and haue grete seruis and grete reste, and gedir grete gold þat oþir mai be holpen bi, and þus haue grete comforth and grete likinge"–and when þe hert is stirred on þis maner, þan liftes he vp þe on fute of likinge vnto worldli coueitise, and, bot if he set it sone doune againe, it will lape him in þe snare. And þarefore, lat him noȝt set his lufe on þis coueitise, | bot þinke on þe paine þat is endeles, to þe whilke swilke coueitise bringes a man.

f. 118ᵛᵃ

6

10

15

f. 118ᵛᵇ

21

25

30

35

f. 119ʳᵃ

---

4 irke] *om., Lat.* fastidium   6 oneli] oneli bot, bot *subpuncted*   17 enogh] enoght, t *subpuncted*   26 þat] *twice, second subpuncted*   36 coueitise] *twice, second ruled through*

'It is wretin: "He þat desires a bishoperike, he desires a gude werke to þe wirship of God". Bot nowe are mani þat desires þe wirshipes, bot þai fle þe trauaile, in þe whilke standes þe heel of saule. þarefore bid þat bishope þat he stand in þe degre þat he hase, and desire no hier,
5 till God will purwai for him.'

Capitulum 3. Wordes of þe modir and maiden, plainli declareinge to þe bishope how he sall execute his bishope office if he will wirshipe God, and of two maner of froite þat folowes verrai dignite, and dubill
10 confusion þat folowes fals dignite; and howe Jesu Criste metes with a verai and a rightfull bishope.

The modir of God saide, 'I will shewe þe bishope what he sall do, and what is þe wirshipe of God. Ilke bishope sulde haue his arrai wele kepid in his armes, þat he sell it noght for siluir, ne len it noght
f. 119rb for frende|shipe, ne l[o]sse it noght bi rekelesnes or slewthe. þis
16 bishopes arai bitokens powere and dignite þat falles to a bishope, as for to giue ordirs, for to make creme, to chasti trespassours. Bot þat he kepe þis in his armes bitokens besi thinkinge howe, and on what wise, he com to þat astate of pouere and dignite, how þat he kepis it,
20 and what froite he hase done in his office: first, þat he take heed wheþir he tuke his bishoperike for himselfe (and þan was his desire flesheli) or he tuke it for Goddes sake and for to [do] wirshipe to God (þan was his desire meritori and medefull). And þan sall he þinke þat he tuke þe bishoperike for to be fadir vnto þe pure men,
25 and [comforther] of saules. For whi, þe temporall gudes are þe gudes of pure men and of saules, and if þai be mispendid in pride, or in lusti lifinge, þe saules of þe pure sall crie to God vengeance vnto þe mispenders.

Two froites suld com of a bishopes dignite, as sais Saint Paule—
f. 119va bodeli and gostli—þat bothe þe bodi and þe saule be glorified | þarefor
31 in blis. Bot he þat hase bishopes clethinge and lifes noght þareeftir, he is worthi dubill blame and shendinge. Also, þat þe bishops power suld not be sold bitokens þat he suld noght entir bi simoni, ne do his office for mone or fauour of a man, ne promote þame þat are of euell liuinge
35 for menis praiers. Also, þat it suld not be [l]ent to oþir bitokens þat þe bishope suld noght make dissimulacion, for oþir menis frendship,

15 losse] lesse, *Lat.* perdere   22 do] *om.*   25 comforther] *om., Lat.* conso-
lator   30 þarefor] þare þarefor, þare *subpuncted*   35 lent] sent, *Lat.* concedi

and let to ponishe sinnes, ne lai on his bake oþir menes charge of sin. Also, þat þe bishop suld noght lose his arai or his miter bitokens þat he suld, in his awen person, do execucion of his office, and noght commit it to anoþir for his bodeli ese and rest, ne he suld noght be rekles to knawe þaime þat are committid to his cure, bot loke beseli þat ilkeane 5 in þaire degre kepe þaime as þai are halden.

'Also þis bishope, be reson þat he is one hird, he awe to haue a birdin and a knight of floures vndir his armes, þat þe shepe þe whilke are nere, and also fer, ren gladli eftir | him for þe gude smelle of þe f. 119ᵛᵇ floures. þis knight of fagote bitokens his gude werkes þat are done 10 opinli, and his preue gude werkes, þat bothe þe shepe þe whilke are nere, of his awen cure, and also þai þat are fere, vndir oþire menes cure, be stirred to lufe God for his gude ensampill; and so sall he be of nobill fame, bothe for his gude techinge and also for his gude liuinge. Bot when þe bishope is at þe ende of his wai, and sall com to þe ȝate, 15 him moste haue somwhat in his hand for to present vnto þe kinge. þarefor he sall haue a voide vessell: þat menes, his hert voide fro all lustes and likinge of manis praisinge.

'And þan sall com and mete with him Iesu Criste þe kinge of blis, God and man, with a grete oste of saintes. þan sall he here þe angels 20 sai, "O þou, oure God, ioi and all gude, þis bishope was clene in his fleshe, manli in his wirkinge. Ilke dai he desired oure compani. þarefore his desire is nowe froitfull, and of his comminge | we are glad and f. 120ʳᵃ oure ioy is encressed." þan sall oþir saintes sai, "O þou, oure God, ʼoureʼ ioy is in þe and of þe, and oþir nedis vs noght. Neuirþelesse, 25 oure ioy is þe more stirred of þe ioy of þis bishopes saule, þat, while he might, he desired þe and þi plesaunce. He bare flourres of swete sauour in his mouthe, þat he encressed oure nowmbir with. And also he bare þaime in his wirkinge, þat gafe comforthe to þaime þat were nere, and also to þaime þat were ferre. þarefore graunte þou him to 30 ioy with vs, and haue þou ioy of [him], lorde, for þou desired so him þat þou died for him." þan, last of all, sall þe kinge sai, "Mi frende, þou hase broght me þi hert voide fro þine awen will, and I sall fill it with mi lufe and blis, and gladnes þat neuir sall ende." '

Capitulum 4m. Wordes of þe modir to þe doghtir of 35
misdesires of euell bishopes, and howe þat mani gettis

---

1 menes] meenes
twice, second subpuncted

8 þe shepe] twice, second subpuncted
31 him¹] om., Lat. de eo

13 and so sall]

spirituall dignite for a gude will, þe whilke bishopes of
euell condicions settis noȝt bi: | and note wele þis
ensampill.

The modir of God spake to þe spouse and saide, 'þou wepis þat
5 God lufes man so mikill, and man loues God so litill. Forsothe, it is so
þat euirilke lorde or bishop desires more worldli wirshipe and riches
þan for to giue ani gude to pore men with þaire handes. And þarefore,
sin þai will noght com to þe feste of weddinge in heuen, þe pore and
þe seke sall com þareto: as I sall shewe þe bi ensampill.

10 'þare was in a cite a bishope wise, faire and riche, and ofte times
praised bothe of beute and of wisdome. Bot he thanked noȝt God of
his witt ne of his fairenes, as he suld. He was greteli praised for
riches, and for þat cause he gaue mikill for fauour of þe world. He
desired gretli þat he miȝt giue largeli for worldli wirshipe. þis
15 bishop had a clerke with him þat thoght þus in himselfe: "þis bishop
lufes God les þan he suld, and his life is gifen all to þe world. þare-
fore, and it were plesinge vnto God, I wald desire his | bishoperike to
do wirshipe to God, and noȝt for þe wirshipe of þe werld, þe whilke
is noȝt bot as an aire; noȝt for worldli riches, for þai are as a charge
20 moste heui; noȝt for reste of fleshe, ne mine awen profite, for I am
halden to be bot in resonabill riste, so þat þe bodi mai abide in
Goddes seruise; bot oneli I desire it for þe wirshipe of God. And all
if I be moste vnworthi wirshipe, neuirþeles, mi will is to profit in
worde and werke, and for to sustene mani folke of þe gudes of holi
25 kirke. God wote wele þat dede were sweter to me, and I had leuir
suffir a grete disese, þan to bere þe charge of a bishop. Bot bi
encheson þat he desires a gude werke þat desires a bishoprike, þarefore I desire þe bishoprike with þe [wirship and þe] charge: þe wirship, for hele of mony; þe charge, for mine awen hele, wirship of
30 God, and hele of mannes saule; and to þat ende, þat I mai dele þe
gudes of þe kirke largeli vnto pore men, freli to enforme þaime þat
dose amise, more beseli to trauaile mi fleshe and sobir miselfe in
ensampill of oþir."
'þis chanon blamet | þis bishope wiseli, warli and preuali. Bot þe
35 bishop toke his wordes heueli, and reproued him opinli and vnwiseli,
seinge þat he suffised himselfe to all his charge. And þe chanon weped
for þe bishopes reproue and trespase, and ȝete suffird pacientli all þat

<hr>

20 I am] *also marg.*   21 be] *twice*   28 wirship and þe] *om., Lat.* honorem
. . . cum onere   29 mony] money

he saide. Bot þe bishop scorned him so þat he was halden bot a fole
and a lier, and þe bishope a gude man and a wise.

'It fell þat þis bishope and þis chanon died bothe, and were called
vnto þe dome of God in þe sight of aungels. And þare was sene a sete
of gold, and bifore þat sete was all þe bishopes arai. þare was mani 5
fendes þat folowed þe chanon for to finde somwhat with him—for of þe
bishope þai were sikir enogh, right as þe whalle in þe tempest kepis
his frye in his wombe for þe stormes. And when þare ware mani þinges
purposed againe þe bishope—with whate entent he toke his bishop-
rike, and what he had done to God for þat at God had done to him, | 10
howe he had keped þe saules þat were vndir his cure—and þe bishop f. 121ra
couthe noȝt answere, þe domesman saide, "Set on his hede filth for his
miter. Put on his handes pike for his gloues, and clai on his fete for his
sandailes. And for his rochet, þat he vsed to pride and to wantones, he
sall nowe haue reproue. And for pride of his meine, he sall now haue a 15
compani of fendis." Also þe domesman saide, "Put on þe chanons
hede a bright crowne as þe son, and gloues of golde on his handes, and
also sandales on his fete, and so clethe him in bishopes clethinge with
all honour." And onone he was so clede, and presented with a grete
oste of heuen vnto þe domesman, as a bishope, with grete wirshipe. 20
Bot þe bishope went done as a thefe that had a rope in his neke, fro
whome þe domesman turned his ein of merci.

'Lo, howe gude will is rewardid! Lo, how mani, for gude will, gettes
grete spirituall dignite, þe whilke þai set at noght þat are called þareto!
All þis was done | in a pointe anentes God, all if þai be shewed bi f. 121rb
proces vnto þe, for a thousand ȝere in Goddes sight is as an oure. It 26
falles ilke dai þat, for cause lordes and bishopes dose noȝt þe office þat
þai are called to, God chesis pore prestes and bellringers þat loues
wele to wirshipe and, as þai can, to plese God; and þarefore þai take
states þat were ordeinede to bishopes. For, treuli, God is like to him 30
þat hanged a crowne of golde bifor his ȝates, and cried on þaim þat
passed þerbi þus: "Of eueri state mai men win þis crowne, and whoso
is best cled in vertuse, he sall haue it." Neuirþeles, wit wele þat if
bishopes or lordes bene wise in worldli wit, God is wiser þen þai, for
he enhies þe meke and lawes þe prowde. 35

'Wit wele also þat þe chanon, þe whilke is praised bifore, tuke noȝt
himselfe his hors ne charged it noȝt when he went to preche, ne he

made noȝt his awen fire when he suld ete, bot he had meine and all þat
f. 121va was necessari to his plesaunce and to his resonabill | sustinance. Also
he had mone, bot noȝt vnto coueitise, for, if he had had all þe gude of
þe werld, he wald noȝt haue giuen one peni for to haue bene a bishope,
5 ne he wald noȝt haue left a bishoperike, if it had bene plesant vnto
God þat he had halden it, for all þe world. Bot he put all his will fulli
vnto Goddes will, redi to his wirshipe or vnwirshipe, as God wald, in
lufe and drede.'

        Capitulum 5. Wordes of Saint Ambrose to þe spouse of
10   praiere made bi gude men for þe pupill, and how þat
        seculer lordes and of hali kirke are vndirstande bi a
        gouernoure, and pride bi tempest, and þe entre of
        trewthe bi þe hauen, and of [callinge of] þe spouse into
        þe spirit.

15 'It is wretin þat þe frendes of God cried somtime, praiinge God to
brest heuens and com downe for to deliuer his pepill. Also, in þe time
þat nowe is, þe frendes of God cries and saies, "O þou mildest God,
f. 121vb we se þe pepull perise in perlious stormes, | for þaire gouernance are
besi to rine in þe landes where þai mai get to þaimselfe moste worldli
20 profite, and þarefore þai lede þe pepill where is horribill wawes, and
þe folke knawes noȝt a sikir hauen. And þarefore mekill is ouir
mischeuousli perishet and full few com to þe sikir hauen. þarefore we
prai to þe, kinge of blis, þat þou sende þe light of þi grace, þat we mai
knawe þe hauen and com þareto, and fle all þe perels.

25 'Be þese gouernoures I vndirstand all þaime þat hase pouere in þis
werlde, owþir bodeli or gosteli. Bot mani of þaime loue so wele þaire
awen will þat þai take no hede of þe perels of saule of þaire soiettes,
bot ledis þaime throwe stormes of pride, coueitise and vnclennes. And
þus mani are perisht. þai com noȝt to þe hauen, bi þe whilke I vndir-
30 stande þe entre of suthfastnes, þat nowe is so derke þat þai sai þe
gospell is bot lesinge. And þus þe simpill pepill is begiled, þat þai
f. 122ra folowe more þame þat | lifes in lustes and likinge þan wordes of þaim
þat preches þe treuthe of þe gospell. Bi þe light þat mi frendes askes, I
vndirstand som speciall reuelacion made vnto men of þis werld,
35 throwe þe whilke þe light of God mai be renewed in menis hertes, and
his rightwisnes thoght vpon. And þarefore it liked vnto God for his

merci, at þe praiers of his frendes, for to call þe into his awen spirit, for þou suld here and se and vndirstand gosteli þinges, þe whilke þou sall tell furthe, eftir it is Goddes will.'

Capitulum 6. Wordes of Ambrose to þe spouse, of a liknes bitwene husband, wife and seruande, how an euell bishop is vndirstanden bi þe husband awowtre[r], bi þe wife holi kirke, and bi þe seruande lufe of þe werld; and of a full fell sentence agains þaime þat cleues more to þe world þan to holi kirke.

'I am Ambrose þe bishope þat aperis vnto þe, spekinge bi likenes, for þi hert mai noght take vndirstan|ding of gostli þinges withoute bodeli liknes. þare was a man þat had a wife semeli and wise, bot his maiden plesed him more þan dide þe wife, and of þat fell thre þinges. Firste, þe wordes and þe dedis of his maiden pleset him more þan his wife. þe second was þat he cled þe maiden in precious cloþinge, and gaue no fors howe euell his wife was araied. þe þird, þat he wald dwell neine oures [with þe maiden] and bot one with þe lawfull wife. þe first oure wald he sit bihaldinge þe maidin, and haue likinge in hir bewte. þe secound oure he wald slepe bitwix hir armes. þe þird oure he loued mikill bodeli trauaile for hir profite. þe fourt oure he tuke bodeli riste with hir eftir werenes. þe fift oure he had mikill vnrest and besines of saule howe he might make purueance for hir. þe sext oure, fro he sawe þat he had fulli plesed hir with his purueance, þan wald he take his riste with hir againe. þe seuent oure bigan to kindill in him þe fire of fleshli luste. þe eghtend oure he fulfilled his luste | with hir in dede. And þe neint oure he left somwhat vndone þat had bene to him likinge for to haue done. Bot in þe tent oure, what oure he was with his wife, he did swilke þinges as he had no likinge in. þan com one of his wife frendes and reproued him gretli for his avowtre, and counseiled him to lufe his wife and comon with hir, and cleth hir honestli, and dwell with hir þe nein oures, or elles he suld die an euell dede.

'By þis avowterrer I vndirstande þe bishop of þis kirke, þat suld be husband to holi kirke, knit þareto with faithe and charite. Bot he loues bettir þis werld þan þe kirke: and so he is one husband in nam and avowtrer in wirkinge. For, first, he makes more of þe fals flateringe of þe world þan of þe jentill spouse holi kirke; þe second, he settis mikill

marginal notes: 5 / f. 122rb / 15 / 20 / f. 122va / 26 / 30 / 35

4 of'] of þe   6 awowtrer] awowtre   16 wald] wald neine   17 with þe maiden] om., Lat. cum ancilla   31 hir] hir in, in *subpuncted*

bi worldli arai, bot he rekes noȝt how febilli þat his kirke be araied, ne
of his awen gostli arai. þe þird is þat he spendis nein oures in worldes
plesaunce and bot one in Goddes seruise.

'þe first oure spendes he in gladship of þe worlde, avisinge himselfe
what luste and what likinge he mai haue þarein. þe second oure he
slepis b[e]twix | þe armes of þe world: þat menes, he lies sekirli in grete
castels, and grete maners with hie towres and hie walles, and wenes he
mai be sikir þare fore God and all his creatures, and he hase þarein
grete gladnes. þe þird oure is þat for worldli profite he will gladli be
besi and trauaile. þe fourt is, when he hase getin mikill gude, he tristis
mikill þareon, and in þat he settis his ristinge. þe fift: he hase mikill
thoght for purueance vnto his lusti lifinge and liking. þe sext oure, he
hase a grete likinge þat he can plese men. þe seuent oure, when he
heris and sees þe likinge þinges of þe worlde, he drawes þaime
desirousli into his awen lust, and kindles in his hertli thoght a grete
luste desire of thaime. þe eghtend, he wirkes in dede eftir he was
sterrid bi lusti desire. þe neint, somwhat he leuis of his likinge for
greuance of his werldli frendes. And in þe tende oure he dose som
þinges þat are of kinde of gude werkes, vnlikandli (for oþir he dose it
for drede of paine | or for plesinge of þe world, and noght for þe lufe of
God).

'Bot þis bishope turn him þe sonner to God, and lufe him and holi
kirke, he sall be smetin as sore as, [b]e likenes, he were smetin þe
whilke fro þe crown of þe heued to þe sole of his fote, in all his parties
of his fleshe, veines and synows were brosten, and all þe bones broken
in sondir, so þat all þe merghe flowet oute and none left within. Right
so I sai moste sikerli, and I swere bi God þe lord, þe wreched saule of
swilke one sall be ponished on slike manere. And loke what paine suld
be to þe hert when þe nere and fere bodeli partes were so hurt: so sall
þe wreched saule, þe whilke is next vnto þe stroke of Goddes
sentennce, b[e] vntrowabilli turmentid, for his consciens sall noȝt lat
him haue no rest, ne no swetenes of God sall dwell with him, bot he
sall euir be in sorowe'.

Capitulum 7m. Wordes of þe maiden, how a bishope
þat loues þe werld is like a bleddir blowen full with aire

---

6 betwix] btwix   11 þareon] þare þareon, þare *subpuncted*   23 be²] he,
Lat. per similitudinem   31 be] bi

and winde, and to a snaile þat [l]igges in filth, and howe
swilke is full contrari to þe bishop Ambrose. |

'It is wretin, "He þat loues his saule in þis werld sall losse it." For-   f. 123ʳᵇ
sothe, þis bishope lufes his saule eftir desire of all his lustes, ne þare is
no spirituall delectacion in his saule. And þarefor he is wele likned to   5
belowes full of winde, for when þe fire is wastid, and þe metall is
melted and ron oute, ȝet leues þe belis full of winde and aire. So, when
he wastid his time and also his might in lustes, ȝet dwelled within him
ane euell will, full of couetise and pride, geuinge to oþir euell
ensampill and occasion of sin: wherefore þat he is now ponished   10
greuoseli in hell. Bot so was it noȝt of Ambrose þe bishope. For his
hert was full of gude will, his etinge and restinge was resonabill, and
blewe fro him all will of sin, spendinge his time both profetabilli and
honestli. He might wele be called þe belis of vertewe, for he heled
woundes of sin with wordes of trewthe, and he warmed cold hertes   15
with his clene ensampill of gude werkes and vertuouse liuinge. He
withdrewe mani fro will of | sin, and so he keped mani fro euirlastinge   f. 123ᵛᵃ
dede. Bot þis bishop, þat I tolde of bifore, I like to a snaile þat ligges in
filth, and puttes his hede in þe erth; so he lai in þe filth of lusti sin,
haueinge his hert on erthli þinges. And þarefore, I bringe thre þinges   20
vnto his minde: first, how þat he held þe ordir of presthede; þe
secound, what bitokens þat worde of þe gospell, "þai haue shepis
clethinge withoute, and within þai are wolues of rauain"; þe þird, whi
temporall gudes brennes so hertli in þaire lufe, and [he] þat [is] maker
is so colde in þaire hertes.'   25

    Capitulum 8. Wordes of þe maiden to þe doghtir, of hir
    awen excellent perfeccion, and of þe euell-mesured
    desire of maistres in þese daies þat are nowe, and of a
    fals answere to a question þat þe glorious maiden askes
    of thaime.   30

    The modir of God saide, 'I had fro mi childhede þe holi gost perfi-
teli with me. [Take] ensampill bi a not, þat, within it, hase a kirnell
and, withoute, a shelle, [s]o þat þer i[s] `noght´ voide | in it. So fro mi   f. 123ᵛᵇ
childhede I was full of þe holi goste, and right as I wex of elde and in
quantite of bodi, so filled þe holi goste me within þat þare was no   35

    1 ligges] bigges   10 and] and of   14 might] mught   24 he . . . is] I
. . . am   32 Take] om., Lat. habere poteris   33 so] no not, not subpuncted
is] I

place in me þat sin miȝt entir. And þarfore I synned neuir, venialli ne dedeli. I was so brenninge in þe lofe of God, and þe fire of God was so feruent in mi hert, þat þare plesed me nothinge bot þe will of God, þat shewed to me his grete charite, insomikill þat he sent to me his
5 messagere to make me knawe þat I suld be þe modir of God. And fro I wist þat þat was þe will of God, I assentid in mi hert, and of a grete charite I spake oute and saide vnto þe messagere, "Be it done vnto me eftir þi worde." And in þat same instans was God within me made man, and Goddes son mi son. And so þe fadir and I had bothe one son,
10 þat was both God and man, and I bothe modir and maiden. Bot fro þe time þat he was conceiued within mi bodi, as he was full of wit, he
f. 124ʳᵃ filled me | full of wit, insomikill þat noȝt oneli I vndirstode þe grete [wit] of maistres, bot also wheþir it com of letterure or elles of þe charete of God.

15 'And þou þarefor þat heres þis, sai to þat maistir þat I aske him thre þinges: wheþir it is leuer to him for to haue his saule presented to God, or for to haue bodeli fauour or frenshipe of þe bishop. þe second: wheþir he is gladder in saule of þe possession of mani nobles þan if he haue right none. þe þird: wheþir it is more likinge to him to
20 be called maistir and sit in wirshipfull place amange wirshipfull men for worship, [or] be called a simpill frere and sit lawest amange þe lest. Lat him take gude auisment of þese thre. If he loue þe bischope more bodeli [þ]an gostli, þan reproues he noght his sin, bot saies to him þat þinge þat likes him. If he haue more likinge of mani nobles þan of
25 none, þan loues he bettir riches þan pouert, and more counseils his
f. 124ʳᵇ frendes to gedir worldli gudes þan | for to leue it. And if he hafe likinge to be called maistir, and loues worldli wirshipe, þan loues he more pride þan mekenes. And þan, as bifore God, he is more like to an asse þan to a maistir. And þan etes he voide strees, to þe whilke letturere
30 and conninge withoute charite is likned. And him wantes clene wit, þat is likned to charite, for cherite mai noȝt be festned in one hert þat is foule. Ne þis maistir sall noȝt excuse him falsli to his profit, and sai þat it is more likinge to him for to present þe saule of þe bishop to God spiritualli, and þat he hase no likinge in mone, ne in þe name of a
35 maistir. For I, þat bare him þat is verrai treuthe, knawe wele if his mouthe and his hert accorde.

'I haue asked of þe maistir thre þinges, to þe whilke if he had

12 me] *Quire catchphrase*, full of witt, *below*   13 wit] *om., Lat.* sapientiam
21 or] and, *Lat.* aut   23 þan¹] and
28 as] as þe, þe *subpuncted*
33 more] more present, present *subpuncted*

answerde treuli, I suld wele haue knawen `it´: for, eftir þe message was
saide to me fro þe mouthe of þe archangell Gabriel, treuthe tuke in me
bothe fleshe and blode, and þe same treuthe, bothe in godhede and
man|hede, was born of me. And þarefore I knewe wele wheþir in þe   f. 124ᵛᵃ
mouthe of men be treuthe or noght. Bot for I knewe þat in þe wordes   5
of þe maistir was no treuthe, þarefor I make him warninge of thre
þinges. First, þat þare is som þinges þat he lufes bodeli and desires, þe
whilke he sall neuir haue. þe second: he sall want and forgo þat þinge
þe whilke he hase nowe with grete worldli gladnes. þe þird: þai þat are
litill in þaimeselfe sall entir þe ȝate of heuen, and maistres (þat menes,   10
þai þat fel[e] greteli and hieli in pride of þaimeselfe) stand withoute;
for þe ȝate is straite.'

Capitulum 9. Wordes of þe maiden to þe spouse, howe
bi sight of þe son, and heringe, perels are eshued.

The modir saide, 'All if a blinde man [see noȝt], neuirþeles, when   15
þe son shinnes, men þat mai loke and see mai flee þe perels of þe wai
with grete gladnes. And all if a de[f]e man [mai] noȝt here, neuirþeles,
he þat mai here, when he heres grete noise abowue, of thoner or oþir, |
he mai flee [fr]o perels where he mai be sikir. And so of tastinge. Som   f. 124ᵛᵇ
mai taste ne sauour right noȝt, as þe dede man. Ȝit þe gude drinke   20
haldes þe swetenes of his sauour, þe whilke þe leuand man mai [taste],
and be glad in his saule, and be made hardi to whilke manli werkes
him likes.'

Capitulum 10. þe modir spekes vnto þe doghtir of
wordes saide to hir, and of perels þat in haste falles to   25
þe kirke, and howe þe principales of þe kirke takes
nowe hede to a lusti lifinge and coueitise of mone, and
of þe wrethe of God sterrid againes þaime.

The modir saide vnto þe spouse, 'Drede þou not þo þinges þat þou
sall see, weninge as þai were of ane euell spirit. For, right as, when þe   30
son is nere, þare are two þinges þat puttes awai þe dirke cloude, þe
whilke are light and warmenes, so with þe holi goste commes hete of
charite and perfite lighteninge of þe faithe, þe whilke | two, as þou felis   f. 125ʳᵃ

11 fele] feli   15 see noȝt] *om.*, *Lat.* non videt   17 defe] dede, *Lat.* surdus
mai] *om.*   19 fro] two   Som] som þat   21 taste] flee, *Lat.* degustans
30 as¹] *twice, second subpuncted*

nowe, suffers noȝt þe feende, þat is likned to a dirke cloude, ne
folowes him noght.

'Send þarefore to him whome I haue named mi messangere. For all
if [I] knawe his hert, his answere and his hasti ende, neuirþeles ȝit sall
5 þou send to him þere wordes. Forsothe, I make it knawen to him þat
þe fundament in þe righte parti of holi kirke is so mikill sliden downe
þat þe werke abouen is riuen and falles perrelousli, so ferefurth þat
some, þe whilke hase gone vndir it, hase lost þaire liues. And þe pilers,
þe whilke suld stand vpright, þai bowe all downe to þe erthe. And [þe]
10 pament is so rent þat blind men falles downe þare, and somtime þai
þat mai see. And for þis skill þe kirke standes perelousli, and is in
point to fall downe. þarefore, I sai bot if þe kirke haue sone helpe,
elles it will fall, and þat fall sall be throw cristendome.

'I ame Goddes modir, and he is mi son. I stode bi þe cros when mi son
f. 125ʳᵇ with paciens chiualrousli ouercome hell, | and with his blode opind
16 heuen. I was in þe hill when mi son stied vp to heuen. I knewe all þe
faithe þat he taght men to com to heuen. And nowe I ame tentinge to þe
praiers of men, as it were þe rainebowe, þat semis to touche þe erthe
with bothe endes: bi þi whilke I vndirstande miselfe, þat with mi praer
20 touches bothe God and man, gude and euell. For I make þe gude man
with mi praier stabill in þe faithe, and I let þe euell of [his] malice.

'And I make knawen, vnto him þat I saide vnto þe, þat on þe to side
of þe erthe rises horribill clowdes againes þe clerenes of þe bowe–bi
þe whilke I vndirstande þaime þat liues in luste of fleshe. And þai are
25 neuir filled of worldli coueitise, no more þan it ware a swelowe of þe
see. þai waste in pride þe gudes of holi kirke. þaire sinnes cries vnto
heuen and are agains mi praiers, as derke cloudes agains þe clerenes
of þe bowe. And so, þare þai suld plese God, þai prouoke and sterris
him to wrethe. |

f. 125ᵛᵃ 'þarefore, woso will þat þe grounde of holi kirke be stabill, and þat
31 blissed vineȝerde, þe whilke is holi kirke, þat Criste with his blode
groundede, be nowe renewed in mekenes and charite, if he þinke himselfe þareto noȝt sufficiant, I, þat ame qwene of heuen, sall helpe him
with all aungells, and take awai febill rotes and barein trees, and set in
35 þe stede fructuouse branches.'

Capitulum 11. Wordes of faithe of þe spouse to Criste,
and howe John Baptest telles hir sekirnes of Cristes

4 I] om.   5 þere] þere hasti, hasti *subpuncted*   9 þe³] om   21 his] þe

speche to hir, and of þe blis of a gude riche man; and howe an vndiscrete bishope for his sacli and euell life is likened to one ape. And þarefor note wele þis ensampill.

The spouse spake to Criste in praiere, and saide, 'O mi lorde Jesu, I trowe so stedfastli in þe þat, if þare lai a nedder before mi mouthe, he suld noȝt entir bot at þi sufferaunce for mi god.' John Baptest answerde, 'He þat apperes to þe is Goddes awen kindeli son, of whome þe | fadir bare wittnes and saide, "þis is mi son." And when I baptized him, þe hali goste aperid vpon him in likenes of a dufe. þe same is in mankinde þe maidens son, and I haue handiled him with mine handes. He it is þat teches þe wai to pore and riche vnto heuen. Bot þou mai aske and sai, "Howe suld a riche man com to heuen, sen þat it is harder þan to a camell for to go throwe a nedill eye?" I answere and sai þat a riche man þat so gouerns him þat þare is no euell-getin gude with him, bot he spendes his gudes wele to þe wirship of God, and he hase leuir lose and leue all þat he hase or þat he wald greue God, and þarefore he besis him all þat he mai to plese God: swilke a riche man is dere to God, and sall com to heuen. Bot þus was it noght of þat riche bishope, for he is like to ane ape: firste, for his clethinge couers not þe parti þat suld be preue; þe secound, for with his fingers he touches filthe | and þan laies þaime to his mouthe; þe þirde, for he hase a mannes visage, bot it was colour of vnresonabill bestis; þe fourt, for all if he haue handes and fete, ȝete he fowles with clai both fingers and handes.

'So þis foltishe bishope, as it were an ape, is sotell in vanitee of þe world, bot noȝt besi in vertuouse wirkinge. He hase clothes, and ordirs of a bishope þat are wirshipfull bifor God, bot his besines is all aboute worldli þinges and fleshli, þat suld noȝt be sene in a bishop for euell ensampill of oþir. What menes fingirs, bot for to shewe with þinges þat are sene, as I, seinge to God in manhede, shewid him with mi finger when I saide, "*Ecce agnus dei*". þan is þe fingers of þe bishop noȝt elles bot his vertuse, throw þe whilke he suld shewe þe rightwisnes of God and his charite. Bot all if his condiscions seme outeward honest, ȝete þai are putt to stinkinge þinges, for þai ende in likinge of fleshe. | Also, he hase a visage: þat is, a saule like to þe shape and liknes of God, bot it is defadid with fals couetise. þe fourt is þat þe ape touches, and

f. 125vb

_5_

_10_

_15_

_20_

f. 126ra

_25_

_30_

f. 126rb

_36_

<hr/>

5 O] O þou, þou _subpuncted_   24 fowles] folows fowles, folows _subpuncted_
31 shewid] shewid inge

defoiles with his fingers and handes, clai: þat menes, þat his affeccion
and lufe is all to þe world and noȝt to Godward. And swilke a man
stintes noȝt þe wreth of God, bot sonner greues him more, and sterres
againes him þe rightwisnes.'

5   Capitulum 12. Howe þe spouse of Criste makes praiers
         for þe bishop forsaide, and of þe answers þat Criste and
         þe maiden and Seint Agnes made þan vnto hir.

The spouse saide þan, 'O þou lorde, þare commes no man in heuen
bot þe fadir drawe him. þarefore, þou mildist fadir, drawe þis bishope
10 to þe. þou son, help him. þou hali goste, fill him with þ[i] charite.' þe
fadir saide, 'If he be stronge þat drawes, and þe þinge þat is drawen
f. 126ᵛᵃ heui, it mai sone fall. And if he þat is drawen be bunden, þan | mai he
nowþir help himselfe ne him þat drawes. And if he be foule and
vnclene þat is drawen, it is þe more wlatsom to drawe him and touche
15 him. On þis wise is þis bishope disposed, as he þat standes and avises
him what wai is best to halde. He standes bitwene þe wai of ioi and of
sorowe. He hase one horror of þe paine of hell, and wald haue þe blis
euirlastinge: bot him þinkes hard to go þat wai.'

þan saide Saint Agnes, 'þis bishope is disposed as he þat stode
20 bitwene two wais. And he knewe wele þe tone of þaim was hard in þe
bigininge, and likinge in þe endinge; þe second is likinge for þe time,
bot þe ende is woundir sorowfull. And he wald gladli wende þe wai þat
is likinge in þe bigininge bot he dredes sore þe ende. And þan he
þinkes of þis manere: "þare is a short path in þe likinge wai. If I couth
25 find it, I might wele be sekir þarein, and when I come to þe ende, I sall
leue it." Bot when he com into þe ende, he fell into þe depe pit, for he
f. 126ᵛᵇ couthe | noȝt finde þe short wai. Bot þare are mani þat þinkes þus:
"Nowe it is hard to liue straite, to leue worldli wirshipes." þarefore þai
þinke, "þe wai is lange; þe merci of God is mikill. þis werld is plesant
30 and likinge, and þarefore it is no harme if I vse þe worldli likinge a
while, for I sall amende me at þe ende. þare is a shorte wai: þat is, contricion and shrift. If I mai haue þis, I sall be saue." Bot þis is a febill
thoght. For þese men dies soner þen þai wend, and þai haue so grete
sorowe in þe ende of þe deede, þat þaire endinge is so sodaine, þat þai
35 can noȝt þan finde medefull contricion. And it is reson þat it be so, for
cause þai walde noȝt seke it in time of hele, bot þai set þe time of merci

of God eftir þaire awen will, ne þai thoght noȝt to make ende vnto þe
time þat þai miȝt haue no likinge in sin.

'Nowe standes þis bishop, and hase bifore him thre leues þat he
chesed. þe first he redis with likinge, bot it lastes noȝt, þe whilke is | þe
lesson of worldli riches and wirsheps þat passes sone awai. þe second 5
is drede of þe paine of hell, and of þe dome þat is to com, þe whilke he
redis with grete ferdnes and drede, bot it lastes noȝt lange. þe þird is
loue of God and gude drede: and þis leef is turned full seldom. For if
he tuke hede what God hase done for him, his lufe suld euir be whike,
and neuir dede ne slokend in his hert.' þan saide þe spouse, 'O þou 10
ladi, prai for him.' Saint Agnes answerde, 'What dose rightwisnes bot
dome, and merci [bot] for to drawe man to God?'

þe modir spake þan and saide þus: 'It sall be saide vnto þe bishop,
"All if God mai do all þinges, neuirþelesse a man moste trauaile himselfe for to flee sin, and to win charite." þare is thre þinges þat sin is 15
fleed bi. þe first is perfite penance. þe second is to þinke at neuir sin
againe. þe þird is: amend him eftir þe consaile ofe God. þam þat loues
God and noȝt þe worlde, þese þre þinges helpes to gete and kepe |
charite–meknes, merci, and besi trauaile to do wele. Of þe oþir f. 127rb
bishope I told þe firste of, I do þe to wit þat him þinkes þe dikes to 20
brode for to skipe or to lepe, þe walle is ouir hie to climbe, þe lokkes
ouir stronge to breke, and þe wilde bestis ouir mighti to hald. þarefore
I stande and abides him. Bot he turnes his heued to þe werkes of thre
companis, to whome he takes grete hede. þe first is dawnsers, to
whome he saies, "Me likes wele to here ȝou: abide me." þe second 25
standes to behald vanite of þe world, and to þat he sais, "Me likes to
see þat ȝe seene." þe þirde restis him, and with þat wald he riste.
What menes þe dawnsinge bot for to go fro one likinge vnto aneoþir,
and so withdrawe mannes hert fro contemplacion of God to þinke on
worldli likinge and of gediringe of gude? For þe standinge menes 30
ouirmekill þinkinge on worldli likinge of fleshe, and rest menis restfull
likinge of fleshe. These companis hase he folowed, and noȝt taken
hede of mi wordes.'

þan saide þe spouse, 'O milde modir, wende no[ȝt] fro him.' þe
modir answerde, 'I wende noȝt fro him vnto þe time erthe ressaiue 35
erthe. If he will brist his bandes, I sall mete with him as a seruand, and

   2 miȝt] miȝt noȝt, noȝt *subpuncted*   12 bot] *om., Lat.* nisi quod   16 to]
twice   31 fleshe] fleshe þe companes hase and of gediringe of gude of þe worlde f. 127va
and rest menis restfull likinge | and of gaderinge of gude of þe world, *marg.* va-cat *and,* f. 127va
after fleshe, *superior* va   34 noȝt] now, *Lat.* noli

I sall help him as a modir.' And þan saide þe modir to þe spouse,
'Doghtir, þou þinkes what suld haue bene þe rewarde of þe chanone
of Orliens if his bishop had bene conuertid. I sai, right as þou sees
erthe bringe furth erbes and floures of diuers kindes, so, if ani man fro
5 þe biginninge of þe werld had stand in þe stat þat he was first sete in,
he suld haue had one excellent rewarde and ane soueraine mede. For
all þat dwelles with God wendes fro one gladshipe vnto anoþir. And
þare is none irkesomnes, for in ilkane of þaim is more and grettir ioi
and likinge.'

f. 127ᵛᵇ   Capitulum 13m. Wordes | of þe modir to þe doghtir,
11   howe þe wordes and werkes of Criste are bitokened bi
             tresori, and þe godhede bi a castell, and sinnes bi
             lokkes, and vertuse bi walles, and þe fairnes of þe world
             and delite to depe pittes; and how a bishop suld haue
15   [him] for þe hele of saules.

The modir spake vnto þe spouse and saide, 'þe bishop walde haue
me in his loue and charite. I knawe a tresoure, and he þat mai gete it
sall neuir be at mischefe, and he þat sees it sall neuir fall `in´ tribula-
cion. And he þat hertli desires it sall haue what at euir he desires with
20 grete ioi and comforth. þis tresoure is closed in a gude castell with
foure lokkes, þe whilke castell hase hie walles and thike. Withoute þe
walles are two depe dikes and brode. þarefore I prai him to lepe ouir
both þe dikes at one lepe, win ouir þe walles at one passe, breke all þe
f. 128ʳᵃ lokkes with one stroke, and þus | mai he present to me þe moste
25 precious þinge. þis tresoure is mi sonnes wordes, and his preciouse
werkes þat he wroghet in his passion, and bifor his passion, as in his
awen incarnacion in mi bodi, and in his blissed bodi on þe awter. Bot
fewe hase nowe minde of his tresoure. It ligges in one stronge castell:
þat menes, in vertuse of godhede þat defendes þe manhede fro his
30 enemis, as a castell defendes þaim þat are within it.
    'þe foure lokkes are foure þinges þat lettis men fro þe homelines of
God. þe first is pride and coueitise of worldli wirshipe. þe seconde is
coueitise of worldli gudes. þe þird is luste of fleshe. þe ferthe is drede,
wreth, enui and reklesnes of his awen saule hele. Bot som sees Goddes
35 bodi and ressaiues it: neuirþelesse, þaire saule are fer fro him. þarefore, if he will com nere to God, him most breke þe lokkes with one
f. 128ʳᵇ stroke. þis stroke is lufe of mannes saule, þat þis | bishop suld haue,

4 of diuers] *twice, second subpuncted*   15 him] *om.*   30 enemis] enenemis

with werkes and rightwisnes, to stire men for to leue þair sinne and to
lufe God, and so might he come to þis tresoure. And if he might noȝt
smith all þat are sinners, he suld be besi on þaime þat are nere him,
and nawþir spare riche ne pure, gret ne small, frende ne foo. For so
dide Thomas of England, þat suffird mikill tribulacion for right-   5
wisnes, and at þe last a hard dede, for he spared noȝt to smith þe bodis
with censures of hali kirke, so þat þe saules had lesse paine. And I
wald þat þis bishope folowed his life, to h[a]te his awen sinnes and
oþir. And swilke a stroke of þe lufe of God suld be herde aboue
heuenes in þe sight of God and aungels. And þan suld mani be con-   10
uertid, and sai, "He hates noȝt vs bot oure sinnes, and þarefore turn
we fro sin, and we sall be Goddes frendes and his."

'þe thre walles þat gose abote þe castell are thre vertuse. þe first is—
leue lusti þinges and take þe lufe of God. þe | second—gladlier to suffir   f. 128va
reproues and harmes for treuth and rightwisnes þan for to [haue]   15
wirshipe and worldli gudes for feininge of þe treuthe. þe þird is—
noght to spare his life ne his gudes for to haue a cristen mannes saule.
Bot take hede what man dose nowe. Him thinke[s] þat þere walles are
so hie þat he mai in no wise win ouir þaime. And þarefore þai come
noght nere to þat preciouse bodi for to dwell þarewith, ne þare saules 20
are noght nere to God. And þare[fore] I bad mi frende þat he suld
wende ouir þe walles at one trine. It is called one trine when þe bodi is
in þe erthe and þe lufe in heuen. þan passes a man lightli þere walles
when for lufe of heuenli þinges he forsakes his awen will, and for rightwisnes will suffir tribulacion and, if nede be, die for þe wirship of God. 25

'þe two dikes are likinge of þe werld and likinge of frenshipe. Mikill
folke wald gladli rest in þe dikes, and rekes noȝt of þe blis of heuen.
And þarefore is þare dikes bothe | brode and depe: brode, for þai hald f. 128vb
folke fro God; [depe], for þai drowne mani into þe depnes of hell. Bot
þan moste he lep[e] i[t] ouer: þat menes, þaim most be defendid fro a 30
mannes hert, and man moste nedeli set his hert vpon heuenli þinges,
and lepe þiddir in his loue. And þan mai he haue þat þinge þat is
moste preciouse, þat is, God and man in one persone. And I sall shew
þe howe þat þe bishope mai present to God a preciouse þinge. When
þat he findes a sinfull man þat hase litill thoght of God and mikill on þe 35
worlde, and he hase pite þat þe saule suld be lost þat God boght with
his blissed blod, and he takes to him two voices, one, þat praies God to

1 men] men to sin, to sin *ruled through*   8 hate] hote, *Lat.* odit   15 haue]
om.   18 thinkes] thinke   21 þarefore] þare   28 þarefore is] þare is
fore is   29 depe] *om., Lat.* profunde   30 lepe it] lepid

haue merci on þe saule, þe second, þat he shewe to þe saule þe perell
þat it is in–þan accordes God and mannes saule; þan, as it were, with
handes of charite, he presentes þat þinge þat mi sone boght full dere.

f. 129ᵣᵃ For I was present when þat nobill knight | mi son went oute of Jerusa-
5 lem for to hald bataile for man, and þat was so hard a bataile þat all þe
sinowes in his armes brast in two. His bake was blo and blodi, his fete
were persed with nailes, his een and his eres were full of blode, his
neke was bowed downe when he gaue þe goste, his hert was shorn in
sondir with a spere, and with grete disese ouircome his enemi, and
10 boght mankinde. And nowe sittis he in blis, and haldes oute his arme
to ressaiue mannes saule. Bot few takes hede vnto him, to present to
him mannes saule.

'Sai also vnto þat bishope, þat, for he wald haue me vnto his para-
moure, þarefore I will gife him mi faithe, and binde me to him in a
15 bonde of lufe and charite. For, right as þe fadir was with þe son in me,
and holi goste with þe fadir and son continuli, so sall he be bunden
vnto þe holi goste. For when þat he loues mi sons passion, and hase
ressaiued his bodi within him, þan is he with God, and God with him.

f. 129ʳᵇ And | when þe bishop and I haue one God, þan haue we one bond of
20 charite, in þe whilke we are bunden togidir. And sai vnto þe bishope
þat, if he will hald trewe cou[e]nand with me, I sall help him whiles
þat he leues, and I sall be nere to him at his diinge, and serue him and
present his saule vnto God, and sai, "O gude lorde God, þis man hase
serued þe and bene lawli vnto me. þarefore I present vnto þe his
25 saule." O þou doghtir, what þinkes a man when he dispises his saule?
Wenis þou þat þe fadir almighti wald haue suffird his son to haue so
grete paine had he noȝt loued mannes saule so wele and ordeined it
vnto his blis?'

Capitulum 14. Wordes of þe modir, þat likens a bishope
30 to a buttirflee, and his mekenes and pride bi two
winges, and þre euels of þe bishop bi þre coloures, and
two desires bi two hornes, his coueitise bi his grete
[mo]uthe, and his charite be þe litill bodi of þe buttirflee.

f. 129ᵛᵃ The modir saide vnto þe spouse, 'þou | art þe vessell þat þe lorde
36 filles and þe maister voides. Neuirþeles, he is one and þe same þat

---

bothe filles and voides. For right as he [þat] wald menge togedir into one vessell wine, milke and watir, and wald, eftir, disseuer þaime againe, ilkone to þe one kinde, dede o maistri, so I, modir and maistres, hase done and dose to þe. Sethen gone a twelmoneth and more, þere were saide vnto þe diuers þinges þat are now menged in þi saule, and if it were sodanli nowe ȝet oute, it suld seme abhominabill þinge of þaim. And þarefor I departe þaim be litill and litill as me list.

'Haue þou noght minde þat I sent þe to a bishope þat I called mi seruant? Nowe we likken him to a buttirflee þat hase brode winges of white, rede and blewe. And when it is towched, it files a mannes fingers. þis worm hase a litill bodi and a mikill mouthe, and two hornes in þe hede, and a priue place in þe bodi þat þe filth gose oute at. þe winges of þis bishope are mekenes and pride. Him semis meke with|oute in his wordes, contenance and clethinge. Bot he is within proude, desirand wirshipes and fauour of men. He demes of mennes dedis, and not his awen. With þere two winges he flies mekli before men, to plese þaime, bot he is proude within, thinkinge himselfe bettir þan oþir. Thre coloures of þese winges bitokens thre þinges þat hides his euell. þe rede coloure bitokens þat he will gladli speke of þe passion of Criste and of his saintes, bot þai are full ferre fro his hert. þe blewe colour bitokens þat he rekkes not outeward of þe worldli gudes, and þat he were dede vnto þe worlde, and all his thoght on heuenli þinges. Bot blewe hase þe coloure of þe heuen, bot it is noȝt so within. þe white coloures bitokens fairnes of condicions and religion in habite, bot it is noȝt within. Right as þe coloure of þe buttirflie is þike and cleues to a mannes fingers, and is noȝt bot poudir, right so his | werkes semis faire, bot þai are vnfaire and vnprofetabille, for þai are not for þe wirshipe of God bot for þe wirship of himselfe.

'His two hornes bitakens two willes in him. One is for to haue esi life in þis worlde, and life þat is endeles in þe tothir: þat menes, wirshipes in þis life and blis in þe toþir. And so him semis for to bere heue[n] in þe one horne and erthe in þe toþir. And þus he þinkes in himselfe: "Sen I ame called a deuote man and meke, whi suld I lede a more straite life? If I haue mi likinge in som þinges, I do oþir grete dedis þat sall excuse me. And sin heuen mai be wone with a draght of watir, what nedis it me to do grete penance?"

'þis buttirflie hase a grete mouthe, and ȝet he hase a grete desire, for, if he had dewoured all þe flies bot one, ȝete desires he to deuoure

f. 129vb

f. 130ra

---

1 þat] *om.*   5 þere] þat þere   28 himselfe] him himselfe, him *subpuncted*
29-30 life in þis] *twice*, in þis life *subpuncted*   31 heuen] heue

þat. So, if he had neuir so mikill, ȝete priueli he desires more, so þat he
f. 130ʳᵇ is neuir full. Also þe | buttirflye hase a priue voidenge of his filth. So
hase he a preve voidinge of his ire and impaciens, þat it be noȝt seen
vnto oþir. Also þe buttirflie hase a litill bodi. So he hase litill charite.'
5 And þan saide þe spouse, 'If he haue ani sparke of charite, ȝet is þare
hope of life and hele.' þe modir answerde, 'He hase swilke a charite as
Judas had when he saide, "I haue sinned, bitraisinge right blode." He
shewed charite, bot he had none.'

Capitulum 15. Wordes of þe maiden to þe doghtir vndir
10   figure of oneoþir bishope, howe he is likend to a grete
            flie þat flies aboute, and his bostefull wordes to þe
            flight, two consideracions bi two [w]inges, and of þe
            maidens [meruallinge] of oþir two bishopes and of
            prechowers.

15 The modir saide vnto þe spouse, 'I shewed þe oneoþir bishope,
whome I called a shephirde. I liken him to a grete flie þat flies aboute
f. 130ᵛᵃ with grete noise, | and bites full sore where he bites, and he hase one
erthcli coloure. So þis bishop, þat suld be a pore man, desires gretli to
be riche. He had leuir hafe his awen will þan be obedient to me. He
20 gose aboute with mani pompos and bostfull wordes, bot fewe are of
God or of swetenes in him. He disputes of charite and of simpilnes of
his degre, bot all is for vanite of þe world. His two winges are two
desires: one, þat he wald gladli gife faire plesinge wordes þat he might
haue þanke of men; þe second, þat he wald all men wirshiped him. Bot
25 þis flie bittes full sore, for with his faire wordes he makes men to hald
þaime in sin, and ceses noght, ne correctes ʿnotʾ as he suld.
'Bot see þat þare is grete deferennce in þese two bishopes. One of
þaime semes withoute pore and meke, þat he mai be called a gosteli
man. þe second wald haue þe worldes gude, þat he might be called a
30 large man. One wald seme as he had noȝt, and neuirþelese he wald
f. 130ᵛᵇ pre|uali haue mikill. þe second wald haue openli mikill, þat he might
be halden manli. And þarefore, eftir þe comon prouerbe, for þai serue
me þat I see noght, I sall rewarde þaim þat þai fele noȝt, for I sall noȝt
approue þaime.
35 'þou hase woundir þat swilke are praised of prechinge. I answere

---

2 þe] þe pre, pre *subpuncted*   12 consideracions] consisideracions   winges]
þinges, *Lat.* alas   13 meruallinge] *om., Lat.* admiratione   30 wald²] wald
noȝt

þat somtime þe euell man spekes to gude men, and þe gud goste is
gifen somtime to þe wordes, bot noght for gudenes of þe [te]chere, bot
fore gudenes of þe wordes þat are saide, and of herers þat heres þaime.
Somtime a gude man spekes to euell men þat are amendid for þe
gudenes of þe speker and þe gudenes of þe wordes. Also somtime a 5
febill man spekes to febill, and ȝete throwe herynge of gude wordes are
þai amendid. And þarefore, doghtir, gife no fors to whome þat euir
þou be sent.'

Capitulum 16. Wordes of þe son to þe spouse þat þe
dampnacions of saules pleses noȝt God, and of | mer-   f. 131ra
ueilous questions of þe ȝonger bishope vnto þe elder,   11
and of þe answers of þe elder againe.

The son saide vnto þe spouse, 'Hopes þou þat þis is shewed vnto þe
for þe shame, reproue and harme of þaime pleses God? Nai, forsothe.
Bot it is for Goddes wirship, and for paciens mai be sene opinli and 15
shewed, and þai þat heres it drede þe dome of God. Bot here a
meruaile. A ȝongere bishope asked þe elder, and þan saide, "Whi hase
þou left þe ȝokke of abedience sen þou was bunden þareto, and, sen
þou was bunden to religion, whi left þou and desired a bishoprike?"
þe elder answerde and saide, "It was hard to me to be vndirloute, and 20
þarefore I desired to be free. þat yoke þat God sais is soft was full bittir
to me; þarefore I soght reste of mi bodi. þe mekenes þat I shewed was
bot feininge, and þarefore I desired wirshipes. And for methoght it was
bettir to bide þan to be biden, þarefore I desired a bishoprike." |

'þan saide þe ȝonger againe, "Whi wirshiped þou noȝt þi see with f. 131rb
worldli honore? Whi gate þou þe no riches bi þi worldli wit? Whare 26
spendid þou oght þat þou had to þi wirshipe? Whi shewed þou þe so
lauli, and wald noȝt do furth as þi state asked?" þan answerde þe elder
and saide, "I did no more wirshipe to mi see, for I hoped ai to come to
a gretter if I made me lawli and gosteli þan if I semed worldli. And 30
þarefore, þat I might haue þe praisinge of men, I made outewarde no
fors of worldli gudes. Also, I besid noght mi wit aboute worldli gudes,
in aventure þat gude men wald haue spoken of me; ne I spendid not
largeli, for methoght it more ese to be with fewe þan with moni, and I
loued for to haue somwhat in cofers."   35

'þan saide þe ȝonger, "Whi gafe þou þine asse swete drinke and

1 somtime] somtime þat some, þat some *subpuncted*   2 techere] chere, *Lat.* doc-
toris   32 worldli²] *twice, second subpuncted*

likinge in swilke ane vnclene vessell? Whi gaue þou þe bishope of þine
hogges mete? Whi castes þou þi crowne vndir þi fete? Whi caste þou

f. 131ᵛᵃ outè þi whete and etes þiselfe cokill? Whi lowsed þou oþir | of bandes
and band þiselfe with fettirs? Whi laide þou heland medicins to oþir
5 mennes woundes, and to þine awen þou laide dedeli medecins?"

'þan he answede and saide, "I gaue þe [asse] a swete drinke and
likinge when I felid me lettird, and, for worldes wirshipe, put me to
trete þe godli sacramentes on þe awter, and leue worldli besines. And
in þat time I was in sin, as God knewe, bot I keped it preue for mannes
10 knawleche; and, noȝtwithstandinge þat I was in syn, I presumed to
take þe sacrament, and so mi awen dome. To þe second I sai þat I
gaue to þe bishop hogges mete, for I gaue lust and likinge to mi kinde
withoute mesure of restreininge. To þe þird I sai þat I put mi crowne
vndir mi fete, for me list do more in sight of men in rightwis dome, þan
15 for þe lufe or wirship of God, ne me list noȝt do þat I bad oþir do. To
þe fift I sai þat, when folke come to me, [it plesed me] for to do þe

f. 131ᵛᵇ same þinges þat þai fortoght and with penance forsoke. To þe | sext I
sai þat when folke com to me, I taght oþir gude liuinge, bot I did noȝt
so miselfe, and þarefore þat at was cause of [l]yue of saule, it made me
20 wers, for I did þe contrari, and I had euir more likinge for to encrese
þe charge of sin [þ]an for to lesse it in me." '

Eftir þis was herd a voice þat saide, 'Thanke God þat þou art noȝt
with þe venemos vessells.' And þan, as fast it was saide, þat one of þe
bishopes was dede.

25   Capitulum 17. Wordes of þe modir to þe doghtir þat
commendes þe life and ordir of Saint Dominike, and
howe in time of his deinge he turned him to oure ladi,
and how in þere daies mani of his freres leues þe token
of Cristes passion þat Saint Dominike gafe þaim.

30   The modir saide vnto þe spouse, 'I tolde þe ȝistirday of two þat
were vndir þe reule of Saint Dominike, þe whilke lufed mi son as his

f. 132ʳᵃ awen derrest lord, and me his | modir bettir þan his awen hert. And mi
son shewed and inspired inwardli to him þat þere was thre þinges in
þe world þat displesed him—þat is to sai, pride, coueitise and luste.
35 For destruccion of þe whilke thre vices, Saint Dominike, with mani

6 asse] om., Lat. asino   16 it plesed me] om., Lat. me delectabat   18 liuinge]
liuuinge   19 lyue] byue   21 þan] and   32 his¹] Quire catchphrase,
moder, below

si[g]hinges and praiere, as a speciall medicine, purchased of mi son a
reule and a maner of liuinge, in þe whilke he ordeined thre gudes
againe þe forsaide thre euels. For againe þe sin of coueitise, he bad þat
his folowers suld noþinge hafe withoute leue of þe prioure. Againe
pride, he ordeinede meke and simpill clethinge in abite, and, againe 5
lust of fleshe, gude abstinens and gude occupacion in spendinge of
time.

'He ordainde also a prioure to kepe pese and vnite and, for he wald
þai had a spirituall token of þe crosse, he empr[i]nted, as it were, a
spirituall rede crosse on þe left arme, by þe hert. And he taght þam to 10
haue continuall minde of þe passion, and for to preche | feruentli þe f. 132rb
worde of God oneli for þe loue of God and hele of mannes saule. He
taght þaime also þat þai suld gladli obei to þair souerains and leue
þaire awen will, suffir pacientli reproues, and noght for to desire bot
straite findinge in mete, drinke and cleþinge, loue þe treuthe and sai 15
þe treuthe, and lete for no fauoure of man.

'When þe time come of his passinge, þat mi son shewed to him in
spirit, he come to me with wepinge teres and saide, "O Mari, quene of
heuen, God chase þe to take mankinde in þe. þou art maiden and
modir most singuler and worthiest, and full mighti, of whome all verrai 20
might was broght furthe. Here me prainge þe, and take mi frereis þat I
haue norishet vndir mi straite scapolori, and ressaiue þaime vndir þi
brode mantelle, þat þe enemi haue no poure agains þame, ne þat he
distruye noȝt þis ȝonge vineȝerde þe whilke þi son hase sett with his
right hand. O mi ladi, be þis scapolori þat hase one pese bifore þe 25
breste, an|oþir bihind at þe bake, I vndirstand two þinges þat I had to f. 132va
mi freres. One was besines, þe whilke I had night and dai, þat þai suld
serue God with sobirnes. þe seconde was–I praide for þaim þat þai
suld desire no worldli þinge þat suld greue God, or harme þe fame of
meknes and pite on þe pepill. And þarefore, sen nowe is þe time of 30
passinge to mi rewarde, I assigne þaim to þe. Teche þou þaime as þi
childir, and lede þaim as þaire modir."

'With þere wordes, and oþir, was Dominike called vnto Goddes blis.
Bot I answerde him againe bi þis likenes: "Mi frende Dominike, for
þou hase loued me more þan þiselfe, I sall defend and kepe þi freres 35
vndir mi wide mantill, and all þat lastes in þi reule sall be saued. Mi
wide mantill is mi merci, þat I warn noȝt to þaime þat askes it. And

---

1 sighinges] sithinges   2 thre] thre þinges, þinges *subpuncted*
9 emprinted] emprnted   11 for to preche] *twice, second subpuncted*   29 þat]
þat þai, þai *subpuncted*   33 was] was called, called *subpuncted*

who þat euir sekis me, þai are defendid bi me." Bot doghtir, what
hopes þu menes þe reule of Saint Dominike? Forsothe, mekenes,
f. 132ᵛᵇ castite, and dispisinge | of þe worlde. Whosoeuir takes to þaime there
þre, and lastes in þaime, sall noȝt be dampned; and þai are there þat
5 holdes þe reule of Saint Dominike. [Bot here a meruaile. Dominike]
assigned his freres vndir mi wide mantill. And nowe are fewer vndir mi
wide mantill þan were þan vndir his straite scapolori, ne som of his
freres, while he liued himselfe, had noȝt his flees: þat menes,
Dominike condicions and maners, as I sall shewe þe bi ensampill.

10 'If Dominike come fro heuen, where he nowe is, and bad vnto a
theefe þat come oute of his den for to sla shepe and distroie þaime,
"Whi calles þou and ledes awai mi shepe, þe whilke, of evident tokens,
I knawe þat are mine?", þe theef miȝt sai againe, "Dominike, whi
chalange þou for þine þat are noȝt thine?" If Dominike answerde
15 againe and saide þat he norished þaime and taght þaime, þe theefe in
cas suld sai againe, "What if þu norishet þaime and taght þaime? Ȝete
f. 133ʳᵃ haue I cherised þaime to mi will. | I haue shewed to þaime ese and
likinge, and þou reuled þaime with hardenes. And þarefore, mo of
þaime heres mi voise þan þine, and rennes eftir me into mi pasture
20 and leues þe. And þarefore þai are mine, for þai hafe a frc will to go
eftir þe or me as þaime liste." If Dominike saide againe, "þai are mi
shepe, merked with a rede merke in þe hert", þe theefe might answere,
"þai are merked [with] mine merke, bot [kutt] in þe right ere. And for
mi merke is more opin and shewen þan þine, þarefor I knawe þaime
25 for mi shepe."

'This theefe bitokens þe deuell þat hase drawen vnto him mani of
Dominike freres, þe whilke are kutt in þe right ere, for þai will noȝt
here þe wordes of liue þat teches how þe wai of heuen is straite. Bot
þai here gladli alloneli þo þinges þat delites þame to do. And fewe are
30 þe shepe of Dominike þat hase þe rede merke in þe herte, for fewe
f. 133ʳᵇ haues þe passion of Criste in minde with charite, or preches | feruentli
þe worde of God, or ledis a gudeli blissed life in chastite and pouert.
And ȝete, as þe pupill sais, þe reule of Dominike is: to bere all þere
þinges on þare bake; to will at haue noȝt in possession, bot at þe reule
35 suffirs; noȝt allonli to leue all outrage, bot, for chastisinge of þe fleshe,
some[time] to abstene fro þinges lefull and necessari.'

5 Bot . . . Dominike] *om., Lat.* sed audi mirabile; Dominicus   17 þaime²] þaime
to, to *subpuncted*   18 þaime] *twice, second subpuncted*   23 with] *om.*   kutt]
om., Lat. incise   36 sometime] some

Capitulum 18. Wordes of þe modir to þe doghtir þat þe
freres heres nowe more gladli þe voice of þe enemi þan
of þaire fadir Dominike, and fewe folowes nowe his
steppis, and how þai þat desires bishoperikes for wirshipe of þe world, and rest or fredome of þameselfe, are   5
noȝt in þe reule of Saint Dominike, and of a fell sentence agains swilke, and of experiens of one dampned
for swilke cause.

The modir spake vnto þe spouse and saide, 'I saide þe þat all
Dominike freres were vndir mi mantille. Now sall þou here þat mani   10
are nowe of swilke condicion þat if Dominike | come fro þe place of   f. 133ᵛᵃ
delites, in þe whilke he is nowe blissed, and cried þus, "O mi wele-
beloued freres, folow ȝe me, for foure þinges are ordainde for ȝou, þat
is to sai, wirshipe for mekenes, euirlastinge riches for pouert, likinge
withoute irksomnes for chastite, and euirlastinge life for dispite of þe   15
world"–vnnethe suld he be herde. Bot, of contrariouse wise, [i]f þe
fende went agains him and cried, "I hight ȝou wirshipes. I haue in mi
house riches. Ȝe sall haue lust of bodi and likinge of þe world"–if þere
two voices sounded nowe in þaire eres, mo wald wende eftir þe theef
þan eftir Dominike. þese takes no heed to Cristes voice, þat sais,   20
"Come ȝe eftir me, and I sall fede ȝou and gife to ȝou miselfe."
'And wit wele þat þo freres þe whilke desires bishoperikes are noȝt
of Dominike reule. Bot he þat takes it on skillfull cause is noȝt
excluded fro Dominike reule. For Saint Austin leuid full welle eftir his
reule before he was bishop, and in his bishophede. He forsoke noght,   25
ne left, reuli | liuinge, all if he went vpward to more wirshipe; for he   f. 133ᵛᵇ
toke it for þe more trauaile, seinge þat he might profite þe pepill, and
noght for ese of fleshe. And þarefore þai þat takes so bishoperikes, for
to profite and helpe þarewith mannes saule, þai dwelle in þe reule of
Saint Dominike, and þai sall hafe dubill rewarde: one, for þe swetenes   30
of þe reule; aneoþir, for þe charge at þai are called to.
'And þarefore I swere bi þe same God þat þe prophetes swore bi,
not for impaciens, bot for witnes of þare wordes, to þe freres, þat
sorowe sall com to þaime þat hase left þe reule of Saint Dominike. For
þare sall come a wode hunter with wode hundes, and þai sall sai vnto   35
þe lorde, "Lorde, þare are mani shepe commen into þi ȝerde, and
þaire fleshe is venomed and þaire flees filed. Thaire milke is noght
worth, and þai are to wilde. Bid has[t]e þaime oute of þe pasture, þat

2 voice] vice voice, vice *ruled through*   16 if] of   38 haste] hase

f. 134ra þai distrue it noȝt, ne þat þe gude shepe be | noȝt filed bi þaime." And
þan þe lorde answerde and saide, "Spere all þe holes þat nane come in
bot þai þat suld, and are restfull and honest. And shote þe oþir with
arrows and sla þaime. And þan sall kepirs come and loke wele [of
5 whilke kinde] þat þai sall be þat sall be ressaiued to þe lordes
pasture." '

þan saide þe spouse, 'A, ladi, be noȝt greued at mine askinge. Sen
þe Pope hase relesed þe sharpnes of þe reule, whi suld þai haue bene
blamed þat þai ete fleshe or oþir þinges of ese?' þe modir answerde,
10 'þe Pope toke hede to þe febilnes of mankinde, and to þe defaute at
þai saide þai suffirde, and þarefore he suffird þaim ete fleshe, þat þai
might be more stronge for to preche, and to oþir gude trauailes, bot
noȝt at þai suld be þe more wanton and more slawe in þe serues of
God: and þarefore I excuse þe Pope.'

15 þan saide þe spouse, 'Dominike ordeined clothes for his freres
f. 134rb nawþir of þe beste ne of þe werst. Whi suld þai þan be reproued | if þai
were gude clothes?' þe modir answerd, 'Dominike, þat endi[tid] his
rule of þe spirit of mi son, bad þat þai suld haue no preciouse
cloþinge, in auenture þat þai wex proude bi þaime, ne þat þai suld
20 haue of þe werste and hardest, in awntir þat þai suld be lettid, bi
hardnes of clothinge, of þaire reste eftir þaire trauaile; bot at þai suld
vse a mene, and noȝt to preciouse for pride and vanite, bot at þai might
kepe þaime fro colde, and might helpe to whi[ke]ne vertuse. And
þarefore we praise Dominike in his ordenance. Bot we reproue his
25 freres, þat þai make þaire clothes more to vanite þan to profite.'

þan saide þe spouse againe, 'Whi suld his freres be blamed for þai
make hie kirkes and bigginges and begis þarefore?' þe modir answerd
and saide, 'When þe kirke is so wide þat it mai ressaiue þaime þat
commis þareto, and þe walles are so hie þat þai let noȝt þaim þat suld
f. 134va entir, and when þai | are so thike þat þe winde sall noght blawe þaime
31 doune, and it raine noȝt throw þe thekinge, it suffices vnto þaime, for
it likes God more a meke hert in a lawe kirke þan one hi kirke and one
hert oute þareof. And þarefore þaime nedis noȝt to fill arkes with gold
and siluir for bigginges, for it was no profit to Salamon þat he bigged
35 so grete places and howses and forgat God, whome he reklest.'

When þis was said and herde, þan þe olde bishope, þat was, cried
and saide, 'A! A! A! Mi mitir is taken awai, and nowe is shewed þat are

---

4-5 of whilke kinde] *om., Lat.* de quo genere 17 enditid] endis, *Lat.* dictauit
23 whikene] whilome, *cf. Lat.* profectum 26 saide þe] *twice*, þe saide *subpuncted*
31 þe] *twice, first subpuncted*

was hid. Whare is þe ho`nora´bill bishop? Whare is þe wirshipfull
prest? Whar is þat pore frere? þe bishop þat was anointed for his
office, and in tokeninge of clennes of life, is now a seruant, and filed
with fatnes of þe dungehell. þe prest þat had pouere to chaunge brede
into God throwe holi wordes, is nowe proued a fals traitur, for he sold 5
him for coueitise þat boght man dere vpon þe crosse. þe pore frere þat
forsoke þe world for pride and vanite now is dampned. Bot nowe | ame   f. 134ᵛᵇ
I compelled to sai þe sothe. þe domeseman þat hase demed me, he
wald haue deliuerd me, with as grete and bittir paine as he suffird on
þe crosse, and it had bene possibill. Bot his rightwisenes, agains þe   10
whilke mai noþinge be, wald noȝt suffir it. And þarefore f[e]l[e] I nowe
rightwise dome.'

    Capitulum 19. Wordes of þe spouse to Criste, and how
    sho is dishesed with diuers maner of þoghtes and sho
    might noȝt put þaim awai, and þe answere of Criste to   15
    þe spouse, whi God suffirs þat, and of þe grete profite
    of thoghtes with detestacion and drede had, and with
    discrecion, and þat a man set noȝt litill bi a veniall sin at
    it bringe not in a dedeli sin: and þarefore beware.

The son spake vnto þe spouse and saide, 'Whi aret þou turbled?' 20
Sho saide againe, 'For I ame disesed with vnprofetabill thoghtes, þe
whilke I mai noȝt put awai.' þan saide | þe son, 'þis is verrai right-   f. 135ʳᵃ
wisnes, þat as þou had bifore likinge in worldli affeccions agains mi
will, so þou haue nowe diuers thoghtes againes þi will. Neuirþeles,
drede with descresion, and hafe trest in me; and wit wele þat when þe 25
hert hase no likeinge in thoghtes of sin, bot withstandes þaime, þai are
clensinge bothe of þe saule and of þe bodi. Bot if þare be a sin þat þou
wote wele is sin, all if it be a litill sin, if þou do it in traiste þat þou sall
aneoþir time abstene þarefro, and of presumpsion of grace, ne þou
takes no penance, ne makes noght amendes in þat at [in] þe is, wit þou 30
wele þat swilke a sin, þe whilke of his awen kinde is bot a litill sin, mai
þus be made a dedeli sin. And þarefore, when ani likinge comis to þi
hert, take heed whereto it will drawe and repent: for man sinnes oft
time of freelte, and þare is no man bot he sinnes somtime venialli.
þarefore God, full of merci, hase ordained a remedie, þe wh|ilke is   f. 135ʳᵇ
forþinkinge for sin and amendinge þareof.   36

1 honorabill] *orig.* horribill, rri *subpuncted*   11 fele] fill   26 no likeinge]
marg., nota   30 in²] *om.*   35 God] God is

'For þare is noþinge þat more greues God and a man: to sin and reke noȝt þareof, ne charge it noȝt, or elles to trist þat þou art so gude þat God will noȝt punishe þe for his wirshipe (as ife he might noȝt be wirshiped withoute þe), or elles to trowe þat he wald suffir þe to do ani
5 sin vnponished for þou hase done mani gude dedis! For wit þou wele, all if þou had done ane hundrethe gude dedis, ȝet might þou noȝt be suffissant to ȝeld to God þat þou were halden for his charite and gudenes. þarefore haue resonabill and skilfull drede with þe, and if þou mai noght lett þi þoȝtes, haue paciens, and besi þe to withstand
10 þaime in þi will. þou sall noȝt be dampned for þai come into þe, for it is noȝt [in] þi pouere for to lete þare comminge. Bot þan it is trespas if þou assent and haue likinge in þaime. And all if þou assent noȝt to þi thoghtes, drede in awntir þat þou fall be pride, for þare mai no man
f. 135ᵛᵃ stand bot bi þe grace | of God, and drede is one entre vnto heuen.

15 'Mani hase fallen into þe gosteli dede, for þai put fro þaime þe drede of God, and haues had shame to shriue þaime of þaire sin vnto man, whare þai shamed noght to sin bifore God. And þarefore, he þat rekkes neuir for a litill sin to aske forgifenes sall noȝt haue forgeuenes. And so, for encressinge of sin to sin, þat sin þat miȝt lightli haue bene
20 forgeuen, of rekleshede and contempt waxes grete sin, as þou per- saiues in þis saule þat is nowe dampned. Fro þe time he had done one veniall sin and remissibill sin, he ekid, of custome, sin vnto sin, traistinge of oþir dedis þat he had done—as if I suld haue demed for þaime þe sin lesse. And so he went furth be custom of vnskilfull
25 likinge, ne amendid noȝt his will vnto þe last point. And þan was his consciens wortheli charged, and he sorowed þat he suld leue þat litill
f. 135ᵛᵇ worldli gude þe whilke he left. And God suffirs a | man to þe last point, if he will turn his will freli fro sin. And for þe sinfull man will noȝt turn his will fro sin, þarefore, at þe ende, þe fende stresses him, for he wote
30 wele þat ilke man sall be demed eftir his will is fonden, and his con- sciens. And þarefore he trauails and besis him, and specialli at þe ende, to blind and combir so þe saule þat it suld noȝt turn to þat þinge whilke is rightfull. And þat suffirs God, for, when a man might, he wald not turn him to God.

35 'Also presume þou noȝt, ne traiste þou noȝt, to mikill, if I call a man mi frende or mi seruant, as I did þis man; for Judas was called mi frende, and Nabugodonosore mi seruant. For, as I saide in mi persone, "Ȝe are mi frendes if ȝe do þat I haue commanded and biden

---

11 in] *om.*   38 frendes] frendes þat folous me and þai mi enemis þat dispises mi commandmentes, *and, exc.* frendes, va-cat

ȝou." So sai I nowe þat þai are mi frendes þat foloues me, and þai mi
enemis þat dispises mi | commandmentes. Take hede of Dauid, of f. 136ʳᵃ
whome I saide I fand a man eftir mi hert. [He] trespased eftir bi
mannessla[u]ghtir. And Salamon, to whome so mikill gudenes was
shewed to, trespased bi vnkindnes. And þarefore þe hest was noȝt ful- 5
filled in him, bot in me, Goddes son. And þarefore I set þis for mi conclusion and finall clause: whoso dose mi will and leues þaire awen, þai
sall take þe life euirlastinge to þaire heretage. He þat wele heres, and
lastis noght in perseuerance of wirkeinge, he sall be as a seruant
vnkinde and vnprofetabill. Also, on þe oþir side, be noȝt in dispaire I 10
call a man mine enemi, for as sone as he chaunges his will to God, he
sall be mi frende. Judas was one of þe twell when I saide, "Ȝe are mi
frendes þat foloues me, and ȝe sall sit vpon þe twelue setes."

'Bot þou mai aske me howe Goddes wordes are treue, for Judas sall
noȝt sit with þe twelue. To þis I answere: | God, þat knawes mennes f. 136ʳᵇ
hertes and þaire willes, called both gude and euell [to] two dignites— 16
him þat dwelles and abides in perseuerence of gode wirkinge to haue
blis, and him þat turnes awai to forgo it. And þarefore, bicause Judas
foloued me, bot noght in full perfite hert, ne he had noȝt perseuerance
vnto þe time of rewardinge, þarefore was he none of þaime þat God 20
ment of. For oneli he ment of þaime þat suld be trewe folouers vnto
þaire liues endes, and he wist wele þat Judas was [n]one of þaime þat
God ment of. He spake as wele of þaime þat were to com as of þaime
þat were þare present, within whose sight are all þinges present. He
spekes of þat is for to come as if it were present, and sometime of þat is 25
present as if it ware to come. And sometime he takes þat as to come as
if it were passed, and þat at is passed as if it ware for to come, for to
make men at be noȝt to besi for to wit þe conseile of þe Tri|nite þat f. 136ᵛᵃ
"mani are called and fewe are chosen". So he þis was called to þe
bishoperike, bot noȝt chosen, for he was vnkinde to þe grace of God, 30
and for cause he is in þe name of bishope, and noȝt in þe dede, he is
rekened with þaime þat wendes downwarde and noȝt vpwarde.'

Capitulum xx. þe modir spekes vnto þe doghtir, how þe
giftes of þe holi goste are bitokend bi þe talent of
beȝant, and howe Saint Benet multiplied to himselfe þe 35

3 He] *om.*   4 mannesslaughtir] mannesslaightir   5 hest] hiest, *Lat.*
promissio   16 to] and   17 gode] gode and euell, and euell *subpuncted, marg.*
va   22 none] one   þat²] þat suld be trewe, *exc.* þat, *subpuncted; marg.* va-cat
23 of¹] of for oneli he ment   as²] as one, one *subpuncted*   28 at] þat

giftis of þe holi gost, and here is shewinge bi what
þinges þe holi spirit or þe euell spirit entir into a
mannes saule.

The modir saide, 'Doghtir, it is wretin, þat "He þe whilke toke
5 fiue beȝauntes wane oþir fiue." What is a beȝante bot þe gifte of þe
holi goste? Som takes conninge, som riches, som homelines of riche
men: and all suld bringe þe dubill winninge againe. As bi ensampill:
f. 136ᵛᵇ in conninge, þai suld bringe againe | conninge in gude liuinge and a
gude techinge, riches and oþir giftes, vsinge þaime resonabli for
10 þaire profites and oþirs. So þat nobill abbot Benet multiplied þat he
toke, when he dispised all þat was passand, and made his bodi to
serue his saule, and set þe lufe of God bifore all oþir þinges. He
purid and kepid his eres fro foule wordes and vaine, his een fro lusti
sightes. He fled into wildirnes and folowed him þe whilke, within his
15 modirs sides, made ioi at þe comminge of his againebier. And all if
Benet had noght gone to wildirnes, ȝet he had, and suld haue,
commen to heuen, for his hert was full of God. And he died to þe
world, bot God called him into þe hill, þat oþir suld folowe his
liuinge bi gude ensampill.

20   'His bodi was as a seke of erthe, in þe whilke was closed þe fire of
þe holi goste, þat put fro his breste þe fire of þe fende. For right as a
f. 137ʳᵃ bodeli fire is kindeld of two þinges, þat menes aire and blaste | of
mannes mouthe, so þe holi goste entirs a mannes saule with inspiracion and gude wirkinge of a mannes selfe, or gude spekinge, þat
25 steris mannes saule to God. Also þe holi gost, when he commes, he
warmes a mannes saule to se God. Bot he brinnes noȝt fleshli. He
shinnes in clernes of sobirnes; bot he puttes no malice in mannes
hert. Bot þe euell spirit birnes in mannes will to fleshlines, and
makes it vnsaueri to gudenes. He blindes þe saule, þat it mai noȝt
30 knawe þe treuthe, for it is euir besi aboute erthli þinges. þarefore þis
fire, þat was in Benet, suld be kindled in mani mennes hertes. God
set Benet in one hill where he kindled mani sparkes, and made of
þaime a grete lowe of þe loue of God, throw þe whilke þai ware
made perfite as Benet was. Bot now þe brandes of Benet are casten
35 downe, and where þai suld haue hete thai hafe cold, and dirkenes for
f. 137ʳᵇ light. Bot and þai were gadird togidir, þan suld þai gife | some hete.'

---

26 warmes] warnes, *and, after* n, *superior* i   27 in²] *twice, first subpuncted*

Capitulum xxi. Wordes of þe modir to þe doghtir, shewinge bi ensampill þe grete perfeccion and magnificens of Saint Benet life, and howe þat a froiteful saule is bitokenede bi a tre, and þe pride of þe saule bi a flintstone, and a cold saule bi a cristall stone, and of thre sparkes þat flies fro þe forsaide cristall, flintstone and tre.

The modir spake and saide, 'I told þe bifore þat þe bodi of Saint Benet was chastised and gouerned, bot it had no gouerninge of þe saule. þe whilke saule was as ane aungelle, þat gaue of himselfe a grete hete, bi ensampill, as if þare ware thre fires: one kindled in mir, þat gaue a swete smell; þe second kindled in a dri mater, of whilke come birnand coles þat shines in brightnes; þe þird kindled in þe oliue, þat gaue l[o]we, light and hete. In þere thre fires vndirstande I thre persones, and in þese þre persones þre states in þe world.

'þe firste is of | þaime þe whilke, for þe loue of God, forsoke þare awen will, and put þaime to pouert and outecastinge for pride and vanite of þe world, and loues clennes. þese men hase kindilled þaire fire in mirre, for riȝt as mirre is bittir, and ȝet it flemis awai fendes and slokenes threst, so þe abstinens of þere men is bittir to þe bodi, and neuirþelesse it slokkenes euell luste, and withstandes þe powere of þe fende. þe second fire is of þaime þat þinkes þus: "Whereto loue whe þe honour of þe worlde, sen it is bot a aire wendinge bi þe eres? Whereto lufe we golde, þat is bot rede erthe? What is þe ende of oure fleshe bot filth and poudir? All is bot vanite þat is worldli. And þarefore I will oneli leue and trauaile to þe wirshipe of God, and þat oþir men, bi ensampill, mai be kindiled in þe lufe of God." þis fire is kindiled in þe loue of God in drie mater, for þe world is all dri and dede to þaime, and ilkeane of þese gifes coles | of rightwisnes and clernes of gude techinge. þe þird state [is] of þaime þat, for þe grete loue of Cristes passion, desires of all þar hert to die for Cristes sake. Thai kindill fire in þe oliue, þe whilke hase grete fatnes and hete when it is kindiled. So þai are fate with þe grace of God, þat þai gife light of conninge, hete of feruent charite, and streng[þ]e of honest conuersacion.

'þese thre fires are sprede fere on brode. þe first is kindiled in heremites and religion, as Saint Jerome discriues, þat was inspirit with

5

10

15

f. 137ᵛᵃ

20

25

f. 137ᵛᵇ

30

35

14 lowe] lawe   30 is] *om.*   32 grete] *twice, first* (gret) *subpuncted*
34 strengþe] strengie

þe holi goste and fande þaire liues wondirfull. þe second fire was kindilled in confessoures and docturs; þe þird in martirs, þat dispised þare fleshe for Goddes sake, and oþir þat wald haue died for Goddes lufe. For to com to þese thre states was Benet sent, and he broght all
5　thre fires into one, insomikill þat þai þe whilke were noȝt wise were
f. 138ᵛᵃ lightened, þai þat were cold ware warmed, and þai þat | were warme ware made more warme. And so with þere thre fires bigan þe religion of Saint Benet, þat ordains euirilke man, eftir þat he is abill, to þe wai of blis. Bot as [of] Saint Benetes sekke come þe swetenes of þe holi
10　goste, bi þe whilke mani places were made to þe serues of God, right so nowe of þe sekke of his freres is þe holi goste cast awai, for þe hete is slokened and quenched, and þe brandes are sparpled, and gifes noþere hete ne brightnes, bot smoke and vnclennes and coueitise.

'Neuirþeles, God hase graunted to me thre sparkes, bi þe whilke I
15　vndirstand moo. þe firste is broght oute of þe berall stone with hete of þe son and brightnes, þat hase nowe festened him in dri mater, þat þare mai be made þareof a grete fire. þe second is broght oute of þe hard flint; þe þird of a barain tre, þat grewe with rotes and leues. Bi þe cristall is vndirstanden man saule, þat is colde in þe lufe of God as
f. 138ʳᵇ þe cristall. Neuirþe|les, he besis him with a gude will to com to perfec-
21　cion and prais God of his helpe. And þarefore his gude will bers him to God and hase gude steringes, þat makes euell stiringes to wax colde. And þan God lightenes his hert, and festenes him in his saule so þat he listes noȝt to liue bot to þe wirshipe of God. [Bi] þe second, þat is flint,
25　I vndirstande pride. What is harder þan pride of him þat wald haue wirshipe of all men (and ȝet wald he be halden meke and called deuote)? What is more abhominabill þan to þinke þat he is best of all oþir, and ȝete will suffir no worde ne techinge of none oþir? Neuirþeles, þare are mani proude men þat prais to God for to do awai
30　pride and ambicioun fro þaime. And þarefore God forthirs þaire gude will, and withdrawes fro þaime þaire pride, and also sometime worldli þinges þat lettes þaime to desire heuenli þinges. Bi þe þirde, þat is, þe baraine tre, is bitokened þe saule þat is norished in pride and
f. 138ᵛᵃ fleshelines to þe | worlde, and desire to haue wirshipes and riches.
35　Neuirþeles, he pulles oute mani stubbes of sin for drede of dede euir-lastinge, and, for þat, God drawes nere to þe saule warde and sendis of his grace, and makes þe tre þat was barein to be fructuouse. And, with þise manere of sparkes, Saint Benetes religion suld be repareld, for it semis nowe all desolate and forfarn.'

6 were²] *twice*　　9 of²] *om.*　　24 bi] *om.*

Capitulum 22. Wordes of þe modir to þe doghtir of a
monke þat had a licherous hert in his breste, and howe
he made apostasie fro God with his awen propir will
and coueitise and coward l[e]uinge of angell conuer-
sacion.   5

The modir spake to þe spouse. 'What sees þou þat is worthi to be
reproued in þis man?' þe spouse annswerde and saide, 'He singes
seldome his mes.' þan saide þe modir, 'For þat suld he not be demed.
þare is mani abstenes for minde þai haue of þaire awen dedis, and ʒete
are þai neuirþeles accepted vnto me. | Bot what sees þou elles in him?'   f. 138ᵛᵇ
þan saide þe spouse, 'He hase noght þe clethinge of Saint Benetes   11
ordenance.' þe modir saide, 'It falles oft time þat a custome þat is
bigon is left for vnknaweinge, and þai suld noʒt for þat be demed. Bot
þare is þre þinges þat he is worthi to be reproued for. First, for his
hert, þat God suld rest in, is as þe hert of a comon woman. þe second   15
is, for he left a litill gude and now coueites a grete gude. He hight to
forsake himselfe, and now folowes he all his awene will. þe þirde, þat
God made him a faire saule as one aungelle, and he suld haue keped
aungell lifinge: bot nowe it is like to one aungell of hell þat fell bi
pride. He is grete amange men, bot God wot what he is in his sight.   20
God is like to a man þat hase a þinge closid in his hand, þat no man
wote what it is till he opin it. So God kepes close what sall fall to himselfe liste.'

Capitulum 23. Answere of þe fadir of heuen to þe
praiers | of þe spouse for sinners, and howe þare is thre   f. 139ʳᵃ
þinges gifes witnes in erthe, and howe þe Trinite of   26
heuen beris witnes to þe spouse, þe whilke is spouse bi
faithe, as all oþir is þat folowes þe right faithe of holi
kirke.

The spouse saide vnto þe fadir, 'O, þou swetest lorde, I prai þe for   30
sinfull folke þat þou will haue merci on þaime.' þe fadir answerde, 'I
here and I wote þi will. þi praer sall be fulfilled. For, as Jon sais in his
gospell, þre þinges are þat beris witnes in erthe (spirit, watir and
blode) and thre in heuen (fadir, son and holi goste). So þre þinges
beres witnes [to þe]: þe spirit þat kepid þe in þi modir wombe, þat þou   35
art Goddes bi þe faith of baptim. þe watir of baptim beres witnes þat

4 leuinge] liuiinge   20 wot] whot, h *subpuncted*   35 to þe] in, *Lat.* tibi

þou arte þe doghtir of Cristes manhede bi clensinge; and þe blode of
Criste Jesu, throw þe whilke þou art boght, beres witnes þat þou art
Goddes doghtir, deliuerd fro þe fendes powere with þe sacramentes of

f. 139ʳᵇ holi kirke. | And we, fadir and son and holi goste, bers witnes þat þou
5   art oures bi faithe, and so are all þai þat haldes þe right bileue of holi
kirke. And in tokin þat þou will do oure will, go and ressaiue þe bodi
and blode of þe manhede of Criste, þat mi son bere þe witnes, þat þou
hase ressaiued his bodi in strengh of þi saule.'

Capitulum 24. þe answere of Criste to þe praiers of þe
10   spouse for þe mistrowinge pepill, and howe God is wirshiped bi þe malice of euell men, all if it be noght of
þaire will ne vertu, and e[n]sampill, bi þe whilke holi
kirke or a saule is vndirstanden bi a maiden, þe ix ordirs
of aungells bi ix brethir of þe maiden, Criste bi a kinge,
15   and thre states of men bi þre kinge sonnes.

The spouse spake vnto Criste and saide, 'O lorde Jesu, I prai þe þat
þi faithe be sprede vnto vncristen, þat þe gode mai more wirshipe þe,

f. 139ᵛᵃ and þe euell mai be amendid.' þe son answerde and | saide, 'þou art
turbled and disesed þat God hase lesse wirshipe þan þou wald. I sall
20   giue þe ensampill þat God is wirshiped of þe malice of euell mene.
þare was ones a riche maiden and wele condeciond, þat had ix breþir,
þe whilke lufed þaire sistir as þaire herte. And ilkone of þaire hertes
had bene [als] in hir. Bot in þat kingdome where þat maiden was it was
þus ordeined, þat whoso wirshiped suld be wirshiped, and whoso
25   spoiled and robed suld be spoiled, and whoso filed a maiden suld lose
his heued. The kinge of þis realme had thre sonnes. þe firste loued þis
maiden, and present to hir shoes þat were gilted, with a girdill of gold,
a ringe on hir fingir, and a crowne on hir hede. þe second desired þe
maidens possession, and spoiled hir þareof. þe þird besid him to haue
30   defoiled hir. þe whilke thre sonnes were taken bi two breþir and
present to þe kinge, and þe breþir saide vnto þe kinge, "Thi sonnes
hase desired oure sister. þe first wirshiped hir and loued hir with all

f. 139ᵛᵇ his hert. þe second robed hir. þe þird | had leuir [þ]an his life hafe
defoiled hir. And in þat point are þai taken þat þai had full wille to
35   haue done þis."
'þan saide þe kinge, "þai are all mi childir, and I loue þaime all
elike. Neuirþelesse, nowþir I will ne I mai do againe right. þarefore

12 ensampill] esampill   23 als] om., Lat. quasi   33 þan] and

I sall deme þaime as [seruantis]. And þarefore þou, son, þat wirshiped
þe maiden, þou sall haue wirship and þe crown with þi fadir." To þe
second I saide, "þou þat robid þe maiden, þou sall abide in prisson till
þe time þou gife againe þat þou tuke. I herd þat þou forthoght þat þou
did, and wald restore it againe, bot þat þou was broght vnto þe dome   5
or þou fulfilled it." To þe þird he saide, "þou, son, þat did all þi
besines to haue defowled þis maiden, ne þe forthoght it noȝt–þarefore, as mani wise as þou besid þe to defowle hir, as mani maner sall
þou be punished." þan saide all þe breþir, "Wirship be to þe, domesman, for þi rightwisnes."   10

'This maiden bitokens holi kirke þat is worthi in faithe and faire | in   f. 140ʳᵃ
condecions. þe firste of þe sonnes bitokens þaime þat loues God with
all þaire hert, þat bringes giltid shone when þai haue verrai contricion
of þair trespas and of þaire reklesnes. þai bringe furth clethinge when
þai take hede to þe commandmentes of þe lawe, and kepis þe consails as   15
þai mai. þai present a girdill when þai þinke with all þaire besines to
liue in charite. þai put þe ringe on þe fingir when þai trowe stedfastli
in þe dome þat is to come, and þe euirlastinge life. þe stone of þis
ringe is stedfaste hope, þat þere is no sin bot it mai be clensid with
penance. Thai set a crowne vpon hir heued when þai haue full charite: 20
and right as þare are diuers stones in þe crowne, so þere are diuers
vertuse in charite. þe heued of þis holi kirke is mi bodi. And he þat
wirshipes þis holi kirke is called Goddes son. þis holi kirke has neine
breþir, þat are neine ordirs of aungels. For in þe life euirlastinge, holi
kirke sall be felawe with aungels. þe[r] aungels lufes holi kirke | right   f. 140ʳᵇ
as it were in ilke of þaire hertes, for holi kirke is not stones and trees,   26
bot rightwis men saules.

'þe second son bitokens þaime þat dispises þe ordinaunce of holi
kirke, and leues in wirshipe of þe world and luste of fleshe. þai leue
vertu and lyues eftir will. Neuirþelesse, at þe ende þai repent þaime,   30
and hase sorowe of þaire misdedes. These men sall be in purgatori
vnto þe time þat þai be reconsiled to Gode bi praiere and oþir gude
dedis. þe þirde bitokens þaime þat rekkes noȝt what commes eftir, so
þat þai mai fullfill þaire will here. And of swilke, askes þare neine
ordirs of aungels right, for þai will noȝt amend þaime with penaunce   35
doinge. And, in þat, þe aungels wirshipes God for his rightwisnes. And
þus is God wirshiped of þe malice of euell men. And þarefore, when
þou sees euell men, haue pite on þaime, and wirshipe God of his

---

1 seruantis] frende, *Lat.* seruis   11 faire] *Quire catchphrase*, in condiciouns,
below   13 shone] shone and   25 þer] þen

rightwise punishinge of þaime. For God suffirs mani þinges be done, as a rightwise domeseman, for þe whilke he is wirshiped bothe in heuen and erthe.' |

Capitulum 25. Wordes of pleininge of þe modir, howe
þe moste innocent lambe Crist Jesu is reklest nowe of
his creature.

The modir pleines hir, and saide, 'I make mi plaint at þe moste innocent lambe was born þis dai, þe whilke couthe alþirbest go; þis dai þat child held his silens þat couthe alþirbeste speke; and þe same moste innocent child, þat neuir sinned, is þis dai circumcised. And þarefore mesemes wrothe, all if I mai noght be wrothe, sen þe gretteste lorde, made a litill barn, is so forgetin and rekleste of his creature.'

Capitulum 26. Wordes of Criste to þe spouse þat
declares þe hie misteri of þe hie Trinite, and howe most
passing sinners getes grace of forgifenes bi contricion
and will of amendinge, and of Cristes answere, howe he
hase merci of all, and of dubill juggement of þaime þat
are to be dampned.

The son saide to þe spouse, 'þou mai aske me, sen þare are thre |
persones in godhede, "Whi are þai noght thre goddes?" I answere þat God is noght bot þat might þat all oþir might commes of, wit and godenes þat all oþir commes of. þe fadir is might and wit, of whome is all oþir, and he of none oþir. þe son is wit and might, euen with þe fadir, neuir departed ne disseuerd fro þe fadir. þe holi goste is might, wit and gudenes of þe fadir and son, euen with bothe, euerlastinge. And so is þare one God and thre persones, for one kinde, one wirkinge, one will, one might, one blis, one powere: and so þare is one þinge in beinge with dist[i]nccion of thre persones, ilkone of þaime all hole in oþir and all in one kinde of godhede, none sonner þan oþir, ne eftir oþir, ne more ne lesse, bot all thre togider, and all one like. þarefore it is wele wretine þat God is merueilous and worthi to be loued of his creatures.'

Bot þan saide Criste, 'Nowe mai I pleine, for I ame litill set bi, for
folke are besi | aboute to do þaire awen wille and noght mine. Bot be

19 þare] *marg.*, þere   28 distinccion] distruccion   34 besi] *catchphrase*, abowte, *below*

þou stabill and meke, and make [þe] noght hie in þi hert if I shewe to
þe þe perels of oþir. Ne tell not þaire names bot it be bedin þe, for [þai
are shewed] noght to oþir senshipe bot to þare bettir and turninge. I
sall shewe þe perels þat þai are in, þat þai mai knawe þe rightwisnes
and þe merci of God. Ne fle þai noght as þai were now demed. For if   5
þe werst man þat liues þis dai wald turne to me with contricion and
will of amendinge, I ame redi to forgife him. And him þat I called
ȝestirdai þe werst man, I will þis dai call him mi frende, if he will
amende him, insomikill þat, if his contricion were lastinge, I will
noght oneli forgife him þe sinne [b]o[t] also þe paine he is worthi for   10
sin; as I sall shewe þe bi ensampill. If þare wer two grete gobetes of
whikesiluir, and þai wald ryn togidir, if þai were so nere togidir þat
þere were bot one point bitwene þaime, ȝet were God of þat might þat
he might let þaime to come togidir. | Right so, if a man were roted so in   f. 141ʳᵇ
þe werkes of þe fende þat he were euen at þe point of perishinge and   15
losinge, ȝit if he will haue contricion and will to amend, he sall haue
merci and forgifnes.

'Bot þou mai aske, þat sen I ame so mercifull, whi I shewe no merci
vnto þe Jewes and painems, som of þe whilke, if þai were taght in mi
faithe, wald die for mi sake. To þis I answere þat I do merci to all   20
pupill, Jewe and paineme, for whosoeuir heris þat þaire faithe is noȝt
trewe ("And þou desire to knawe þe trewe faithe"), or whoso trowes
stedfastli þat þai trowe þat thinke þe whilke is beste, ne þare is none
oþir taght no preched to þaime bot þai do þair vttirmaste might for to
come to þe knawleche of treweth–þe dome of swilke men sall be in þe   25
esier merci.

'For þare is thwo manere of domes, one of þaime þat sall be saued,
and aneoþir of þaime þat sall be dampned. þe dome of þe cristen þat
sall be dampned sall be withoute merci, and þe paine euirlastinge,
with derknes | and euell will firme and obstinate againe God; to þaime   f. 141ᵛᵃ
þat sall be saued, ioi and blis in þe sight of God, festened endelesli in   31
Goddes lufe. Bot þe fals cristen, painems and Jewes sall be excluded
fro þe[r]e compani. For, all if þai had not þe trewe faithe, ȝet,
neuirþelesse, þai had a consciens þat shewed vnto þaime þat þare was
one God, and bot one, whome þai suld haue wirshiped, and whome   35
þai greued and offended. And þai whose will was to haue done gude
and flede sin, þai sall haue les paine þan þe euell cristen. Bot þai sall
noȝt haue comforthe of blis, ne þe sight of God, for þai ressaiued neuir

1 þe] om.   to] to oþir, oþir subpuncted   2-3 þai are shewed] om., Lat. osten-
duntur   10 bot] for   31 of] twice   33 þere] þese

baptime' (and þat, for somþinge withdrewe þaime, þe whilke is hid fro
vs, and alloneli knawen to þe preue dom of God). 'Bot þai þat hase
hertli soght God, and nowþir left ne letted for no trauaile ne drede, ne
losse of gode ne wirshipe of þe werld, bot þaire lettinge passes mannes
5 freelte to ouircome, I sall rewarde þaime as I did to Corneli and cen-
f. 141ᵛᵇ turio eftir | þaire faithe and gude will askes.

'For þare is one maner of vnknawinge and ignorance of malice,
oneoþir of pite and of difficulte. Also þare is one baptime of watir,
oneoþir of blode, and þe þird of perfite will. And to all þese God takes
10 hede, þat knawes all hertes and rewardes ilk man eftir his desert. Ne
þe lest gude dede þat is done passes noght vnrewarded, for I, þat was
born and broght furth withoute biginninge of þe fadir, and in þe ende
ame of times temporalli born, knawes wele þe desertes of all creatures,
and I ȝelde to ilkone as þai are worþi. þarefore þou arte mikill haldin
15 to God þat þou art born of cristen folke and in time of grace. For þere
was mani þat wald haue had and sene þat at is profird to þe cristen, bot
þai gat it noȝt.'

> Capitulum 27. Praiere of þe spouse to oure ladi for
> Rome, and for þe innumerabill multitude of holi
20   martirs þat restes þare, and of thre degrese of perfec-
f. 142ʳᵃ   cion of cristen, and of a vision þat | þe spouse had, to
> whome Criste aperid and declared it.

The spouse saide vnto þe modir, 'O Mary, I beseke þe of helpe, and
I prai þe for þe moste excellent cite of Rome. I se bodeli þat mani
25 kirkes, in þe whilke þe bodis of mani gude saintes restes–som are
bigged, bot þe hertes of þe dwellers and gouernours of þaime are fere
fro God. Gete vnto þaim charite. For I haue herd sai in writinges þat
ilke dai in þe ȝere hase seuen thousand martires. And all if þair saules
had neuir þe lesse blisse in heuen if þair dedis were dispised in erthe,
30 ȝet I prai þe þat more wirship be done to þi saintes and to relikes of
þaime, þat þe pepill hafe more deuocion to þaime.' þe modir answerd
and saide, 'And þou met [þe erthe] ane hundreth fete on brede and
one hundrethe on lengþe, and þou sewe it full of whete; if it grewe so
thike þat þe naile of a finger might noȝt be set bethwene, and ilkea
35 corne broght furth ane hundreth cornes–ȝet were þere mo martires
f. 142ʳᵇ and confessours | in Rome, fro þe time þat Petir come to Rome with

---

32 þe erthe] *om., Lat.* terram

meknes vnto þe time þat Pope Celestine left his see of pride and went
to solitary lifinge againe.

'Of þo martires and confessoures I speke þat prechid þe verrai faith
againe misbeleue, verrai meknes againe pride, and þe whilke died for
suthefastenes of faithe, or elles were in gude will for to die. Petir and 5
oþire were so brinninge in charite þat þai wald gladli haue died for
euirilke man if þai had might. Neuirþelesse, þai kepid þaimeselfe fro
reproue of þaime þat þai prechid vnto, for þai lufed bettir hele of
saules þan þaire awen life or wirshipe. And þarefore þai ware wele
avised, and went furth warli and preuali for to win mo saules. And ȝet 10
were noȝt all gude bitwene Petir and Celestine, ne all euell, bot þare
ware thre diuers degrese: þat menes, gude, bettir and best.

'In þe first degre were þai þat thoght þus: "We trowe all þinge þat
holi kirke biddes. We will begille no man, bot þat we haue dissaiued
we will amend it. And we desire of all | oure hert to serue God." And f. 142ᵛᵃ
like vnto þese in þe time of Romille were þe founders of Rome, þe 16
whilke thoght þus eftir þe faithe þat þai had: "We vndirstand and
takes knawlech of creatures þat þare is one God, maker of all þinge.
Him we will loue bifore all oþir þinges." And mani oþir thoght þus:
"We haue herd of þe Ebrews þat þe verrai God shewed him to þaime 20
bi opin miracles. And þarefore, if we knawe in whame we might
ground vs, we wald gladli do þe best and serue God." All þese were as
in þe first degre. (And þai þat hase resaiued þe faith, and in wedlake
and oþir gude disposicion dwelles þerein ai, bi ordinance of holi kirke,
þai are in þe positife degre.) 25

'Bot þai þat leues all þaire awen will and worldli gudes for Goddes
sake, and hase shewed, to oþir, gude ensampill of lifynge with wordes
and werkes, and set bi noþinge so mikill as Criste, þai ware in þe comparatife degre. And þai þat gaue þaire bodies to þe dede for þe loue of
God were in þe superlatife degre. Bot where sall we finde in þese 30
degrese nowe moste feruent charite? | Forsothe, knightes, doctoures f. 142ᵛᵇ
and religious are halden to be in þe comparatife and superlatife
degrees, for þare is no life more straite þan knigh[th]ed, if it be kept
eftir þe first ordinance. For if a monke sall were a coule, a knight sall
were a haburgeon þat is mikill harder. A monke sall fight agains his 35
fleshe, bot a knight sall fight againe armed enemis. And if a monke
make abstinence, a knight liues in continuall drede of his life. þarefore
knighthede of cristen men were noȝt ordainede for worldli wirship
and couetise, bot for to strenghe þe treuthe and sprede obrode verrai

9 wirshipe] wirshiped   33 knighthed] knighed

faithe. þarefor knighthed and religion suld be in þe comparatife degre
and superlatife degrees. Bot all grese nowe hase made apostasie fro þe
state of þaire first ordinance, for charite is turned into couetise. For if
a man profird now a florene þat þai suld hald þaire tunges, þai had
5 leuir lat þe treuthe perishe or þai wald lose a florene.'

þan saide þe spouse, 'I sawe mani ȝerdes and gardins on þe erthe, |
f. 143ʳᵃ and mani roses and lelis amange þaime. And in a brode place of þe
erthe I sawe a felde of ane hondreth stepis of lengþe, and as mani on
brede. In ilke stepis was sawen cornes of whete, and ilke corn had ane
10 houndrethfald froyte. Eftir þis I harde a voice sai, "Rome, Rome, þi
walles are broken, þi ȝates are withoute kepinge, þi vessell are [s]old,
þi wine, þi sacrifice, þi encens are brente. þarefore þare commes
noþinge oute of þe holi place þat is of swete sauoure." '

þan saide Criste vnto his spouse, 'þe erthe þat þou sawe bitokens
15 euirilkea place where nowe is cristen mennes faithe. þe gardins
bitokens   þe   places   where   holi   saintes   toke   þaire   crownes.
Neuirþelesse, amange þe panems, and in Cherusalem, were mani
chosin to God, þe whilke places are noȝt nowe shewed to þe. þe feld
of one hundreth fete bitokens Rome, for þare are als ʽmaniʹ martirs in
20 Rome as in a grete parti of þe werld eftirward, for þat place is specialli
chosin to þe loue of God. þe whete þat þou sawe bitokens þaim þat bi
f. 143ʳᵇ chastissinge of þaire | fleshe, or contrision of innocent lifinge, are
comen to heuen. þe roses bitokens þe martirs made rede with
shedinge of þaire awen blode. þe lillis bitokens confessoures þat had
25 and teched þe faithe.

'Bot nowe mai I speke to Rome as þe prophet spake to Jerusalem
"þat sometime dwelled in rightwisenes, and þe princes þareof luffed
pees." Bot nowe it is turned to rusti colu[r]e, and þe princes of it are
menslaers. Wald God, Rome, þat þou knewe þi daies. þan suld þou
30 morn and noght be glad. Sometime was Rome wele colourde with rede
blode of martires, and set togidir with þe bones of saintes. Now are
Rome ȝates desolate, for þe kepers are all bowed to couetise. þe walles
are pute done, for þai take no hede of perishinge of mennes saules; bot
þe clergi and þe pepill, þat are þe walles, is sparpled aboute [bi] lust
35 and likinge of fleshe. þe vessels, þat menes þe sacramentes, are nowe
dispised and set at noȝt, for þai are gifen for worldli fauour and coue-
f. 143ᵛᵃ tise. þe auteres are desolate, for þai þat suld occupi þaime are | voide of
charite. And all if þai haue God in þaire handes, þe hert ne þe lufe is

---

11 sold] fowled, *Lat.* venduntur   28 colure] coluie   30 Rome] Rome no,
superior mark to no   34 bi] *om.*

noȝt to him, for it is filled with couetise. And þe holi place, þe whilke
bitokens desire of þe sight of God and his blis, is nowe turned to luste
and vanite of þe world.

'And so is Rome nowe as þou hase sene, þe auters desolate, for
nowe it is spendid in þe tauerns þat suld haue bene spendid on þe 5
pore and to þe wirship of God. Neuirþelesse, wit þou wele þat fro
Petres time þat was so meke vnto þe time þat Boniface stied vp into þe
[se]te of pride, saules withoute nowmbir went to heuen. And ȝet Rome
is noȝt withoute some þat lufes God. And if þai had helpe þai suld crie
to God, and he suld haue merci.' 10

Capitulum 28. Informacion of þe maiden to þe spouse
of þe maner 'of' lufe, and of foure citees in þe whilk is
founden foure manere of charitees: þe whilke of þese
sall propirli be called perfite charite.

The modir saide vnto þe spouse, '[Wheþir] lufes þou me?' Sho 15
answerde, 'Ladi, teche | me to lufe, for mi saule is filed with fals lufe f. 143ᵛᵇ
and begiled with venom, þat it kannoȝt knawe trewe lufe.' þan saide
þe modir, 'I sall teche þe. þare is foure citees, in þe whilke is foure
maner of charites. Neuirþelesse, all suld not be called charitees, for
þare is no charite propirli bot where God and mannes saule are 20
confedered in verrai anehede of vertu. þe first is þe cite of preuinge,
þat man take hede of his awen freelte, þat he gete him vertu and come
vnto blis. Bot in þis cite is inordinate lufe, when þe fleshe is loued
more þan þe saule and temporall gude more þan gosteli, vice
wirship[ed]—and vertu dispised—when it is more swete to a man þan 25
þe blisse of heuen, when a man [þat] sall die is more wirshiped þan
God. þe secound is þe cite of clennes, where filth of þe saule is
weshen awai. It was likinge to God to ordein swilke places, in þe
whilke þai þat suld be crowned suld be clensed of þat at þai had trespassed. In þis cite is fonden lufe, bot noȝt perfite, for 30

[Loss of leaf containing end of III. 28, beginning of III.
29: missing material supplied from Ju.] |

God is louyd by hope of captiuite to be losenyd, but not of feruent f. 95ʳ
affeccion, for þe irkesumness and bittirness of satisfaccion of synne.

8 sete] cite, *Lat.* sedem   15 wheþir] for, *Lat.* numquid   lufes þou] *trsp.*
21 confedered] confededered   25 wirshiped] wirship   26 þat] *om., Lat.*
moriturus

The iiide cety is the cety of sorow, where helle is. In þat is foundin
loue of al malis and onclennesse, alle invie and obduracion. In þat
cyte, God regnys by his ordinat rightwosness and by dew mesure of
peynes and be refreynyng of malice. Like as some ar dampned for
5 more and somme for lesse, so þer peynes and rewardes ar ordeyned.
Alþough all þat be dampned ar sperin in derkenes, ȝit alle are not in
oon maner of derkenesse. Derkness differis fro derkness; hogsumness
f. 95ᵛ fro hogsumness; hete fro hete. God has disposid | in rightwosness and
mercy þat thei shal nat be ponyschid alike in helle. They þat has
10 synned of wilfulness and of fre[y]elness, and of ony odir wise, þey shal
be ponyschid after þer synne, or elles, but yf God disposid al thinges
in number and mesure, the dewle wold neuer haue mesure in
ponysching. The iiiite cite is of ioye. In þat is perfit loue, and ordinat,
for non thinge is desirid but God and for God. þat þou may come to
15 þe perfeccion of this cite, the behouys to haue a iiii-fold cherite: þat is
to sey, ordinat, clene, trewe, and perfite. Ordinat cherite is where the
body is lovyd alonly to sustinauns, the word to no superfluite, thi
neyboure for God, þin frend for clennes of liff, þin enmy for þe reward
of God. Clene cherite is, by þe wheche synne is not louyd with vertu,
20 be the whech shrewd custom is contempned. Verry loue is, whan God
is lovyd with all herte and will, whan the honour and dred of God is
thought before in all dedis, whan of trust of good werkis non sinne is
doon, whan ony man wisly mesuris himself þat he faile nat of ouyr-
mech hete, whan of cowardness and ignorauns [he] bowys not to
25 synne. Parfitt cherite is, whan non thinge is so swete to man as God.
þis beginnys in þis present liff, and is endid in heuen. þerfore loue þis
good, perfite cherite, for he þat has it not xal be purgid. For, like as is
oon God, so is oon feith, on bapteme, oon perfeccion of ioye and
reward. þerfore he þat desiris to come to oon God, he must haue oon
30 wil and oon cherite with oon God. þerfore thei are wrecchis þat thus
seys, "Yt is inow yf I be þe leste in heuen. I will not be a perfitt man." O
onwigthty thinkyng. How may þer be an onperfite man, whereas alle
are perfite, som of innocensy of liff, sum of innocencye of childhod,
and som of feyth and good wil?'

35 [III. 29] A lovinge of þe spouse to þe virgine, conteyning the similitude of Salomon temple, and godhed vnyte with manhed, and how
prestis templis ar peynted with vanyte.

'Blissid be þu, Mary, the modir of God, the tempel of Salomon,
whos walles were gilte, hos roff was shinyng, and þe pament made

10 freyelness] frethelness   22 of¹] *partially erased*   24 he] *om.*

with precious stonys. All inward thingis are redolent and delectabil to
see. Thou art like Salomon tempel in all manerys: in þe whech very
Salomon sat. So þu, blissid maydin, art the temple of þat Salomon þe
wh[e]che made pees betwen God and man, þe wheche reconsilid
synneris and gaff liff to ded men. Thin liff was the pament, and besi 5
hauntyng of vertuys. þer wantid in þe no one honeste, for all was stabil
in the, all thinge meke, all thinke deuoute and perfite. The wallis
of þe tempil was iiii-cornerid, for þu was neuir troblid with repreff,
neuer prowde of worshipp, neuir inquiete by inpaciens, nothinge
desiringe but honoure and loue of God.   10

[Cl continues]

[þe image] of þe tempill was hetinge of þe holy goste, þat lift vp þi   f. 144ra
saule so mikill þat þare was no vertu bot it was fuller in þe, and perfiter
þan in any oþir creature. In þi tempill rested Goddes son, when with
grete swetnes to all þi parties he was man in þe. Blissed þe þou Mari,
in whome grete Gode is made a litill childe, and he þat is euirlastinge is 15
in þe made man and creature. And þarefore, ladi, for þou arte moste
mighti and moste milde, I prai þe luke to me and haue merci on me.
þou art modir of Salomon, bot noȝt of him þat was Dauid son, bot of
him þat was Dauid lord and fadir. Also, þe child sall gladli here þe
modir. And þarefore aske of þi son þat slepid in þe, þat he wake so   20
with me þat no likinge of sinne prike me, bot þat I haue a stabill contricion for trespase. þe loue of þe worlde be it dede in me, lastinge
paciens and fructuose penance be ai in me. I haue not of vertu for me
bot one worde: þat is, "Mari, haue merci one me"; for mi tempill is
contrari | to þine. For mine is dirke with vices, claide with lichery, f. 144rb
rotin with wormes of coueitise, vnstabill for pride, febill for vanite of 26
þe worlde.'

þe modir þan answerde and saide, 'Blissed be God, þat hase gifen
þis grace to þi hert to bringe furth þis gretinge to me, þat þou might
vndirstand what gudenes is in God and what swetenes. Bot whi   30
likkens þou me to þe tempill of Salomon, sen I ame his modir þat noȝt
had begininge, ne sall haue endinge, a[s] it is saide, þat he nawþir hase
fadir ne modir: þat is, Melchesedech? He was a preste, and to a
preste falles a tempill, and I ame modir to þe soueraine preste, and

---

4 wheche¹] whche   11 þe image] *om., Lat.* picture   19 þe²] *twice, first with*
superior cancellation mark   22 dede] dedede   32 begininge] begiminge   as]
þat

maidene. I am modir of kinge Salamon, and of þe pesibill preste. Mi son in mi tempill cled him with gosteli prestes cloþinge, in þe whilke he made sacrifice for þe world. In þe kinges cite was he crowned with a full sharpe crowne, and withoute þe cite, as a campion, he entird þe
5　feld and had þe victory. Bot nowe I mai pleine, for mi son is forgetin of

f. 144ᵛᵃ | prestes and kinges. Kinges hase þaire ioi in þaire grete palais, of grete coste and wirship of þe worlde. Prestes are proude of þaire gudes and possessions. Bot [als] one tempill painted with gold said bifore, [so] are þe tempils of prestis painted with vanite and coriouste of þe
10　worlde. Simoni is as kinge. þe arke of testament is withdrawen; þe lanterns of vertu are done oute; þe borde of deuocion is desolate.'

þan saide þe spouse, 'Modir of merci, haue merci one þaime and prai for þaime.' þe modir saide, 'Fro þe biginninge, God hase so loued his, þat noȝt alloneli þai are herd of þaire praiere for þaimselfe, bot
15　oþir are also herd and feli[s] praier of þaime. And, þat praiere be herd for oþir, are two þinges nedefull: þat þai be in will to leue þaire sinne, and to trauaile in gude liuinge. To all þat hase þere two sall mi praier profite.'

f. 144ᵛᵇ
21

Capitulum 30. Wordes of Saint Agnes to þe spouse how
sho sall lufe þe modir vndir figure of a floure, | and
howe þe glorious maiden declare[s] Goddes pite againe
vnkindenes of vs and euell.

Saint Agnes saide vnto þe spouse, 'Doghtir, loue þe modir of merci. Sho is like to a floure withoute fadinge, whose figure is like to a swerde
25　þat hase two sharpe sides and one smale point. And þis floure passes oþir, bothe in lengþe and brede. So Mari is þe floure of floures þat grewe in þe vaile of mekenes, as it were in þe vaile of Nazareth. Bot sho sprede vnto Liban, for scho passes all pure creatures in wirship and powere.

30　'Sho had two sharp sides, þat was hertli sorowe in passione and deinge of hir son, and stedfast standinge agains þe deuell. Swilke sorowe it was as he prophecied þat saide, "þare sall passe a sharpe swerde", for so mani strokes scho suffird to hir hert as hir son had woundes. Also þis ladis merci had a grete brede, for it spred ouir þe

f. 145ʳᵃ world, for sho | was so mercif[u]ll þat sho had leuer suffir all desesse þat
36　sho might or mannes saule had perished. And nowe, as sho is with hir

3 for] fro　　8 als] *om.*　　gold] gold is　　so] *om.*　　15 felis] felid
21 declares] declare　　35 mercifull] mercifill

son in blis, sho forgetes noȝt hir merci, bot spredis it ouir all. And right as þe son lightenes and warmes abowen and binethe, right so þare is none so euell, þat will aske merci, bot he sall finde swetenes in Mari. Also, sho had a small pointe. þat was meknes, þat sho plesed God with, when sho saide vnto þe angell þat sho was Goddes handmaiden. 5 And ȝet sho was chosen to be ladi bi þis mekenes; sho consaiued Goddes son, and is nowe in þe hier trone, for sho loued God. þarefore wende furth and hals þe modir of merci, for now sho commes.'

þan aperid Mari and saide, 'Agnes, þou hase nowe saide þe sub-stantife. Sai now þe adiectiue.' þan answerde Agnes and saide, 'If I sai 10 fairest and moste vertuose wordes, þat accordes to none so wele as to þe, þe whilke art modir of hele.' þan saide þe modir to Agnes, 'þou hase saide | sothe, for I ame most miȝti, pure creature. And to þi sub- f. 145rb stantiue I sall put one adiectiue. þou hase sorow þat þis is þe comon worde amange men: "Liue we eftir oure luste, for God will be lightli 15 plesid; take we oure likinge in þe world, for it was made for men." Trewli, doghtir, þis spekinge commis noȝt of charite, ne it drawes noȝt to charite. And ȝit God forgetis noght his charite, bot shewes euir pite agains man vnkindnes. He is like to a smith, þat makes a grete werke. Somtime he hetis his iren, and somtime he lattis it be cold. 20

'So God, þat made all þe werld of noȝt, shewed his charite to Adam and þaime þat com of him, bot þai w[e]x cold, and dede mani greuouse sinnes. And þarefore, when merci was shewed and benigne warneninge went tofor, God shewed his rightwisnes in diluui, þat was called Noye flude. Eftir þe whilke, he made [t]rette with Abraham and 25 shewed him tokens of his loue. He broght furth his progeni in tokens and meraclis, and gaue þe pupill | lawe of his awen m[ou]th, and con- f. 145va fermed his biddinges and commandmentes with open tokens. And ȝet þe pupill wex cold againe, to so grete wodenes þat þai wirshiped fals goddes. Bot ȝet God, for to helpe his pupill, he sent his awen son to 30 shewe þat mekenes is þe verrai wai vnto heuen. Bot nowe es he forgetin of mani folke: and ȝet shewes he his merci. For, firste, he sent þe flode called diluuy. And sithen he did þe childir of Israel abide fourti ȝere befor he wald bringe þaime into lande of biheste—and he might haue broght þam in fourti daies if he had wald: and þat 35 tareynge was to shewe þaire vnkindnes and his rightwisnes.

'Bot if þare be ani þat þinkes, "Whi turmentes God his pupill? And whi es þe paine euirlastynge, sin a mannes life is not euirlastinge?" þis

22 wex] wax   mani] mani 'a'   25 trette] frette, *Lat.* fedus   27 mouth] might, *Lat.* ore

is grete presumpsion to aske. For God is euirlastinge, þarefore is his rightwisnes and his rewarde euirlastinge. For, had he noȝt shewed his rightwisnes in þe aungels þat trespassed, howe suld his right haue bene knawen? And, bot he might haue made man, and eftir haue

f. 145ᵛᵇ deliuerde him | of disese, howe suld his merci haue bene knawen? His
6 werkes is euirlastinge, for he is euirlastinge. He knawes all þat is, was and sall be. And þarefore, mi frendes suld abide in mi lufe, and noght be disesed, all if þai se worldli men haue welefare in þis world. For God is a nobill lawnder, þat puttes a clothe þat is noȝt clene in swilke
10 place of þe water whare, thrugh mouinge of þe water, it mai be clenner and whitter, and ȝete sho takes heede þat þe watir drowne noȝt þe clothe. So God suffirs þaim þat he loues in þis werld be in disese of tribulacion and pouert, þat þai be clenner and more abill to blisse. And ȝit he kepis þaime, þat nowþir to grete disese ne heuenes fordo
15 þaime. And þarefore oft he comfortes þaime.'

Capitulum 31. Wordes of Criste to þe spouse, techinge þe best ensampill of a leche and a kinge, and how Criste is vndirstanden bi þe leche, and howe oft times, þai þat men wene is dampned are saued, and againewarde.

f. 146ʳᵃ   þe son saide vnto þe spouse, 'þare come a | leche, of fer cuntre and
21 vnknawen, vnto a contre where þe kinge gouernd naw[t] bot he was rewled bi oþir and he was gouernd, for his hert was as þe hert of one hare. And þare he semed, in his trone, as he had bene a crowned as. þe pupill of þe realme gaue þame to glutery, and forgat right and honeste,
25 and hated all þat counseld þaime to þe gude. þan þis leche presentid himselfe to þe kinge and saide þat he was of a land of likinge, and come for to see seknes of men. þe kinge had woundir of his chere and of his wordis, and saide vnto him, "I had two men in prisson, and ȝete I haue þe same men, þat sall tomorn be dede and heded. One of þaime
30 mai vnnethes drawe his brethe. þe oþir is stronnger and fatter. Go to þaime into prisson, and avise þe, of þaire chere, whilke of þaime is of þe bettir compleccion."

'And when he had sene þaime, he saide to þe kinge, "þe man þat þou sese is stronge is more like to dede and to die, ne he mai noȝt liue.

f. 146ʳᵇ Bot I haue gode hope of þe oþir man, þat he sall liue." þan | saide þe
36 kinge, "Wharebi wote and knawes þou þat?" þe lech answerde, "For he is full of euell humors and winde, ne he mai noȝt be heled. Bot þe

14 fordo] for to do   21 nawt] nawþir

toþir is anentisht, and with gudnes of aire he mai be heled." þe kinge saide, "I sall call þe grete men and þe wise of mi realme, þat þai mai se þi wit, and þou mai be praised of þaime." þe lech saide, "Nai, do noȝt so, for I knawe wele þat þi pupill is coueitouse of vaineglorie, and þai will haue envye at me. And þarefore I will shewe in a priue place bitwene þe and me þat I can, for I coueit noȝt opinli to shewe mi wit bot in priuete. And it is noȝt ȝit time of helinge while þe sone be in his miȝt in þe middai, and þe winde be at þe southe." þan saide þe kinge, "Howe mai þis be in mi land, where þe sone shinnes noȝt commonli, and þe winde is comonli in þe northe? What suld þi witt serue þe of? I see þou hase wordes ynowe."

'þan saide þe leche, "A wise man suld noȝt be sodaine. Bot for I will noȝt þat þou sai þat I ame vnkinde, and haue me in suspecion, gife me þere two men at mi liste,| and I sall lede þaime to þe ende of þi realme, whare þe aire is holesome and acordinge, and þan sall þou wit þat mi wordes are sothe, and what þai are worthe." þan saide þe kinge, "We are occupied in oþir þinges and more profitabill. We will noȝt be lettid for þi seruise, þat will do vs bot litill gude. We haue oure liste in þat at we see, and þat hald we. We take no heede to þat at is to com. Neuirþelesse, take þou þare two men, and if þou shewe any grete þinge in þaime, we sall wiriship þe, and make oþir to wirishipe þe." þan tuke he þe two men, and had þaime to gude aire, bot þe one died, and þe oþir was refreshed and leuid.

'This lech am I, þat wald hele man. I send mi wordes into þe world, and amange oþir I see two seke men, to whome I shewed mi rightwisnes and mi merci. On, as I shewed, was preuali þe fendes for euir, and neuirþelesse him semed outeward gude, and his werkes semed rightwis. þe toþir was opinli euill, bot abill to be | helid, all if men demed him opinli euell. Bot right as þe deuell bi litill entird vpon him, so bi litill and litill he was putt fro him, þat when he come to þe dome with him, þe domesman saide, "þou hase clensed him and windowed him as if he had bene whete. Nowe langes he to me, for þe confession and knawinge of his trespas. Wende awai þarefore fro him. And o, þou blissed saule, come to me and see my ioy and blisse with þine gosteli yen."

'And þan he saide to þe oþir saule, "For þare was in þe no trewe faithe, and þou shewed þe as þou had bene treue, þarefore sall þou noȝt haue þe mede of þame þat were trewe. þou asked whi þat I wald dye for þe, and whi þat I mekid me so lawe for þe. þarefore I answere to þe

27 semed²] semed wer

nowe þat þe faithe of holi kirke is trewe, þe whilke drawes saules vpwarde to heuen. And mi passion and mi blode ledis þaime bothe to

f. 147ra heuen, and mi passion to God. þarefore thine vntreuthe and | þi vaine loue puttis þe downe to noght in regarde of gosteli þinges þat are euir-

5 lastinge." Bot þat þe fende went noȝt oute, þat all men sawe, was for þis werld is a litill foule cote in rewarde of þe dwellinge place of God; and þarefore he went so[k]ingli as he com inne.'

Capitulum 32. Wordes of þe maiden to þe spouse shewinge in figure howe God chase hir amange oþir to be
10 modir and þe hauene of heele.

The modir saide vnto þe spouse, 'A man fande a magnete, þe whilke he tuke vp with his awen hande and kepid it in his tresori. And be þat he broght þe ship vnto a sekir hauen. On þe same wise mi son soght preciouse stones–þat menes, his saintes–bot he chese me for to be his

15 modir, þat he might bringe men bi me to þe hauen of heuen. For right as þe magnete drawes þe yren, so I drawe hard hertes vnto God. þarefore be þou noȝt turbled if somtime þi hert be hard, for it is fore þi mor blisse.'

f. 147rb Capitulum 33. Wordes of þe son to þe spouse | bi þe
20 whilke he shewes howe he demis eftir a man is
in[n]eward and noght eftir þat he is outewarde bi
ensampill.

The son saide to þe spouse, 'þou hase wondir of two men. One was as a square stone, þe second as a pilgrim of Jerusalem, and nawþir com

25 to þat at þou wende. þe first to whame þou was sent was a square stone, stalworth in his awen conceites, bot somwhat dowtinge as Thomas. He tasted þe wine, bot he dranke noȝt of it. þe secound bitokens him þat is in habit of religiouse profession. Bot in maners and condicions he is apostata. He is in dignite a preste, bot he is seruant of

30 syn. He is in nam a pilgrime, bot in his entent he wauers aboute, for he went oute agains obediens and statutes of hali kirke, and he is filed with heresi, insomekill þat he trowes þat þe bishope þe whilke is to come sall restore all þinges as it is shewed bi his writinge. And

3 and²] *Quire catchphrase*, þi vaine, *below*   7 sokingli] ?sobingli   15 men
bi] *twice*, bi men *cancelled*   18 mor] modir, *Lat.* maiorem   21 inneward]
inreward   25 first] first come, come *cancelled*

þarefore he sall die sodainli, and, bot he be ware, he sall be felawe to
þe fadir of lesinges. And þarefore þou sall noȝt be disesed, | all if som   f. 147ᵛᵃ
þinges be saide derkli, or elles for þat þe whilke is saide falles noȝt
eftir þine entent. For Goddes wordes mai be vndirstanden on diuers
maner, and I sall shewe to þe when it sall fall, for I ame verrai God of   5
Ierusalem, and I will be to þe felawe of þine iourne.'

Capitulum 34. Wordes of þe modir to þe doghtir in
figure, how þe saule is tokend bi a ringe, þe bodi in
clothe, and howe þe saule awe to be purified bi discrecion and þe bodi bi discrete abstinence.   10

The modir saide, 'Yf þare be a ringe gifen to one, and it be straite
vpon þe finger and þou aske counsell at þi enemy, he will bid þe cut þi
fingir and make it mete to þe ringe. Bot þi frende will counsell þat þou
make þe ringe more with one hamir. Also, if þou suld clense a lordes
drinke throwe a cloute, and þou asked counsell of þine enemye, he   15
wald bid þe cut of all þat were foule of þi clothe. Bot þi frende wald
bid þe weshe it and make it clene, and so drawe þe drinke þarthrugh.
So suld it be in goste|li þinges. Bi þe ringe is vndirstandin þe saule and   f. 147ᵛᵇ
bi þe clothe þe bodi. þe saule þat suld be on þe finger, of gold, large
with þe hamir of discrecion; þe bodi suld noȝt be slaine bot be clensed   20
with abstinence, þat þe wordes of God mai go throw it.'

To þe wirshipe of one God in trinite of persones, and of þe
blissedest maiden Mari, modir to þe fadirs son of blisse, þus endes þe
þirde buke of heuenli reuelacions graciousli shewed to gloriouse
Bride.   25

6 iourne] *superfluous mark of contraction above, reading* ioururne   8 saule] saules
13 mete] mete it meke, it meke *cancelled*   20 bodi] bodi þat, þat *cancelled*
23 Mari] Mairi

[BOOK FOUR]

In full meke traiste of þe fadirs might, þe sonnes wisdome and þe holi
gostes gudenes to gife graciousli helpe in perseuerans, here biginnes
þe ferthe buke of heuenli reuelacions, bi þe gude will of oure moste
gloriouse God, his most graciouse modir, and oþir blissed saintes
5 shewed to saint Bride.

Primum capitulum. Wordes of saint [Ion þe] ewangeliste to þe spouse, howe rewarde is ordeinede for ilke
werke, and howe þe Bibill is moste ʻexcellentʼ. |

f. 148ra   There apperyd to þe spowse a persone, whose here semed [kut]te
10 abowte wyth reproue. Hys body was all naked and anoynted wyth oyle.
Bote he had no scham of hys nakednes, bot he sayd to þe spowse, ʻHoly
write sais þat þare sall no gude dede be vnrewarded. þis writynge þat
ȝe call holi is þe Bibill, þe whilke shynes wyth vs as þe sonne, and is
bryghter þan gold. It brynges forth more þane one hundrethfolde
15 froyte. As gold passes all oþir metalles, so it passes all oþir wrytynges,
for in it is taght and wirschipped verray God. þere ar þe dedes of
patriarkes broght vnto mynde, and þe visions of profetes ar schewed
þare. And for no werk is wythouten rewarde, here what I say.
      ʻThis kynge is a traitoure of saules, a wastoure of riches and a
20 robber. Ryght as þere is no wers traytoure þan he þat bytraies his
frende þat traistes hym, so þis man has betraysede, louynge wrang-
wysly euell men, in harmynge and doynge wronge to þe gude men,
ouirpassynge by dissimulacion, and noȝt chastisynge defawtes.
f. 148rb   ʻþe commonalte of his land lay, as it had | bene, in hys bosom, þe
25 qwylke he betraysed euel and spoyled. For he suffirde some wyth
wronge take oþir mennes gude, and he put heuy charges on oþir, and
wold noȝt amend wronges, and he was slawe in doynge of rightwisnes.
Also, þere is no wers theef þan he þat stelis fro hys maistir, þe whilke
gifes hym þe keis and puttes all in his kepyng. So þis kyng takes þe keis
30 of power and honour of God, bot he wastes þe gudes þat God sent in
þam.
      ʻþarfor, bycause he lefte somwhat for my lufe þat hym lyked, I coun-
sell hym thre thynges. First, þat as he, of whame mynd is in þe

4 modir] god modir   6 Ion þe] *om.*, *Lat.* Johonnis (*sic*)   8 excellent] *Quire*
catchphrase   9 kutte] owte, *Lat.* circumcisi

gospelle, þe whilke left hogges mete and come agayne to his fadir, so
he dispyse riches and wirschipes of þe worlde, þe whilke, in rewarde
of euirlastynge godes, are bot hoges mete, and wyth mekenes and
deuocion come agayne to hys fadir God. þe secunde is þat he suffir þe
dede bery þe dede, and folow he þe hard and strayte way of Cristes 5
sufferaunce. þe third: þat he leue þe heuy birden of syn, and go þat
wai þe whilke in þe bygynnynge is hard, and gladsome in þe ende.

'And þou þat sese me, vndirstande wele þat I am he þe whilke
perfytely hase | knawen þe golden scripture. And throw knawynge f. 148ᵛᵃ
þarof, I eked itt. I was made naked schamefulli. Bot for I suffird it 10
paciently, God cled my soule wyth clethynge of euirlastynge life. I was
anoynted wyth oyle. And þarfor I haue ioy þat may noȝt be tald. And,
eftir þe modir of mercy, I dyed þe esiest dede, for I was made custos
and kepar of Goddes modir. My body is in place of moste riste, quiet
and sekirnes.' 15

Capitulum 2. A merueylouse and notabill visione of þe
spowse, þe whilke Gode hymselfe expownes to hir, in
þe [whilke] he lykkenes þe cristen, þe paynems and also
þe frendes of Gode.

þe spowse saw, as it had bene, two balanses standynge besyde þe 20
erth. And þe heght of þame towchid þe clowdes, and þe serkles of
þame perched þe heuene. In þe firste balaunce was a fische, and þe
skales war scharpe as a rasoure. His sight was venomous as þe basiliske. He had a mowthe as a vnicorn þat ȝett oute venome. His eres
war scharpe as a spere and peses of iren. In þe secund balaunce was 25
oneoþir beste þat had a skyne as hard as flynte, a gret mouth | ȝetynge f. 148ᵛᵇ
oute brynnynge flammes of fire, browes as scharp as a swerde, hard
eres, oute of whome come moste scharp arrowes as it had bene oute of
a stronge bente bow. And eftir þis apered thre companys in þe erthe.
þe firste was litill, þe second was lesse, þe third was leste. And þare 30
come a voys fro heuen þat said to þaime, 'O my frendes, I thirst full
sore þe herte of þis wondirfull beste, yf þar be any þat wald for charyte
gife it to me. Also, I desire hertly þe blode of þis fische, yf þar war any
þat wald brynge it to me.'

And answerd a voys, as it had bene of all þe firste company byhalfe, 35
and saide, 'O þou lord, maker of all thynge, how may we brynge vnto
þe þe hert of ȝone best, sen hys skyn is harder þan þe flynt? And if we

6 and] and þai, þai *subpuncted*   18 whilke] *om.*   19 þe] *twice*

come nere to hym, we sall be brynt wyth flame of fire þat comes oute of
hys mouthe. If we se his eyn, we sall be periste wyth sparkes of arrowes
þat comes oute of his eyn. And ʒitt, if any hope were to haue þe beste,

f. 149ra who suld wyn þe fische þat has skales scharper þan spere | poyntes?

5 His eyn blyndes vs. His mowth ʒettis oute dedely venom.' And þane
answerd a voys and said, 'Frendes, þe best and þe fische semis not
abill to be ouircomyn of ʒou. Bot ʒit he may throw helpe of þat is
almiʒti. And to hym þat will assay, I wyll gyue wytt and strengis, and,
to hym þat makes hym redy to dye for me, I sall gyfe hym myselfe in

10 rewarde.' þan said þe firste company, 'Fadir, þou arte gyfer of all
gude. We ar maste of þe and of þi werke. We sall gladly gyfe oure hert
for þi wirschipe. Oþir þinges þat ar wythoute oure bodi we sall
ordayne and dispose to þe sustenance of oure flesch. And, for it semes
to vs þat dede of body is hard, and bodely seknes is heuy, and we haue

15 litill connynge, þarfor gouern vs wythin and wythoute, and take gudely
þat we ofir to þe, and ʒelde vs agayne as þe likes.'

þan saide þe second company, 'We knaw oure febilnes and we take
hede of þe vanite and vnstabilnes of þe world. And þarfor we sall

f. 149rb gladly gyfe þe oure herte, and oure will we sall putt into þese mennes |

20 handes, and we wyll noʒt haue of þe worlde.' þane said þe third company, 'Lord, we sall gyfe þe oure herte, and we ar redy to dye for þe.
þou gyfe vs witt, and we sall seke þe way to fynd þe hert of þe beste.'

þan com þar a voys from heuene and said, 'Frend, if þou wald fynd
þe hert of þe best, pers þi handes in þe myddes wyth a persure. þane

25 take þe eyeliddes or þe browes of þe whale, and lay to þi eyliddes wyth
stronge pike, and take a pese of steel, and lay it to þi hert, so þat þe
moste brede þerof be nerreste to þi herte. And close þi mouth, and
hald in þi breth, and so wend bo[l]dely agaynes þe beste. And when þu
arte comyn to itt, take his eres in þi handes and þe arrowes sall noʒt

30 dissese þe. þan blaw on þe beste wyth all þi breth, and þe flawmes þat
comes fro his mouth sall noʒt harm þe, bot þai sall turne agayne on þe
beste and bren itt. Bot bewar of þe scharpe poyntes of þe swerdes þat
comes oute fro þe bestes eyn, and kepe þi eyn wele wyth þe liddes of

f. 149va þe qwalles eyn. And take þe pese of steele, and pers | þe hardnes of þe

35 skyne of þe beste. And if þe hardenes breke, þan sall þe herte be
wythine. And if it will noʒt breke, bot þe beste happely disseses and
hurtes þe man, þan sall I hele hym, and, if he be dede, to gyue to hym
life agayne.

8 assay] *twice*   14 bodely] bodely thynges   27 be nerreste] *twice, first sub-*
puncted   28 boldely] bodeli, *Lat.* audacter

'Also, he þat wald brynge me þe fische, he suld go to þe seesyde, and
haue ane nette in hys handes, made noȝt of thredes, of gud bras, and
he sall go into þe watir vp to þe knees, and festyn hys fete where þar is
hard grauel wythowte clay. þane sall he couer þat eye þe whilke is to
þe fischwarde. He sall take on his arme a sheld of steel for bytynge of   5
þe fische. þane sall he sprede his nett ouer þe fische warly, for cuttyng
þarof. And if he fele þe fische, he sall warly streche þe nete oute
abowen hym. And if he hald his net ouer [h]yme ten owres þe fische
sall dye, and so sall he brynge it to land. And þan sall he loke on it with
þe eye þat he closed byfor, and he sall opyn itt on þe bakesyde, where 10
moste is of þe blode. Bot ȝitt if it so be þat þe fische wyn away fro þe
man and hurte hym, I am mighti to hele hym, and he sall noȝt haue
losse of hys trauel.'

þan said God, 'þese tua balauns betokens as mikel as | if a man   f. 149vb
saide, "Spare and suffir. Abyde, and haue mercy." For, as a man þat 15
saw anoþir do wronge, and warned hym to leue, so I, God and maker
of all, sometyme in manere as a balance, comes donewarde and stirs a
man to þe gude. I spare hym and proues hym by tribulacion. Somtyme
I wende vp and liȝthenes mannes saule wyth my grace, as þe scales of
þe balauns sometyme gose vp and sometyme downe. þe bonde vp to 20
þe clowdes bytokens þat I wyth my grace visetes and haldes vpe both
þe gud and þ'e euele', both frend and fo þat wyll turn þame fra þe
euel. þe beste betokens þame þat has taken baptym. Bot when þai
come to ȝeres of discrecion þai turned all to worldly thynges and toke
no heed of gostely. þe fisch bytokens paynems, þat wauers in stormes 25
of luste. þaire faith and þaire vndirstandynge of God is wondir litill.
And þarfor I desire þe herte of þe beste, and þe blode of þe fische. þe
thre companys ar my frendes. þe firste ar þai þat takes þair nedfull
sustinance of þe world. þe second leues þair awne wyll. And þe thirde
wyll full gladly, for þe loue of God, dye.' | 30

f. 150ra

Capitulum 3. A merueylouse dialoge bytwene Gode
and þe spowse, and of a kynge and right of his eritage in
þe realme, and of hys successours, of what some may
make clayme, and of what noȝt.

'O, lorde,' saide þe spowse, 'be þou noȝt wroth if I aske a questione. 35
I haue herd tell þat nothynge suld be getyn ne halden wyth wronge.
þar is a kynge þat occupies a lande; and some sais þat it is right, and

3 festyn] festyin   8 hyme] tyme   19 liȝthenes] liȝthtenes

some sais þat it is wronge. And it is wondir þat þou suffirs þis.' þan
said Gode, 'Eftir þe flode called diluuy come, of þame þat were
þerein, one kynde. And of þat went some into þe este–of whome some
come into Sweci–and some come to þe weste–of whome some come
5 into Denemarke. And of þame som tilled þe erth, and some dwelled
amange watirs in iles. And ilke of þame held hym payed of þat at he
come to, as it fell bytwyne Lothe and Abraham, for þat at ilkeone
chesid was his awne: as it was wretyn, "*Si tu ad dexteram vadis, ego
sinistram tenebo*"–þat menys, "If þou go to dwelle as in þine awne, I sall
f. 150ʳᵇ go to þe lefte hand." And so eftirward come | kynges and domesmen
11 þat held þame payd of þair termes, not oþir desirynge.'

þan saide þe spowse, 'Suppose þat a kynge aliene any parte fro hys
kyngdome, may his successoure aske it agayne?' God answerde, 'In a
kyngdome þe crowne was langynge to a kynge, and þe pepill, takynge
15 heede þat þai miȝt noȝt stand wythouten a kynge, thay went and
chesed on and gafe hym þe crowne to were for hys tyme, and to kepe to
his lawfull successoure. Yf a kynge þan þus chosen wald aliene any
parte þat langes to þe crowne, forsoth þe kynge þat is to com may and
aw to make clraym and chalange, for þe croune awe to suffir no
20 damage, ne þe kynge may noȝt aliene þe crowne, bot it were happely
for resonabill cause for hys dais onely. What is þe crown of a kyngdome bot þe kynges riall powere? þe kyngedome is noȝt elles bot þe
pupill þat is soiet to hym. þe kynge is kepar of þe kyngdome and of þe
pupill, and þe sauer of þame. And þarfor þe kynge suld on no maner of
25 wyse minouse, or waste, or lessen hys kyngdome fro hys successoure.'

þan saide þe spowse, 'What if a kynge were stressid to aliene a parte
f. 150ᵛᵃ of þe crowne?' þan | said God, 'Yf two men were at debate, and þe
grettir wald noȝt acord bot a fynger of þe symplere were cutt of, whose
were þe fyngir eftir it were cutt of bot þe mannes fro whome it was
30 cutt? Right so, if a kynge were stressid by takynge, or elles oþir nede, to
aliene a parte of kyngedome, he þat were his successoure might aske it
agayne. For þe kynge is not lord of þe crown bot rewler and keper
þarof, ne nede makes noȝt law.'

Scho saide, 'What if a kynge had granted to a lord a parte of hys
35 crown? Might noȝt þat be claymed agayne eftir dede of þat kyng?' þe
lord said, 'Ȝis, forsoth. þat land aw to returne to þe lawfull ayre.' Scho
said agayne, 'What if a parte of þe crown were wedeset for det, and he
to whome it were wedset had taken þe froytes many ȝeres; and so be

---

4 Sweci] þe Sweci   5 some] sonne   21 crown] crown bot þe kynges, *exc.*
crown, *ruled through*

dede of hym it were occupyed of oneoþir to whom it was neuir
graunted, ne layde in wede? Bot he comys to occupy alonely by some
occasion; ne he wille not leue it bot he take þe mone. What suld be
done in þis case?' þe lord saide, 'If one had a gobed in his hand and
said to hym þat stode byside hym, "This is | thyne. þarfor, if þou will   f. 150ᵛᵇ
hafe it agayne, gyue me so mony powndes", forsoth, þe pondes aw to   6
be gyfen: for when a land is occupyed by might and p[es]ibly
posseste, it sall wysely be clamed and broght agayne þare it suld be, þe
harmes alowed. Now forsoth, as a kynge chosyn and sett vpon a stane
schewes insomykyll þat he is lorde of þe ouir partes of þat realme, so   10
þis land in þe lawer partes, both be right of heretage, by purchase and
agaynbyeng, langes to þe realme. þarfor þe kyng kepe he þat he hase,
for eles happely he sall lose his lordschip and be made soiet to þe
crowne.'

þe spowse saide agayn, 'O þou lord, be not euel payde þat I aske ȝet   15
onys. þare is a kynge þat has two sonnes and two kyngdomes. In `þe´
tone realme falle[s] þe eleccion by þe right of heretage; in þe toþir be
þe fauour of þe pupill. And þis semis agayns right.' þan said God, 'In
þe chesers ar thre inconuenyentes, and þe ferthe is ouirpassynge: þa[t]
is, mysordeynd loue, feyned wisdome, flatterynge of foles, and   20
mistrayste on Gode and þe comonte. And þarfor þair chesynge was
agaynes | ryghtwysnes, agayne Gode, agayns gude lyfyng, and agayne   f. 151ʳᵃ
þe comon profyte. And þarfor, [for] pes and profite of þe communes, it
is gude þat þe elder brothir go to þe kyngdome þat fallis by heretage,
and þe ȝonger to þat at falles by eleccion; or elles will fall harme to þe   25
kyngdome, þe comonte sall be desesed, debat sall ryse, þe childir sall
noȝt acorde, and so þair kyngdomes sall be no kyngdomes. For it is
wretyn þat þai þat are in gret astate sall be chaunged fro þair places,
and sympill sall be lyft vpe to þame. Lo, I tell þe ensampell of two
kyngdomes. þe first is distroyed, for þe rightwys ayre is noȝt chosyn: 30
and þat made defawte of þe chesers and þe coueitise of hym þat
desired þe kyngdome. And þarefore þe kyngdome sall noȝt com to þe
first prosperite þat it was inne, ne to þat gode astate nawþir, to þe right
ayre be sett vp, þat is of succession of þe fadirs syde or elles of þe
modirs.'
                                                                         35

7 pesibly] partibly, *Lat.* pacifice   17 falles] falle   19 þat] þar
23 for] *om.*

Capitulum 4. Wordes of God to þe spowse of two
spirites, gode and euell, and of a wondirfull and profitabill batayle þat sprange in þe saule of a certayne lady,
bytwyne inspiraci[on] of þe gude spirit and þe euell. |

f. 151ʳᵇ   Gode saide vnto þe spowse, 'Thoghtes are sent into mennes hertes
6 of a gode spirit, and he stirris man to desire heuenly thynges, to thynke
what is to come, and noȝt for to lufe worldely þinges. þe euel spirit
stires to loue þat a man sees. He alleges synnes as litill of charge, and
sekenes as heuy to suffir, and purposes ensampill of synfull: for
10 ensampill of synfull men makes a man to deme þat syn is light, and
enflawmes hym to luste. Bot þe gude spirit sais þus to hym: "Riches ar
chargeows. Wyrschip of þe world is as þe aire, lustes of þe flesche as a
dreme. Worldly lykynge is sone passynge, and þer[to] worldly þinges
ar bot vanite. þe dome þat is to come mai noȝt be flede, and þe tor-
15 mentour is hard. And þarfor it is heuy to me to gyfe so strayte
rekenynge for þis passynge riches, to take a sp[ir]i[tu]all schame for
light ayre, to suffir longe dissesse for a schort lykynge, and for to gyfe
rekenynge to hym þat knawes all thynges or þat þai be. And þarfor it is
mor sikir to rekyn for few þen for mony."

f. 151ᵛᵃ   'Bot þe euell spirit sais agayne, | "Gode is myld, and lightly wyll be
21 plesed. Take bo[l]dely þat þou may gett. Gyfe largely, for riches is
gyfen to þe þat þou may be praysed in þe pupill, and gyfe to þame þat
askes þe. And yf þou leue riches, þan sall þou be seruant to þame at
serued þe. þou sall be sett at noght, for þe pore man passes furth
25 wythoutefurth wythouten wyrschype. It is hard to lyue eftir new cus-
tomes and ponysh þi flesche: and, þarfor, hald þine astate vpon þe,
for, yf þow chaunge, men will say þat þou art vnstabill." Bot þe gud
spirit brynges to þe saule this mynde: "Two thynges ar euirlastynge:
heuen and hell. And þa þat loues noȝt God ouer all thynges sall noȝt
30 haue heuen. And he þat loues God ouer all thynges sall noȝt haue hell.
Heuen is full of ioy and blyse, and helle is full of sorow and malice.
Oure lady and þe sayntes suffird penance for to come to þe blysse, and
despyte also. Wharfor it is bettir betyme to leue þe vanite of this world
þan to abyde vnto þe laste ende, in awnter þat, when dyssesse of þe
35 sekenes trauelles þe sore, þe mynde of þi trespas fayle, and þai sall
haue þi gude þat rekkes of þe noȝt." |

f. 151ᵛᵇ   'Bot agayn þis sais þe euell spirit, "We may noȝt be like to Criste or

to his modir or to oþir saintes. It is enoghe to lyfe comonly furth and
ask forgyfnes of synne, for it is bot a foly to take anyþinge vpon vs and
þan faile." Bot þane sais þe gude spirit, "All yf þow be noȝt worthi to
be likkened to saintes, ȝett sall þou besy þe to folow þame in gude
lyfynge and God sall helpe þe. For ofte tyme we se þat þe same way   5
þat a riche man gose, þe pore man folowes hym in. And sometyme to
þe same inne comes þe pore man where þe riche man is herberd: and
þat is for he gose þe way þat þe riche man ȝede. So, all if þou be noȝt so
gode as saintes were, neuirþelesse, folow þame, and þou may be
holpyn wyth þaire medes, as a pore man is refresched wyth þe releue   10
þat a riche man leues in of hys grete welefare. Two þinges suld stire þe:
one is pride of wirschipes þat lightly wyll begyle a man, anoþir pouert
of my frendes þat lokes eftir helpe. And þarfor will I leue þis world."

'Bot þan þe euell spirit sais þus, "Mercy is best, and to þat | þou may f. 152ra
ay com. Bot to leue þe world is bot foly, for þou wot noȝt yf þou may bere 15
pouert and dissese." þan answerd þe gud spirit and said, "O þou hase
herde told of Elizabeth, þat was þe kynges doghtir of Hungary, þat was
noriste in grete delytes and nobilly wedded, bot scho was eftir right pore
and law. And ȝitt had scho more comforth in hir pouert þan euir scho
had in wardly wyrschipe or riches." þan said þe euell spirit, "þou may   20
be tempid and fall to lechery and so be sclandirde." Bot þe gud spirit
sais, "God is willi to helpe me, and I will do my besines." ' þan said God
to þe gud spirit, 'Warn þat lady þat will leue þe world for me þat I
comaunde hir to take heed vnto [þre] þinges: first, þat scho brynge to
mynde to what wirschip I chese hir; þe secound, what cherete I schewed 25
hir in hir weddynge; þe þirde, how gudeli þat God has kepid hir. Also
take heed, firste, þat þow sall gyue a rekenynge of all þe gudes þat þou
has had. þe second is þat þe tyme is schort. þe third 'is': God spars no
more a lady þen a seruant. And þarfor, I conseill þe, first, þat þou do
pennance for þi | syn and loue God wyth all þi hert. þe second, amend þe f. 152rb
þat þou may fle purgatory, for þar ar perdons and forgyfenes of synnes, 31
and rawnsons of mennes saules by þe blode of holy men.'

Capitulum 5. Wordes of Saynt Petir to þe spowse of þe
grete desire þat he had for to saue folke, and of informacion þat he makys to þe spowse, and of grete merueyles   35
þat ȝet sall fall in þe cite of Rome.

---

7 man¹] man folowes hym in, *exc.* man, *ruled through*   14 þou] *twice* 24 þre]
two, *Lat.* tria   27 þat¹] þat þe tyme is schort, *exc.* þat, *subpuncted*

Saint Petir said vnto þe spowse, 'Doghtir, þou has likened me to a plowe þat makes wyde furres and drawes vp þe rotes. And þat is sothe, for I was so feruent agaynes vices, and so besi to conuert þe pupill, þat I wald noȝt haue spared my trauell to haue turned all þe world and I

5 had myght. God was so swete to me þat `it' was to me gret heuenes to thynke oght bot on God. And þarfor, when it come to my mynde how I had denyed hym, I wepid sore. I made couenant and sware þarto þat I suld rathir dye þan forsake God. And ȝit at þe voce of a woman I denyed hym. And þis was þe cause–for I was þan lefte to myselfe. þan

f. 152ᵛᵃ wist I wele þat I was noght of myselfe. þan com to mynd þe | gudenes

11 of my God, þat nawþer for payne ne for dred of dede wald I denye þe faithe ne þe trewthe, ne forgett my Gode. So ryse þou vp by mekenes and aske mynde of God, and I sall helpe þe.

'Sometyme þis cite of Rome was cite of campions, and þe stretis

15 were strwed wyth gold and siluer. Bot now þe preciouse saphir stones ar turned into clay. And of þe few folke þat dwelles þarin, þe riȝt eye is put oute, and þe right hand is cutt of. Todes and edders dwelles wyth þame, so þat meke bestes may noȝt come omange þame. Bot ȝit sall þere be gaderd þeder fyshes as swete as þai were before, all if þai sall

20 noȝt be so many. And wormes sall be changed into lo[mbe]s and lions vnto dowues. And ȝit in these dais sall it be herd, "Leue þe viker of Petir": *hoc est, viuat Petri vicarius*. And þou sall se hym wyth þine eye. I sall pers þe hyll of delytes, and þai sall come done and sit in it, for God will be made mykyll aboue all oþir in mercy and rightwysnes.'

25   Capitulum 6. Saint Paule telles a gude story to þe spowse, how throw þe prayeris of Saint Steuen he was called to ryght faith, and of a wolfe he was made a lombe, and how it is gude to pray for all. |

f. 152ᵛᵇ Saint Pawle saide to þe spowse, 'þou likened me to a lion þat was

30 norished emange wolues and deliuerd fro þame. Sothely, I was a rampand wolfe, bot God made me a lambe; first, [for] his gret gudnes, and þe second, throw þe prayer of Saint Steuen, wose prayer I deserued, for I had no likynge of his payne, none envye at his ioy, bot I walde þat he had bene dede, for methoght þan þat he had no suthfast

35 byleue. Bot wen I saw hym passyngely willi to suffir penance, I prayed wyth all my hert þat hys bittir payne suld turne hym to blysse. And

---

5 it] is   10 þe] *twice*   20 lombes] lions, *Lat.* agnos   26 of] *twice*
31 for] *om.*

herefor was his praye[r] profetabil to me, and throw his prayer was I
made a lombe of a wolfe. And þarfor it is gude to pray for all, for one
rightwis mannes prayer is helpe to þame þat ar moste worthi to resayfe
grace. Bot now þis nobill man is forgetyn, and of þam þat suld moste
hertly thynke on hym. Thay brynge hym broken vessell, and voyde 5
clay and abhominabill. And þar'for', as it is wretyn, þai sall be cled
wyth dowbill confusion and schame and castyn owte.'

Capitulum 7. A merueylowse visione of a saule þat suld
be demede | and of diuers accusacions, and oure lady
answers, and how þe same visione is expouned. In þe   10
whilke exposicione heuen is vndirstonden by a palace,
Cryste by þe sone, þe maiden by þe woman, þe fende be
þe Ethiope, one angell by þe knyght, and of 'two' places
of paynes vnremediabill and thre remediabill, and oþir
maters of suffragyes.   15

There was schewed, to one persone þat waked in prayer, a palayce,
in þe whilke were folke clede in whyte shynnynge garmentes; and
ilkane of þam had þair awn propir place. And þe principall place was
fillid wyth þe sone, wondirfully bright, schynand in lengþe, brede and
depenes. And þar stode a mayden beside þe sete crowned wyth a 20
preciouse crowne. And all þat were abowte wirschip þe son wyth
mirthfull and melodious songes. þan was þare sene a blake Ethiope,
ferdefull to loke vpon, full of envye and wreth, þe whilke cried þus to
þe domesman: 'Rightwys domesman, deme þis saule to me. He sall
bot a wyle suffir me ponyshe þe body wyth þe saule, whyle þai be 25
departed.' | þan saide one, as he had bene a knyght, wele armed, on
þis manere, 'Here ar þe gude werkes þat he has done vnto þis oure.'
þan saide a voice, as if it had bene fro þe sone, 'Here is þe vice more
þan þe vertew.' þe Ethiope answerde, 'þarefor, be right, he suld be
knyt wyth me.'   30
þe knyght said, 'þe mercy of God is redy to all vnto þe laste pont.
And ȝett þe saule and body ar togydir, and he has hys wyt wyth hym.'
þe Ethiope saide, 'He dide more hys gude dedis for dred þan for loue,
and þe synnes þat he shraue hym of war wyth litill contricion. And, for
he had no verrey contricion, þarfor sall hys synnes be opynly schewed 35
befor þe domesman.' þe knyght said, 'He hopid for to haue verray contricion byfor hys dede.' To þe whilke þe Ethiope answerde, 'þou has

1 prayer] prayes   24 Rightwys] righthtwys

gedird togidir all þe gude dedes þat euer he dide, and all hys gude
thoghtes, and þai all ar noȝt like to a werray contricion. And þarfor is
he noȝt worthi to come in heuen. Wherefor I haske þat he be wyth me
in paynes of hell.'

5 þane stode þe knyght still and answerd noȝt. Bot þare come a gret

f. 153ᵛᵃ company of fendes, as | þai were sparkes of a grete fire fliand abowte,
and cried vnto þe domesman, þat was like vnto þe sone, 'We knaw þat
þou arte one God and tre persons, and was wythouten bygynnynge
and sall be wythouten ende, ne þar is no oþir God. þou made aungell

10 kynde of þi might, bot we fell vnto pride, envye and malice, and so þi
righttwisnes put vs oute of heuen vnto þe fowle derke depe pit of hell
for oure malice. And þere is so mikyll rightwisnes in þe þat, if þi modir
þat þou lufid moste, and neuer synnyd, had synned dedely, and were
dede wythoute contricion, hir soule suld neuir come in heuen, bot it

15 suld be in hell wyth vs. And þarfor, domesman, deme þis saule to be
ponyshed wyth vs.' Eftir þis was herd a voce, as it had bene of a
trumpe, þat all were still; and þe voyse saide on þis manere, 'Lystenes
all ȝe angells, saules and feendes, what Goddes modir spekis.'

þan aperid oure lady bifore þe sete of þe domesman and said þus.

20 'Ȝee enemys, þat pursewis agayns mercy and loues noȝt rightwysnes,
all yf þare be defawtes in þis saule þat lettid hym to come to heuen,

f. 153ᵛᵇ neuerþelesse, se what is vndir þe mantill.' And þan scho ope|ned both
þe sides of hire mantill, and schewed þam a litill kirke, and þere semid
monkes; and on þe toþir side of þe mantill aperyd men and wemen,

25 religiouse and oþir, þat were Goddes frendes. And all þai said to
Gode wyth one voyce, 'Mercifull lord, haue mercy.' þan saide þe
maiden, 'Holy write sais þat whoso has perfyte faith, he may flit hilles.
þarfor þe voces of þese þat ha[se] faith, and serue God with brinnand
cherite, whame he prayed to pray for hym, suld be herde, þat he come

30 noȝt in hell, bot þat he come to heuen, syn he desired noȝt bot heuenly
þinges for all hys gude werkes. þe terres þat he has weped, and þe
prayers þat he has made, wethir þai may noȝt gett hym contricion wyth
cherite befor he dye? And þarto sall I put my prayers wyth þe prayers
of all þe saintes þat ar in heuen, whome he wirschipe[d] speciali.'

35 And þan saide þe lady, 'Ȝe fendes, I bid ȝou take heed what ȝe see.'
þan cryed þai all at ones, 'We se þat as þe rayne stintes þe wynd, so þi
prayers plesses God to haue mercy.' þane come a voys fro þe sone þat
said, 'For þe prayers of my frendes, he sall haue contricion byfor hys

28 hase] haith   34 wirschiped] wirschipe   35 fendes] frendes, *Lat.*
demones

dede, so þat he sall noȝt come | to hell, bot he sall be clensed in purga-   f. 154ʳᵃ
tory wyth þame þat suffirs þere greuous paynes. And wen þe saule is
clensid, it sall haue mede in heuen wyth þame þat had fath and litill
cherite.'

And when þis was saide, þere was schewed to þe spowse a ferdfull   5
place and derke, wyth ane hote brynnynge ouen, and in þe fire were
fendis and saules. Abouen þe qwilke ouen stode þis saule þat we haue
spokyn of, in likenes of a man, by one side of þe ouen in a ferdful
likenes, and þe fire semyd to wende vp bytwyne his fete till it come
abouen hys hede, and þe pores stode full of brynnynge fire. His erres   10
semed as þai had bene two belwes, and it semyd þat þai blew oute all
þe brayne oute of þe hede. Hys eyn were turned, and semid festynd
into his nodill behynde. Hys mowthe was opyn, and hys tonge drawen
oute at hys nesethirles, and it hange downe to hys lippis. Hys teth were
as þai had bene iren nayles festynd to þe palace of þe mowth. Hys   15
armes was so lange þat þai hange downe to hys fete. Both hys handes
semed to haue bene in brynnyng pike and grese. Hys skyn semed as a
cloth spottide wyth fowle blode, and þat skyn was so colourde | þat it   f. 154ʳᵇ
was heuy to loke on. And þere come oute of it whytir and foule mater,
as oute of a rotyn wownde, and þe werste stynke þat myght be felid.   20

þan saide þe saule fyue tymes, wyth teres, alas: 'First, alas þat I lufid
God so litill for hys gret vertewe and hys grace. Also, alas þat I dred
noȝt ryghtwysnes of Gode as I suld. Also, alas þat I lufed luste and
lykynge of my flesch. Also, alas for my worldely riches and my pryd.
And alas þat euer I saw ȝow, Lowes and Jon!'   25

þan saide þe aungell to me, 'I wyll expowne and declare þis vision
to þe. þe palace bytokens heuen. þai þat were clede in white bytokens
aungells and holy saules. þe son bytokens Criste in his godhede. þe
woman bytokens maiden Mary; þe Ethiope, þe fende; þe knyght, þe
gude angell; þe ouen, hell. þat þe ouen is full of fire bytokens þat all   30
þe world may noȝt make so horribill fire. In þis ouen are herd voces,
and all begynnyng wyth sorow and [so] endes. Also þis fire brinnes in
euerlastynge derkenes. And neuerþelesse þai haue noȝt all elike payne
þat are þarin. þe derknes þat is abouen þe ouen is called Lymbus, þe
whilke is a place of | þame þat suffirs no bodely payne, and ȝet is all   f. 154ᵛᵃ
one hell. Aboue þis is þe gretteste paynes of purgatori; and wythoute   36
þat is oneoþir place, where lesse paynes er, for þere is defawte of
strenth and fairenes, as of a man were seke. When þe sekenes is away,
he is seke, ȝete feles he no sekenes in payne, bot hym wantes strenth

while he be couerde. So þai feile no payne þat ar in þis place. þe
thirde place is aboue, and is noȝt of payne elles bot desire of
commynge to Gode.

'In þe firste place aboue derknes, where I saide is purgatory, in
5 gretteste payne, þere is tormentynges of fendis, and þere is schewid
lykenes of payne: wormes venomose and wilde bestis, grete hete and
grete colde, derkenes and confusione. þere hase some saule lesse
payne and some more, eftir at þai had amend not þaim at þaire
passynge. In þe toþir place where is defawte of strenth, sall þe saules
10 dwelle till þai may get helpe of prayers of holi kirke, or of oþir gostely
speciall frendes: for þe more helpe þat he hase, þe sonner he sall be
recouerd and deliuerd of þat place and broght to þe oþir place, where
f. 154ᵛᵇ is no payne bot desire | of comynge to þe presens of þe blisfull Trinite
and hys sight. Witt þou wele also þat some dyes in þe werld so clene,
15 ryghtfull, and innocent þat þai wend onone to þe sight and presens of
Gode. And some makes so amendes þat þai go to þe place where þai
fele no payne; and some to þe place of desirynge of gode. And all þe
saules þat are in þere thre places are holpen throw þe prayer of holi
kyrke and almosdede of oþir frendis. And right as hongry man hase
20 lykynge of þe mete þat comys to hys mowth, and þe thirsty of drynke,
þe naked of clothynge, þe seke of ryste, so þe saules has ioy and
gladnes of þo gude dedes þat are done here for þame. And blissed be
he þat helpis in þis werld saules þat are passed, wyth prayers and oþir
gud werkes, or trauayle of þair body, warethrow saules eftir þair pas-
25 synge ar clensid or deliuerd.'

þan were þer herd mony voyces oute of purgatory, saynge, 'Lord Jesu
Criste, rightwys domesman, sende þi charite to þame þat has spirituall
f. 155ʳᵃ power in þe world, þat we may be holpyn of þair | syngyn, redynge and
offerynges.' Bot aboue þe place where þere voyces war herde where oþir
30 voyces of many, and saide, 'Mede be vnto þame of Gode þat sendes vs
helpe in oure nede.' And in þat howse þat þai were in, it semyd to be
mornynge and sprynge of þe day—and owte of þat sprange a grete voyce,
'Lord God, of þi grete power, þou graunt ane hundrathfold rewarde in
þe worlde to þame þat helpis vs, wyth þair gude werkes, to come to þe
35 light of þi godehede and þe sight of þi visage.'

Capitulum 8. Wordes of þe aungell to þe spowse of þe
payne of þe saule demed by God in þe oþir chapiter,

13 þe presens of] *twice*   27 Criste] Criste i, i *subpuncted*

and of remission of þe same payne for he sparyd his
enemys byfor hys dede.

þe aungell saide to þe spowse, 'þe saule þat þou herd dome ofe is
in þe moste greuouse payne of purgatori, for it knawes not ȝett
wheþir it sall come to reste eftir þe purgatori, or elles þat it is 5
dampned. And þat is þe rightwysnes of Gode, for he had a gret wytt
and discrecion, and he vsed it all to þe werld and noȝt to gostly
þinges. And so he forgatt God while þat he lyued. And | þarfor hys f. 155ʳᵇ
saule suffirs now hete of fire and also tremelynge for cold. It is blynd
throw dirknes and ferde of þe horribill sight of fendes, and defe for 10
criynge of feendes; hongry and thirsti; clede wyth senschipe. Bot ȝett
has God gyuen it one grace, þat it sall [noȝt] come in þe towchynge
of fendes, onely for þe wirschepe of Gode, bycause þat he forgaue
hys enemys grete trespas, and made frenschipe wyth hys hede enmy.
And also, what at he did or hyght of hys gudes, and fullfillid of hys 15
riches þat were wele bygetyn, and namely þe prayers of gode men,
lesses hys payns, and refreshes hym. Bot þe godes þe wylke he gaue
þat were not wele getyn are helpe in special to þaime þat first aght
þaime dewly and lelly, yf þai be worthy to be holpyn.'

Capitulum 9. Wordes of þe aungell to þe spowse of þe   20
dome of Godes right agayne þe forsaide saule, and þat
satisfaccion suld be made in þis lyfe for þe saule in
purgatori.

þe aungell sayd to þe spowse, 'þou herd how, for þe prayers of gude
men, he had contricion byfor hys dede, | þat kepid hym fro helle. Bot f. 155ᵛᵃ
he suld be ponysched in purgatory by sex eledes. þe firste was for he 26
loued not Gode for his dede and dissese þat he suffird for þe hele of
mannes saule. þe seconde was þat he luffed noȝt his awne saule as a
cristen man suld, ne thanked noȝt Gode of hys cristendome, and þat
he was neþir Jew ne panym. þe third, þat he wiste wele what God wald 30
þat he had done, bot he had litill will þarto. þe forthe, þat he wald do
þat at God forbed hym. þe fifte was þat he was rekles of grace, and
schraue hym noȝt so tendirly as he suld. þe sext, þat he toke to litill
hede in þe resayuynge of Goddes body, ne lefte noȝt hys synne for
wirschepe of þat body.'   35

3 þe¹] Tþe   12 noȝt] *om.*   14 hys¹] for hys, for *subpuncted*   18 aght]
þat aght, þat *subpuncted*

þan aperyd a man clede in shynyng whyte, as it had bene a prestis awbe. He was girdid wyth a girdill of lyne, and a stole of rede abowte hys neke and vndir his armis, and he sayde þus. 'þou þat sees, take heede. For ȝe þat are in þe world, ȝe may noȝt so clerely vndirstande
5 þe might of Gode as we þat are wyth hym, for in a poynt we see þam in God. I was one þat þis saule wirschep[ed] wen it was demyd to purga-
f. 155ᵛᵇ tori. And þarfor I haue getyn grace | of God for hym, þat, if any will do for hym þat I sall say, þe saule sall be delyuerde oute of payne to one place where he sall suffir no payne, bot as it were a man þat had befor a
10 gret seknes and were deliuere þarof, and of all þe desessy werke of it, and lay still wythoute strenth and miȝt. Neuirþelesse, he suld be [glade] þat he wiste in sekeirnes þat he suld come to life. And þarfor, as þou herd þat þis saule cryed fyfe tymes, "Alas", so sall he now haue fyue þinges to hys comfort.
15 'þe first alas was þat he loued God so litill. And þarfore þat he [be] delyuerd fro þis, be þar gyfen for hys saule thirty chales, in þe whilke þe blode of Criste be offird for itt. And þe second alas was for he dred noȝt God. And for to asoile hereof, be þer chosen thrity prestes deuote, and ilkeane of þame synge thirti messis, ix of ma[r]tirs, ix of
20 confessours, ix of all halows, one of þe angeles, one of oure lady, and one of þe Trinite. And pray þai hertly þat God forgyfe and turne hys rightwysnes into mercy. þe third alas was for pride and couetyse. And
f. 156ʳᵃ for þis sall þare be taken therty pore men, | whose fete sall be mekely weshen. And þai sall haue mete and siluer and cloþis, and þai sall pray
25 hertly to God þus, and also þai þat weshes þame, þat, for hys mekenes and for hys hard passion, he forgyfe to þe soule all pride and couetyse. þe ferde alas was for lichere. And þarfor suld be gyfe a maiden into one abbay of religion, and a wedow also, and a damysell to mariage and husband, wyth resonabill gude þat is necessary to þaire lyuynge:
30 for þer ar thre lyues in þe world þat God will be sustened and halden. þe fiffte alas was for he did many synnes in deseseynge of oþir, and in speciall for he made bytwene two, byfor spoken of, mariage in degrees of blode forbed, and agayne ordinance of holi kyrke and leue of þe Pope: more for hys awn selfe þan for heuen, for þe whilke defawte
35 mony holy martirs dyed, þat swylke þinges suld noȝt be suffird in holy kirke. Bot for to clens hym of hys syn, wold one go to þe Pope and tell hym of þis syn, bot not þe persone, and tel how he was repentant in þe

6 wirscheped] wirschep   12 glade] *om., Lat.* gauderet   15 be] *om.*
19 martirs] matirs   23 men] *twice; Quire catchphrase,* men whose fete, *below*
31 fiffte] firste, *corr.*

ende, bot did not her his pennance, and he wil resaue "what penance
þe Pape wyll gyfe þat I may suffir", were þere no more penance gyfen
hym bot one Pater noster, it suld pr[o]fyte þe saule to forgyfenes and |
lessyng of purgatori payne.'   f. 156ʳᵇ

Capitulum 10. How Criste pleyned on þe euell men of   5
Rome vnto þe spowse, and of a fell sentence þat was
gyfen agayns þame yf þai dye in þair synnes.

Criste saide þus, 'O, Rome, þou rewardes me vnkyndely for þe gret
gudenes þat I haue done to þe. Thre wayes þere were, by þe whilke I
walde haue come to þe, and þou has sett lettynge in þame. In þe firste 10
way þou has hanged vp one heuy stone abouen my hede, for to breke it
þarwyth. In þe secound þou has sett a sharpe spere, þe wylke suld noȝt
suffir me to come to þe. In þe thirde þou has made a depe dike, into þe
wilke I suld falle vnwarly and be distrued. þere ar vndirstanden on
gastely maner, for I speke þam to þe dwellers in Rome þat ar euell, bot 15
noght to my frendes.

'þe firste way in þe wilke I was wont to come to mannes hert is þe
drede of God. Bot on þis is hanged a gret stone of hard presumpcion,
for þai dred noȝt þe commynge of þe righttwys domesman, whome no
man may agaynstande, bot [sais] þus: "If þe drede of God to me ward 20
be comynge, þe pre|sumpcion of my herte sall breke it." þe secund f. 156ᵛᵃ
`wai´ was gude counsaile þat I sent vnto mannes herte. Sometyme þat
comys by schryuynge, sometyme be gode prechynge and techynge.
Bot þan he settis a spere agayns me when, of grete likynge, he
trespas[es] agayns me, and thynkes stedfastly to continewe in hys 25
synnes. And þis spere lettes a man þat he may noȝt come to grace. þe
third way is lightenynge and inspyrynge of þe holi goste, when a man
vndirstandes what I did for hym, and what I suffird. In þe whilke [way]
a mane makes a depe dike, when he thynkes þus, "It is enoghe to me to
thynke on my lykynge, and þat will I folowe."   30

'þus do þai of Rome to me. þai life noȝt as cristen men suld, for þai
haue no more charite to me þan þai were feendys, þe wilke has leuere
suffir þaire wrechednes wythoute ende, and halde þaire malice, þan to
se me, and be to me warde in my blyse. On þe same wyse ar þai þe
whilke will noȝt take ne resayue my body þat is on þe awter, eftir myne 35
awn ordinance, sacred of brede; whose takynge and resayuynge is

3 profite] perfite   5 Criste] Cristen   20 sais] om., Lat. dicens
25 trespases] trespas   28 way] dike, Lat. via

f. 156vb sufferan helpe agaynes temptacions of þe fende. O full | wreched ar þai
þe whilke, wan thay ar hole of body, sette lesse [bi] and more refuses
þat helpe þan þai do poyson, for cause þai will noȝt refreyne þameselfe ne sese of synnynge. þarfor I sall come to þame be anoþir way þat
5 þai knaw noȝt, and, right as þai sett þre obstak[l]es, þat I suld noȝt
come to þame, so hafe I ordeyned thre þinges in þaire way whose
bitternes both lyue and dede thay sall taste.

'My stone is sodayn dede and vnavised, þat smytes þe saule fro þe
body. And þan sall all thynges þat he had firste ioy in be left behynde,
10 as þe saule allonely sall come to dome. þe secound is my spere, þat is,
my rightwysnes, þe wilke sall put þam so fer fro me þat þai sal neuir
taste of my gudenes, ne sall not se my blisse þat I made þame and
boght þame vnto. þe third is my dike, þat menys þe derkenes of helle,
þat þai sall fall so fer þat all my aungels in heuen, and all sayntes, sall
15 dampne þame, and all þe feendys and saules in hell sall curs þame.
Bot þis I say of þame of what degre, religiouse or seculers, clerkes or
lewyd men, woman or barnes, þe whilke are comynge to þat age þat |
f. 157ra thay knaw God and hys gudenes, and how he has forbed all syn, and
ȝet þai excluded fro þame þe loue of Gode and settes noȝt by his
20 drede, bot puttes þameselfe wilfully for to syne. Neuerþeles, I haue
ȝett þe same will þat I hade when I hange on þe crose, for I am þe
same persone þat I was when I forgaue þe theef, þat asked mercy, all
hys synnes. And to þe toþir theefe þat dispised me, I opynd helle ȝates,
where he suld endlesly be ponyshed for his synnes, and to þe firste I
25 opned heuen ȝates. And so am I ȝet redy to haue mercy.'

Capitulum 11. Wordes of Saynt Agnes vnto oure lady of
loueynge and blyssynge, and how scho prayes oure lady
for þe doghtir, and of þe comfortabill and swete
answere of þe lady to þe spowse.

30 Saynt Agnes saide to þe modir of mercy, 'þou may wele be called þe
mornyng þat Jesu þe verray son lyghtned. I call þe noȝt mornyng for þi
grete kyn, ne for þi grete riches or honours, bot for þi mekenes, for þe
light of þi faithe, and for avow of þi chastite. þow art þe tokenynge of
þe verray son. þou art þe gladnes of þe rightwis men. þou art putter
f. 157vb away of feendis, | and þou art comforthe of þe synfull. þarefor I pray
36 þe, for þe weddynge þat God made wyth þe, graunt [þi doghtir] to

2 bi] *om.*   5 obstakles] obstakes   34 þe^2] *twice*   36 þi doghtir] me,
Lat. filiam tuam

dwelle in lufe of þi son. þis weddynge was made in þe when God was
knyt to man in þe, wythoute lessyng of hys godhede, and in þe maidenhede of moderhede wythoute losynge of chastite. þow art modir and
þe doghtir of þi maker. þou bare hym temporally, þe whilke was
broght furth of his fadir wythoute ende. þe holi goste fulfilled þe, and 5
God, þat was borne of þe, was in þe or his messagere come to þe.
þarfor, lady, do þi mercy vnto þi doghtir, thi sonnes spowse.

'Scho is like vnto a pore woman þat dwelled in a vale, and had no
whik thyng bot one henne; and scho loued þe lorde þat dwelled in þe
hille so wele þat, whateuir scho had þat bare life, scho offird it to þe 10
lorde in þe hille. To whome þe lord said, "I haue plente of all thynges.
Me nedis noȝt of thyne. Bot happely þou gyfes me swilke smale
thynges, for þou wald hafe bettir thynges of me agayne." Scho sayd,
"Nay, lord, bot I gyfe þe it, for þou lattes so pore a creature dwell so
nerhand þi hill; for I ame wirschiped of þi seruantes; | and þarfor þat   f. 157ᵛᵃ
litill þat I haue I gyue þe, in token þat if I had bettir, bettir wald I gyue, 16
and for I wald noȝt be funden vnkynd to thy gudenes." þe lord said,
"For þou hase swilke a loue and charite to me, I sall lift þe vp into my
hille, and I sall gyfe þe necessarys in clethynge and fode." So is now þi
doghtir disposid. For þat scho had lyuynge–þat was þe lufe of þe 20
werld and of childir–scho forsoke it and lefte it to þe. þarfore it sittes
to þe for to puruey for hir.'

þan saide þe moder to þe spowse, 'Doghtir, stand stabilly. I sall
pray my son to set þe in þe hill were, thowsandes of thowsantes, angels
serues hym. For if þou reken all þe men þat were fro Adam to þe laste 25
þat sall be born in þe ende of þe world, for euirylkea man þare are mo
þan ten aungels. þis world is like a pot. þe fire vndir þe pot and þe
askes are þe frendes of þe werld. Bot Godes frendes are þe beste mete
in þe pot. þerfor, when þe tabill is redy set, þan sall þe gude mete be
broght to þe lorde, þe pot sall be broken, and þe fire sall be slokened.' 30

Capitulum 12. Wordes of þe moder and mai|den vnto   f. 157ᵛᵇ
þe doghtir of þe reuolucion of Godes frendes in þis
werld, now in gostely tribulacions, somtyme in consola-
cions; and what is spirituall tribulacions and comforte;
and how Godes frendes may temporali be glad.   35

The moder of God said, 'þe frendes of God bose sometyme, in þe
werld, be in tribulacion spirituall, and sometyme in gostely comforthe.

27 pot²] pot and þe mete in þe pot þerfor, *exc. first* pot, va-cat

Gostely consolacione is inspirynge of þe hali gaste, takynge heed of þe
gret werkes of God and meruayles of hys gret paciens. Gostely tribulacion is when vnclene thoghtes distrubes þe saule agaynes mannes will,
when a man hase dissese in saule þat God is noȝt wirschiped as he
wald, and for gostely hyndirynge and þe harme of saules, when a man
is constreyned to thenke on temporall thynges agayns hys will. Also a
man þat Gode loues may be comforted in temporall thynges, as in
gude wordes of edificacion, of honeste pla[is] þat none vnhoneste is
in: as þou may se be ensampill. For if þi fist were euirmor closed to-
gidir, owþir þe synows suld be drawn to|gidir or þi hand suld wax
febill. Right so in gostely thynges, if he were ay occupyed wyth contemplacion, owþir he suld wax febill throw pryde, or hys blysse suld be
lessed, for þe feruoure wald noȝt wax.

'Also, Godes frendes sometyme hase comforth throw þe grace of þe
holy goste; sometyme þai are disseshed of Goddes sufferynge, so þat
by dissese þai may knaw þair trespas, and by rotes pull þame away,
and plant þere, insted, froyte of ryghtwysnes. Neuirþelesse, God
mesurs þe temptacions of hys frendes so þat þai turne þe suffr[yng]es
to profyte. þarefor, for þou arte called into þe spirit of Gode, besy þe
noght to witt þe longe gudenes of Gode. For right as a shipehird
drawes and correctes hys shepe wyth a handfull of flowres into þe
hows, and þan he spers þe dore, and all yf þe schepe ryne here and
þare, neuerþeles þai wyn noȝt oute, and so þai fall to and etes hay and
waxis tame, right so is it done wyth þe. And þarefor, þat thynge þat
was sometyme harde vnto þe ys now esy ynoghe, insomykyll þat
nothynge likes þe now bot Gode.'

Capitulum 13. Wordes of Criste to þe spowse shewynge
what manere of teres is plesant to God | and how, and of
what thynges, almouse sall be gyfen to pore men, and
for cristen saules of þame þat are dede, and of þe con-
sayle of Criste to þe spowse.

þe son sayde to hys spowse, 'þou wondres þat I here noȝt ȝone
mane þat þou sees hase many teres and gyues mykyll gode to pore
mene. I answere þe. Where two wellis rynnes togidir, and þe tone be
drouy and toþir clere, þe clene watir is fyled wyth þe drouy. So þere
are teres þat comes fro tendirnes of kynde or of disese of þe world, or

elles of drede of þe payne of hell, þe whilke teres are drouy and clay, for þai come noȝt of charite. Bot þo teres are swete to me þat comes and sprynges of þe lufe of God and of hys grete godenes, and for his awne syne: þe whylke teres lyftes þe saule fro erthly thynges to heuen, and brynges a man furth to þe life euerlastynge. And þis is a spirituall bryngynge furth fro vnclennes to clennes. Bot þe body brynges furth fro one vnclennes to oneoþir. He wepis þe harmes of hys body; he suffres gret trauayle for þe world. Bot þees terres brynges noȝt to blysse. Bot þai brynge to blysse | þat sprynges of þat for þe whilke God is [noȝt] greued and þe saules [noȝt] harmed.

'As anentes þe seconde, þat is, almosdede, I say þat if þou suld by a cote to þi son of þi seruantes siluer, þe cote wyth ryght were þi seruantes. Ryght so, gostely, he þat takes of þame þat are vndir hym, or of hys neghbours gode, to gyue for his frendes saules, he greues Gode more þen he dose profite to þam, for þe gude turnes to þaire profite þat aw þe gude. Bot for þi frend þou sall do gostely gude and bodely gude. Firste, gostely gode: prayyng to Gode mekely, for þat pleses God full mykyll, as I schew þe by ensampill. Whoso wald present þe kynge wyth a grete some of silluer, thay þat were abowte wald say þat it were a faire present. Whoso wald com and tell þe kynge a Pater noster, he suld be scorned. Bot it is agaynward anemptes God. For whoso wyll offir to God a Pater noster, it were to hym more plesand þan a grete weght of gold, as it was schewed in Saynt Gregore, þe whilke, wyth his prayer, delyuerd þe emperour Traiane.

'Also þu sall sai to him, "Frende, one þinge I counsell þe, and one thynge I pray þe. I counsell þat þou oppin þi eyn of | þi herte, and take heed to þe vnstabillnes and vanite of þis werld, and how þe lofe of Gode is vaxen colde in þi herte; and how greuous is þe ferdefull dome þat is to com; and drawe þe lufe of Gode into þi hert, ordeynyng þi tymes, þi godes, þi werkes, thy loue and thy thoghtes to þe wirschipe of God, lessyng noȝt of þi lufe for any worldely thynge. þe seconde is þat I pray þe to aske of God in þi prayers þat he, þat all may, gife th[e] paciens, and fulfill þi herte wyth hys blysfull charite." '

Capitulum 14. Wordes of comforte þat Criste said to þe spowse when scho was putt in fer, bydynge þat scho suld noȝt drede for þat scho had sene and herde, and

f. 158ᵛᵃ

5

10

15

20

25

f. 158ᵛᵇ

30

35

---

4 whylke] whylke lyftes, lyftes *subpuncted*   10 noȝt[1,2]] *om.*   11 þe seconde] *marg.*, nota bene   þou] þou do, do *subpuncted*   28 how] *twice*   32 the] thi

how þe fende is vndirstandyn by a serpent and lyon, bot
þe consolacion of þe holi goste is vndirstanden by þe
tonge, and how it sall wythstand þe feende.

The son saide vnto þe spowse, 'Why dredes þou, and why art þou so
5　besy, for þe feende sendys somethynge amange þe wordes of þe holy
goste? Herd þou tell þat a man kepis his tonge hole þe whilke puttes it
f. 159ʳᵃ　amange þe lions tethe when he is greued? | Or elles hase þou owte sene
þat a man sekys swete hony of þe neddir tayle? Nay, forsothe. þe
feende is called a lyon for hys malice, and one neddyr for hys bygylling
10　sleghtes. þe tonge is þe comforth of þe holy gaste þat aperyd in likenes
of tonges. To put þan þe tonge bytwene þe lion tethe menys noȝt elles
bot prechynge and spekynge of þe wordes of þe holy goste for
praysynge and fauour of man. And þarfor, he þat gyfes hym to prayer
for plesynge of men, fro hym sall be taken þe comforthe of þe holy
15　gaste. And, forsoth, he sall be betyn of þe deuell [as] of one neddir and
be deseyued. For all if swilke wordes be Goddes wordes, ȝet passe þai
noȝt owte of þe mouthe of charyte and loue of Gode. Bot he þat settis
hym holy to plese Gode, and settes noȝt by worldely lustes, he sall
noȝt be dissayued, for þe feende dare noȝt come nere to hym for þe
20　presens of þe holy goste.

'Also, he sekes hony of þe neddir tayle þat wald haue gostely
comforth of þe feendys suggestions. For hym had leuer be dede þan to
conforthe a saule wyth a worde þat suld brynge to euerlastynge lyfe.
Bot dred noȝt, for God þat has bygon hys gudenes wyth þe sall
f. 159ʳᵇ　perfor[m]e it to a gude ende. Bot ȝet be|war of þe fende, for he is lyke
26　to one honde þat is vncowpeld, and if he come to þe warde wyth hys
temptacions, as it were, for to byte þe, putt agayn hym som harde
thynge to hurt hys teth wyth. þis hard þinge sall be charyte and
kepynge of þe commandmentes, þe wilke will distruye þe felnes of þe
30　feende þat he may noȝt disese þe, for he persayues þat þou has leuer
suffir all contraryous thynges þan to contrary Goddes wille.'

Capitulum 15. Wordes of Criste to þe spouse shewynge
whi gude men are trubbild in [t]his lyfe and euel ˋmeneˊ
hase prosperite. And he proues by ensampill þat spiri-
35　tuall thynges are vndirstanden by temporale, and whi

1 vndirstandyn] vndirstandynge　　　15 as] *om.*　　　25 performe] perforne
33 this] his　　mene] m

Gode tolde noȝt byfor þe certayn howres and tymes þat
thynges suld fall in, syn ylka moment and houre hase
knawynge to hyme.

þe son spake vnto þe spouse and said, 'þou wonders why my
frendes are diseshede in þe world, and my enemys wirscheped. I 5
answere, my wordes sall be vndirstandyn both bodely and gostely. þe
tribulacion of þis werld is a lastynge vp to blys. And þe | welth of þis   f. 159ᵛᵃ
werld is to hym þat mysvses it, and grace also, a wendynge downe to
payne. þerfor I tell þe ensampill. þer was as it had bene a moder þat
had two sonnes. On was born in a mirke prisson, and had no knawlech 10
ne experiens bot of derknes [and þe milke of the modir. Anodir is
borne in a streith place. . . . The modir sais to him þat was born in pre-
soun, "Yf þu wold go forth fro derkeness], þou sall haue likand mete
and a softe bed, and a more siker place." And wen þe child herd þis, he
went furth. Bot had þe modir hyght hym gret thynges, as grete howses 15
and faire hors, he wald [noȝt] haue gone forth, for he knew noȝt bot þe
modir mylke and derkenes. So God sometym hyghtes smale thynges to
make men for to com to grettir.

'þan saide þe modir to þe oþir son, "What profyte, son, is it to þe to
dwell in þis lityll tofall? Do my consaile, for I knawe two citees. In one 20
is ioy and blysse wythoute ende; in þe toþir ar men of bataile." þan þe
son went oute and saw þe cite where men were caste done and
defoyled wyth mennys fete. Som were made naked, and som were
slayne. Neuerþelesse, all held þame still and all played, and nowþir
straue ne debatid agayns þam þat keste þam downe. þan answers þe 25
modir, "þis cyte þat þou sees is bot a suburbe to þe cyte of blys, and in
it proues | God þame þat sall wend vnto blysse. And eftir he sees þam   f. 159ᵛᵇ
more hertly wirke and wake in trauayle, to þam he bygges more worthy
mansion of blysfull rewarde." Bot þan answerde þe childe, "It is hard
to take defoyle and nawþir speke na do agayne. It is bettir to me at 30
turne agayne to my holet or tugurry and tofall." þe modir saide, "Yf
þou turne agayne to þi tofall, wormes and venomouse serpentes sall
sprynge of oure derkenes and stynke, þe whilke ar horribill to þe for to
here, and þai will bite þe full sore. And þarfor dwell noȝt wyth þame."
þan þis son fell by litill and lytill vnto hys modirs will. 35

'Right þus dose Gode. Somtym he [h]ightes bodely thynges and
gyfes þame, for to stire men to gostely þinges, þat men be þe more

11-13 and þe milke . . . fro derkeness] om. (haplography); supplied from Ju, f. 107ʳ
16 noȝt¹] om.   36 hightes] lightes, Lat. promittit

stirred to lufe hym for þe gyfetes he gyues þam, and by a spirituall vndirstandinge of swilke gyfetes þai presume þe lesse of þamselfe. For þus dide God to þe childir of Israel. Fyrst he hyght þam and gafe þam temporall gudes and schewed þam many meruayles. And so he leryd
5 þam to vndirstande gostely thynges þat þai saw noȝt. Eftir what tyme God spake vnto þe prophetes more derke wordes and harder to vndir-
f. 160ʳᵃ stand, and he mengyd | amange ioyfull wordes and lykynge, when he hyght þame at þai suld com agayn to perpetuall pees, and all þer places suld be reparaled agayne; by þe whilke byheste thay noȝt
10 allonly vndirstode bodely thynges bot gastely also.

'Neuirþeles, þou may aske of me why þat God wald shew þam bodely thynges and vndirstande by þame gostely, sen he myght haue made þame to vndirstanden gostely thynges wele ynow and clerely?' To whilke Criste saide þat þe folke of Israel were wondir charnell, ne
15 walde ne couthe noȝt desire bot temporall thynges, and þarfor by temporall he broght þame to vndirstande spirituall. And for þat cause he taght þame on many maners, þat for þair byleue þai suld haue mede. And þai þat did wele suld haue þe gretter mede, and þe more feruoure to loue God; and at þai þe whilke were slaw suld be stirred to
20 þe gude; and þat trespassours suld more gladly leue thair synnes; and þo þat were in tribulacion suld haue þe more paciens; and þai þat were stedfast suld haue þe gretter blys. And þarfor God hight to fleschly men noȝt only gostely thynges, for þan wald þai haue bene full slaw to serue Gode, ne he wald noȝt hyght þam onely bodely |
f. 160ʳᵇ thynges, for þan had þar bene no deference bytwene man and beste.
26 þarfor Gode hyght þam bodely thynges to þe body, and gostely thynges to þe saule, and schewed many meruayles fro heuen, and he schewed vnto þame ferdefull thynges and domes to kepe þam fro syn. And þus mengyd he gostely thynges and bodely.

30 'Right on þe same manere God now schewes gostli þinges bi bodili liknes, and to God be giuen all þank and worschepe. What is þe wirschepe of þis worlde bot wynde and trauayle, and lettynge of gostely comforth? And tribulacion is disposynge to vertew, and medecyn of grete sekenes. þarfor, doghtir, my wordes may be vndir-
35 standid of many wyse. And þat is for gret wytt, and noȝt for chaungeabilnes of me. And I gyfe to my frendes verray vndirstandynge of my wordes.'

---

25 beste] beste and man, and man *subpuncted*   34 may] by may, by *subpuncted*

Capitulum 16. Wordes of þe maiden to þe doghtir,
shewynge how þe deuell somtym vndir þe skyn of
deuocyon ledys and disayuys som creaturs, bryngynge
þe euell amange þe gude to distrubill þam; and how
indulgences are gyfen; and how þe disposi[ci]on of holy   5
kyrke is vndirstanden by a gander and God by a hen,
and [w]h[o] is worthy to be callid Godes chekyns. |

þe modir said vnto þe spowse, 'Why has þou herberd þis man þat is   f. 160ᵛᵃ
so grete a speker? Hys lyfe is vnknawyn to þe, and hys maners and
condiscions are worldly.' þe spouse answerd, 'For I wende þat he had   10
bene gude, and for I wald noȝt þat a strange man were putt away.
Neuerþeles, had I wetyn to haue greued Gode in þat, I wald no more
haue herberd hym þan one neddir.' þan saide þe modir, 'Thy gude
entent and will hase kepid and refreyned hys tonge and hys hert, þat
he has noȝt moued ne stirred ȝou to perturbacion. þe feende þat is   15
wyly hase broght a wolfe in a schepe skyn, and he myght gett somwat
for to disese ȝou.' þan saide þe spouse, 'Vs thynke þat he is a meke
deuote man and of grete penance, and gladli visete[s] gud men, and
abstenys fro syn.'

þan answerd þe moder of mercy, 'When men etys a gose, þai leue   20
þe feddirs, for þai ar noȝt holesome, bot abhominabill to þe stomoke.
þe ordenance of holi kyrke is, as it were, a gose. þe body of Cr[i]ste is,
as it were, þe swete flesch of it. þe sacramentes are [as] þai were þe
inder party. þe wynges bytokens þe vertuse of martyrs and con-
fessours. þe feders byto|kens þe indulgens and perdones. þarfor he   f. 160ᵛᵇ
þat comys to þe indulgens, and will noȝt leue hys olde custom of   26
synne, he hase þe fedirs bot noȝt þe flesch, for þai do hym no profyte.
Bot he þat comes to þe indulgens in þat entent þat he fle synne, and
restore þat he has t[a]ken wyth wronge fro oþir, and will amend to
þame þat he has harmed þam, and will lyue furth gude lyfe, and put   30
fully þer will in Godes will, both in tribulacion and welthe, and take
no heed to þe wirschepes of þe world–þis man sall haue indulgens,
and be lyke to one aungell in þe faythe of God. Bot he þat wald be
clensyd of þat at he hase done, and will noȝt leue hys euell custome,
ne restore þat he hase mysdone, to þis man auayles þe indulgens as   35
feders, for wyth þame he gettis contricion and confessione, wyth þe

2 of] of þe   5 disposicion] disposion   7 who] he   14 refreyned hys
tonge] *marg.*,   nota   bene   18 visetes] visete   22 Criste] Crrste
23 as²] *om.*   29 taken] token

wylke he flyes owte of þe fendis dawnger, yf he wyll putt to a gud will
to do wele eftir.'

þan saide þe spouse, 'A, moder of mercy, pray for þis man þat he
may gett grace of þi sone.' þe modir saide, 'þere lyes byfor hys herte
5 on hard thynge as it were a stone, þat lettys þe grace to entir. God is as
f. 161ʳᵃ it were one hen þat warmes hyr eggys, | of þe whilke are broght furthe
qwhyke birdes. And all þat are vndir hyr takes hete of hir, and noȝt þai
þat are wythoute. Ne þe modir brekes noȝt þe shelle, bot þe bird
fandes to breke it wyth hyr bylle. And þan þe modir takes itt and kepis
10 it. Ryght so God, wyth hys grace, visetes þam þat þinkes on þis
manere: "We will abstene fro syn. And als mykyll as we may, we will
trauayle to perfeccion of lyfynge, and we will noȝt do þat at sall greue
God. Bot we will folow wyse men counsayle, and noȝt folow þe
styrynges of oure flesch ne oure awne wyll." þere men sall hafe com-
15 forth of God. And þai þat þenke þat þaire litill deed, þe whilke þai
haue done, is worthi gret thanke and mede, and þai will noȝt trauayle
ferrer to perfeccione, bot þai excuse þaimselfe by freelte and mys-
lyueynge of oþir, these are not Goddes chekens, for þai haue no will to
breke þe hardnes of þe herte, bot þai wald longe lyue, þat þai myght
20 contynew in synne. Bot so did not gude Zachee, ne Mary Mawde-
layne, þat gafe all þair partyse of þair bodyse to God for to make
amendes for þaire syn, and þai [set noȝt] by worldly wirschepis. And
þis is þe more sikyr payrty þat þai chesid.' |

f. 161ʳᵇ   Capitulum 17. Wordes of gude informacyon of Saynt
25   Agnes to þe doughtir for to lyue wele and beware of an
           euell and vnkynde lyfe to Gode; and how paciens and
           gostely strengþe is bytokened by a chariet, and be þe
           foure whelis is vndirstonden thes foure vertuese: þat is,
           to forsake perfytly all thynges for Gode; mekenes; to
           lufe Gode whysely; and to brydill þe flesche discretely.
30

Saynt Agnes spake vnto þe spowse and saide, 'þou saw þe lady
Pride sit in hir chare.' þan sayde þe spouse, 'I saw it, and `I´ held me
still in pees. For where mekenes suld be, þare I saw boste. What
menes prowde and bostefull shewynge bot wastynge of þe gyftes of
35 Gode and forgetynge of þameselfe, and agrewynge of þe dredefull
dome.' þan saide Agnes, 'Thanke Gode þat þou arte delyuerde of it.

---

21 God] God bot, bot *subpuncted*   22 set noȝt] *om.*, *Lat.* descenderunt in ...
contemptu

Bot I sall shew þe a chare þat þou may sikerly rest in: þat is, strenth
and paciens in dissese and tribulacion. For yf þou be stirred to pride,
set þi herte stedfastely in mekenes; and yf tribulacion come, hald þe
fast in paciens.

'þe firste whele of þis chare | is a perfyte wyll to leue all warldly   f. 161ᵛᵃ
thynges for Godes sake, and to desire noght bot God. þare is many þat   6
loues worldly gudes for þat ende at kepe þame fro disese, and þat þai
want noȝt þat is profetabill to þame and likand. Bot þis wheile gose
noght as it suld do on þis manere. For yf pouert com, þai desire plente;
and, agayns aduersite, thay desire welth. Thay gruch agayns lawlines,   10
and þai desire wirschipes. They desire to haue þer fredom agayns þe
will of þair sufferaunce. Bot I sall say what wheile gose to Godes
plesaunce: þat at desires noȝt to haue of hys awn, ne is noȝt hye inwyth
ne greued in aduersite of tribulacion. þe second wheile is mekenes,
þat a man hald hymselfe vnworthy in þe sight of Gode for hys synnes,   15
and for to thynke continuly [þar]on. þe third wheyle, þat is for to lufe
Gode wysely: þe whylke þou dose yf þou behald þi synnes and hate
þame, and haue sorow for neghbore synnes, and ioy of hys welefare,
and desire þi frendes life, noght for þi profyte, bot þat þou may serue
God and drede for to greue hym; and loue þam moste hertly þat þou   20
sees | moste feruent in þe lufe of God. þe fourte is discrete refreynynge   f. 161ᵛᵇ
of hys flesche, as a weddid man þat thynkes þus: "I will refreyne me fro
luste of my fleshe, þat I greue noȝt hym þat is maker of my fleshe, and
þat I may lyfe as I suld. I pray Gode of hys helpe." A man of religion
suld thynke þus: "þe fleshe wald draw me to lustes; tyme and stede   25
and elde, to lykyng. Neuerþeles, wyth þe grace of God I wyll noȝt syn
for þe profession þat I haue made and þe schortenes of luste. I sall gyfe
a rekenynge of all my dedes, and þarfor I will noȝt greue my Gode, ne
gyfe ne euell ensampill to myne euen crystene. And þat I be noȝt for-
sworne, I will noȝt syne."   30

'Bot he þat is in honours and lykynges of þe world, he suld þus
thynke: "I haue plente of gode and þe pore hase defawte, and
neuerþelesse we haue both one Gode. And whi sulde I haue þis state
bot onely by þe gudenes of Gode? For my fle[s]he, as hys, is mete to
wormes; and delytes drawes occasion of sekenes and losynge of tym.   35
þarfor I sall refreyne my fleshe, þat þe wormes wax noȝt by me to fat,
ne þat I waste noȝt my tyme, ne þat I distruye noȝt | swylke thynge as   f. 162ʳᵃ
pore men suld lyfe wyth." And he þat does þus, he may be called bath
confessoure and martir. For a kynde of martirdome it is to be amange

16 þaron] on   26 elde] helde, *Lat.* etas   34 fleshe] flehhe   hys is] *trsp.*

delytes and vse þame noȝth, to be in wirschepe and set noȝt þarby, to
be grete in mennys reputacion and noȝt to make of hymselfe. þis
wheile pleses God.

'þe leder of þis chaer is þi gude aungell, and þi reen is besy kepynge
5 of þis. Bot þe chaere of pride is inpaciens againe God in deminge his
priue dedis; also, impaciens agains his neghboure in maliciouse per-
sewinge, and agains himeself in schewynge of þe preuetes of hys herte.
þe firste wheile of þis chare ys couetyse of wirscheps, puttynge hymselfe byfor oþir, and dispisand þame at are sympill. þe second is
10 vnbuxumnes to þe commandmentes of Gode, þat makes hym vnskylfully to excuse hys trespas, and to defende hys malyce by presumpcion
of herte. þe third wele is couetyse of worldely gudes to spende at hys
wyll, and þat makes hym to forgett hymselfe, and slaw to þe lofe of
Gode. þe ferth is vnskyllfull lufe of hymselfe, þat excludes fro hym
15 reuerence and drede, and makes hym to take no heede of þe dome and
f. 162ʳᵇ hys ende. þe ledir of | þis chare is þe feend, þat makes a man glade and
hardy till all þat hys herte desires. þe two horses þat drawes þis chare
are hope of lange lyfe, and will to laste in syne. þe brydell and reyne of
þis is shame of shryft, and þis drawes a man oute of þe ryght way vnto
20 þe payne of hell.'

Capitulum 18. Wordes of louynge of þe doghtir to þe
mayden, and þe gostely answere of þe maiden to þe
doghtir, and of many graces graunted to þe doghter.

The spouse saide, 'A, Saynt Mary, blyssed be þou euerlastyngly, for
25 þou art modir and mayden, clene wyth aungels, full of faith, and clene
byfor þi chylddynge, and in þi childyng, and eftir: [clener] þan angels,
full of faith wyth apostills, full of sorow of herte wyth confessoures.
Ȝay! and þou passes confessours in abstinens, and maydens in
chastite. þarefor all creatures blysses þe, and þe makere of all
30 creatures is made man in þe. Bi þe, þe ryghtwys receyues grace, þe
synfull forgyfenes, thay þat were dede lyfe, and he þat was exilede is
broght agayne.'

f. 162ᵛᵃ þan | answerde þe mayden and saide, 'It is wretyn þat wen Petir
bare wyttnes to my sone þat he was Godes son, he saide agayne,
35 "Blissed arte þou, Symon, for fleshe and blode shewed noȝt þis to þe."
So I say þat þis reuelacione is noȝt shewid to the by any fleshly thynge,
bot by hym þat was wythouten bygynnynge. þarfor be meke and I sall

16 of] twice   26 clener] om., cf. Lat. pre angelis purissima

be to þe mercyfull; Jon Baptiste sall be to þe swete; Petir sall be to þe
mylde; and Paule als stronge to þe as it were a champion. þan sall Jon
say to þe, "Doghtir, sit on my kne"; Petir, "Doghtir, opyn þi mowthe
and I sall fede þe wyth mete of swetenes"; Paule sall cleth þe in þe
armoure of charite; and I þat am modir sall present þe to my son.   5

'Bot þis may be vndirstandyn gostely. For in Jon, þat is, þe grace of
Gode, is vndirstanden obediens. Jon was ryght swete. Firste, he was
ryght swete to þe fadir and modir for þe singulare grace Gode gaue
hym. He was swete to man for hys singulere prechyng, and he was
swete to Gode for holines and obedyent lyuynge. Obediens sais, "Com   10
vp, and þou sall haue hye thynge for þi mekenes. Leue now þat hase
bene bittir, and | þou sall haue swete thynges. Leue þine awn wyll, and   f. 162ᵛᵇ
it sall be fulfilled. Despyse erthely thynges, and þou sall haue heuenly
thynges. Despyse waste, and þou sall haue plente and spirituall
gudes."   15

'In Petir is vndirstanden faith. For as Petir was stabill to hys lyues
ende, so sall þe faithe of haly kyrke laste wythouten ende. þis faith
byddes þe opyn þine mowth, þat menes, þe vndirstandynge of þi
herte, and take swete mete, þat menes, Godes body in þe sacrament of
þe awter; full vndirstandynge of þe new laue and of þe old, wyth þe   20
exposicion of docturs, þe gronde of all vertuese. So sall þou fynde in
þe faith of haly kyrke. In Paule is vndirstanden paciens. He was
feruent agayns þame þat inpugned þe faithe. He had ioy in tribula-
ciouns and paciens in sekenes, and to hys lyues ende he lastid in
charyte. Thys paciens sall arme þe wyth gude ensampills of þe paciens   25
of martirs and oþir holy men, and þis paciens sall make þe myld,
mercyfull and feruent to heuenly thynges. þan, for þe conclusion, hym
þat obediens norysses in mekenes, gode faith fedis in swetenes, and
paciens armes in vertuese, þe modir of mercy | sall brynge to hyr son,   f. 163ʳᵃ
þe whilke sall crowne hym wyth endeles swetenes of blis and gladnes.'   30

Capitulum 19. Wordes of þe doghtir to þe laydy of praysynge and commendacion of þe ladys bewte, and of þe
answere þat oure lady gaue agayne, and how þe son
lykened þe modir to a goldsmyth.

The spouse saide to þe modir of mercy, 'O, þou swete Mary, new   35
bewte, and fairnes in light of moste clerenes, com and helpe þat mi

11 thynge] thyngees, es *subpuncted*   17 kyrke] kyirke   20 and of þe] *twice*,
of þe and of *subpuncted*   25 ensampills] emsampills

vnclennes be clensed and my charite be kyndled. Thy clennes gyfes
thre thynges vnto þe heede. Firste, it clenses þe mynde, þat þe wordes
of God may entire. Also, it gyfes þat, wen þi wordes are herde, thay be
halden in mynde. And þe third, þat þai be taght furth wyth a gude
5 wylle. Also, þi fairnes gyues thre thynges to þe hert. First, it takes away
all heuy charge of slewth. Also, it gyfes charite and mekenes, and it
gyfes to þe eyn terres. þe third, it gyfes to þe hert feruour of swetenes.
A, lady, þou arte a preciouse bewte, for þou arte gyfen to þe seke in
help, to þe heuy in solace, and to all in mediatrise. And þarfor may all
f. 163ʳᵇ men crye, "Com, þou preciouse fairhede, and lighten | our derkenes.
11 Take away our reproue. Com, þou swetest fairehede, and lesse oure
bittirnes, lowes oure bandes, and clens oure faithe. Patriarches
desire[d], and profytes spake byfor of þe, and all þe sayntes in heuen
has ioy of þe."'
15 þan saide þe modir, 'Blyssed be God, my fairhede, þat hase gyfen
þe grace to speke swylke wordes. Wherefor I say to þe þat þe euerlastyng Goddes fairehede sall comforte þe and teche þe meruayles, and
enflawm þe wyth hys charite. þarfor trayste in Gode, for when heuenly
fairehed is shewed, all worldly bewte sall sesse.'
20 þan said þe son to þe modir, 'Blissed modir, þou arte lyke to a
goldsmyth þat hase made a faire werke, þe whylke all þat sees it
prayses it, and are glad of it. In token of þaire gladenes, ʻowþirʼ þai
offir preciouse stonys or gold, þat þe werke may be perfurned. So þou,
my derly lufed modir, þat helpes all to ryse wyth gude wyll vnto Godes
25 plesance, and þou forsakes not ne leues none voyde fro þi comforthe,
þou may be called þe blode of Godes herte, for as by blode is all þe
f. 163ᵛᵃ partyse of mannes body whykynd, so by þe are men made whyke | fro
syn and lyuely and fructuose to Gode.'

Capitulum 20. Informacyon of Saynt Agnes to þe
30 doghtir how scho suld noȝt turne bake ne passe ouere
ferre forwarde, and of haldyng of mesure in abstynens,
and what continens is acceptabill vnto Gode.

Saynt Agnes sayd, 'Doghtir, stande stabilly, and go noȝt bake, for a
byttyng neddir lyges at þi heles. Ne passe no ferrer þan þu sulde, for a
35 sharpe spere poynt standys byfor to wounde þe. What menys goyng
bake bot a man repent þat he hase done any penance, and þarfor he

wyll turne agayne to lustes? And þat wyll drawes `a´ man fra all
gudnes. Ne þu suld not go to fere: þat menys, þu suld [not] ponisch
þiselfe ouere þi miȝt, or set þe to folow oþer aboue þi miȝt. For þe
fende, of envie, steris a man to fast overe his miȝt, and folow more perfeccion þan he mai dele with, and þan to leue for schame of men, and 5
so for indiscrecion to schort hys days. And þarfor do þou eftir at þu
mai, and gouerne þi lyfe eftir þe counsayle of wyse men þat dredis
Gode, and kepe þe fro bytynge of þe neddir, þat þou leue noȝt gode
dedys, ne | þat þe spere poynt pryke þe not: þat is to say, coueyt noȝt to f. 163ᵛᵇ
hye vertu þat is abouen þi myght.   10

'For som wenes to wyn heuen by þair awn meretes and gude dedis,
and God kepis þame fro fandynges and temptaciouns of þe feend by
hys pryue godenes. Some wenys to make aseth to God for þair trespas
by þair awn werkes, and þe error of þame is dampnabill. For yf a man a
hundreth syth cut asondir hymselfe, ȝit myght he not make asyth for 15
one dedely synne. And also God gyfes wyll and myght, hele and gude
desire, riches and blysse, and all thynges are in hys hand. þarefor
mannes mede is noȝt in regarde of hym.

'Also, haue no wonder at þat lady, þe whylke com to þe indulgens,
was defoyled. For som woman kepys chastite (bot þai loue it noȝt), for 20
þai haue no gret stirrynge. Bot if þar were profird to þame grete
mariage þai wald take it; bot þe smale mariage þai set at noȝt. And
þarfor of þair chastite rysis sometyme pryde and presumpesion. And
þarfor God suffirs þame fall sometyme, as þis woman hase done. Bot
yf þar be any þat th[y]nkes | þat for all þe world scho wald noȝt onys be f. 164ʳᵃ
filed, scho sall not be lefte. And if God, of hys preue counsayle, suffir 26
swylke one to fall agayns hyr wyll, scho sall ryse agayne in more
mekenes.

'For God is as one egyll þat sees of ferr. And yf he see oght ryse fro
þe erth, sone he smytes it downe. And if he se any wenomouse thynge 30
agayns hym, as it were an arrow he smytes throw it. And if any filth fall
fro abouen vpon hym, he shakes it son fro hym. Ryght so dose God. If
he see mens hertes, of freelte of fleshe and fandyng of þe feende,
agayns þe wylle of þe saule, ryse vp agayns God, as fast by gode
inspiracion and compuncion and penans he dose it away, and makys 35
hym to turne agayne to Gode. Also, if þe venom of coueytyse entire a
mannes hert, he smytes it agayn wyth þe arow of charite. And if any

2 not²] *om.*   13 pryue godenes] *marg.*, nota   22 þai¹] þai set at noȝt, set at
noȝt *ruled through*   wald] wald noȝt, noȝt *subpuncted*   25 thynkes] thankes; *Quire*
catchphrase, þat for al *below*

filth of pryde or of lichery haue filede þe saule, by gode stabyllnes of faithe and hope he castes it away, þat þe saule be noȝt obstynate in synne. And þarfor, in all thynge take heede of þe mercy and right-wisnes of God.'

f. 164rb

5   Capitulum 21. Wordes of þe spowse to God of hys mag-
      nificens, and vertu, and how oure lady comfortes hyr by
      ane answere, and | 'howe' þe seruantes of God þat are
      gude suld noȝt sese of prechyng of folke, wheþir þai be
      turned or noȝt.

10   Saynt Bryd said vnto Gode, 'þou art like to a flowre þat growes by thyselfe in a feld, þe whilk giues, to þaim þat comes nere, swetenes in tastynge, comforte to þe brayne, lykynge to þe sight, and strenth to þe body. So þai þat comes nere to þe, thay are faire in lefynge of syn, wyse in folowynge of þi wyll, and rightwys in folowynge of þi wyrschype.
15   þarfor, gode God, gyfe me grace to loue þat lykes þe, to wythstand temptacions manly, to sett noȝt by þe world, and to hold þe stabill in mynde.'

      þan saide þe modir, 'This gretynge gate vnto þe Saynt Jerom, þe whilke lefte fals witt and come to trew wysdome, despysed worldely
20   wirschepe and wan God. þat was a blyssed Jerome! And þai are blyssed þat folowes hys techynge. He was louere of wydowes; he was þe [m]irrour of gude lyfers; he was techer of all trewth and clennes.'
      þan saide þe modir to þe spouse, 'Say what is þat þat trubbilles þi

f. 164va
      herte.' Scho saide, 'If it so be þat one be gode | þamselfe, what nede is
25   it to be besy aboute oþir, syn it falles not to his astate to teche?'

      þan saide þe modir, 'This thoght blindes a mannys saule, þat he forgettes hymselfe. And it hase many fro Gode. þe feend lettys þe gude men to speke to euell men, þat þai make þame noght for to haue com-punccion of syn. He lettys þame also to speke to gude men, þat þai gett
30   noȝt a hier degre. For if a gude man vse gude techynge, [he] makes hym to haue gretter mede and hier place in heuen, as he, þe tresorere of þe qwen Candace, þat red þe prophete Isay, suld haue had þe lesse payne in hell: bot Philipp come and taght hym þe right way to heuen, and lift hym vp to a blisfull place. So was Petir sente to Cornely, and
35   had Cornely died befor, he suld haue had sum refreshynge for hys gude faithe. Bot Petir drowe hym to þe ȝate of lyfe. So Paule come to Denys, and broght hym to blis.

      22 mirrour] nirrour   23 to] *twice*   30 he] or   32 qwen] qwen of

'And þarefor þe frendes of Gode sall noȝt wax irke in Godes seruyse, bot be besi þat an euell man be amendide, and a gude man come to hyer perfeccion. For if þare were a man þat wald do all hys myght to turne all folke to Criste, all if right few or | none were con- f. 164ᵛᵇ uertide, he suld haue þe same mede as if þai were all conuertid, as by 5 ensampill: yf two mene [were] hired olike to delue in one hille, and þe tone fand gold and þe toþir fand none, neuerþelesse, as by a couenant, þai suld haue elike reuarde, for þai had bothe elyke gude will and elyke trauell, as Paule þat conuertyd mony and oþir apostills þat were of as gude will. þarefor suld noȝt a man sese, a[ll] if few receyued þe 10 wordes of Gode. For ryght as þe thorn kepis þe rose, so þe prikkynge of þe feend is profitabill to þame þat are chosyn.'

Capitulum 22. How in dayes þat are now þe malice of
man passis þe [s]light of þe feend, and how men are
now more redy to syn þan þe feend to tempt, and of 15
dome agayns swylke, and how þe freendes of God awe
to trauayle sadely in prechyng, and how god
inspir[ing]es com vnto hys frendes.

The son saide to þe spouse, 'If I myght be disesed, I myght now say me forthynkes þat I made man. For man rennys now | willfully as a best f. 165ʳᵃ into þe net, for he folowes all hys luste. Ne it is noght now to blame þe 21 fende, for man is more hasty to syn þan þe fende is to drawe man. As houndes þat are cowpled, when þai see þair pray thai ryne byfor þe leder, for þai are customed þareto, so men þat are customed in syn hyes þam faster to syne þan þe feende hyes hym to fande and tempt 25 þame. Ne it is no wonder, for it is full lange sene þe kyrke of Rome, þat is heued of þe world, plesyd God wyth holines and wyth gude ensam-pill of lyuyng as it did sometyme. And þarfor all þe oþir partys are febill, ne men takes no heed how Gode, richeste of all, is made so pore to teche þere worldely þinges to be dispisede, and heuenly þinges to 30 be loued and desired.

'Bot þat a man þe whilke is pore of kyn is made riche of fals riches— þat wald ilkea man folow, bot few wald folow þe pouert of Criste. þarefor sall þar come a tillman þat sall [noȝt] be besy abowte þe erthe ne þe fairehede of body, ne þat sall drede þe manas of man; ne it sall 35 take heed of mennes personnes. Bot he sall caste done þe body to

6 were hired] hired for   10 all] and   14 slight] flight   18 inspi-
ringes] inspires   com] *marg.*, coming   34 noȝt] *om.*

f. 165rb wormes, and he sall send | þe saule where it hase deserued. And þare-
for warne my frenndes þat þai be war and besy. For þis sall not abyde
to þe laste end of þe world, bot in þese dais it sall fall, and many þat
lyuen sall se it. For wyues sall be wydowes and childir fadirles, and
5 likyng of men sall be wythdrawen.

'Neuerþelesse, whoso will turne þame to me by mekenes, I sall
resayue þame, and whoso will wirke rightwysnes sall haue myselfe.
For it is skyll þat þe house be clensid into þe whilke þe kynge sall
entir; and þe glas also, þat þe drynke mai be schewid; and þe whete
10 commes soner fro þe cafe þat þe bred sall be made. And þan, ryght as
eftir wynter comes somer, so eftir tribulacion sall I sende comforthe to
þame þat will be meke and desire heuenly thynges. And to some I will
do eftir þat prouerbe: "Smyte hym in þe nek, and he sall ren[n]e"–for
tribulacion sall make a man to hye. And to some I sall do eftir þat
15 worde: "Opyn þi mouth, and I sall fullfill it." And to some I sall say,
"Come, ȝe sympill idiotes, and I sall gyue ȝou mowth and wysdome,
f. 165va þat gret spekers sall noȝt wythstande ȝou." And | þus I haue done in
thees dais. And grete men hase sodanly passed away, for þai wald noȝt
do my byddynges.'

20   Capitulum 23. Wordes of John ewangeliste vnto oure
      gloriouse lady of one þat was dissayued of þe feend, and
      þe answere of oure lady agayne, and what `one' is þat at
      is in þat plite, an[d] how both gode spirit and euell may
      be knawen by seuen tokens.

25 Saint Jon euangelist said vnto Goddes modir, 'Take heed how þis man
is dysesed of þe feende, and of þe spirit of lesynge, clethynge hym in a
schepe skyn, and wythin hase a lyons herte. He hase wytnes of wykked
spirit þat he is all feyned, for he aspires to be myghty agayns þe myght
of þe fadir, to haue wytt agayns wisdome of þe son, and to haue heet,
30 bot oþirwyse þan þe holy goste hetys. And þarfor pray þi son awther
þat he be son wythdrawn, or þat he be meked and amend hym.'

þan saide þe modir to Jon, 'Here, þou maiden, not woman bot man.
It liked God to call þe owte of þe world wyth þe softest dede eftir me.
f. 165vb For I in my passynge | lay as I had slepid, and in my wakynge I woke in
35 blis and ioy euerlastynge. And þat was for þe grete sorow þat I had in
þe dede of my son, when þou was next to me of all apostels, and my
son shewed þe moste tokens of loue. And my sonnes passion was

13 renne] renewe, *Lat.* curret   16 idiotes] idiotestes   23 and¹] an, *rest erased*

moste bittir to þe, and þou lyued langer þan any of þi brethir and was
in deyng of þame all, and so sory as if þou had bene a martir. And
þarfor, eftir me, þou passid wyth þe lighteste dede.

'Bot I will tell my doghtir how it is wyth hym þis þat we spake of.
For he is þe seruant of þe feende, þat is like to a mi[nte]r; for, firste, he 5
smytes and blowes hys mone, when he drawes hys seruant to hys wyll.
þan smytes he his prynte in hym when he bringes his euele will to
dede, and when he has done it, þan is he full mone of þe feende. Bot
wit þou wele þat Goddes mone is fyne gold, for it is bright, soft and
preciouse. So many saules þat hase þe prynt of Gode is briȝt throw 10
charite, soft in paciens, and preciouse in continuanse of gode lyuynge.
Swylke a saule is blawn wyth vertu; it is proued wyth many tribula-
cions to knaw þe selfe and þe gode|nes of Gode, and so it is meker and f. 166ʳᵃ
more perfyte by þat. Bot þe mone of þe feend, it is owþir copir, þat is
like to golde, bot it is harder þan gold–so þe fendes seruant thynkes 15
hymselfe gode and demys oþir besyde hym, and is harde in pride and
noght softe in paciens and mekenes–or elles þe mone of þe feend is of
lede, þe whilke is fowle and to softe: so þe seruand of þe fende is fowle
wyth synne, and vnstabill as þe lede, redyer to synne þan þe fennde to
stire hym þarto. 20

'Slike one is he þis, foule irke of þe obseruance of his religion. He
besyd hym how þat he might plese men by feined holines to norysch
his fleshe, and for to com to wirsch[e]pes þat he sall neuer haue. Bot
right as, when a man fyndes any new mone, he gose to a wyse man þat
can skylle of þe prynte and of þe forme, so suld a man, if he fynd in hys 25
saule any mone of þe feende, he suld go to som man of discrecion, to
be counseild wheþir þat it be gode or euell.

'Bot my doghtir, take hede þat by seuen thynges þou may knaw þe
gude spirit fro þe euell. Firste, þe gude spirit makes a man to sett noȝt
by þe world, ne by þe wirschipe | of it. þe seconde is þat he makes þe f. 166ʳᵇ
saule to lufe wele Gode, and to haue no lykynge in fleshly lustes. þe 31
third is, he sendes a man paciens and likynge in Gode. þe firthe, he
stires his saule to lufe his frende and enemy, and to haue compassion
of þam. þe fifte, he stires to all chastite. þe sext, þat he makes a man to
triste in Gode in all dissese, to haue likynge in aduersites. þe seuent, 35
he stires a man to couet and desire gretly to be white and noȝt fyled
wyth þis werld. Contrary to þes, dose þe euell spirit oþir seuen þinges.
þe firste, he makes þis world to seme swete, and he stires hym to be
irke of heuenly þinges. þe second, he makes a man to desire worldly

5 minter] miror, *Lat.* monetarii   23 wirschepes] wirschpes

wirscheps, and to forgett hymselfe. þe thirde, he stires a man to hatred
and impaciens. þe firthe, he makes a man grucchand agayns God, and
bold and hardy to synne. þe fyfte, he makes a man to excuse hys synne,
and noȝt to charge it. þe sext, he [inspi]res to lightnes and vnclennes.
5 þe seuent, he gyfes a man trayste of lange lyfe, and shame to shryue
hym. Be þarefor besy and ware of thy thoghtes, þat þou be noȝt
deceyued of þis euell spirit.' |

f. 166ᵛᵃ   Capitulum 24. Oure lady telles þe spowse how Goddes
              seruantes sall gouern þame agayns impacyent men, and
10   how pride is bytokynd 'be' a tonne.

The modir saide, 'Where a ton of wyn waxis warme and bygynnes to
boln, þare comes vp fame and exalacions þareof, somtyme gretter,
sometyme smaller, and it falles sodanly downe agayne, and þai þat are
aboute and sees it wote wele þat it is of þe strenth of wyne or of þe ale.
15 And þai þat laies þaire nose to þe wyne, or elles þaire nese or þare
brayne is moued. So, gostely, som mens hertes bolnes throw pride and
vnpaciens. And þai wote wele þat it is of vnstabilnes, or elles of þe
flesche. þarefor þai suffir wordes paciently, knawynge þat eftir
tempest comes reste, and for paciens is more þan he þat wynnes cytes,
20 for it ouercomys man in hymselfe. Bot þai þat are impacient takes þis
wyn, þat menys wordes of oþir. þarefore when [ȝe] see oþir impacient,
put ȝe, throw Godes helpe, kepynge to ȝoure mouth, ne leue ȝe noght
þo gude þinges þat ȝe haue bygon for wordes of vnpaciens, and here as
f. 166ᵛᵇ | ȝe herd noȝt, puttynge God a[l]way in ȝoure sight and beynge
25 pacient.'

Capitulum 25. Wordes of maiden Mary to þe doghtir,
þat a man suld noȝt set to fulfill desires of his fleshe, bot
he sall mesurabily norysh hys body wyth thynges necessary.

30   The modir saide, 'þou sall be as a spouse; þi body as one asse þat
nedys mesurabill mete þat it wax noght to wilde, and discrete chastisynge þat it wax noghte prowde, and continuall betynge þat it i[t] wax
noght slaw. For þus stode þai þat [k]e[s]te there clothys for Godes
sake, and euerilke oure were redy at Godes will when he wald call

4 inspires] charges, *Lat.* inspirat   10 be] to   20 takes] and takes
21 ȝe] þai   24 alway] away   32 it²] is   33 keste] lefte, *Lat.* strauerunt

þame, for þare was no lange way bytwyne þame, for þai had hym ay present; ne þai had no heuy charge, for þai sett noȝt by þe world. And þarfor wythouten lettynge þai flowe to heuen.'

Capitulum 26. Wordes of ammonycion of þe maiden to þe doghtir what vertuouse dedis are worthy heuen and 5 whilke noȝt, and of grete mede of `ob´ediens.

'Here is mony flowres of a tre, bot ȝet comes noȝt all to profyte. So þere is many

[Loss of a leaf containing rest of IV. 26, IV. 27-30, beginning of IV. 31. Missing material for chs. 26, 31, supplied from Ju]

vertuos werkis. Neuirtheles, all deserue nat the reward of heuen but f. 112ʳ they be don discretly. To fast, to pray, to go pilgrimage, alle be dedis of 10 vertu. But yf thei be don with soch a wil þat man beleuis to come to heuen by mekenes, but he haue discrecion in al thingis þei vayle but litil to euerlastinge joye. As yf þu see ii men, oon vndir obediens, anodir at his liberte. He þat is in his liberte fastis: he shal haue a simpil reward. Yf he þat is vndir obediens etis þat same fastinge day flesch, 15 after þe ordenans of his rewle and obediens, he þis shal haue dobil reward, oon for his obediens, anodir for delaying of his desire and not fulfelling his will. þerfore be as a wiff whech first makis redy the boure before her husband come. þe secund, as a modir [þat] ordeynis clothis before the child be born; the iiide, as a tre þat ferst beris floures and 20 þan bringes frute. The iiiite, be as a clene vessel to reseyue abil drinke or it be put in.'

[IV. 31] | These be the wordis of the modir to the doughtir preuynge f. 113ʳ be exsample þat prechoris of God are not less crounnd in the sight of God allthough thei turne nat the pepil be there predicacion. 25

The modir of God seis, 'He þat heyris a laborer to labor, seinge to him, "Fecche quyksonde fro the see, and seke in euery berde[n] yf þu finde ony peece of gold"–hys reward is no les þough he finde noon as though he fonde meche. So it is with him þat laboris in word and dede to þe profite of soulis. 30

6 obediens] bediens, *orig.* bbediens   19 þat] *om.*   27 berden] berde, *Lat.* onere

[Cl continues]

f. 167ʳᵃ His mede sall neuer be þe lesse þat he conuertes none þan [if] he conuerte many. As þe maister said be ensampill, he þat wendes to bataile
at þe biddynge of his lorde, and fightys wyth gude wyll and is
greuousely hurte–neuerþeles he takes no presonare–he sall haue
5   neuerþelesse his couenant. So for euirilkea gude word and werke þat a
man dose for þe loue of God, and to wyn menys saules, þai sall be
crowned, wheþir som be conuertid or none.'

Capitulum 32. þe moder shewes how infynite hir mercy
is to synners and hir louers.

10   The modir of mercy saide, 'þare is noȝt so synfull a man in þe world
þat will turne hym and lufe my son of hert, bot I am redy to com to
him, as a modir to þe childe to hayls hym, saiand þus: "Son, what will
þou þat may plese þe?" For if a man had deserued þe dippest pitt of
hell, and he had will to amend hym, forsakinge wordli wirschipes and
15   lustes of flesch and he held hym paide of his nedefull sustinance, he
and I suld sone be accorded. þarefor say to him þat writes songes in
f. 167ʳᵇ wir|schepe of me, noght for [hi]m[self]e bot for him þat is worthi all
wirshepe, þat I sall rewarde hym gostely. For right as a sillabe hase
vpon hym mony notes, so God wyll gyfe hym, for euerilkea silabe þat is
20   in þe sange, a crowne, and it sall be said of hym, "This is þe maker of
þe songe for no worldely gude, bot for Godes sake." '

Capitulum 33. þe spouse spekys of þe cite of Rome,
purposynge vndir forme of question þe comfort, deuocion and gode olde ordinance of þame of Rome, both
25   clerkes and lewed men, and why now all þat is turned
into desolacion and abhominacion.

The spouse compleyned þe cite of Rome of þis manere: 'A, lorde,
how wreched is now þis cite both gostely and bodely, þat sometym
was, one both wyse, so blysfull and so worthy. For þai þat suld be
30   defenders of it are now þe robbers þarof. And, for þat, þe house is
desolate þat sometym was wirschyped wyth gloriouse mirakels and

---

1 if] *om.*   10 modir] modir saide, saide *subpuncted*   17 himselfe] me, *Lat.*
suam

holy saintes bones. Temples are destroyed and þe closours is taken away; and þat som[tyme] serued to men is now opyn to beestes and hondes. | Also, it is desolate gostely, fore many gude ordinance þat mony gude holy pope made by inspiracion of þe holy goste, to þe wirschepe of Gode and hele of mannes saule, are now fordone, and many abusions, by stirringe of þe feende, are putt in þaire stede. It was ordeynd in holi kyrke þat whosoeuer suld take holy ordirs and be auaunsed in holi kyrke suld be clene of lyuynge, deuote in Goddes seruyse, gyue god ensampill both in lyuynge and techinge to oþir. Bot [nowe] is þis abusione broght in, þat prouandres are gyuen to men þe whilke, all if þai be not weddid men, neuerþeles þai ar not honest, and haldes concubynes in house wyth þame. Prestes, dekyns and sub-dekyns sometyme had horroure of vnclene lyuyng. Bot now som of þame are glad to se þaire lemmans go gret with child amang oþir, ne hym shames not of þat. And þarfor þai may bettir be called lyons of þe feende þan clerkes of holy kyrke.

'Also, Saint Benet and oþir holy fadirs ordaynde reweles wyth leue of popes and made abbays, where abbotes and monkes suld serue Gode night and day. And it was a ioy to here þam both night and day, and many | synfull where amendid and turned to gode life by þe praer of þame and gude techinge, and saules in purgatory were releysed of paynes be þaire praere. And he þat best kepid his rewle was moste sett by. And þan mygth a monke be knawyn by his abite. Bot now abbotes will not dwell with þaire brethir in þair abbays, bot abowte in castells and maners. And þarfor religion amange þame perysese, and þaire abbays gose downe, and gode serwise is laide, and þare gude mene hase no daynte of þame, and þe febill ar noȝt amendid by þame. And like it is þat litill ese þai do to þe saules in purgatory. And in þis cite are some þat hailses þaire awn childir with expressynge by worde þat þai are thaires. And vnneth may þai be knawen be þar abyte, for þai haue schort kirtels, straite sleues, and swerdes hangande be þar side, and some bers armour vndir þair kirtil, þat þai mai more hardeli full-file þere luste.

'Also, somtyme þere were holi men þat left gret riches for loue þat þai had to pouert, and þai made rewles of forsakynge of propirte. Thay fled all maner of pride, and cled þame in pore clethynge. þai | flede luste of fleshe, and þai and þaire brethir were called mendynantes: whose rewles popes confermed and had þame in daynte. Bot now þai

2 somtyme] som   10 nowe] *om.*   11 all] þe all, þe *subpuncted* 30 þai¹] *subpuncted*   38 whose] *twice, first subpuncted*

f. 167ᵛᵃ

f. 167ᵛᵇ

f. 168ʳᵃ

are turned fro entent of Austyn, Domynyke and Fraunces, þat made
þaire rewles throw þe inspirynge of þe holi goste. For þare are many
called riche men þat hase noȝt so mykyll mone ne iowels as þai haue,
eftir þe fame is of þame. And þarfore agayne þe rewle som of þame hase
5 propir, and settes not by pouerte. þair abytes is as fyne as if þai were
bishopes. Also, Saint Gregori and oþir saintes bygged places, were
wemen were closede þat vnneth suld be sene. Bot now þer ȝates ar
comon to lewed and leryd, and sometyme be n[iȝt], as þair sistirs liste.
Also, it was ordayned þat þaire suld no siluer be taken for herynge of
10 shryftes. Bot now riche men will gyfe as þame thynke, bot þe pore men
sall noȝt be herd vnto þe tyme þat þai make couenant wyth þe
penitanser.

'Also, it was ordeynde þat þe lewyd folke, at þe leste anes in þe ȝere,
suld be schryuen and howseld, and clerkes and religiouse ofter. þe
f. 168ʳᵇ second, þat þai | þe whilke myght noȝt leue chaste suld be weddid. þe
16 third, þat all cristen men suld faste þer lenten and imber dais and
vigils, bot if þai be excused by sekenes or oþir disese. þe fourt, þat
men suld reste on þe haliday. þe fifte, þat þe cristen man suld not dele
wyth vsur. Bot now, agayns þe firste, þare are mony of full age dede in
20 Rome þat were ʻneuerʼ shryuen ne hoseled. Agayns þe seconde, men
leues þare wyfes and takes concubynes. And some haldes togider boþe
wyfe and concubyne. Agayns þe third, men in Rome þat are hole in
lentyn etys fleshe, and few fastes to one male. Agaynes þe ferthe, þai
breke þair halidayes. Agaynes þe fifte, now are cristen men more
25 coueytouse and more vsurers þan þe Jewes. And agayn all þere was
ordeyned cursynge. Bot now men rekkes no more of cursyng þan of
blyssynge. And þat is, for prestes latys þame, in tym of cursynge, to
entir into þe kyrke; ne þai, ne oþir men nowþir, flees þair company as
þai suld do. And þarfore it is no wonder yf I call Rome ane vnhappy
30 cyte, for þar is many oþir abusions þat are vsede þarin, and, bot þai be
f. 168ᵛᵃ amendid, it is | no drede of peryshynge of cristen bileue, bot swylke
one come þat loues God ouer all thynge and his neghbour as hymselfe,
and do away all oþir abusions.'

35   Capitulum 34. A vision of þe spouse of diuers paynes
          ordeyned for a certayn saule, and how þat all þo kyndes
          of paynes, [y]f þe saule had turned byfor dede, suld
          haue turned to þe same into grete ioy and blysse.

8 niȝt] neþ, *Lat.* noctibus   as] *twice*   21 takes] takens, n *subpuncted*
22 concubyne] concubynes, s *subpuncted*   23-4 þai breke] *twice, second subpuncted*
36 yf] of

þe spouse þan said, 'Methoght þat I saw men standyng and makynge ropis. And oþir makes redy hors. And oþir made sheris, and oþir made galowes and oþir. [þan] aperit a maiden somwhat greued as to my sight, and asked me if I wiste what þis ment, and I saide nay. þan saide scho to me, "Thes are gostely paynes ordeyned to þat saule þat 5 þou wote of. þe ropis are ordeyned to bynd, þe hors to drawe þe saule, þe sherys to clepe þe eyn, þe eres, þe nese and þe lippis, þe galowes to hange it on." Bot I was gretly dysesed for þe saule. þan saide þe maiden to me, "Be not disesed. For if þe saule will, he may зet briste þe ropes, caste downe þe hors, make þe sheris to melt as wax, and 10 remowyn þe galowes. And it may take зet so mykell | charite þat all þe f. 168vb payne sall turne to mede and to honoure to hym, insomykyll þat þe ropis wyth þe wylke he suld haue ben bonden sall turne hym to girdils of gold. And for þe hors þat suld haue drawen hym, aungells sall lede hym byfor Godes sight. And for þe sheris, he sall haue gude smell to 15 his nese and gude taste to his mouthe, clere sight to his eyn and likynge melody to hys erys." '

Capitulum 35. þe spowse shewes hir desire vnto Jesu
Criste of saluacion of saules, and what answere hir is
gyuen agayne in spirit, and how þat owtrage of mete 20
and drynke wythstandes visitacions of þe holy goste.

þe spouse saide, 'O þou swete Jesu, maker of noзt of all þat is, wald Gode men knew þe hete of thi spirit, for þan suld men desire heuenly þinges and dispise þe world.' And in spirit it was onone answerde, 'Excesse and superfluite of herthely þinges wythstondes 25 þe visitacions of þe holy goste, for superfluite and outrage in metes and drynkes, and callyng of frendes þarto, lettys þat þe gude goste waxis noзt swete | in thaire hertes. Exces of gold and siluer, and f. 169ra presiouse clethenge and plente of rentes, lettys charite to be kyndilled in þair hertes, and exces in m[e]ne, hors and bestis, lettys aun- 30 gels to comm nere at serue þame. And þarefor, þai knawe noзt þe fawtes þat þai haue, þe whilke loues God.'

Capitulum 36. Gode shewes to þe spouse how þat religiouse men entird somtyme into þair monasteris throw

3 þan] om.   as] after aperit   30 mene] mone, Lat. famulis

a gudely charite and drede of God, and now `fals´ reli-
giouse men gose fro Gode into þe werld for pride and
wikked couetyse.

Gode saide to þe spouse, 'Here now how my enemyse dose agayn
5   þat at my frendes were wonte to do. My frendes entird places of religion wyth discret drede and charite. Bot þai þat are now in religion
gose agayn into þe world wyth grete pride and for coueytise, to haue
þair awn will and þair lustes. And þai þat dyes in þis will, right will þat
þai feile no parte of blis, bot payne in helle. Wit þou wele also þat men
10 of religion, þe whilke agains þair will, and for charite, takes of þameselfe for to be prelates, ar noght in þe nowmbir of þe oþir. Also
f. 169ʳᵇ   knygh|tes were sometyme redy to shed þair blode and gyue þar liue for
rightwisenes and for þe right faithe. Bot þai haue now leuer dye for
pride, or for coueytise and envye, þan lyfe eftir Godes commande-
15 mentes. And þarfor þai sall haue þer rewarde, dwellynge wyth fendes.
And þai þat serues me sall haue, for þer rewarde, þe blise þat is
endeles.'

Capitulum 37. Criste askes of þe spouse how þe world
stondes, and how scho answers and likkenes it to `ane´
20 opyn seke to whilke all rynnes in haste, and of a fell and
rightfull sentens of Criste agayne þe worldly liffers.

The son asked of þe spouse how þe world standes now. And scho
answerd, 'It is as a seke þat all men rynnes to, as gyfynge no fors
whydir þai go.' þan saide Gode, 'þerfor it is right þat I go wyth my
25 plowe vpon all þe folke of þe world, and þat I spare none, olde no
ȝonge, riche ne pore, bot þat I make þer houses [vo]ide and wythoute
dwellers. And ȝet sall I noȝt make on ende.' þan saide þe spouse, 'A,
f. 169ᵛᵃ   lorde, haue þou [noȝt] dedeyne all | if I speke. Lorde, send som of þi
frendes and warne þam of þair perelles.' þan saide he, 'It is wretyn þat
30 þe riche man þe whilke was in hell, and had no traiste of his hele,
asked þat som might be sent to warne hys brethir þat þa perysch noȝt.
And it was answerde vnto him þat nai, "for þai haue Moyses and þe
prophetis, of whome þai mai be lernid." So sai I nowe. þai haue
techinge of þe gospell and þe sawes of þe prophetis. þai haue en-
35 samples and techinge of doctours. þai haue resone and vndirstandinge.

Lat þaim kepe þaim, and þai sall be sauide. Bot to mi frendis I wil
sende as me list to schew to þaim.'

Capitulum 38. Criste taght þe spouse þat scho suld
haue no faith in `dremes´ wheþir þai were heuy or
gladesom, bot to beware of þame, for þe fende mengys   5
in dremys falshede wyth trewth, and how many
erroures ryses vp now in þe werld, and why þe prophetis erred noght.

Criste saide vnto his spouse, 'Why art þou so glad for likynge
dremys and so heuy for oþir? I saide þe þat þe feende is envyouse, and   10
he may do right noȝt bot at þe sufferance of God. I saide also þat he is
fadir and fyn|der of lesynge, and ofte tymes mengys trewth wyth   f. 169vb
falshede. And þarfor I say þe þat þe feende slepis not, bot gose faste
abowte and sekys occasion. And þarefor beware, for he is full sutell in
connyng, and by tokens outefurthe he knawes what is wythin. Some-   15
tyme he sendes to þe herte þinges þat ar likynge, to make þe at haue
vnskyllfull ioy. Somtyme he sendes heuy þinges, [to] make þe at haue
vnskylfull heuynes: and þat he does to make þe to leue þi gude dedes
þat þou suld do, and to be slaw and heuy. Sometyme he sendis disese
to a mannes hert þat wald fayne plese þe world. Bot þou may aske why   20
þat I suffir þe fende wyth hys lesynges begyle men. To this I answere
þat it is for þe myslyuynge of clerkes and lewt men, and for þai mysvse
þe grace þat is graunted to þam. And for þat cause God suffirs mekyll
þat elles suld noȝt fall. Bot þe prophetes lufed God and spendid wele
þe grace þat was graunted þame. And þerefore þai were noȝt deseyued   25
in þair spekynge, as oþir fals prophetes were, and ȝet are.

'Bot witt þou wele, þat ryght als þou | sall noȝt trow all dremys, ryght   f. 170ra
so þou sall [noȝt] dispise all dremyse. For sometyme Gode suffirs þam
þat are bade haue knawynge of þinges, þat þai may wytt þe ende to
amend þame, and sometyme he enspires to gode men in slepynge to   30
knaw þinges, þat þai loue Gode þe more. And þerfor, as ofte as any
þinges commes to þi hert, wepe þam wele and comon wyth som wis
man, or elles leue þame. For if þou set þi hert on þam þou may be
begylled and to gretly trubbild. þarefor luke þat þou be stabill in þe
faith of þe Trinite, and lufe Gode wyth all þine herte, and be obeynge   35
to all þinge to Gode. Be noght presumptuouse, traistynge ouermykyll

4 dremes] drem   5 fende] fendes   17 to] om.   28 noȝt] om.
31 þe] twice, first subpuncted

of þine awn witt; bot in all þinges haue a drede of þi Gode, and putt þi
will in Godes will, and be redy to do all þat at God will þou do. And
þan sall no dremys disese þe, for, if þai be gladsom, charge þame
noght bot if þai be to þe wirschipe of God; and, if þai be heuy, putt
5 þame in Godes wille.'

þan saide þe moder of God, 'I am moder of mercy. I ordeyn clothis
to þe doghtir when scho slepes, and mete when scho is cled. And to all
f. 170ʳᵇ þat trauayles | trewly I ordeyn a crown and all oþir gude.'

> Capitulum 39. þe moder spekes to þe son of þe spouse
> 10   and þe son answers to þe modir. Also þe moder tellis
> what is bytokened by þe lion and þe lambe, and how þat
> Gode suffirs many þinges fall for vnkyndenes of man
> þat suld noȝt elles fall.

The modir saide to hir son Jesu of þe doghtir, and saide, 'Oure
15 doghtir is a lambe, þe whilke puttes hir hede in þe lions mouthe.' To
whome þe son answerde, 'Modir, tell what þis menys, þat þis spouse
may vndirstande.' þan saide þe modir to hir son, 'þou arte þe lion of
þe kynde of Juda. þou arte þe lambe wythoute spote þat Jon shewed
wyth hys finger. He puttes his hede into þe lions mouth þat committes
20 all hys will vnto Gode, ne will noght do bot þat he suppose will plese
God. Bot he sekis blode of þe lion þat haldes hym noȝt payde of þat
state þat God has sett hym in, bot besyd him for oþir agayns þi
plesaunce. Bot right as þe kyndely mete of þe lambe is hay, so a man
f. 170ᵛᵃ suld hald hym paid | of sympill state. And God suffirs many þinges fall
25 vnto a man for þaire vnkyndnes þat suld noȝt elles fall. þarefor,
doghtir, gyfe þi will to Gode. And if þou trespas, ryse agayn be
penance, for it is a gude wesher of spottes, and contricion makes þe
saule white.'

> Capitulum 40. Criste declaris to þe spouse whilke is a
> 30   cristen dede, and how a man dies wele or euell, and
> how þe frendes of Gode aw noȝt to be disesed all if þai
> se somtyme þe seruantes of God dye bodely and
> cruelly.

Criste saide to þe spouse, 'þe departynge of saule and of body of
35 þame þat hade bene gude lyuers ys noȝt propirly called dede bot a

15 lions] lioons   20 bot] *twice*

slepe, for þai are in euirlastynge lyfe. Bot þat sall be called dede when
þe saule is departyd fro þe body and gose to endeles payne. Bot a
cristen dede is to dye as I dide wilfully and paciently wythoute gilt. My
frendes and I are noȝt to be dispisede for we suffird harde dede, and
for we suffird so for to shewe in worde and dede þe way to heuen, and 5
how besy men suld be to amend þame, sen þai þat were chosen of God
| suffird so hard for to com to heuen. And witt þou wele þat he dyes   f. 170ᵛᵇ
euell þat hase lyuyd euell, and dyes in will to syn, and wald lyfe langer
to continue his syn. Bot he þat loues Gode wyth all his hert, and owþir
is trubbild wyth sekenes or oþirwyse, and settis noght by þe dede bot 10
þankes God of all, he dyes wele. And now sall I brynge þe to mynde
two persones, þe whilke to mannes dome had bittir dede and dis-
pitowes, and, had [it] noȝt bene of my gret mercy þat þai had þat dede,
þai had noȝt bene sauyd. Bot for God ponyshes noght twyes for one
þinge, þarfor com þai to þe crowne. And þarfor Goddes frendes suld 15
noght be heuy if þai be dissessed bodely, and dye here a bittir dede, for
it is ane happy thynge to be disesed and turbeld in þe world and so be
excused of purgatori þat is mekill more greuouse, and where a man
may nawþir fle ne serue thanke for his sufferaunce or trauaile.'

Capitulum 41. þe moder teches þe doghtir how prestes   20
þat hase power may asoile, and of resayuynge of
Goddes bodi.

þe modir saide, 'Go to him þat | hase powere to asoile þe, for, b[e]   f. 171ʳᵃ
þe porter neuer so mesell or lepruse, and he haue þe keys he may als
wele opyn þe ȝate as he þat is hole wythoute sekenes. On þe same wyse 25
it is of absolucion and of þe sacrament of þe awter. For what þat euer
þe preste be in hys awne lyuyng, and he haue lawfulli office and
powere, he may asoile of synnes. And þarefor þare suld none be dispised. Bot neuirþeles I warn hym of two þinges. One is þat he sall not
haue þat þinge þe whilke he loues fleshely and desires. þe secounde is 30
þat his life sall be shorted. And right as a pismawre called formica
wyth besines, both by night and day, gettis sometyme bot one corn,
and ȝet when he comes nere his hole, it falles fro hym and he dyes
wythin, þe corne abydynge and dwellynge wythoute, so when he
bygynnes to come to þe ende and froyte of his trauaile he sall dye. O! 35
And for his ouervoide trauaile he sall be ponyshed.'

12 dede] dede bot þankes God of all, *exc.* dede, va-cat   13 it] *om.*   23 þat]
Quire catchphrase, hase power, *below*   be] by

Capitulum 42. þe modir techis how hir frendis are two
posterns by þe whilke ar vndirstanden god maners,
gode werkes, and gude wordes.

f. 171rb   þe modir saide, 'My frendes ar two posterns þat oþir | folke may
5 entir by. And þerfore it is gude to be ware þat þare be no sharpe
thynge for to lett þame. þese posterns bytokens gude maners, gude
werkes and gude wordes, þat suld be shewed in my frendes. And
þerfor beware of scornfull wordes and fowle wordes to lett þam at
walde entir to Goddes serwyse.'

10   Capitulum 43. þe moder telles þe doghtir how euell
curates ar likned to a worme þat gnawes þe tre rote.

þe modir saide, 'þese men ar like to a worm þat rekkes not if þe
froyte faile, so þat he may gett þe rotes of þat þat is next to þe erth. So
þai reke noȝt yf þe saules peryshe, so þat þai mai haue þe worldely
15 gude. And þarfor, by þe ryghtwysnes of my son þai sall sone be wythdrawn. Ne þer dome sall be lange drawen of lite, bot it sall com to
þame horribill, and þai sall be pryued þaire delites and suffir on harde
confusion endelesly bot if þai amende.'

    Capitulum 44. Criste shewes to þe spouse how þe body
20   is bytokned by a ship and þe world by a see, and how þe
f. 171va   will is for to brynge saules vnto heuen | or to helle, and
how ertly bewte is likened to glas.

The son saide, 'Here þou. He þat is in þe see suld not drede whyls
he is wyth hym þat may lett wyndes and stormes, and thay sese at his
25 biddyng. So some are in þis world as it were a shepe to brynge þe body
ouir þe watirs of þis world, som to comfort and som to tribulacion: for
a mannes fre wille may helpe to bringe þe saule to heuen, and some to
hell. And þarfor þe wyll þat desires right noght bot Goddes wirshype
and for to serue God pleses God; and wyth þat will hym likes gladly to
30 dwell and to sese all tempestes of þat wyll, and make þe saule restefull
fro lustes of fleshly desires. For all þe bewte of þe worlde and of þe
body is like glas, paynted wythoute, and, wythin, full of erthe. Bot
when þe glas is broken, it is bot a litill blake erthe. So þe bewte of þe

world and þe fleshe, when be bodi is dede, it is abhominabill. Bot he
þat chastises his fleshe here, he may leue in pees and riste in God, and
God is wyth hym to brynge hym to þe heuenes blisse.'

Capitulum 45. þe spouse | compleynes befor þe souer-   f. 171vb
ayn maieste for cause þat foure sistirs, doghters of Jesu   5
Criste hye kynge–þat menys meknes, abstinens, continens and charite–are comen to noght and oþir foure
sistirs, doghtirs of þe feende–þat is to sai, prid and lust,
superfluite and symony–are called ladys.

The spouse saide, 'I pleyne byfor þe maieste of Gode þat þere were   10
foure sistirs, a kynges doghtirs, þat asked parte of þe heretage. þe first
hight mekenes in all þinges; þe seconde, abstinens fro all vnhoneste.
þe þirde is continens wythoute superfluite. þe ferth was charite. Bot
þere foure are now dispised and foure oþir sett in þair steddis þat were
broght furth vnlawfully. þe firste is pride to plese þe world, þe   15
seconde is luste, þe third is waste and superfluite, þe ferthe is symony:
for men rekkes noght how þai com to þe worldes gude. þere foure are
euer agayns Goddes commandmentes and destroys vertuse, and
bringes men to sorow and payne.'

Capitulum 46. þe spouse monyshes and warnes a cer-   20
tayn lorde to make asethe of | gudes wyth wronge getyn,   f. 172ra
and whatkyn sentence þe angell gafe agayn hym.

þe spouse saide to a lorde, 'It is rede in þe Olde Testament how þat
a kynge dis[ir]ed þe vyneȝerde of a man, and he wald haue gyfen pryse
þarfor; and, for he wald noght sell it þat had it in possession, he toke it   25
fro hym wyth wronge, and þarfor he was ponyshed, and þe qwene also,
wyth foule dede, ne þaire ayres had neuir ioy þarof. þan, sen ȝe are
cristen men, ȝe aw to knawe þat Gode is as mighti now as he was, and
as rightwys. And þarfor be ȝe wele ware þat ȝe haue noȝt of any
mannes thinges wyth wronge, or agayns his will, or stressand hym to   30
selle, or noȝt to pay hym, þat as fell a dome sall be on ȝou as fell apon
þe qwene, and ȝoure ayres neuer to hafe profite þarof. And þarfor I bid
þe by þe passion of Jesu Criste, þat boght þi saule whyth his blissed
blod, þat þou lose noȝt þi saule for none erthly gude þat sone will

1 bodi] bodis   24 disired] disesed, *Lat.* desiderasse   30 thinges] subpuncted   wyth] *twice*   31 þat] *marg.*, hase

passe, bot restore agayn þat þou has gettyn wyth wronge to þame þat
f. 172ʳᵇ suld hafe it, and are harmed by þe. God is wittnes to me þat | I write
not to þe [of] my hede, for I knaw þe note, bot of grete compassion, for
one certayne persone [w]akynge in prayere herd one aungell say thus:
5 "þou bere, bere, þat now is ouerhardy agayns God and rightwisnes, þi
will ouercomes in þe thi consciens, þat now þi consciens is stille and
thi will dose all. Bot sone sall þou to þe dome, and þare sall þi will be
still, and þi consciens sall speke, and þou sall suffir right dome.'

Capitulum 47. þe son teches þe spouse how [w]e sall
10 beware of temptacion of þe fend, and how þe fende is
vndirstonden by one enemy and God by one hen, his
powere and wisdome by þe wynges, his mercy by þe
fedirs and þe men by chekens.

Cryste saide, 'Yf þine enemy knoke at þi ȝate, þou sall noȝt be hasty,
15 as gayte þat rennes to þe walle, ne as þe ram þat rynnes agayns his
felowe. Bot ȝe sall be as birdes þat, when þai see abouen þam fowles þat
will harme þame, þai flye vndir þe modir wengis to hyde þam. þis
f. 172ᵛᵃ enemy is þe fende, þe whilke knokes at mannes saule sometym | wyth ire
or bakbittynge or misdemynge or sum oþir vice, or dome of ȝoure euen
20 cristen. Ȝe sall not ryn as gayte (þat is to sai, ȝe sall not haue euell dome
of ȝoure neghboure, for ofte tymes he þat is euell today sall tomorn be
gude) bot ȝe sall stand and meke ȝoureselfe. Ne ȝe sall not be as rammes
feghtand, þat is, gyfynge euell wordes for euell wordes, bot ȝe sall stand
stifly and kepe ȝou fro reprouabill wordes, and hald ȝou in paciens, for
25 þat will lightly be loste in wordes. He shewes hymselfe vnstabill and
light and vayne, and losis þe mede þat he suld haue for his paciens. Bot
þe wynges of þe modir of þe birdes bytokens þe myght and þe power of
Gode, for he is like one hen þat kepis hir birdes fro þe feendes temptacions, and calles þaim with gude inspiracions. þe feders is mi merci þat
30 saues all þaim þat will come þerto, and defendes all þaim þat traistes
þereon, for I defend þaim with mi miȝt, and I fede þaim with mi merci,
and I hode þaim with mi paciens, I visit þaim with mi comforþ, and I
reward þaim ane hundrethfolde with my charite.'

Capitulum xlviii. þe son telles þe spouse of a certayn
35 kynge, how he suld encrese þe wyrschipe of Gode and

3 of] om.   4 wakynge] makynge   9 we] he, Lat. debemus

charite to saules, and a sentence apon hym if he do it
noght. |

The son saide, 'If he will wirschip me, hym moste firste lett my   f. 172ᵛᵇ
vnwirshipe: þat menys, þat þe commandmentes þe whilke I haue commanded, and my wordes þe whilke I haue spoken, be not dispised.   5
And he þat will lufe me, hym byhoues lufe þe saules þe wylke I haue
boght wyth my blode of my herte. And if he will haue more riste and
gretter lordeschipe and more helpe of me, he moste besy hym to wyn
agayn Jerusalem where my body lay. Say vnto hym þat I made hym to
be crowned, and þarfor he suld þe more folow my will, and wirschipe   10
me and loue me. And if he will noȝt, his dais sall be shorted, and þai
þat loues me sall be departid fro hym, and his kyngdom sall be
depairtid in many partis.'

Capitulum 49m. A vision þat þe spouse hade vndir
figure of hali kyrke, and of exposicion of þe same, in þe   15
whilke is called þe maner þat þe 'Pope' suld hald in his
awn lyfynge, and to cardnals and to oþir prelates, and
specialy of his mekenes.

It was shewed vnto þe spouse þat scho was in a gret qwere, and þare
aperyd a gret bryght son, and two places for þaim þat | suld preche,   f. 173ʳᵃ
one on þe son side, and þe toþir ofer fro þe son. And two bemys went   21
fro þe son [t]o þe two places. þere was herd a voice fro þe place of þe
left sid þat saide, 'Haile kynge wythouten ende, maker and gaynebyer,
and ryghtwis domesman. Se! þi vicare þat sittes in þi see hase broght
agayne þi sete into þe olde stede where Petir þe firste Pope sate þat   25
was prynce of apostils.' þan answerde a voyce on þe ryght side and
saide, 'How may he entir into holi kyrke? þe holes of þe dore ar full of
ruste and erth. þe postis are bowid downe to þe erthe, for þare is no
place to þe crokes. þe pament is all turned vp, and full of pittes þat
hase no gronde. þe couerynge is spred ouir wyth pike, and brynnes   30
wyth wild fire and brunstone. Of þe blakenes and thikenes of þe
smoke, and of þe pittes and þe droppynges of þe couerynge, all þe
vales ar filed and fowle to loke to, as it were mengyd wyth foule blode.
Wherfor it sittes noght to Godes frende to dwelle þerein.' þane saide
þe voices vnto þe left side, 'Expowne and declare þis.'   35

10 crowned] crowned þarfor, þarfor *subpuncted*   16 Pope] þore   20 for]
fro   22 to] of   29 and] and is all, is all *subpuncted*

þe vois answerde, 'þe Pope is vndirstanden bi þe postes, and bi þe
holes þat þe dore turnes in is vndirstonden meknes, þat suld be voide
f. 173ʳᵇ fro alkine pride. Bot now þere is so grete superfluite, | and riches þat
are keped for pride, þat mekenes is away and all turned to pride. And
5 þerfor it is [no] wondir þat þe Pope, þe whilke is vndirstanden be þe
postes, is bowed downe to worldly þinges, þat is vndirstanden bye þe
erthe. þarfor, hym bose take verray mekenes in aray of hors, and gold
and siluer both in vessell and oþir, kepynge to hymselfe þat at is nedefull, and þe remland gyfe it to þe pore, and speciali to þame þat lufes
10 Gode; and kep[e he] to hym m[e]ny acordynge to hym, and to defend
hym and holi kirke, and to execucion of þe ryght.

'By þe crokis is vndirstandyn cardnales þat puttes all þair besines to
worl[d]ly coueytise, pride and luste of fleshe. þarefore þe Pope suld
take one hamir in his hande and bow þame to his will, and lett þame of
15 þaire superfluite in mete, clethynge and aray, and wyth Godes, and
gode, counsell and charite stire þame to þe gode. And if þai will not
obeye, take þe hamir, þat is to sai, sharpenes of rightwisnes, and stres
þam þarto. In þe pament are vndirstanden byshopes and seculer
f. 173ᵛᵃ clerkes, whose couetise hase none ende, | and of whose pride and
20 lichorous lyuynge comys swylke a smoke þat both gud aungels, sayntes
in heuen and men in erth hase horror þareof. Thys may þe Pope
amende yf he will take fro þame þe superfluite þat þai haue, and
charge euirilkea bishope to amend þe lyuynge of hys clergi, and
amende þair awne lyuynge and be chaste, or elles take fro þame þair
25 prouandres, for it 'is' more plesynge to God þat þar be no mese saide
ne songe in þat place þan þai wyth vnhoneste handes handill Godes
body.'

Capitulum 50. A vision þat þe spouse hade of þe dome
of many personnes þat were lyfynge, in þe whilke scho
30 herde þat if men amended synnes God suld gyfe esyer
dome.

þe spouse saide, 'Methoght as a kynge had sittyn in hys see of
dome, and ilkea man lyuyng had stondyn byfor hym, and ilkeane of
þame had two stondynge by hym, one semynge a knyght armede,
35 oneoþir as a blake creature. Byfor þe dome stode a pulpit, and on it a
bill. And I herde þe domesman sai to þat armed knyght, "Kall byfor þe

5 no] om.   10 kepe he] kepis   meny] many, Lat. famulos   13 worldly]
worlly   30 God] twice, first subpuncted

dome all þat þou serued to." And on|one all called by þair name fell
downe. But some lay langer þan some or þe sawles were partide fro þe
body. And I herd many þinges þat I might not take in mynde. þan
saide þe domisman to me, "Yf men amend þam, I will mese my dome
and make it esi." And I saw þar many demyd, some to purgatory and   5
some to euirlastynge payne.'

Capitulum 5[1]. A merueyllous and a ferdefull vision
þat þe spouse had of one saule þat was presented byfor
a juge, and what was funden agayne it, and of þe dome
of it, and how it answerde agayns þe selfe, and what   10
paynes were assigned to purge it.

þe spouse saide, 'Methoght I saw a saule presentid to þe dome by a
knyght and a blake Ethiope, and it was saide to me, "þat at þou sese
was fulfilled in þat saule in þe tyme of partynge fro þe body." þis saule
stode abouen sorowfull and nakid, and methoght þat it was answerde   15
in a boke to all þinges þat þe saule saide. þan spake þe armed man
þus: "Domeseman, it is noȝt right þat þo synnes þe whilke are clensed
by shryft be rehersed vnto reproue." | þan was it answerde fro þe boke
of ryghtwysnes, "þer folowed neþer contricion ne makynge amendes
as he had hight and it was bidden hym, and for cause he wald not when   20
he miȝt, he is now ponyshed." þan bygan þe saule to wepe as it suld all
tobristen. Bot þer was no voice herde, all if þe terres were sene. þan
saide þe domesman, "þi consciens declares now þi synnes þat were
not amendid." þan cried þe saule lowde, "Wo is me þat I haue not
done eftir þe commandmentes of God as I was lernyd, and I dred noȝt   25
þe dome of God." To whome it was answerde fro þe boke, "þerfor
þou sall now drede þe feende."

'þan said þe saule all tremland and whakynge, "For I had no lufe to
Gode, þarfor did I litill gude." To whome it was answerde agayne fro
þe boke, "þarfor sall þou now be nere to þe fende, for he drow þe nere   30
to hym wyth fandynges." þan saide þe saule, "Now I vndirstand þat all
þat I dide was eftir þe fendis stirynge." To þe whilke it was answerde
fro þe boke, "þe fende sall rewarde þe wyth tribulacion and sorow."
And þan saide þe saule, "I clede my bodi, fro þe hede to þe hele, wyth
pride and many vayn arayes and | prowde, of þe whilke som I broght
vpe and in som I folowed þe costom of þe contre. I weshid my handes   36
and mi visage not onely for to make þame clene bot þat I suld be

praised of oþir." To þe whilke it was answerde fro þe boke, "It is þe
kynde of þe feende to rewarde þe in payne." þan saide þe saule, "I was
redy to speke vnhoneste, for I wald plese, and I desired all þat þe
whilke was not shamefull to þe worlde." To þat it was answerde fro þe
5 boke, "þarefore þi tonge sall be drawen oute, and þi teth sall be
croked, and þou sall noȝt fele þat suld like." þan saide þe saule, "I had
gret likynge þat many folowed me and myne ensampill in wirkynge."
To þe whilke it was answerde fro þe boke, "All þat folowed þe in syn
sall be ponyshed wyth þe, and for ylkane þat folowed þi new fyndynge
10 and comes to þe, [þou] sall now haue a new payne."

'þan methoght þat þar was a bande bonden abowte his hede so faste
and sore þat þe forhede and þe nodell mete togiddir. þe eyn were
hingande on þe chekes; þe eres as þai had bene brent with fire; þe
f. 174ᵛᵃ brayne braste oute at þe nesethirles and hys eres; | þe tonge hange
15 oute, and þe teth were smetyn togyddir; þe bones in þe armes were
broken and wrethyn as a rope; þe skyn was pullid of hys hede and þai
were bunden in hys neke; þe breste and þe wombe were so clo[n]gen
togiddir, and þe ribbes broken, þat one myght see þe herte and þe
bowelles; þe shuldirs were broken and hange down to þe sides; and þe
20 brokyn bonys were drawen oute as it had bene a thred of a clothe.

'And þan said þe blake Ethiopes, "Now are þe trespasses of þis
saule in party ponyshed. And þarefor putt vs now togiddir for euermore." þan answerde þe knyght þat was armed. "O ryghtwyse domesman, þis saule at þe laste of worldli lyfe thoght þus: 'Wald God gyfe
25 me spase of lyfe, I wald gladly amend my trespas and neuir syn more,
bot trewly to serue Gode all my life tyme.' " þan was it answerde fro þe
boke, "To swilke thoghtes at þe ende sall not hell be gyuen. And
þarfor," þe domesman saide, "for my passion it sall be saued and com
to blis eftir þat it is purged in purgatory." '

f. 174ᵛᵇ   Capitulum 52. A ferdfull vision of þe spouse | of a man
31   and a woman, and in þe exposicion ar mony wondirs.

The spouse saide, 'It was shewed to me as a man whose eyn were
drawen oute and hange on his chekis by two synows. He had eres as an
h[ou]nde and nesethirles as an hors, a mowthe as a wilde wolfe,
35 handes like þe fete of ane ox, fete as a wolter. And þar was shewed a
woman by hym whose here was as breres. Hir eyn were in þe nodill of

10 þou] *om.*   17 clongen] clogen   34 hounde] hynde, *Lat.* canis

þe hede, here eres were [k]ute away, hir nese was full of filth, hir lippis were like neddirs teth, hir tonge was a venomose tonge, hir handes were as fox tailes, hir fete were as scorpions. And when I had sene þis, noght slepynge bot wakynge, I saide, "What is þis?" And a swete voice saide vnto me, "þare are shewed vnto þe in þese bodely liknes, for to 5 shew þe gostely vndirstondynge of þam þat are þus defetid in þair saules, by þe feendys disfigurynge, fro þe schape þat God mad þam in.

' "þe two synowes bytokens firste þat he trowed Goddes | endeles   f. 175ʳᵃ
beynge, and þe second þat his awn saule suld euer be awthir in blisse or in payn. By þe one eye suld he haue taken hede to fle syn, and by þe   10
oþir how þat he suld haue wroght Goddes werkes. Bot þaire eyn are drawn oute, for he wald noght do wele for þe blisse of heuen, ne fle euell for þe payne of helle. By þe hondes eres is vndirstonden desire of wirshipe of hymselfe more þan of God, as a honde knawes bettir his awn name þan his maistres or any oþir. Also he hase `a´ hors nese-   15
thirles, for right as a hors, when he has made filth, puttes his nose þarto, so he had swete likynge of syn þat stynkes byfor God, and also in þe þinkynge þarof. Also ryght as `a´ wolfe, wen his mouthe his full, ȝet he desires to swalow þat is beside hym, so, wen he had ynogh, he desired euermore to [haue] of oþir menys. Also, right as a ox files wyth   20
his fete þat he is angird wyth, so he, wen he was in ire, rught noȝt what he dide to be vengid. Also, right as a grype, þat he gettis in his clees he streynes it, and ȝet for he | may noght sometyme hald, for pure sorow it   f. 175ʳᵇ
fallis away fro hym, so he thoght to haue halden oþir mennes gude euir, bot his strenth fayled at his dede, and þan fell all away fro hym.   25

' "Also, þat þe womans [h]eres semed as breris: by þe here þat is in þe hight of þe hede is vndirstonden hir will. And for hir will was more sett on þe world þan on God, þarefor þai semed as breris, þat are prikand as þis world is. þat hir eyn semyd in þe nodill of þe hede bytokens þat hir inwarde vndirstondyng was all set fro þe gudnes of   30
God þat God had shewed hir and done for hir. Hir nesethirles were full of filth, for þat swete sauour þat suld haue gone to þe hede, to haue comfort it of þe gudenes of God, it was all sett on luste of fleshe. Hir lyppis were as a neddir teth, and in þe tonge a venomose tonge. þe neddir closis his teth to kepe his tonge, bo[t] ȝet þare comes a wikked   35
aire oute. So sho sperred hir lippis fro gude shryft, to kepe þe luste of syn, bot ȝet þe sauour of syn stinkes byfor Gode and all þe angels of heuen." '

1 kute] oute, *Lat.* abscise   13 desire] desires, s *subpuncted*   20 haue] *om.*
26 heres] eres   35 bot] bo   36 gude shryft] *marg.*, nota

Capitulum 53. Oure lady telles to þe spouse | how scho
is redy to defende ilkea wedow, ilke mayden, and ilke
weddid wyfe whome scho sees stonde in ryghtfull purpose.

5   þe modir saide vnto þe spouse, 'þou prayes God þat þi childir suld
plese God. Forsoth, þis is a gude praiere. For if sho þat is a modir wyll
plese my son, and lufe him ouir all oþir þinges, pray for hirselfe and
hir childir, I will help hir to haue effett of hir praier. And so will I do a
wedow þat will kepe hir wedowhede to þe wirshipe of my son. And so
10 will I do a maiden. For I was moder and maiden and, as it were, a
wedow, for my son had none erthly fadir. And þarefor I will defend
þam and draw þam to my son þat are in þo thre states.'

Capitulum 54. þe moder telles þe spouse of gostely
spirituall birth of one of þe werste synners, to þe whilke
15 birth he `was´ broght throw praers and teres of gude
men.

þe moder saide to þe spouse, 'Se ȝon child of teres þat is now born
gostely. For ryght as a childe þat comys oute of þe modir wombe, firste
comes | oute þe hede, sen þe handes, and eftirwarde þe remland of þe
20 body, so haue I done to ȝone child of teris for þe teris and prayers of
my frendis. And þarefor he moste be noryshed gostely to gude prayers
and werkes and gude counsels, and kepit wele þarin. And þe same
woman þat I said of to þe, and sent þe to, sall pray for hym and kepe
hym gostely, and loke þat he haue all þat hym nedis vnto his bodi, for
25 he was so fer fallen into dedely synnes þat þe fendes ordaynd þaim to
resayue hym to helle. Bot he is now deliuerd oute of þer handes, and
new born and gostely broght furthe.'

Capitulum 55. þe moder telles þe doghtir how scho will
loue a certayn child for þe prayers of Goddes seruantis,
30 and arme him wyth þe spiritual armoure.

þe modir saide to þe spouse, 'Haue mynde þat þe kynges doghtir
fand Moyses vpon þe watir, and sho toke hym for hir son, and in
Storys it is wretyn þat þe same Moyses by birdes ouircome venomose

6 sho] sho had, had *subpuncted*   17 child] childir   26 oute] oute þer, þer
subpuncted

neddirs. I am þe kynges doghtir of þe kynred of Juda. I fand þis child
in þe stormes of teres | þat were wepid for hym in þe arke of his body,   f. 176ʳᵃ
and þai sall noryshe hym þat I saide to þe of, to he come to eld, and
þan sall 'I' arm hym to wyne land of þe kynge of heuen, so þat it sall be
saide of hym, "He lyued as a man and dyed as a gyant, and come to   5
dome as a gude knyght." '

Capitulum 56. þe modir teches how a man suld not be
heuy for þe chastysynge of God.

þe modir saide þat a man suld not be heuy for worldly disese, for
sometyme þe fadir betys þe child wyth a softe strawe.   10

Capitulum 57. þe moder tellis to þe doghtir how Rome
sall be purged, firste wyth sharpe iren, þan wyth fire
and þan wyth 3okkes of oxen.

þe modir saide, 'Rome is a feilde where popill and cokill hase
growed, and þerfor it moste be clensid wyth a sharpe iren, and þan   15
wyth fire. þan it sall be tillid with a 3oke of oxen. þarefor I sall do to
3ou as he dose þat remous plantes fro one place to a oþir. For, trewly,
to þat cite is ordaynd swilke a payne as if a juge saide, "Take of all þe
skyn and drawe all þe blode oute of þe fleshe. Kut all þe fleshe in|to   f. 176ʳᵇ
gobetes and breke þe bones, þat all þe mergh flowe oute." '   20

Capitulum 58. Criste telles to þe spouse a figure, wyth
exposicion of it, and how Criste is vndirstanden be þe
lord goynge on pilgramage, his body by tresoure, kirke
by þe house, prestes by þe kepers, whome he wirsheped
on seuen wyse and þai turned seuen vertuse þat þai   25
suld haue into seuen vices.

Criste likened hymselfe to a pilgrame þat had ben ferr and comyn
agayn to hys awn cuntre wyth ioy. He had preciouse tresoure þat wald
hele blerid eyn and comfort þam þat were heuy, hele þame þat were
seke, and raysed þe dede to lyue. And to kepe þis tresoure, he made a   30
grete hows, and seuen grese þerin þat he went to þe tresoure vpon: þe
whilke tresoure he gafe to his seruantes to see and to ordeyn fore, so
þat men myght se his kyndenes and his seruantes trewthe. Fell eftir

27 hymselfe] hym hymselfe, hym *subpuncted*   32 ordeyn] ordeynd

proces of tym þat þis tresoure was not set by, ne þai come not in þe
house. þe kepers wex slaw, and had forgetyn þe kyndenes of þe lorde.

f. 176ᵛᵃ þan asked þe lord his counseill | what he suld do. And one of hys
counsaile answerde and saide, 'It is wretyn þat domesmen and kepers
5 of þe folke þat were rekles were comandid to be hanged agayn þe son.
Bot mercy and dome, both is thine: þou spars all, and of ilkone þou
hase mercy.'

'I ame þis lord, þat went in pilgramage when I toke mankynd and
come into þe world, all if I were in heuen euer in my godehede, and in
10 erth. I faght `so´ mightyly in erth þat all þe synows of my handes and
my fete were brosten. And when I stied vp wyth my manhede to heuen,
I left a preciouse tresoure and memoriall, þat is myn awn body. And
ryght as þay in þe alde law were glad of þe arke where manna was and
þe tabils, so suld man now haue ioy of þe new law, þat is of my body,
15 for it is trewth þat þe oþir was figur of it. And I ordeynde þe house of
hali kirke to kepe it wythin wyth reuerence, and prestes to be gostely
kepers þarof: and in þat þai are abouen aungels. Ouer þis I gafe
prestes seuen wirshipes, eftir seuen degrese.

'Firste, þai suld be clen and honeste of lyuyng. For if þe prestes of
f. 176ᵛᵇ þe olde law in tym of þair sacrafice and þair scr|uyse suld noȝt medill
21 wyth wemen (and þat was bot þe shelle, and my body is þe kyrnell), so
mikill þe more suld prestes of þe new law continualy be clene and
honeste for to continualy serue me, as þe kirnell is swettir þan þe
shelle, and noþinge þat is vnhoneste suld com ner Gode. þarfor, in
25 tokyn of þis, þere here is kut in þe bygynnynge. In þe second degre
suld be mekenes, for wyth mekenes is þe heuen thirled, and þe fende
þat is prowde putt away, and by þis hase prestes þe offyce of aungels,
þat is, to ouercome fendis and put þam away. In þe third degre is connynge of Goddes lawe. And þarefor þere are guyen þam a boke in þere
30 hande. In þe ferde degre suld be besy kepynge of þe gostely tempill of
Gode, þat is, mannes saule, and in tokyn of þis are gyfen to him keys.
In þe fifte suld be pouert, to be not besy abute wordli gudes, bot hald
þam payd of þat at is nedefull to þame. In þe sext suld be besines in
preching and techynge of þe pupill. In þe seuent suld be mediaci
35 bytwen God and man. Bot now I pleyn þat þere degrese are caste |
f. 177ʳᵃ downe, for pride is now loued for meknes, lichery for clennes, þai take
no hede to þe law of Gode, and þe auter is forgetyn for coueytyse.
Goddes wisdome is halden bot foly, ne þai reke not of þe hele of

---

13 arke] arke þat   where] were, *superior* h *inserted erron. after first* e   34 medi-
aci] *marg.*, ?medici

mannes saule. And ȝit þis suffises noȝt to þam bot yf þai caste away my cloþis.

'I shewed to Moyses in þe mont swylke clothis as prestes suld vse, noght for þat at þare is swilke cleþinge in heuen, bot for gostely þinges may not be shewed bot in likenes of bodely. And þarefor I shewed bodely clethynge, þat it be knawen and wiste wyth what reuerence and clennes it is nedefull þai trete my verray body, sen þai þat hade bot onely þe shadow and þe figure had so mikyll clennes in cloþing. And þerfor, as þere were seuen manere of clothynge þat langed to þe preste, so suld þare be seuen vertuse for to clethe þe saule. þe first suld be contricion and confession. þe second suld be lufe of chastite; þe third paciens in disese for þe lufe of Gode. þe fourt suld be: set noȝt by þe praysynge of man, bot for to do all for þe wirshipe of Gode. þe fift is abstinens fro lustes of fleshe wyth verray mekenes. þe sext is mynd of Goddes gudenes, and drede | of hys domes. þe seuent is lufe of God aboue all oþir, and perseuerance in gode wirkynge. Bot now are þes clothys changed, for shryft is turned to excusacion, chastite into ribbaldery, paciens into besines abowte worldly profyte, þe wirshyp of God into worldly wirshipe, mekenes into pride, and agayns þe clothe of lufe of Goddes gudenes and drede of his domys, presumpcion; and perseuerance in Goddes lufe into þe sone turninge into syn. And þarefor, as says þe prophete, I sall come wyth indignacion and disese, and make þame to vndirstonde and for to haue knawynge.'

þan said þe modir of mercy, 'Blissed be þou, my son, for þi ryghtwysnes. I speke to þe þat knawes all for þis present spouse, þe whilke may noȝt knawe spirituall þinges bot throw bodely likenes. þou saide in þi godehede, or þou toke mankynde of me, þat, if ten ryghtfull men were funden in þe cite, þou wald spare and haue mercy on all oþir þat were in þe same for þe ten. þarefor spare þou þam þat are not gude, for þare is now mony ma prestes þan ten þe whilke pleses þe in þe offerynge of þine awn | body. þat I pray, þat is þe modir of þine manhede, and þat same prayes all þi chosyn derlynges.'

þan saide þe sone, 'Modir, þou sees þat I spare on thre maneres for thre godes þat comes of my body, þat I shewed byfor in my traitour Judas. Firste, I shewed my grete paciens, for I wiste þat he suld betraise me, and ȝet I put hym noȝt away fro me. þe second, þat when he com to take me, I shewid my myght, when at one worde of me þai fell all downe. And þe third, I shewed my witt when I turned all þer malice to hele of mannes saule. Right so I shewe now mi paciens, for

f. 177rb

16

20

25

30

f. 177va

35

---

17 excusacion] execusacion, *second* e *subpuncted*

I suffir me now as wele be handild of one euell man þat is a preste as of
a gude. þe second, I shew my myght, for þe offerynge of my body dose
gode, whatsoeuer þe preste be. þe þird, it prophytes þame þat offirs it,
be þai neuer so euel, for right as, at one worde, þai fell down, right so,
5 when þis preste sais þis worde, "*Hoc est corpus meum*", þe fendes flyes
away, and dare noȝt come agayne yf þare be no wille to syn agayne.
And þus my mercy is redy to suffir all þinges, all if my ryghtwisnes crye
f. 177vb vengeance. And | ȝet I sall sende my wordes abowte, and þai þat will
do eftir þame sall ende þer life in lykynge and swetenes, and þai þat
10 will noght here sall be disesed wyth seuen mischefys in þe saule and
seuen in þe body.'

Capitulum 59. Criste telles þe spouse how a preste is
holden to haue thre þinges: firste, to sacre Godes body;
also, clennes of body and saule; also, to puruay for his
15 paryshe; and he is halden to haue buke and oyle; and
how he is ane aungell and more.

þe sone said, 'A preste suld sacre Goddes body, he suld be clene
both in body and saule, and also he suld puruay for his paryshens yf he
haue any. And if he haue none, he suld haue a will to do it. Also, he
20 suld haue a buke, in token þat he suld teche both bodely and gostely:
bodely, for to kepe hymselfe fro luste of his fleshe and fro couetyse of
þe worlde: gostely, in techynge þam þat ar noȝt connynge, and chas-
tysing of þame þat ar fawty, and in forthirynge of þame þat are gude.
And he suld also haue oyle: þat menys, swetenes of prayere and gude
f. 178ra ensampill, mercy in chastisynge. I tell þe | þat þe name of a preste is
26 gret, for he is Goddes aungell, and mediatur bytwyne God and man,
and hys offyce is more þan þe aungell, for he handils God.'

Capitulum 60. Wordes of þe spouse of thankefull
makynge of praiers byfor Gode.

30 The spouse saide vnto God, 'Be noȝt wrothe þat I speke to þe as a
wownded man to his leche. þe wownded man sais, "Haue none
horrour of me, for þou arte my brothir." Also I speke to þe, as he þat is
heuy to hym þat will comfort hym, and I say, "Dispise me noght, bot
ese me wyth þi comforth." And also I speke to þe as a pure man to þe
35 riche, and sais to þe, "þou riche man, þinke on me, for I peryshe for

6 dare noȝt] *marg.*, nota bene   12 spouse] *twice, first subpuncted*

hungir and colde." So say I. Almyghty and best of all, take heed of my
wondes of syn fro my yowtheede, þat I haue hurt my saule wyth, and
wastid my tyme and my strenth þarefor. þou arte well of all gudenes
and best leche. þarfor towche my saule wyth þi hand of þi mercy, and
wyth þi gudenes comeforth my saule.'   5

Capitulum 61. How þe fend aperyd to þe spouse at þe
lauacion of Cristes body, makynge resons þat it was
noȝt Goddes body þat was lyft. Bot | onone a gude   f. 178ʳᵇ
aungell of God comforth[ed] hir. And how Criste compelled þe fende to say trewthe, and how Goddes `bodi´   10
is taken as wele of þe euell as of þe gude; and a gude
remedy agayns temptacion of mystrowth in þe sacrament of Goddes body.

The fende apperid to þe spowse at þe leuacion of þe mese. 'Trowes
þou, fool, þat þis kake of brede is God? It wald haue bene wastid and   15
consumed longe sen, all if it had bene a hill of all hilles. Ne þere wald
none of oþir wise men of þe Jewes, to whome God had graunted hys
gret witt, trowe it. And trowes þou þat God wald suffir hymselfe to be
handild of so vnclene a preste as he þis is? For he is myne at my will,
and I sall take hym onone to myselfe.' þan aperyd a gud aungell to hir 20
and saide, 'Doghtir, answere noȝt þis foole, for he is fadir of lesynges.'
þan onone come Criste hymselfe and saide to þe fende, 'Why trublis
þou my doghtir and my spouse? My doghtir I calle hir for I made hir,
and my spouse for I boght hir, and I haue knyt hir to me wyth charite.'
þan answerde | þe fende, 'I am suffird to trubbill hir, and I do it for I f. 178ᵛᵃ
wald lett hir at do þe serues.' þan saide Criste, 'þat shewed þou well,   26
and more þou wald do yf þou were suffird. Bot as ofte as scho wythstandes þe, as ofte scho wynnes a new crowne.

'Bot þu þat saide þat I suld longe sithen haue bene consumed, all if
I hade bene a passynge hyll, if I hade bene eytyn, answere to þis.   30
Scripture bers wyttnes þat when þe pupill was in perysheynge,
Moyses raysed vp a serpent of bras, and þe sight of it helid all þat were
hurt of oþir neddirs. And þou wot wele þat þis was noȝt of myght of
bras, ne of þe likenes of þe neddir, ne of gudenes of Moyses, bot onely
of þe preue vertu and might of God.' þe fende answerde, 'It is sothe.   35
þis vertu was of noþing elles bot onely of Goddes preue vertu, and of
gude faith and obeynge of þe pupill to þe commandment of Gode, þe

1 all] I all   9 comforthed] comforth   10 bodi] *from* godis bodi, *marg.*

whilke pepill trowed stedfastely þat Gode þe whilke made all þinges of noght myght do what som he liked.' þan saide God agayn, 'When Moyses ȝerde was turned into a neddir, þat was noȝt of þe gudenes of Moyses, þe | whilke of hymselfe was bot a frele man, and all his gudenes hade he of God.' þe fende saide, 'It is sothe. Moyses of him-selfe was frele, and of God ryghtwis. And byfor þat God bade, þe ȝerde was bot a ȝerde, and at þe worde of Goddes biddynge, it was made a neddir, and þat was onely throw Goddes myght.'

þan saide Gode to þe spouse þat sau all þis, 'Right so it is now in þe sacrament of þe awter. For in þe bygynyng brede is put on þe awter, and þan it is bot brede. Bot eftir þis worde be saide, "*Hoc est corpus meum*", of a preste, eftir þe maner þat holi kirke has ordaynde, it is þe verray body of Criste, þe whilke body resayues and tretis as wele þe euell as þe gude, bot noȝt to þe same effect. And þere þe fend saide þis body myght be [filede] by þe vnclennes of þe preste, þat is opinli fals, for it mai no more be filede bi þe preste vnclennes þan a kei is filede of þe handelinge of a messell man, or god confecciouns loses þer strengþe for a seke man beris þaim in a wessill: for in trewth þai hald þair vertu whosoeuir bere þame. So þis sacrament may noȝt be filed of þe malice or euell of þe mynystir, ne bettird of þe | gude man, bot whosoeuer offir it, it is ay one.

'Also he saide þat þis preste suld sone dye. þat know[es he] by sotelte of his kynde, and of owtwarde causes. Neuerþeles, he may noȝt take hym away bot it like me to suffir it. And þat he saide þat he had stynkand partys of hys body and an houndes hert, þat is for filth of his bodi and lichery, and for his wrekefull hert. Also þe fende saide þat þere was none of þe wise men of Jewes þat wald trowe Cristes bodi on þe awter: þat is for þai haue loste þair ryȝt eyn, þat menys þe gosteli vndirstandynge þat þai suld haue to hele of þaire saule. Bot þou spouse, I bid þe þat if any thoght com in þi herte of my bodi, go sone and tell it to some gostely wyse man, þe whilke are stabill in þe faithe and trewe. For þis was þe same body þat was born of þe maiden, and myselfe þat dyed on þe crose and rose fro dede to life. And ryght as I shewed me to my discipils in anoþir likenes þan I had byfore, so I shewed me in þe sacrament of þe awter for mede of þam þat trowes as þai suld it.'

---

15 filede] *om., Lat.* fedari   16 kei] kai, a *subpuncted, superior* e   20 of þe²]
Quire catchphrase, god man bot wo so euer, *below*   22 knowes he] know

Capitulum 62. Gode blamed a certayne preste beriinge
one þat was dede in paciens, and how Criste sall com to
euell prestes wyth | seuen bodely and gastely mischeuys.

f. 179ʳᵇ

þe spouse herd how a voyce saide to a preste þat beryd a dede
man, þe whilke had liggyn thre ȝere seke in his bed, 'Why presumys 5
þou to towche þis dede man? þi handis are full of blode. Why cryes
þou for hym to Gode? þi voice is like a froske voice. Whi arte þou
besi to plese þe domesman for hym, sethen þi dedis are like to a
traitur and noght to a deuoute preste? þarefor þe vertu of my
wordes, and his gude byleue, and his gret sufferaunce, sall brynge 10
hym to blisse, and noght þi werkis.' þan saide þe spirit to þe spouse,
'His handes are all blody, for all his werkes are to luste of flesche,
and þarefor he may not helpe þis dede man by his dedis, bot by þe
vertu of þe sacramentes. Bot gude prestes helpes þame þat are dede
both throw vertu of þe sacrament and also throw þaire awn gudenes. 15
His voys is like a froske, for it is all of þe mude and filth of fleshe,
and þarfor it wendes noght vp to God, þe whilke loues a meke voys
of contricion and confession. Also, þe condicions are of jogulers. He
is called a jogulour þat con|fermes hymselfe to þe condicions of f. 179ᵛᵃ
worldly men. What elles is his songe bot þus: "Ete we and drynke 20
we, and vse we delites. It is ynoghe to vs to com to heuen ȝate"? And
ilkan of þam sais, "I kepe noght to be perfyte." þis is a euell voys.
For þare may none com to þe ȝate of blis bot if he be perfite, or elles
perfytely purged, and, wyth þat, perfitely desire it.

'And þare, as I saide, wyth seuen scourges þai sall be priued of all 25
þat þai loued. Thai sall be put owte fro þe sight of God, and þai sall be
demyd in his wreth. þai sall be gyuen to fendis, thay sall suffir
wythoute ryste, þai sall be dispised of all men, and þai sall haue nede
of gude and plente of all euell.' þan saide þe spirite to þe saule of hym
þat was dede, 'A, saule, haue ioy and gladenes, for þi faith has departid 30
þe fro þe fende. Thy mekenes has shorted þi longe way of purgatori.
þi paciens has broght þe to þe hauen of blis. And my mercy sall brynge
þe to þe crown of blis.'

Capitulum 63. How þe deuell, apperynge to þe
spouse, wald haue bygylid hir by resons in þe faith of 35
þe sacrament of Cristes body, and how Criste helpid
þe spouse and compellid | þe fend to say þe trewthe of

f. 179ᵛᵇ

þe sacrament in presens of þe spouse, and þe maste
profitabill informacion to þe spouse of þe same sacrament.

The fende apperyd to þe spouse wyth a longe bely and saide, 'I rede
5 þou leue to trowe swylke þinges as þi wit will not com to, and trow
swilke þinges as þi witt shewes to þe. For sees þou wyth þine eyn, and
heres wyth þi bodely eres, þe brekynge of materiall brede in þe oste.
þou has sene it caste oute fro it was resayued, be towched vnhonestely
and fall downe to þe erthe, þe whilke I wald noght suffir of myselfe.
10 Mykyll more God will noȝt suffir swilke vnworthines be done to hym.'
þan saide þe spouse to þe manhede of Criste, 'A, lorde Jesu Criste, I
thanke þe for all thi gudenes, and specially for thre þinges. Firste, þou
cleþis my saule wyth penance and contricion, and wyth þam þou dose
awai mi sinnes þat are greuous. þe seconde, þat þou fedis my saule
15 wyth þi loue, and mynde of þi passion. þe third is for þou comfortes
f. 180ʳᵃ all þat calles on þe. þerefor, lorde, haue mercy | of me, and stabill me
in gude faithe, for, all if I be worthi to be gyled, ȝet I traiste þat þe
fende may no more do þan þou will suffir hym, and þi sufferance is
neuer wythoute comforthe.'
20 þan saide Criste to þe fende, 'I bid þe sai, þat þis spouse may here
and vndirstand, of Thomas, when he handled my body eftir my resurreccion. Wheþir it was gostli or bodeli? If it was bodeli, how com I to
þe disciples, þe ȝetes beynge sperde and noȝt opyn? And if it were
spirituall, how myght I be sene and handild?' þe fende answerd, 'Eftir
25 þe resurreccion þou was bothe bodely and gosteli, for þi bodi was
glorified, and þarefor might þou entir and be where þou wald.' þan
saide Criste to þe fende, 'When Moyses ȝerde was turned into þe
neddir, wethir was þat a verray neddir wythin and wythoute, or elles
bot þe likenes of a neddir? Also þe twelue skeppis of relefe, wheþir
30 were þai brede or likenes of brede?' þan saide þe fende, 'All þat was in
þe ȝerde was þe neddir, and þat was in þe lepis was verray brede: and
þat was onely throw þi myght and þi vertu.'
f. 180ʳᵇ þan saide Criste, 'Sen I ame als myghty now | as I was þan, why may
I noght make my verray body to be now in þe handes of prestes, sen
35 þat it is no more trauaile ne maistry to my godehede þan þe oþir? And
þarefor now, fadir of lesynges, as þi malice is alþirmoste, so my charite
is abowue all charites. And þarfor, if one of his malice wald bryn þis

---

5 leue] leue swilke, swilke *ruled through*   23 þe²] ȝe þe, ȝe *subpuncted*
27 Criste] *twice, second subpuncted*   29 of²] of bere lepis of, *exc. second* of, *subpuncted*

sacrament, aneoþir wald defoile it vndir fete, nowþir of þame defoyles
me, þat ordeyns all þinges as me likes. And þarefor, doghtir, trow þou
þat I ame Criste, reparalare of lyue, verray trewthe and endeles
powere. And, forsothe, if þou traiste wele and haue stedfaste faith þat I
ame verrayli in þe handes of þe preste, eftir þat he haue saide þe 5
wordes þat I ordeynde, þou takis my verray body wyth my godehede
and manhede in þe forme and likenes of brede.'

Capitulum 64. þe modir telles þe doghtir how hir son is
likened vnto a pore vplandis man, and for what cause
persecucion is gyfen both to gode and euell. 10

þe modir saide, 'My son is like on husbandeman, þe wilke is so pore
þat he hase | nowþir ox ne as, bot he went to þe wode and broght home f. 180ᵛᵃ
trees of diuers werkes, and he broght home ȝeredes þat were nedefull
to bete his childir wyth when þai trespaste, and for to warme hym wen
he was colde. So my son, þat was lorde of all, was wonder pore in man- 15
kynde. He bare vpon his bake þe bitter crose, and wyth hys blode
clensid oure syn. He chase to hym vertuouse men to stire men at loue
Gode, and amange all oþir he broght some ȝerdes, þat are louers of þis
werld, and by þame are Goddes childir gretely persewyd. And all for
informynge of þam and encressynge of mede, and for þe pacient suffir- 20
ynge þat þai haue, Gode sendis þame comforthe, þat þai wax more
warm in þe loue of Gode. Bot when þe childir are bete, þan are þe
ȝerdes castyn in þe fire and brent. So sall þe wykked persewers of gode
men be casten into euer brinnande fire bot þai amende þame.'

Capitulum 65. þe modir by wordes of admonicion 25
shewes to þe doghtir how Goddes frendes suld not be
irke ne sese of trauaile in prechynge for þe grete reward
þat þai sall hafe. |

The modir saide to þe spouse, 'þou suld [be] as a voide vesell abill f. 180ᵛᵇ
to be filled, bot it suld not be so wyde þat all thynge flowed oute þat 30
were putt þarein, ne so depe þat it had no gronde. By þis vesell is
vndirstande þi bodi, þe whilke is þan voide and empti when it hase no
lusti thoghtes. þan it is mesurabill wyde wen þe fleshe is wysely
chastide, so þat þe saule be meke to vndirstand gostely þinges, and þe

29 be] om.

body kepid in plite to trauaile. Bot þan it is wythouten gronde when þe
body dose no abstinens and folowes þe lustes of it. Bot som sais,
"What is þat to me of any oþir? It is ynogh to lyue myselfe." þis worde
displeses Gode, for he þat knawes þe treweth and will not tell it is gilty
5 of þe trewthe.

'þare was a lorde þat had a castell þe wilke was stronge, and þere
were fowre þinges þarein. One was mete þat will not rote, bot puttes
away all hungir. þe seconde was gude watir þat puttes away all þriste.
þe thirde was gude smell þat puttes away all venomose þinges. And þe
f. 181ʳᵃ fourte was armour to ouercome all his enymyse. It fell þat while | þe
11 lorde was besi in oþir þinges, hys castell was bysegid, and, wen þe
lorde wiste it, he sent one to cry vpon his knyghtes, and say, "I will go
for to deliuer my castell; and he þat folowes me wyth gude will, he sall
be wyth me in wirshipe and honour. And he þat is slayne sall be raysed
15 agayn." Bot he þat went to cry cryed not so besily as he suld, and
þerfor þere was a nobill knyght þe whilke, for he herd not of þe crye,
come noȝt þere. Neuerþeles, eftir, he was rewarded for his gude will.

'This castell is holy kirke, and in it is mi sonnes bodi, and plente
agayns houngir, and watir of þe wise gospels. þere is þe sauoure of gode
20 ensampill of gude liuers, and þere are þe armys of my sonnes passion.
þis castell is now bysegid, for þare are mony þat lyues agayn þe
techynge of my son, and rekkes not of þe blis of heuen so þat þai may
haue þair lustes here. þerefor some frendes of my son suld be abowte to
'wyne' holi kirke and chasty þame þat are euel wyth gude will.'

25 Capitulum 66. þe modir telles þe doghtir how temporall gudes posseste discretely noyes noȝt bot 'if' þe
entent of þe possessoure be wronge. |

f. 181ʳᵇ þe modir saide, 'It disese[s] noȝt if one prike wyth o nedill or one
iren in a mannes clothis, so þat he negh not þe flesche. Right so,
30 worldly gudes noyes noȝt þe saule yf þai be trewli getyn, bot if þe herte
be set on þame. And þarefore kepe wele þi herte and þine entent. For
right as a recette of a watir myln sometyme haldis þe watir and sometyme lattis it ryn, so, when thoghtes comes in þi herte, late þame þe
wilke are vayne passe away, and hald þame still in þi mynde þat are
35 gude, as it is wretyn: "þe law watirs fletis furth and þe hye watirs stode
still as a walle." þe law watirs are fleshely thoghtes and worldely, and
þe hye are gostely thoghtes.'

28 diseses] disese   29 negh] neght, t *subpuncted*

Capitulum 67. Criste telles to þe spouse þe magnificens
of hymselfe, and how all þinges has abydynge eftir hys
ordinance bot þe saule of a synner.

þe son saide to þe spowse, 'All þinges are rewled by my ordinance,
as I sall shew þe by thre þinges. First, in þat at woman beris a child 5
and noȝt þe man. þe second, bi þe froite, for swete tres beres swete
froite, soure tres soure froit. And þe þird, bi þe bodis abouen þat
haldes | þaire cowrs of þe son and þe mone and þe sternes, as it is f. 181ᵛᵃ
ordeynde. Right so it is ordeynde what sall come of þe resonabill saule
of man, ne to þat ordinance is nothynge lettynge bot mannes fredome. 10
For all if Gode hase ordaynde all saules to saluacion of entent of hys
makes, ȝet may a man, of fredome of hys will, chese weþir he will be
saufe or dampned.

'And þerefore, right as þe woman berys þe child, so a gude saule,
þat is Godes wife, brynges furth gude werkes þat are plesynge to 15
Gode. Also it is shewid in trees, as in swete froyte and bittir. Wherefore in þe date are two þinges: þe froyte þat is swete, and þe harde
stone. So where þe holy goste will dwell is þe froyte swete, and so grete
strenth þarein þat swilke ane hert is noȝt broken with grotchyng in
aduersite, ne vnskylfully glad for none prosperite. Bot where þe thorn 20
of þe fende is, þere is þe froyte rede wythoute, and, wythin, full of
sharpenes. So in luste is a short and a sone done likynge wythoute-
furth, and, wythin, sore prikynge in consciens. þe third is þat | man is f. 181ᵛᵇ
set of God in certayn cours þat he suld hald, as þe planetes are aboue,
and if he moue hymselfe amys, it is defaute in his will and noȝt by þe 25
cours of resone þat Gode hase set hym in. And þarefor, kepe a gude
will and rewele þe wyth þe reson, or elles I ponyshe, for I do no
wronge to any.'

Capitulum 68. þe modir tellis to þe spouse how þe
fende is like a fox, and how wyth many maner of temp-   30
tacions he bygyles man, and þam next þat he sees
profite in gudenes.

The modir saide to þe spouse, 'þe fox is a whily beste, and he feynes
hym somtym to dye, and as he were sometym slepand, and so he
makes þe birdes for to com nere hym, and þan he takes þame and slaes 35
þaim. And also þe birdes þat liȝtes doun [and] ristes vnder trees on þe

10 ne] none   16 trees] teres, *Lat.* arboribus   36 and²] *om.*

erth he takes. Bot þai þat haldes þaim abouen þe fox mai noȝt disese.
þis fox is þe fend þat persewes gude men. And he feynes hym to slepe
and as he were dede, for to stire man to folow hys liste, and so drawe
hym more baldely to syn. Somtyme he intrikes so a man þat he makes
f. 182ʳᵃ hym to wene þat syn be vertu, as | when he dose rightwys dome for
6 coueytise. And if a man make hymselfe meke for to plese men, þan it is
pride. And also a man semys pacient, and is noght so, when he hase a
priue entent for to venge hym when he may com þerto. And sumetyme
þe fende sendes to a man tribulacion and fandynges to make hym heuy
10 and slawe in þe seruys of Gode. Also, sometyme when a man is comyn
to grete eld and wenys þan to be sikir, oft tym he bygilis hym owþir
wyth desire of lange life or elles he makes hym to want þe sacramentes
at hys deynge and forgett þame, or elles noȝt for to trow in Gode, ne
for to ordeyn for þe gude þat he hase getyn. And so when he entirs hys
15 graue, he ledys no corn wyth hym into hys bern, for he leyues all his
trauailes to profyte of oþir byhynde hymselfe, for cause þat he þe
whilke geddirs not his froyte to hymselfe in tym of h[er]ueste, he sall
not hafe profite of his sede þat he sew. þarefor, þai þat are gentill
birdes, and blissed of þe lorde, þe whilke slombirs noȝt ne slepis vndir
f. 182ʳᵇ trees of worldly lustis and desires, bot wyth | meke knawyngc of þame-
21 selfe and hope of þe helpe of Gode, as it were wyth two wynges, þai
flye vnto heuenly contemplacion and gostely thoghtes, and so sall þai
þan passe oute of danger of þe wikked fox throw þe wynges of meke
confession and help of Gode.'

25   Capitulum 69. Criste techis þe spouse how gude condicions and gude werkes of clerkes are bytokynd by clere
watirs, and euell werkes by turbild watirs.

þe sone saide, 'By thre þinges it may be perseuyde if þe watir of a
well be noȝt gude. Firste, by þe coloure; also, if it be clay, and if it be
30 continuli ʿstandingeʾ and noght moue; and if it take filth and caste
noght oute. By þere watirs I vndirstande maners and condicions of
clerkes, þat suld be as swete as wellis to drynke of, and clere agayns þe
filth of syn. þerefore þe propir coloure of a clerke suld be mekenes.
For where pride is, þere is þe coloure of þe fende. For ryght as a
f. 182ᵛᵃ mesell man þat drawes watir of a well makes þe watir | abhominabill to
36 þame þat seese it, so files pride þe werkes of a clerke. Also þan is þe

---

17 herueste] honeste, *Lat.* messis fructuose   he] þat he, þat *subpuncted*
30 standinge] fandynge

watir drouy as clay when a clerke settys [noifull ensampill of couetise to
oþir]. Also, þat clerke is vnclere as a watir þat resayuys filthe þe wylke
luffis lustis of hys fleshe both in wille and dede, and castis it noȝt away
by contricion and shrift. For right as a smyt is fowle and a spot, wereeuer it be in þe body, and special in þe visage, so þe filth of syne suld 5
be hatid of all men and speciali of clerkis. And forþi, þo clerkes are
chosyn to me, þe whilke are meke and clene in thameselfe, and teches
oþir men by word and gud ensampill.'

Capitulum 7[o]. þe blissed modir tellis to þe spouse þe
ordir of þe passion of hir blissed son, and of þe fairnes 10
and bewte of þe faire son.

The modir saide, 'In tyme of passion of my son, teres were in hys
eyn, and all hys body swete for drede of paine. And onone he was
wythdrawn fro me, ne I saw hym no more to þe tyme he suld be broght
furth to be scourged. And þan was he caste downe to þe erth so felly 15
þat his hede toke so harde to þe | erthe þat his [tethe] were smyten f. 182ᵛᵇ
togydir. And þai smote hym so dispitusly in þe neke and þe visage þat
I might here it, standynge of ferre. þan þai made hym to do of his
cloþis, and he went willfully vnto þe piller, and he bilapped it in his
armeis. þai band hym þerto, betynge hym faste wyth scourges þat had 20
prikkes hoked agayn, and so þai drowe down þe fleshe throwoute all
þe body. And þe firste stroke went so sore to my herte þat I swowned.
And when I com agayn to myselfe I saw his body all torent. And þan
said one, "We will slo hym wythoute dome." þan went he to þe piller
and lawsed hym, and toke vp his clothes, bot þai gaue hym no tym to 25
cleth hym agayne, for þai drowe hym furth, þat I myght folow hym by
þe steppis of blode fro þe place þat he was scourged in till he com to
þe place where he was done on þe crosse. And þan wyth hys kirtill he
wypid hys visage full of blod.

'þan was þare a hamer and foure nayles redy, and so he was made 30
naked agayne all þe body, saue a litill clothe to hyde hys preuy partis.
þe crosse | was festynd, bot þare was right noght þat hys hede might f. 183ʳᵃ
ryste vpon, as he was blody. þan he turned hys bake to þe crosse, and
firste he sprede furth hys ryght arme, þe whilke was onone festened.
þan þai drow vp þe oþir arme till þe synows all tobraste in drawynge 35

1-2 noifull ... oþir] *om., corr. against Lat.*   4 were(*of* wereeuer)] *marg.,* where
9 70] 78   10 passion] passioion   16 toke] toke to þe herd, *exc.* toke, *sub-*
puncted tethe] *om., Lat.* dentes   20 prikkes] prikekes   26 myght] myght noght

of it to þe oþir hole. þan drowe þai þe fete and layde þam on þe
crosse, festynynge þame throw þe harde bone wyth two nayles vnto þe
crosse. Bot I at þe firste stroke fell in swowne, and when I woke
agayne, þan saw I my son hangynge on hye, and herde men spekynge
5 togiddir þus: "Was he þis a thefe or a robber or a lier?" Some
answerde agayn and saide, "A lier." þan toke þai a crown of thorn and
putt it faste on his heued, till it come to þe middis of þe forheued. þan
þe blode ran downe by hys visage and filled his eres, his eene þen and
his berde, þat þer was not almoste sene on hym bot blode, ne he might
10 noght see me þat stode faste by þe crosse or þe blode was wyped away
fro hys browys.

'And þan he comendid me to hys discipill Jon, wyth a voice þat was
fer owte of hys breste. þan lyft he vp hys heued, and hys eyn full of
blode and teres, and saide, "God, my God, why has þou forsakyn me?"
f. 183ʳᵇ And | I myght neuer, whyll I lyued in þis erthe, forget þat voice. For he
16 saide more of compassion of me þan for hys awne payne. þan come þe
coloure of dede on hym, and þe chekis fell to þe teth, and men might
tell all þe ribbes in hys side, his wombe clongen to his bake and all hys
body trembild. þan fell I for fant[n]es downe to þe erthe. And his
20 mowth was opyn, þat men might se hys teth and his tonge. Hys chin
was fallen on hys breste, and hys eyn were vnclosid and þe body hange
lawse. His knees were bowed to þe one side and his fete to þe oþir.
þan saide som þat stode abowte, "A, Mary, now is þi son dede." And
oþir s[a]ide, "Lady, now is þe payne of þi sone at a end, to his grete
25 blis."

'And a litill tyme eftir, þai opynd his side wyth a spere. And when þe
spere was drawen oute, on þe heued of it was þe colour of blode, all
browne, þat I might see it was hys hert blode, þe whilke sight perchid
my hert so sore þat it was wondir þat it braste noȝt. And þan abode I
30 while þai toke done his bodi, and þat was to me a gret liking þat I miȝt
f. 183ᵛᵃ touch his bodi and se his wondes and | wype þe blode away. þan kissid
I hys mowthe and his eyn. His armes were so stife þat I might noght
bow þame to lay þame on hys breste, bot on his wombe. þe knees
might noȝt be drawen downe.

35 'Bot he was, befor, so faire in visage þat ilka man þat saw it had
likynge þarein, and if þai were in any hertly heuynes thai had comforth. And þe gude men had, ouer þat, gostely likynge. And þai þat
were bad, for þe tyme þat þai saw hym, were þai neuir so heuy, þai
were comforth[ed], insomykyll þat þai were wont for to say, "Go we

and se Mary sone, þat we may be so longe esyd." When he was twenti
ȝere in age, he was fulli at mannes state in strengþe and gretenes of
body. He was large of persone, noȝt fleshely bot bony. þe here of his
browes and his berde were awburne hew. þe lengþe of hys berde was
þe lengþe of a palme of a hand. He had a mene and a streyte oute 5
forhede, a nese nowþir to grete ne to small. Hys eyn were clere, so þat
hys enymys had likynge to behold hym. Hys lippes were thike anogh
and redyse. His chyn was noȝt to longe. | His chekis were skilfully f. 183ᵛᵇ
fleshely. Hys skyn was white menged wyth rede. He wente euen vpe.
On all hys body was no spot, as þai bare witnes þat sawe hym bonden 10
naked at þe piler. þer was on hym no vermyn ne skall, ne oþir
vnclennes.'

Capitulum 71. How Criste askid certayne questions of
þe spouse and how sho answerde, and how Criste
spekes of thre states, maydenhede, wyfehede and 15
wedowhede.

þe son saide to þe spouse, 'Answere me to foure þinges þat I aske
þe. Firste, if a man gyfe his frende a palme fructuouse tre, þat were set
nere hys howse, for þe comforthe þat he hade of þe sight and þe
sauoure of it, and he to wome it were gyuen aske of hym þat he might 20
se[t] it in a oþir place þat were more fructuose, suld he let hym to flit
it?' Sho saide, 'Ya, for helpe of his frende.' 'þe seconde is, if a mannes
fr[e]ndes had gyuen þair doghtir, a maiden, wyth hyr assent to a ȝonge
man, if þai asked þe man if he wald haue hir or noght, and he answerd
noȝt þerto, wheþir ware þat maiden weddid or noght?' | Scho saide, f. 184ʳᵃ
'For þe man saide noȝt his entent, sho is noȝt weddid.' 'þe third: a jen- 26
till ȝonge mane stode amange thre maidens and saide whosom of
þame saide þe worde þat stirred hym to moste lufe, hir wald he beste
lufe. þan saide þe firste maiden, "I lufe þis ȝonge man so wele þat or I
were filed wyth anoþir I suld dy." þe seconde saide, "Or I suld speke 30
one worde þat suld greue hym, I wald suffir all maner of payne." þe
third saide, "Or I suld se any dispite of hym or harme, I had leuer suffir
þe moste harme þat I might." ' þan saide þe lorde, 'Tell me whilke of
þes thre is moste worthy to be louede.' þan saide sho, 'Meþinke þat
þai loue all one elike, for þai were all of one will to hym.' þan saide þe 35

---

3 þe] þe browes, browes *ruled through*   4 berde[1]] berde was þe lengþe of a palme of a
hand *and, exc.* berde, va-cat.   21 set] se, *Lat.* ad transplantandum   22 helpe of]
twice, of helpe *subpuncted*   23 frendes] frondes   35 all[2]] *twice, first subpuncted*

lorde, 'þe ferthe is: þare was a man þat asked counseile at his frende of whete þat he h[a]de, and was wondir plentewouse and fructuouse, wheþir þat he suld saw it or ete it, for he had grete hungir. þan sayde hys frende, "Wyth somewhat elles may þou abate thi honger. Where-
5 for, [for] þe profite þat will come þareof, I rede þou saw it." '

f. 184ʳᵇ   þan saide Criste, 'These foure thynges falles to þe. Thy | doghtir is, as it were, þe palme tre, whome þou whowed and gaue vnto me. And þerefor I will sett hir where me likes. And it is noȝt acordynge þou gruche, sen þou assentid þat I suld haue hir.' þan þe lord saide agayn,
10 'þou gaue me þi doghtir, bot I haue noght shewed to þe wheþir it is more likynge to me þe maidenhede of hir, or of hir wifehede.' He saide also, 'Maidenhede is gude, for it is like to aungells if it be deuote and lawli, and ȝet may it so be þat a wyfe or wedow may be euen in mede wyth a meke maiden. I set ensampill of Susan, Judith and Tecle, þe
15 whilke thre were euen in mede, for þai had all thre olike entent, and ȝet þai were noȝt like in lyuynge. Susan, when scho was falsly turbild wyth hir fals accusours, sho had leuer haue dyed þan haue brokyn hir spousale. Judith, when scho saw what dispite was done to me and to my pupill, scho put hirselfe in perell of dede to amend it. Tecla had
f. 184ᵛᵃ   leuer haue suffird hard paynes þat | þai cowth haue putt hyr to þan
21 haue saide one worde þat suld haue greued me. And for þai thre hade one will to me, þarefor þai were euen in mede. þarefor þi doghtir, wheþir scho schall be wyfe or maiden still, sho pleses me yf hir will and desir be to me. It is bettir þat þe body be wythoute and þe saule
25 wythin þan þe body closede and þe saule wauerynge abowte. þarefor þi doghtir sall haue thre þinges, hows, cleþinge, and mete, to hym þat sall haue hir.'

Capitulum 72. Criste tellis þe spouse of two sistirs, Mary and Martha, and of Lazare raysed fro dede, and how þe
30 spouse and hir doghtir were vndirstandyn by þe two sis-tirs and þe saule by Lazare þer broþir, and worldly pros-perite by þe Jewes, and how Criste shewed more mercy to þam þan to þe sistirs of Lazare, and how grete spekers and litill wirkers gruches with gude lyuers.

2 hade] hide, *Lat.* habeo   5 for] *om.*   11 He] to he, to *subpuncted*
13 lawli] lawlilly   15 all] *twice, second subpuncted*   16 in] in mede, mede *ruled*
through   17 brokyn] brorkyn   21 haue¹] haue þai, þai *subpuncted*
24 desir] desiir

Criste saide to þe spouse þat þer were two sistirs, Mary and Martha, þe whilke had Lazare to þaire broþir, 'whome I raisede fro dede to life, and he was more besy to serue me eftir þan byfore, | and so f. 184ᵛᵇ was his sistirs also. On þe same wyse raysed I to þe and to `þi´ doghtir ʒoure broþir, þat menes, ʒoure saule, þat was foure dais stynkand. 5 One was brekynge of my commandmentes; þe second, shrewed custome; þe third, likynge of þis world and luste of syn. Bot fowre þinges þare were þat moued me to rayse hym. Firste, for he was my frende while he liued. þe second was þe lufe of his sistirs. þe thirde was meknes of Mary in weshyng of my fete, an þe ferth was þat þe blis 10 of my manhede suld be shewed. Bot þere fowre [were] noʒt in ʒou, for ʒe loue more þe worlde þan þai dide, and þerefore I do more merci to ʒou þan I dide to þaim, as mikill as þe gostli is more perlious þan þe bodely. And þarefor, sen my mercy gose byfor ʒoure gude werkes, resayue ʒe me as ther sistirs did. Loue me and triste in me, and haue 15 no shame to lat it be knawen to oþir þat ʒe lufe me, and þat ʒe dispise þe world. And þan sall I rayse ʒour broþir: þat menes, I sall defende ʒour saule fro þe enemys of it, as þe Jewes ware to Lazare: by þe wylke Jewes are vndirstandyn thay þat will speke wele and grete, bot þai do litill eftir þat speche. For þer are now many prechours þat | will speke f. 185ʳᵃ holily and holi of me, bot þere commes no froyte þerof. For allonli a 21 blawynge makes noʒt a fire bot þere be wirkynge þerto, and, if nede be, for to put þaire life for þaire techynge.'

Capitulum lxxiii. Techynge of þe maiden to þe spouse in what wyse sho sall noʒt be turbild for a knyght   25 shewed to hyr as dede.

It was shewyd to þe spouse of a knyght þat suld haue bene dede, for whome sho was disesed, for he asked helpe. Bot þe modir of mercy bad hir þat sho suld noʒt be disesed bot helpe hym wyth prayer, for it was noʒt now tyme to hyr for to knaw wheþir he was dede or noght.   30

Capitulum lxxiiii. Wordes of Criste to þe spouse, and how Jhon Baptist loues Criste in presens of hyr, makynge deuote prayers for þe cristen, and in speciall for one certayn knyght, and how throw his prayers þe

2-3 fro dede] *twice, first subpuncted*   4 þi] i *erased*   11 were] *om.* 15 ther] thre in] ine, e *subpuncted*   19 are] are ar, ar *subpuncted*   27 was] *twice, second subpuncted*   34 knyght] kynght

same knyght was spiritalli armede by þe handes of þe
glioriouse maiden oure lady, and of Petir and Paule, and
what bodely armour bytokens, and of deuote prayers.

f. 185rb   Criste saide to þe spouse, 'I haue gyuen þe of my | grace, þat þe
5   fende suld hafe no power ouer þe.' þan saide Jon Baptiste to Criste,
'Blissed be þou, oure blis and our likynge, for it is no wondir all if we
loue þe, for þou art maker of vs, and so þou shewed grete loue to vs.
þou art onely Gode, ne þere is, ne was, ne sall be, non oþir God bot
þou. þou was þe trewe byheste of þe prophetes, of whome I made ioy
10   in my moders wombe, and eftir my birth I kn[e]w þe perfytly, and
shewed þe to oþir wyth my fynger. And it is no meruaile þat we loue
þe, for þou loues þi louers. And also þou, [þat] art maker of all, shewis
loue to þame þat has dedeyn of þe. þerefor, my lorde, we whome þou
makes riche in þiselfe prayes þe þat þou gyue of oure spirituall riches
15   to þame þat hase none: þat as we haue ioy and trest in þe and noȝt in
oureselfe, so oþir may haue.' To whome Criste answerde, 'þou art a
souerayn membir to þe hede, and set nere þareto. Neuerþelesse, þe
chekis are nere to it and more worthy. I ame þe heued, and my modir
f. 185va   as it were þe chekis. þan aun|gels, þou and oþir apostils are, as it were,
20   þe principall bones of þe bake, for ȝe loue me and þam þat loues me.
And þarefor þat I sayde is siker: "ȝe sall do þe same werkes þat I do",
for ȝour will is my will.'
     Eftir þis John Baptiste broght furth a knyght þat semed halfe dede,
and saide, 'Lorde, þis is he þat heght to fight for þe, bot he may noȝt,
25   for he has no armour, and he is seke. And I am halden to helpe hym,
both for deuocion of hys eldirs, and for hymselfe loues to wirshipe me.
Wherefor, lorde, for þi awne gudenes, gyfe hym clothynge of knyghthede, þat his nakedenes be noȝt shewed.' Criste saide, 'Cleth hym as
þe likes.' þan saide Jon Baptiste, 'Come, sone, and take of me þe firste
30   clethynge of þi knyghthede, þat is, a dublet, for riȝt as a doublet is
softe and esy to bere, so þi gostely doublet sall be swetenes in þe loue
of Gode, and to haue a softe affeccion to hym for þe gudenes þat he
hase done, and for mynde of þi synnes, þe whilke he has forgyuen.'
f. 185vb   þan come Saint Petir and saide, 'Jon hase gyuen þe a | doublet. Bot
35   I, þat sometyme fell and rose agayne stronger, sall gyue þe ane haubergeon of godly charite and loue of Gode: for right as an haubergeon is
made of many lynkes and rynges, so charite defendes fro many dartes

---

10 knew] knaw   12 þat] *om.*   27 þi] þe þi, þe *subpuncted*   30 dublet]
dublet as.

of þe fende, and makes a man abill to suffer diseses þat are likly to fall. þis hawbergeon suld be softe and shynand as of gold: softe throw pacient sufferyng, and bright throw gude wisdom and discrecion. Also it suld be stronge as stele, for he þat hase charite suld be stronge in þe faith, and myghtily wythstande þam þat inpungnes it, ne he suld noȝt 5 let for no worldly profite ne feyne for no bodely ese, ne for no dede if nede were. And if þare be many rynges in þis haburgion, neuerþelesse þere are two principall. þe firste is to þinke of what a man haues resayued of God, and kepe his commandmentes. þe seconde is refreinynge of his awn will for þe loue of God.' 10

þane come saynt Paule and saide, 'Sone, I sall gyfe þe a paire of plates: þat menes, charite to þi neghbour. For ryght as plates are made of many peces and knyt to|giddir wyth nayles, so loue of mannes negh- f. 186ʳᵃ bour knyttes togiddir mani vertuse: firste, to haue sorow þat þai þe whilke were boght wyth þe blissed blode of Criste cannoȝt lufe hym as 15 þai suld; also, to haue sorow þat hali kirke, þe wilk is þe spouse of Criste, is noȝt in þe wirshipe þat it suld be in; also, þat þare is so few þe whilke hase mynde of þe passion of Criste wyth compassion and charite; also, to be besy þat none be occupyed wyth euell ensampill; also, to pray for oþir, and to gyfe þame gladly of þi gude. þe nayles þat 20 knyttes þer peses togydir sall be gode comfortabill wordes in þe lufe of God, and also to þame þat are disesed; also, to defende þame þat are disesed agayn right; to viset þe seke, and ranson þame þat are prissond; to lufe trewthe, and go noȝt fro right for nothynge. þese plates had I on when I was seke wyth þe seke and stedfastly byfor 25 kynge and prynce I spake þe trewth. For helpe of my euen cristen I was redy to dy.'

þan come þe modir of mercy and saide to þe knyght, 'Son, what wantes þe?' He saide, 'One helme to my heuede.' þan | saide þe modir f. 186ʳᵇ of mercy to þe aungell þat was his kepere, 'Shewe furth what gude 30 dedes þis man hase done.' And he saide, 'Bot litill. Neuerþelesse, some gude dedis I haue þat he hase done, all if þai be few. For sometyme he dide almows dedis for Goddes sake. And he saide orisons and left his awene will somtyme, and prayed God þat he myght leue þe loue of þis world and lufe Gode hertly.' þan saide þe modir, 'We most 35 do þan as a goldsmyth, þat hase to make a gret werke of gold. Yf he haue noȝt enogh of his awne, he borows at hys neghbours. Bot to a werke of clay he borows ne gold. þerefor all saintes þat are in heuen

---

16 sorow] sowrow, *first* w *subpuncted*　　26 trewth] trewth byfor kynge and prynce, *exc.* trewth, *ruled through*　　37 noȝt] noȝt of, of *subpuncted*

sall helpe wyth me to gett one helme to þis knyght. þis helme is a will
to plese onely Gode, for, ryght as one helme defendes þe heued and
kepes it fro strokes, so o gude wyll, þat is set oneli vpon Gode, kepis þe
saule þat þe fandynges of þe fende sall not disese it. þis helme had
5 gode Saint George and Maurice, [a]n[d] oþir, and þe theefe also þat
f. 186ᵛᵃ hange on þe crose, [wythoute] þe whilke þare may no mane | set no
gude grounde ne come to haue þe crowne. In þis helme suld be two
holis byfore hys eyn, þat are discrecion of what he sall do, and wharefor, and auysement [and] sight of þat at suld be left.'

10 þan saide þe modir to þe knyght, 'Son, what wantes þe?' And he
saide, 'Armour to my handes.' 'þe ryght hand þat suld hald þe swerde
is ryghtwysenes. And þerto langes fyfe vertuse in stede of fyfe fyngers.
þe firste is þat he gyue none euell ensampill in worde ne dede. þe
seconde is þat whateuer he do, do it onli for þe wirshipe of Gode. þe
15 third is for to noght leue þe right nowþir for frende no fo, bot opynly to
do þat þe whilke is ryght. þe fourt is for to be in gude will to dye for þe
right. þe fifte is not onely to do ryghtwysenes bot also to loue it: þat is,
to ponyshe men eftir þai are worthi. Bot ȝet moste hym take heed þat
hase þere fife fyngers, and þe swerde in his hande, þat he sharpe it not
20 in wreth and vnpaciens, ne þat he make it noȝt to dule wyth fleshly
f. 186ᵛᵇ affeccion, þat it be not smyten fro hym at vnwares, | ne þat he make it
not blake wyth lythernes.

'þe left hand is gud praier, þe whilke hase fyfe fyngers. þe firste is
stedefaste trowthe in þe articles of þe faithe, and to trow stedefastely in
25 þe techynge of hali kirke. þe seconde is to amende þat he hase mysdone and will to syn no more. þe thirde is þat fleshely lufe be turned
into gostely. þe fowrt is, not to will lyfe in þis werld bot for to lere at
wirshype Gode, and amend hym of hys sinnes. þe fifte is noȝt to triste
on hymselfe, bot euermore to drede Gode and abyde hys will: so þat
30 þe right hand halde þe swerde of ryghtwisnes agayn trespassours, and
wyth þe left hand of prayer he aske helpe of Gode.'

þan ordayned oure lady armour for hys fete. 'þe firste fote of þe
saule is for to will noȝt greue Gode, all if þare suld neuer payne folow
þarefore. þe seconde is to wirke þe gude and do it. All if it were saide
35 to hym þat he suld be dampned, ȝet for þe loue of Gode suld he wirke
gude. þe knees of þe saule are gladenes and strengh of gode wille. For
f. 187ʳᵃ ryght as þe knees are bowed eftir þe mouynge of þe fete, | so suld þe

5 and²] one, *Lat.* et   6 wythoute] *om.*   8–9 and wharefor] *after* auysement
9 and²] *om.*   16 gude] gude in, in *subpuncted*   37 fete] *Quire catchphrase*, so
suld, *below*

will of þe saule be rewled eftir Goddes will, for a man suld gladly and
stalwortly do þat þat God wald þai did. And ȝet if a man walde do
wele, and is lettyd by þe fleshe þat he may not do it so gladli as he
wald, ȝet sall he haue mede: firste, for it was more besines to hym,
bycause he hade lettynge by þe fleshe, þe whilke he ouercome. þe 5
seconde skill is, for he hase not so mykyll comforth within, and ȝet he
dose it neuerþeles. There two fete, þat is, to will noȝt syn, and will to
do þe gude, nedis dowbill armour, þat is, wise takynge of þe worldly
gudes, and desire to com to heuen.'

þan saide oure lady, 'Son, for þou hase noȝt hade þis armour, þare- 10
for pray we martirs and confessours þat has plente of þis riches þat þai
will helpe þe.' There sayntes saide, 'Lady, blissed be þou, for all
thynges are at þi will. þou may do what at þe likes.' þan saide þe
modir to þe knyght, 'The moste haue a sheld, and þareto falles two
þinges. þe first is strenth, þat it be stronge and brode: strange of þe 15
lefte arme; next þe hert. Agayn luste of þe fleshe, take hede of þe |
wondes of Jesu Criste. Yf pouert greue þe, take heed of þe dispite and f. 187ʳᵇ
pouert þat Jesu suffird. And yf þou be stirred to desire wirshepe or
lange life, take hede of þe bittir disspites and dede of Jesu, and þan sall
þi sheld haue strenth of perseuerance and brede of charite. þe 20
seconde þinge is þe coloure of þe sheld, þat sall be wite one þe to side,
in tokenynge of clennes, and þe oþir side sall be rede in tokyn of þe
shame þat a man suld haue to do syn. And þare to suld be in þe sheld
in mynde of Cristes passion. And when þe fende sees þis knyght þus
armede vndir þis sheld, þai will fle and noȝt come nere, for he hase 25
many aungels and saintes in his company.'

þan saide þe modir, 'Vs moste haue a couerynge to kepe armour fro
rayn and ruste, þe wilke sall be charite to God, for to dye for hym if
nede be, and to be besy for a mannes euen cristen. For þis charite
couers all syn, it kepis all vertuse, it mesys all þe wreke of God, and 30
f[r]ayes þe fendes. þis | is white wythin in clennes, and bryght f. 187ᵛᵃ
wythoute wyth gude vertu.'

þan saide þe modir, 'Son, þou moste haue hors and sadill. þi hors
sall be þi baptym. For ryght as ane hors bers a man in his wai, so
baptim brynges a man and spedis him to heuen. This hors hase foure 35
fete. þe firste is þat þai þe whilke are baptized are deliuerd fro þe
fende, and bonden to þe commandmentes of Gode and hys seruys. þe

10 for þou] *twice, second subpuncted*   16-17 þe wondes ... heed of] *twice (first,*
hede) *and* va-cat *to* yf pouert ... wondes of Jesu Criste   31 frayes] flayes, *Lat.*
deterret

seconde is þat þai are clensid fro originall syn. þe third is þat þai are
bicomen þe childer of Gode and þe aires of heuen. þe ferde is þat
heuen is opyn to þame. Bot þare ar mony þe whilke, wen þai come to
ȝers of discrecion, þai bridell þis hors and ledis hym a wrange way, as
5 wen þe fleshe or þe worlde is set byfor Gode. Bot if a man suld sit
sadly in þe sadill of baptyme, hym moste haue two stiropes, þat falles
to prayer. þe firste is þat he sall thanke God for he made hym and
boght hym, and ȝet wen he had trespaste he suffird hym and broght

f. 187vb hym to penance and forgyfenes: "And þarefor I can not bot | one
10 worde, 'Haue mercy on me, Gode, eftir þi grete mercy.' " þe seconde
stirope suld be a knawyng of hys awn freelte, and of þe gudenes of
Gode, and þanke hym of þame.'

þan aperide þare as it had ben a hors wyth all hys hernes ouergilt.
And þan saide þe modir, 'þis harnes bytokens þe gyftes of þe holi
15 goste, þe whilke are gyfen in baptym, as forgyuenes of originall syn,
ekynge of grace, þe holi goste in wed, þe gude aungell in kepynge, and
heuen to heretage. þese are gyuen in baptym, weþir it be gyfen of a
gude mynistir or of euell. Son, take now hede þat þis aray of a gostely
knyght, and he þat is clede þus, he sall take to his mede euerlastynge
20 wirshepe and life wythowte ende.'

Capitulum lxxv. þe spouse wyth wordes of gret louynge
of Criste and his modir makes prayer, and how þe
gloriouse maiden and modir, in hir answere of gret
comforth, proues by ensamples expowned þat oft tymes
25 God throw his ryghtfull dome makys his vertu to be
more opyn by lesynge of þe fende, and howe bi tribula-
f. 188ra cions | entirs þe [man] to spirituall goddes.

þe spouse saide to Criste, 'Blissed be þou, for by þe we are boght
out of thraldome and led vnto all holso[m]nes, and aned to þe blisfull
30 [v]nyt[e]. And þarefor, all if I be ashamed of my wrechednes, ȝet I ame
glade þat þow, þe whilke wald ones dye for oure hele, sall no more dye
agayne. Allonely þou was byfor worldes, in whose pouste is bath life
and dede. Allonely þou arte Gode, ryghtwis, almyghti and to be drede.
And, þarefor, be þou blissed wythoute ende. Bot what sall I sai of þe, o
35 þou blissed Mary, þe hole hele of þe werld? þou art like to one frende
þat made anoþir frende fynde and see a preciouse þinge þat he hade

loste. By þe is all sorow abatid, joy encressit, and all þe saule of man kynddilled agayne in gladnes. þou, souerayn swete modir, shewid to vs Gode, whome þe worlde had firste [loste]. þou bare hym in tyme, þe whilke was broght furth of hys fadir wythoute bygynnynge, of whose birth both ertly þinges and heuenli makes singulere ioy. þare- 5 for, | I pray þe, my swetteste lady, helpe me þat my enemy be not glade f. 188ʳᵇ of me, ne wyth hys fraudes haue no powere to ouerset me.'

þe modir answerde, 'I sall helpe þe. Bot whi art þou turbild? All trewth is of Gode, and all lesynge is of þe deuell, for he is fadir of it: throw þe whilke, Gode of his preue dome makes sometyme hys vertu 10 more opyn to knaulege, as I shew sall by ensampill. þare was a maiden þat loued hir housband wondir tendirly, and hir housband hir, so þat Gode was plesed and þair frendes gladded. Bot þair enemy had envy þareat, and thoght þat he wald let it, and caste þe lettynge on þis maner: "I knaw wele þat an housband and his wyfe 15 commes togiddir on thre wyse, owþir by lettirs, or by speche, or by comuninge of þair bodis. Bot I sall stope þe way wyth thornes, stokkes and hokes. Also, I sall make gret noys and criynge, þat þai speke noȝt togidir. And I sall set kepynge þat þa comon noȝt to-gidir." Bot þe housband was more slye and wise þan þe enemy, and 20 he | saide to hys seruantes, "My enemy layes for me desaytes. Go ȝe f. 188ᵛᵃ and aspi, and lat hym trauaile. Bot eftir hys trauaile cry vpon hym, þat oþir may wyt and be more ware of hym."

'Right so gostely lettirs, wyth þe whilke God and mannes saule comes togidir, are prayers and syghynges of gude men. For, as bodyly 25 lettirs shewys þe affeccion and þe will of þe hert, so prayers wendes to Gode, knyttynge Gode and mannes saule togidir in a bonde of charite. Bot þe fende is abowte to lett men to pray, somtyme by flesly thoghtes, somtym by worldly occupacions. Also he lettys men þat þai be not herde for oþir synfull men, sendyng vanite into þaire thoght, ne þai 30 will not aske þat at is more profitabill to þe saule and brynges to blis. þe speche þat a man suld haue wyth Gode suld be penance and con-tricion, bot þe fende with hys cryinge wald let þat, when he sendes þere manere thoghtes into a mannes hert: "I am tendir. Why suld I ponyshe my body? All may not be perfyte. It suffices to me þat I be a 35 man of comon ly|uynge. If þou bygyn and eftir leue it, men will do bot f. 188ᵛᵇ scorn þe, and Gode is mercyfull and will not lose me þat he boght." And with siche criynge is God lettyd, þat he hase no lykynge to here

man. Bot God and mannes saule er knyt togidir when þe saule desires
onli heuenly þinges, and is in gud lofe to Gode and man.

'Bot þis lufe is lettid by foure þinges. Firste, þe fende stires a man to
do somwhat agayns þe will of God þat hym þinkes is not of gret
5 charge, bot ȝet þat likes hym. þe seconde is þat he leue somwhat þat
he suld do, and þat for loue of men, or elles for drede of þe worlde. þe
thirde: þat he makes man þat he liste not do gude, and forgett þat he
suld do. þe fourt is to make a man besy in worldly þinges, or myrthes
or heuenes þat are vnskillfull. And þus he stirres to forget Gode. þe
10 whilke foure lettis þe saule to haue homely spech wyth Gode. Bot God
brekes þe snares of þe feende, when þat he sendes to a mannes hert to
f. 189ʳᵃ þinke þe gude, and gladly to wirke it, and fle euell. He lettys | þe cry-
inge of þe fende when þat he sendes contricion to a mannes herte, and
lettys hym to shryue hym of hys syn wyth will to amend hym. Also,
15 sometyme he cryes agayns Goddes frendes, when he sendes vaynglory
to þer herte of þere gude dedes, or when he sendes þame vnskilfull
drede, þat þai dare noȝt reproue syn as þai suld. And þarefor in all
swilke maner of lettynge of þe fende ys þe moste helpe to sai to Gode,
"Lorde, I pray þe helpe, for þou mai shende my enemy." '

20   Capitulum lxxvi. Wordes of þe mayden to þe doghtir,
       shewynge how þe frendes of Gode are now few in þes
       daies, assigned ilke state, bothe clerkes and lewed men,
       and whi riche Gode loued pouert and chase pore men,
       and for what ende riches were spedefull 'to' holy kirke.

25 þe modir saide to þe spouse, 'Why art þou turbild?' þe spouse
answerde, 'For I drede þat I sall be sent to þame þat are harde of hert.'
þe modir saide, 'Whereby knawes þou þame?' Sho answerde, 'I can
noȝt discerne, ne I dar not deme. For two men were shewed to me.
f. 189ʳᵇ One semed | wondir lawly and holy. þe oþir semyd large and
30 couetouse of wirschipes. And þere ententes were noȝt like þere
werkes, and þai haue stonyd me full gretely.' þan said þe modir, 'Of
þo þinges þat are opyn, it is lefull to deme, to þat entent at haue compassion and be abowte to amend it. Bot of dowtus þinges, for to deme
of what entent þai are done, langes noȝt to þe. Bot wit þou þat þai are
35 Goddes frendes þe whilke are ferde for to greue hym, and þe whilke

2 lofe to Gode] *twice, (second,* lufe), *second ruled through*   18 of²] es of, es
subpuncted   20 þe²] þe spouse, spouse *ruled through*   32 þat²] þat what, what
subpuncted

þankes hym ay for þat he hase sent to þame, and kepis to haue no
waste. Bot it is full herde to fynde any swilke. Bot he is worthy to be
called a kynge þat gouerns hym as did Job, þat kepis hym in
mekenes as did Dauid, þat hase loue to his lawe as Phynees, he þat
is myld and abidynge as Moyses was. Also he is worthi to be called a 5
duke of Godes folke þat hase triste in Gode, and drede, as Josue, þat
loues more his lordes profite þan his awn, as Joab, and he þat is
zelatur of þe lawe and lufe[s] his pepill, as Judas Machabeus. Swilke
a duke | is like to one vnicorn þat hase one horn in his hede, and   f. 189ᵛᵃ
vndir it a preciouse stone. þis horn is a manly hert, to fight for þe 10
trewth and þe faithe. þe preciouse stone is charite, þat suld dwelle
stably in his hert.

'Bot dukes are now like licherows gayte þat fightes for þaire luste,
[more] þa[n] to þe vnicorn þat fightes for charite. Where sall we now
fynde one kynge þat taxis noght hys pupill to may[n]ten his pride,   15
and þat haldes hym payde of þat þat langes to his crowne, and
restoris agayn þat he hase taken wyth wronge, or þat mayntens þe
ryght for þe lufe of Gode and his wirshipe? Also, what lorde haldes
hym payde of þat was left to ȝou or hym in heretage, and departes it
as he sulde, takynge to hymselfe eftir hys astate, and releueyng þe 20
pore wyth þe remlande? Also, clerkes, þat are not bot almos folke, if
þai lyfe of þat at is gyuen þame, for of pouert is þe grounde of holy
kirke–so þat God suld be clerkes heretage, for þai suld lyfe of
Goddes offerynges, no þai suld noȝt make no ioy of þe worlde ne of
þe fleshe.   25

'Ho|pis þou noȝt, doghtir, þat God might haue chosyn kynges and   f. 189ᵛᵇ
dukes to haue bene his apostills? Bot þan sulde holy kirke by þaire
heretage haue bene riche if God had wald it miȝt hafe ben so. Bot
riche God com pore man into þe world, for he wald shew erthli
þinges not stabill in abydynge, bot sone passynge away, and þat man 30
suld lere by ensampill of hym þat was his lorde to be not ashamed of
pouert, bot for to desire at haste towarde his lorde verray heuenly
riches. þarefor it was þat he wald wyth a pore fishere begyn þe ryght
faire disposicion and settynge of holi kirke, þe whilke was bygon in
thre þinges: in feruour of faith, in pouert, and wirkynge of vertu and 35
miracles, þe whilke thre were in þe apostill Saynt Petir. For he hade

---

4 to his lawe] *twice, second subpuncted*   8 lufes] lufe   14 more þan] þat
15 maynten] mayten   19 heretage] *marg.,* Nota hic   28-30 haue bene . . .
erthli þinges] *over erasure, also in marg.* (*var.,* haue; *binding cuts off* li *of* erthli)
29 riche] riche erthli   32 desire] desiire

feruoure of faith when he prechid opynly, and wyth a fre voys he
knawleched his Gode and was redy to dy for hym; he had pouert
when he went about beggynge and trauellynge wyth hys handes, and
so fede hymselfe. Neuerþeles, he was riche in gostely þinges, when
5   he bad þe halt man ryse and go, and þat miȝt noȝt no erthly prynce
haue [done],

> [Loss of a leaf containing end of IV. 76, IV. 77-8, begin-
> ning of IV. 79. Missing material supplied from Ju]

f. 134ᵛ   to hom he had noudyr gold nen siluer to geue. But whedir Petir myght
not a getyn siluer whan he reysid ded men and he had wold? Yis, forsothe, but he dischargid him fro þe berden of riches þat he might þe
10   more redily enter heuen. The iiide was effecte of meraclis, for, þe hi
and gret meraclis left, seke men were helid be þe shadow of Petir.
f. 135ʳ   þerfore Petir had with him þe vertu of perfeccion, whech is to be | con-
tent with nessessary thinges. þerfore his tunge is made the key of
heuen, and his name is blessid in heuenys and in erdes. And what
15   mervel wheche has put to God þer part and þer joy, how myght God
be fro them? Therfore, vndir Siluester and odir, temporal goodes were
gevyn to þe chirch. The wheche holy men longe tyme d[isp]endyd to
þer nede and þe seruauntes of God and help of poore men. þerfor wet
wel þat soche are the frendis of God þat ar content after Goddes dis-
20   posinge and, þough þei be onknowyn to þe, my sone sees them, for
oftyntymes in hard metall is foundin gold, and ought of a hard flint-
ston is getyn a sparke of fyre.'
f. 137ʳ   [IV. 79] | A notabil informacion of levinge made of Cristes spouse to
a serteyne deuoute clerke, in þe wheche many good thinges are
25   conteyned.

'Louyng and joy be to allmyghti God for al his werkis. Euerlastinge
honour be onto him whech has begunnyn to make his grace with the.
We se þat, whils þe erde is coueryd with snow and frost, what sedys be
sowyn in yt, it is inserteyne þat they may not burgoun but in fewe pla-
30   cis wheche be made hot with þe sonne bemys. And ther corne and
floures springis, þat men may knowe of what kynde þei are and what
vertu. Likewise, mesemys, all þe

---

5 noȝt no] *marked for cancellation, caret mark*   6 done] *om.*   17 dispendyd]
deuydid, *superior* denyed, *Lat.* dispensabant

[Cl continues]

werld is couerd wyth coldenes of pride, couetyse and lechery, inso-   f. 190ra
mykyll þat men may persayfe bot few by þaire wordes or by þaire
werkes þat are Goddes childer or of Goddes byhalue. Bot ryght as
Godes frendes thanked God when þai saw Lazar raised fro dede to
lyue, so Goddes frendes may haue gret ioy when þai se any man resyn   5
fro any of þes thre synnes, þe whilke are dede euerlastynge. And ryght
as Lazar was hatid of two pupill, þat were bodely enemys and gostely,
ryght so þai þat are ryssen fro syn to be chaste, pore and meke, are
hatid of prowde men, couetouse and licherouse, and also of fendes, for
wykked men are ay aboute to disese þame wyth euell wordes and euell   10
dedis, to lett þame for to wirke gode werkes. Bot remedy agayns þis is
to suffir mekely þese wordes and stynt noȝt to do þe gude. Also, þe
fende wald make þame to turne agayne to syn, and if he may not bringe
þat aboute, he besis hym to make þam vndiscretli to wake or to fast, for
to make þame ouerfebill. Bot agayns þe firste, þe beste remedy is | 15
hertly contricion and ofte shryfte. And, agayn þe seconde, is to be   f. 190rb
rewled wyth þe counsell of som discrete man, and not to take of þameselfe, all if he þat gyfes þe consaille be not so wise as he þat askes it.
For God, of hys gret witt, sall enspire hym þat sall gyfe þe consaile, yf
þai haue both gude will to do þe plesynge of Gode.'   20

Capitulum lxxx. A profitabill and discrete informacion
of þe maner of lyueynge, how prestes suld spende þaire
gude.

The spouse teched a clerke on þis maner: 'I rede þe to dwell in one
inne nere þi kirke, and hald bot a seruant, and all þat þou resayues of   25
þi rentes besyde þi nedefull spendynge, pay for þi dettis, for it is no
skill to gyfe plenteuously to frendes or pore men, and leue þi dettes
vnpayed. Bot when þi dettes are fulli paied, þat at leues ouer þi nedefull spens, gyfe it to þe pore and to þe nedy. And haue honest cleþinge,
noȝt to pride nawþir in shape ne in preciouste. Hald þe paide wyth   30
two changeinges of þi clethinge, one for þe feste | dais, aneoþir for þe   f. 190va
comon dayes, and so of oþir þinges þat þou hase. And what þou hase
more, chaunge 'it' owþir to pay þi dettes or to gyfe it to þe pore. Dwell
one ȝere in þe kirke of oure lady as in a cloyster, and if þu wer in before

---

1 werld] d is werld, d is *subpuncted*   23 gude] *marg.*, nota   33 it^1] t *of*
chaunget

on prude wise, dwell fra henseforwarde in godli obediens in mind of þe mekest maiden. And if byfor tyme þou stirred any of þame þat are in clostir to euell wyth vnhonest wordes, drawe þam now wyth gude wordes to þe lufe of Gode. And if þou shewed byfore euell ensampill,
5 shewe now gude.

'Ordeyn þi tyme both by night and by day to þe seruys of Gode. And als sone as þou heres þe bell rynge, ryse and knele downe fyfe sythis, saynge a Pater noster and ane Aue ilke tyme in þe mynde of þe fyfe wondes of Jesu and compassion of oure lady. Begyn þan matyns of
10 oure ladi and oþir deuote prayers, to þe tyme þat all be gedird into þe where to synge. And it is bettir þat þou come wyth þe firste þan wyth þe laste. Luke þou walke not vp and downe, as it were wauerynge in þi
f. 190ᵛᵇ disporte, when þou sais þi oures, for þat | is token of an vnstabill saule, vndeuoute spirit, litill charite and litill deuocion.

15 'When Goddes seruys es done, þan may þou speke of worldly and bodely þinges, and take honest consolacion and comforte, and when þou comes to þi mete and þe grace is saide, firste speke of Gode and his gude modir to edificacion and profite of þame þat are at þe mete. And when þou ryses of þi mete and hase saide þe graces, þou may
20 occupy þe a tyme in þinges þat are necessary to þe or comfortabill. And þan go eftir to som place and knele done and say fyfe Pater noster, and fyfe Aue, for þe wondes of Criste and þe sorow of oure lady, þe whilke scho had in tyme of hir sonnes passion. And þan, eftir, oþir stody or rede, or ryste þi body or pray, or elles in nedfull consolacion
25 spend þi tyme to euensange tyme, þat þou may be more strenge to serue Gode. And þan go to euensange, and say it deuotely, or elles synge it. Than say þi Placebo and Dirige. And at þi soper do as is saide
f. 191ʳᵃ þou suld do at þi mete. And or þou go to þi bede, | say fyfe Pater noster and fyfe Aues knelynge, and slepe ynoghe an no more.

30 'And euerilkea Fryday, say þe seuen psalmes and letayne, and gyfe v penes in þe wirshepe of þe fyfe wondes. Fast all þe Lentyn and Aduent, and all oure lady euens to brede and watir, and þe apostils euens to fyshe, and ilke Friday onely to brede and wyne and, if þe list bettir, drinke watir. Sonday, Monday, Tuseday, Thursday, þe whilke
35 are noȝt byddyn fastynge, ete fleshe, and þe Settirday fishe, and oyse to one mele. And, my welebelouyd broþir, thre þinges makes me to tell þe þis maner of gouernance: firste, þat þe fende begyle þe noȝt to wast þiself sodandly, throw þe whilke þou suld noȝt eftirward serue þi

18 of] þere of, þere *subpuncted*   30 Fryday] frayday, *first a subpuncted*

Gode as þou were holden; þe second, for if men of þe werld persayued
þe, þat þou failed for ouermykyll abstinens and trauayle, þai suld be
ferde to take on þame swilke gostely labours in Godes seruyse; þe
thirde, for it plesis God more þat þou do it of counsell of þes þan of þi
awn hede, for þe mede of mekenes.'   5

Capitulum lxxxi. Answere gyuen to þe spouse by oure
lady | of thre men for whome þe spouse suld send   f. 191ʳᵇ
[praier] to God, and whilke teres are meritori and
whilke noȝt, and how Goddes charite is encresed by
mynde of Cristes mekenes, and of drede.   10

The modir saide to þe spouse, 'þe man þat þou prayed me firste
fore, if he leue one syn for drede, he puttes ten agayn for wirshipe of
þe werlde. þou askes for oneoþir þat he haue here tribulacions for
hele of his saule. Bot his will acordes noȝt to þine askynge. For he
wald haue luste and wirschype of þe world, and riches, and no gostely 15
pouert, and þerfor hys saule is stynkynge byfor me, and þe gude
sau[c]es of tribulacion sall he not fele to his mede. Of þe thirde man
þat þou sees teres in hys eyn, it is of hym as a mirke clowde þat wendes
vpe fro þe erth, and þan it comes downe agayne, somtym owþir in rayn
or in snawe or in haile. Ryght so a man þat lyfes in lustes to hys eld, 20
and þan for drede of dede he þinkes on his syn and will leue it, | bot for f. 191ᵛᵃ
þe custome þat he hase of syn, he will lightly fall agayne, he will wepe
watir for losse of frendes or worldely gudes, or of hys bodely hele: þe
teres þat comes þan are erthely; or elles, þat he wepe for perell þat his
body is in, or for drede of dede or paynnes of hell, and noght for hys 25
vnkyndenes to Gode; þe teres are as snaw þat will sone melt fro thoght
of þe hete of luste to com to þame. Bot when it is so þat a man þinkes
how swete þe land is þat euer sall laste, how swete þe blissed body of
Criste is, what gudenes he has shewed to man, þan wendes þe lufe to
þe herte and makes it to sorow þat he hase bene so vnkynde to his 30
Gode. þan comes teres þat may be likenede to þe dewe, [and] makis
þe froyte of þe erthe.

'Neuerþelesse, it is gude to drede for two þinges: for somtyme drede
drawes þe hert to grace, by ensampill as yf þere were a goldsmythe,
and laide clene golde in his balaunce, and þan come a colier and saide, 35
"Sir, I haue cole conabill to þi werke. Gyfe me at þai are worth." He

---

8 praier] *om., Lat.* intercedebat   17 sauces] saules, *Lat.* salsamenta
31 and] *om.*

f. 191vb gyues hym of þat clene golde for his | coles, and he takys þe golde to
hys lyuynge. Right so dedis and werkes þat are gyuen withoute charite
are like to coles. Charite is likened to golde. þarefor, he þat dose a
gude werke for drede, and hase a will to wyn hym mede to his saule
5 wyth þe dede, God will accep[t]e þe dede for to forthir hym sonner to
grace. And þus may he dispose hymselfe in parte to gete grace. þe
seconde gude þat comes of drede is for als many synnes as a man leues
for drede, he sall be fre fro paynnes answerand to þe synnes in hell.
And neuerþeles, [yf] he haue no charite, þai are noȝt abill to brynge
10 hym to heuen. Ȝet if þer be one þat þinkes he wald euer life in þis
werld, þe charite of Gode is noght in hym, and þarefor he synnes
dedely and he sall be dampned to hell. Bot þere sall he not brin for
þat, bot he sall sitt in dirkenes, for he for drede lefte syn, ne he sall fele
no blis, for he had no charite. He sall sitt as a blynde man and dome,
15 and wythouten hand and fete, and he sall take litill heede of þe payne
of helle, and as litill of þe blis þat is in heuen.' |

f. 192ra Capitulum lxxxii. Criste telles þe spouse what a deuote
saule awes to haue.

Criste saide to þe spouse, 'þou suld haue a likande mouthe, clene
20 eres, chaste eyn, and a stabill herte. Right þus suld þi saule be dispo-
side. þe mouthe of þe saule is þe thynkynge þat suld be honest in þe
selfe, and of my passion. It suld be rody throw charite þat is warme,
and whike by gude wirkynge. It suld haue two affeccions, as it were
two lippes. One suld be to loue heuenly þinges; anoþir, charge noȝt
25 worldely þinges. þe neþir parte is to þinke what þe body sall be when
it sall be departed fro þe saule. And þe ouer palase suld be drede of
gret dome. þe tonge sall be thoght of þe mercy of Gode, þat sall sometyme be mengyd wyth thoght of my ryghtwisenes. þe eyn sall be gude
thynkenge of my gudenes, and of þe fendes felnes and falsenes. þe
30 eres sall be clene, for þai sall here no vnhoneste ne ribaldry. þe herte
sall be stabill in sufferynge dede, and nede were, for þe faithe.'

Capitulum lxxxiii. Criste teches þe spouse how sho suld
loue hym as a gude seruant. |

f. 192rb Criste saide to þe spouse, 'I loue þe as a lorde his seruante, as a fadir

3 dose] doses   5 accepte] accepe   9 yf] *om.*   13 drede] he drede, he
subpuncted   26 saule] body saule

hys son, and as husband his wife. þe lorde sais to his seruant, "I sall
gyfe þe mete and drynke and cloth, and esy trauaile." Yf þe seruant
be gude, he will say, "I will sereue þe gladlyer þan any oþir." þe
fadir sais to his son, "All þat langes to me is þine." And þe son sais
agayne, "Fadir, all þat longes to me and þat I haue, I hade of þe.   5
þerefore I will not go fro þe." þe husband sais to his wyfe, "My ryste
and my comfort is in þe", and sho sais agayne, "I will dye or I go fro
þe." I ame', saide Criste, 'þe husband of þe saule, and wythoute me
it suld haue no comforte. And two þinges langes to vs: godes to oure
sustinance and a son to be oure aire. Oure gudes sall be gude   10
vertuse. þe son of þe saule sall be reson, and þe seruant suld be
affeccione, not to lusti bot to nedefull seruys of þe body. I loue þe for
þi ryste and þi comfort is in me, and for þou hade leuer suffir þe
dede or þou wer departed fro me. Also, I lufe þe as a fadir lufis his
son, | for I haue gyfen þe fre will, and also I lufe þe as a seruant, for I   f. 192ᵛᵃ
haue sente to þe all þat was nedefull to þi body.'   16

Capitulum lxxxiiii. Criste telles of thre men þat were
supplantid for wommen, and he likenes þam.

'It is rede of thre þat were begyled with wimmen. One was a king
þat smetin was of his lemman in þe visage when he wald not lagh   20
with hire. He þis was a crowened asse: one asse for his foly, and
crowned for his dignite. þe second was Sampson, þat, notwytstand-
ynge all his strenge, he was ouercomyn with a woman, for he had ane
hares hert: for faintes he miȝt noȝt chasti a woman. þe þird was
Salamon, like to a basiliske, þat is a cocatrise, þat was slain be a   25
womanse visage, as þe basiliske bi sight of a miror, and so was his
witt ouercomen.'

Capitulum lxxxv. Criste telles þe spouse of two leues of
a boke, and of þe wrytynge of it.

Criste telles þe spouse of two leues þat are wretyn: 'In one was   30
mercy, in þe oþir was ryghtwisnes. Bot who þat will forsake þe
vanite of þis world, my spirit sall make hym feruent in loue. And
when he is redy to dye for me, þan sall | he dwell in me and I in hym.   f. 192ᵛᵇ
Ryghtwisnes sais, "Whoso will not amend hym while he has tyme,
bot turnes hym fro Gode, þe fadir sall noȝt defende hym, ne þe son   35
helpe, ne þe holi goste warm hym." þerefor now is gude to take tent

to þe lefe of mercy, for þere was one þat toke no heede þerof, and
coueyt[ed] to be aboue all oþir, and in þe night he was soudanly
slayne.'

[Capitulum lxxxvi]. þe modir of mercy said, 'I am like to a floure, of
5 þe whilke þe bee takes grete swetenes, and ȝet þere leueis swetenes.
So I gate grace to all, and I ame euer full of grace. And my derlynges
are like to bees, for all þair besines is aboute my wirshype. Thay haue
two wynges. One is lufe of charite; anoþir is obediens. They haue
tribulacion instede of þaire tonge, þe whilke kepis þame þat þer
10 vertuse be not taken fro þame, as þe tonge kepis þaire bodis.'

Capitulum lxxxvii. Criste telles þe spouse how sho suld
haue clene membres, and likenes þam to loue.

f. 193ʳᵃ   Criste sais to þe spouse, 'I saide | to þe þat þou suld haue clere eyn,
þat þou might se þe euell þat þou hase done and þe gude þat þou hase
15 left. þi mouth, þat is, þi mynde, suld be clene fro all euell. Thy lippes
suld be wille to leue all þe world for me, and will to dwell ay wyth me.
þai suld be rede by clerenes of charite and gude wirkynge. þi left arme
is mynde of þe gudenes þat God hase shewed þe, and þe riȝt arme is
feruent lufe to me, so þat þou will not greue me for all þe world. And
20 bitwix þe armes wyll I gladly ryste. þere ribbes þat kepis þe hert are my
frendes, þat þou suld lufe more þan þi bodely frendes for my lufe, for
my charite birnes and will noȝt be slokend, bot it makes my saule
warme, and strengþs it, as þe bird called fenix, þe whilke, in þe eld of
it, gedirs togidir stikkes in a hye mount, and þai are kyndeled at þe
25 hete of þe son. And þis bird flies into þe fire, and of þe askes of it ryses
vp anoþir of þe same kynd: so þat þe saule þe whilke is brent in my
lufe ryses better and stronger þan it was before.'

Capitulum lxxxviii. Criste telles þe spowse þat all
f. 193ʳᵇ   þinges þat are made kepis | his will bot man, and of
30   likenes bytwene man and shyppes in þe see.

þe son saide, 'I ame maker of all spirites, both gude and euell,
rewler and gouerner, and all þinges þat are in heuen, in erthe and see
folowes eftir mi will bot onli man. For ryght as a shepe at hase loste þe

2 coueyted] coueyt   4 Capitulum lxxxvi] om., space of one line for chapter title
13 saide] Quire catchphrase, to þe þat þu, below   20 þere] also marg.
33 folowes] fowlowes

stere and þe maste waueris here and þere, so man þat is wythouten
me, þat am verray stere, is vnstabill to he come to þe ryghtwysnes of
dede. Bot þe shipe of religion has his stere. He hase his maste, and þat
is þe law of God þat is vpryght. þe chefe anker is paciens. þe second
anker is gode wille to serue God, bunden wyth faithe and hope, as it   5
were two ropes, þat kepes þe shipe stabill in þe loue of God, and kepis
it fro þe watir of dissolucion and vanite. And in þis shipe are my
frendes redy to saile to heuen.'

    Capitulum lxxxix. Criste telles to þe spouse þe maner
    þat a gastly knyght suld kepe in batale, and how he sall   10
    prai and treste in Gode.

  Crist saide, 'He þat will feght gostely, traiste in me and noght in |
hys awn strenght. He þat mystrastes my gudenes, þinkyng þus: "Yf I   f. 193va
take vpon me to refreyn my fleshe in fastyng or to labour in wakynge, I
may nowþir continu in abstinens ne haue perseuerance, for God   15
helpis me noght"–it is ryght þat swilke a man faile and falle. þerfor he
þat will fight gostely, traiste he þat in my grace he may brynge þat to a
perfite ende. Also, haue he gude will to wirke þe gude and leue þe
euell, and, if he fall, to ryse agayne, and ofte to pray þus: "Lord God
almighti, þat ledis all men to þe gude, I haue ofte tymes wythdrawen   20
me fro þe by my synnes. I thanke þe þat þou hase broght me agayne to
þe ryght way. þerfore, mildfull Jesu, I pray þe þat hange on þe crose,
blody and sorowfull, þat þou haue mercy on me, and for þi fyfe
wowndes, and for þe swerde þat went to þi hert, wouchesayfe to kepe
me þis day, þat I fall in no syn. Also, þou gyue me myght to wythstande 25
þe fandynges of þe fende, and if I fall, to ryse agayn." Also pray on þis
manere: "A, lord Gode, in whome is al myght, þou gyfe me strenght to
wirke gude werkes, and for to haue perseuerance | in gudenes."   f. 193vb
  'And þan to make a clene confession–þe whilke is a gostely swerde.
For, eftir þe propirte of a swerde, confession polyshes and discusses   30
wele a mannes consciens, in what whyse, how gretely, and whar þat he
hase trespast. And loke þat þare be no ruste of sham ne of hydyng
þerein, ne say non oþir wyse þan it is. þe whilke swerde of shryft sall
haue ii sydes. One is will to syn no more. þe toþir is will to mend þat is
mysdone. þe poynt of þe swerd is contricion þat þe fende sall be slayn   35
wyth. þe pomel is þe gret mercy of God. þe hilt is warenes of presumpsion, þat o man presume not more þan he suld do. Hald fast þe

3 stere] stere and þat is þ

swerd of confession wyth drede of losyng of grace. And þarefor þe
handill of þis swerde is thoght of þe ryghtwis dome of Gode and of his
mercy. And þan sall he be keped fro presumpcion and also dispaire.
þe habergeon sall be abstinens, not onely fro metes and drynkes, bot
5 also fro vices of glotory and lichery of þe sight and oþir wittes þat Saint
Benet has bedyn men ware fro, and do þam noȝt. And to fulfill þis is
f. 194ᴿᵃ nedefull to kall my moder | to helpe. þe helme of þis knyght sall be
perfite hope, þat hase two holes. One is forethoght of þat at suld be
done, and oneoþere is to fle þat `at´ suld noȝt be done. þe shelde is
10 paciens, þat suffirs all þe strokes þat comen.'

Capitulum xc. Criste telles to þe spouse how his
frendes are a[s] his arm, and he, as a gude lecch, cuttes
away rotyn fleshe and transforme[s] þame vnto hymselfe.

15 Criste saide, 'My frendes are as my arme, in þe whilke are fyfe þinges.
þe firste is þe skyn, þan fleshe, blode, bone and mergh. Bot I do as a
surgen þat cuttes away all þat is dede. So I take away fro my frendes þe
worldly coueytise and lustes of fleshe, and I putt to þame helpe of my
myght, as it were mergh, for ryght as wythouten mergh is no strengh in
20 þe arme, right so wythouten my might is mannes might noȝt. And þis
mergh is in þe bone þat is sade. So sall my frendes knaw my myght and
besy þam to wirke þe gude wyth a lastyng will. þe third is þe blode, þat
bytokens a gude will; and þe fleshe paciens, þat is softe of þe selfe; and
f. 194ᴿᵇ þe skyn bytokens lufe, in token | þat þai suld lufe noþinge so mykyll as
25 me. And þan I knyt þam fulli to myselfe, and hase þame all in me.'

Capitulum xci. Criste warnes þe spouse to make hire
meke in foure wise.

Criste said to þe spouse, 'On foure wise suld þou meke þe: firste, to
þe grete men of þe werld, for, bycause þat man wald noȝt kepe þe obe-
30 diens of Gode, þerefor he sall stand vndir þe obedience of man. þe
second is to pray for þam þat are in syn, þat God deliuer þame oute
þereof. þe third is þat þou be meke to my frendes, thynkynge þou art
noȝt worthi to comon wyth þame. þe ferde is, meke þe to þe pore
folke, cleþinge þame and seruynge þame, and weshyng þer fete.'

2 thoght] grace thoght, grace *ruled through*   9 at] a   12 as¹] at
13 transformes] transforme   27 wise] wise et ideo

Capitulum xcii. Criste warned þe spouse to haue perseuerance in vertuse, folowyng þe life of sayntes.

Criste saide to þe spouse, 'I saide þe þat my frendes are myne arme.
My godehede is as it were þe mergh, for wythouten it may no man life.
Mi manhede is bones, þat suffird so stalworthli, painfulli, passion. þe 5
skyn is my moder | and þe sayntes of heuen, þat prayes for þe synfull to f. 194ᵛᵃ
couer þer syn, as þe skyn coueres þe fleshe. þe blode þat is stirrynge in
þe body is my gode goste þat stires þam to all gude: and þus am I knyt
to my frendes.'

Capitulum xciii. Criste commandes iii þinges to þe   10
spowse, þat sho desire noþing bot nedefull sustinance
of mete and cleþinge, ne spiritual þinge bot at þe will of
Gode, ne be not heuy of noþing bot of syn.

Criste saide to þe spouse, 'Thre thynges I bid þe. Firste, coueyt no
worldly þinge bot mete, drynke and cloþinge. þe second, couete no 15
gostely þinge bot at my will. þe thirde is þat þou sall not be heuy for
noþing bot for syn, and for drede of my dome, as I sall shew þe be
ensampill. þere was a man and come to a abbay, and thoght þus:
"Firste, I wald noȝt trauayle. þe second, I wald fare wele wythoute
besines. þe iii, if I war stirred to lichery I wald flee þe dede if I myȝt be 20
any sleght." And agayn þes thre he was desesed on thre wyse: first
wyth wordes and | betynges, and he was constreyned to trauayle. As f. 194ᵛᵇ
anentes þe seconde, he had a gret mischefe of mete and of cleþynge.
And anentes þe third, he was so gretely dispised of oþir þat he had no
likynge of lichery. 25

'When tym com of hys profession, he thoght þus: "I may noght be in
þe world bot I trauaile. þerefor me is bettir to be still h[e]re and
trauayle for þe lufe of Gode." And for þat will I sent to hym my mercy
wyth my ryghtwisnes, þat he suld be clensid and com to euerlastyng
blis. And þerefor, as sone as he was profest, he was smetyn wyth so 30
grete sekenes þat he myght nowþir se no here, and all his lymmes
failed hym. He was naked, and when he wald haue etyn, he myght
noght. And he was sa anentysed and wastid, or he dyed, þat he lay as it
had bene a stoke. And when he was dede, he was broght to þe dome as
he had bene a theef, for he wald haue bene in religion at his awn will, 35

19 I wald²] I wald not *twice*, not, not, *subpuncted and ruled through*   27 here] hire

bot he was taken to mercy. Befor his dede he was noȝt fully clensid in
f. 195ʳᵃ   þis life, and þarefor he is now in purgatory, where | he is now ponyshed
so greuously as if þe bones 'wer pressed' and þe margh ran oute. A,
what sall þai þan suffir þat all þair life ligges in syn, and þerto hase all
5   þair will! Thay say, "Why died God, or what profite com of his dede?"
Lo, so vnkynde þai are. Bot for þai haue broken þer faithe þat þai
hight in baptym, þai sall come to þe hard dome, and I sall not leue þe
leste poynt þat þai trespaste agayn þer religion vnponyshede.'

Capitulum xciiii. Criste teches þe spouse faire orisons
10   to say when sho dose on hir clothis, and gose to þe
[b]ord, steryng hir to meknes and honeste.

Criste saide to his spouse, 'Fairnes withowte bytokens fairnes
wythin. And when þou dose þi howde or þi cap on þi heued, say þus:
"A, lord God, I þanke þe þat þou has noȝt distruyd me in mi syn. And
15   for my vnclennes I am not worthi to se þe. And þerfor I couer my
heued." ' þan saide Criste, 'Lechory is so fowle to me þat if a maiden
haue full will to do þe deed of lichory, sho is no maiden in my sight,
bot sho chaunge þat will. Also when þou couers þi forhede, say,
f. 195ʳᵇ   "Blissed be þou, | lord, þat made me to þi likenes. Hafe mercy on me,
20   for I hafe not keped my bewte to þi wirship. þerefor I couer my forheued." And when þou dose on þi shone, say, "Lord, gyfe me grace þat
I may go in þine commandmentes, and kepe þame". And in all oþir
cleþinge, loke þat þou be meke. And wen þou sall go to þi mete, say,
"Lord, I beseke þe to gyfe me grace so to take of mete and drynke þat
25   my kynd may be sustenyd, and noght to take outrage." Also, when þou
sall go to þi bede, say, "Lord, I beseke þe to gyue my body reste, and
kepe my saule fro þe feendes power and his dissaytes." '

Capitulum xcv. Crist shewes to þe spouse whilk is þe
armour of a euell man.

30   Criste likkens hymselfe to a kynge þat standes redy to þe bataile.
And þe fende standes armed agayns hym. And or he meked hym, he
had leuer suffir as mony mischeues as þare are motes in þe son. 'Now
þe feend comes wyth his oste. His baner is raysed. þe sheld is on þe
shuldir. þe hand is at þe swerde, bot it is noȝt drawen. In þis bannere

are glutry, lichory | and couetyse. þe helme is hardnes of hert, for þai   f. 195ᵛᵃ
take no hede of þe filth of syn, ne of þe paynes of hell. One hole in þe
helme is luste of fleshe. þe toþir is plesyng of þe werld, for þer to
makes folk besy in þe world. þe sheld is falshede þat þai excuse þair
syn wyth, and puttes it on þe freelte of þe fleshe. And þarefor þai aske   5
no forgyfenes. þe swerde is will to laste in syn, þat is noȝt ȝet drawen,
for þare malice is noȝt ȝit at one ende. For þai wald euermor lyfe, so
þat þai myght euermore haue þair luste in syn, and þai haue grete
likyng of þat syn þe whilke þai haue done. And þerfor is now a voice
herde in my company: "Smyte now!" And þe swerde of my ryght-   10
wisnes sall destroye þere bodys, and fendes sall take þair saules and
wythoute reste ryue þame.'

Capitulum xcvi. Criste declares to þe spouse certayn
poyntes spoken of byfore.

Criste saide to þe spouse, 'I saide þe þat `þere´ were bot two fete   15
bytwyne my enmys and me. One is rewarde of þe gude dedes þat I hafe
| gyfen þame. And þerfor, fro þis tyme sall þare shame be shewed, þar   f. 195ᵛᵇ
likyng sall be lessid, þar sorow sall be newed. þe second fote is þere
malice þat is not ȝit fulfilled, bot when þe body and þe saule sall be
departed. þer swerde is will to syn and not to leue, so þat þai may frely   20
syne. Bot wo is þame bot þai amend þame, for þaire vndoynge is now
at þe hande.'

Capitulum xcvii. Criste telles þe spouse how a deuote
saule þe whilke be pride hase loste þe hete of deuocion
and holy meditacion may couer it agayne by meknes.   25

Criste sent by hys spouse to a prelate on þis manere. 'þou arte like
to a whele of a myln þat standes stille and gryndes noȝt. So þi will suld
be moued at myne ordynance, bot it is noȝt moued at my will, ne takes
no hede to my passion, and þerfor is þer no gostely mete þat sauers þi
saule. And þerefore briste þe stoppyng of þe watir, and lat it haue þe   30
cours, þat þe myllen may turn and þe corn grynde. þis watir is þe
grace of Gode þat is stoppid with pride and | ambicion. And þerfor   f. 196ʳᵃ
take mekenes, for by it sall swetenes of þe hali gaste flow into þi saule,

9 likyng] likyng þerin, þerin *ruled through*   27 of] *twice*   28 myne] myne
ne takes no hede, *exc.* myne, *ruled through*   ordynance] ordyinance, i *subpuncted*
33 flow] folow

and þan sall þi will be rewlid eftir me, and þou sall deme þi awn
werkes. And þan my passion and holy saintes lyfynges sall sauer þe,
and þan sall þou witt how þou arte halden to þe saules þat are com-
mytt to þi cure. Bot for þou arte vpwarde [o]n þe whele by myght and
5 wirshipe, it makes þe to prowde. þerefor come downe and meke þe,
and pray meke men to pray for þe, or elles I sall send to þe mi ryghtwisnes, and I sall ponyshe þe for myskepyng of saules þat I boght wyth
my blode.'

Capitulum xcviii. Of fowre maner of blamynges þat
10 synners suld be prikked wyth.

Criste saide, 'þare is one blynde on þe one eye, oneoþir halt on
one fote, þe þirde deefe on one ere, þe fourte casten down to þe erth.
þe blynd is he þat is lerned in þe commandmentes of God and in
holy mennes lyues, and takes no hede to þame, bot of likynges of þe
15 werld. And þerefore þere bose be shote to hym a darte, and say to
f. 196ʳᵇ hym þus: "þou arte like to | Lucifer, þat desired þe grete hynes of
Gode, and for he desired oþirwyse þan he suld he fell into hell, and
so sall þou bot þou leue þe likyng of þe werlde sen þat þou knawes
þe law of God." Also, he is halt on þe to fote þat is s[a]ddid of his
20 syn, and ȝet is besy on þe worldly gudes. To hym it sall be said on
þis maner, as it were a darte þat were shote: "þou makes þe besy for
ese of þe body þat wormes sall ett, bot þou forgettes þi saule þat
euer sall lyue."

'Also, he is deefe into one ere þat will gladly here gude wordes of me
25 and of saintes and, als gladly, vnhoneste wordes and worldly. To hym
it sall be saide, as if a darte were shote to hym, "þou arte like to Judas,
þe whilke herd Goddes wordes wyth one ere, and þai went away by þe
oþir. þerfor spere þin eres fro vayne wordes þat þou may here angels
synge." Bot he ligges casten downe to þe erthe þat is bonden in bandes
f. 196ᵛᵃ of syn, and he þinkes | þat he wald gladly amend him, bot to hym it sall
31 be saide þus: "þe tyme of þis lyfe is short as a poynt. þe pyne of hell is
euerlastyng, and also þe blys of heuen. þerfor þinke not heuy to suffir
penance and disese to come to þat blis of heuen. For ryght as God is
mercyfull, so is he ryghtwys." And þerefor he þat takes his arow in hys

4 on] and   7 for] for myspe, myspe *ruled through*   18 þe likyng . . . þou
knawes] *twice*, (*second*, likynge, world)   19 saddid] soddid, *Lat.* penitet
24 Also] also in (*or* also iii)   25 To hym] *twice, first subpuncted*   27 wordes]
wordes þat þou may here aungels synge bot he ligges casten, *exc.* wordes, *cancelled*
29 downe] *subpuncted*

hert and will amend, to hym sall be sent oyle of my grace þat sall hele
all his lymmys and his wowndes.'

Capitulum xcix. Criste pleynes both on Jewes þat
crucyfied hym and of cristen þat dispices hym and his
ryght and charite, and his commandmentes and   5
cursynges.

The modir saide, 'þat tyme my son was takyn, he bowed downe to
kys Judas, for Judas was short of stature. And some prikked him, and
some drewe hym by þe here, and some spit on hym.' þan saide Criste,
'I am as a worme þe whilke liggis in þe wynter as it were dede, and   10
men treden on þe bake of hym. So dide | þe Jewes wyth me and   f. 196ᵛᵇ
dispised me. And so dose now euell cristen men, þat haldis all bot
vanyte þat I did for þame. þai trede, as it were, on my bake wen þai set
more by men þan by me. Ne þai set not by þe tyme of my merci, for þai
sai, "Whiles þat we are here, do we wat vs liste, for wen we go hens we   15
sall haue heuen. For God wald neuer haue made vs and boght vs so
dere yf he wald hafe loste vs, or elles endlesly ponyshed vs." And
þarfor sall þai fele my ryghtwisnes, for, ryght as þe gude sall be
rewarded, so sall þe euell be ponyshed. þai dispice me when þai take
no hede of my kyrke, þat is to say, of cursynge, and þarefore, ryght as   20
þai þat are opynly cursed are depart fro oþir, so sall þai be departe fro
me endelesly, and þai sall se me com as domesman.'

Captilum cm. Criste likkens þe spouse to a pipe of þe
holi goste, by wome þere is made a swete noys in þe
world. þerfor he will sho [be] siluered wythoute and   25
gylted glitterand within. |

Cryste likened þe spouse to a pype þat was syluered wythouten, and   f. 197ʳᵃ
gilted wythine. 'For so suld þow,' he saide, 'be siluerd wyth gude
maners to þe wirshipe of God and gude ensampill to þi neghbour. þou
suld be as gold wythin, wyth verai mekenes to plese God. And þan, as   30
þe piper lappis vp his pipe in sendale to kepe it clene, so suld þou
wyth þe loue of Gode. þe second is þat he makes it a case to kepe it in,
þat it be not stoln. So suld þou be clene keped, both in will and werke
in gudnes, fro all euell company, for þai change gode maners. þe loke

1 hele] be hell hele, be hell *ruled through*   25 be] *om.*   26 gylted] gylted it
w, it w *subpuncted*

suld be besy kepynge of þi wittes fro þe deseyte of þe fende. þe key
moste be grace of þe holy goste þat sall opyn thy herte.'

Capitulum ci. þe modir shewes how þe hert of hir son
is swetest and clennest, and so habundant of charite þat
5 if a synner stode at þe ȝates of losyng and cried to hym
with will to amend hym, he suld onone be deliuerd: to
þe wilke hert of God a man mai com by mekenes of trew
contricion, and besy mynde in deuocion of his passion. |

f. 197ʳᵇ The modir saide, 'My sonnes herte is swete as hony to hym þat
10 takes [þogh]t of his gudenes in makynge of man, and of þe trauayle of
his pacien[c]e in his passion and dede. Also, he is clen as any well, for
þere is no vertu ne gudenes bot of hym, as of a plentewouse well. His
mercy is so grete þat if a synfulle man were at þe poynt of peryshyng,
and he wald turne hym to Gode wyth will to amend hym, God wald
15 resayue hym. Bot þer are two wayes to com to Gode. One is mekenes
of verray contricion. þe seconde is mynd of my sonnes passion, þe
whilke softes mannes hert, and makes hym to rynne to Gode wyth a
gude chere.'

Capitulum cii. It shewed to þe spouse in vision þe
20 dome of one religiouse [s]oule befor Criste juge, for
whome oure lady prayes, and whome þe fende accuses
euele.

Criste saide, 'To a domesman falles nyne þinges: þe firste, to here
f. 197ᵛᵃ besely; þe seconde is to avyse hym | wele of þat þat is purposed to hym;
25 þe thirde, a wile to deme ryghtwisly; þe ferde, to take gude heede why
þe strife is; þe fyfet, how longe þe strife has lasted. þe sext is to take
heede of þe wittnes, and wheþir hase mare ryght. þe seuent is to be
noȝt hasti in demynge, and to drede noght for to gyue a ryghtwise
dome. þe eghten, take no heed, ne here noȝt prayers ne gyftes; þe
30 neint, to gyfe ryghtwis dome to ryche and pore, sib and frem[d]e.'
þan saide vnto Criste, verray domesman, a man of Saint Austyns
religion, and pleyned on þis manere on anoþir: 'Lorde, þou called þis
man to ryste, and he has forgetyn it. His obediens was feynned. His

7 of¹] *twice*   10 þoght] it, *Lat.* considerare   11 pacience] paciene
12 well] well is, is *subpuncted*   15 One is] onone his, on, h, *subpuncted*
20 soule] foule   30 fremde] frembe

name is done away. His werkes ar noght.' þan answerd þe domesman,
'He is noght present here to answere.' þe fende saide, 'I will answere.
þou called hym fro stormes and tempestes of þe worlde to riste, and I
called him fro vertu to a depe dike. His obeyng was to me, for he sett
noght by þe callynge. þe hyeste vertu is contricion and confession, for   5
he þat kepes | þes two comes to þi maieste, fro þe wilke I kest hym   f. 197ᵛᵇ
downe when I made hym to syn, and contenu it to his lyues ende. þes
dike þat I broght hym to is awowtry, lichery, glotony and couetyse. þat
is wonder depe, for it will noght be filled. His name was monke, and
suld haue ben to kepe hym fro euell, and for to bere þat at is lefull to   10
oþir. Bot þat he hase forgetyn, and he is now called Saule, for, ryght as
Saule left obediens of God, so he brake his obediens, for he wald noȝt
do bot at his awn will. And his werkes were eftir my will, for all if I
synge no mese, ne do oþir þinges þat he dose, neuerþelesse, all þat he
dose es eftir my will: for when he synges mes he presumes to þe auter,   15
and of þat presumpcion he is filled full of malice. And oþir þinges þat
he dose, he dose þame to praisynge of man. And wen me liste he
turnes his bake to me, and when me list he turnes his bely.'

þe modir saide, 'Two striues amange þameself, and in þame are
two spirites: | in one a gude spirit, in þe oþir a euell spirit. þer strife is   f. 198ʳᵃ
for þat þou boght wyth þi blode, þe one for to sla, þe oþir for to   21
wheken. In one of þame is obediens and lufe, in þe oþir is hate and
pride. þerefore, my son, be dome gyfen.' þe son answerde, 'I sall make
ryghtwis dome.' þe modir saide, 'My frende plenes noȝt. It is enogh to
hym to haue þe substance of his body. Bot I þat ame his lady pleynes   25
þat malice suld noth hafe þe ouer hande.' þe sone answerd, 'I sall do
whateuer þou will. Bot, as þou knawes, bodely dome sall go byfor
spirituall dome, and or syn be done sall no man be demyde.' þe moder
saide, 'O son, all if we knaw clerly all þinges, ȝete I aske for hir þat
standes here what bodely or gastely dome sall be to hym þis.' þe son   30
answerde, 'þe bodely dome is þat þe saule passe sonne fro þe body,
and dede folow it. Spirituall dome is þat þe [saule] sall be hanged on a
gybet in helle, þe whilke is noȝt of ropes bot of þe hatteste brynnynge
fire, for he has forsaken þe condicions of his floke.'

Capitulum ciii. When þe spouse prayed sho saw in | 35
vision how Saint Denys prayes to oure lady for þe   f. 198ʳᵇ
realme of Fraunce.

5 þe²] h þe, h *subpuncted*   28 or] oþir, *Lat.* nisi   32 saule] *om.*

Qwhen I was in praying, I saw how Saint Denyse spake vnto þe
maide Mary and saide, 'Whene of mercy, þou arte þat persone to
whome is gyuen all mercy, and þou arte maide þe moder of Gode for
þe hele of wreches and of synfull men. Haue merci on þe rewme of
5 France, þe whilke is þine, for þou arte wirshiped in it one specialle
wise. And it is myne, for I ame þare patron, and in me þai triste.
Forsoth, þou sees how mani saules perisches euerilke oure, and þe
bodis of men are striken down as bestis. Bot þis is more heuy, for þe
saules falles doune to helle as it were snawe. þerefore, sen þou arte
10 ladi and helper of all, comforth þaime and prai for þaime.' þe modir of
God answerde, 'Wende forth to my son, and here we, for hir sake þat
standes here, what he sall answere.'

Capitulum ciiii. þe moder of God, wyth Saint Denys
and oþir saintes, prayes hir son for þe realme of France,
15 and for `sesinge´ of were bytwyne two kynges, of Frauns
f. 198ᵛᵃ and England, likenyng þame to two | ryght fers bestis.

þe modir spekes to þe son. 'It is wretyn þat I was called blissed, for I
bare þe in my wombe. And þou answerd þat he was also blissed þe
whilke herde þi wordes and kepe[d] þame. And þarefor, son, bycause I
20 am sho þat hase kepit þi wordes freshe in my hert and mynde, þarefor
I thynke on a worde þou said to Saint Petir when he askede if he suld
forgyfe hym þat had trespaste to hym vnto seuen tymes, and þou
answerd agayne and sayde þat he suld forgyfe vnto seuenti times seuen
sithes: vndirstandynge by þat þat as ofte as a man mekes hym wyth
25 wyll to amende hym, as ofte þou arte redy for to forgyfe and graunt
mercy.' þan answerde þe son, 'I bere þe wytnes þat my wordes were
rotide in þe as sede þat is sawen in a gude fat erthe, þe whilke gyfes an
hundrethfauld fruyte. So þi werkes are likynge and fructuose to all
pupill. And þerefor aske what þou will.'
f. 198ᵛᵇ   þan saide þe modir, 'I pray þe wyth Denys and oþir | sayntes whose
31 bodys restes in þe land of þis realme of Frauns, and þe saules are in
heuen, haue mercy of þis kyngdome. I se as it were two fell bestis, and
moste fers of þer kynde. One coueytes to swelowe all þat he may gete,
and þe more he etys, þe more hungry he is, ne his hungir is as neuer
35 filled. þe seconde beste couetes to be aboue all oþir and to stye vpe
þerto. þes two bestes has thre euell þinges. Firste, þere vois is ferdfull.

15 sesinge] lesyng   19 keped] kepe   21 he] he w, w *ruled through*
36 vois] voiys

þe seconde, þai are full of perlious fire. þe thirde, ilkeane of þame
desires to swelowe oþirs hertes, and one wald entir to bite þe herte of
þe oþir in þe bakeside, and so throw byttynge he wald sla hym. þe
seconde has a bone byfor þe breste of þe oþir, desirynge so to entre
into þe hert. And þe ferdfull voices of þe bestes is herd full fere, þat all 5
oþir bestes comes to þam. Bot all þat comes wyth opyn mowthe sall be
brent wyth þe fire of þese two bestis, þat þai fall downe to þe dede. Bot
þai þat comes wyth þare mouthe closede sall be reft | and priued þere f. 199ʳᵃ
fleses, and þai sall go away naked.

'Bot þese two bestes are vndirstandyn by kynges of Frauns and 10
Yngland. One of þame is not filled, for he makes werre for couetise. þe
oþir kynge wald be aboue hym, and þerefor þai are both full of fire of
wreth and of couetise. þis is þe voice of þer bestes: "Take gold and
worldly ryches, and spare no cristen blode." Ylke of þere bestes
desires þe dede of þe oþere, and þarefor ilke wald haue þe oþir place 15
to noye hym. Bot he sekes to noye in þe bakeside, þe whilke wald his
wrange were harde as ryght, and þe oþers ryght were hard and saide as
wronge. Bot he þat comes on þe breste side knawes þat hymselfe hase
ryght, and þerefore he dose mykyll wronge, gyfynge no fors of þe los of
oþir, ne in hys ryght hase no godely charite, for he has pride and wreth 20
wyth his right, and þerfore þe oþir hase les ryght. þerfore he brynnes
in coueytise. þe bestes þat comes wyth opyn mouthe er þai þat comes
for couetise. And þai þe whilke are called kynges fylles þere mouthes
wyth gold, for þai are werray proditowrs. þai caste plente|ously gold f. 199ʳᵇ
and money in þe mouthes of þame, and so þai wald be at bataile, 25
where þai fall to dede: whose godes are lefte byhynd þaim, and
wormes gnawes þere bodys bered in erthe, and fendes þair saules. And
so þere two kynges betraises mony saules fro my son, þe whilke boght
þame wyth his blode. þe bestes þat were refte and spo[il]ed of þere
fleshe are simpill men, þe whilke haldes þaim paide and walde liue of 30
þaire awen gude, þe whilke also of þat entent gose to bataile, for þai
wene þat þai hafe riȝt wherel. And ȝit is þere flesche reft fro þaim, for
þair bodys are slayn and þare saules are taken into heuen. þerfor, son,
haue mercy.'

þan saide Criste, 'Modir, for þou knawes all þinge in me, sai, in 35
hereynge of þis spouse þat standes here, what skyll or ryght is it þat
þes kynges be herde.' þe moder answerde, 'I here thre voices. þe firste
is þe voices of þer kynges, of þe whilke one þinkes þus: "If I had myn

---

11 werre] *second* r *subpuncted*   29 spoiled] sposed   32 þaim] þaim þaine
(*for* þaim þame)

awen, I wald noȝt charge all if I hade none oþirs gude. Bot I d[r]eede
to lose and wannt alle." And of þis fere, by þe whilke he dredes reprofe
f. 199ᵛᵃ of þe worlde, he turnes hym to me and sais, "O | Mary, pray for me."
þe oþir kynge þinkes þus: "Wald God I were in my first astate. I ame
5 werey." And þarefor he turnes him to me. þe seconde is þe voice of þe
comonte, þat ilka day prays for pese. þe thirde is þe voice of þi
derlynges þat sais þus: "We wepe noȝt þe bodys of þame þat are dede,
ne pouert, ne for oþir harme, bot we wepe for þe saules þat peryshes
ilkea day. And þerfor, lady, pray þi son þat þe saules may be saue."
10 Wherefor, son, haue merci on þame.' þe son answerde, 'It is wretin,
"To him þat knokkes it sall be oppind; to him þat calles it sall be
answerde; and to hym þat askes it sall be graunted." Bot riȝt as ilke
mane þat knokkes is wythoute þe dore, so þes kynges are wythowte þe
dore, for þai haue noȝt me wythin þame. Neuerþeles, for þine askynge
15 it sall be opynd.'

Capitulum cv. [Criste] shewes by what mene he will þat
pes be made bytwene þe kynges of Frauns and Ingland:
to þe whilke ife þe kynges will not assent, þai sall be full
greuosly ponyshed.

f. 199ᵛᵇ   þe son sais, 'I ame kynge moste to be drede and wir|shyped. þere-
21 for, for þe prayers of my modir, I sall send my word to þe forsaide
kynges. I ame verray pees, and where pees is, certayne þer am I. And
þerefor, yf þose kynges two of Fraunce and Ingland wille haue pees, I
sall gyfe þame perpetuall pees. Bot verray pees may noȝt be hade bot
25 trewth and ryght be loued. þerefor, for one of þo kynges hase ryght, it
pleses me þat pes be made be mariage, and so þat þe realme may come
to þe lawfull aire. Bot I will þat þai haue one herte and one will in
defence of cristendome, wen and whare it may beste be to my wirshipe. Also, I will þat þai lay downe þe intollerabill taxis and takyng of
30 þer sogettes gudes and fraudulent adinuencions, and þat þai lufe
bettir þe saules of þame. And þerefor, if þe kynge þe wilke haldes þe
realme will noȝt obeye, witt he moste sikirly þat he sall noȝt fare wele,
ne haue prosperite in his dedis. Bot he sall ende his life in sorow, and
f. 200ʳᵃ þe real[m] sall be lefte in tribull and tribulacion, and his sone | wyth
35 hys ʿgeneraciouneʾ sall be in ire and reprofe and confusion, þat all

---

1 dreede] deede   2 lose] lose drede   15 Criste] *om.*   22 ame] ame
werray kynges, werray kynges *ruled through*   30 adinuencions] andinuencions
33 life] lifee   34 realm] reall   35 generacioune] gouernance, *Lat.* generatio

pupill sall haue wonder þerof. And if it so be þat [þe] king þe whilke
hase riȝt will obei, I sall help him and feght for him. And if he will noȝt
obei, he sall not come to his purpose, bot a ioyfull bygynnyng sall haue
a sorowfull endyng. Neuerþelees, when men of Fraunce takes to þame
verray mekenes, þan sall þe kyngdom come to þe ryght aire and gude 5
pees.'

Capitulum cvi. Criste biddes þe spouse charge not
brekynge of abstinens, for it is no syn if it be done be
obediens of þe spirituall fadir; and he stirres hir to
stand stabill and to wythstand temptacions, and to haue 10
gude will to perseueraunce in gudenes by ensampill of
Mary, Dauid, Abraham.

Criste saide to þe spouse, 'þou suld noȝt be ferde to ete foure sithes
on þe day, att þe suffirynge of þi gostely fadir to whome þou awe
obediens, bot stand stiffly as a knyght þat is wowndede in bataile, and 15
wowndes agayne greuously his enemys. So be þou stabill in gudenes
with a gude will, for þan smytes þou þe fende, | when þou assentes f. 200rb
noght to his fandynges bot withstandes þame: as, to withstande pride
by mekenes, and lichery bi clennes. And þan is þi will resonable, when
þou puttes þi will holely in my will. For Lucifer, for cause he wyth- 20
stode noȝt, bot onone assentid, þerefor he fell. Also, Judas had no
stabilnes, for he fell in dispaire and slow hymselfe. Ne Pilate had no
gude will, for he had more likyng to plese þe Jewes þan to delyuer me.
Bot þe firste gude, þat is, withstondynge of euell, had my modir, for
sho assentid neuer to euell. þe seconde gude, þat is, stabilnes, had 25
Dauid, þat was pacient in aduersite and fell not in despaire. þe third
gud, þat is, perfite will, had Abraham, þat left his cuntre at my
biddyng, and wald haue offird his son: þe whilke thre is nedefull to þe.'

Capitulum cvii. Criste stirres þe saule to kepe euere
pure contricion, gudely charite, stabill obedience, and 30
he condempnes þaim þat settis noȝt by þes, and he
gyfes gude | counsaile to a spirituall man. f. 200va

One aungelle aperyd, to whome oþir angells saide, 'Frende, why
offirs þou to oure lord a defe note?' He answerde, 'I ame assigned to
kepe saules, and ȝet am I euer in presens of God. And if I offir noȝt þe 35

1 þe¹] om. 3 haue] haue and, and subpuncted

note of swetenes, neuerþeles I offir to hym a key of fyne golde, a vessell
of silluer, and a crowne of precious stones. þe key bytokens verray
contricion, þat opyns þe hert of Gode and brynges þe synfull man
þerin. þe vessell is charite þat makes God to reste in mannes saule. þe
5 crowne is gladsom obediens and stabill. þes thre sekes God of mannes
saule. Bot now I pleyn on þis saule, for it hase putt away þe key of contricion. þe vessell of charite is bittir, for þere is luste of fleshe. þe
crown of obediens is putt away, for þere likes hym noght bot his awn
will.' And þan saide þe aungell to Gode, 'Lo, þe key, þe vessell and þe

f. 200ᵛᵇ   crowne þat þis saule is noȝt worthy to haue.' Bot wen þe aun|gelle
11 brake þe note, þan was it full of erth, and in þe middis lay a worme. 'þe
shell of þis note is one harde herte þat is broken in þe deynge and is
funden full of worldly desires, þat are bot erthe. þere is one neddir þat
is þe worme of þi consciens.'

15   þan saide Criste to þe spouse, 'þis man is like a man þat passed
forby aneoþir man þat stode still, and when he come nere hym, he said
to hym þat stode, "Sir, þere is a lettyng bytwene vs. Tell me þe way, for
I se þat þou arte mighti wythoute comparacion. þou art suthfast and
beste, and none oþir is gude bot of þe." þan saide he, "Frende, I sall
20 shew þe thre ways, and all to one ende. þe firste is stony in þe entre
and bygynnyng, bot þe ende was esy, and sharp in þe bygyning, bot þe
ende was light and softe." þan saide he, "Shewe me þat way, and I sall
gladly go it, for I se perell in þe tareyng, and gret profite in it." ' þan
saide Criste, 'I ame he þat standis still, for I am ay stabill in miselfe.

f. 201ʳᵃ   And he commes ner þat loues me ouer all þinge. | I turn my visage
26 when I send hym comforte in me, and, when he hates þe world and
lustes of fleshe, I shew hym gostely thre ways: þe firste, þat he suld be
bouxom to God and to his souerans-and he thoght þat his prelate was
hard and noȝt as he suld be. þan I shew to hym þe seconde way, þat he
30 suld flee lichery and gluttry, for clennes and abstinens wald brynge
hym to verray obediens. And if he thoght, agayn þat, he might noght
fast, for his kind was febill and him most hafe solace bodeli, þan I
shewed 'him' þe þird wai, þat him most hafe paciens in disese for mi
sake. And þat will bringe hym to abstinens and so to obedeens. And
35 þan, he thoght, þat will he noȝt do, "For if I suffir reproues, I sall be
halden bot a fole, and if I be sympilly arayed, oþir will scorn me." '
       þan saide Criste, 'þis man will be pacient, so þat he lose noȝt of his
will. And þe feende is abowte to make hym blynde and dom, to bynd
his handes and his fete, and to lede hym to helle. Firste, he makes hym

25 þinge] *Quire catchphrase*, I turne my, *below*

blynde when he makes hym to þenke þus: "God boght me wyth his
passion. He will noȝt lose me. | He will not so straytely ponyse syn, for f. 201ʳᵇ
he is full mercifull." þus he makes hym blynde in þe faith. For sen I
say in my gospell þat I will haue rekenynge of ilkea word, mykill more
I will haue a rekenyng of werkes. And also, þe ryche man was beryd in 5
hell, noȝt for robbery bot for mispendynge of his gudes. Also, he
makes hym dome, when he þinkes þat men may noȝt life now as holy
men did before, and in þis failes his hope þat he suld haue, for I ame
als myghty now to gyfe grace as I was byfore. þan byndes þe fende his
handes, when he dose his werkes more for thanke of þe world þan for 10
my wirshipe. Bot þan he byndes his fete, when his lufe is more sett on
þe world þan on me. And þan þe feende byndes his hert, when he settis hys will to euell, and to dwell þerin. Bot þan he ledis hym to
derkenes, when he sais þus: "I gyue litill wheþir þat I go to hell or to
heuen." Bot wo is hym þat comes in þat derkenes! Bot if he will | turn f. 201ᵛᵃ
agayn, I will resayfe hym as a mercifull fadir dose hys son. Bot ryght as 16
a fadir will noȝt streyne his son to take a wife agayns his wyll, no more
will `I´ streine him to me agains hys will, bot wyth þe gude will of hym
he may wyn to þe lufe of me, for ryȝt as a querreour þat will gete
stonnes, first he puttes in smale instrumentes, and þan gretter, right so 20
I desire firste a gude will, and where I fynde þat I putt plente of my
grace. And so sall my lufe com to þe saule where a gud will gose byfor.'

      Capitulum cviii. Criste telles þe spouse þat thre sayntes
      plesed hym specially, þe maiden Mary, John Baptist,
      and Mary Magdalane, and he comendes þe abstinens 25
      þat þes thre held in mete, drynk and clethynge.

    Criste saide þat þere were thre þat plesid hym byfor all oþir: 'My
modir', quod he, 'John Baptist, and þe Magdalane. Mi moder was so
clene in hir birth þat þer was herd a voice as it had bene fro hell þat
saide, "þere is a mai|den broght furth so vertuously þat þer is none f. 201ᵛᵇ
swilke on þis halfe þe sete of Gode. Scho will briste all oure snarres 31
and oure malice, and oure vnclennes may neuer do agayns hir more
þan a sparke of fire in a grete rynnyng watir." Also, when John Baptiste
was born, a voice saide as it had bene fro hell, "þer is a wondirfull
child born. Yf we go agayns hym with pride, he will noȝt here vs. If we 35

---

  1 blynde] bly blynde, bly *subpuncted*   5 werkes] ilke werkes, ilke *subpuncted*
13 hys] hys derkenes, derkenes *subpuncted*

profir hym riches, he turnes his bake on vs. And if we profir hym
lichory, he shewes hym as a dede man þat myght noȝt fele." Also wen
þe Magdalane was conuertid, þan saide þe fendes, "How sall we do?
We haue lost a fat pray. Sho wheshes hir so white wyth terres þat we
5 dar not luke on hyr. Sho couers hir so wyth gude werkes, and sho is so
warme and feruent in seruys of Gode, þat we dar noȝt com ner to hir."

'Thes þre had þair bodys soiet to þair saules, and ȝet þai hated noȝt
þair bodys, bot þai tuke on esy fude for to sustene þame. þai had
f. 202ʳᵃ cle|thyng, noȝt to pryde bot to couer þaim with, and beddes to rist
10 þaime on. And neuerþelesse, if þai hade wittyn to haue plesid me, þai
wald gladly haue suffird and takyne bittir þinges in mete, and thornes
in cleþing, and haue liggyn wyth[in a hill of amptes]. Bot ryght as þai
refreyned þair bodys fro þat þe whilke was vnlefull, right so þai gafe to
þair bodys þat at was nedfull. Bot þou may aske me why þer thre fastid
15 noȝt as holy men somtim did, þat ete bot ones in þe weke. To þe wilke
question I answere: for þo holy men fastid for thre skilles. þe firste was
to shewe my grace and my myght, þat, ryght as I sustene þe saule
wythoute bodely fode, so I may susten þe body and it like me. þe
seconde skill was for to gife oþir ensampill þat bodely disese helpes a
20 man to heuen. þe third was for to fle syn, bycause þat to grete norysh-
yng of þe fleshe drawes men to payne, and þerfor, þat men suld lere of
me þe maner of lifynge, all if I might hafe lyfed wythouten fode,
f. 202ʳᵇ neuerþelesse ȝett I toke þat at was nedefull to | my bodely sustinance,
and noght to superfluite.'

25   Capitulum cix. Mari modir teches how a spirituall man,
           fro he be turned and conuertid throw labour of
           penance, charite, contricion and paciens, awes to bi
           agayn gude dedis byfore loste, and one [swilke] wise
           etchewe þat he offir noȝt to God defe notes.

30   þe modir said þat Mary Magdalane offird notes to God, 'þat is to
sai, gud werkes. Bot omange þame were some defe, for sho was longe
tyme in syn, bot þat tym was eftir holpyn wyth besy trauayle and
paciens. Bot John Baptiste offird notes as þai had bene full, for fro his
ȝouth he serued Gode holely. þe apostill[s] offird notes as þai hade
35 bene halfe full, for þai had longe tyme bene inperfite byfor þer conuersion. Bot I, þat ame Goddes modir, offird mi notes all full and swete as

12 wythin . . . amptes] wyth beddes, *Lat.* in tumulo formicarum   28 swilke] *om.*
34 apostills] apostill

hony, for all my life I was in grace, and kepid þarein. þarefor I say þat
þe tyme þe wilke is passed in syn suld be boght agayn wyth gude
trauaile | of penance, contricion, charite and paciens.'

Capitulum cx. Criste techis þe spouse þe difference
bytwene a gude spirit and illusion of þe euell spirit, and
how it sall be answert to bothe.

Criste teches þe spouse how sho sall knaw his spirit fro one euel
spirit. 'My spirit, þat is gude and warme, stirs þe to lufe allonely Gode,
to be meke and to dispice þe worlde. þe euell spirit is cald, for he
makes þe lufe of Gode, inalsmykyll as he may, to wax cold, and it is
hote also, for he stirres a man to luste and to pride and to fulfill his awn
will. At þe bygynnyng, he comes as he were a frende and comfortour,
bot, at þe last, he byttes as it were a hound, and is aboute to gildir a
man. And þerefore when he comes sai to him, "I will noȝt of þe, for
þine ende is euel." Bot when þe gude spirit commes, sai to him,
"Kindell þe lufe of God in mi hert. And all if I be vnworþi to haue þe,
neuerþelesse I haue mikill nede of [þ]e. And þerefore com to me, for I
ame noȝt wythouten þe." '

Capitulum cxi. Criste spekys to þe spouse of þre laues:
of holi kirke | lawe, þe emperours and þe comontes. Bot
he warnes hir þat sho life eftir þe fourt, þe wilke is spirituall in mekenes, stedfast bylefe and perfite charite.

Criste saide to þe spouse, 'þere are thre laues. One is of þe hali
kirke, oneoþir of þe emperour, þe third of þe comonte. [All] of þes
laues are wretyn in skynnes of dede bestes. Bot þer is oneoþir lawe þat
is wretyn in þe boke of life, and þis will neuer away. Ilke lawe suld be
ordaynede to þe hele of þe saule, and to fulfill Goddes commandmentes, and for to fle euell. In þes thre lawes is wretyn one worde: þat
is, "to take a þinge". Bot for hym þat suld take a þinge, one of þes foure
were nedefull: to hym oþir a gyft þat is gyfen is gyuen for lufe, or for
homelines, for eritage or for seruyse. And so it is of gostely laue: þat is,
to vndirstonde and knaw Gode and to loue hym. And in þis law are
gostely riches, þat are getyn on foure maners: first by lufe, in case þat
he hase noȝt deseruede it; þe second is for eritage, for

4 difference] diffeerence   17 þe] nede   19 laues] *marg.*, lawes
24 All] *om.*   30 hym] hym þat   34 for²] for man is

[Loss of a leaf containing end of IV. 111, IV. 112-13,
beginning of IV. 114. Missing material supplied from
Ju]

f. 150ʳ I be myn manhed and myn passion bought heuen to man and openyd
it to his heritage. The iiide spiritual honour is purchasid for diuision,
þat is, whan a man departis him fro all delectacioun of carnal delites in
abstinens and pouerte, and the vision of the word for þe vision of God.
5 The iiiite spiritual honour is purchasid for þe werkis of humilite and
seruitute, as whan a man leuys in þe seruise of God and paciens as a
f. 150ᵛ knyght | in batayle. þerfore, doughtir, seke to obteyne spiritual honour
be cherite, þat is to sey, nothinge to loue as me. Seke be heritage, in
beleuyng stedfastly þe thinges þat þe chirche biddis. Seke be werkes
10 of humylite, doynge alle thinges for myn honour. þu art callid in myn
lawe, and þerfore þu art boundyn to kepe myn lawe. Myn lawe is to
leve aftir myn wil. As a good clerke leuys aftir þe laue of the chirch, so
thou leve aftir the lawe of myn humilite, conformynge the to myn
frendis. Al temporal lawe tendis somdel to þe honour of the word, and
15 sumdel to þe contempt of it. Min lawe tendis to heuenly thinges
alonly, for before me and aftir me no man vndirstondis fully what, and
hou glorious, is the suetnes of þe heuenly kingedom, as I knowe and as
he to whom I wyl reuele or shewe.'

f. 151ʳ [IV. 114] | Crist monyshis his spouse þat she bewar of þe conuersa-
20 cioun of wordly thingis, the whech is the deulys rost. The sone spekis:
'Take hed to the deulis rost, þe whech þe deul rostis with the fire of
lecherie and coueytise. Whereas fatnes is leyd to þe fyre, þer must
drop sumqwat; so, of þe conuersacioun of wordly thinges, sum synnes
procedis. Alþough þu knowe nat the consciens of men, ȝit þe owtward
25 signis shewys what is within þe soule.' The modir spekis. 'Alle þin
dede is resonabil, and intent is right, for all þat thou does is done to
þat intent of þe honour of God. Many seruis God in dede, bot þer
intent is corupt, as þu may vndirstonde by exsampil. þer is a serteyn
best callid a bere. Whan he is hungrid and sees his pray, he fixis on fot
30 on his pray and he lokis where he may set the todir, þat his pray go nat
fro him til he has etyn. This bere with his pray sekis neydir gold ne
siluir ne redolent herbis, but alonly a hid place or preuy and sekir, þat
he may hold his pray. So many peple seruis me with prayours and
fastingis for dred, and þei considere þe horribyl peyn of hell, and also
35 myn gret mercy, and as a bere thei set all þer intent on

17 heuenly] heuuenly

[CI continues]

esy life, and eftir to fle payne, bot þai take no tent to þe passion of my f. 203ʳᵃ
son, þe whilke is þe preciouse tresore of þis werld, ne þai take no tent
of þe lyfynge of holy men þat hase bene before as preciouse stonnes,
ne þai toke no heede of þe gudenes of þe holy goste þat is als swete as
erbes, bot onely þai take hede to þair luste, and how þai may moste 5
frely vse þere syn. And þerfor, doghtir, loke þat in all þi werkes thyne
entent be to plese Gode, or elles is it noȝt profitabill to þe.'

Capitulum cxv. Criste telles þe spouse of delyuerans of
a man þat was trauaild wyth þe feende.

Criste saide to þe spouse, 'I ame like to a mane þat sais to his iailere, 10
"þou hase in þi house þre wardes. In þe first are þai þat sall be dede.
In þe second are þai þat sall be mayned and in þe third þai þat sall be
bett and þe skyn pulled of þame." þe iayler sais to hym, "Lorde, whi
bides þou so longe of þi dome?" þe lorde saide, "I bide of þame þat
sall be dede þat þai `þat´ are gude may be þe better, and þai þat are 15
euell may drede and be more | ware; also, þat þai þe whilke sall be f. 203ʳᵇ
ponyshed by losyng of any lym may haue, eftir þat þai haue done,
sorow of þair euell; and also þai þat sall be bett be more ware." þis
iailere is þe fende, þat ponyshes saules eftir þai haue trespaste, and
power is gyuen hym of þis mannes saule, and on what party I sall shew 20
þe. For ryght as þe body hase bones, mergh, fleshe and blode, so þe
saule suld haue thre þinges, mynd, consciens and vndirstandyng.

'Also þe body hase thre resaites. þe firste is þe herte, þat hase vpon
hym a thyn skyn, to kepe þat filth come not to þe hert. For if þere com
any filth, as faste moste hym dye. þe seconde is þe stomoke. þe third is 25
þe bowles, þat clenses þe body. Right so þe saule hase his thre
resayuynges. þe firste is hertly lufe of God, for if þere were any euel
lufe in þe hert it will sla þe hert. þe secound is as a stomoke, þat is, a
wise ordeynyng of a mannes tyme and his werkes, for ryght as þe mete
is difíed in þe stomoke, so suld a man ordeyn hys tyme and hys | werkes f. 203ᵛᵃ
to þe wirshipe of Gode. þe third are þe bowels þat clenses þe mete, by 31
þe whilke is vndirstandyn contricion þat clenses þe saule.

'Also þere are oþir thre partys: þe hede, þe whilke bytokens charite,
for þere are all gostely gudes closed, as þe fyfe wittes are in þe heued.
And as a man may noȝt haue life when þe heued is away, ryght so a 35
man is dede gostly þat wantis charite. þe oþir parte is þe handis, þe

whilke bytokens faith. For ryght as in þe hande er mani fyngers, so þere
ar mani articles langynge to þe faith; and right as a man wirkes wyth his
handes, so þe holi goste wirkes in þe saule by faith. þe third party are þe
fete: and þat is hope, þat a man wendis furth wythall to Gode. Bot þe
5 [s]kyn þat is vpon þe bodi bitokens comforth of God, þe whilk stabils þe
saule, þat it faile not throw fandings of þe feende. And þe saule of þis
man ȝet may be holpyn, bothe for my kyndenes, and also for prayers of
my saintez and derlynges in erth. Bot he moste do thre þinges: first, gyue
f. 203vb   agayn þat he hase fa[l]sly gettyn. Also, he | moste be asoyled of þe court
10 of Rome; and þat he be noȝt howsilled to he be asoylede.'

Capitulum cxvi. Criste pleynes on paynems and Jewes,
and moste of þe euel cristen men, for þai resayfe noȝt
deuotely þe sacramentes, ne þay knawlege noȝt Godes
benefices.

15 Criste saide, 'Som trowes þat I ame noþir God ne man, as þe
payne[m]s; som, þat I am God bot not man, as þe Jewes; and some, þat
I ame God and man, as þe cristen. Bot I pleyn on þame, for I
ordaynde in haly kirke seuen sacramentes, and none takes hede of
þame. For þai are taken wyth pride, þai are kepid in vnclene vessell,
20 and þai are gyuen wyth coueytise. Also I pleyn þat man is vnkynde, for
if he wald noȝt loue me for I made hym, he suld haue loued me for I
boght hym.'

Capitulum cxvii. God metis onone wyth þam þat
desires hym, and he comforthes þame as a gudely and
25   milde fadir. |

f. 204ra   It fell þat one red þe Pater noster, and þan herd þe spouse a spirit
say, 'þou sall haue eritage wyth þi fadir.' þe manhed said, 'þou sall be
my tempill.' And þe hali goste saide, 'þou sall haue no fandynges bot
þat þou sall wele wytstonde, for þe fadir sall defende þe, þe manhede
30 sall stand by þe, þe hali goste sall warme þe. þerefore, ryght as þe fadir
helpis his son þat berys a grete byrdyn if he se hym ouersett, and as þe
modir hase rewth on þe child wen sho sees hym wepe, so am I redy to
come and mete wyth þame þat calle on me, for I will gladly come nere
to þame þat will com toward me.'

5 skyn] kyn   9 falsly] fasly   15 noþir] noght þaire   16 paynems]
paynens   28 my] in my

Capitulum cxviii. Criste telles to þe spouse how `þe´
fadir drawes þam to hym, and comfortes þam in
gudenes whome he sees change gladly þair euell will
into gude will, wyth desire to amend þat is euell done
byfore.   5

Criste saide, 'He þat will be in my felishipe, hym moste turne hys
will to myne, and forþinke þat | he has misdone. And þan sall my fadir   f. 204rb
draw hym to perfeccion, for my fadir drawes hym þat will turn þe euell
will to gode, and amend þat is mysdone. Bot how drawes þe fadir?
Forsothe, fortheryng a gude will in þe gude, for, bot þe will be gode,   10
þe fadir will noȝt drawe.' þan saide Criste, 'To some I ame so colde
þat my way pleses þam noght, and to some I ame so warm þat, wen þai
suld do any gude dede, thayme thynke þat þai are in þe fire. And to
some I ame so swete þat þai kepe ne desire noȝt bote me.'

Capitulum cxix. þe modir telles of seuen gude þinges   15
in Criste, and of seuen contraryes.

þe modir saide, 'My sone hase seuen þinges. For he is myghty, as he
þat ouercomes all oþir. He is witty, for none may comprehende hys witt,
no more þan if he wald drawe þe watir all oute of þe see. He is moste
stronge, for he may noȝt be stirred, no more þan one hill. He is   20
vertuouse as any erbe. He is faire as | þe bryght shynnyng son. He is   f. 204va
ryghtwis as a kyng þat may noȝt be turned fro þe ryght. And he is moste
louand, for he gafe hymselfe for hys seruand. Bot agayns þes suffird he
seuen oþir contraryes. For agayns hys myght, he is made as a worme.
For his witt, he is haldyn as a fole. For hys strengh, he was bunden as a   25
child in credill. For his fairnes, he was like a mesell. For hys vertu, he
stode naked and bunden. And for his ryghtwisnes, he was halden a lyer,
and agayns his louandenes, he was vnkyndly dede.'

Capitulum cxx. Criste telles to þe spouse of spirituall
delectacion and fleshely.   30

Criste saide to þe spouse, 'þere is two maner of likynges, one
bodely, oneoþir gostely. Bodely is wen nede dryues to take bodely
sustinance. And þan suld he say þus: "Lorde, þou gyue me grace þat I
trespas not in takynge of þis mete and drynge. Also, I pray þe to gyfe

1 þe²] þ

f. 204ᵛᵇ　me grace so to ordeyn for þes erthly þinges | þat I may gyue to þe a trew
reknyng." þe gostely likyng is, when þe saule has likynge in Goddes
gudenes. Bot somtim þere is, as it were, a skyn bytwene God and þe
saule, when he has swetenes in oþir þan in me. Bot þat is broken,
5　when þe drede of Gode is lastyng in þe thoght, and þe saule has no
likynge bot in Gode.'

Capitulum cxxi. þat þe vertu of abediens and of kepyng
of rewly lyfynge makes a monke, and noȝt þe owtwarde
abit: and how verray contricion wyth purpose of
10　amendynge deliuers þe saule fro þe powere of þe fende.

þe fend was constreyned by God to tell what felle to a verray
monke, and he said þat a verray monke suld be kepar of hymselfe. His
abyt suld be obediens and kepyng of hys profession. For ryght as þe
body is cled wythoute, so suld þe saule be clede wythin wyth gude ver-
15　tuse. 'For þe outwarde clothe makes noȝt a monke, bot þe vertuse þat
f. 205ʳᵃ　is wythin. Bot swylke a monke | is fled away, and onely a lyknes is lefte,
when he thoght þus: "I will haue my luste." Bot he flow away fro me',
saide þe fende, 'when he knew hys trespas, and purposed wyth
Goddes grace to amende hym.'

20　Capitulum cxxii. þat one irksom manys life in gudenes
and dissolute is as it were a strayte perlyous bryge, fro
þe wilke, bot if he skype son into þe shipe of pennance,
þe fende will depely drowne hym.

Cryste saide, 'He is my heued enemy þat settis noȝt by me, bot will
25　do his awn will and hys luste. He is like to a man þat is vpon a narow
bryg, and on þe lefte hand is a depe pitt, and if he fall þerin, he may
noght ryse. One þe ryght syde is a shipe, into þe whilke if he lepe he
may be safe. þis brige is þe short life, where some are verray slawe and
idill, and trauayls noȝt besely in gude werkes as þai suld do. þis brige
30　is perlious, and will bere a man perliously for short tyme, for þe dede
f. 205ʳᵇ　makes ende of þis life, and | þan sall man, if he draw to þe lefte side,
and dye in will to continu his luste, fall into þe pitt of helle. Bot if he
will þan lepe into þe shipe of holi kirke, and be in will to amend hym,
and so turn hym to þe ryght side, he sall be sauede. Bot hym bose haue

12 of] þer of, þer *marked for cancellation*　　20 irksom] irksomnes　　21 as it
were] *twice*　　fro] for

mykyll trauaile in purgatory, and be holpyn þere wyth besy prayers
of holy kirke and gude dedis of his frendes.'

Capitulum cxxiii. How Criste defendes his spouse,
whome modir, fadir, sustir and broþir wald haue
chaungid fro his lufe and fro chaste matrimone.   5

Criste saide þat he is as it were a man þat had weddid a spouse
agayns þe fadirs will, and modirs, þe brethirs and sustirs. 'þe fadir
sayde, "Gyue me my doghtir agayne, for sho is of my blode." þe modir
saide, "Gyue me hir agayne, for I noryshet hir wyth my milke." þe
sistir saide, "Gyfe me hir, for we were noryshed and broght vp   10
togider." þe broþir saide, "Gyfe me hir, for sho suld be at my gouer-
nance." þan answerd þe husband, | and saide, "Fadir, and if sho be   f. 205ᵛᵃ
born of þi blode, I will now fille hir wyth my blode. Modir, þou fede
hir wyth þi milke. I sall now fede hir wyth my lufe and my delite.
Sustir, if sho were noryshed eftir thyne vse, sho sall nowe be noryshed 15
eftir my manere. And, broþir, if þou haue gouerned hir till now, I wyll
forward gouern hir eftir my rewle." Right so, my spouse, if lust of
fleshe will call þe agayne, þan thynke how I will fill þe wyth my lufe
and charite. Yf þi modir, þat menes, besines of þe worlde, call þe
agayne, thynke þat I will fill þe wyth my comforth. Yf þi sustir, þat is, 20
euell custome, call þe agayn, leue it and do my biddyng. And if þi
brothir, þat is, þi awn will, will come agayne, thynk how þou hase
bunden þe to me.'

Capitulum cxxiiii. How Saynt Agnes set on þe spouse a
crowne of seuen preciouse stones.   25

Saynt Agnes saide to þe spouse, 'þou sall haue a crowne of seuen
preciouse | stonnes. þe crowne is prouyng of paciens made in þe fire of f. 205ᵛᵇ
tribulacion. þe first stone is jasper, þe whilke cleres a mannes sight.
And þis putt he in þi crowne þat saide on reprouynge wyse it were
bettir to þe to spyn þan for to entirmette þe of visiones and writynges. 30
þis clerid þe sight of þi saule to se heuenly þinges. þe seconde stone is
saiphir, þe whilke is of þe colour of heuen, and kepis a mans lymys in
plite. þis put he in þi crowne þat maliciously bakbyttid þe byhynde.
Neuirþeles, þis kepis þi hert in plite fro pride. þe third is þe emeraud,
þat is grene and faire. And þis puttes he in þi crowne þat lied on þe, for 35

15 sho sall nowe] *twice* (*second*, now), *second subpuncted*

þe sufferynge of lesynges makes þe saule faire. þe ferthe is þe mar-
garyte, þe whilke is faire and lightes þe herte. This put he in þi crowne
þat reproues þi frende in þi presens, for he set harde to þi herte, and
ȝete þou kepid paciens, and þou kepid þi saule white fro desire of
5 vengeans. þe fifte stone is called topasi, þe whilke kepis a man chaste.

f. 206ʳᵃ This | put he in þi crowne þat waryed þe, and þou blyssed hym agayne,
for þe whilke þou had grete grace of Gode. þe sext is þe adamant, þat
will not breke. And þis was put in þi crowne when þou was hurt in þi
body, and þou suffird it in paciens. þe seuent is cherbukill, þe whilke
10 gyfes a grete light. So þe paciens þat þou had when one come and told
þe þat Charles þi son was dede, all if it was fals, it made þe bryght and
light in þe sight of Gode. And þerefor, stand þou stabill, and wyn þe
mo stones.'

Capitulum cxxv. þe modir of Gode telles þe spouse a
15 faire figure of seuen bestes, by þe whilke foure maner of
euell men and thre manere of gude men is vndirstanden.

The modir spake of seuen bestes. 'þe firste hase grete hornes, of
wome he hase grete pride, and þerfore he fyghtes gladly wyth oþir
20 bestis. þe second is a litill best, þe whilke hase one horn, and vndir þe
horn a preciouse stone. And þis beste may noȝt be taken bot by a
f. 206ʳᵇ mayden, þat | he gose to. þe thirde is a beste þat hase no iunctures, and
he gose to ryste hym at a tre þe whilk is kut to þe myddis, and he falles
þerwyth. þe fourt semes a meke beste, for he dose no harme wyth his
25 fete ne hys hede, bot þai are all mesell þat feles þe breth of it. þe fifte is
dredefull in all places. þe sext dredis noȝt bot his awen shadow. He
dwelles þerfor gladly in hidels. þe seuent dredis nothyng, and it hase
foure meruailous condicions. þe first is gret comforth wythin hymselfe. þe seconde, he is neuer besy for hys mete. þe third, he standes
30 neuir, bot euir rynnes. þe ferthe is þat he restes hym in hys wendynge.
'þe firste beste bytokens hym þat is proude of worshipes, bot for his
awn slawnes he is lightly taken bot if he be ware betyme. þe seconde
bytokens hym þat is proude of precious stone of chastite, and þerfor
hase dedeyn of oþir, for he will be taken of pride þat semes honeste, as

---

9 paciens] paciens þat þou hade when one come and told, *exc.* paciens, *ruled through*
cherbukill] cherbubill *or* cherbukill   22 þat¹] *twice*   26 sext] shext
32 bot] for for bot, for for *ruled through*

it | were of a maiden. Bot þe taile of pride is shame and dethe. þe   f. 206ᵛᵃ
[þi]r[d] beste bytokens hym þat is dry wythoute iuncture of perfeccion, and þerfor, wen þai wene moste to haue þair ese in þe world,
þai fall þerefro. þe ferthe bytokens hym þat is proude of anythynge,
for he will file all þat delys wyth hym, as meselry dose wyth hym þat   5
communes with þe mesell. þe oþir thre sall be shewede in þaire
tyme, for þe first, [a]s Thomas, was a foure-cornerd stone, wele
polishede. þe seconde is as golde in þe fire, and as it were a pipe
giltide, kepid wele in a faire couertoure. þe third is as a tabill
depaynted, aptede to resayue colours. Bot if any of þe oþir foure will   10
turn þame to me, I sall go to þam and ese þame of þair charge, and if
þai will noȝt, I sall sende eftir þame a beste, swyfter þan þe tigir, þat
sall distroye þame foreuer.'

Capitulum cxxvi. Oure lady spekes to þe spouse of a
bishope, for whome sho prayed, and sho teches how   15
verray and trewe | byshopes suld liue and gouern þair   f. 206ᵛᵇ
soiettis.

þe modir of merci saide to þe spouse, 'What sall we do to ȝone
blynd byshope? He hase thre þinges. Firste, he bises hym to plese
mene more þan Gode. He loues þat tresoure þe whilke thefes may   20
stele, bot not þat tresore þat angels kepis. Also, he loues hymselfe
more þan hys neghbour, and more þan his Gode.' And þan, as it
hade bene in þe same moment of tyme, þe spouse saw sex balanses,
and thre were ryght heuy and thre were ryght light. And þe modir
saide to þe spouse, 'All if þis bishope hafe thre euell thynges saide   25
befor, ȝete he hase a grete drede, and þat will brynge in charite. Ȝone
thre heuy balanses bytokens hys dedis þat he hase done agayns
Godes wyll, þe whilke drawes done hys saule to helle warde, and þai
semen thre for euell loue, spekynge and wirkynge, þe whilke eftir þe
manere of balanses drawes hym down to þe werlde. And þe oþir thre   30
light balanses were shewed | to þe as bi a lightnes goyng vpwarde.   f. 207ʳᵃ
For somtyme he thoght on God, sometyme he spake of hym, and
some[tyme] he wroght þe gude. Bot þai were noȝt so oft tyme
vpwarde as þe oþir were donewarde, for he did noȝt þere so hertly as
he dide þe oþir. And þerfor þe fendes has hym now by þe fete, and   35
þe snare is redy.'
    þe spouse saide, 'A, lady of pite, put þou somewhat vnto þe balans.'

2 þird] ferthe   7 as] is   16 and²] twice   33 sometyme] some

Oure lady saide, 'Agnes and I abyde if þe bishope will oght thynke on vs. Neuerþelesse, ȝete sall we do as thre frendes, þe whilke sittis by þe way for to telle it to þair frende, and saide, "Frende, þis way þat þou wendes is not siker, ne þe ryght way, for theues are þareine, þe whilke
5 will sla þe wen þou wenys to be moste siker." þe seconde saide, "þis way semys a plesand and a likand way, bot þou sall fynd it eftirwarde full sharpe." þe thirde saide, "Son, I se þi sekenes displeses þe noȝt. If I gyue þe counsell, be not vnkynde, and I sall helpe þe." Ryght þus will Agnes and I do to þis bishope, and, if he will here þe firste, þe seconde
f. 207ʳᵇ sall shew hym þe | wai, and þe third sall bryng hym to þe kyndome of
11 lyght.'

þa[n] it was shewed to þe spouse what þinges were sent to enforme þe bishope. 'Bot', þe modir saide, 'all if God may do all þinges, neuerþelesse, a man moste trauaile hymselfe to flye syn and to gete
15 grace. Bot þe firste þing þat is nedefull to fle syn is to haue trew sorow of all þat bytes þe consciens, and will to do þame no more, and, fro he be shreuen of þam, to amend þame eftir þe counsell of wise men. Also, hym moste pray God to helpe hym to put away all euell likynge and will of euell. Bot a man moste haue iii þinges yf he sall take grace: first,
20 þat he sett noȝt by lessyng of worldly wirshype; also, sett not by disese of þe world; and also, set not by bodely sekenes. For when charite is in a man, he settis noȝt by tribulacion, ne by þe worldly gudes ne by þe worldly wirshipe. þe seconde þinge þat brynges charite and grace to a man is to do almos dede of þat þe whilke leues eftir his nede spens, for
f. 207ᵛᵃ elles sall þe pore | men crye vengeans if þai be priuede, and þe
26 bishopes men wax proude of þe godes þat pore men suld haue. þe third is besy traualynge to kepe charite. For say a man one Pater noster in charite and for to gete charite, it likes Gode, and he will gyfe hys charite to swhilke one.'

30 þan saide þe modir to Criste, 'þou art stronger þan was Dauide þat slow hys enemy wyth a stone, for þou come nere þine ennemy and cast hym downe. Sen þou arte strongest in fight, I pray þe, teche þis bishope to fight, þat he may sit amange þame þat are victorious and hase shede þair blode for þe.' þan answerde Criste, 'It is wretyn þat
35 þare commes none to me bot ïf my fadir drawe hym. Bot if he be stalworth þat drawes, and it be stronge þat it is drawen wyth, if it be heuy þat is drawen it will breke. Also, if it be bunden and may not help itselfe, or elles it be fowle, it will lett þe drawynge þerof. And if a thynge

1 and] *subpuncted*   12 þan] þat   31 come] come in handes come
32 teche] teches

suld be drawen, it moste be clene and wele ordeynde. Bot, modir, for
ȝour prayer sall þe | way be shewede to þe byshop þat he suld go.'   f. 207ᵛᵇ
    þan saide þe modir to þe spouse, 'Yf þe bishope will go þe way of þe
gospell, þat is þe way of pouerte, thre thynges ar nedfull to hym or he
take þe way. Hym moste firste do away þe grete charge of couetyse,   5
and hald hym paide of þat is nedefull to hys astate, and gyfe þe superfluite to þe pore for þe wirshipe of Gode. For so dide Marke þe
bishope, þat putt fro hym þe charge of couetise, and he wiste noght þat
it was a charge to þe time þat he had taken þe ȝok of God. þe second is
þat him most be kiltid redi to 'go', as Tobi fand þe angell redi in his   10
wai: þe whilk angell bitokens a prest, or elles a bishop, for a prest suld
be clene as an angell, for he sacris Godis bodi, and handils God, þat
angels sene and wirship. þerefore ilka prest suld be beltid wyth þe
girdill of rightwisenes, to shewe oþir þe way of trewthe and ryght, ne
for to leue it noþir for threte ne for dede, hauyng euirmore a treste in   15
Gode. þe third þat he suld do is þat hym moste ete brede and drynke
watir, as Hely þe prophet did of þe brede þat he fand at his heued, in
strenghe of þe whilke he traueld fourty days. þis brede is bodely | gude   f. 208ʳᵃ
and gostely gude: bodely gude for gude ensampill of oþir; þe gostely
gude is strengh in saule to þe lufe of Gode and seruys of Gode. þis is   20
þe brede of charite, and wyth þis moste hym haue watir, þat is, continuall mynde of þe bittir passion of Criste, as for to thynke how þat he
prayed þat þe bittir passion suld be putt fro hym, and how þe dropis of
blode come oute of hym, how þat he stode byfore Herode and Pilate,
and how þe blode and watir come oute of his side.   25
    'And when þe bishope hase þes þre, þan sall he dispose hys tyme
þus. Firste, when he wakes in þe night, he sall thanke God of all his
gudenes, first þat he made hym, þan þat he boght hym, and þan þat he
takes no vengeance of hym for syn. Aftir, when he ryses, he sall say,
"Lorde, þe whylke of þi grace hase called me to þis astate, þou kepe   30
me stabill in my herte to þe, þat I be noȝt proude of my cleþing, bot
onely for to vse it for þe astate þou has called me to. And ryght as my
habit withoute is wirshipfull, so be þe clethyng of my saule vertuose in
þi sight." þan sall he say his | seruys. And when his mes is done, do   f. 208ʳᵇ
þan þat langes to his office, and euermore þinke on þe merci of Gode   35
and his wirshipe. And when he sall go to his mete, thinke þus: "Lorde
Jesu Criste, ryght as þou will þat þe body be sustende of bodyly mete,
so þou gyfe me grace to fede it þat it faile not for defaute of mete, ne

    16 þat¹] is þat, is *subpuncted*   18 bodely] *Quire catchphrase*, gud and gostli, *below*
19 for] *twice, first subpuncted*

þat it wax noȝt rebelle for ouermykyll exces." At þe mete, þan haue his
honeste mirth for his gestis comforth, and beware þare be no bak-
byttyng ne fowle wordes, ne stirryng to syne, bot on any wyse þat þare
be somwhat saide to þe wirship of Gode, and edificacion of þame þat
5 are þare. And eftir mete disporte hym wyth hys frendis and his menȝe
onestely, for þat will make hym more freshe for to serue Gode, so þat it
be discretly mesured and noȝt wanton. Also he sall teche his meneȝe
þe loue of God, and ʽofʼ no wyse mayntene no viciouse man þat will
noȝt amend hym.
10 ʽEftir þis say he his seruys, and at his soper þinke as at mete. And
f. 208ᵛᵃ when he suld go to his bede, þan sall he þenke | on hys werkes on þe
day. And if all it be noȝt as it suld haue bene, aske merci and forgyuenes wyth will to amende it. And when he liggis downe, say þus:
"Lord, þou kepe me and gyue me grace so to reste my body þat it faile
15 noȝt in þi seruyse, ne þat my saule be filed, ne my body." And if oght
falle be illusion, or oþirwyse, clens it on þe morn by shrifte, for
sometyme a syn þat is veniall, by wilfull forgettyn and contempt was
dedely. And luke euerilke day þat he be shreuen to a preste wyth will
to amend hym.ʼ
20   þan saide þe modir, ʽI sall warn þe bishop þat he cleth hym wyth
paciens agayns þe malice of men, and falshede of þe werldely per-
sewynge, and he sall kepe þe ten commandmentes agayn þe prikynge
of syn. Also, he sall desire blis endeles, and set noȝt by þe welth of þe
werld more þan is nedefull to hym. Bot þan commes thre enemys
25 agayns hym. þe firste is fandynge of þe fende, þe whilke sais þus to
hym: "Whi suld þou m[e]ke þiselfe? Why puttes þou þiselfe to so |
f. 208ᵛᵇ mykyll trauaile? Will þou be holier þan oþir were byfor þe? What hase
þou at do of oþir mennes dedes?" þe seconde enemy is þe werld, þat
stirres hym to be arayd as oþir are. þe third wald haue hym to hye
30 wirshipes. In all þir sall he take hede þat þe fleshe will faile, þe world
sall pas, dede will come, bot we wot noȝt when. þerefore he sall take
heede what he sall haue, for he sall haue a mytir, in token þat he is
heued aboue þe pupill, for to ordeyn his clergi at informe his folke and
amend defautes. This sall be kepid besily. And o none wise vse
35 symony. Ne he sall noȝt say bot þe trewth and Godes worde, for it
semes noȝt to a messyngere for to be dome, ne to wise men for to be
blynde, bot for to luke wele aboute hym, and so suld þe bishop do.
And he suld gyfe to God fully his herte voide fro worldly þinges, and
onowred and arayed with vertuse of gudenes.

4 of²] *twice*   26 meke] make   30 þir] oþir

'And þan, when he passes oute of þis werlde, þe aungels sall present
his saule to Gode and sai, "A, lorde, þis was þe bishope þat was clene
in his fleshe. He keped his presthede. He | was besy in prechynge and   f. 209ʳᵃ
waker in hys office, stalworth in his wirkynge and lawly in his beringe.
And þerfore we present hym to þe." And þe holy saules in heuen sall   5
say, "Lord God, we haue ioy of þis bishope, for he bare a floure in hys
mouthe with þe whilke he called furth his shepe. He bare a floure in
his handes wyth þe whilke he fede þame." And þan sall God say, "A,
my frende, þou hase presentted to me þi hert, and þou desired þat I
suld fille it. þerfore come þou to me, and I sall fill it wyth myselfe, for 10
þou sall be in me and I in þe, where blis sall neuer haue ende." '

Capitulum cxxvii. Oure lady, mayden Mary, telles to þe
spouse prayng for ane heremite, or þat þe heremites
body was beryd þe saule was in heuen.

þe modir aperid to Saint Bride when sho prayit for a gude heremite 15
þe whilke was passed fro þis werlde, and saide to hir, 'Dog[h]tir, witt
þou wele þat þe saule of þis heremite my frende þat þou prayes fore,
onone as he was dede had entre[d] into heuen if he had had in his |
deyng a perfite desirrynge for to haue comen to þe presens of Gode,   f. 209ʳᵇ
bot for he had not þat full desire, þerefore is he now kepid in þe place 20
of purgatory, where he hase no payne bot onely desiryng of comyng to
God. Bot witt þou wele þat or his body, þe whilke is now vpon þe erth,
be beryd, his saule sall be in blis.'

Capitulum cxxviii. Oure lady answers to þe spouse
praiyng for one heremite, þat was in doute wheþir he   25
suld ay abide in wildirnes, or sometyme go oute for
edificacion of oþir men.

þe modir saide to þe spouse, 'Say to þat olde preste þe heremite,
þat prayed þe to pray for hym, to wit wheþir it were more plesyng to
God þat he held hym onely to his contemplacion, or elles þat he of 30
charite went omange men to gife þame gostely counsels-say hym on
my bihalue þat it is more plesynge vnto God þat he go sometyme
omange men to stir þame to more hertly lufe of Gode, and to informe
þame to þe gode, | þan for to dwell stabilli in deserte in his contempla- f. 209ᵛᵃ
cion, and more medefull to hym, so þat he do it noȝt wythoute lefe of 35

16 Doghtir] dogtir   18 entred] entre   in his] *twice*

his souerayne and at his counsell. And say to hym þat I will þat he take
vndir his gouernance all þe heremites and nonnes and recluces þe
whilke were vndir þe gouernance of my frende þe hermite þat is dede,
for it is Goddes will. And þan sall he be þair fadir, and I sall be þair
5 modir, þat will be vndir his counsell.'

Capitulum cxxix. Criste aperis to þe spouse, and
expownes to hir clereli a vision þe whilke sho had two
ȝere byfore, of a beste and a fishe, of þe whilke it is
spokyn byfore in þe second chapitir of þis ferthe boke.

10 Criste said to þe spouse, 'I saide þe byfore þat I desire þe hert of þis
beste and þe blode of þe fishe. þe herte of þe beste is þe saule of a
cristen man, þat is more likyng to me þan any worldly þinge. þe blode
f. 209ᵛᵇ of þe | fishe is perfite loue to God. And þerfore þe hert suld be offird to
God wyth clene handes, and þe blode in a clene vessell, for right as a
15 preciouse stone wirsheps þe rynge, ryght so clennes wirships a
mannes werkes.

'Bot he þat will present to me þe hert of ane obstinate cristen man
þat rynnes in syn, hym moste pers his handes wyth a persoure. þe
gostely handes is fastyng and praynge and oþir gude dedis, þe whilke
20 are nedefull to þe saule as bodely werkes are nedefull to þe sustinans
of þe body. Bot þes gostely handes moste be persid wyth þe drede of
Gode, for, ryght as þe persure makes þe holes redy to þat at sall be
putt þere, so þe drede of God makes way to charite, and drawes Gode
to helpe. Also, he suld kepe and defende hys eyn wyth þe browes of þe
25 whalle. þe eyn suld be knawyng of gudenes of Gode and knawyng of
hymselfe. þe eyeliddis are nowþir harde as bone ne soft as fleshe, and
f. 210ʳᵃ þat bytokens þat a man suld not be to hardy for þe merci of God, | ne to
dispaire for þe ryghtfull dome, bot þinke here on bothe.

'þe third þinge þat is nedefull, to hym þat sall turne one hard-hertid
30 man, is to lay a plate of stele vpon his breste: þat is to say, to haue in
mynd þe grete passions of Criste, for Criste sais þat he was a pes of
stele strongly betyn oute on þe crosse, as steel is on þe stethi. Also, his
nesethirles suld be closed, for right as throw þame commes a mans
brethe, so by mannes desires and ȝernnynges entirs life or dede into
35 mannes saule. And þerefore þai suld be wele keped, þat þai þe whilke
is euell be not lange dwellyng in þe saule, for, ryght as one euell ayre
þat entirs to þe herte is cause of dede, so euell desires and þoghtes þat

5 þat will be] *twice, first subpuncted*   15 ringe] ryinge

dwellis in þe herte makis þe gostly dede to entir. Also, þis beste bose
be takyn wyth two handes. One is gostely wit, to knaw þe kyndenes of
God and þe desayte of þe world. Oneoþir is gude ensampill in lyuyng,
for it suffise noȝt, to þe turnynge of synfull men, gode prechyng bot if
þer folow þerewyth gude lyuyng.   5

'þe skyn of þis beste is hard | as flint, by þe whilke I vndirstand   f. 210ʳᵇ
feynyng of rightwisenes. For be a man noȝt gude, ȝete he wald be
called gude. And þerefore he feynes tokens of gudenes to be praysed of
men, and so of praisyng þai wax proude and hard as flynt, for þere is
no resone þat is made to þame, ne blamynge þat is set on þame, þat   10
may make þame to amende þame. And þerefore moste Goddes
seruantes smyte þame wyth þe melle of Goddes ryghtwise dome, and
putt to þame þe fire of charitefull prayinge, as Saynt Stephen praied,
and þat helpis many. þerefore he þat persis his handis of his gostely
wirkynge, and kepis his eyne wyth thynkeyng of þe merci of God and   15
his rightwisnes, and kepis his hert wyth mynde of þe passion, and
ordeyns his desires wele, | and þus presentes to me þe hert of þe beste,   f. 210ᵛᵃ
I sall gyue hym full likand tresor, and comfortabill to þe ai, swete to þe
ere, and blisfull to þe vse.

'þe fisch þat we spake of bytokens þe paynems, whose scales are so   20
harde þat noþinge may entir: þat is to say, þere syn is so vsed þat þai
will noȝt here speke agayn it. And, þerfor, he þat will bryng me þe
blode of þis fishe, him bose sprede hys nett, þat is, his prechynge, þe
whilke sall noȝt be made of rotyn thredis of philosophers spekynges,
or of coryous endyttynge, bot of sympilnes of wordes and meke   25
lyuynge. þe prechoure moste beware þat he pas noȝt þe knees in þe
watir: þat is to say, he sall noȝt sett his entent to þe gudes of þis werld,
þat is vnstabill as þe watir, and he sall set his fete faste, þat is, his affeccion, in God þat euer is stabill and lastynge.

'He sall be blynde of þe one eye. þis eye is drede of bodely dissese,   30
þat þe prechoure sall putt fro hym, for he sall trest fully in Gode, and
drede | noȝt bot Gode. þe oþir eye þat sall be opyn sall be compassion   f. 210ᵛᵇ
þat he sall of þame haue in þat þat þai are of mankynde, and to luke
þat he may haue to lyue on, and noȝt to be constreyned to bege his
lyuelade, for þat suld make hym to be euell payde of his conuertyng;   35
and to se þat he be enformed both by gude techynge and gude ensampill in cristen lawe. þere are some cristend þat gose amange þe

6-9 by þe whilke ... hard as flynt] *twice* (*second*, be, vndirstande, feyinge, þerefor,
feines, takens, praised, wex)   22 agayn] and agayn, and *ruled through*   28 is
his] his his, *first* h *subpuncted*   33 of²] *also marg.*

paynems, and hase a likynge to sla þair bodis and to wyn þair temporall gudes. Bot þis is no likynge to me. And þerfore he þat will
wende to þe paynems, putt fro hym all coueytise and all worldly drede,
and haue will to wyn þayre saules, and to lyue or dye for þe loue of
5 Gode.

'Also, he suld haue a shelde of stele: þat menes, verray paciens. For
riȝt as a shelde defendes a man fro þe strokis, ryght so paciens kepis a
man, þat he be noȝt hurte wyth bodely disese. þis shelde sall be
shapyn by ensampill of my paciens, þat was of stronge stele in þe dede
10 þat I suffird, and þe reproues on þe crosse. And beside, what wondir is
it if he [suffre] þat

> [Loss of a leaf containing end of IV. 129, whole of
> IV. 130: missing material from ch. 129 supplied from Ju]

f. 161ʳ is worthi iugement? þerfore he þat is defendid with paciens, he openys
his net vpon the fishe and holdis him x owris above þe watir, and he
schal haue þe blood of the fish. What ar þes x ouris but x counselis
15 whech ar to be don to a man þat is conuertid? The first is to beleue
myn x commandmentes, the wheche I gave to þe pepil of Ysrael. The
iide is þat he shal take and worship þe sacramentes of myn chirch. The
iiide, he owis to be sory for his sinnys don, and to haue perfit wil to do
no moore. The iiiite is þat he is boundyn to obey myn seruantis, what
20 they bid them do, onythinge ageins þer wyl. The vte is to contempne
all ill customs wheche are ageyn God and good manerys. The vite is
that he shal haue desire to drawe to God all þat he may. The viite is
þat he shal shew trew humylite in his werkis, shonynge yll exsamplis.
The viiite is to haue paciens in aduersite, not grocchinge ageins the
25 iugementes of God. The ix is þat he shal not here or haue them with
him þat are ageins þe cristen feith. The xte is to pray God, and [he]
shal desire personally, þat he may perseuer in þe loue of God. Ho þat
is turnyd fro synne and holdis and kepis þese x counselis, he shal deye
fro þe loue of the word, and he shal quekene to þe loue of God. Whan
30 þe fisch, þat is, þe synner, is drawin forth fro þe watir of lust, and pur-
posis to kepe the x counselis, he shal be openyd in þe bac wheras
f. 161ᵛ habundans of blood is. What betokenys þe bac? Good | werke with
good wil, þat must be don aftir þe plesure of God, for oftyntymes a
good dede is done of men, but the intent and wil of the doer is not
35 good. þis will wold be doon away, and myn grace takin to and ekid

11 suffre] *om*.   26 he] *om*.

with prayoris, and made perfit with myn good wil and werke and myn
swetnes. Behold, on þis wise the blood of þe fisch is to be presentid to
me. He þat presentes it so to me shal haue a good reward: euerlastinge
brightnes schal lytyn his sowle. And his helþe shal be newyd with-
owtyn ende.'   5

[Cl continues]

In wirshipe of hym þat is þe endeles crowne of rewarde to all vertuose   f. 211ʳᵃ
perseuerence, one God in trinite of persons, here endis þe fourte boke
of heuenly reuelacions graciously shewed throw þe fre godenes of þe
same gloriouse Gode, of þe same clennest mayden and mekest modir
to þe son of þe hye fadir, and of blissed saintes in heuen, to þe   10
syngulerly loued and chosyn spouse of our sauiour Jesu, Bride, pryncesse of Neryce in þe realme of Swene. *Deo gracias*.

---

11 and] god and, god *subpuncted*

[BOOK FIVE]

Prologe into þe fift boke of heuenly reuela[c]ions.

The fifte boke of heuenly reuelacions is worthely intitild þe boke of questions, bycause þat þe proces of it is by manere of questions: to whome þe lorde, Criste Iesu, gyues in his awen personne merueylous
f. 211rb answers and solucions, | þe whilke were shewed to þe forsaide lady
6 Bride on wonder wise, as hi[r]selfe by mouthe and by confessoures tolde vnto mony.

It fell in a tyme, when sho, wyth honeste menye and seruandes rydynge towarde a castell of hir awn, had hir mynde in prayer lift vp to
10 God almyghti, on swhilke wise þat sho was rauysht in spirit, and in manere aliende fro bodely wittes, suspendid in extasy of gostely conte[m]placion. In þe whilke tyme sho saw in spirit a leddir festynd into þe erthe, whos heht towchede þe heuen; and in þe hight of þe leddir þat was in heuen, sho sawe Criste Iesu sittynge in a merueylous
15 trone, as a juge demynge, at whose fete stode mayden Mary; and aboute þe trone a infynyt oste of angels and copiose multitude of oþir saintes. And þe forsaide Bride sawe, in þe middes of þe leddir, a certayne personne of religion whome sho knewe wele, þe same tyme
f. 211va lyfyng in body, a man þat had grete connynge in þe fa|culte of
20 diuynyte, and ȝit was fulle of diseyte and malice of þe feennde. þe same man semyd moste impacient and vnrestefull in his berynge, and so he semed more to be a fende þan a meke religious.

þe same lady Bride saw in þat tyme all þe thogthes of herte, and inwarde affeccions, of þe same religiouse, and howe he purposed his
25 ententes vnto Crist juge sittinge in þe trone bi þe maner of askinge o questions, and one vnrestfull and vnsittinge wise. And þan herd sho and saw in spirit how Crist þe juge, on þe most mild wise and honeste, answerd compendiouseli to ilka question. Amange þe answers þe maiden Mari somtim menged wordes to þe ladi Bride, as it sall be
30 talde wythin. þis lady lastide in þis rauyshynge till sho come to hir castell called Watezeny, kepynge all þis boke in þat tim in mynde, and when hir seruantes toke þe bridill of hir hors and moued hir to awake owte of þat trauns, sho come agayn to hirselfe, and was heuy þat sho was priued swilke a swetenes as sho had bene ine. Neuerþeles, all
35

1 reuelacions] reuelaions   2 þe] in þe   4 whome] wohome   6 hir-selfe] hisselfe   12 contemplacion] contenplacion

þis boke of questions abode in hir as it hade bene grauen in mar|bill,
þe whilke sho wrote onone in hir awne tonge, and hir confessoure
translatid into Latyn.

Thus endes þe prolouge.

In þe honoure and speciall louynge of Iesu, þe hye fadirs wisdome 5
of blis, here bygynnes þe fifte boke of reuelacions, intitild þe boke of
questions, to þe whilke þe same hyeste wisedome Jesus is juge and
answerer, shewed to þe same gloriouse Bride, Princes of Nerisse in þe
realme of Swene.

     þe first interrogacion þe whilk was purposid vnto þe 10
     juge.

'þow domesman, þou gaue me a mouthe: whi suld I not speke what
me liste? þou gaue me eyn: whi suld I noȝt se and byhalde þo þinges
þat likes me? þou gafe me eres: whi suld I noȝt here þo þinges þat delites me? þou gaue me handes: whi suld I noȝt do wyth þame þinges 15
þat is me lefe? þou gafe me fete: whi suld I noȝt walke wyth þame eftir
my awen will?'

Answere of þe juge.

Criste þat was domesman and sat on | þe trone, whose maner of
haueyng in continanse and chere was maste honeste and mild, 20
answerd and saide, 'Frende, I gafe þe mouthe for to speke to my wirshipe, and þinges profitabill to body and saule. I gafe þe eyn to se gode
and chese it, and to behald euell and fle it. I gaue þe eres to here
wordes of trewthe and honeste. I gafe þe handes to werke gode workes
and holesom to þe saule, and I gafe þe fete, wyth þe whilke þou suld 25
renne and fle fro þe loue of þe world vnto gostely reste, and to me þi
maker and thyne agaynbyer.'

     The seconde interrogacion made vnto þe domesman.

The same persone of religion purposid and saide, 'þou Criste,
suffirde þe moste bittir payn for me: whi suld I noȝt þan desire 30
wirshipe and be proud in þe world? þou gaue me temporall gudes:
why suld I noȝt do wyth þame what me likes? þou hase gyfen bodely
membris to me: whi suld I noȝt moue and vse þaime eftir mi awen

---

8 of Nerisse] *twice* (*second*, nerice)   25 þe²] þe handes, handes *ruled through*
33 mi awen] mi awen my

liste? Why gafe þou lawe and ryghtwisnes bot for to take vengeaunce?
þou ordey|ned rest: why suffirs þou þan vs to haue and fele swilke
werynes and tribulacion?'

Answere o[f] þe domesman eftir ordir.

5   The domesman awnswered, 'Frende, of my grete paciens I suffir
mannes pride, þat mekenes may be wirshipet and my vertu opynly
shewed. For pride come neuir of me, bot of fyndyng of þe fende, and it
ledis into hell: bot mekenes, þat I taght in werke and ensampill, indede
ledis to heuene. Also, þe worldly godes are gyuen and graunted to man
10 by me þat he suld haue resonabill vse of þame, and throw þame to loue
þe maker of all, and noȝt to lyue eftir his fleschly wille.

'Also, þe body hase his partis to vse vertuosely, and to shew þe
entent of þe saule, for þai are instrumentis of þe saule. Also, lawes
and ryghtwisnes are ordayned of me þat charite suld be kepede wyth
compassion, and Goddes aned suld | be amang men wyth gude pees
16 and acorde. Also, I hafe graunted bodely reste to refreshe þe body
wyth, þe whilke suld elles be ouer faint to serue þe saule in vertu.
And, for þe fleshe wald be to wilde bot it were chastised, þerefor
sende I sometyme tribulacions, þe whilke suld gladly be taken for
20 amendment of it.'

þe þird purposyng vnto þe juge.

þe same man of religion saide to þe domesman, 'Whi hase þou
gyuen vs bodely wittes, if we suld noȝt leue and vse þam eftir luste?
Whi suld we noȝt take metis and drynkis at oure liking, and oþir
25 delites also, sen þou hase graunted and gifen vs þaime? Whi hase þou
gyuen vs fredome bot if we suld haue oure awen will? And whi gaue
þou to man and womane kynde wythin þame, bot if þai suld vse it eftir
þe desire of flese? And whi hase þou gyuen vs herte and will, bot if we
myght loue as vs liste?'

30   þe þird answere of þe juge.

þan answerde þe domesman, 'I gaue | mane witt to knawe wyth
t[h]o wayes þat ledis to life, and to fle þo wayes of dede. Also, I gaue
man metis and drynkes þat was nedefull to his bodely sustinaunce,
and þat he suld þe more strongly wirke þe plesaunce of me and of þe
35 saule, and noght to shende þe body wyth glotonye. Also I gaue man
fredome of will for to encrese his mede in my seruyse, and to chese my

4 of] to   10 loue] loue and to loue   14 suld] suld noȝt, noȝt *subpuncted*
26 -dome bot if] *twice (second*, it *for* if), *second ruled through*   32 tho] two

seruys byfore his auen will. Also, I gaue man and woman kynde wythin
þame þat þai suld brynge furthe froyte as I haue ordayned in lawe, in
tyme and place on resonabill cause. Also, I gaue man herte and will,
þat he suld loue me his Gode þat hase done moste for hym, and þat his
likynge sulde be in me þat made hym.'   5

þe modir of mercy saide, 'Doghtir, þou moste haue fyfe þinges
wythin, and fyue wythoute: a clene mouthe fro bakbittynge; eres
closed fro wayne wordes; chaste eyn; handes to wirke þe gude, and to
wythdraw þe fro worldly conuersacion. Also, þe bose haue wythin þe a
feruent lufe to | God, and a wise desire of hym. Will þou gyfe of þi   f. 213ʳᵃ
worldly gudes wyth gude entente, resonabli to fle þe world and   11
mekely; and for [to] abide my byhestis paciently.'

The fourt asking of questions.

þan purposed þe man þat spake byfore þus, 'A, domesman, whi
suld I seke eftir þe wisdom of God, sen I haue a worldly wit? Whi suld 15
I be heui and wepe, sen I haue plente of gladnes and ioy of þe world?
Also say me why þat I suld haue likynge in ponyshyng of my fleshe,
and bodely dissese. And whi suld I be ferde, sen I haue strengh
enoghe? Whi suld I obey to oþir, sen my will is in myn awen propir
power?'   20

þe fourte answere.

The domesman saide, 'He þat is wise to þe worlde is blind to me his
Gode; and þerfore, it is nede [t]o seke wit fro aboue wyth mekenes.
Also, he þat has þe wirshipes of þe worlde, hym bose haue many
besines: and þerefore, it is nedefull to pray hertly and to wepe sadely 25
þe trespas þat he dose; for worldly | besines hase many bittirnes þat f. 213ʳᵇ
ledis to helle; and þarefore, þat he go noȝt wronge by þame, it is gude
to wepe and morne. Also, it is full mekill profete to be glad in sekenes
and tribulacion of þe body, for þan will merci come nere hym, by þe
whilke he may come nere to þe life ay lasteand. Also, ilke man þat felis 30
hymselfe stronge, wit he wele þat he has it of me, and I ame stronger
þan he; and þerefore, it is gude to hym to drede þat I take not fro hym
his strenghe. Also, whoso hase fredom in his hande, be he ferde and
knaw he wele þat þare is no gude thynge þat bringes so sone to hell as
a selfe-will, and þare is nothynge þat brynges so sone to heuen as for- 35
sakinge of propir will.'

1 byfore] by byfore, by *subpuncted*   3 Also I gaue man herte] *twice*, va-cat *to first*
8 wayne] *marg.*, vayne   12 to] *om.*   23 to] so

The fifte askyng of questions.

þe same persone byforesaide aperid and saide, 'O, þou domesman, why made þou wormes, þe whilke may do harme and no profite? Also, whi made þou wild bestis, þat dose harme and noyes man? Why

f. 213ᵛᵃ suffers þou sekenes | fall to m[e]nnes bodys? Why suffirs þou wi[k]ked
6 souerayns to dises to seruantes? And whi is þe body so tormentid in poynt of dede?'

þe fifte answere.

Criste saide, 'I, God and juge, made of noght heuen and erthe, and
10 all þat is in þame, and nothyng withoute resonabill cause, ne withoute likenes of spirituall þinges: for ryght as saules of saintes are like to holi aungels þat are in life and blis, right so þe saules of wikked men are like to fenndes, þe whilke are in euerlastynge dede. þerefor I answere þe whi I made wormes: þat was, to shew my wit and my might; for, all
15 if þai may noye, þai may noȝt noye bot at my souerans, and for syn of man þat wald noȝt be obedient vnto Gode: and þerefor it was ryght þat he suld be dissesed of þat was bynethe hym, for all þinges are at my will.

'Also, I made wild bestis, þat were in þair kynde full gude, and I

f. 213ᵛᵇ made þame soiet to man, þat man suld more hertly lufe me. | Bot now
21 þai disese men, owþir for amendment of þam and knawleche of trespas throw þair ponyshynge; or elles þai dissese þame þat are gude, to clensyng of þame and encressynge of vertu. Also, sekenes falles to a mannes body; þat is, fore a man suld be ware of exces, and þat he lere
25 paciens.

'Also, euell souerayns are suffirde, þat þai þe whilke are my frendes be proued be paciens. As þe gold is proued in þe fire, right so, of malace of þe euell, þe saules of þe gude are purged, and taght to wythdrawe and abstene fro þat at þai suld noȝt do; and I suffir euell men,
30 þat are þe fendes eres, for to disseuir þame fro þe gude whete, and þat þe malice of þame þe whilke are euell be fullfilled.

'Also, a mannes body is ponyshed in dede, for it is ryght þat a man be ponyshed in þe same by þe whilke he synned by; and, for þe body has vnskilfulle likynge, þerfore it sall be ponyshede wyth payne and
35 tribulacion resonably ordeynede. For som men, in þis life, begynnes |

f. 214ʳᵃ þaire dede þat euere sall laste in helle, and oþir endes here þere dede, and begynnes ioy þat euir sall be lastand.'

5 mennes] mannes   wikked] wilked   20 lufe] lufe þame, þame *ruled through*
28 euell] euell wille, wille *subpuncted*

Reuelacion made to Bride, in þe whilke oure lady sais
þat he þe whilke desires to tast godely swete hym moste
first take some bittirnes.

The modir saide, 'No saint had ne hase swetenes of spirit bot he þat
[f]irste suffird bittirnes. þerefore, woso will haue swetnes of blis in 5
tyme to come, flye he noȝt þe bittirnes of life þat is present.'

þe sext purposyng in question.

þe forsaid persone aperid and saide, 'O domesman, whi commes
one child oute of his modir wombe on liue and hase baptime eftir, and
aneoþir dies in þe modir wome? Also, whi hase þe gude man mekill 10
aduersite, and þe euell man all his liking? Also, whi falles þe pestilens
and hunger, and oþir noyfull þinges þat ponyshes þe body? Also, whi
commes dede soddanly, þat men knawes noȝt? Whi suffirs þou men
þat are full of wreth and malice go to bataile wyth will for to venge
þame?'   15

þe sext answere.

The domesman answerd and saide, 'Thy askynge, | frende, commes   f. 214ʳᵇ
noȝt of charite bot of my sofferauns. And ȝete I will answere þe by a
likenes. All þe strenghe þat a child hase in þe wombe is of þe kynde of
þe fadir and modir. And some tyme þat matir þat is consayued, for 20
some indispocicioun of sekenes in þe fadir or modir, is febill and noȝt
so stronge þat it may abide, wherefor it is hasti to dede. Also, þere
falles many þinges by reklesnes of þe modir; and oft tyme falles
swhilke þinges by my pryue will and rightwisnes. And I do my merci
wyth swilke childir, for all if þai sall neuir se my visage, ȝete þai sall 25
neuir fele tormentynge payns, and so þai sall be nerrere mi merci þan
payne.

'Also, it is skille þat gude men hafe þat þai aske vpon reson. Bot
þere is none ryghtwis frende bot if he desire to be partiner of þat
disese þat I suffird in þe world; and þerfore, takyng heede what I had 30
done for þame and hight þame, and what malice is in þe world, and
how disese makes a man to fle syn, þerefore, þai desire sonner disese
þan welth. And herefor I suffir þame | somtim haue tribulacions, þe f. 214ᵛᵃ
whilke, all if some take with grucchynge, ȝet I suffir þame to haue it,
and not wythoute cause. Ne I forsake þame noȝt in þaire disese, bot I 35
ame wyth þame in comforthe.

5 firste] criste, *Lat.* prius   21 indispocicioun] indispociciomn

'For right as a childe þat is ȝonge, if þe modir chastis hym, will gruch, bot when he commes to mannes age he thankes þe modir, for hir chastisyng makes hym to be of gude condiscions, right so, all if my frendes somtyme gruch with diseses, ȝet sall þai þanke me eftirwarde
5 þat I suffird þame to be a short tyme in tribulacions and disese, for to haue euerlastynge mede for þair paciens. Bot euell men, þat coueytes noght to fare here bot eftir þair lustis, þerefore þai haue here þair welth for a litill while, for oþir thanke ne mede gete þai none. And ȝet I suffir not ilkean euell man haue here plente, bycause I will þat þai wit
10 þat gudes of þe worlde are in my powere and noȝt at þair will.

'Also, I ponyshe a mannes body here wyth pestilens and hungir and
f. 214ᵛᵇ oþir disese to | gyfe hym eftirwarde þe more mede. And somtym I ponyshe hym in þat he loues beste of þe world, þat he suld haue his likyng in me, whome he suld loue best of all þinges. Also, I suffir dede
15 come sodanly, for if a man wiste þe tyme of his dede he wald noȝt serue me for lufe bot for drede, and he suld faile in hymselfe for drede: and þarefor, þat a man suld ay beware and loue me, and for man left þat at was sikir, þerefor is he ponyshede in þat at is unsikir.

'Also, I suffir hym to go to bataile þat is full of wrethe and enuye, for
20 swilke a man þat has will to noye his neghbore is like to þe fende, and he is þe fenndis instrument. þerefore I dide þe fende wronge if I suld, wythoute ryght, reue fro hym his seruant; and þerfor, as I vse frely my seruante in my plesaunce, so ryghtwisnes will þat I suffir þe fende vse his seruande; and so I suffir hym to be at þe fendis stirrynge, sen hym
25 had leuer folow hym þan me.'

The seuent purposyng of questions.

f. 215ʳᵃ   þe same persone asked þe juge, | 'Whi is on þinge called faire, and oneoþir foule? Whi suld I hate fairenes of þe world, sen I am faire and of gude kinred? Whi suld I noȝt hald myselfe bettir þan oneoþir, sen I
30 am richer and more wirshipfull þan oþir? Whi suld I noȝt lufe to be praised, sene I ame worþi? And suld I noȝt take rewarde if I do profite to oþir?'

The seuent answere.

þe domesman answerde, 'Frende, faire and foule of þe werld is as
35 bitter and swete. þe filth of þe world, þe whilke is dispite and aduersite, is, as it were, bittirnes, þe whilke is profitabill to gode men. þe

---

12 hym] hyne hym, hyne *subpuncted*   23 fende] fendes   27 juge] *Quire*
catchphrase whi is one, *below*

prosperite of þe world is, as it were, fairnes, for it is soft, plesaunt, and
also fals and dissayuande. þerefor, he þat will fle þe fairnes of þe
world, and leue þe softnes þereof, he sall noȝt come to þe filth of helle,
ne taste of þe bittirnes of it, bot he sall com to my ioy.

'Also, þou had of þi fadir filth, and in þi modir wombe þou was as a   5
dede þinge and vnclenne. Whi suld þou þan be proude of kyn? It was
noȝt in þi power to be broght furth into þis world of pore or of riche, bot
onely of my | godenes: and þe same mater þat þe pore and þe bonde is,   f. 215ʳᵇ
arte þou. þerefore, put þe noȝt to dispise þe sympill man beside þe; for
þe hier kyn þat þou arte commyn of, þe more drede suld þou hafe, for þe   10
more þat I haue gyuen to þe, þe more sall þou gyfe rekeninge of.

'Also, þu suld noȝt pride þe of riches, for if þu hafe more riches þan
is nedefull to þi sustinance, þou sall gyue a straite rekenynge þereof.
And if þou spend þam in pride, or elles kepe þam fro þe pore and
nedy, þou sall at þe dome haue als mikill sorow and penans as þou   15
hase now likynge in þame. And þerfor, for to be proude of þes worldly
gudes is bot harm to þe.

'Also, þu suld noȝt lufe to be praised, for sen þu hase no gude of
þiselfe, bot all þe gudenes at þou hase is of me, whi suld þu couet to be
praised for þat at is noȝt in þe, ne is noȝt þine? And þerefore, riȝt as of   20
God is all gudenes, so to him suld be giuen all praysynge; and, as þi
God gifes to þe all temporall gudes, strenghe, hele, consciens and discrecion, all wirshipe suld be thoght to hym.

'And, as towchynge rewarde, if þou stand to Goddes rewarde, for
þat at is full litill, þou | sall haue full grete rewarde; bot he þat will   f. 215ᵛᵃ
algatis haue his rewarde here, it bose nedis be short, for þe tyme þat is   26
here is shorte, and he sall losse þe rewarde þat wald euir laste.'

The eghten purpossyng made be forme of question.

The same persone aperid and saide, 'O þou domesman, I aske of þe:
whi suffirs þou fals goddes be set in temples and to haue þe same wir-   30
shipe þat langes to þe? Whi makes þou noȝt þi blis to be sene of men
in þis werld, þat it might be þe more desired? Whi are þi angels noȝt
sene in þis life? And sen þe pains of hell are so horribill, whi are þai
noȝt sene in þis life, þat men miȝt fle þaim? Also, sen fendes are so
foule, whi are þai noȝt sene in þis lyue, so þat no man suld haue liste to   35
folow or consent to þame?'

---

1 fairnes] fairnes of þe world   4 of²] þereof, þere *subpuncted*   com] come
þere, þere *subpuncted*

The eghtende answere.

The domesman answerde, 'Frende, I am God, maker of all, and I do no more wrange to þe euel þan to þe gude, for I am þe self ryghtwisnes. And þerefor it is right þat þe entre of heuen be þe stabill faith,

f. 215ᵛᵇ resonable hope, and | feruent lufe and charite. And þat þe whilk is
6 moste in a mannis hert, þat loues he most tendirli, and þat wirshipes he moste hertli. þere fals godes þat are in temples are more loued of þaire wirshippers þan am I, for þai lufe þame for hope of worldly welth, and my loue is for gostely gude. Bot if I distruyed þame, I dide wronge to
10 þame þat wirshepes þame, for þan suld I lett þame of vse of þaire fre will, and I may do no swilke wronge to gude ne to euell. (Bot in sothefastenes, þare is no verray God bot one, fadir and son and holi gaste.)

'Also, whi blis is not now sene, I answere: my blis is so grete þat, if it were sene in þis life, mans body suld faile to wirke bodely werkes, and
15 his wit suld be lettid fro þat at it suld do. Also it is hid for a tyme, þat it be more hertly desired, and þat mannes mede may growe of þat desire, and so þe endeles sight of it sall be more ioyfull.

'Also, my saintes are noȝt sene in þis life, for þe freelte of man myght noȝt bere þe sight of þame. Also, if þai were sene clerely, men |
f. 216ʳᵃ wald wene þat þaire blis were gude, and þai wald wirshipe þame as
21 Gode: and so suld my wirshipe be gyuen to my creature. Also, þe payns of hell are not sene wyth bodely eyn, for þan suld man for pure drede fare as he suld dye, and also þan wald men serue me more fore drede of payne þan for loue, and so suld þai lose þaire mede. And
25 þerfor, right as holy saules knawes not þe swetenes of blis till þe saule be departid fro þe body, right so may noȝt þe payne be felid or þe saule be departid fro þe body.

'Also, if þe fendis were sene in þaire horribill likenes, a mannes body þat sawe þame suld tremill for drede, and his wit suld faile, ne
30 his fete suld not suffise to bere hym vp. And þerefore, þat þe saule be kepit in state þat it sulde be in, and þe body be abill to my seruyse, and þe fendis malice be refreynid, þerefore will I noȝt þat þai be sene.'

f. 216ʳᵇ A reuelacion in þe whilke Criste spekes to his spouse Bride, techynge by likenes of a trewe | leche and a fals
35 mannessleere þat a man, þe whilke resayues with hymselfe synners, if he gyue þame helpe or mater of

---

13 sene] *twice, second subpuncted*   14 suld] *twice, first ruled through*   20 gude] *marg.*, gode

synnyng, and so þai dye in þair syn, God sall aske of his
hand þe spirituall dede of þo saules: and he bad þame
sese of syn, and stird þame to vertuse, and so þai be
amendid throw his techynge, he sall haue a grete thanke
of Gode.   5

Criste saide, 'If a grete fisician com into one howse to a seke man, he
can se by tokens wythoute what sekenes he hase; and if he gyfe hym
medcyne, of þe whilke he dyes, he sall be blamed of his dede. And if he
do his medsyns for worldly rewarde, he sall noȝt be rewardede of me.
And if he do it for my sake, I sall rewarde hym. Bot if þare be any þat is   10
no maistir, and he supposes þat his medcyn will do gude to þe seke,
and so he gyues to hym wyth gude entent, þis man sall not be blamed
of his dede, all if þe seke man dye–bot he sall be blamed | of his foly   f. 216ᵛᵃ
and of his presumpcion, and if þe seke man hele, he sal not be
rewarded as a maistir, bot he sall haue aneoþir rewarde, for he had   15
noȝt connyng of þe crafte.

'þe vndirstandyng is þis: þai are seke gostely þe whilke in pride and
coueytise folows þaire awn wille. þan if any þat has auctorite and suld
be gostely leche comfort þame in þe syn, if þai dye þerein, he sall be
blamed for þaire dede, and þameselfe also, for þai had fre will þat was   20
noȝt stressed. Also, if he hele þame of fleshly loue, he gettis no
rewarde of me, bot he teche þame and helpe þame, and withdraw
þame fro euell for charite. þan sall I gyue þame grete rewarde. And if
þare be any þat sall wot noȝt if he sall profite, and he suppose þat it
sall not greue God his doynge, if þai dye, he sall noȝt be blamed of þe   25
dede, ne he sall noȝt haue full rewarde as he þat it fell to. Bot ȝit if þai
lyue, for his doynge he sall haue lese payne.'

þe neynt purposyng vnto þe juge by for[m]e of ques-
tion. |

þan spake þe same persone byforsaide. 'O þou domesman, whi arte   f. 216ᵛᵇ
þou noȝt euene in þi gyftes and in þi gyfyng of þi graces? For þou   31
enhaunced thi modir Mary aboue aungels and all oþir creaturs. Whi
hase þou gyuen to þi aungels kynde spirit wythouten fleshe, and put
þam in þi blis of heuen, and þou hase made man one vesell of erth, and
he is born in wepyng, lyues in trauell, and dies in sorow? Whi hase   35

8 he¹] he hase   13 his²] his dede, dede *subpuncted*   21 noȝt] noȝt wit, wit
subpuncted   27 lyue] lyue oute, oute *subpuncted*   28 forme] fore   34 in]
twice, second subpuncted

þou gyfen man witt and resone, and not to bestis? Whi hase þu gyuen
bestis lyue, and to som oþir creatures none? Whi is þer not light on þe
night as wele as on þe day?'

The neynt answere.

5   The domesman saide, 'I loued my modir aboue oþir creatures, for
in hir was funde a speciall shewyng and jowels of vertuse. For ryght as,
when þaire are many trees laide aboute a fire, þat is sonest in fire þe
whilke is most abill to bryn, right so, when þe fire of loue of God was |

f. 217ʳᵃ   shewed to þe worlde, and Gode wald be man, þere was none so abill

10   ne so besy to take þis grace and fire of loue as sho was. And God knew
þat not onely at þat tyme, bot, or euir þe werld was, he wiste it. And
right as þare was none like to hir in lufe of God, right so þer was none
þat so grete grace was graunted to, ne so grete wirshepe.

'Also, to þe secund question, I made spirites in fre will, and þai, þat

15   stude eftir mi will, to hafe ioi of mi blis. Bot som hade pride þat I had
made þame in þat kynde, and moued þare fredom of will vnskillfully
to euell, notwithstandynge þat þai ware made gode, and þerfore þai
fell. And som of þe spirites held þame vndir me, and þerefore I haue
confermed and stabild þam for euer. And it is grete skill þat I, God, þe

20   whilke ame a spirit, haue spirites to serue me þat are swyfter and
soteller þan oþir creatures.

'And for my company suld noȝt be lessed, I made man to serue me
in þair stede and he wald. Bot if man had saule and no fleshe, he might

f. 217ʳᵇ   noght deserue to wyn þat hye blis, | and þerfore is þe body knyt to þe

25   saule. And I suffird man to be dissesed and haue sekenes, þat he wax
noȝt proude, and þat he coueyte no restynge here, bot desire þe blis
þat he is made to. And þerefor, his entre to þis werld is wyth wepyng,
and also his endynge and his life is trauaylous.

'Also, to þe third question: all þinges þat ar made bineth man are

30   made ouþir to profite of mane, or to his nedefull sustinance, or to his
mekyng, or elles to his comforte. Bot if all bestis had vndirstandyng
and reson as man, thay suld rather do man harme þan profite at his
nede, ne þai walde noȝt be obeyng to hym as þai suld, ne dredyng
hym, bot onely obey to God and drede hym.

35   'Also, to þe oþir question: þinges þat may not fele are ordeynde to
mannes serues; and, might þai fele, þai wald not bow so redely to
mannes hand as þai do now. For all þinges ware made to mannes
solace, þe aungels aboue to his kepyng (and with þame hase he vndir-

f. 217ᵛᵃ   standynge), and all þat is byneth hym is made | to his helpyng.

38 kepyng] kepyng also þou asked why, *exc.* kepyng, *ruled through*

'Also, þou asked why it is not alway day. To þe whilke I answerde by ensampill. A chare hase whelis to drawe it, and þe hyndir whelis commes eftir þe for whelis. Right so, gosteli, þis world is a grete chare, chargid with trauayle and besines. Fore cause man loste Paradise, þe place of ryst, þerefore is he now put to þe place of trauaile. þat þe charges of þis world þe more suld esily be born, þerefore God of his endles mercy ordeynde þe changeynge of þe warlde. And þerfore was þe light made, þat man in his trauaylyng suld haue helpe and þinke on þe light þat euir sall last. And, for man may noȝt euirmore endure bodely trauale, þerefor is þe night ordayned for riste and for to haue will at come to þat place where neuir sall be night ne dirkenes.'

Reuelacion made to Sante Bride, in whilke Criste hyely commendes and praises all partes of his modirs body, likenyng þe same membres vnto sere vertuse. And he telles how sho was moste worthy a quenely crowne. |

Criste saide vnto his modir, 'I ame kyng crowned in godhede wythoutyn bygynnyng and endyng. I haue myselfe, þat ame as a crowne þat was kepid to hym þat most hase loued me. And, modir, þis crowne, þat is myselfe, drowe þou to þe: for aungels and santes bers wittnes þat in þe was most brenyng loue and moste clene chastite. And þerfor aboue all oþir þou plesid me.

'þi heued was bright shinyng as golde, and þi here as þe son bemys, for þi clene maidenhede þat is in þe, hede of all vertuse, and withdrawyng of all vnskilfull mouynges, wyth þi mekenes, plesid me. þarefor arte þou crowned quene—quene for þi clennes, and crowned for þi dignite.

'Thi forhede was wondir white—þat bytokens clennes of þi consciens. þi eyn were wondir clere in þe sight of my fadir: for in þe gostly sight of þi saule he sawe all þi will, and þat þou desired not bot hym and at his will. þine eres were opyn as þai had bene full clere wyndowes, when þe aungell Gabriell | tolde þe my will, and I toke mankynde in þe. þi chekis were coloured wyth white and rede, for þe gude fame of þi wordes and þe fairnes of þi maners plesid me and my fadir so mekill þat hym liste not turn hys eyn fro þe.

'þi mouthe was bright as a brynnyng lawmpe and shynnyng wythoute, for þi wordes are brynnyng within wyth þe techyng of Gode, and þai were shynnynge withoute with sobirnes and informynge of

20 was] was and, and *partly rubbed*   22 þe son] *twice, first subpuncted*

gude vertuse. A, my der modir, þe likynge wordes of þi mouthe drowe
me to þe, and þe warmenes of þi swetenes, for þi wordes are swettir
þan hony or þe honycombe.

'þi neke is ay raysede vpe, for þe ryghtwisnes of þ[i] saule reches vp
5　to me at my will, for it was neuir bowede to euell. Bot as þe neke bowes
with þe heued, so was all þi wirkyng at my will. Thi breste was full of
swetenes, for I, þat am God, rystid in it, and dranke milke of þi pappes.
Thi armes were faire be obediens and suffrynge of trauailles, for right
f. 218ʳᵇ　as þou | handilled my manhede with þi bodely handes, so I with my
10　godehede ristid bytwene þine armes.

'þi wombe was moste clene as iuory, for þe stabilnes of þi consciens, and þi faithe, sesed neuir, ne was defouled wyth disese. þi fete
were clene weshyn in swete erbes, for þine affeccions were likyng to
me, þe whilk were of gude smell by gude ensampill to oþir. And here
15　come I downe to riste in þe, and herefor, my der modir, þis crowne of
my godhede was gyuen to none bot to þe, for allonely in þe I toke mankynde.'

The tent purposyng in forme of question.

þan aperid þe forsaide persone and saide, 'O þou domesman, sene
20　þou arte moste mighti, most faire, and moste vertuose, for þou arte
wythoute comparison brighter þan þe son, whi wald þou cleth þe in
swilke a seke of mankynde? Also, how closes þi godhede all þinges
wythin þe selfe and may noȝt be closid? And how contenes and haldes
f. 218ᵛᵃ　it all þinges, and may noȝt be haldyn? Also, whi wald þou | be so lang
25　tyme in þe maydens wombe, and not as fast passe oute þareof as þou
was consayued? Also, sen þou art almighty and present in ilkea place,
whi wald þou not apere in þe 'schap' þat þou was in at thretty ȝere?
Also, sen þou had no fadir of Abraham kyn, whi wald þou be circumcised, and sen þou was consayued and born withoute syn, whi wald
30　þou be baptized?'

The tent answere.

Than saide þe domesman, 'Frende, I answere þe by ensampill. þere
is a kynde of grapis, and þe wyne of þame is so stronge þat it gose oute
fro þe grapes withoute stresse or pressynge, and þarefor he þat awe þe
35　grapes abidis not þe rypyng of þame, bot he takes byfor a vessell and
settis it vndir, and so þe vessell abiddis þe grape and not þe grape þe

vessell. And if þare `be´ many vessels, þat `at´ is next to þe wyne is
sonnest filled. þis grape is my godhede, þat is so full of wine of charite
þat all þe company of aungels is filled wyth it. Bot man | throw his   f. 218ᵛᵇ
dissobeysance made hymselfe vnabill to it. Bot wen my fadir saw his
tyme, he sent me his son into a vessell, þat was, into þe maidens   5
bosom, for sho had moste feruent lufe to Gode, and so sho was moste
nere to resayue me, for sho had so grete desire to me þat it was neuir
houre þat sho ne coueyted to be my seruant.

'And þarefore resayued sho þis nobill wyne, þat had in it thre
þinges. First, strengþe, for withoute tochynge of man, I come furth. þe   10
second was faire coloure, for I come fro þe hye heuen. þe third, it had
gret softenes, and will make one dronkyn. þis wyne am I, þat come in
mankynde, and þat was skill, þat liklynes in kynde suld make asethe
eftir þe maner of trespas. And þarefore toke I purpose in manhede to
be with man; and þe charite of þis maiden temperd my felnes; and by   15
hir was shewed my lufe to man. And in so pure aray I shewed myselfe
to shende þe pride of þe fende.

'Also, þe godehede is a spirit, | and where it will be, it is, and þere is   f. 219ʳᵃ
nothynge may lett it, for it hase all vertu and all might, and þerefore
þer is noþinge þat may comprehende it: and it may comprehende all   20
oþir.

'Also, to þe thirde, wit þou þat for I haue ordeynde to euirilkea
kynde his manere, his ordir, and his tyme of furth commynge–þan if I
þat ame maker of all kyndes had comyn furth of my modir wambe
sonner þan I did, I had done agayne kyndely ordinance of bryngyng   25
furth of childir: and þan wald þai haue said þat I had no verray body of
mankynde. And þerefore I wald fullfill in myselfe þat I ordeynde in
oþir.

'Also, to þe ferthe, I wald not shewe me in so grete quantite in tyme
of my birth as eftir, when I was therty ȝere of age, for meruaill and   30
wondiryng of men, and also for þe prophetis hade saide before þat I
suld be a childe, and laide amange bestis, and to be soght of kynges
and offird vp in þe tempill. þerefor, to shewe my verray manhede, and
to fulfill þe | prophetes spekyng, was I born in quantite as oneoþir   f. 219ʳᵇ
child.   35

'Also, `to´ þe fifte: all if I were not of Abraham kynd be my fadir, I
was of his kynde by my modir, and wythouten syn. þerefore, to fulfill
þe lawe þat my fadir had ordeynde was I circumsised. Also, I was baptized, for it `is´ skill þat he þat makes a lawe, go byfore oþir in þe way

---

1 at] as it, *with superior marks*   20 þer] *marg.,* þer f   23 ordir] *also in marg.*

to lere oþir. Bot in þe ald lawe was þer a fleshely lawe, þat was circumcision, þe whilke was þe shadowe of þe new lawe. Bot nowe is comyn
þe treuth þat it was shadow of, in my commyng. And þis way is þe
more esy way, þat is, baptym, for it is openyng of ȝates of heuen.

5   'In tokenyng þereof, when I was baptizede, þe heuen was opynd, þe
fadirs voyce was herde, and þe holy goste was sene in likenes of a
coluer; and I was þere, verray man. And sen þat I ame verray trewth
and hase broght my laue of baptyme, skill it is þat I suld take it
f. 219ᵛᵃ   myselfe, noȝt for my syn, bot for to shewe þat whateuir þai be in | man-
10   kynde þat resayues þis baptym as þai suld, þai are made childir of
grace and of þe lyue euirlastynge.'

A reuelacion shewed to Saint Bride, in þe whilke Criste
teches hir noght to be besy aboute worldly riches bot to
haue paciens in tyme of tribulacion.

15   Criste saide to þe spouse, 'Be wele ware, for þe werld will sende to
þe, firste, besines for riches to begyle þe. Bot answere and say, "Riches
are sone passynge, and þe more a man hase of þame, þe more a man
hase to gyue rekenynge of. I reke noȝt of þame, for þai will noȝt go
with þaire possessoure, bot at his nede leue hym." The second seruant
20   þat þe worlde will sende is losse of catell and of gudes. And to þat
seruant say, "He þat gafe riches tuke þame away: he wote what is þe
beste: be his will done." þe thirde seruant is þe dissese of þe worlde,
and to þis say, "Blissed be þou, gode God, þat suffirs me be turbild,
for þou suffirs me be desesed here for to spare me in tyme to come. I
f. 219ᵛᵇ   byseke | þe of paciens and strengþe to suffir þame." þe ferthe is
26   reproue of þe world, and to þat say, "Onely God is gode, and to hym
be all wirshipe. I ame worthi to be reproued. Wirshipe wald stir me to
pride, and þerfor I set noȝt þareby." '

The elleuent purposyng in forme of question.

30   þan saide þe same man, 'A, lorde, sen þou arte both God and man,
why shewed þou noȝt þi godhede as wele as þi manhede, and þan suld
all haue trowed in þe? Also, whi wald þou noȝt make þi wordes be
herd at ones in one poynt, and þan nedid þame noȝt haue bene
prechid in diuers times? Also, whi wroght þou noght þi werkes in one

---

13 bot] *also in marg.*   20 þat¹] þat is   is] his   23 gode] gud *in marg.*

oure? Also, whi shewed þou þe noȝt in þe might of þi godhede in tyme
of þi dede? And whi shewed þou noȝt þi felnes on þine enemys?'

The elleuent answere of Criste juge.

Criste answerde, 'To þe firste, my godhede is gostely and my man-
hede bodely, þe whilke were neuer disseuerd ne de|parted, fro þai   f. 220ʳᵃ
were knyt first togidir. And þare is so grete fairenes, perfeccion and   6
clerenes in my godhede, þat a clere eye myght noȝt se it. For right as
þe son, when it shynes bright and most clere, wald shende þe eyn, so if
a man lyfyng here saw my godhede, þe whilke, wythoute comparison,
is brighter þan þe son withoutefurthe, his body wald melt and relent   10
as wax dose agayn þe fire, and þe saule suld haue so grete ioy þat þe
body suld turn to askis.

'Also, I may noȝt shewe my godhede to man lyfeyng here, for I saide
þat man suld noȝt life bodely life and se my godhede. For þai þat
herde bot one voyce, and sawe þe hill smokande, saide: "Lat Moyses   15
speke to vs and noȝt to our lorde." And þerfore schewed I myselfe to
man in liknes of man, and mi godhede was hid, þat I suld `not´ slai
man, ne make him ferde.

'Also, to þe second: as a man takes his fode by proces, so my wordes
were spokyn in diuers tymes, and noȝt sodanly, to profite of þame þat   20
vndirstandes þame. For right as bodely mete is sustenauns to þe body,
so are my wordes to þe saule. And right s[o] it was skill and reson þat
þai þe whilke trowed in me | suld se here be diuers tymes þare awn   f. 220ʳᵇ
malice.

'Also, to þe third: it was ordeyned and shewed to þe prophetes þat   25
`I´ suld com in mankynde and suffir dede. And þerefore it was my
fadirs wille þat I suld take swilke a body þat I might trauayle with fro
morn to euen, fro ȝere to ȝere, to þe ende of my lyue here, þe whilke
body I toke wythoute syn, like to þame þat I suld by agayn. Also, to þe
fourt: I fulfilled all þinges þat were wretyn of me to þe leste poynt. And   30
þerfor, in my deyng I hid my godhede in my manhede, for elles had I
noȝt bene dede, ne rissen eftirwarde fro þe dede, with my glorified
body, ne stied vp to heuen. And also, if I had commen whike down of
þe cros and shewed my myght of my godhede, þai suld noȝt haue
trowed þereon, bot þai wald haue saide þat I did it by þe fendes craft.   35
And þerefore, þat man suld be deliuerd of his bondes, I was bonden;
and þat he þe whilk was gilty suld be saued, I giltles hange on þe cros
and dyed on it.'

5 fro] for, *Lat.* a principio   22 so²] as

f. 220ᵛᵃ Reuelacion shewed to Saint | Bride, in þe whilke Criste
teches hir þat in spirituall life throw perseuerant trauayle
in mekenes, and mighty withstandyng of temptacions, a
man commes to ryste of saule and endles blis, by ensam-
5 pill of Jacob, þat serued for Rachell. And he shewes howe
þat many ourecommes strongely temptacions in þe
bygynnyng of þair conuersion to spirituall life, som in þe
middes, and som at þe ende. And þarefor a man suld euir
be in drede, and trauaile to perseuerans in godenes.

10 Criste saide, 'It is wretyn þat Jacob serued for Rachell, and hym
thoght þe dayes were fewe for þe grete lufe þat he had to hyre, þe
whilke lessed þe [þ]outh of his trauaile. And wen he wend to haue had
his purpose, he failed. Neuerþeles, he sessed noȝt of his trauaile till he
come to his purpose. Right so þere is many þat trauayles in prayer and
15 oþir gude dedis for heuenly þinges. And when þai wene to com to
reste of contemplacion, þai are disesed wyth fandynges and tribula-
f. 220ᵛᵇ cions þat growes vpon | þame: and þat is more for to proue and clens
þame, and make þame more perfite. Bot som hase temptacions in þe
bygynnyng of commyng to gostely lyueyng, þe whilke are saddid in
20 perfeccion into þe ende: som are gretely tempid in þe middis and
aboute to þe ende of þaire gostely lyueyng, and þat is for þai suld noȝt
triste on þameselfe, bot ay besily pray God, as Laban saide: "First sall
þe elder doghtir be takyn" (as if he say[de], "Firste trauaile besily and
þan sall þou haue ese.")'

25 þan saide Criste, 'I set þe ensampill of two personnes. One in þe
bygynnyng of his turnyng was gretely temptid, and he withstode, and
profited, and fand þat he soght. þe second was gretely temptid in his
eld with temptacions þat he knewe not in his ȝouthe, insomykill þat he
had almoste forgetyn þe godenes þat he had done byfore. Bot
30 neuerþeles, he stode to þe consell of gude men, ne left not of his
trauaile, all if it were noȝt so whike as it was byfore. Bot þus, wyth gude
techyng, he com to reste.'

f. 221ʳᵃ The twelfet purposyng in | forme of question.

þan saide þe man byfore spokyn of, 'Why wald þou more be born of
35 a maiden þan of aneoþir woman? Whi wald þou noȝt shew by opyn

---

8 euir] neuir   9 in] *twice, first subpuncted*   12 þouth] ȝouth   19 lyue-
yng] lyuenyng   23 sayde] say

tokyn þat sho was modir and maiden, and whi shewed þou to so fewe
þi birth? Whi fled þou to Egipte and suffird þe innocentes be slayne?
Whi suffird þou þiselfe to be blasphemed, and falshede to ouircome
þe trewthe?'

The twelft answere.   5

The domesman saide, 'Frende, I am God, and so clene is nothyng.
And þerefore I chase a clene maiden þat was not filed, for in hir was
neuir stirryng to luste. And for maidenhede is þe fairest path to heuen,
and wedlake is, as it were, þe hyeway, þerefor I chese to reste in a clene
maiden. For, right as Adam was made of þe erthe, þat in maner was   10
mayden, for it was no3t þan filed with blud, ri3t so wald I be borne of a
maiden þat was no3t filed in þoght ne dede.

'Also, to þe secound, tokening and witnes þat mi modir was
[maiden] was þe witnessinge of Joseph, þe whilke was ke|per of hir   f. 221ʳᵇ
chastite, and oþir mirakell wald I no3t shew to þat þan þe prophetes   15
spekynges, for þe mistiry of takyng of my manhede I hid fro þe fende.
And þat was on skylle why þat I shewed not to all folke þe tyme of my
birth and my bycomyng man, þat I might sodanly in mekenes ouircom
þe pride of þe fende.

'Also to þe third, I flede into Egipt for to shewe þe febilnes of man- 20
kynde, and to fulfill prophecies, and for to gyue ensampill to þam þat
were to com eftirwarde, for somtyme it is nedefull to fle persecucion
for þe bettir þat is sometyme folowyng. Also, I suffird innocentes be
slayne, for to shewe þe malice of men agayns me, and for þe gretter
mede of þame, and for shewynge of my dede þat was to com.   25

'Also, I suffird me to be blasphemyd, for I ame like Dauid, þe whilke
wen he fled his sone, one warid hym, and he suffird it. One skill was, for
he had hope of his turnyng agayn. Anoþir skill, for he wiste þat he was a
fole, þe whilke | cursid hym. Right so ame I pursewed and put oute of   f. 221ᵛᵃ
mannes saule, þat suld be my kyngdome, and I for þaire foly suffir, and 30
for I abide þe turnyng of þame agayn to me to þe laste poynt of þaire life.
Bot to þe last, men trowes now bettir falshede þan trewth, for þai loue
bettir þe world þat is fals þan me þaire God þat is verray trewthe.'

A reuelacion shewed to Sant Bride in þe whilke Crist
commendes ofte shryuyng, þat a man losse not þe grace   35
of God þe whilke he hase.

---

8 for] þerefor, þere *subpuncted*   heuen] heueuen   9 -way] way to heuen, to
heuen *subpuncted*   14 maiden] *om., Lat.* virgo   17 þe] *twice, first subpuncted*

Criste saide, 'Where is [fire] in one hows þere moste nedis be a hole
þat þe smoke may voide oute at. Right so, woso will hald þe hali goste
and my godly grace, hym bose haue continuall shryft, by þe whilke þe
smoke of syn may passe away, for elles my spirit and my grace will not
5 abide þare.'

A reuelacion in þe whilke Criste shewes what þe com-
monyng of þo men is like þe whilke hase all þaire delite
in erthly and fleshely likynge and not in heuenly, and
f. 221ᵛᵇ   how þai sall be cast away | fro þe sight of God.

10 Criste saide, 'He þat songe þus, "Lorde, deliuer me fro þe wikked
man", his voice was in myne eres as two stones had smetyn togedir.
His herte cryed to me with thre voices. þe first is, "I wald hafe my wille
in my hand, to slepe and ryse and speke as me liste. I will haue silluer
in my purse, and go softly clede." þe second voice is, "þe dede is not
15 to hard, ne þe dome is not so fell as þai say. þarefore haue I my likyng
in þe werld. Lat þe saule go where it may." þe third voice þis: "God
wald not haue boght man bot if he wald haue gyuen hym heuen. What
made hym to dye bot for to bryng vs to blis? I knaw not of heuen bot by
herdsa[y], and wheþir þat be trew þat is wretyn or not I wot neuir. And
20 þarefor, I wald fare wele ay here."
'Bot to þe firste voice I answere,' sais Criste, 'thy way gose not to
heuen, ne þou loues not heuenly þinges. þarefor helle is opyn, and,
sen þou loues þat is bynethe, þou sall ga downe.' To þe second he
f. 222ʳᵃ   saide, 'þe dede sall | be harde, þe dome sal be ferdfull. þou sall noȝt
25 mowe fle bot þou amend þe.' To þe third he answerd, as it sall be
saide, 'All my werkes I wroght for lufe, þat þou suld haue turned to me.
My werkes are dede in þe and my wordes are heuy to þe. þarefore sall
þou haue turmentis and company of fendis, for þou turnys þi bake to
me, and puttes vndir þi fete my mekenes.
30 'þou takes no hede what I suffird on þe crosse for þe, for I was on þe
crosse as a man þat were smyten throw þe eye with a knyfe, and ȝit my
payne was mekill sorer þan þat. Also, I was on þe cros smyten throw
þe herte with þe swerde of sorow; and ȝet more sore for my modirs
sorow þan for myne awne. Also for sorow of disese all þe partes of my
35 body, both within and withoute, trembild; and ȝet left I not ne went
noȝt away bot hange still and dyed on þe cros.'

1 fire] *om., Lat.* ignis   19 herdsay] herdsaw   23 To] tho, h *subpuncted*

The thirtende purposing in forme of question.

þan asked þe forsaid man þus: 'O þou domesman, why is þi grace withdrawen sonner fro som, and som are suffird lang to be in malice? Whi is grace | gyuen to som in þaire ȝouthe and taken from som in þair f. 222rb elde? Why are some gretly disesed, and som are withouten any disese? 5 Whi are som wele witted and hase grete vndirstandyng, and som er lewde as þai were assis? Whi are som hard hertid in syn, and som hase grete comforth? Whi hase euell men grettir welth in þe worlde þan gude men? And why is he called to God in his bygynyng and oþir in þe ende?' 10

The thretende answere.

The domesman answerde, 'Frende, for a man folows his awn will more þan myne, þarefor skilfully are taken fro hym þe giftes of grace; and, for many are vnkynde and kan not thanke for þat I haue done to þame—bot þe more kyndnes I shewe þame þe more vnkynde þai are 15 agayne—þarefor withdrawe I my gyftes fro þame, for elles þai suld haue harder dome for mysevsyng of my graces.

'Also, I suffir many in þaire malice, for somewhat þai do þat is suffirabill, bycause þat þe oþir dose profite to oþir, or elles þai are ensampill to oþir for to beware of syn, as I | suffird Saul in his trespas f. 222va and Dauid in his. Bot Saule left me and toke one wiche of his consaile. 21 Dauid when he was blamid amendid hym and arette his disese to his synnes, and suffird paciently his chastisyng. þarefore, in sufferyng of Saul was shewed my godenes, and his vnkyndenes. Bot in þat at Dauid ame[n]did hym is shewed his mekenes, and myne forgyuenes. 25

'Also to þe thirde. Fro som I withdrawe grace in þare eld, for at þaire ende þai are not kynde, ne in þaire life besy to kepe it, as Salamon. And for þat cause at his ende he loste grace. And þarefor, when one is rekles and will noȝt knaw how grete a gifte is grace, fore his reklesnes it is taken fro hym. Also it is sometyme taken away, to 30 make oþir to be more ferde to losse it, when þai see oþir þat hade grete grace fall þarefro.

'Also, I suffir som to be disesed more, and some les, to teche þame for to turn fro syn, and þat þai þe whilke are disesed here be comfortyd in tyme to com. Also some are withouten disese, and þat is, for þai 35 cannot bere disese | withouten gruchyng, and þat suld be cause of þe f. 222vb harder dome to þame: and some are not worthi to be disesed, and some are not ponisht here, bot þaire ponishyng is kepid to eftir þis life.

13 of] of god, god *subpuncted*   25 amendid] amedid

And some are in tribulacion here and sekenes fro þai are born to þai passe oute of þis werlde, and þat is for þaire mede, yfe þai hafe paciens.

'Also, for þe fourte: euirilka man lifand in þis werld, þe whilke hase
5 vse of reson, hase suffisant wit to lere þe way vnto heuen. Neuirþeles, þare is many þat hase no reson elike, and þat is somtyme of my suffryng, oþir to profite of þame or elles to more meke beryng of þame. Somtyme it falles for vnkyndnes and fandyng, and somtym for defaute of kynde and pryue synnes, and somtym for þe fleyng of grete synnes.
10 'Bot witt þou wele þat þe hyer witt a man hase, and he be rekles to rewle hym wele, þe harder sall be his dome, for with connyng itt is nedefull to haue gude lyueyng. Petir and Jon in þaire ȝouthe were

f. 223ra sympill of beryng, and ȝet þai come to verray knawynge | connyng; bot þai come noȝt to verray wisdome for defaute of gude lernyng, and
15 þerfor þai leryd noȝt to þaimselfe bot to oþir. Balaham had conyng bot no gude lifynge, and þerfore þe asse blamyd his foly. And þerefore connyng is not plesynge to me withoute gude lifyng.

'Also, why þat som are obstinate in syn, as Pharao, þe skille is, for he wald noȝt conforme his wille to Goddes wille, and þerefore obstinasy
20 is noȝt elles bot withdrawyng of my grace, and I withdraw it for man gyues noȝt to me þat he hase fre, as fre wille of hym, as þou may lere by ensampill. þare was a man þat had twa feldis: one was telid, and oneoþir lay still and did no gude. þan saide his frend to hym, "Whi tilles þou noȝt þi feldes, or elles latt þaim to onoþir?" He answers,
25 "One of þe feldes, do I neuir so mekill þerto, it brynges noȝt furthe bot euell wedis, þat euell bestis etis: and þe more þat I do to it þe more wilde it is. And if it bryng furthe a litill whete, þe remlande is bot cokill, þat I set noȝt by. þarefore it is bettir to leue it vntilled, fore þan

f. 223rb sall noȝt | bestis com þare and hide þaim; and ȝit will þe gre[s]s of it, if
30 it be not tilyd, do gode, inalsmykill as þe bittirnes of it sall make þe bestis þat tastes þareof to haue more daynte of gude pastur. þe oþir felde is tilid: one party þat was stony is mendid with fattnes, and þe oþir þat was moste is dryed, and þat at was dry is moysted."

'I ame like to þis man. þe firste felde is fre mouyng of manys will,
35 whilk þat is more agayns me þan eftir my will. þus did Pharao, þe whilke, for all þe tokens þat I shewed hym, lastid in his malice agayns me. And þarefore I shewed vpon hym my ryghtwisenes. þe oþir feld is

1 fro] for   9 and¹] and witt, witt *subpuncted*   12 lyueyng] lyuenyng
13 knawynge] *Quire catchphrase*, conynge, *below*   29 gress] grees, *Lat.* herbe
31 gude pastur] *margin*, Nota bonum verbum   32 one] þe one, þe *subpuncted*

puttyng away of his awn wille and obeyng to my will: and þat herte, if it
be drye, it sall abyde þe rayne of my grace: and if [it] be stony by impaciens and hardnes, it sall suffir clensyng and amendynge; and if it be
moiste by disposyng vnto luste of fleshe, it sall be ponyshede with
abstinens. And of swilke a saule haue I grete likynge. þarefore obsti- 5
nasy com of an euill wille, for all if I walde all were saued, neuerþeles, |
þame moste wirke eftir my will, yf þai sall be sauyde. Bot þat all hase f. 223ᵛᵃ
noȝt elike of grace, þat is of my preua dome, þat dose to euirilkeone
eftir he will take. þere is many þat takes þe gyfte of grace, þe whilke
were enoghe to þam to wirke withall, bot þai lefe it, and some with- 10
drawes þaim fro syn fro drede of payne, or for þai haue no time þareto,
or for þai haue no lust þarein.

'Also, if I gyue oneli to mi frendes þe worldly gudes, þai þat were
euell wald fall in dispaire and þe gude walde wax proude. Bot I gife to
all, for þat all suld loue me. Also, I call som in þe bygyninge and som 15
in þe ending, for I ame like to a modir þat sees in hir childir hope of
life, þe whilke dose, to some, more stalworth þinge, and to som softer;
and to þat childe sho hase no hope to, sho has compassion, and ȝet sho
dose þat sho may. Bot if þe childir wax þe wers and febiler by þe modir
medcyns, wherto suld sho trauell hir? þus do I to men, for to him þat I 20
see haue a gude wille and feruent, and will be stabill, to hym gyue I
grace in þe | bygyning, and it laistis to his ending. Bot he þat hase f. 223ᵛᵇ
leued euell, and besis hym to do welle, he sall haue grace at his ending.
Bot he þat is vnkynde is not worthi to com to þe modir pape, ne to
haue grace.' 25

A reuelacion in þe whilke Criste shewes to his spouse
how sho is deliuerd fro þe house of þe worlde and syn,
and sho is now comyn to dwelle in þe house of hali
gaste, and þarefore he warnes 'hire' to conforme hir to
þe same spirit throw perseuerans in mekenes and 30
deuocion.

Criste saide to þe spouse, 'þou arte sho þat was norishit in a litill
house, and come eftir to grete mennes company. In a pore house are
thre þinges: foule wallis, mekill sote, and smoke. Bot þu art broȝt to on
house wher is clennes withouten filth, hete withouten smoke, and 35
softnes withouten desese. þis pore hous is þe werld, wher pride and

2 it²] *om.*   17 stalworth] stalworth life, life *subpuncted*   20 suld sho] *twice,*
second subpuncted

gettyng of gude and welth in syn makes walles foule, for þese distrues
þe gude werkes þat suld hald vp a man. þe smoke is lufe of þe werld,
þat blyndes so mans een, with þe whilke he suld se gostely, þat he
knawes not | þe trewth. þe sote is luste þat files foule, all if it be likyng
5 for a while. Fro þis arte þou withdrawen and broght to þe dwellyng
place of þe holi goste, þat is in me, and [I] in hym. And also he hase þe
in hymselfe, and þarefor, sene he is moste clene, moste stronge, and
moste stabill, conforme þe to hym with stedfaste mekenes and
deuocion.'

10   þe fourtend purpossing in forme of question.

þan purposid þus þe persone byforesaide. 'O þou iuge, whi suffirs
þou bestis desesed, sen þai haue no reson, ne sall haue no life eftir þis?
Whi is all born in disese, sen þare is som þat synned noȝt? Whi sall þe
child bere þe fadirs trespas, sen he couth noȝt syn? Whi falles þinges
15 ofte tymes vnauisely? Whi dyes a gude man ane euell dede, and
agaynewarde?'
þe fourtend answere of Criste.
þe domesman saide, 'Frende, bestis suffirs disese, for all if bestis
ware made for man, and when man synned agayns his maker, þe bestis
toke deordinans and left | þe seruys þat þai sulde haue done to man
21 and wex rebell to hym. And for þis deordinans bestis suffirs both
sekenes and oþir deseses. Also, bestis suffirs ofte tymes for þe defaute
of kynde, and somtyme for mannes syn, as when þo bestis þat man
lufes, and suld be to his helpe and to his solace, are disesed. þan suld
25 man take hede what hymselfe is worthi to suffir, sen vnresonabill
bestis suffirs for his syn.
'Also, all þinges are broght furthe with disese for mannes trespas,
for when man misbare him to me his God, mi rightwisnes wald þat
oþir creatures, þe whilke suld haue bene solace to him, be disesed
30 with him.
'Also, childir are ponishet not for þair fadirs gilte, bot for þaire
awen, for when þe firste man had loste þe clennes of innocentry, he
was put oute of Paradise and wappid in filth. And all þat is taken oute
of a foule vessell, þat towches þe vessell, is foule. And so þe child bers
35 his awen syn. And for to retourne agayn þis innocentry, I haue
ordeynde baptym to clens man of syn. Neuirþeles, sometyme | it is so

6 I] _om._ 35 agayn þis] þis agayn þis, _first_ þis _subpuncted_ 36 sometyme]
sometyme þe childir are, _exc._ sometyme, _subpuncted_

þat þe son folowes þe fadirs syn, and þan are þe fadirs synnes ponyshet in þe son, and sometyme þe childer are ponishit for þe fadirs syn vnto þe þirde or þe fourte generacion, for þare is none of þame þat amendid þe fadirs trespas, or elles þai folow þe fadir in his trespas.

'Also, God sendes somtyme þat at he moste dredes, and I withdrawe 5 fro þe gude man þat he loues, and þat he leste wenys I send hym, and þat he desires I withdrawe fro him, for I wald þat man euirmore drede me, and loued me byfore all oþir þinges.

'And also, an euell man dyes somtime a gude dede, for he dide somtyme gude dede, þe whilke God will rewarde him here fore; and þe 10 rightwis man trespasses, for þe whilke God wille ponyshe a man here, fore þere passes no trespas vnponisht, and gude liue makes a man to com to blis. Also somtyme þai þat are euell desires a gude endinge, þat þai hafe for þaire rewared, and þe rightwis man hase a harde passinge for his mede, þat right [as] in his lifyng he hase bene besy in gettinge of 15 vertu, so, | in his endinge, he sall flye to blis: as it is wretyn þat a lion f. 224vb slowe þe prophete þat obeyd noȝt to þe biddyng of God, bot he ete not of his bodi, bot kepid it, in tokenynge þat his vnkyndenes was ponysht, bot his gude liueing was shewed in þat at he ete note of his bodi. And þerefor be ilkeone ferde for to discusse my domes, for as I am incom- 20 prehensibill in vertu and miȝt, so ame I ferdefull and to be drede in my counsels and domes. And some þat wende for to haue taken and comprehende me in þaire wisdome, þai failed of þair entent, and fell fro þaire hope.'

A reuelacion in þe whilke Criste biddes þe spouse to be 25 not turbild, all if his wordes þe whilke he shewes in reuelacions be somtyme dirke, somtyme doutefull, and somtyme vncertayn, for þat is Goddes preuay right, and oþir causes to be assigned.

Criste saide to þe spouse, 'Wondir þe noght if I say somwhat more 30 dirke and somwhat more plain. Mi wordes mai be vndirstandin on diuers maners. | For right as in þe olde lawe I said many þinges þat f. 225ra suld more be vndirstandyn gostely þan bodeli, as of tempill of Dauid in Ierusalem, right so hafe I saide many þinges to mi frendes, þat mai be vndirstanding on diuers maners þat men mai be lerned eftir, eftir 35 þaire astate. Bot þat I say mani þinges derkely is for I will kepe mi counseill till I þinke at shewe it, and for to make men godely for to

15 as] *om.*		37 till] till þat, þat *subpuncted*

abide mi wille. I haue hight many þinges þat I haue withdrawen for mannes vnkyndenes, and þare are many þinges saide bodely þat suld be vndirstandin gosteli.'

þe fiftende purposing in forme of question.

5   þan purposed þe persone byforesaide þus: 'Whi are þare so mani þinges made þat no profite is in? Whi are not þe saules sene þat dwelles in þe bodi `when´ þai passe oute fro þe bodi? Whi are not þi frenedis ai herde when þai prai? Whi are many lettid þat wald do euell? Whi is þe fende oft present to some, and to some neu[i]r more? Whi 10   trespas þai þat hase þe spirit of Gode?' |

f. 225ʳᵇ   The fiftend answere of Criste.

þe domesman saide, 'Frende, man is like to a childe þat is norishede in a prisson of derkenes. If a man sai to him, "þare is light and sternes withoute", he trewes it noȝt, for he saw neuir none. Right 15   so, fro man had loste and lefte þe light of vertu, he hade no liking bot in derkenes, eftir þe comon speche, for "he þat is vsed to euell, him þinkes þe euell swete". Bot I am like to a man, þat hase some place to his solace and walking, and som to [þ]e kepyng of his household, and som for his bestis, both wild and tame. And some þare are of strengþe, 20   and some for his counsell, and some for chastissing of defautes. Right so ordaynde I som places for wilde bestis and [fo]ules, som to fill mannes desire, som for acordinge of þe elementes, some for ponish-inge of sinne and for cause of my preuai counsell: and all þis are ordaynde for man.

25   'þe bee is a litill beste, and ȝitt can take more profite of þe herbes þan any man can. þe froskes and þe neddirs, þe breris and þe nettills, f. 225ᵛᵃ   are þe | outecastes of bestis and of erbes, and, neuerþeles, þai are profitabill to him þat can wirke with þame. And ilke þinge þat lyues knowes kyndely with what þing it suld be sustened: and all þinges þat 30   are made wirshipes me. And þerefore mane, as mikill as he is fairrer þan oþir creatures, so mykill he suld þe more lufe me.

'Also þe saule, for it is a pure gostely þinge, it may noȝt be sene with bodely een bot by bodely likenes.

'Also, I ame like to a modir, þe whilke will not graunt hir child 35   swilke þinge as he askes agayns his profit, bot sho chastis him if he wepe. Right so I put ouir and grauntes noȝt ay to my frendes þat þai

<hr>

7 when] and what, and *subpuncted, superior mark over* what   9 neuir] neur
18 þe] be, b *subpuncted*   21 foules] saules, *Lat.* auium

aske, for I wote bettir what is þaire profite þan þaimselfe. For Paule
and all oþir praied, and ȝit I graunt not to þame þaire asskynge, for, all
if þai were vertuouse, ȝett þere was somwhate to clens in þaime. And
for to mak þaim more feruent in lufe to me and more meke in þaimselfe, to gete þaim more mede, I put ouir þaire asking, and for to proue 5
þaire stabillenes.

'Also, I suffir þame þat are euell. For right as a man þat has two
sonnes, and þe tone | of þame is wonder buxum, and þe oþir not so, þe   f. 225ᵛᵇ
fadir disposes him to withstand þe malice of his sone, þat he do no
euell, and þe bettir son puttes he to grete besines to stir þe euell child 10
to amende him: right so som[tyme] I let þame þat are euell to trespas,
for some gude dede þat þai haue done: and þarefor, þat þai be noȝt
sodanly taken to payne, I let þame of euell þat þai wald do.

'And also, þai þat are gude are somtyme disesed for ensampill of
oþir, and for encressyng of þair awne mede, as Job befor his disese was 15
gude, and of his paciens men toke ensampill. And neuerþeles, þare
wiste none whi I suffird him to be dispised bot miselfe.

'Also, he þat has mi spirit and my grace may sin, for ilka man hase a
fre will. Bot when he stirs his will agains me, my spirit gose fro him, or
elles he is chastised to ʿheʾ amend his will, as Balaam wald haue werid 20
my pupill, bot ȝet I wald noȝt suffir him, all if he were euell, for sometyme he spake þe gude, not of himselfe bot of mi spirit.

'Also, þe fende, of mi suffering, | trauals som mens saules, and he   f. 226ʳᵃ
blindes som mens consciens, and he trauells som mens bodis. He
trauels þaire saules þat giues þame to vnclennes and misbyleue. Bot 25
he turbles þaire consciens and þaire bodis, þe whilke are here purgede
for certaine sinnes, and ȝet are vexit, þe whilke vexacion falles to
childir as wele of painems as of cristen, and as wele to maidens as to
men: and þat is ouþir for defaute of fadir and of modir and defaute of
kynde, or elles for to [fr]ay oþir and make þame to be ensampill and so 30
to meke oþir, or elles þat þai haue gretter blis for þair paciens.

'Also, mani swilke þinges fals to bestes, owþir for ponishing of men,
or elles for mistempering of þaire kinde. And þarefore I suffir þe fende
be nerrer to some, oþir for meking of þame, or for to make oþir here to
beware, or elles to make þame more besi to seke me, or elles for geting 35
to him of more mede, or to clens sin here, or elles þat þaire paine
begin here for sinne and laste withouten ende.'

11 somtyme] som   20 he²] his, is *subpuncted*   29 and of modir] *over correc-*
tion, also marg.   30 fray] slay, *Lat.* terrorem   37 begin] be gifen, fe *sub-*
puncted, marg. gyne

f. 226rb

A reuelacion in þe whilke Criste shewes to | Saint Bride
where and whi þe wordes of his reuelacions were tolde
hir in spirituall vision, and what þai profite principalli.

Criste saide þat be kinde might be made a helefull drinke: of þe
5   colde iren, and þe harde stone, and þe drye tree, and þe bittir erbe.
'And if þou aske how it might be, I answere: if a pese of steel fell on a
hille of bronstone, oute of þe steel suld come fire þat suld brin þe hille;
and of þe hete of þe fire suld þe oliue, þat were dry withoute and moste
within, springe oute of þe fatnes, þe whilke if it fell on a bittir erbe
10   vndir it, þat suld wax swete of þe oile of þe oliue, of þe whilke might be
made one holsom drinke.
'Right so dide I gostely. þi hert was to mi lufe cold as stele, in þe
whilke was hid bot one litill sparke of loue, when þou thoght þat I was
worthi to be wirsheped aboue all oþir. Bot þi herte fell on þe hill of
15   bronston when þe werld wax fraward to þe, and þi husband, whome
f. 226va   þou loued mekill, died | fro þe. For þe likynge of þis werlde mai wele
be likened to one hill of bronstone for grete stinke of luste and
birninge of paine.
'Bot when þou left þe loue þat þou had vnto þe werlde and set fulli
20   all þi loue on me, þan felle þis sparke on þe olyue tree, þat is to sai,
wordes of my gospels and holi mennes lifynges, þe whilke are within
þameselfe full of swetenes, all if beforetime þai were drie to þe, fore
þai sauerd þe noȝt. Ȝet now þai are liking to þe and right swete.
'Bot þan fell moister fro þe oliue on þe bittir erbe when mi loue
25   plesid þe, and þe wordes of mi reuelacions were shewed to þe. Bot þan
one cried vpon þe hill and saide, "By þis drinke is þe thirste slokind,
þe colde man made warme, he þat is turbled is gladed, and þe seke
takes his hele." I þat ame verrai Gode makis þis crie of þe drinke and
mi loue.'

30   The sextende purposing bi forme of question.

þan aperid þe same `man´ spoken of byfor and saide, 'O juge, whi,
f. 226vb   eftir þe worde of þe gospell, sall þe gaite be pute | on þe lefte hand, and
þe shepe on þe right? Also, sen þou arte þe son of God, euin with þi

---

7 of¹] *twice*   12 was] was on litill sparke of lufe, *anticipating l. 13*, on litill *sub-*
puncted; marg., to my luf cald as stele in þe whilk was hide bot on litil spark of luf to mi
lufe cald as, *repeating ll. 12–13 and, exc.* sparke of luf, *ruled through,* (*second* to mi lufe cald
as *rubbed*)   31 man] oste *and caret mark*

fader, whi is it wretin þat noþir þou ne þine aungels kn[a]wes þe oure
of þe dome? Whi is þare so grete varians amange þe gospilers, sen þe
holi goste spake in þam all? Whi delaye[d] þou so lange þine incarnacion, sen þare suld come so grete profite þerof? Whi sendes þou noȝt
þi prechoures throw all þe worlde, sen a mannes saule is bettir þan all 5
þe worlde?'

The sextende answere of Crist.

The domesman saide, 'In my godehede is nowþir bodeli right hand
ne lefte hande, bot þai are saide by a likenes. For by þe right hand is
vndirstanden þe hyenes of mi blis, and by þe lefte hand, wantting of all 10
gudenes and gude. Ne þare sall be nowþir bodely shepe ne gaite, bot
by þe shepe, þe whilke are innocent, are vndirstanden þai þat is clene
fro malice of sin, and by þe gaite, þe whilke are vnclene bestis, is
vndirstanden þai þat | are foule in sine.   f. 227ra

'Also, to þe second, wit wele þat in þat at I ame man, I knew not þe 15
oure of þe dome, for it is wretin of me, inalsmikill as I ame man, þat I
profited in witte and age: bot insomikill þat I ame God, I ame one substance, one will with þe fadir, and knawes als mikill as mi fadir: and
allonely þe godhede knawes þe oure of þe dome.

'Also, to þe third: it is wretin þat þe holi goste has mani maner of 20
wirking, for he is like a man þat hase a balauns in his hand, and ofte
times lais in and takes oute till þe time þat both þe scales be acorded.
And he þat hase of custome to del[e] with þame acordes þame on othir
maner þan he þat hase þame not of custome. Right so þe holi goste is
þe maner of a balauns, now wending vpe in þe herte when þe minde is 25
lifte vp bi deuocion and bi hertli fauo[u]re and clere knawing of God
and vndirstanding. He wendes downe when he suffirs þe herte be
occupied with idill thoghtes. And þerefor it is nedefull to mesure | þe f. 227rb
liuing eftir þe wille of þe holi goste, if þe saule be euen set to God.

'Bot I, Godes son, prechid in diuers places and had diuers maners 30
of herrers. Som of þame were sotell of witt, and some were simpill. To
þe simpill I spake plaine þinges, and to þe sotell I spake hie þinges,
and, to þaim for to wondir one, sometime I spake misteli and sometime I rehersed againe þat I had saide before, and somtime I ekid to
þat I had spoken, and sometime I saide les. And þarefor, it is no 35
wondir if þe gospilers wrote diuers.

'Bot all was trew þat þai wrote, som of þame bi worde, and some sett

1 knawes] knwes   3 delayed] delaye   16 is] *over correction, also marg.*
23 dele] delth, *mark under* h   26 fauoure] fauoire   30 diuers¹] diuers
maners, maners *subpuncted*

þe sentence and not þe wordes. Some wrote as þai hade herde, and some as þai saw. Some wrote eftir þat at was done byfore, and som wrote mykill of mi godehede, and som of mi manhede. And ȝet ilkone of þame wrote as þe holi goste techid þam. Bot admit þou þe gospilers
5 of hali kirke, and none oþir.

'Also, to þe fourte, I abode or I toke mankinde, þat man suld first be
f. 227ᵛᵃ lerned in | þe lawe of kynde, for in þat was mannes lufe shewed, eftirward in þe lawe wretin, by þe whilke man vndirstode and knewe his sekenes. And þan it was skill þat þe leche suld come when þe sekenes
10 was persaiued greuous.

'Also, to þe laste: a mannes saule is worthier þan all þe worlde, for it is a gostly þinge and euen with aungels, and it is more nobill and worthi, for it is made to likenes of þe trinite to liue withouten ende. And þerefore suld man liue more worthili þan any oþir creature þat is
15 worldeli. Bot sen man is so worthi, and so indowed with resone, and if he leue resone, what meruel is it if I ponishe him? Bot I sende noȝt mi prechours alle aboute, for I knawe þe hardnes of som men hertes, þe whilke is aboute to mantene þare syne and noght to turn þame. And þerefore, þai are noght [worthi] to here mi prechours. Wherefor, I
20 spare þe trauells of mi frendes, þat þai trauaile not in vaine ne be to greteli turbilde.'
f. 227ᵛᵇ   þan saide Criste to þat man of religion: 'A, frende, I ende now | mi answers to þi thoghtes, and þou sall ende þi life. Now sall þou witt and finde what þi eloquens, þe whilke is bostefull, and mannes fauoure,
25 sall do þe. O full wele had þou bene if þow had taken hede to þi profession and kepid þi wowe.' And þan saide þe spirit to þe spouse, 'Doghtir, þis personne, þe whilke hase asked so many questions, liues ȝit in bodi. Bot he sall not liue fulli one day to ende, whose thoghtes and affeccions are shewed to þe þus by likenes for þe saule hele of
30 many oþir.'

A reuelacion in þe whilke Criste biddes þe spouse þat
sho be not turbild in hirselfe, all if he shewe not his
rightwisnes onone vpon þe grete synner, for he delais
his sentens, for it suld be shewed openli to oþir.

35 Criste saide to þe spouse: 'Be noȝt disessed þat I abide paciently þe synfull man, for it is hard to brene euirmore. And þarfo[r] I abide þe

16 resone] resone and drawe   ponishe] *twice; marg.*, what meruil is it if
19 worthi] *om., Lat.* digni   36 þarfor] parfo

laste poynte of ponishynge. Also, mi wordes sall be shewed with merci
and rightwisnes, and growe and | bringe furth fruyte in þe worlde. Bot f. 228ʳᵃ
be þou noȝt disesed, all if þat man þou wote of haue ȝit no grete triste
to mi wordes. For he is like to a brinning lawmpe when þe mache
commes nere to þe oyle. Right so is he abill to ressaiue þe grace of 5
God, for mi wordes sall perfitely sinke in his saule. þe fire of þis
lawmpe is þe holi goste, þat kindles þe lawmpe of his herte to trauaile
in mi wirshipe, and to resaiue fatnes of grace and of his wordes.'

The fadir spekes to Saint Bride and enformes of þe fiue
vertuose places in Ierusalem, and what grace pilgrames 10
resaiues þat visetes þame with meke deuocion.

God þe fadir saide þere was a lorde to whame his seruant spake þus:
'Lo, þi land is tiled and þe rotes of þe wedes are taken vpe. When sall
þou þerefore sawe þi sede of whete?' To whome þe lorde saide, 'All if
þe rotes be taken vpe, ȝete þe old stokkes are lefte, þe whilke moste in 15
þe sawing tyme of þe ȝere with raines be law|sed.' þan saide þe f. 228ʳᵇ
seruant, 'What is þan to do bytwene þat tyme and heruest?' þe lorde
answerde, 'I knawe fiue places and whosoeuir in clennes, mekenes and
feruent charite commes to þame, þai sall haue fiuefalde fruyte.

'In þe first place was a vessell closed and noȝt closed, litill and noȝt 20
litill, full of light and not full of light, empti and not voide, clene and
not clene. In þe second place was a lion born, þe whilke was sene and
not sene, herd and noȝt herd, towched and noȝt towched, knawen and
vnknawen, þe whilke was halden and noȝt halden. In þe third place
was a lambe klipped and not klipped, wownded and noȝt wownded, 25
criing and not criing, sufferring and not suffiryng, deing and noȝt
deyng. In þe fourt place was pute a neddir, þe whilke lai and lai noght,
[moued] and moued not, herd and not herde, sawe and noȝt sawe,
felid and not felid. In þe fifte place was one egill þat flied and not flied,
þe whilke come to a place, fro þe whilke | he neuir passid, þe whilke f. 228ᵛᵃ
restid and noȝt restid, was renewed and noȝt renewed, was glad and 31
noȝt glad, wirshiped and noȝt wirshiped.'

þan saide þe fadir, 'þe vessell þat I spake first of was Mari, þe
doghtir of Joachim and modir of þe manhede of Criste. Sho was closed
fro þe fende and noȝt closed fro God; and right as a beke of rininge 35
watir, if it pase noȝt furth in one side, it sekis beseli, on oneoþir,

---

28 moued¹] *om., Lat.* mouebatur   and²] *twice*   29 felid²] felid þe whilke come
to a place, *exc.* felid, *ruled through*   35 rininge] riminge

passing furth, so þe fende, þat is beke of all vices, wald haue funden
entre and furth passing throw Maris herte, bot he might noȝt, for sho
was so closed fro his temptacions þat he might neuir bowe hir to þe
leste veniall sin, fro þe grace of mi spirit had flowed into hir so plen-
5　teuosli þat it had all fulfilled hir.

'Also sho was a litill vesell in a laweli feling of hirselfe, bot sho was
not litill ne small in þe charite and loue of mi godhede. Also sho was
voide and empti fro all sin and luste, bot sho was not voide of vertuse
f. 228ᵛᵇ　and gudenes. Also sho was full of light of all perfeccion: bright | to
10　heuen, to saintes, aungels and to mi son. Bot þe werld held hir noȝt
light, for sho dispised all worldli wirships, riches and delites. Also,
scho was all clene, in hir awen persone conceiued withouten sin; ȝet
sho was vnclene in þe rote of Adam þat sho sprange of. And herefor,
whoso commes to þe place where Mari was borne, he sall be made
15　clene vnto my wirshipe.

'þe second place is Bedlem, in þe whilke mi son as a lion was born:
þe whilke was sene and halden as man, bot not as God, for in þe godhede he was vnvisibill. þe þirde was þe place of Caluari, where mi son
as a innocent lambe was wownded and dede in his manhede: bot he
20　was wondirli vndedeli in his godhede. þe ferth was þe place of sepulcre of mi son, þe erthe in þe whilke he was berid, in þe whilke þe manhede lai dispised and set at noȝt, as a serpent: bot þe godhede was in
ilkea place. þe fifte place was þe Mownte of Oliuete, in þe whilke mi
son in his manhede flied vp into heuen as one egill, þe whilke anentes
f. 229ʳᵃ　his god|hede was euir þare. And whosoeuir commes to þese fife places
26　in clennes and with perfite will, he sall deserue and taste and se how
swete I am his God. And, forsothe, when þou commes to þese places, I
sall shewe þe mo þinges.'

In þe wirshipe of thre personns in godhed, and two kyndes in þe one
30　persone of þe sone, here endis þe fifte boke of heuenli reuelacions
inti[ti]ld þe boke of questions, graciousli shewed to blissid Bride,
Princes in þe realme of Swene. *Deo gracias.*

[BOOK SIX]

Throw þe stedfast triste in þe graciouse helpe of oure gloriouse God in trinite of persones, godeli inclined vnto oure simpill vnworthines by mercifull praiers of þe mildest maiden and modir, with all oþir aungels and saintes, here byginnes þe sext boke of heuenli reuelacions shewed vnto þe blissed Bride, princes in þe realme of Swene. *Deo* 5 *dicamus gratias*.

Primum capitulum. þe modir of God shewes to þe
spouse | and telles hir of þe bewte of hir son Criste, and f. 229rb
how Jewes, when þai were heuy, comforted þameselfe
throw þe sight of his sembland. 10

þe modir saide to þe spouse, 'I ame qwene of heun, whome mi sone loues with all his hert. þerefor I counsell þe þat þou loue noþinge so wele as him, for he is so likand þat he þe whilke hase him mai noȝt desire bot him; he is so faire þat whosoeuir ses him mai wele se þat nowþir þe elementes ne oþir þinges are noȝt in rewarde of him and of 15 his fairnes; insomikell þat when I norishet mi son, he had so grete bewte þat whosoeuer loked on him had comforthe and gladnes. And þerefor þe Jewes wald sai amang þameselfe, "Go we to se Maris son, for we sall haue comfort when whe behald hym." And all if þai wiste noȝt þat he was God, ȝete þai had grete gladenes in | his sight. Also, he f. 229va was so clene of bodi þat he had neuir no maner of vermyn ne oþir 21 vnclennes in his bodi.'

Capitulum iim. Criste telles þe spouse of one þat had
euell lifed, bot in þe dede he had will for to amend him
yf he suld langer haue liued, þe whilke will saued him 25
fro helle: bot ȝett he went to horribill purgatori.

Criste saide, 'He þat now is seke, fore whome þat þou praies, he was ouer softe and ouer esi to himselfe in his liue, and he led a life all contrarious to me. Bot sai to him, and he will amende him if he liue, I will do him grace. Be he þarefore moued and stirred to haue will of 30 amendynge, for grete merci makes me to haue compassion of his bittir paines.' Neuerþeles, þe same persone was dede bifor þai sange prime,

22 his] his or

and þan Criste aperid and saide againe to þe spouse, 'Now mai þou see how rightfull I ame in mi dome. þis man þat was disesed in þe

f. 229ᵛᵇ sekenes come to mi dome, and all if he be demed to grace | for his gude will, ȝete him bose be in purgatori and suffir swilke paine or he be fulli

5 clensid, þat þare is no man in erth may þinke how harde þe torme[n]tes are. And what hopis þou þan þat þai suffir sall þat hase all þare will in þis werld and in noþing are disesed?'

       Capitulum iiim. þe spouse [sawe] a fende with confu-
       sion fle fra a deuote man in time of his praiere, whome
10   he had greteli turbild. And on angell declares þe vision.

þe spouse sawe þe fende stande, and his handes bunden, byfore a deuote man in his praier, and when he hade standen þare a litill while, he made sodanli a horribill noyse, and was confusede, and so for shame went awai. þan saide a gude aungell to þe spouse, 'Ȝone fende

15 turbild greteli þis man, bot he might noȝt ouercome him as he wald. þarefor his handes are bunden. And it is Goddes wille þat, for he withstode manli þe fende, þarefor þat fende sall noȝt haue his will of

f. 230ʳᵃ him, notwithstanding þat | he hase traiste þat he sall ouercome hym. Bot in þis oure sall þe fende be ouercomen for euir. And þe man sall

20 ilke day haue more and more of þe grace of Gode. And þerefore þe fende cries, for he has loste him þat he was so besi aboute to ouercom.'

       Capitulum iiii. Criste saide to þe spouse þat ilke ver-
       tuouse and wis man preche bo[l]deli þe gracious
25   wordes þat are contende in ther bokes to all þat desires
       to knawe þame, and he sall haue God to his rewarde.

Criste saide to his spouse, 'þe wit þat is of me is more precious þan all þe gold of þe werlde, and with þis wisdom haue I filled him þat þou prayes fore. And þarefor I will þat he preche mi wordes bo[l]deli, noȝt

30 oneli to þame þat will gladli here þame, bot also, as a bold knight, preche he my grace to þame þat will noȝ[t] here it. Also, him bose be pacient for mi loue, knawyng þat I ame his lorde þe whilke suffird all reproues. Also, I will þat he spare no more þe riche þan þe pore, ne be

6 tormentes] tormetes   8 sawe] *om. Lat.* videbat   18 þat¹] *twice*
24 preche] preches, s *subpuncted*   boldeli] bodeli, *Lat.* audacter   25 ther] thre,
superior mark   29 boldeli] bodeli   31 noȝt] noȝ

aferde o none, for I ame in him and he in me. Who mai noye him |
when I, almighti, ame with him? I sall giue him for his trauaile a   f. 230ʳᵇ
preciouse rewarde: non ertheli þinge or bodeli, bot mine awen selfe in
whome is contined plente of all maner of gudenes.'

Capitulum vm. Criste blames ypocrites in religion þat   5
are presumptuose and proude, þe whilke scornes
simpill men and diseses þame with þe hornes of detraccion, et cetera.

Criste saide, 'I ame maker of all and noȝt made. I haue longe time
turned mi sight fro þis place for þe wikkednes of þaim þat dwelles   10
þarein. As þe firste funders beside þame to profite fro vertu to vertu, so
þat nowondais passes fro euell to euell, and ilkane wald be byfor oþir
in gladnes of syn. Bot þe prayers of mi welebeloued modir inclines me
to haue merci, notwithstanding þat of þe werste kinred are ȝet lefte
certaine rotes, as I sall shewe þe bi likenes. þare was a sheperd saide   15
to his maistir, "Sir, in þi feld are a fewe restfull shepe, bot þare are
amange þame topis and rammes, þe whilke diseses þame | with þaire   f. 230ᵛᵃ
hornes, and þaire hedes are noȝt worthe. þe skinnes are roten, þe
fleshe and þe entrels stinkes." þan saide þe lorde, "þat mi milde
shepe be kepid fro disese, kut of þe hedes of þe rammes with a sharpe   20
iren. Pulle of þe skinnes, and cast away þe bodis and þe entrels into þe
feld to birdis þat knawes not what is clene and what is foule." '
    þan saide Criste, 'I ame þis lorde, þat hase some sympill seruantes,
as þai were shepe, amange whome is som, as þai were horned rammes,
þe whilke firste reues fro þame þaire wolle, for with þaire scorninges   25
and þaire bakebittinges thai withdrawe þame fro gude fame, and þan
þai caste þame downe to þe erthe, taking fro þame þaire gudes, be þe
whilke þai suld be halden vpe. And somtime þai hurte þame in þaire
bodis. And þerefore þare hede, þat menes, þaire pride, sall be ponishet in mi dome with þe sharpe swerde of rightwisnes. þaire skinnes,   30
þat is þaire fals feyning of ypocrisi, sall be refte awai, and þe fendes
sall make | þe saule naked fro all gode. þe fleshe þat was gifen to luste, f. 230ᵛᵇ
and þaire entrels, þat is, þaire thoghtes and þaire affeccions þat were
stinking for lufe of þe werld and of sin, sall be wownded of fendes, and

3-4 in whome] *twice, first subpuncted*   15 certaine] *twice, first subpuncted*
19 entrels] entrels are roten and, *exc.* entrels, *subpuncted*   20 rammes] rammes þe
whilke disese man with þaire hornes, *exc.* rammes, *ruled through*   29 and þere (*of*
þerefore*)] also marg.*

withoute merci brin in fire and in endeles paine. And þarefor, while
þai haue time, bid þame lai downe þaire hedes of pride and take
mekenes, and leue þaire ipocrisi and take þe skine of verrai simpilnes;
refrein þe fleshe fra lustes and þaire entrels of þaire thoghtes also, and
5 take penance. For elles I will shewe þame rightfull ponisheyng, and
commit þame to þe power of fendes, with whome þai sall mowe done
noþinge bot encrese euell to euell.'

Capitulum vim. Criste reprehendis beningli þe spouse
o[f] one vnpaciens þat sho had, and teches hir to be not
10 worthe, ne noȝt to answere to þame þat prouokes hir, to
þe passion of þe saule be sobird and pesid.

Criste saide to þe spouse, 'I ame both þi maker and þi husband.
þou hase nowe t[r]espast in þi wreth on foure maner. First, for þou
f. 231ʳᵃ was | impacient in þi hert at wordes were saide; and I suffird hard
15 betinges and answerd not one worde. þe second, þou answerde with a
hie voice, sharpe and reproueing; and I was festined with nailes to þe
crosse, and ȝete opynd I noȝt mi mouth. þe þird, for þou dispised me
be þine vnpaciens, for whos lufe þou suld haue suffird pacientli. þe
fourt, for þou gaue euell ensampill to þat neghbour in þi vnpaciens.
20 And þarefor, if þou be stird and prouoked, oþir answere noȝt or elles
abide to þe passion of wreth be gone, and þan answere with softenes
and sobirnes, and by no wai shew no token of wrethe.'

Capitulum vii. Criste warnes þe spouse to speke to one
dekin, þat he preche þe worde of God with feruoure of
25 spirit, teching þe seke and reproueinge þe incorrigibill,
and putting his saule [to dede] if it be nede for þe saule
hele of oþir.

Criste said, 'I ame þi God, maker of all þinges, all if I be rekelest
and noght set bi. Sai to þat deken, for whome þou praies, and whome |
f. 231ʳᵇ þou wote wele has loued me, on þis wise: "Sen þe dekens office is putt
31 vnto þe, þou has taken auctorite of prechinge, to lerne þame at are
simpill and to reproue þame þat are euel. For so did I and also mine

9 of] bot, *Lat.* de   10 worthe] *also marg.*   13 trespast] tespast
16 reproueing] reprouening   19 þat, þi] *also marg.*   25 reproueinge]
reproueninge   26 to dede] *om., Lat.* morti   28 þinges] þinges for whome
þou praies and whome þou wote wele hase lufed me, *and, after* þinges, va-cat
30 dekens] denkens

apostels, þe whilke wente abowte to mani a place for þe winning of one saule, and for þe hele of saules þai offird gladeli þaire liues. And þerfore þi office is for to preche, and it is noȝt to þe acordinge to hald silence fro preching, foralsmikill as mi enmis are abowte the, whose cursid glotonye is as odious to me as if þai ete fleshe on Gude Fridai. 5

'þai are like to a vessell þat is opin at both þe endes, þe whilke wald neuir be filled all if all þe see were putt þerein. And fro þat þai fall vnto licheri, and þai put fro þame þaire gude aungels, and takes to þame fendes. þai stand in mi where noȝt for to plese me, bot þat þai be noȝt blamid of oþir. And so þai seme religiouse, bot trewli þai are fals 10 liers. þai dissaise þe saules þat þai haue þair lyueing ofe, | for nowþir f. 231ᵛᵃ in liueing ne in praiere þai make asethe. And þarefor I swere in mi trewthe þat, bot þai amend þame, I sall suffir þame a while in þaire luste, and þan sall I lede þame a wai fulle of full prikand thornes. And I sall make mi seruantes take hed opon þame, þat þai sall nowþir ash- 15 ape on þe right side ne left, bot þai sall go throw þe prikyng þornes. And right as a dede bodi falles downe vnto þe erthe, so sall þaire saules fall into hell, and þai sall be so ouircharged with paynnes þat þai sall neuir rise.'

Capitulum viii. Criste geues boldnes to þe spouse to 20
reproue certayne religiouse of grete sinnes, amange
whome sho was herberd, and he latis hir wit þat all if
þai be euell paide of hir blamyng, ȝet sall scho haue hir
mede and þanke.

Criste saide to þe spouse, 'O spouse, þou boȝt ofte times þus: "Sen 25 mi God is God of all creatures and suffird pacientli his traiture, whi suld I his creature not suffir pacientli þaim at dwelles with me? For elles | it mai happe `þat´ of mi blaminge þai sall be þe wers." To þe f. 231ᵛᵇ whilke I answere: þou suld do as a gude knight, þe whilke dwelles amange þame þat are trespasoures vnto his lorde. For if he mai noȝt 30 amend þame, ȝet suld he lett þame with þe lordes wirshepe. Right so speke þou hertli and tell þame þare trespas, and all if þou profite noȝt to þame, ȝet sall þou haue þi mede. For þe apostils prechid to many þat wald noȝt be conuertid, and ȝet þair mede was neuir þe les, for some were þe bettir. 35

'þarfore latt þame witt þat, bot if þai amend þame, I sall shame þame byfor all angels and saintes, for cause þai take on þame þe abit of

3 þi] sen þi   11, 12 lyueing, liueing] lyuening, liuening   27 I] I noȝt

religion and liued noȝt þareeftir. þai are in mi sight as theues þat takes oþir mennes gudes, for þe gudes þat þai haue is godes of oþir men þat are gude liuers. And þarefore þai sall be smiten with my swerde and kut in sondir, fro þe hede to þe fote. I sall fille þame full of buyling fire
5 þat sall neuir sloken, for I warned þame and þai wald noȝt here; I sent
f. 232ᵃ mi wordes to þame and þai dispised þame and sett | þame at noght, mekill more þan panims wald haue done. And bot þai amend þame, I sall nowþir spare þame for mi modir praier, ne for prayers of mi saintes, bot als lange as I sall be in heuen and blis sall þai be in paines.'

10   Capitulum ix. Criste telles þe spouse how abhominabill
      a preste is þat singes his `mes´ in dedeli sin, and how
      fendes are homeli with him in time of singyng, and of
      his paine if he amend hym noȝt.

      Criste sais to þe spouse how fowle was, and abhominabill, a certaine
15 preste for whome sho praied, for cause he sange mese in dedeli sine.
'When he gose to þe awter', sais Criste, 'he is sett aboute with fendes, and his saule is dede bifore me. When he castis on his amitt, fendis blindes hym, þat he suld noȝt haue minde how fertfull it is to com to myne awter in sin. When he dose on his albe, þan clethes he him with
20 hardenes of hert, for he þinkes þat his syn is not greuows, ne þe payne þat is ordaynde þarefore so hard as it sal be funden. When he dose þe
f. 232ʳᵇ stole abowte his | neke, þan puttes þe fendes on him a heuy ȝoke, þat is, liking of sin, so þat he has no contricion þareof. When he dose on his fanone, þan likes noȝt him to wirke a gud werke for þe plesing of
25 God. And when he beltis him, þan bindes he his wille to þe fende. And when he dose on þe chesabill, þan clethes þe fende him in misbileue.
'And when he sais "Confiteor", fendes answers and sais, "We are witnes þat þis confession is like Judas confiteor, fore he sais one with þe mouth and oneoþir with his hert." When he gose vp to þe awter,
30 þan I turn mi visage fro him, of whome þat euir he sai mes. And when he sacres and sais þe wordes of consecracion, þan flees þe fendes away. Bot when he resaiues mi bodi, þe compani of fendes commes againe. And wald he þan sai with contricion and wille to amend him, "Lord, for þi passion and þi loue þat þou hase to man, forgiue me my
35 sinnes", I suld help him, and þe fendes suld noȝt com againe to him.
f. 232ᵛᵃ Bot þat will he noȝt do. And þarefore sall he noȝt | come at mi awter in heuen, where is blis, and holi angels and saintes are fede. þarefor in

33 wille to amend] *marg.*, nota bene

gladnes I ame a verai pellicane, for I sall gife mi awn blode both now
and in time to come to all þame þat loues me. Bot he þat I spake of sall
be fede as þe egill fedes hir birdis, and leues þam euirmore hungre. So
þe fende fedis him with luste for a time, bot he sall euir haue hongir
eftir. Neuirþeles, whille he liues, and he will turn him, he mai haue   5
merci.'

<blockquote>
Capitulum x. þe modir of God telles þe spouse what
benefice all creatures resaiues of hir, and how a saule
þat sho praied for, and by what suffrages, might be
deliuerd fro purgatori.   10
</blockquote>

'I ame qwene of heuen, modir of merci, gladnes of þe rightwis and
þe entre of sinners to God. þere is no paine in purgatori bot it is þe
more esi to suffir for mi sake. þere is non so wered ne cursed þat will
leue his syn and þinke on me bot he sall be þe more eseli tempted of
fen|dis þan elles he suld be throw mi merci. Ne þare is none so fer fro   f. 232ᵛᵇ
God, and he will call on me and turn againe to Gode, bot he sall haue   16
merci.'
    þan saide þe same ladi, 'Foralsmikill as I gat merci of mi sone, I will
tell þe how þat he [þat] was dede, for whome þou prays hertli, mai be
holpin of þe vii hurtes þat mi son spake to þe of. First, he sall be saued   20
fro þe fire þat he suffirs for licheri, if ani wald giue for his saule a
maiden to one husband and a persone of woman to religion, and þe
thirde þe whilke wald stande in wedowhede, for he greuousli sinned in
licheri, breking his spousehede. þe second hurt was in glotonye, and
þat on thre wise: firste, for he did outrage in quantite of eting and   25
drinking; þe second, for pride and shewing of himselfe he araide ouir-
mani meses; þe third, for he sat ouirlange at mete and left vndone þe
werke of Gode. Bot if a frende wald finde þre pore men a twelmonthe,
and euirilke dai giue þame swilke mete as he ete, and se þam | ete   f. 233ʳᵃ
euirilke dai as sone as himselfe ete, þan sall he find ese for his lang   30
sitting at mete; also, if he gife þo þre cleþing and bedding eftir þat þai
hafe nede.
    'And also, for he sinned in pride, take in oþir vii pore men, and
weshe þair fete ilka woke ones be seuen ʒer, and while he weshes þer
fete þinke þus: "Lorde Jesu Criste, as þou was taken of þe Jewes, þou   35
haue merci of him. Lorde Jesu Criste, as þou was bonden to þe piler,

---

13 wered] *marg.*, nota   16 call] call againe, againe *subpuncted*   19 þat²]
om.   29 and¹] and he, he *subpuncted*

þou haue merci of him. Lord Jesu Criste, þat was demed falsli, þu hafe
merci of him. Lord Jesu Crist, þat was naked and cled in cleþing of
scorn, þou haue merci on him. Lord Jesu Criste, þat was so bet þat
men might see þi ribbes and all þi bodi bludi, haue merci on him.
5 Lord Jesu Criste, þat was buffeted and dispised, þou haue merci on
him." þe seuent time sai, "Lorde Jesu Criste, þat was spred on þe
crosse, and þi he[n]de and þi fete persed, and þine hede prikked with
thornes, þine eyn full of teres, þi mouthe and þi eres full of blude, þou
haue merci on him." And þus when þai are all seuen weshen, what dai
10 þat þe liste, in ilke weke by seuen ȝere, and in þe weshing of ilkeone,
f. 233ʳᵇ one of there forsaide praiers be deuoteli thoght–giue þame | þan mete,
and prai þame mekeli to prai for his saule. And þis sall be done for him
for cause his þirde sin was pride.

   'þe ferthe, he synned in slewth on þre wise: in going to þe kirke; in
15 seking of perdone; and in seking of holi places. For þe firste, his
frende suld go to þe kirke, and euirilke moneth do sai a mes of
requiem for his saule. And for þe oþir, seke pilgramage for his saule,
and also sende þe offering to places of hali saintes for his saule;
rewarde him for his trauaile þat gose for him. The fift, þat he is brint
20 for his vainglori, for þe whilke som frende sall gedir þe pore folke þat
are nere him, one time in þe moneth throwoute one ȝere, into þe kirke,
and do sai one mes of requiem for his saule; and pray þaim, or þe
messe bigin, þat þai prai hertli for his saule. And eftir þe messe giue
þame mete and drinke, so þat þai be glad of þaire fare, and his saule be
25 glad of þaire praiers.

   'þe sext, þat he is ponisht for his det. Bot at his ende he hade will to
f. 233ᵛᵃ amend and make asethe for þe leste ferþing, | and þarfore was he
saued, or elles had he bene dampned. And þarefor þai þat hase owþir
his gude or his lande, paye his dettis, and prai þame þat it be forgiuen
30 him þat it was so lange taride: and, bot þai pai, þai sall bere þe charge
of his dett and be ponisht þarefore. And þan send to places of religion
for to prai for his saule, and to sai messes openli, in þe couent, of
requiem for his saule. And þan send to all parishe kirkes þat he had ani
gude in, to sing bifor þe parishyng openli a mes of requiem, and bifore
35 þe mes sall þe prest prai þe pupill þat, if he trespast againe ani of
þame, þat þai will forgiue it to him for Cristes name.

   'þe seuent is for he was a domesman, and committed his power to
wikked vikars. And þarefor is he now in fendis handes. Bot neuirþeles,
for it was noȝt his will þat þai suld do wrange, he mai be

───────────────

7 hende] hede, *Lat.* manus   30 him] þame him, þame *subpuncted*

holpin bi þe blissed bodi of mi son on þe auter, for in þat is þe fadir
wirsheped in spirit, and mi son, and þe hali gast, of all þe compani of
heuen. And þarefore sall þare be saide of ilkea solempnite of mi son |
one mes: as of his natiuite, one of circumcision, one of þe Epiphanye,   f. 233ᵛᵇ
one of Corpus Cristi, one of þe passion, one of þe pasche, one of þe   5
ascension, one of þe holi goste; and, in minde of me, one of euirilk of
mi festes, and neyn in þe wirship of nein ordirs of aungels. And when
þe messes of þe aungells are in singing, þere sall neyn pore men be
clede and fed, þat he so plese þe aungels þat has takin cure of his
kepinge. And þan sall þare be done one generalle messe for all þat are   10
dede, þat þai with him, and he with þame, may haue gude reste.'

Capitulum xi. þe modir warnes þe spouse þat sho hafe
euir minde of þe sorowfull passion of Criste, and how
þat all þinges were turbled in þat time.

The modir saide vnto þe spouse, 'In þe deing of mi son, all þinges   15
were turbled. For þe godhede, þat left him neuir, in þe time of his
deing, semid to haue compassion of him, all if it might noȝt suffir
payne ne sorow. My son suffird sorow in all þe partis of his bodi and in
his herte. | And þe saule, all if it were vndedeli, ȝete it suffird gretli in   f. 234ʳᵃ
þe departing fro þe bodi. þe aungells had compassion, and in maner   20
suffird disseses of his paine, all if þai be inpassibill: bot, with þat, þe
grete ioy of þe profite þat suld com of þat passion. All þe elementes
were disesed. þe son and þe mone withdrawen þ[er] 'light' [in]
tokening of compassion. þe erth tremlid, þe stonnes braste, þe graues
were opynde in tyme of þe dede of mi son, and þe panems were dis-   25
esed where þat euir þai were, for þai had no[w] maner of prikkyng at
þair hertes of sorow, and þai wist noȝt fro when it come. Also, þai þat
did him on þe crosse were disesed, and þe wikked spirites bothe. Also,
þai þat were in Abraham bosom were disesed, so þat þai had leuer be
in a part of purgatori withouten ende þan for to se swilke a oþir sorowe   30
on þaire lorde. Bot þe sorowe þat I his modir hade, when I stode bi
him, kan no man tell. And þarefor, doghtir, þinke on mi sonnes pas-
sion, fle þe vnstabilnes of þe werld, and worldli blis, þe whilke | as   f. 234ʳᵇ
floure sone fadis.'

6 of e (of euirilk)] also marg.   21 be] be vn, vn subpuncted   23 þer] þ, rest
rubbed   in] om.   26 now] no

Capitulum xii. þe modir sais þat sho is like to þe hyue
of bees, for þat heuenli bee, þe son of God, has fillid hir
with hony of þe moste swetenes, bi þe whilke no venom
is with vs.

5   þe blissed maiden spake to þe spouse of God. 'þou sent greting to
mi son, and þou likkened me to a behiue. Forsoth I ame so, for mi bodi
was in mi modir wombe as a tre bifor þe saule was knit to it. Also eftir
mi dede þe same bodi was a tre, for mi saule was departid fro it, vnto
þe time þat God lift vp þe saule with mi bodi [v]nto his godehede. And
10 I am a beehiue, in þe whilke þat nobill and gentill bee, Goddes son of
heuen, made his dwellinge place. And in me was a swete honicombe
sotelli wroght with gude werkes, abill to ressaiue þe honi of þe swete
grace of þe holi goste. And þis was filled when Goddes son com with
might of his godhede and loue of mankinde, and clennes withouten
f. 234ᵛᵃ filth into mi bosom. And right as a bee, | he hase a tange, with þe
16 whilke he smites noȝt bot he be greteli offendid and moued. And, forsothe, men hase euell rewarded him for his profitabill trauale. For
whi? For his might and powere he is betraised into þe handes of sinners. For his loue and charite he is dongen and betin. For his innocent
20 lifyng he was naked and scourged. Blissed, neuirþeles, be þat bee þe
whilke made me his hyue, and put in me so grete plente of swetenes
þat it flemis awai þe poysyne of þe fende fro all þat tastis mi swetenes.'

Capitulum xiii. Criste warnnes þe spouse to spende hir
time eftir þe will of God, and þat sho haue euirmore
25 will to stand in þe seruise of God, and 'þink' on heuenli
þinges, and so to chasti hir bodi þat it mai rise to blise
for to com.

Criste sais to þe spouse, 'þou aw to haue thre þinges: first, to go
eftir mi will, and þat dose þou when þou ordeyns all þi time eftir mi
30 will, and dose at þou mai to mi plesing. þe seconde is þat þou sall
f. 234ᵛᵇ stande to mi wirshipe: þat is, when þou hase | will to dwell allwai in my
seruise. þe third is þat þou sall sit and take hede what blis is in heuen,
and set þi thoght þare. And þan sall þou haue, eftir, oþir thre þinges.
Firste, þou suld be weddid to me, and with me to dwell in wele and
35 wo. And þarefor, all þat þou mai of gudes þat are left to þe, geue þame

9 vnto] and to   18 his] his profite, profite *subpuncted*   25 þink] thoght,
with superior mark   34 to¹] to haue, haue *subpuncted*

vnto þe pore, for so mai þou plese me. þe second is to þinke þus: "Mi
husband Criste loues me, and þarefor I sall do him all þe wirshipe þat
I mai, and drede him bifor all oþir." þe third, thinke þus: "Mi husband sall neuir dye, ne his riches sall neuir faile. þerefore I loue him,
and I will dwell with him withouten ende."'   5

Capitulum xiiii. Criste telles þe spouse how he made
one aungell norishe hir as a child in spirituall life, and
vertuouse and oþir gude maters.

Oone aungell saide to God, 'þou assigned me to þe keping of þis
spouse. And first I drewe hir to me with one appill. And þan I saide to   10
hir, "In a appill is bot a litill sauoure. þerefore ȝet com with me, and I
sall giue þe 'þe' swettest wine." | And so I drewe hir furthe, and broght   f. 235ʳᵃ
hir to þe gode þat ay wald laste.' þan saide Criste to þe spouse, 'He
chereste þe with one appill, when þou þanked me of all at þou hade,
and þoght at þou had all of me. And ȝet had þou no grete fill of me.   15
And þarefor þou tastid of mi wine, when þou þoȝt þat þe gladnes of
þis werld was shorte or noȝt, and þou sett þi hert on þe blis þat euir
sall last. And ȝet þou restid noȝt þare, bot þou thoght þat in me, þi
Gode, is all godenes, and þou lefte all for me. þan was þou with me,
and I made þe mi spouse.'   20
þan saide Criste to þe aungell, 'I will þat þou kepe furth mi spouse
fro þe fende. Ordein hir clothes of gude wertuse. Fede hir with mi
wordes. For I haue done to þis spou[s]e as a man will do to his frende
þat he will for loue take prisonere. He prais him to com to his hous,
and when he is within he shewes him noght neddirs and wilde bestis,   25
for þai wald f[r]ai him, bot he sais to him, "Frende, I loue þe, and
þarefore I haue takin þe, þat mi prissonyng mai be more liking to þe
þan þi fredom." Right so, doghtir, I take þe prisonere to mi lufe | fro   f. 235ʳᵇ
luste of þe world and þe perels þarof. And þarefor be glade, for þe
spirit þat broȝt þe hider sall bring þe to blis, and he þat broght þe to a   30
gude biginning sall bringe þe to a gude endinge.'

Capitulum xv. Criste likenes men of grete conning þat
are euell liuers to comon 'wommen' and drinkers of
wine. Ȝet mai þai haue merci if þai will conuert and turn
to godenes.   35

Criste plened to Sant Bride of a man þat sho praied for, for he left
his thoght of God and lokid ouirmekill to þe werld and on þe boke, in
þe whilke is wretin þe lawe of þe kirke. And sho saide, 'Lorde, is noght
þe law of þe kirke þi lawe?' Criste answerde, 'It was mi law als lange as
5　mi seruantes rede it for me. Bot now is it red for winning of þe werldli
gude, and noȝt for mi wirshipe. And it is red in þe hows of plaiers at þe
dise, where common wemen and gloterows wine-drinkers are moste.
A common woman has mani wordes. Sho is light of continans and
proude of arai. Right so are þai þe whilke suld teche þe lawe. þai
f. 235ᵛᵃ　speke gladli vnhoneste | wordes, bot þai will not oppin þaire lippis to
11　þe wirshipe of me. þai are so light þat þe lewed men are shamed of
þair manners, and þai drawe oþir to euill by þaire euill ensampill. þai
desire to be praised and wirshiped, to gete mekill gude, and to be
prowdeli clede. Mi wordes and mi commaundmentes are bittir to
15　þame, and mi liue is abhominabill, as þai þinke, and so are þai to me
as comon women, þe whilke is moste in reproue: and so are þai to me.
'Sw[i]lke are now þe maistres of þe lawe. þai haue no shame, ne are
not sorowfull, for sin. And for all þis, if þai red wele mi lawe, þai suld
wele wit þat þai were most halden to be chast and meke, and gude
20　liuers. And þarefor sai to þame þat hase erred þat þai turn againe, and
I will resaiue þame and mete with þame for to saue þame, as þe modir
will go to þe lambe þat hase erred fro þe floke when sho hers his voice.
And right as þe lambe þat hase gone wille commes to þe modir when it
heris þe voice of þe modir, right so suld þai turn to me, for I boght
f. 235ᵛᵇ　þame and | I will gladli ressaiue þame, as þe fadir of whome þe gospell
26　makes minde, to his son when he com againe.'

Capitulum xvi. One sant telles þe spouse þat, if a man
died for Goddes sake ilke dai ones, it were [noȝt] suffisant thanking to God for þe blis of heuen; and he
30　telles horribill painnes þe whilke a woman suffird for
luste of fleshe in hir liue dais.

One saint of heuen saide to þe spouse, 'If I had, for ilkean oure þat I
liued in þe world, ones bene dede and leuid againe, ȝet might I neuir
fulli haue thanked God for his kindenes, for þat his louing is neuir
35　oute of mi mouthe, ne his ioi and blis is neuir oute of mi saule and mi
sight and mi heryng.' And þan bad God telle þe spouse of penance þat

7 and] and in, in *subpuncted*　　9 þe¹] *twice, first subpuncted*　　17 swilke] swlke
28 noȝt] *om.*

one dede woman suffird. And þan þe saint saide, 'For þe pride þat sho
hade in þe partes of þe bodi, are now hir hede, hir armes, hir handes,
and hir fete smetin with one horribill lightening. Hir brest is prikked
throw þe fleshe, as it were, with one vrchon skin. Hir armes and þe
oþir partes | þat sho halsed men with are as þai were two neddirs vmbi-   f. 236ʳᵃ
lapping hir and eting hir continuli. Hir wombe is disesed as if þere   6
were a stake dreuin in by þe neþir parte. Hir theis and hir kneis are
cold as ise and hard as stone, and mai noȝt be bowed. Hir fete þat bare
hir aboute to euell, and to drawe oþir to euell, standis, as it were, vpon
a rasur sharpli sherand.'   10

Capitulum xvii. Mari teches þe spouse how sho sall
answere þe fende in time of his fandinges, and how
thoghtes diseses not if þai be withstandin.

The modir saide to þe spouse, 'If þi enemi stire þe to loue þe
worldeli gudes, sai to him, "þe gudes of þe werld sall sone fall, and þe   15
lufe of þe werld endes in sorowe, and so dose þe lust of þe fleshe." '
þan made þe modir þe fende for to sai, in presens of þe spouse, þat he
was made gude of God, bot of himselfe he fell, and his will is ai to
euell, and þe likinge of þis werld had neuir gude ending ne sall haue.
þan saide þe modir, 'Whi hase þou no powere vpon þis spouse?' þe   20
fende answerde, 'For I kan neuir depart þe blode of þe lufe of God | fro   f. 236ʳᵇ
þe blode of hir hert.' þan saide þe modir, 'Whi will þou noȝt lat hir
liue in riste?' þe fende saide, 'For if I mai not sla hir with dedeli sin, I
sall disese hir with som veniall sin, and if I mai noȝt do þat I sall kaste
on hir skirt mi mantill, and I sall send hir mani thoghtes to tari hir.'   25
þan saide þe modir, 'And I sall help hir, þat all þo þoghtes sall be
casten at þi heued, and sho sall so encrese hir mede. For as ofte times
as sho assentes not to þame, bot castes þame againe to þe, sin sall be
forgeuen hir, and hir crowne sall wax in mede more preciouse.'

Capitulum xviii. Criste likenes religious men ⸌þat⸍   30
thankes not God mekeli of grace þat is geuen þam: in
þe whilke is mani notabilitees.

Criste saide, 'þare is som like to a nedi man þat hase grete threste,
and commis to a gude man and prais him of drinke, to whome þe gude
man gifes of þe beste þat he hase. And when þe pore nedi man hase   35

30 þat] and, *superior mark*

tastid, he sais, "Me likes noȝt þis drinke, ne I thanke þe noȝt þare-
f. 236ᵛᵃ fore." And so he castis it in his eyn. Bot þe | gode man wipis his eyn,
and suffirs to he come bifore þe domesman. Right so dose mani men of
religion to me, for in þaire disese þai aske me comfort, and I giue
5 þame of mi best wine, þat is, grace of þe holi gost, and so I comfort
þame in þaire disese. Bot eftirward þai are full vnkinde and castis it in
mine awen eyn, when þai lefe me and drawes toward þe lufe of þe
worlde, and waxis proude of þe helpe þat I hafe shewed þame. And so
did he þat þou knawes of, þe whilke set mi grace and mi comfort at
10 noȝt. And þat mai þou see be sauour of him, for, als lang as he serued
me of all his hert, þere was a nobill smell in his cloþinge. And þat was
no wondir, for þe aungels, þat are full of vertu, are euirmore aboute mi
frendes. Bot for his will is chaunged, þare is no swete sauour aboute
him. Neuirþeles, I abide ȝet pacientli, to loke if he will com againe to
15 me, and elles at þe grete dome I sall accuse him of his vnkindnes.'

Capitulum xix. Criste pleins of men þat settis þaire
f. 236ᵛᵇ liking in delites of þis werld | and settis noȝt bi þe blis of
heuen, and he likenes þair prayere.

Criste saide to þe spouse, 'He þat þou kennes, and singes þus:
20 "Lorde, deliuer me fro euele man", his voice is in mine eres as it were a
whistill of a rede. His hert cries to me with thre voices. þe firste sais, "I
will haue mine awn will, to slepe and rise when me liste. I sall fill mi
bodi and ete wele and drinke wele. I will haue siluir in mi purs, and
softe cleþing to mi bake." þe second voice is, "Dede is noȝt sa hard as
25 þai sai, ne þe dome is noȝt so fell. Prechours sais mani þinges to make
men ferde and ware; [la]t þe saule go where it mai." þe þird voice
saide, "Gode hade neuir made me bot if he wald giue me þe blis of
heuen, þat he made to me; ne God wald neuir haue suffird so hard
paine, for what profite is þat to him at lose me? I will haue here ioi and
30 liking. I couete none oþir heuen, for I ken it noȝt bot bi herdsai."
'To þe first voice I answere, "Frende, þi wai is noȝt to heuen, ne mi
f. 238ʳᵃ passion sauers noȝt to þe. For þou lofes noȝt | þat at is aboue, þarefore
sall þou go binethe to helle." To þe second voice I sai þat "Hard dede
sall com, and fell dome, þat þou mai noȝt fle, and bittir paine, bot þou
35 amend þe." To þe third I sai, "Broþir, all þat I did for þe was for to
make þe like to me. Bot now is mi loue slokind in þe. All mi werkes
semis to þe heui, mi wordes foli and mi wai right hard. And þarefore,
bot þou turn again to me, þou sall dwell with paine and compani of

26 lat] bot   go] go it

fendis, for þou hase giuen mi liuerai awai, and taken mine enemis liuerai on þe."

'Behald, spouse, and se þat þai, þe whilke suld be mi frendes, are turned fro me, ne þai take ne hede what I suffird pacientli for þame, and how I stode on thre wises for þame: first, as a man þat had a sharpe swerde prikked throw his eyn, and as his hert were persed þrow and all his limes tremled. First, mi passion was as sore, of pennance þat I suffird in mi bodi, as is þe prikking in þe eye. Also it was als sorowfull as mi hert is bi smiting throw with a swerde. And all þe partis of mi bo|di tremild for drede of dede and suffiringe þareof. And ȝet dispice þai all þese and sete þame at noȝt.

'I ame as a woman þat trauals with child, þat has grete thoght how hir barn sall be born and cristend. þus haue I done to man as a woman. I broght furth man, þrow mi passion, fro þe derkenes of helle vnto þe dai and light of endles gladnes. I fede him with mi gude wordes. Bot he as one vnkind sone takes no hede of his modir penans, for he dispises me, and to mi wondes ekis diseses. For he, þrow sin, departes himselfe fro me. He giues me mater in þat at is in him to wepe, for he knawes mi will and dispises it and dose agains his consciens ([þare]for he sall haue depper paine in hell for dispising of mi commandmentes fro he knaw[s] þame); and he ekis vnto mi wondes disese, for he is glad to do þe euele. Also he giues me stones for brede; þat menis, he giues me hardnes of hert instede of contricion. And for his dispite I mai pleyne as a modir on hir vnkinde son, | for I b[r]oght þame fro derkenes to light be mi passion, and fede þame with milke of mi swetenes. þai set right noȝt by all þis. And þarfore I sall raise againe paine, and dem þam eftir þai haue deserued.'

Capitulum xx. þe modir of God teches þat a man þe whilke hase contricion and wille to amend him, all if he be cald in deuocion and þe lufe of God, he sall gete him hete of besi meditacion of Cristes passion, and he sall `suke´ of þe pappes of maiden Mary.

þe modir saide to þe spouse, 'I am as a modir þat has two sonnes. þe first is contricion for þat is misdone. þe ii is will to amende all þat is misdon. Bot þese childir are right colde, for þai hafe no inward desire to loue God. þan saide I to mine awen son, "Mi son, louyng and

---

1 awai] awai on þe, on þe *ruled through*   20 þarefor] for   21 knaws] knaw
24 broght] boght, *Lat.* peperi   33 to] *twice*

wirshipynge be to þe for all þat þou hase loued me. I haue two oþir childir. Haue merci on þame and helpe þame, for þai are full colde." Mi son saide againe, "Modir, I sall sende on sparke of fire, of þe whilke þai mai make a grete fire. þis sparke is consideracion, minde

f. 237ᵛᵇ and thoght of mi passion. And | whosoeuir will thinke on hertli how I

6 was taken, smetin, spit on, and scourged, so þat þe fleshe was reuin with þe scourges, and how þat mi sinows braste, and I cried on þe crosse and ȝeldede þe goste, if he will ofte blow with his hertli þoght at þis sparke, mai he þan be warmed, and soke mi modir pappes: þat is to

10 sai, he mai com to þe drede of God and obediens, þat mi modir had perfiteli. For all if sho sinned neuir, ȝete was sho ferde to greue God." ' þan saide þe modir, 'I ame sho þat neuir disobeied God. And þarefore sall I sende to mi frende, þat þou praies for, loue to God and obediens to all his commandmentes.'

15   Capitulum xxi. Howe oure ladi for one of hir dede
       seruantes praied, and how Crist answerd þat þo þinges
       [þat] were done for him by his predesessours profite
       him bot litill, and þe cause.

þe modir of merci saide to hir son, 'Son, þi bodi is offird þis dai for þis

20 mannes saule. I prai þat it be profite to him and haue merci on him.' þan

f. 238ʳᵃ saide þe son, 'I ame like to a man þat boght a litill feld of fife | fote for a grete prise, and þare was grete golde hide in þis felde. þis man is þat felde, þat hase fiue wittes. He was boght with mi preciouse blode. And in it was tresoure, þat is, his saule made bi þe godhede. Bot it is with-

25 drawen now fro þe bodi, and oneli þe erthe left.' þan saide þe modir, 'Haue merci on him for mi praiers. For ilkea dai he saide owres of me. Ne putt not to him þat his successours hase noȝt done þaire deuere, and hase so trespassed, for þai make ioy, and he wepis and is ponisht.' þe son saide, 'Modir, þat þou praies for sall haue thre maner of merci. First, he

30 sall be deliuerd of þe handes of þe fendes, for þai sall leue and neuirmor come nere it. þe second is þat he sall be putt fro þe more paine to þe lesse. þe þird is þat þe aungells sall comforth him. Bot is he noȝt ȝitt all deliuerd. Bot throw þi praier, bi mi merci, he sall be clene deliuerd.'

       Capitulum xxii. How Criste ressaiues a certaine
35   bishope vnto his merci þat was naked of gude liueing

7 on] *twice*   9 be] *twice, first subpuncted*   17 þat] *om.*

and new turned to contricion and holi purpose, and
how Criste clethis him in merci and enformes him. |

Criste saide to þe spouse, 'þat prelate for þe whilke þou praied me   f. 238ʳᵇ
is turned againe to me on thre wise. First, as a naked man; also, as a
man þat had a swerd in his hande; and as he þe whilke haldes vp his   5
handis to aske forgiuenes. þe apostels prayed for him, bot þai had bot
litill grace for him, for, fro he tuke þe dignite of mi kirke, he was contrarious to me. Neuirþelesse, for þe praiers of mi modir, I turn me to
him as a modir to þe childe þat was loste. I sall cleth him with gude
vertuse, for he þinkes now þat of himselfe he hase no gude, and if he   10
wiste how he might plese me he wald gladli do it, for he hase done
bifore bot few gude dedis. þe second, he had a swerde in his hand,
when he thoght þat þe dome suld be fell, and þat he might not flee it,
bot he putt him fulli at mi will. þan changed I þe felnes of mi swerde to
forgiuenes. þe third, he held vp his hand, when he þoght þus: "Lord, I   15
knaw mi trespas, bot I trist helpe in þi gudenes, for þou forsoke noȝt
Paule | þat persewed þe, ne Mawdelaine þat was full of sin. þarefore,   f. 238ᵛᵃ
lord, I turn me to þe, and I prai þe of merci."
'For this thoght sall I put to him þe hand of mi merci, if he put fro
him all pride and hienes and take meknes; also, if he departe fro him   20
couetise, and giue, of his gudes, part to þe pore; also, if he be noght
rekeles in his cure, bot amend his soietts, and teche þam to fle sin and
ressaiue þame gudeli þat will amend þame, and chastise þame þe
whilke will noȝt amend, awþir with bodeli pennans or elles with
paynge of moneye. And beware þat he do noȝt þat for couetise, bot þat   25
he turn þat moneye to swilke vse as he sall gife God a rekenyng of. Bot
fro þe time þat he þe whilke is ponisht has paied his moneye, and he
will not amend him, priue him of his benefice and his astate. For so do
I. For, first, I chastise þame with tribulacion and disese, and if he will
noght amend him, bot turn againe, þan take I fro him mi merci, and I   30
ponishe him eftir mi rightwisenes.' |

Capitulum xxiii. Oure ladi aperid to þe spouse praiing   f. 238ᵛᵇ
hir son for a grete lord whom sho likens to a theefe, to
whom Criste telles his greuowse sinnes, and how throw
hir praier he hase done to him grete graces, and whilke   35
þai are.

19 to] to þe, þe *subpuncted*   20 meknes] mekens   23-4 þe whilke] *twice,*
first subpuncted   35 he] *twice*

þe modir praied hir son for a gret man whome sho likenes to a theefe. þan saide þe son, 'Modir, he hase done þre grete thiftis. Firste, he has robbid mine aungels, for [bi] his vnhonest wordes and his euel ensampill he hase withdrawen mani saules þat suld haue bene in
5 compani with aungels. þe second is, for he has robbid mani mennes bodis, for he hase bene cause of slaing of mani men, and so he hase reft þaire liues fro þaire bodis. þe þird is þat he hase spoyled mani men fro þaire gude and so done mani wranges to men. And with þese he has þre euell condicions. First, he hase grete couetise of þe worldes gudes.
10 þe second is, for he trespast in spousale, for cause þat he vses it oneli for luste. þe þirde, he is so prowde þat he wald men were like to him.

f. 239ʳᵃ And þarefor, modir, þou sees mi right|twisnes, þat when þe modir of Jon and James come and askid me þat one might sit on mi right hand, and þe oþir of my left, I saide þat he þat more trauailed and more
15 mekid himself, he suld sit on mi right hand. Bot how suld he þis sit þare, þe whilke has no3t done for me bot all agains me?'

þan saide þe modir, 'Son, I see þi rightwisenes þat is ferdfull, bot I go to þi merci þat is softe and gudeli. þis theefe mai no3t be saued bot bi þi mercy, for he is like to a childe, þat, all if he haue mouthe, eyn,
20 handes and fete, 3et can he not speke, ne he canno3t disseuer þe brightnes of þe fire fra þe brightnes of þe son. Ne he canno3t go with his fete, ne wirke with his handes. Right so þis theefe, fro his 3outh-hede, hase growen to werkes of þe fende. His eris were stoppid to þe gude, his eyne were blinde to godnes, his mouth sperrid to Goddes
25 loueyng, his handis febill to gude werkes. Bot with þe one [fote] he stode in two steppis. þe fote was desire of amending. One stepe was when [he] thoght of þe hard paine of hell. Oneoþir was sorow for losing of þe blis of heuen. And þarefor, mi swete son, for þi gudenes,

f. 239ʳᵇ and as I | bare þe of mi bodi, haue merci on þis man.'
30 þan saide þe son, 'Modir, for þre þinges þat he had I sall giue him oþir þre. First, for þe purpose þat he had to amend him, I sende to him mi frende þat sall shewe to him þe wai of liue. þe second, for þe thoght þat he had of þe paine of helle, I haue geuen to him more knawleche and vndirstandinge of it þan he had before. And þe þirde, þat was
35 sorow, þe whilke he hade for losing of þe blis of heuen, I haue giuen him grace to hope for to com to þat blis.' þan saide þe modir, 'Son, blissed be þou for þi rightwisenes. Bot I beseke þe of þi merci. Do to him grace for mi sake, and for loue of þi seruantes, þe whilke praide me

---

3 bi] *om.*   12 righttwisnes] *Quire catchphrase*, twisnes, *below*   25 fote] *om.*,
Lat. pede   27 he] *om.*

for to prai for him, and for þi spouses sake þat praies for him.' þan
saide Criste, 'þou arte modir of merci. þou bowes me ay to hafe merci.
Aske what þou will, for þine askyng mai noȝt be warned.'

þan saide þe modir, 'I aske firste þat þou will graunt to him festen-
ing of his fote þat standes in two steppis. And graunt | to him þi blissed f. 239ᵛᵃ
bodi, for it is hele to seke, and for it is þe swetest emplastir þat mai be 6
felid. Graunt þarefor him to ressaiue with feruoure of charite. For þe
second, I aske þat þou shewe him what he sall do and how he mai
plese þe. þe þirde is þat þou giue him rest of þe brining of his fleshe.'
þan saide þe son, 'Modir, þine asking mai noȝt be denied, and þare- 10
fore I will be auised, noght for þere is chaungeing in me, þe whilke mai
noght be vnstabill, ne for þat þou sees noght all þinges in me, bot I
abide for mi spouse þe whilke is here, þat sho mai be disposed to
vndirstand mi witt.'

        Capitulum xxiiii. Criste biddis þe spouse yf þe þeefe of 15
        whom it is spoken will take þe sacrament of þe awter,
        loke þat he haue contricion bifore of his misleuinge,
        with will to amend him. And he teches oþir gude
        remedis, how he mai reconseill himselfe againe to God,
        aungells, saintes and to oþir gude men. 20

    Than saide þe modir, 'Mi blissed son, I aske þe ȝet for ȝone theefe.'
þe son answerde, 'Modir, for ȝour loue, I sall do him merci.' þe mo|dir f. 239ᵛᵇ
saide, 'Son, graunt me grace to him, and þi bodi, for he is hongry and
voide of gudenes, þat he might be strenkþed.' þe son answerde, 'Right
as a child þat wanttis mete dyes bodeli, so he þis mai noght leue gosteli 25
bot he be fede with gosteli fode. And þarefore he moste haue þre
þinges. þe firste is contricion of þat þe whilke he hase misdone; also,
will to haue to amend him and neuir to turn againe; and him moste
trauaile for defens of þe faith and holi kirke, if nede be, as he traualed
byfore for þe profite of ane erthli lord, and to drawe all þat he may vnto 30
mi seruise, as he drewe bifore men for to serue þe world. And I sall
rewarde him with þe life þat is endeles.

    'Also, foralsmikill as he hase greued þe aungells and robbid bodis
fro þe saules, him moste make to sing all one ȝere euirilke dai one

---

    2 merci] merci, do to him grace for mi sake and for loue of þi seruantes þe whilke
prayed me for to prai for him, *and, exc.* merci, *ruled through and* va-cat   7 him to
ressaiue] *trsp.*   12 noght²] all þing in me noght, *exc.* noght, *ruled through*
25 wanttis] wanttis witt, witt *subpuncted*   34 moste] moste to, to *subpuncted*

messe, where þat him likes, of all halows, for þe aungels are plesid by
þe offiringe of mi bodi. Also, fore þat he hase robbid oþir mennes
gudes, him moste giue againe, as fere as he kan witt, to þame þat he
f. 240ra hase gude of with wronge. And pray | þame of forgiuenes. And for he
5 can noȝt make asseth to all þat he has trespaste to, he sall do make a
awter in som kirke, where þat him liste, and endowe it sufficientli to
one preste to liue on withouten ende, for þame þat he harmed. And he
suld meke him to þame þat he had trespast to, and aske þaim forgiuenes. And if he here oþir commend him of þat he did þe whilke was sin,
10 haue no liking þarein, bot aske God forgeuenes þat euir he had likyng
in ani euell, and þan suld he sai, "I prai ȝou, breþir, prai for me, þat I
fall neuir againe." Also, for þat he had luste of fleshe, make resonabill
abstinens, and if he here mi wordes and fulfille þame, he sall be saue,
and elles he sall giue a rekeninge of þe leste ferthinge.'

15   Capitulum xxv. Fro þe time þat þe spouse had reuela-
           cion of þe theefe spoken bifore, Crist saide to hir, þre
           ȝere eftir, þat bot he amendid him, he suld be dampned
           with one horribill sentens in his kinne and in his gudes:
           as it fell, for he wald noȝt amende him.

f. 240rb   Criste saide to þe spouse, 'I talde þe of ȝone þeefe a | faire songe.
21 And now I sall tell þe of morning, for, bot if he turn him þe soner, he
sall fele mi fell rightwisnes. His dais sall be shorted. þare sall no froyte
dwelle of him. þe riches þat he has gedird sall be scailed, and he sall
be demed as a theefe, and as a child þe whilke dispices his fadirs
25 biddinges.'

           Capitulum xxvi. Criste biddes þe spouse þat a certaine
           king for whome sho praies dispose him to reparell þrow
           counsell of wise spirituall men þe walles of Jerusalem,
           þat menis, holi kirke.

30   Criste saide to þe spouse, 'I pleine me firste þat þe walle of Jerusalem, þat is, mi kirke, is distroied. þis walle is þe bodis and þe saules
of cristen men, of whome holi kirke suld be bigged. Bot þare walles are
fallen, for all men er more besi to fulfill þaire awen will þan mine. þai
turn þame fro me, and wille noȝt here mi wordes, for þai þinke þame
35 heui, and mi werkes foli. Mi passion is abhominabill to þame, and þai

2 þe] þe of   22 mi fell] *twice, second subpuncted*

sai þat mi liueing is noȝt abill to be fulfilled. Also, I pleine þat þe
vessell | of mi hows are born into Babilone; þat is to sai, gude liueing of f. 240ᵛᵃ
clerkes and men of religion is now turned to pride of þe werlde and
þaire awn liking. Mi witt and mi lore is halden vanite. þe hight þe
whilke þai made to me þai haue broken. þe gude lawes þat þaire 5
predecessours kepid þai haue left, and þai make þame lawes eftir þaire
awen will. Also, I pleyn þat mi commandmentes are noȝt kepid. And I
said to him þat asked me how he suld haue þe liue euirlasting þat he
suld kepe þe commandmentes. Bot now þai are forgetin.

'And þarefore sai to þe kinge þat þou praies fore þat he gedir 10
togedir spirituall men, and besi hym eftir þaire counsaill to reparalle
þe wall of þe kirke: þat menis, þat mi wirshipe be halden, faith be
strenkþed, charite encressed, and mi passion had in minde. Besi him
þat clerkes and religious turn again to mekenes, and lichours to
chastite, and couetouse clerkes to worldli dispising, and so þai awe to 15
gife othir ensampill of gode liueing. And so besi he him þat mi com-
mandmentes be kepid, for, trewli, mi kirke | is passed so fer fro me, þat f. 240ᵛᵇ
were noȝt þe praiers of mi modir, þer were no hope of forgiuenes. Bot,
amange all astates of lewid pupill, knightes hase made apostasye
ferreste fro me, whos perell and paine is shewed to þe bifore.' 20

Capitulum xxvii. Criste forbeddis þe spouse to here
gladli nouelles or werkes of werldli men, or batails of
lordes, bot take sho hede to þe wondirfull werkes of
God. And he blames þame greteli þat are ouir besi for
riches and wirsheps. 25

Criste bad his spouse þat sho suld noȝt be besi to here batails and
dedis of worldli men, for his werkes are gretter þan þairs (and þarefore
take hede of his dedis), for þai sall all be demed bi him: 'for þe worldli
mennes besines is to win worldli wirshepe, to gedir grete riches, and to
make þaire aires grete. Bot I swere be mi godhede and manhede þat, if 30
þai dye in þat will, þai sall neuir com in þat land was hight in figure to
þe childir of I[s]rell. Bot right as þai died bodeli dede, r[i]ght so sall
þai dye | gosteli. And þai þat dose mi will sall haue þe land þat euir sall f. 241ʳᵃ
laste, þat is, þe kingdome of heuen, where þai sall be fulfilled with þe
swetenes of mi loue, þat passis all þe honi of þis werld. Bot mine 35

1 liueing] liueing, n *subpuncted*   2 liueing] liuening   4 hight] hight of
16 liueing] liuening   18 no] noȝt, ȝt *subpuncted*   32 Isrell] Irell   right²]
rght

enmis sall neuir taste of it bot þai turn þame to me. And wald þai þinke
what I hafe done for þame, how þat I haue giuen þame all þat is nedefull to þame! I suffird þame to hafe wirshipes, and frendshipes, bot þai
wald noȝt þinke þat in þaire wirshipes þai suld haue done me reuer-
5 ens, and haue bene godeli to þe pore and simpill. Ne þai wald noȝt
þinke to spend þer riches amange þame þat had nede, to kepe þame
fro sin, bot þai put þer will bifor mi lawe. þai þinke þat þai haue neuir
enoghe of þaire worldeli wirsheps. þai geue þame to lustes and likyng
of fleshe. þarefore, bot þai amend þame, þai sall neuir com to þe land
10 þat is withouten ende.'

Capitulum xxviii. How a saule is dampnid for greuose
sinnes, and for he wald noght haue sorow and compassion of Cristes woundes and passion, and how that
saule is likened. |

f. 241ʳᵇ   There was gadird in heuen a grete compani, and Criste saide, 'Ȝone
16 saule is noȝt mine, for it gaue no more fors of þe wownde of mi side
and mi hert þan if his enmis suld haue bene persed throwe. Ne it gaue
no more fors of þe woundes of mi handes þan if a þin clowte had bene
ryuen, ne of þe wowndes of mi fete þan of þe bittinge of a soft appill.'
20 þan saide he vnto þe saule, 'þou asked me oft time in þi liue whi þat I
died in mi bodi. And I aske þe, wrech, whi art þou dede in þi saule?'
þe saule answerde, 'For I loued noȝt þe.' þan saide Criste, 'þou was
to me as a dede born childe, of whome þe modir hase als mikell payn
as of þat þe whilke is whike. Right so, as bittir painnes suffird I for þe,
25 and als mikill gaue I for þe, as for one saint in heuen. Bot right as a
dede born childe tastes noȝt þe swettenes of þe modirs milke, ne comforth of hir wordis, ne warmenes of hir briste, right so sall þou neuir
taste of þe swetenes of mi blis, ne þou sall noȝt be comforted of mi
f. 241ᵛᵃ wordes, ne þou sall noȝt | fele þe warmnes of mi charite. Go þarefor to
30 leue in euirlasting dede, for þou wald noȝt liue in gude liue.'
   þan saide Crist to þe compani þat was with him, 'þis saule was like
to þre þinges: first, to þame þat folowde me in mi preching, of malice
to take me in mi wordes. þai saw þe miracles þat I wroght, and mi
liueynge, and þai herde mi wisdome, bot, for þaire werkes were euell
35 and noght according to mi werkes, and I reproued þam of sin, þai had
envie at me and hatid me. Right so þis saule folowed me noȝt for lufe
bot for sight of men. He sawe mi werkes and had envye at þame. And

2 I¹] þai, þa *subpuncted; marg.,* I

þat was of his malice, þat he might more freli folow his lustes and his awn will. Neuirþeles, his consciens saide þat he did omis. He wist wele þat I was lord and maker of all þinges, a[n]d ʒit he was wrothe with mi wordes, for I reproued his sin. þe second is þat he was like to þame þat slow me. þai wende þat I suld noʒt haue resin againe, for þai wend þat I had bene oneli man. "Right so", saide þis saule, "I mai do what me likes, for God sall neuir rise to þe dom so felli as men prechis, for he | wald neuir haue boʒt man so der if he wald haue lost him, and he wald neuir so lang abide of vengeance as he dose, if sin greued him so sare as men telles." þe þird is þat he is like to þaim þat kepid þe sepulcre and armed þame. Right so, he armed him with hardenes of hert, þat mi wordes, and my frendis wordis, might noʒt entir to his hert to amend him, bot he thoght þat he wald withdrawe him, þat he suld here no gude wordes, in auenture þat he had bene stird to haue left his luste.'

      Capitulum xxix. It is beden to þe spouse þat sho take oft   15
      þe bodi of Criste, and it is tolde what were figurs of þe
      bodi, and what grete vertuse cumys to a deuote saule
      þat oft takes it.

Criste bade þe spouse þat fro þat dai sho suld dispose hir to ressaiue ofte times his blissed bodi, for he sais þat þe profete was sent to a woman, þe whilke fede him with þe mele, and itt failed not whils God sent raynes vpon þe erth. 'I ame þe prophete, and mi bodi is þe melle þe whilke is þe fode of þe saule. And it is euer elike grete. Bot bodeli mete, when it | is broken, it waxis soft and wastis awaie, and fedis bot a while. Bot mi bodi dwelles ay hole. It is noʒt wasted, bot ay lastis þe same, and it fedis for euir. And mekill more þan þe bodi waxis in bodeli strenghe, þe saule takes strengþe in eting of mi bodi, þe whilke was figured by þe fode þat oure fadirs had in desert, þe whilke had all gude sauoure.'

      Capitulum xxx. Criste biddes þe spo[u]se þat sho con-   30
      ferme hir will to Goddes will both in time of prosperite
      and aduersite, and what þe will is like to.

Criste saide to þe spouse, 'Sai me what maner of wille þat þou hase.' And þe aungell hir kepir saide, 'As it is wretin, be þi will done in heuen and in erthe.' þan saide Criste, 'þat is it þe whilke I desire. Spouse',   35

    3 and²] ad   30 spouse] spose

saide Criste, 'þou moste be as a tre þat is wele rotid, þat nedis noȝt to drede, first, þe moldewarp wroting, ne, eftirward, þe grete blastes of winde, ne þe hete of þe sonne. Þe rote of þi saule suld be a gude will, of þe whilke comes mani gudes and vertuse, as braunches of þe tre.

f. 242rb Bot þis rote bose be grete and stalworth, and wele | festynde. So suld þi
6 will be stronge [a]n[d] pacient in suffering, grete in þe lufe of God, and depe growen in mekenes.

'And þan suld þou noȝt drede þe moldewarpe, þat bitokens þe fende, þe whilke gose aboute preuali to begile mennes saules, as þe
10 moldewarpe dose in þe erthe. And if he finde þe will impacient in diseses, he sheris it in sondir, for he makes þe to desire someþinge agains mi wille, and so he kuttis þi will fro mi will. And riȝt as þe tre dries and falles if þe rote be harmed, so all þi vertuse falles if þi wille be noȝt pacient. Bot if þi will be stronge and pacient, þe fende mai
15 wele stir þe, bot þou sall noȝt fall fro þi vertu for him. And if þou fall somtime of sodayne passion, at vnwisement, rise vp again bi pennance and contricion. Þe second is þat if þe rote be wele festined, it nedis noght to drede þe grete blastis of wind. So if þi wille be wele festened to mi wille, þan sall þe blastis of þe world noȝt disese þe, ne
20 mannes reproue, ne þi worldli putting downe, ne sekenes of þi bodi.

f. 242va For þou sall þinke þat I do noght withouten | cause. Þe þird is þat a tre, þe whilke is wele rotede, sall noȝt drede þe hete of þe son: þat menis, a gude will sall noȝt wax dri fro þe loue of Gode for all þis werlde, ne for lufe of it, ne for suggestion of þe fende.

25 'Þarefore, þat man þat þou þinkes vpon now is a gude tre, for his cheefe will is þat mi will be done. He had þre þinges, pouert in riches, sekenes in his limmis, and defaute in conning. And it was mi will þat if he stode pacientli in þese þre, he suld haue euirlasting plente, endeles hele and trew knawyng and sight of God. Bot now his will is turned
30 agains mi will, for he is heuy of pouert, he is angry in sekenes, and all for defaute of conning. And þarefor he sall haue nowe at his will more plente of worldli gudes, more conning, and more set bi. And þarefor, now it is gude to him to be ware when þe fendes temptacion cumys, for þe cheefe rote is broken, þat is þe gude wille, for if þe lufe of þe world
35 wax warme and he wende to couetise, and if he gruche in disseses and
f. 242vb besi him of wirships | of þe werlde, and how þat he mai plese all men to be halden gude, þan will þe tre fall, for þe rote is hurt.

'Bot I ame like', saide Criste, 'a gardenere, þe whilke hase mani

---

5 bose b (*of* be)] *also marg.*   6 and¹] in   30 will] will þat if he stode pacientli in þese þre, *exc.* will, *ruled through*

barayne trees in his ȝerde and fewe gude. And if I kutt away all þe
euell, þare will be a grete deformite in mi ȝerde. And if I kut awai all þe
gude, þe ȝerde will be noȝt. Right so, if I take oute of þe kirke all þe
gud men, þere were no liking of it, and if [I] take sodanli all þe euell
awai, þan were þere a grete deformite, and þai wald serue me not for   5
lufe bot for drede. And þarefor I will do as gude graffer þa[t], when his
graffes has taken rote, þan he kuttes awai all þat is drye. Right so sall I
make some to growe in mi loue, and þan sall I kut awai þaim at are
euell, and cast þame into þe fire, and þus sall I clens mi gardin.'

Capitulum xxxi. þe spouse sawe how þe fende and a   10
saule stode togedir in dome, and whi þe saule was for-
juged.

It was shewed to þe spouse þat þare stode bifore þe dome two
fendes like in all partes. þere | mouthes were opin as þai had bene   f. 243ra
wolues. þaire eyn was brining as fire. þaire eres hanged downe as   15
hondes. þaire belis were side. þaire handes were as þe fete of a griffon.
Thaire thies were withouten iunctures, and þaire fete kut of by þe
middis. þan saide one of þame, 'Domesman, deme þis saule to me, for
it is now like to me, bot þou made it like vnto þe. Also deme him to me,
for we haue one taste and whe haue bothe one will.' þan saide þe   20
domesman, 'How is he like to þe?' þe fende answerde, 'As we are like
in oure oþir and uttir partes, so we are like in oure dedis. For we haue
eyn, bot not to se þe gude. We haue eres, bot noȝt to here þi wirshipe.
Oure mowthes are opin to speke þat at will grefe þe. His handes are
like a griffon, for what he might gete he held [it] to his dede, and langer   25
wald if he had langer lifed. His beli hangis side, for he was neuir filled
with couetise and likyng. His brist is colde, for he hase no lufe to þe.
His thies are withouten iuncture, for his will was ay fro þe, and so was
mine. Oure fete are kut of, for oure affeccions | were turned fro þe to þe   f. 243rb
world and luste of fleshe. Oure tastes were like, for þi swetenes wald   30
we noȝt of, ne we wald noȝt taste how gude þat þou art. Bot sen it is so
þat we are þus like, deme vs to dwelle togidir.'

þan saide one aungell, 'Lord God, I haue bene besi to kepe þis
saule, and it wald noȝt obey to me. And þarefor I left it as a seke þat is
empti and tome. þis saule held þi wordes bot lesinges, and þi dome   35
bot falshede, and set þi merci at noȝt. He held his spousale, bot noȝt

4 I] *om.*   6 þat] þan   16 þe] þaire   17 iunctures] juiunctures
25 held it] helded

for þe lufe of þe, bot for flesheli lufe þat he had to his wife. Also, he herde messes and was in Goddes seruise not for deuocion bot for mennes speche, and for þou suld gife him hele of his bodi, and worldeli riches and wirshipes, and kepe him fro vnhape. Bot, lord, he
5 was rewarded more in þis worlde þan euir he serued. þou gaue him faire childir, hele of bodi and riches, and kepid him fro vnhape. And þarefore now I leue it voide of all gudenes.'

þan saide þe fende, 'Domesman, sen þou hase rewarded þis saule
f. 243ᵛᵃ ane hondrethefolde more þan it serued to þe, I | aske þat it be demed
10 to me, for we are both in one will and one assent.' þan saide þe domes-man, 'Lat þe saule tell what is þe entent of it.' þe saule saide to þe domesman, 'þou art so odyous to me þat I had leuer be in þe paine of hell withouten ende þan to be in blis to þi comforte.' þe fende saide, 'Euen swilke a wille haue I.' þe domesman saide to þe saule, 'þi wille
15 is þi domesman, and þat dome sall þou haue.'

Bot þan saide Criste to me, 'þis saule is wers þan þe theefes saule. þe voices of men cries vengeaunce. þe aungels turns þam fro it. þe saintes flees it.' þan saide þe fende, 'þarefor deme vs togidir.' þe domesman saide, 'And þis saule in þe last point of his liue wald haue
20 asked forgifenes with will of amending, it suld not haue commen in þi handes. Bot for he lastid to þe ende in euell, þarefor sall it now be with þe. Neuerþeles, if it dide ani gude, þat sall restreine þi malice, þat þou sall noȝt punish it so sore as þow walde.' And þan made þe fende grete ioy, and þe domesman saide to hym, 'Sai, þat þis spouse mai wit, whi
f. 243ᵛᵇ þou makes so grete ioi.' And þan | saide þe fende, 'þe more þat I
26 ponishe þis saule, þe more am I ponished. Bot for þou boght it with þi blode and gaue þiselfe þarefore, and þat I haue desaiued it to folow me and leue þe þat loued it so wele–þarefor make I ioy.'

þan saide þe domesman, 'þi malice is grete. Bot loke aboute þe and
30 see.' And þere went a saule vp to heuen as bright as a stern. And þan saide Criste to þe fende, 'What will þou giue to haue ȝone saule at þi wille?' þe fende answerde, 'All þe saules þat are in helle. And ȝete if þare were one piler fro þe erthe to þe heuen all full of swerd poyntes, I wald go vp to þe ende of it so þat I might hafe ȝone saule in mi
35 powere.' þan saide Criste, 'þi malice is grete. Bot if it were possibill, I wald ȝete die againe or I wantide one saule.' And þan said Criste vnto þat saule, 'Come, mi derling, vnto mi blis þat þou hase desired. I sall giue þe miselfe þat ame all gode.'

23 punish] punisht

Capitulum xxxii. Criste telles þe spouse how fadirs and
modirs þat enformes þaire childir in worldli condicions
to gete wirshipes, | worldli blis with pride, er bitakind to
a serpent.

f. 244ra

Criste saide to þe spouse how þat a man þe whilke sho knewe was 5
like to a neddir, for his modir taght him loue of þis worlde, and how he
suld com to be grete in þis werlde. 'He makes mani fare heghtes to
men to drawe þam to him. He spares noȝt his bodi ne his liue to be
halden manli. He dose mikill disese to oþir þat are byside him, for fro
som he takes þaire gudes, and fro some þaire liue. He auentures him 10
to debate with grete, and he spares noght hali kirke, ne hase no minde
of mi passion. Bot he sais on þis manere, "If I sall be dampned,
whereto suld I do gode? If I sall be saued, God will lightli forgiue me."
Bot wo sall him be, bot he sonner amend him! And wit þat wele, þat
his modir, þe whilke hase lerned him, sall noȝt haue hir desire, ne þat 15
kinredyn–ne þat neddir kindeling–sall haue prosperite in þis worlde,
bot sho sall die in sorowe, and all hir kin sall be forgetin.'

Capitulum xxxiii. þe fadir spekis to þe son þat he is like
to one husband þe whilke loued so mikill his wife þat
for hir lufe he | wald be putt on þe crosse, and sho loued
þe awowtrer and slewe þe husband.

f. 244rb
21

The fadir saide to þe son þat he is like to one husband þe whilke
hase weddid a new wife þe whilke is faire, and he loues hir as himselfe.
'þis wife is mennes saules, whom þou, mi son, hase weddid to þe, þe
whilke are to þe bot one wife in faithe and charite, all if þai be mani in 25
nowmber. þai are broght into þi chambir when þou bringes þame to
þe kirke. Bot þere is mani of þame avowtres, for þai loue þe world
more þan þe. þai haue sperd þe dores of þi chambir: þat is to sai, þai
haue putt awai þaire gude will þat þou suld entir bi into mannes saule,
and þai do þe will of þine enemy. And noȝt oneli þai leue þi will, bot 30
þai þinke also, when þou arte slepinge, for to sla þe: þat menes, þam
þinkes þou slepes, for þa[i] are noȝt punished in þaire syn. Also þai
þinke at sla þe when þai set noȝt by þe blissed bodi, wheþir þai take it
or þai leue it, ne þai trowe noȝt þareon as þai sulde. Bot þou sall leue
all þese avowtres and chese | to þe a chaste wife, þe whilke is semeli in
sight and honest in maners: þat menes, þou sall chese to þe clene 36

f. 244va

32 þai^i] þar   33 þai^i] þai þinke, þinke *subpuncted*

saules full of deuocion and charite, þe whilke will endelesli dwell
with þe.'

Capitulum xxxiiii. þe modir of God declares bi ensampill to þe spouse how sho purchased of hir son, at
5 þe prayer of all gude liuers of þe world, þe wordes of
þis heuenli boke, þrow whilke wordes curs is hight to
þe proude and benison to þe meke.

þe modir saide, 'Mi son is like to a king þat hase one cite, in þe
whilke are seuenti princes, and in ilkeone of þaire lordeshipes is bot
10 one trewe man; þe whilke trewe men gedird þame togidir, and wrote
to a ladi þat was homeli to þat kinge, and prayed hir þat sho wald pray
þe king to sende to þaim þat were noȝt trewe som wordes of forgeuenes, and by þe whilke þai might be stird to trewth. Sho praied, and þe
kinge answerde, "All if þai be worthi noþing bot dede, ȝet for þi
f. 244ᵛᵇ praiers I will sende to þame two wordes, as two lettirs. In þe | first lettir
16 are thre wordes. þe first is dampnacion, þe second pouert, þe third
senshipe and shame, þe whilke þai are worthi. In þe second lettir was
wrctin, "Whosocuir will mckc him sall hafc gracc and liuc." When
þese lettirs was broght to þame, some saide, "We are as stronge as þe
20 king. We will defend vs"; som saide, "We gife nowþir of liue ne of
dede"; and som saide, "þese lettirs are bot feyned. þa come neuir of
þe kinges entent." Bot þe trewe men wrote oft againe to þat ladi and
saide, "þes men trowes noȝt þaire wordes, and þarefor aske of þe
kinge to sende þame some speciall token þat þai knewe." þan saide þe
25 king, when he herde þis, "Two þinges falles to a king: his croune, bot
þat mai none bere bot a king; þe second is his shelde, þe whilke stintes
debate. And þere two sall I sende þam."

'þis king is mi son, þe whilke is kinge of blis. þis worlde is þe cite, in
þe whilke are seuenti maner of spechis and tunges. And in ilke of þese
30 tunges mi son hase one frende. I ame þe ladi þat is homeli with þis
f. 245ʳᵃ kinge. And mi frendis, þat sees þ[e] mischefis of þe | worlde, bisekis
me to prai mi son for to saue þo men þat are þarein. And he sendes
ofte times, at mi praier, bothe manas and profer of merci, and, eftir, he
sent his crowne: þat menes, he giues powere to þe gud liuers to scorn
35 þe malice of þe euell fende. And also he sent his shelde, in tokening of
pees of hertes.' þan saide þe kinge to his modir, 'Blissed be þou,

15 In] I in, I *marked for cancellation* 31 þe¹] þat 32 þat are] *twice, first sub-*
puncted 33 manas] manans

modir. I giue þe powere of mi crowne and mi shelde. þou arte full of
merci and drawis mani sinfull to me, and blissid is he þat seruis þe, for
he sall neuir be forsakin in life ne dede.'

þan saide þe modir to þe spouse, 'It is wretin þat Jon Baptist went
bifore þe face of mi son, and 3et all men sawe him no3t, for he was   5
mikill in diserte. So go I bifore þe ferdefull dome of mi son with mi
merci. And þarefor sai on mi bihalue to him þat hase þe crowne þat,
when he felis himselfe aniþing lettid of his feruour in deuocion, sai
þus: "Lord fadir, with þe son and holi goste, maker of all þinges, þe
whilke sent þi son into þe wombe of þe maiden Mari, command þis   10
euell spirit þat he go awai and disese þis creature no langer." Also, | sai   f. 245ʳᵇ
to him þat hase þe sheld þus: "þou hase oft time made me messingere
to mi son for þe. Now prai I þe, go to þe hede of þe kirke." And bid
him, when he sall com into Fraunce, bifor all þe principalles of
Fraunce, he sai þes wordes: "God, þat is one with þe fadir and holi   15
goste, þe whilke for loue of man come into maiden Mari, and saw þe
spere and þe sharpe nailes bifore him, þe whilke cheese for to dye, and
suffir his hede and his fete be persed in paynefull wise, he knit 3ou in
one lufe and charite"; and telle þame of þe blise of gude men and of þe
paines of euell men.'   20

> Capitulum xxxv. Criste tellis þe spouse how þat one
> deuote monkes saule was purgid in his liue bi sekenes
> of bodi, and how in likenes of a stern he saw his blis
> bifor his dede; and how aneoþir saule of a man of
> religion was dampned; and whi þe euell religiouse are   25
> suffird.

The son saide to þe spouse, 'þou sees þi[s] monkes saule bright as a
stern, for he loued me in his life ouer all þinges, and he kepid his
obseruans. þis saule was shewed to þe | also or he died. It was like þan   f. 245ᵛᵃ
to a stern, for it was wele clensed in þe bodi bi sekenes, and it was   30
brennyng in mi loue. þarefor it was shewed in likenes of a stern, for
when he was in purgatori of bodeli disese, he had so grete a loue to me
þat him þoght all þat he suffird right no3t. And þarefore is he now with
me in blis. Bot þou sall see oneoþir saule þat þe fende hase grete
power vpon. þou sawe his dome bifore, bot now sall þou see his paine   35
be bodeli likenes, for þou mai no3t elles vndirstande þe sodaine
wirkyng of God.'

12 þat] þat he   27 þis] þi   29 died] died as, as *subpuncted*

þere come seuen fendes byfor þe prince, and þe first was prince of
pride, and saide þus: 'þis saule is mine, for he was so prowde þat him
þoȝt none like to him, and he wald haue bene aboue all oþir, as I
walde.' þe second was þe fend of coueitise, and saide, 'He wald noȝt
5 sai, "I haue enoghe." ' þe third fende, of vnbuxumnes, saide, 'It wald
noȝt obey to God bot þe fleshe, and þarefore it is mine.' þe ferde
fende, of glotony, saide, 'It vsed vntimes in etinge and drinkyng and
f. 245ᵛᵇ did owtrage.' þe fende of vainglori saide, 'His singing was for | þanke
of man, and þarefor he lifte vp his voice.' þe sexte fende, of propirte,
10 saide, 'He suld haue bene pure and had no propirte, bot he was as besi
as he might to gedir gude withouten leue.' þe seuent fende, of dispite
of religion, saide þat he wald noȝt liue eftir his statutes of religion bot
right as him liste.

þan saide þe prince of fendes, 'þou spirit of pride, entir into þis
15 saule, as if it had, to þe sight of þame þat are here, bodeli lims, and
streyne his hede so sore þat þe braine with þe eyn go oute, and all þe
mergh oute fro þe bones. Entir, þou fende of coueitise, into it, with hete
þat is wers þan ani venom or welling lede, and fill þe partis of him, for
his hert wald neuir be filled. þou spirit of vnbuxumnes, entir into his
20 hert as a sharpe swerde, for he was disobeing to God and his profession. þou spirit of glotony, go to and gnawe his hert with þi tethe, and
leue noȝt one morsell hole. þou spirit of vaineglori, go into him, and
late him neuir haue riste. And for þe grete likyng he had in his sange,
f. 246ʳᵃ lat noȝt nowe | come oute of his mouthe bot "Wo" and "Allas". þou
25 fende of propirte, reue him now all disporte, and lat him haue noȝt bot
bittirnes and sorow. And, spirit of dispite of religion, for his mispend-
ing of his time, entir into him, and loke þat time com to him of
mischefe þat neuir sall haue ende.' þan com þare anoþir fende and
saide, 'I haue parte in þis saule, for he was a preste and leued noȝt as a
30 preste suld do.' Oneoþir fende saide, 'He wald noȝt bere his crowne to
þat ende þat he suld for þe crowne of blis.' þan saide þe prince of
fendis, 'For þe wirshipfull name of prestes sall he now be called
Sathan, and for þe crowne of blis, þat he dispised, he sall haue a token
of euirlasting reproue.'

35 þan saide God to þe spouse, 'These twa were both of one profession, bot þaire rewardes are noȝt like, for þaire lifynge were noȝt
both one. And I shewe þis to þe þat þe gude man mai be þe more
strange, and þe euell man amendid. Bot men of þis profession are
turned fer fro me, for I gaue þame powere to preche mi wordes, bot

noȝt to plesing of men, and to gete þameselfe riches. þai shewe noȝt
mi rightwisnes, bot þai coloure sinnes, | and so þai make men to lie still   f. 246ʳᵇ
in sine and noȝt to repent þame. Also, I bad þat þai suld haue pouert
and mekenes. Bot if þai be pure, þai gruche and sais, "How sall we
liue? Also, if we be meke, all men will dispice vs." And þus are þai   5
disaiued, and gedirs riches and waxis prowde. Also, I bad þame trauaile
þaire bodis and do abstinens, and þai sai againe þat, if þai wirke or
trauaile or faste as þaire predecessours did, þai suld faile, and þarefor all
þat I walde þai dide, þai caste it awai and turnes þame fro me.

   'Bot I sai þe in sothefastenes þat, were not two þinges, I suld noȝt   10
leue one hows standing of þairs. One þinge is þe prayer of mi modir
and of þere patrone, þe whilke prais for þame continuli. þe second is
mi rightwisnes for helping of oþir, for bi þe preching and singing of mi
seruis takes oþir men deuocion and stirryng to þe gude, all if þameselfe fall downe into þe depe pitt, for þai serue me for worldli profit   15
and noȝt for þe blis þat is euirlasting. And if þare be any gude, þai are
full fewe, as one amange ane hondreth.' |

Capitulum xxxvi. Criste telles to þe spouse for wilke   f. 246ᵛᵃ
thre causes þe holi goste was sent into apostels, and
how he entres noȝt into men full of pride, couetise and   20
licheri, and how G[o]de will þat þe wyne of his wordes
be first birled to his frendes and to oþir.

   Criste saide to þe spouse þat he sent þe holi goste vnto þe apostels,
firste, for þai had will to kepe þame chaste; also, for þai had verrai
mekenes; and also, all þaire desire to God. 'And þe holi goste come to   25
þame as a grete sodaine raine and filled þam full of liking. Also, he
com as a fire and filled þame full of warm[n]es of loue. And he come to
þame in likenes of tounges, and filled þame full of wit to speke mi
vertu, for þaire hertes were clene of sin and voide fro euele. For he will
noȝt com to þame þat are fowle with filth of sin. For þere are þre fowle   30
vessels. Som are foule of mannes filthe, as þai þat are fulle of couetise,
þat makis mani to stinke bifor me. Som are full of bittir sede þat no
man mai taste, as þai þat are licherus men. I mai noȝt suffir þaim ne
dwelle with þam, for I am verrai clennes. And som are | fulle of rotin   f. 246ᵛᵇ
blode and wheter, as prowde men, for it distruys a man within him-   35
selfe, and puttes fro him mi grace, þe whilke is þe liue of þe saule.

   'þarefor, he þat will be filled of þe grace of mi goste, him moste

2 and so þai] *twice, second subpuncted*   21 Gode] gude, *Lat.* Cristus
27 warmnes] warmes

haue thre vessels. One is a gude will to withdrawe him fro all vanite; also a will to verrai mekenes; and a full desire to all gudenes. And for þare come ane to me with þare vessels, I fillid him with gosteli wit, and made þat he was clere to vndirstande gosteli þinges. I filled him with mi charite, and made him more brenning in mi lufe. And also I gafe him a discrete drede to drede me and noght elles. And þerfor he sall haue þe swetenes of mi ioy, and he sall here mi wordes, and þat sall make him more besi to taste of mi swetenes.'

Capitulum xxxvii. Oure ladi telles þe spouse how foure manere of folke sendes gretinges, and how þai are rewardid.

þe modir Mari saide, 'Foure maner of men gretis me: firste, þai þe whilke hase left all þaire awen wille and þaire consciens in mi handes, and all þat þai do þai | mene to do it for my wirshipe. þat gretyng is to me as it were a swete likand drynke. þe seconde are þai þe whilke dredis payne, and þarefor þai withdrawe þaimselfe fro sin: to whome I sall gife, if þai abid and life in mi seruise, lessing of drede and encressing of charite. þe þirde ar þai þat spekis enoghe of my wirshipe, bot for none oþir cause bot for þai wald haue herthli welth and wirshipe, and of þaim haue I no danteth, for I send þat maner of gretyng againe, as a presaunt not plesaunt. þe ferth are þai þe whilke feines þame to be gode, bot þai are euell vndir. þai þinke if þai trespas preuaili þat I ame mercifull and sone will gette þame forgifenes. þe gretyng of þere maner of folke is to me as a vessell of siluir withoute and fulle of filth within, of þe whilke a man may noȝt fele þe sauoure. Swilke is som bi wille to sin.'

Capitulum xxxviii. Criste tellis þe spouse of þe tokens of þe gude spirit and euell.

Criste saide to þe spouse þat 'He þe whilke hase þe gude spirit hase all gude, for þe gude spirit is `God´, my blis and þe swetenes of saintes. And he | þat hase þe euell spirit hase all euell, for he hase þe fende, þe whilke is payne and all euell. And right as a gude man whote not how, or fro whens, þe swetenes of þe gode spirit and þe gudenes of God commes to hym, right so þe euell man kan noȝt persaife fro whens

10 sendes] sendes to   12 saide] saide spouse, spouse *ruled through*
14 þai²] *Quire catchphrase*, mene to do it, *below*   19 haue] haue no, no *ruled through*

commes þe euell leuynge while he is here. Bot wo sall þai be þat
folowes þe euell spirit.'

Capitulum xxxix. How þe spouse saw a fende bringinge
befor Goddes dome seuen bokes againe a certaine saule
of a knight, and þe gude angell broght furth bot one 5
boke, and how þe saule was saued, and to what paines it
was demid to purgatori to domesdai, and Criste tellis
thre remedies by þe whilke it mai be deliuered byfore.

þare apperid a fend in Goddes dome, þe whilke helde a knyghtes
saule all tremilling as it had bene a whaking hert, and saide þus to þe 10
domesman: 'Here, my prai. þine aungell and I hafe folowed þis saule
aboute fro his bygyninge to þe ende, he for to kepe him, and I for to
dissaiue him. And now is he fallen in mi handes, and þare is noȝt at lett
me for to haue it | bot þi rightwis dome. For I hafe one buke full of his f. 247ᵛᵃ
sinnes, þe name of þe whilke boke 'is' [vnbux]umnes, and in it are 15
seuen bokes, and in ilka boke ar thre columpnes, and in euirilkea
columpne, at þe leste, a thousand wordes.

'þe first boke hight pride, in þe whilke are þre columpnes. þe first is
gostli pride in consciens, for he hade pride of his gude liuynge, þat he
wend he had bene bettir þan oþir and more wise. þe second columpne 20
was pride of worldli gudes, as of his mene, cloþing and oþir þinges. þe
þirde was pride of bewte of bodi, of kin and of swilke oþir. þe second
boke was coueytise. þe first columpne was gosteli couetise, for he þoȝt
noȝt þat his sinnes were so greuous as þai were, and þerefore he
desired heuen vnworthili, for he was noȝt fulli clene. þe second was 25
þat he desired to be grete in þe world to make his name grete and his
kyn. þe third columpne was þat he besid him to be abouen oþir, and to
gete him worldli gude. þe þirde boke was enuye. þe firste columpne
was personali to þame þat had more welth and gude in þe worlde þan
he. þe second was þat, of enuy, he toke oþir menes gudes | þat had lese f. 247ᵛᵇ
þan he, to holde þame lowe. þe þird columpne was þat he noyed his 31
neghbour both preualy and apertli in worde and dede, and stird oþir
to do þe same.

'þe fourt boke: auarice. þe firste columpne was gosteli auarice, for
he wald noȝt tech oþir þat he couthe to þer comforte and profite, and 35
so þai þe whilke had nede of gude counsell were noȝt holpin by him.

15 vnbuxumnes] umnes (*rest erased*), *Lat.* inobedientia   35 þer] oþer, o *subpuncted*

þe second columpne was þat he wald noȝt accorde þame þat were at
debate. þe þirde columpne was in his gudes, for it greuet him to gife
one peny for þi loue, bot for þe world he wald gladli spende. þe fi[f]t
boke was slewthe: þe first columpne, þat he was slawe to kepe þi com-
5 mandmentes, and for ese of his bodi he lost his time. þe seconde
columpne was slewth in þoȝt, for, when þi gost send any compunccion
into his hert or gosteli likyng, he withdrew his þoȝt þerfro, and in þe
werld had he grete liking. þe þird columpne, þat he was slawe in
praiynge and in gud spekinge, and redi to vaine wordes and vnhonest.
10 'þe sext boke was wrethe. þe first columpne was þat he was wrothe
f. 248ʳᵃ for þat at no profit was in. | þe seconde columpne was þat he did
harme to his neghboure in his gudes. þe þird was þat he turbild his
neghbore. þe seuent boke was luste. þe first columpne was vnskilfull
spilling of kinde, bi vnhoneste treting and bi halsinge and kissing and
15 handillinge, all if he knew so none oþir woman bot his wife. þe second
is stiringe to sin bi spekinge, as his wife to more luste and oþir to euell
þinkinge. þe þirde is þat he norished his fleshe so delicatli, and
ordained to it ouir mani daintes, and sat to lange at his mete, and in
taking mor þan wald haue sustende þe kinde.' And þan he saide,
20 'Domesman, mi bukes are full. Deme þis saule to me.'

Bot þan com þe modir of merci `and´ saide to the fende, 'I þat ame
þi ladi comandes þe to telle me, firste, if þou wote all þe þoghtes of a
man.' þe fende answerde, 'Nai, for I knawe none bot þame þat I may
knawe bi tokens outeward, or elles be disposicion of kynde.' þan saide
25 oure ladi, 'Telle, þou fende, if þer be anyþinge þat mai haue awai þat
at is wretin in þi boke.' And he saide, 'Ȝaa. Charite mai haue it awai.'
f. 248ʳᵇ þan said þe modir, 'Sai me, fende, if þare | be so sinfull a man in all þe
worlde, þe whilke mai noȝt haue forgifnes while he leues.' þe fende
answerde, 'Nai, if he will turne him to God and dwell stabli with him.'
30 þane saide þe modir of merci, in hereinge of all þat was þare, 'þis
saule, in þe ende of his liue, þoȝt þus: "þou modir of merci, I ame
vnworthi to pray to þi sone for mi gret sinnes and many þat I haue
done in greuinge of him. I loued more mi luste and þe worlde þan I did
him. And þerfor I pray þe, þe whilke is full of merci, to gete me merci.
35 And I hight þe leleli þat if I liue I will amend me, and loue þi son ouer
all þinge. And of one þinge I sorowe and morne, þat I dide neuir
noþing to plessinge of þine son, mi God and my maker. þarefor I
beseke þe, milde ladi, for I dare turn me to none oþir, þat þou will

3 fift] first   22 firste] firste þe þoghtes of a man, *exc.* firste, *ruled through*
31 merci] merci in hereing of all þat was þer, *exc.* merci, *ruled through*

haue merci on me." And þis was his wordes and his wille at his passinge.' þan saide þe fende, 'Of þis þoȝt wist I noȝt.' þe domesman
saide to þe fende, 'Loke what þou findes in þi boke now, and say it
openli, þat all mene | may here.' þan saide þe fende, 'I finde noȝt now   f. 248ᵛᵃ
in my bokes, of all þe seuen þat [I] rehersed, saue þe tokens of þame.'   5

    þan saide þe domesman to his gude aungell, 'Where is þi boke of
þ[e] gude werkes of þis saule?' þe gude aungell saide, 'Mi boke is
obediens, and it hase seuen columpnes, and it is euirmore in þi sight.
þe first columpne is baptime. þe second is abstinens fro sin and luste.
þe þird is praier and gude purpose. þe ferthe is almus dede and   10
werkes of merci. þe fifte is hope. þe sext is faithe. þe seuent is charite.
And, lord, þis boke is in þi presens.' þan cried þe fend, 'Allas, allas, I
ame begilled!' þe domesman saide to þe modir of merci, 'þou hase
wonne þis saule with rightwisnes.' þan saide þe fende, 'In hell sall not
þis saule com, for þis dedeli synns are awai, ne in heuen he mai noȝt   15
com or he be clensed.'

    þe domesman saide, 'For he synned in sight on þre maners, þere-
fore he sall þus be punished. First, he sall se his sinnes, þan þe fend in
his horribill likenes, and wreched paynes of oþir saules. Also, he sall
þus be punished: first, in his hereinge. Firste, he sall here sorowyng, | 20
for he herd gladli his awen praysinge. He sall here scornyng of fendes,   f. 248ᵛᵇ
and he sall here shames and reproues. Also, he sall be punished in
felynge, for he sall be brint in one hote fire within and withoute. Also,
he sall suffir grete colde for his breninge coueitise, and he sall be in
fendes handes to he be als clene as golde, þe whilke is clensid in þe   25
fire.' And þan saide Criste, 'Eftir þat þi will was in þe werld, þereeftir
sall þi tyme be in purgatory, bot if it be shorted be mi grace and helpinge, for he þat wald be oute of þe werld, and desires of all his herte to
be with me, he sall be clensid in þe world, and com to heuen withouten paine eftir þis life. Also, he þat dredis paine and wald liue langer   30
to amend his lifynge, he sall haue light and esi paine in purgatory. Bot
he þat wald euir, to þe ende of þis world, liue, all if he do no dedeli sin,
ȝete for þat will he sall be ponished to þe dai of dome.'

    Bot þe modir of merci asked of hir son, 'What miȝt helpe to short
þat lange time?' And þe son answerd þat, 'Thre þinges. First it is to   35
restore againe þat þe | whilke he hase with wrange of oþir menes, to þe   f. 249ʳᵃ
lest ferthinge, as bi þe praiers of gude men or bi almus or aseþinge
againe of þe same gudes. þe second is plenteuouse almus dede, for it
slokens þe fire. þe þird is bi offeringe of mi bodi on þe auter.' And þan

5 I] *om.*   7 þe¹] þi   23 felynge] fellynge, *first* l *subpuncted*

said þe modir, 'Son, þe gude dedis þat he dide sall nowe ese him. And
þarefor I pray þe þat for þat he did to me þat he mai be esid. He fastid
þe euynes of my festis in wirshipe of me. He saide office of my matins
and oures, and he helped to sing my seruise. And þarfor I prai þe þat
5 one of þe painnes of his sight, þat is, þat he se no horribill fendes, be
forgifen him; also, þat þe felinge of þe heui colde be forgyfen hym.'
þan saide þe son, 'Modir, þi will be done.'

And þan come furth one of þe saintes and saide, 'Lorde, þis saule
serued me deuoteli in his liue. He fastid in wirshipe of me and did me
10 and oþir saintes mekill wirshipe. And þarefore I pray þe þat þou
refreshe him in one paine, and þat is, þat fendes haue no powere to
blind his consciens, to make him to wene þat he sall neuir be deliuerde
f. 249ʳᵇ ne come to blis. And þis were a grete | paine to him. And þerfore, at our
praier, graunt him þis grace, þat what pine euir he suffir, it sall
15 haue ende.' þan saide þe domesman, 'þis is verray rightwisnes, for he
somtime withdrew his consciens fro gosteli knawyng in his life.
Neuirþelesse, at ȝour praiere it sall be done.' þan saide his gude
aungell to þe domesman, 'Sometime þis saule did my will, and þerfore
I prai þe haue merci one him.' þe domesman saide, 'We will take
20 awisment of þis.' And þan þis vision vanished away.

Capitulum xl. Foure ȝere eftir þis biforetolde vision, þe
spouse sawe þe same saule presentid to dome þat befor
was demid to purgatory to þe dai of dome, and how
God deliuerd alltogedir it fro þe grete horribill paines.

25   þe spouse saide, 'In þe fourte ȝere eftir þis, apperid befor þe jugge a
faire ȝonge man with þis saule halfe clede, and þat ȝonge man, with
oþir, saide vnto þe domesman, "Lord, þis is þe saule þat we praied þe
fore." þan saide þe domesman, "If þare were a chaer full of corn eres,
f. 249ᵛᵃ and þere were many men, and ilkeone toke one | ere, þe fulle chare
30 suld be lessed. Right so, mony teris and werkes of charite hase comen
byfor me for þis saule. þerfore þou, þat was his aungell, take and lede
him now to þe kyngdom where euir is ioy and neuir sorowe." ' And
þan it was shewed to þe spouse in likenes of a bright stern wendynge
vp into heuen. 'þarefore se what gude praier dose, for þis saule suld
35 haue bene in purgatori to þe day of dome, had noȝt gode praier bene,
and it was deliuerd þrowe gud praier within foure ȝere. "Bot", þe
domesman saide, "þat time sall com in þe whilke I sall make rightfull

6 him] him þan saide þe son, *exc.* him, *cancelled*   14 pine] pyine

jugement againe þe kynrede of þis dede man, for þe generacion of it gose vpward with pride, and to þe rewarde ordeinde for pride it sall go donwarde." '

Capitulum xli.

Criste saide of a kyng of Sweci vnto þe spouse þat he was bot a child, as it was wele shewed by his gouernance and his grete oste: 'For victori standes in þe vertu of God and noȝt | in mannes miȝt ne wit. þat was shewed in Dauid, þat was a childe and slew þe geaunt so strange and so wise in bataile. þe skill þat I saide þe þat he is a childe is þis. A childe, when he sees two appils, and one be faire withoute bot [þe opir] more freshe within, he cheses þe faire withoute and leues þe bettir. So þe kinge loues a grete oste, bot he takes neuir hede of þe grete coste, and what mischeue þai sall be in, or þai com againe, for hungur. Bot wald he take a litill oste and traiste vpon me, and do with gude auisement of reson, he sall spede wele.'

Capitulum xlii. þe modir of God is glad of hirselfe þat sho loues God to þat ende þat God be loued and wirshipid, and sho desires to þe spouse heuenli cloþing of vertuse.

The modir saide to þe spouse, 'I tell, noȝt for miselfe bot for þe wirshipe of my son, þat I was besi to plese him.' þan saide þe modir to hir son, 'Son, I pray þe geue þi spouse hir mete and preciouse cleþinge, for sho is doghtir and spouse to þe, þe whilke is kinge of kinges. þerfor geue hir þe cloþinge of vertu. Also, geue hir þe moste | likyng mete, by þe whilke I mene þine awn bodi, þat was figured by þe paschalle lambe, and þe whilke is streng[þ]e againe all seknes. þe þird, geue hir a more feruent spirit of þe holi goste, þe whilke is fire þat will noȝt be slokende.' þan saide þe son, 'Hir moste do thre þinges or sho haue þese þre biforsaide. Firste, hir moste haue mekenes, and wit wele þat it commes noȝt of hirselfe. þe secounde, hir moste haue þankeynge to me þat geues hir þaime. þe þirde is drede þat sho losse noȝt þe grace þat I haue geuin hir.'

5
f. 249ᵛᵇ
10
15
20
f. 250ʳᵃ
26
30

---

4 xli] xli. þe modir of god is glad þat sho loues god to ende þat god be loued and sho desires to þe spouse heuenli cleþing of vertuse, *antic. ch. title to VI. 42 (see below)*   10-11 þe opir] *om.*   15 reson] reson and   26 and] againe and, againe *ruled through*   strengþe] strengie

Capitulum xliii. þe spouse was dissesid, for sho made
noȝt glad obediens vnto spirituall fadir, to whome
Criste saide þat, and sho had perfite purpose to obeye,
all if þe will some[time] were contrarious, ȝet sho suld
5   haue mede.

þe son saide to þe spouse, 'Whi art þou heui?' Sho saide, 'For two
þinges. First, for I ame noȝt so buxum as I suld be to mi spirituall
fadir, ne sa glade in disese; þe second, for I se tribulacion fall to þi
frendes, and þine enemis are þaire maistirs.' þan saide Criste, 'I ame
f. 250ʳᵇ in him þat | þou art bunden to obey to, and ilke time and oure þat þou
11   liues þine awen will, it sall be to þe clensinge of sin and encressinge of
mede. And, as for þe seconde, I answere bi ensampill. If two men fight
togidir, and one caste his armoure fro him, he mai lightli be ouir-
commen of him þat kepis his armoure still. Bot mine enemis euirilke
15   dai castes fro þame þaire armoure. For þre maner of armoure are
nedefull to bataile. þe firste is þat sall bere a man, as his hors. þe
seconde is þat þe whilke sall defende him, as his swerd. þe þirde is þat
at kepis þe bodi, as ane hawbirgeon. Bot mine enemis hase loste þe
hors of obediens, þat suld bere þame to all gude. þai haue caste awai
20   þe swerde of drede of God, þat suld kepe þe bodi fro luste and þe
fende fro þe saule, and þai haue caste fro þame charite, þe whilke is
riste in all fandinge and softenes in dissese, as þe haubirgeon is keping
of þe bodi. Bot mi frendes haldes þame vpe on þe hors of obediens, for
þai are redi at mi wille, þai drede me, þai suffir gladeli all disese for mi
f. 250ᵛᵃ lufe, þai | strengþe þameselfe with wit and paciens, and þai are stronge
26   in gude wirkinges. And so mi frendes are armed agains my enemis for
þaire mede.'

Capitulum xliiii. Criste likens himselfe to a maker of a
glas vessell, þe whilke cesis noght to make newe
30   wessell, all if þe olde be broken. And he likens him also
to a bee.

Criste saide, 'I ame like to a glassier þe whilke makes mani vessells
of askes, and all if he breke mani, ȝete he makes furth till he haue his
[nowmbir]. Right so I make man of a foule mater and, if mani breke fro
35   me bi euell lifinge, ȝete I sese noȝt to þe time þat þe places fro þe
whilke aungells fell be fulfilled.

1 sho] som sho   4 sometime] sonne   34 nowmbir] *om.*, *Lat.* numerus

'Also I ame like to a bee, þat wendis oute fro þe hiue to a faire floure
in sight to loke on, bot when he commes nere he findes it drie, and þe
sauour of it chaunged. Bot þan he sekis to oneoþir þat is somwhat
sharpe and esi of smelle, and þare he festenes his fete, and takes þe
swetenes of it and beris to þe hiue. This man ame I, þe whilke come   5
oute of þe hiue of heuen when I toke mankinde. I chese to me a | faire   f. 250ᵛᵇ
floure, þat was þe kinde of cristen, þe whilke hase a faire name, bot þer
lifyng is noȝt accordinge þareto, for þai are drie, baran and bittir to
me. And þarefore þai sall fall. And I haue chosen a oþir erbe, þe
whilke is somwhat sharpe, þat are þe panems. Some of þame hase   10
gude will to turn þame to me, and þai wiste howe. Bot I sall sende
þame helpe, and þai sall leue þaire bittirnes and, of loue, wax swete to
me, and I sall bring þame to mi hiue, þat is, to þe blis withouten ende.'

> Capitulum xlv. Criste telles his modir þat men þe
> whilke are gosteli blinde may, on þre wise, recouir   15
> þaire sight and se God, and he telles certaine erroure
> of men.

The modir of merci saide, 'In þre þinges haue I compassion of man:
firste, þat he hase een and sees noȝt his awen blis þat is endeles; þe
second, þat he hase so grete loue to þe world, þe whilke sall laste bot   20
short while, and forgettis þe merci þat is so mekill. Also, I haue compassion þat þou, Criste, mi son, is so greteli forgetin, and all þat þou
hase done for | man.'   f. 251ʳᵃ
þe son answerde and saide, 'All men þat hase consciens mai see þat
in þe world I ponishe sinfull men, and if I suffir bodeli defautes be   25
ponished bodeli, mekill more þe saule, þat neuir sall haue ende, sall
be ponished endelesli. Bot þai will noȝt se þis þat hase þaire een
turned to þe likinge of þe world. Bot right as þe owle makes mirthe on
þe night, riȝt so take þai hede to þat þe whilke is noȝt lastinge, and
leues þat þe whilke will neuir faile. Also, man mai take hede if he will   30
þat sethen þe planetes, trees and erbes are faire and likand, þat he is
more faire and likand þat made þame, and he is mor worthi to be
loued. Bot men demes all amis; for he takes noȝt hede how God made
him vpright to gosteli þinges, and he bowed himselfe done to þe erth.
And þare sittis his þoght, and ȝete sall þat sone faile. Also þai mai take   35
hede, if þai will, both for cours of planetes and oþir þinges, þat God
set and ordainde all þinges in ordir, and þai kepe þair ordir bot man
oneli, for he hase sperde his eyn of reson þat he suld ken God with.

f. 251rb And þat he shewes | wele when he þinkes þat þe sternes makes a man
gud or euell, and arettes welth of prosperite, and disese of aduersite,
all to fortune as it were euen with God.'

þan saide þe modir to þe spouse, 'Here is a place of religious
5 persones set vpon ise, þe whilke somtime was set vpon clene gold. And
vndir it is a gude grete pite. And when þe son byginnes to wax warme,
þe ise will relent, and þe place sall fall into þe pite. And þarefore, gude
sone, haue merci on þame. And sen alloneli þat þou art God, and all
þat is is purueide by þi gudeli stabbilnes, ne a man is nowþir gude ne
10 euill throw destany, fortune or w[i]rkinge of þe heuenli bodis, bot
throw þi grace and þaire awen fredome, I pray þe þat þi rightwisnes
mai be knawen, so þat þi drede be encressid in men, and also þi merci
be opinli shewed by som of þi seruantes, for to encrese gladenes and
comforte of þe in þi deuote derlinges. Also I prai þat þi name be
15 wirshiped, þat dulle and slawe men mai be kindelled in þi lufe.' þe son
f. 251va answerde, 'When [m]i leue ladi praies, hir moste | be herde. þarefor,
be it as þou wille.'

Capitulum xlvi. þe spouse praied oure ladi to gete hir
þe perfite loue of God, and sho telles how it mai be
20   getin, declaringe certaine wordes of þe gospell.

þe spouse saide to þe modir þat sho desired to loue hir son and to
leue all oþir lufe. þan saide þe modir, 'þou moste þan hald in þi
minde sex wordes þat are saide in þe gospell. þe first is, "Go, sell þat
þou hase and giue it to pore men, and folowe me." þat is to mene þus—
25 he sellis all þat kepis ne coueites not more þan is nedefull to one bodi,
and all þat he haues more, he gifes it þe pore for Goddes lufe. And if
he be in a state þat hase nede of monye, kepe oneli so mekill as is
nedefull to him and to his meine. For þus did Sant Gregore and mani
a gude kinge, þat were as pore in þer herte as þai þat leued at ones all
30 þat þai had, and wente on begginge, for þai occupied þaire possessions to þe plesance of God, and were in will continuli to haue left
þame if it had bene plesinge to God.

f. 251vb 'þe seconde word is, "Be noȝt thoght|full ne besi for tomorn." þat
menes, serue God and traiste þat he, þe whilke fedis and clethis
35 birdes, wille fede and clethe þe, whome he boght with his blode. And
if þou hafe none oþir, aske for þe lufe of God þat þe whilke is nedefull
to þi fedinge and cleþinge, ne leue not þi lerninge ne prayinge to take

10 wirkinge] wrkinge   16 mi] I   praies] praiers

oþir bodeli trauals for þi leueing. þe þird word is, "Thake hede howe þe sparrows are fede, for mekill more sall þe fadir of heuen fede his seruantes." þe ferde worde is, "Gife swilke þinge to God þat langes to him, and swilke þing to þe worldeli kinge as falles to him." þe fifte worde is, "Firste amange all þinge, be besi for þe kingedome of God." 5 þe sext is, "All ȝe þat are hungre cum to me, and I sall fede ȝou." '

Capitulum xlvii. þe modir techis þe spouse not to be irke of wordes of God to sai to þame þat will noȝt here.

þe modir saide to þe spouse þat sho suld noght lett to sai Goddes wordes to þame þat hade no gret will to here þame. 'For shame and 10 paciens þat one hase for þe loue of God coloures wele þe saule, and þe suffryng of euell wordes clothes þe saule | right as it were in faire f. 252ʳᵃ cleþinge. And he þat trauailes his bodi, for þe loue of God, in techinge of oþir gettis grete swetenes to his saule. þe frendes of Gode suld do right as a man þat sees his broþir ligge vndir one hill þat is in point to 15 fall. He will caste at þame smale stones, and hit þame softli, to make þame to be ware, þat þe hille fall noȝt vpon þam. Right so Goddes frendes suld smite þame þat ligges in syn with gude wordes, and make þame to rise fro sin, þat þai be noȝt loste. For right as, when mi son stied into heuen, þere were few þat trowed it, and þarefor he sente his 20 apostils to preche it, so are þare nowe fewe þat kepis þat command- ment of þe loue of God and of þi neghbore. And þarefore it is nede to sende prechours amange cristen men to teche þam to loue God abouen all oþir and þi neghbour as þaimselfe. And þerfor, mi frendes go þai now to preche þe cristen as þai went first to preche þe hethen. 25 For, as it were somtime impossibill to hem at com to heuen þe whilke herd þe right faithe and kept it noȝt, so it is impossibill to þe cristen for to haue heuen if þai | die withouten Goddes lufe and charite.' f. 252ʳᵇ

Capitulum xlviii. Criste likenes himselfe to a potecari þe whilke makes holesom drinke.   30

Criste likenes himselfe to a potecari, þe whilke makes holesom drinkes, 'and all commes to drinke, bot some likes it wele and some noght. Right so it is of gosteli drinke, þat is, þe grace of þe holi goste. To þame þat will leue sin it is right likinge and swete, and to þame þat will not leue it semis bittir and noȝt likinge. And ȝet, if a man wald 35

3 ferde] ferde is

drinke þereofe, it suld gife him mekill gosteli strengþe, and comforte
him againe temptacions. And miselfe ame þe apotecari þat ordeyns þis
drinke for mannes hele, and whoso will desire it with charite sall haue
enoghe of it.'

5   Capitulum xlix. Howe brekinge of faste somtime throw
       obediens is meritori.

The modir set þis ensampell, þat if þere were a man þe whilke wald
faste, and neuerþelesse he had desire to ete, and he wald withstande
his appetite, saueynge for þe biddinge of his soueraine, at whose
f. 252ᵛᵃ biddinge he awe him obediens, if he ete, þat etinge | were more mede-
11 full to him þan to abstene him and faste, and worthi more rewarde.
'Right so mi fadir and modir had þere comminge togiddir by
Goddes biddinge when I was conceyued, and þerfore it is suþfast and
trewe þat I was consaiued 'withouten originall syn', and riȝt as mi son
15 and I sinned neuer, so þere was no wedding more honeste þan þe
weddinge fro þe whilk I com and was broght furthe.'

       Capitulum l. þe modir telles þe spouse how noþinge
       plesis more Gode þan [he] be loued of man souerainli,
       and þat is shewed by ensampill.

20 þe moder saide to þe spouse þat 'Noþinge plesis God so mekill as
þat a man loue him aboue all oþir þinges, by ensampill of a woman þat
was a panim, þe whilke þoght in hirselfe on þis maner: "I wote of
whate mater þat I ame, and I wote wele þat I had neuir mi bodi ne my
wittes of myselfe, for I se oþir vnresonabill bestis by me, and of miselfe
25 was I noȝt made in swilke a bodi as I hafe, no more þan þai are. And
þerefor I ken wele þat þere is some oþir þat made both þame and me.
f. 252ᵛᵇ Bot sen he made me in so faire a shape, | and I wiste what he were, had
I neuer so many husbandes, I wald leue þame all and go to him. And if
I hade brede in mine hande, and all mi childir cried for bred, and he
30 hungird, I suld giue him brede befor þame all. Also, I haue possessions, and if I wiste þat it were plesinge to him, I wald leue þame all."
'And þan sent God, of his gudenes, one of his frendes to enforme hir
and set his godenes and grace in hir hert, þat when þe frende taght hir

5 xlix] xlvix   13 conceyued] conceyued withoute orriginall sin, *exc.* conceyued,
subpuncted   14 consaiued] consaiued neuer, neuer *subpuncted*   18 he] *om.*
29 for] fro   32 gudenes] gudenes and grace in herte, *exc.* gudenes, *ruled through*

þat þare was bot one God, maker of all þinge, þe whilke is and was withouten ende, sho saide þat sho trowed it right wele. And þan he taght hir howe þe same Gode toke mankinde of a maiden and þat he prechid to þe pupill. þan praied sho to teche hir what þo wordes were, "For I will leue myne awen will to fulfill þame." þan he tald hir of his 5 passion and þe crosse and his vprisinge, and þan sho saide with teres, "Blissed be þat gude God. And if I loued him bifore, for he made me, I ame now more bonden to loue him, for he boght me with his blode. And with all þe partes of mi bodi I will | serue him, for he suffird in all   f. 253ʳᵃ his partes for me, and all mi hert I will sett on him." '   10

þan saide þe modir to þe spouse, 'Doghtir, loke whate rewarde þis woman gate for hir maner of louinge, and þarefore loue þu wele God.'

Capitulum li. How a man sall answere to thre enemis of
þe saule.

Criste saide to the spouse, 'þat man whome þou knawes hase þre 15 enemis. One is nere to him wheþir he slepe or he wake, and he sees noȝt him. þe second is homeli to him, bot he hatis him. þe þirde is noȝt hameli to him. þe firste is þe fende, þat temptes of pride and oþir sinnes. And agains him þou moste haue þis scourge: "O þou fende, þou gaue me neuir gude. Whi suld I bow to þi will? Criste calles me to 20 liue, and þou art besi to lose mi liue. þarefor I will fle þe and folow him." And he þat, waking ouþir slepyng, answers þe fende þus, he sall chase him awai fro him. þe second enemy are a mans worldli frendes, þe whilke sais to him, "þou mai noȝt liue so straite. þe moste for þi awen profite lat mani þinges passe | ouir. Also, if þou be to meke and   f. 253ʳᵇ lawli, men sall despice þe. Gete þe riches and make us riche, and take 26 wirshipe vpon þe, and þat sall be oure comforte." Againe þis enemy sall þou make a þike walle, þat þou here him noȝt. þe walle sall be a gude will, so þat þe had leuir be pore with trewthe and rightwisnes þan haue all þe riches of þe worlde with wronge, and leuir suffir 30 reproue in mekenes þan any wirshipe with pride. And þerfor sai vnto þis enemy, "I prai þe þat if þou se me do aniþinge þat is greuing to God, warne me þereof, and þan þou arte mi frende." þe þirde enemi are þai þat rekkes neuir what shame ne harme þat þai haue, so þat þai mai come to welth and worldeli wirshipes. Againe þis enemy, haue a 35 stronge corde, þat is, charite to suffir what God will sende, and

16 slepe] shlepe, h *subpuncted*   18 him] him bot he hatis him, *rep.* l. 17
22 þus] þus slepinge, slepinge *ruled through*   29 with] *twice*

þane all þe harme þat þi enemis walde do þe sall turne to wirshipe.
And þus þou mai haue helpe againe þine enemis.'

Capitulum lii. A wondur siȝt of þe spouse, of þre
wemen in heuen, purgatori and in helle.

f. 253ᵛᵃ   þe spouse saide to Criste, 'O, my sweteste God, it is | a wondir þinge
6   þat þou dose with me, for, when þe likes, þou slombirs mi bodi, and
liftes vp my saule to se and here and fele gosteli þinges. þi wordes are
wondir soft to my saule, and more likeinge þan any mete. þai entir into
mi saule, and so I ame, of þi wordes, both filled and hungre. I ame
10   filled, for me likes noȝt bot þame, and I ame hungre, for I desire so
holeli to here þame. And þarefore, lorde, helpe me to do þi will.' þan
saide Criste, 'I do as a kinge þat sendis wine to his seruandes, and
biddis þaim drinke of it, for it is holesome and will hele sekenes, and
make heuy men glade, and strengþe hole men. And þe vessell þat it is
15   sent in is clene. Right so I sende mi wordes bi þe, whilke is a vessell
accordinge, and þerefore speke þame boldeli where and when mi
spirit biddis þe.' þan saide þe spouse, 'Lorde, I ame a sinfull creature
and vnwise to swilke werkes.' Criste answerde, 'Who sulde haue
meruaile if a lorde toke of his money or metall, and of some made a
20   crowne, of som cuppis, of som ringes to his awen vse? Right so it is no
wondir if I do mi wi[ll] with mi seruantes, and vse þame to mi
f. 253ᵛᵇ   wirshipe, not|withstandinge þe kindeli vndirstandinge þe whilke is
gretter in one þan in oneoþir. And þerfor be þou redi at mi will.'
þan saide þe modir, 'þe proude wemen of þe kingdome of Swene,
25   þat sais, "Our progenitours left vs grete possessions and faire maners.
Whi suld we lawe vs to any simplere? And oure modirs were grete of
arai and in grete wirshipe. Whi suld we noȝt folow þame and teche
oure childir to do þe same?"–þere wemmen takes no hede howe þat
mi son, þe whilke was lorde of all, was so meke and so simpill in
30   cloþinge. þai loke noȝt on his visage, howe blodi it was when he hange
on þe crosse, and howe he was pute to þe dede amange thefis. þo
proude wimmen are like to one þinge full of hote fire þat birnes all þat
it hittes on. So þese wemen pride, by euell ensampill, brennes þam þat
shewes it. I am like a modir þat shewis þe ȝerde to þe childe and to hir
35   seruantes. þe childir are ferde for greuing of þe modir, and þe
seruantes are ferde for betting. And þus þai bothe dose gode and flies
f. 254ᵗᵃ   euell and harme. | So I, þe modir of merci, wille shewe vnto þe, and to

5 it is] *twice*   21 will] witt, *Lat.* voluntatem   26 were] *twice*

oþir, þe rewarde of sin, þat þe gude liuer loue God þe more hertli, and þe euill, 'for' drede of paine, fle sinne, and þus I shewe merci bothe to þe gude and to þe euell.'

þan were þere sene thre wemen, a modir and hir doghtir and hir nece. þe modir and þe nece were dede, bot þe doghtir semid on liue. It semid þat þe modir rose vp of one depe 'dirke' pitt. Hir hert was drawen oute. Hir lippis were cutt awai. Hir chin tremeled; hir tethe chattird. Hir nesethirles were etin; hir eene hinge bi two stringes doune on hir chekes. Hir forhed was dimpled in and þere was a mirke hole, and in þe shede of hir braine was wellinge lede and pikke. Hir neke was wreþin all aboute; hir breste was opyn and full of wormes. Hir armes were croked and hir handes were knottid as nailes. Hir rigg bone was broken ilke juncture fro oþir, and a lange neddir was cropin into hir stomoke and ete it continuli. Hir theis and hir leggis were full of thornes, and hir fete were like to a tode fete.

And sho saide to hir doghtir þat liued, 'Here, þou uenomous doghtir. Wo is me þat euir I was þi modir! For I put þe | in þe nest of pride, in þe whilke þou wex warme till þou com till age, and þou hase wastid þi time. As ofte times as þou turnes þine eyn with pride fro þat I teched þe, as ofte is wellinge venom caste in myne eyn. As ofte as þou spekis proudeli þat þou lerned of me, so ofte I swalowe þe bittirest drinke þat may be made. And as ofte as þou heris, with likinge, praisinge of þi bewete and shape, and how þou mai com to wirshipe of þe worlde, as þou lerned of me, as ofte þer commes a birnand winde throw both my eres, þat wo is me, pore and wrechid: pore, for I haue no gude; wrechid, for I ame full of all euill. As ofte as þou folows my sinnes at mi techinge, so ofte haue I a newe paine.

'A, doghtir, whi art þou proude of þi kinne? Was no3t þe filth of mi bowells þi pelowe? þe vnclennes of mi blode was þe cloþinge when þou was born. Se howe þat my wombe, þat þou lai in, is etin with wormes! Bot whi pleine I on þe? I haue more mater to pleine of miselfe. Bot þre þinges tormentes me euir in my þoght. þe firste is þat God made me to þe blis þat is endeles, and I ordeynde my|selfe to euirlastinge paine. þe seconde is þat he made me faire as one aungell, and I haue made miselfe like to þe fende. þe þirde is þat in my time I made one euell chaunge, chesinge for a shorte likinge in sin to fele now euirlastinge paine in hell.'

And þan sho saide to þe spouse, 'þou sees no3t of my paine bot in bodeli likenes. Bot and þou sawe it and me in þe likenes þat I am in,

f. 254rb

f. 254va

2 for] fro

þou suld die for drede. For all my limmes are fendes, and þe scripture
is trewe þat sais right as gude men are þe limmes of God, so are sinfull
men þe limmes of þe fende. Bot þat þou sees my fete like to þe tode
fete is for I stode still, to myne endinge, in sin. Mi legges and mi thees
5 are full of thornes, for all mi will was sett vnto luste. þe bones of mi
rigge bone are all oute of juncture, for mi wille was noȝt festined to þe
wille of God. þe neddir þat entirde mi stomoke was for my luste was
grete and mi wille was noȝt discretli tempird nor ordainde. þarefor I
[am] now full sore betin. þat mi breste is opin and gnawine with
f. 254ᵛᵇ wormes is for I lufed þe werld and likinge | of mi fleshe more þan
11 Gode. Mi armes ar, as a knife heft is, croked, for I desired longe liue in
sin, and in mi werkes I drede noȝt þe dome of God.
    'Mi handes are as nailes, for I did noȝt mi besines to kepe þe com-
mandmentes of God. Mi neke is wreþin aboute, for I hade no likinge
15 to folowe þe wordes of God, bot all of vanite and sinne. Mi lippes are
cutt, for þai were full slaw to Goddes seruise and redi to speke of filth
and sin. Mi chin tremils and mi tethe chattirs, for all þat I did to mi
bodi was for to forþir mi bewte. Mi nesethirles are rotin away, for I had
grete likinge to be in company, and now ame I putt to shame. And
20 mine een hanges vpon my chekes for pride þat I hade in þame of
fairnes, and þerfor mi forhede is a pite of dirkenes. Ine mi braine is, as
it were, wellinge lede and pike, for my consciens was all turned t[o]
luste, and I had no minde of Cristes passion, with þe whilke man was
broght fro paine, and mi herte was ay heuy to gudenes. Also mine eres
25 are stoppid with stones, for I had no will to here gude werkes bot euell,
f. 255ʳᵃ and if | I did any gude dedis, þat was for drede of þe paine of helle, and
for speche of þe world, and noght for þe loue of God.'
    þan saide hir nece þat was doghtir to hir doghtir (sho spake to hir
modir þat was oliue), 'þou scorpion mi modir, þow taght me þre
30 þinges with þi mouthe. þe firste was for to life flesheli. þe second was
to spend largeli mi gudes to þe wirshipe of þe world. þe þirde was to
take mi bodeli riste. And now for þe firste I haue loste gosteli likinge;
for þe second, I ame now shent and shamed; and for þe þirde, I am
now turbild and all oute of reste. Also, of þi dedis I lerid thre þinges:
35 firste, to do some gude dede, bot noȝt to leue mi sin, and þerefor, mi
drinke is now as it were hony mengid with venom, þe whilke shendes
me. þe second was to cleth me proudeli to þe bewte of mi bodi, and

9 am] *om.*   11 Gode] gode as   22 to] tu   25 are] was are
26 if] *Quire catchphrase*, I did any, *below*   28 sho] ssho   29 mi] *twice, first sub-*
puncted

þerefore I ame now cled and couerd þat I mai noȝt see þe fairenes of
heuen. þe þird, I lernid to fulfill all mine awen will, and leue þat at was
plesing vnto God, and þerfore I am left of þame þat loued God, and
put to fendes.

'Also, I lerned of þe oþir þre | þinges. þe firste was of pride, þat I   f. 255ʳᵇ
wende neuir suld haue had enede. Bot I finde nowe þat þe ende of   6
pride is wo and sorowe. þe seconde was vnbuxumnes to Goddes commandmentes. And þarefore bose me nowe be bowand to pains and
tormentes. þe þird was þat I wende to haue hade longe liue, and so
continude mi sin and at þe laste had repentance. Bot dede com on me   10
sodandli, and vnnethis had I any time to clens me. And þarefor I ame
now punishet greuoseli. þerefor, modir, wo is me, for all þat I lerid of
þe with likinge, I bie it now full sore with harde ponishinge.'

þan saide þis damisell þat was dede to þe spouse, 'It semes to þe
þat mi hede are, as it were, a blaste of thondir within and withoute; my   15
neke and mi breste pressed amange sharpe prikkes; mi armes and mi
fete as þai were longe neddirs; mi thees and mi leggis rennand as a
watir of a beke frosin at þe fete. And ȝete is þare a bittir paine. For if
þare were a persone, and all þe wais within were spered and stoken to
þe hert, and þe hert bigan to bolne with wind, he | wald fare as he wald   f. 255ᵛᵃ
tobriste, right so I ame euirmore in poynt to briste for þe winde of   21
pride þat I bare in my herte.

'Bot neuirþelesse I ame in þe wai of merci, for in my sekenes I
shraue me as wele as I couthe, and þere come to mi minde þe passion
of Criste, and how þat I miȝt mak asethe for all þat I hade done. þan   25
fell I into teres, and with þe eyne of mi consciens I beheld þe gudenes
of God, and I saide þus: "Lorde, verray Goddes son, born of maiden
Mari, haue merci on me. And trewli, if I might liue, I þinke to amend
mi leuinge." And þan I gat one sparke of þe fire of charite. And now
ame I lefte in þe fendis handes to be clensed or I mai come to þe clene   30
aungels.' þan saide sho, 'I mai soner be deliuerd of paine bi gode
praiere, for right as, if þare were one balauns, and in þe one scale were
lede þat is heuy, and þe oþir empti, þe more þat were pute in þe empti
scale, þe soner it suld raise vp þat heui scale, right so þe deper þat one
falles in sin, þe more greuoseli he is ponished. And þarefore þe more   35
praiere and þe more gude þat is done for þat peresone, and þe more
almose dede | of gude þat is wele getin, þe sonner it sall be deliue[r]d;   f. 255ᵛᵇ
and þat makes me to com euerilke dai nerer and nerer to God.'

7 vnbuxumnes] vmbuxumnes   19 stoken] stokend   35 he] *twice*
37 deliuerd] deliued

Capitulum liii. Criste reproues prelates þat are proude
of þaire prelaci, and telles how þai suld bere þame.

Criste saide to þe spouse, 'I, God and man, gafe ensampill to oþir
how þai suld do when þai were prelates. For all if I hade no defaute in
5 miselfe, ȝete I suffird paine on þe crosse, and I com to serue and noȝt
to be serued. So suld a prelate be meke. And ȝete he mai lerne of his
awen defautes to haue compassion of oþir mens defautes. And loke þat
he gife none ensampill of euell to his soiettes, for þare is na þinge þat
so mikill greues God as defaute of prelates. For if Heli þe prest had
10 chastised his sonnes and standyn stifli in himselfe in Goddes seruise,
as Moises and Phinees did, his kinde [and] he had bene saufe. Bot for
he did noȝt so, bot wald plese flesheli his sonnes, þarefor he left his
minde in tribulacion, and to þame þat come eftir him in confusion.'

Capitulum liiii. Criste telles þe spouse whatkin a
wildirnes | þis world was bifore his comminge, and of
seuen wais þat led vnto þe pite of þe worlde, and how
he, fro he was man, shewed þe wais to heuen, and he
commendes wordes of þis boke.

Criste saide, 'Befor mine incarnacioune, þis werlde was a wildirnes,
20 and in it was one stange full of foule drouy watir. And all þat dranke
þerof thrested sore, and it made þaire eyn blerid. Beside þis stange
stode two men. One cried, "Drinke hardeli, for it is bot foli for to
coueite greteli þat þing þe whilke is noȝt certaine." And þere were
seuen wais to þe stange. In þis world men are as in wildirnes, þat leues
25 reson and liues as bestis, for þai will gladli shede blode. þai are as
baraine as trees in wildirnes: so are þai withoute froite of rightwisnes.
In þe whilke worlde was a foule stanke, þat was pride, couetise and
oþir sinnes. þe vii wais are þe seuen dedeli sinnes. þe one mane þat
cried bitokens þe docturs of þe Jewes lawe, þe whilke were coueitouse,
30 bot þai cried þat merci suld com. þe second man was þe doctoures of
þe paynems, þe whilke criede, "Take ȝour | luste whils ȝe liue here."
'þane come I and toke mankinde, and preched opinli þat þa þinges
were fulfilled þat God hade hight and Moises hade wretin: "Com to
me and I sall geue ȝou heuenli þinges þat will euir laste. And loke ȝe
35 com bi seuen waies þat I shewed." þe firste, þat was pouerte; þe
second, obediens. þe þirde was fastinge, þe fourte was prainge, þe

    1 þat] twice, first subpuncted   11 and²] om.

fifte was suffiringe of reproues and diseses. þe sext was trauaile and sorowe, and þe seuent was painefull and shamefull dede. I shewed bi myne awen self þees waies, and mi frendes went longe time in þame. Bot nowe þese waies are lefte. þe kepers slepis. And þerefor I sal rise and sai to mi frendes swettir wordes þan þe dactill, softir þan hony, 5 more preciouse þan golde, and þai sall haue, for þe kepinge of þame, tresore þat sall laste withouten ende.'

Capitulum lv. þe modir sais þat i[t] miȝt wele be called þe golden oure in þe whilke sho was conceyued: in þe whilke conceyuinge Goddes charite wroght more þan 10 luste of fleshe, and obediens more þan þaire awen desire þat was fadir and modir. |

þe modir saide, 'When mi fadir and mi modir com togidir in matri- f. 256ᵛᵃ moyne, þai ware more stirred by þe will of God þan by þair awen wille. þe oure þat I was conceiued in is þe golden oure, for þan was bigin- 15 ninge of hele, and derkenes was turned into light. Bot mi con- ceiueynge was knawen vnto fewe, for right as þe lawe `of´ kinde went befor þe lawe wretin, and in it was wilfulle chesinge of gode and euele, and eftirwarde, in þe lawe wretin, were mani þinges forbedin, right so God suffird his frendes doute of mi concepcion, to him liked at shewe 20 it opinli. For it was wondirfull as þe ȝerd þat florished withoutine moistur.'

Capitulum lvi. þe modir telles bi what hir birth is bi- tokende, and how it was biginninge of hele, and sho pleynes of certain wommen. 25

þe modir saide, 'When mi modir bare me I passed furthe by þe comon place, for it was noȝt accordinge þat any suld be born oþirwise bot mi son, makere of kinde, þat wase born as him leste. When I | was f. 256ᵛᵇ born, þe feendes þoght þat I suld do þame mekill harme, for I was so wele strenthed with grace þat þare was noȝt in me als mekill a place as 30 þe poynte of a nedill in þe whilke sin miȝt reste. And þarefore þai mad mekill sorow. Bot Goddes frendes, þat lange time had abidin, saide, "Make we mirth, for þe light is born throw þe whilk þe derkenes of vs sall be lightened and oure desire be performed." þe aungels saide with

8 it] I   9 in²] *twice*   27 suld] suld passe, passe *ruled through*
30 mekill] mekill as

grete ioy, "Sho is born in erth bi whome oure felaws places sall be restored." ' þane saide þe modir to þe spouse, 'I was þe ȝerde of whome sprange þe floure þat kinges and prophetes desired. And when I wex of elde, þat I couthe ken mi maker, I had a grete lufe to him, and

5 he kepid me with his grace þat I assentid not to sin, for þe lufe of God, and besi techinge of mi fadir and modir, and honeste conuersacion, were with me. Bot I pleine on þe woman þat takes no heede of mi birth, bot leuis alltogidir eftir þair fleshe þat sall faile. And þarefore þe spirit of clennes wendis fro þaime.' |

Capitulum lvii. þe modir tolde þe spouse þat hir nedid
11 noȝt to haue bene purified bot for sho wald life in lawe
eftir lawe.

þe modir saide to þe spouse, 'Me neded noght to haue bene purified as oþir wemmen. Bot mi son wald þat lawe and prophecie suld be ful-
15 filled. Bot `at´ þe dai of mi purificacion mi sorowe was incressid of Symeon wordes, when he saide þe swerde of sorowe sall pers my hert, and mi sone sulde be sett in token to whome it suld be saide nai to, and þat sorowe went neuir oute of mi herte till þe time þat I was takin vp in bodi and saule, all if I were ofte times comforted bi þe holi goste. And fro
20 þis dai mi sorowe was sexfolde. First, as ofte as I held mi childes hede and fete and wappid him in his cloþis, and þoght on þe woundes þat he suld suffir in þame. þe second was als ofte as I herd þe lesinges and þe reproues þat mi son suffird. þe þird was when I sawe mi son bonden and scourged and hanged vpon þe crosse. þe ferth was when I handild mi
son or he was laide in þe grafe, for I þoght þat I walde haue bene | berid
26 with him. þe fift was for þe longe tareynge þat I had in erthe, for þe grete desire I had to be with him, eftir þat he was stied vp to heuen. þe sext was of þe sorowe þat I sawe vpon þe apostils and of oþir of mi sonnes frendes. Bot ȝete, in all þese, I hade þe grace of Gode within me, and mi
30 will was ai eftir Godis will, and so was mi sorowe and mi comfort mengid togidir vnto þe time of mine assumpcion.'

Capitulum lviii. þe modir shewes howe þat it was noȝt
`one´ of hir leste sorowes þat sho flede with hir son into
Egipt, and herd how Herode persewed innocentes for
35 his sake.

11 wald] *twice*

þe modir saide to þe spouse, 'I haue tolde þe of mi sorowes, bot зet
it was noзt þe leste sorowe when I fled with my sone into Egipte, and
herd of þe slaynge of þe innocente childir, and how Herode pursued
mi son. Bot þou mai aske what mi son did all þe time till he com to his
prechinge and passion. I answere, as þe gospell sais, þat he was vndir 5
gouernans of his fadir and modir. And зet he did mirakles in his
зouthe, for kinges soght | him, and at his cominge to Egipte þe ydoles f. 257ᵛᵃ
and fals goddes fell doune to noght. Aungells shewed þame to him and
serued him. þere was neuir filth on him, ne his here lai neuir wrannge.
And when he wex of more age, he went with vs on þe feste dais into þe 10
tempill of Ierusalem, and eftirwarde, when he was of more age, he
trauailed with his handes onest werkes þat were accordinge, and he
talde vs mani comfortabill wordes, so þat we were full of likinge of his
wordes. We were in pouert and disese, and he gafe vs no gold bot ai
stird vs to paciens. And þat was nedfull to vs, somtime we had of oure 15
trauaile; sometime we abode with paciens. Also, sometime he
comonde with wise men of þe laue, and dispotid with þame openli, þat
þai hade grete wondir of his coninge. It fell in a time þat I þoght of his
passion and was right heuy. And þan he saide to me, "Modir, trowes
þou noght þat I ame with mi fadir and mi fadir with me? It is mi fadirs 20
will, and mi will, þat I sall suffir dede to bringe mankind to blis." And
oft times we sawe a wondirfull light a|boute him, and Joseph and I herd f. 257ᵛᵇ
aungels singe with him. And euell spirites miзt noзt abide his
presens.'

>Capitulum lix. þe modir telles to þe spouse what sho 25
>felid onone eftir concepcion of hir son, and what
>Elizabeth and sho felid at þair metinge, and how ane
>aungell comforted and taght bothe Joseph and hir.

The modir saide to þe spouse þat sho felid in hirselfe woundir
þinges and stiringes fro sho had conceiued Criste, and how þe childe 30
made grete mirth in þe wombe of Elizabeth when þai mete togedir
beside a wele. And Joseph thoght himselfe vnworthi to serue hir fro þe
time sho had conceiued, [b]ef[o]r þe time þat þe aungell tolde him þat
sho had conceiued of þe holi goste, and it was Goddes son þat was
within hir. And fro þat time sho had conceiued, scho gaue hir 35

2 when I fled] *twice, first* (flede) *subpuncted*   3 innocente] innocentes
4 com] com home, home *subpuncted*   5 answere] answerde   32 fro] and fro
33 befor] eftir

continuli to praier, wakinge and redinge, saue certaine time þat sho
gaue to hir wirkynge. And all þat left ouir hir nedfull sustinance, þai
gaue it to þe pore. 'And', sho saide, 'Joseph was trewe keper to me, and

defender of my | maidenhede. He desired noght bot heuenli þinges,
5 and he besoght God þat he sulde neuir die or þe time he saw Goddes
will fulfilled in me, his spouse. And, for he obeied so greteli to þe will
of God, his blis is now full grete.'

Capitulum lx. Howe Saint Jerom dowtid noȝt of hir
assumpcion, and howe þe modir comendes Saint
10 Jerome.

þe modir saide to þe spouse, 'Saint Jerome dowtid noȝt of myn
assumpcion, bot, for God had noȝt made opine reuelacion þereof, he
saide þat he had leuer trow godli þan to determyn presumptuoseli þat
þinge þe whilke was noȝt opinli shewed of God. Bot doghtir, as I
15 saide, Jerom was a louer of widows, a folower of holi monkes, and a
defendere of trewth. And he gat to þe þat praiere with þe whilke þou
gretis me. And now I sai þat Jerom was a tendir trumpe þat þe holi gost
spake in, and he was warmede with þat fire þat com on me and on þe
apostils vpon Witsondai.' þerefor *Deo gracias* so sai we ai.

Capitulum lxi. Howe þe modir shewes þe trewthe | of
21 hir assumpcion.

þe modir said to þe spouse, 'Haue minde how I excused Jerome of
myne assumpcion. And nowe sall I tell þe `þe´ sothe of þe same
assumpcion. Aftir þe time þat my son was stied to heuen, I stirred
25 many saules to him. I visited þe places þat he suffird in, and his dede
was so freshe in my minde þat, weþir I ete or I dranke, or what elles I
did, it went noȝt oute of mi minde. And so mi wittes were withdrawen
fro werldeli þinges þat I was enflawmid with newe desires and mengid
with sorwes and gladnes. Neuirþelesse, I mesured so mi soroues and
30 gladnes þat I reklest noþinge þat longide to God, ne in conuersacione
of man I set not bi delitabile þinges, ne desirede riȝt not bot necessari
sustinance. Bot þat mine assumpcion was noght sone taght, ne
preched to many bi Goddes ordinauns, for mi son sawe þat mennes
hertes were hard to trowe his ascension, and þerefore, till it was wele

rotide in mennes hertes, he wald noȝt lat myne assumpsion be opinli
prechid. For while þai had dowtid his ascension, þai wald me|kill haue   f. 258ᵛᵃ
dowtid mine assumpsion.'

Capitulum lxii. þe modir telles howe one aungell tellis
hir þe time of hir assumpsion, [a]n[d] of eght owres.   5

The modir said, 'It fell on a day eftir my sonnes ascension certaine
ȝeres þat I was heuy in miselfe, for þe grete desire I had to com to mi
son. And þan aperid a bright aungell and said to me þat mi son warned
þat time was commen in þe whilke I suld go bodeli to mi son, and take
þe croune þat was ordained to me. To whome I saide, "Knawes þu þe   10
dai and þe oure þat I sall passe?" þe aungell saide, "þi sonnes frendes
sall come and beri þi bodi." þan went þe aungell, and I disposid me to
mi wenedinge, and went aboute þe places þat I was wont. It fell on a
day þat mi saule was lifte vp in contemplacion so full of ioy þat it might
vnneth rest in itselfe, in þe whilke gladnes and ioy it was departid fro 15
þe bodi. Bot what wirshipe was done to it, and what it sawe, sall þou
noȝt wit till þat time þat þi bodi and þi saule be departed. þan come
my | sonnes frendes and berid me in þe vale of Josaphat with multitude   f. 258ᵛᵇ
of aungels, as þai were motes in þe sonne. Bot þe whikked spirit durst
noȝt com nere. And fiftene dais lai mi bodi bired in þe erthe, eftir þe   20
whilke, with multitude of aungels, it was taken vp into þe heuene.

'And þis nowmbir is noȝt withoute grete mistery, for in þe seuent
houre sall be generall vprisinge of bodis, and in þe eght sall þe blis be
fulfilled both of saules and bodis. þe first oure was fro þe bygininge of
þe world to þe time of Moises lawe. þe second was fro Moises to þe   25
incarnacion. þe þird was when mi son ordainde baptim, and sobird þe
hardenes of þe olde lawe. þe ferth was when he prechid. þe fifte was
þat he died and rose and proued his risinge. þe sext was when he stied
into heuene and sent þe holi goste. þe seuent is when he sall com to þe
dome. And in þe eghtand sall all prophecise be fulfilled, and perfite   30
blis sall be to þe gude liuer, where God sall be sene as he is in his blis.'

Capitulum lxiii. Wordes þat Criste bad þe spouse write
| to Pope Clement, for to reform pees bitwene kinges of   f. 259ʳᵃ
France and Ingland.

---

2 wald] wald noȝt, noȝt *ruled through*   5 and] one   19 whikked] whilkked,
l *subpuncted*   21 it was taken] *twice, and* va-cat *to second*

Criste bad þe spouse write þese wordes to þe Pope Clement: 'Rise vpe and make pees bitwene þe kinge of Frauns and Ingland, þat are two perelows bestis, traitoures of menes saules, and com þan into Ytaly and preche þe worde of God and þe ȝere of hele, and se þe
5 stretis holi, þat þai are spred with þe blode of mi saintes. And right als þou went vp bi all þe degrees at mi makinge, so sall I do þe com done gosteli bi all þe degrees, þat þou sall finde it in þi bodi and þi saule bot þou obei to mi biddinge. And I sall seke of þe how slawe þat þou hase bene in þe reforminge of þe pees of þose two kinges, and to wheþir
10 parti þou hase bene more clined. And it sall not be forgetin how pride and desire of honoures hase sprongen in þi time and encresid. þerefor, rise vp or þe last oure com, and amend þi reklesnes, for þi consciens sais þat it is resonabill and charitefull þat I bid. And wer ne mi paciens were, elles suld þou haue fallen ferrer þan ani of þi
f. 259ʳᵇ pre|decessoures felle.'

16   Capitulum lxiiii. Howe a lorde weddid a wife and
        bigged to hir on hows and ordeinde seruantes, maidens
        and mete, and what it bitokens.

Criste saide to þe spouse, 'Wo sall be to þame þat will noȝt amend
20 þame of þer sin, bot leuin in coueitise, for pouert sall rise on þame, and shame and reproue, bot þai meke þame, and þan sall þai find grace.'
Criste saide þat þare was a lorde and weddid a wife, and bigged hir one hows, and ordeynde hir seruandes and maidens and mete and
25 drinke. And þan he went on pilgrimage. And when he com againe, his wife was diffamid, his seruandes were vnbuxum, and þe maidens were defolid. And he broght his wife to þe dome and his seruandes, and þe maidens put he to preson.
'I am þat lorde þat weddid mannes saule in faith and lufe. I bigged it
30 a hows þat is þe bodi. þe first seruand is þe sight, þat was as it had bene a werkeman to see þe gode and resaiue als frendes, and to se þe
f. 259ᵛᵃ euell and put it awai als one enemi. þe | seconde was heringe, and þat was as porter, þat suld opin þe ȝates to þe frendes of þe saule and spere þame to þe enemis. The þird is tastinge, þat is als a leche þat
35 kepis fro excesse and vnholesome metes, and also þat it be noȝt to litill, for drede þat he mai noght serue his God. þe firde is touching,

1 Pope Clement] *blotted*   19 spouse] spouspe   23 bigged] bigged in

þat suld be kepid fro vnhoneste. þe fift is smellinge, and þis is as it
were a spensere to gife þat at his holsome and leue þat at is euell.

'þe first maiden þat suld be with þis ladi suld be drede of greuinge
of hir housband, þat am I. þe seconde suld be deuocion to be besi in
plesinge of him. þe þird sall be sobirnes in maners. þe firth sall be 5
paciens in þat þat it is noȝt all at his flesheli will. þe fifte sall be
chastite, and þat in worde, þoght and dede. þe mete of þe saule suld
be minde of þe gudenes þat God had done–þarto, minde of þe ferdefull dome, and likinge in his loue and his commandementes to fulfill
þame. And þan þe saule sall be faire in kenninge of reson, for it hase 10
[bene] graunted [þat] with þe aungels, and it is made to þe likenes of
þe trinite. Bot if it be set to folllowe þe lustes of fleshe, þan it is f. 259ᵛᵇ
diffamed, and þan þe een seen þat þat is euell to þe saule, þe eres
heres vanite, and so of oþir wittis. And reson is put awai and paciens,
deuocion is loste, and gosteli fode is noȝt set bi. And þerefor of swilke 15
a saule it mai be saide, þat it is tributer to þe fende.

'Swilke one is his saule þat þou sees nowe dede, and þe fende haldis
him on niene maners: first, for he wilfulli assentid to sin; þe second,
for he held noȝt þe hight of his baptim; þe þirde, for he set noȝt by þe
grace of his conferminge; þe ferde, for he sete noȝt bi þe time of his 20
penans; and þe fifte, for he drede noght mi domes; þe sext, for he toke
no hede of mi pacient suffirynge; þe seuent, for he toke more heede to
mannes biddinges and counseils þan to mine; þe eghtend, for he
þanked me noght for þat at I did for him; and þe neynte, for he had no
minde of mi passion. And þarefor he suffirs now neyne paines. Firste 25
is þat all þat he suffirs is with euell will. þe seconde, for þat he forsoke
me, all creatoures nowe hase orrowre of him. þe ferd are | birninge and f. 260ʳᵃ
thirst. þe fifte is ferdenes of fendes. þe sext is wantinge of þe sight of
God. The seuent is dispaire of forgifenes. þe eghtende is bittir bittinge
of consciens. þe neinte is colde and wepinge. 30

'Neuerþelesse, for two godenes þat was in him–first, he traisted
vpon mi passion and spake againe þame þat spake euell of me; anoþir
is, þat he loued mi modir and saintes and wirshiped þame with
fastinge–for þaire praiers he mai be saued: first, for he held þe faith of
holi kirke; þe seconde, by þe offirynge of mi bodi; þe þirde, for praier 35
of saintes þat are in heuen; þe ferthe, for þe gude werkes þat are done
in holi kirke; þe fifte, by þe gude praiers of þaim þat liuen; þe sext, bi
almos dede; þe seuent, bi pilgramage; þe eghtende, bi pardon þat is

11 bene, þat] *om., cf. Lat.* participat cum angelis   13 to þe] *twice, first subpuncted*
22 mi] im-

granted of þe Pope and bishopes; þe neint, bi doinge of penance of
oþir for him, þat he suld haue done in his liue.'

Capitulum lx`v´. Criste likens þis worlde to a ship trauailed in grete tempestes.

5   Criste likens þis world to one shipe trauailed with grete tempestes,
f. 260ʳᵇ for þre partis he likens to þre | eledes: 'þe first parti, þat is, þe elde fro
Adam to mine incarnacion, and þis was time of patriarches and
prophetes; þe medis parti, þat is broddest, bitokens mi comminge þat
was in grete mekenes; þe þird parti, þat is þe hinder parti, bitokens fro
10   mi deinge to þe dome, and in þis ende of þis elde sall Antecriste be
born, bi mi suffirauns, or a werid woman and one werid man. Bot þe
time of þis Antecriste sall noȝt be as þe frer hase wretin þat þu sees his
boke, bot in one time vnknawen, when whikkednes sall be in plente.
Bot som of þe panems bifore þat time sall turn to þe faithe.'

Capitulum lxvi. Criste telles what made one monke to leue his abbai.

Criste saide to þe spouse, 'Wit þou wele þat impaciens made þe
monke to leue his first abbai and go to þe oþir. And for he com curst
into Jerusalem, þarefor was he dissaiued. Rede his bukes, and þou sall
20   finde þaim full of pride, for þare is wretin in þame þat Petir and Paule
saide þat he was worthi to be Pope, and þat he suld be togidir Pope
f. 260ᵛᵃ and Emperoure, and when þat he had nede, he | fand at his heued
golde and monee vnkenid, and oþir þinges. And wit þou wele þat all
þeese are of þe fende þat desaiues him. And þerefore say him þat he
25   sall nowþir be Pope ne Emperoure, and, bot he turn son againe to his
ordir als a meke monke, þat he sall dye sone and noȝt com to blis with
gude men.'

Capitulum lxvii. Whilke two maner of men comis to heuen bi þe gospell.

30   Criste saide þus: 'I saide in þe gospell þat two þinges mai bringe a
man to heuen: one, if he meke himselfe as one childe; oneoþir, he þat
withstandis his lustis and chastis hymeselfe, þat he greue not Gode,
and traistes to com to heuen bi þe merci of God, and noȝt of his awen

1, 21 (twice), 25 Pope] *blotted*   6 eledes] eleldes   22 at] lat, l *partially erased*

rightwisnes. Bot þat frere þat ete noþinge in Lenton, and did vndiscrete abstinens, wenis of his rightwisnes to win heuen. And þai were done for pride more þan for mekenes. I miselfe set amange men and dranke, to giue ensampill to oþir to take þe nedefull sustinance, and þanke God of it.'

5

Capitulum lxviii. Criste spekes againe men of holi kirke þat misvses holi kirke | godes.

It was shewed to þe spouse as it had bene one cardinall, þat was dede, had setin on one beme of tre, and bi blake folke were ordeinde foure chambres þat his saule moste passe bi. In þe first were clothis of diuers kindes. In þe second were vessell of golde and siluir. In þe þird were diuers metis and drinkes. In þe ferth were hors and oþir bestis. And when þe saule was led throw þe firste chambir, it had wondir grete cold, and it cried, 'Allas, þat euir I loued faire cloþis so mekill for mi wirshipe of mi bodi, for now I ame pu[t]e vndir þe fendes fete.' And when it passed þe second chambir, it felid one cuppe of rinninge pike, flawminge on euirilke side. And þan it saide, 'Allas withouten ende, for likinge þat I had in drinkes [of] delites, for now moste me fill me on ȝone standinge pike.' And when it was led throw þe þirde chambir, it felid bittinge eddirs, and when it was led throw þe ferth chambir, he herd orribbill noise, as it had bene of thundir, and þan it cried for ferdnes, 'How rightwisli am I rewarded.'

10

15

20

And þan was þere herd one uoise | þat saide, 'What! þinkes a man in erthe wheþer þat God be a gabber, þat saide þat man guld gefe a rekeninge of þe lest ferþinge? Ȝis, and of þe lest time of mete and drinke, þoght and spechis, sall he giue a rekeninge, bot it be assoled, or it be weshin awai with contricion and penans. And wit it wele þat clerkes and cardenals þat etis and entirs þe almos of oþir men, and make þame proude of þaire almos, sall gife a hard rekeninge for þame þat aght þo gudes, criinge vengean[s]e in mi sight. I dowid holi kirke, for þai suld more restefulli serue me. Bot now þai are proude, and prais noȝt as þai sulde. Bot I, of mi grace, haue merci on þe saules þat som[time] gaue þame to holi kirke, and I sall deme þose clerkes full harde.'

25

30

15 pute] pure, *Lat.* deprimar 18 of] *om.* 30 vengeanse] vengeange
33 somtime] som

Criste biddes a certaine confessoure howe he sall assoile.

Criste bad þe spouse bid to one gude confessoure assoile all þat commes to him with contricion, to one com þat Criste bid not be
5 assoiled of him. 'Bot bid him beware of opin domes of þe kirke.'

Capitulum lxx. Criste blamis parishe prestes þat dare
f. 261ʳᵇ   noȝt assoile of þe preǀuai sinnes for sendinge aboute.

Criste saide, 'Two spottis are in mi kirke. One is þat fewe are assoilled bot for mone. Oneoþir is, þaire parise prestes dare noȝt
10 assoile of all pr[e]uai sinnes, bot sendis þame aboute to bishopes, till oþirwhile þat at was preue be opinli knawen. And þerfore he þat hase of mannes saule loue and tendirnes suld be wele ware þat noþir fore schame ne hardnes þai suld make men to dye in sinne.'

Capitulum lxxi. Criste tellis of one penetansere, þe
15   whilk, all if he be euell, his absolucion is neuer þe wers.

Criste saide of one penitansere þat he was mesell, and he dar awntir him vpon simpill pure folke als one glede, bot noȝt vpon grete, and he was proude als one lion. 'Neuirþelesse, þe absolucion þat he giues, bi þe auttorite of mi kirke, is as verray absolucion os of one gude preste.
20 Bot sai him þat he sall neuir haue ioi of þat at he desires': for þe dai þat he was made one archibishope he died.

f. 261ᵛᵃ   Capitulum lxxii. þe spouse sawe | a vision fro þe castell
of Saint Aungell, and who suld be possessoure of þat place.

25   þe spouse sawe nerehand as it had bene Sainte Petirs in Rom, to þe castell of Aungell, and fro þe castell of Sainte Spirites, and to Sainte Petir kirke as it hade bene a plaine felde, and a stronnge walle aboute it, and abowte þe wall dwellinge-places. And þan scho herd one voce sai, 'þat Pope þat louis mi kirke, als I and mi frendes hase loued it, sall
30 browke þis place with þe purtenance.'

6 lxx] lxxi   10 preuai] pruai   25 sawe] *twice*   26 þe] *twice*

Capitulum ʼlxxiiiʼ. How a man cried as he hade bene
wode, and whi þat sin sone done is ponished withouten
ende.

It fell at þe prechinge of Maistir Mathi, þat made þe prologe of þis
buke, þat one squier cried als he had bene a wode man, ʼ3if mi saule   5
com no3t at heuen, late it go als one beste. It is longe to þe dome, and
before þat time sall neuir saule [see] heuen.ʼ And when þe spouse herd
þat, sho saide, ʼA, lorde, kinge of blis, þou arte full mercifull and
pacient. þa þat will feen erne praised, and þae þat will sai þe sothe are
reprouede. And þerefore, lord, gife þis maistir | streng[þ]e and feruour   f. 261ᵛᵇ
to speke.ʼ þan was shewed, in one visione to þe spouse, heuen opin   11
and hell birninge, and one voice saide to hir, ʼSai to þi maistir þat [I]
and none oþir is his againebier and maker. And þerfore bid him
preche hardeli þat saules þat are clensid, and in þe blise, sees þe
visage of God.ʼ Sone eftir þis, sho sawe hell, and sho was full ferde.   15
And one voice saide to hir þat sho suld no3t drede. þan saide sho, ʼA,
lorde, sethin þou arte moste mercifull, how sulde þou ponishe endelesli him þat trespasses no3t endelesli?ʼ þan saide þe spirit of God, ʼI
take hede to mannes will, and for mannes [will] was, might he euir
haue bene here, euer to haue sinned, þarefore sall he euer be   20
ponished.ʼ

Capitulum lxxiiii. How a man is holden to chasti his
meine, and againe experimentes.

It fell þat þe spouse was herberd in one towne, and þare ware
brint of hir gere and of hir men gere, and Crist saide to hir, ʼþis is   25
for þou suffirs in þi meine pride and loue of þe world, and þat þu
reproues þame no3t, for þou wald no3t be halden heui to þam. And I
tell þe, it is | noght enogh to perfeccion þat a man amende himselfe,   f. 262ʳᵃ
bot also þat he amend, in þat at in him is, oþir, and nameli his
meine. For þat at þou mai amende, and leuis for fauoure o man to   30
do it, it sall be put on þe as sinne. Also, he þat dwelles in þis place
failes in þe faithe, for he trowes þat all þinges b[e] reweled bifor
time, and also he vses experimentes bi wordes of þe fende to drawe
fishes oute of þe stanke. Warne þat he leue, or þe fende þat he
serues sall haue maistri on him.ʼ And sho told him, and he sete it at   35

7 see] _om._   10 strengþe] strengie   12 I] _om._   15 shoⁱ] shcho
19 will²] _om._   28 is] _twice_   enogh] enoght   30 o] o a   32 be] bi

noght, and sodanli in his [bed] was his neke wreþin aboute and
he dede.

Capitulum lxxv. Wordes blaminge a jangeland frere,
and againe sotell sophisticall disputtinge.

5   The son saide to þe spouse, 'Sai to þat jangelande frere þat time sall
com þat þare sall be one saule, one hird, one faithe, one clere knawinge of God. And many þat are called sall be reproued. And mani
[þ]a[t] hase done þaire besines to be cald sall haue, for þat, more
f. 262rb   mercifull ponishinge, bot þai sall noȝt com in blis. | And sai to þat frere
10   þat it is more to þe hele of his saule þat with mekenes he saide his
Pater noster þan for a vaine name to disp[u]te so sofisteli of soteltees.
And bid him thinke whi he com to religion, for he sall sone ete his
brede in oneoþir place. Neu[i]rþelesse, if he will chaunge his will,
God will mese his sentens.'

15   Capitulum lxxvi. Whi þe feende had maistri in a
certan place, and how men suld trow in þe sacramentes.

It fell þat þe spouse was herberd one night in one place whaire
fendes made noise, bot þer was none noise of hem in hi[r] presens.
And when sho was in hir praier, sho herde one uoice sai to hir, 'þai þat
20   dwelt beforetimes in þis place, and þai þat dwellin þarein nowe, are
wirshipers of fals goddes, and þai go noght to þe kirke bot for shame of
men, ne þai will noȝt here Goddes wordes, and þarefore þe fende hase
maistri in þis place. Bot gedir togedir all þat dwellis in þis place and
oþir, and bid þi confessoure sai þis wordes. "God is one and thre, bi
25   whome all þinges are made. þe fende is his makinge, þat mai noȝt
f. 262va   remoue one strawe bot at þe | suffirynge of God. Bot when ȝe loue
more erthli þinges þan God, and walde be riche agains þe will of God,
þan þe rightwisnes suffirs þe fende haue power vpon ȝou. þarefor
trow ȝe in God, and leue ȝour gifinge milke to eddirs and ȝoure sacri-
30   fice to fendes of ȝoure brede and ȝour wine. Ne sai noȝt þat fortune
makes all þis, bot þat God suffirs it, and trowe stedfasteli vpon þe
sacrament of þe auter, and in þe sacramentes of baptim, confirmacion
and aneling. And þan sall þe fende fle fro ȝou.' And also son as þai

---

1 bed] *om.*, *Lat.* lecto   7 mani] mani paines with grace (*? antic. l.* 9, mercifull
ponishinge)   8 þat¹] and   11 dispute] dispite   13 Neuirþelesse]
neurþelesse   18 hir] his   24-5 bi whome] *twice*

saide þat [þai] trowed, and hight amendinge, þere was herd one voice
fro vte of þe oyn, þa[r] he was wont to answere, þat said, 'þere gete I
no more place.' And so he went awai and was noȝt herd þereeftir.

Capitulum lxxvii. Howe one þat sange mes and was
noght ordeinde preste was ponisht, and þerfore saued,   5
and how þe faithe of þame þat tuke sacramentes
[helpid].

Criste saide to þe spouse when sho praied for one þat had songen
mes and was noȝt ordeinde preste, and was demid be þe domesman to
be brinte (and if he had noȝt bene | ponished he suld noȝt haue bene   f. 262ᵛᵇ
saued, and how his penance broght him to contricion, and so drowe he   11
to grace and rest). And Criste saide, 'þou mai aske me whedir þat þe
folke þat tuke sacramentes of him, þat wend þat he had bene a verrai
preste, and wend þat I had bene in his handis, be dampned for þat. I
answere þe and sai þat þaire faithe sauid þame, and þe faithe of þe   15
fadir and `þe´ modir stode þam in stede þat were baptiste of him, for it
was noȝt þaire defaute.'

Capitulum lxxviii. How a woman was traualed with a
fende and þan, eftir, `helid´.

þare was one woman trauailed of one fende, þat sometime hir   20
wombe wex grete, as sho suld trauaile of childe, and somtime it was so
smale as sho had had noȝt þarin. þe spouse asked Criste what þis
might mene, and he saide þat right as, amange þe gode spirites, one
was more he and sotell þan oneoþir, 'right so amange þe euell spirites
one is more maliciouse þan oneoþir. In þis kingdome of Sweþer are   25
þre | maner of fendes. One is birning als fire, and þat hase his lorde-   f. 263ʳᵃ
ship in glotterous men and dronken. þe second is maister of þe bodi
and þe saule, and þe þirde is þe feende of licheri, and he had mastri of
þis womman, for sho let for no shame to shriue hir or þe time þat scho
resaiued mi bodi. And þerefore bid hir shriue þat sinne þat hase bene   30
longe hide, and mi frenndes pray for hir, and lat hir resaiue mi bodi of
one gud prestes hand, þat with praiers and teres sho mai be helid.'
And when þis was done, þe womman was hole.

1 þai] om.   2 þar] þat   answere] answerede   5 þerfore] þerfore fore,
fore subpuncted   7 helpid] om., Lat. profuerunt   19 helid] feled   23 as]
as þe, þe subpuncted   26 þre] Quire catchphrase, manere of, below

Capitulum lxxix. Howe þe fennde gat a childe of a
womman þe whilke was noȝt wele cristened.

þare was a child of þre ȝere olde þat restid noȝt bot when þare was
colde watir castin on it. And þan saide Criste to þe spouse, 'þe feende
5 tuke to him one bodi of þe aire, and com in opin likenes to þe modir of
þis child, als he had sinned with hir in lichori. And ȝet þe child was
getin of þe kinde of þe fadir and þe modir. Bot for þe childe was noȝt
wele cristened, bot als [bi] womman þat knowes [noȝt] wordes of þe
f. 263ʳᵇ sacrament þai | sai, þarefore þe feende hase power of him. þarefor do
10 cristen þe childe in þe name of þe fadir and þe sone and þe hali goste,
and he sall be saufe. And bid þe modir þat sho shriue hir wele, and
when þe fende commis to hir ward, sai þus: "Jesu Criste, Goddes son
of heuen, þat was born of þe maiden Mari for hele of man and done
vpon þe crosse, and now regnes in heuen and erthe, þou haue merci
15 on me." ' And þus þe woman was helide.

Capitulum lxxx. A knight asked a wich how it suld fall
bitwen men of þe kingdome of Sweici.

þare was a knight þat asked of one wiche howe it suld falle bitwene
men of þe kingdome and þe kinge of Sweþir, and it fell pees als sho
20 saide. And þan saide Criste to þe spouse, 'þat it fell als sho saide was
of mi suffirauns, for þe misbeleue of þe pepill. Bot bid þe kinge þat he
put oute of his rewme all swilke maner of womman þat delis with
wikkid spirites, for þai dissaiue mani mennes saules, and makes þam
to greue God. And þat is no woundir, when þai will witt more þan God
f. 263ᵛᵃ will þat | þai wit, or be riche againe þe will of God. For þe fende kennis
26 bi tokens owtwarde whareto þe hert is inclined, and þareto he traualls
with his helpers to drawe man, and so to leue on his wordes and
begile man.'

Capitulum lxxxi. How þe painems sall be conuerted
30 and þe cristen sall serue þame.

Criste saide to þe spouse, 'þe painems sall be turned, and þe

8 bi] om.   noȝt] om.   9 þai] þan, second minim subpuncted   10 cristen þe]
twice, þe cristen subpuncted   13 born] twice, first subpuncted   22 put] put hir
26 is] twice, first subpuncted   27 and¹] and to, to subpuncted   30 sall] sall be
conuer, be conuer ruled through

cristened sall be þaire seruandes, and þe scripture sall be fulfilled þat sais, "þe folke þat vndirstandes noȝt sall blis me." And þai sall singe, "Ioy and blis be to þe fadir and to þe sone and to þe holi goste, and ioy be to all his saintes." '

Capitulum lxxxii. How þe spouse come to one ile by   5
shipe.

It fell þat sho suld com to one ile by ship bi night. Sho was wonder warme, and all hir seruandes so colde þat vnnethe þai might suffir it. And Criste said to hir in hir praiere in þe mornyng, 'Men hase litill traiste in me to kepe þame fro colde, þat clethe þame with mani   10 clothis. And, neuirþelesse, þare is no kindeli hete bot bi me. And if men wald sett þaire traiste on me, I suld giue þame hete both to þe bodi and to þe saule, | and make þame faire in þe sight of saintes.'   f. 263ᵛᵇ

Capitulum lxxxiii. How one was in purgatori fourti wintir, for he restored noȝt againe misgetin gude bi his   15
progenitours.

[Þ]are apperid one to þe spouse þat had bene fourti wintir in pur-gatori for his sinnes, and for he restorid noȝt againe þe gudes þat his progenitours had taken of oneoþir mannes, and he wist it, vnto þe time þat one of his successours restorid it againe to þame þat suld haue it.   20 And þan said Criste to þe spouse þat 'þai þat haldin wittingli fro oþir þat at falles to oþir sall noȝt com to mi riste, to it be restorid. And þe almos þat is geuin of gudes þat are euell getin availes noȝt to þame þat gifes þame, bot þai turne to þe prophet of þame þat aght þame. Bot þai þat hase will to restore againe to oþir men, and þai wiste of it, þai   25 sall noȝt be punishet þerfor.'

Capitulum lxxxiiii. A faire vision þat þe `spouse´ had of a prest þat sange his messe first on Witsondai.

The spouse sawe, in þe handes of one preste þat | sange his firste   f. 264ʳᵃ mes in one Witsondai in one abbai, in þe time of þe eleuacion, a fire   30 come fro heuen vpon all þe awter, and in þe prestes handes sho sawe a lambe, hauinge a mannes visage all birninge. And one voice saide to

15 bi] m (or in) bi, m subpuncted   17 þare] Aare   19 it] twice, second subpuncted   27 spouse] spoue   32 visage] visagage

hir, 'þus com þe hali goste all þis dai vnto þe apostils.' And eft sho
sawe againe in þe prest hand a wonder faire childe, þat saide, 'Blissed
be ȝe all þat are of gude bileue, and to þaime þat trowes noȝt I sall be
domesman.'

5   Capitulum lxxxv. How sho sat at mete with a bishop
           and grete lordes, and felt a stinke of a cursed man.

It fell þat þe spouse sat at mete with one bischope and oþir grete
lordes, and scho felde a wondir stinke, als it had bene of rotid fishe,
and none felid þis sauour bot sho. And þere com one man þat was
10 cursed, bot for he was a grete man he set not þerbi. þan saide Criste to
þe spouse, 'þus stinkith cursinge, and is perilous to mannes saule als
þe stinke of fische is to þe bodi. And þerefor bid þe bishope ponishe
swilke, þat oþir be noȝt filed by þame.'

f. 264ʳᵇ   Capitulum lxxxvi. How þe spouse felt within hir | hert
15   as it had bene a whik childe.

It fell on þe Cristemes night þat þe spouse, with one passing glad-
somnes of hir hert, felid as it had bene a whike childe sterringe in hir
hert. And at þe hye mes, þe modir of merci apperid to hir and saide,
'Doghtir, right as þou wote noȝt how þat gladnes and stirynge com so
20 sodanli to þe bi þe sonde of Gode, so þe comminge of mi son to me
was wondirfull and sodaine. And also sone as I assentid to þe aungels
message, I felid in me a wondirfull whike steringe child, with a gladnes
þat mai noȝt be saide. And þerfore haue comforthe, for þis gladfull
stiringe sall laste with þe and incres in þe, for it is þe comminge of mi
25 son into þi herte, and þou sall shewe to mi sonnes frenndes, and mine,
oure will.'

          Capitulum lxxxvii. Howe Jon euangeliste apperid to þe
           spouse and talde þat he wrote þe apocalipes.

Maistir Mathi, þat made one glose vpon þe Bibille, praied þe
30 spouse þat sho wald witt if Jon þe euangeliste made þe apocalips, and
of þe time of Antecriste. And in hir praing apperid to hir one enointed
f. 264ᵛᵃ all ouir with oile | with a grete lightenes, and saide, 'I, John euangelist,
wrote þe apocalippes at þe inspiringe of God.' And þan saide Criste to

6 lordes] lordes and petenti, and petenti *subpuncted*

þe spouse, 'So Maistir Mathi had wretin, by þe inspiring of me, þe gosteli vndirstondinge of holi write. And sai to him þat þare are mani Antecristes, bot how þat he sall com þat he askes eftir, he sall wit bi þe.'

Capitulum lxxxviii. How vengeaunce was taken of a
man of religion.   5

It fell þat on grete man of religion saide to Maistir Mathi þat it miȝt noȝt stand with scripture þat Criste wald leue þame þat had forsaken þe worlde and shew his preuatees to so grete a woman. And when þe spouse herd þis, sho praied to God to shewe þe trewth. And þan herd scho Criste sai, 'Ȝone iangeland man of religion desires noȝt me for 10 vanite of his coninge. Bot I sall gife him one buffett, and he sall wit wele þat I ame God.' And sone eftir he died in þe peralisi.

Capitulum lxxxix. Criste biddis þe spouse to take þat at
is nedefull to þe bodi.

Criste saide to þe spouse, þat had febild hirselfe with | wakinge and f. 264ᵛᵇ
fasting, þat sho suld take þat at were nedefull to þe bodi, þat þe saule 16
were noȝt lettid fro gosteli þinges.

Capitulum xc. Of a monke þat broght furth *Uitas
Patrum*, with whome God was euell paied.

One monke broght furth bifore þe kinge of Swein and his counsell, 20
in presens of þe spouse, *Vitas Patrum*, and shewed how þat mani, of vndiscrete abstinens, ware begilled with penance. þan saide Criste to þe spouse, 'Forsoth, þere was neuir none of mi frenndes so desaiued þat loued me. Bot þose þat had pride of þair abstinence, and thoght þai suld be bettir þan oþir, and wald noȝt obei to meke consaile, þai 25
ware dissaiued. And for þis monke hase broght þis buke againe me, I sall bringe mi buke of rightwisnes againe him, for he is full fer fro his profession.'

Capitulum xci. How a woman ʽwasʼ gostli holpin by
oure ladi.   30

þare was shewed to þe spouse a woman sittinge, and þe one fote

21 þe] þe kinge, kinge *subpuncted*   29 was] wa, *superior mark*

f. 265ra held vp Saint Petir, and þe oþir oure ladi. | And þan saide þe modir
and ladi to þe spouse, 'þis womman þat þou knawes had som[time]
will to sin, bot nowþir steed ne time, and þat made þe prayer of Saint
Petir þe apostill. And somtime sho had steed and time bot no will, and
5 þat made I. And þerfore counseill hir to do some mekenes and
penance in hir cloþinge, and b[e] meke.' And þan Saint Petir saide to
þe spouse þat sho suld go to þat woman and witt if sho wald fulli be his
doghtir. And sho saide, '3a.' And he saide þat he suld puruai for hir as
for Peronell his doghtir. And as fast sho changet hir lifinge, and was
10 seke term of hir life, and at hir endinge sho saw Saint Petir þe apostill
com in, all in bishope arrai, and þan Saint Petir þe martir, in one frere
prechoure abit. And þan sho saide, 'Now I se þam þat I haue loued,
and traiste in þaire helpe.' And þan sho cried, 'Blisse[d] be God; I
com.' And so sho 3eldes þe goste.

15   Capitulum xcii. How Criste apperid firste to his modir,
          and whi þe spouse hase temptacions in hir elde þat sho
          hade noght in hir 3outhe. |

f. 265rb   þe modir saide to þe spouse, 'þe saules þat mi son deliuerd oute of
helle ware in one place þat was knawen oneli to mi son. And whare þat
20 euer he was, or is, ern ioi and blis, als he saide to þe theefe: "Todai sall
þou be with me in Paradise." Also, mani saintes þat were dede in
Ierusalem rose with him, and þe saules stied vp with him, bot þaire
bodis abiden in erth to þe generall resurreccion. And to me his modir,
to comforthe me, apperid mi son first, all if it be no3t wretin so, for þat
25 is for mi mekenes þat it is no3t wretin. And als I was comforted þis dai,
so sall I fro þis dai furth comforthe þe.
     'þou wondirs greteli whi þat þou has temptaciouns now in þine
elde þat þou had no3t here in þi 3outhe no in þi wifehede. I answere
þe þat þat is to make þe to witt þat þou art no3t of þiselfe, ne no3t mai
30 withouten helpe of mi son. For þere is no sin bot þou had fallen
þerein, had no3t bene þe helpe of mi son. Bot I sall tell þe thre
f. 265va remediis againe temptacions. þe first is, when þou art temptid | in
thoght, sai þus: "Jesu, God son, maker of all þinges, helpe me þat I
haue no likinge in euell þoghtes." And if þu be temptid to speke, sai,
35 "Jesu, God son, þat held þi tunge befor þe domesman, kepe mi tunge

fro wikked spekinge." And sai also, "Jesu þat was bunden, gouern all mi werkes to a gude ende."

Capitulum xciii. Of a gude man of Swene called Israel,
and how to desire gouernance, for pride is euell.

It fell in þe kingedome of Swen þare was a man hight Israel, and þe 5
kinge wald haue hade him to hier gouernance, and he forsoke it, for he
wald haue went to haue his dede for þe beleue on Goddes enemis.
Oure ladi called þe spouse and saide, 'A man þat is rightwis and gude
suld be drawen to charite to take gouernaunce, or elles wikked men sall
haue it and rightwisnes be lefte. Bot for to desire hie wirshipe and 10
grete gouernans for pride is euell, for þai are tirantes. And þerefor bid
Isral mi freende take his gouernans vpon him for þe wirshipe of God,
and hafe in his mouthe þe wordes of sothefastenes, and take no hede to
mannes personne. For I sai | þe þat it sall be saide of him þat he went f. 265ᵛᵇ
oute of his cuntre manfulli, he wirshiped Goddes modir herteli, and 15
he serued God treweli.' For sone eftir he went againe þe mistrowers,
fro he had gouerned diuers ȝeres right wele, and he come into Almaine
to a cite þat hat Rigensis, and þere toke he sekenes. And when he felid
þat he was nere dede, he went into þe cathedrall kirke, where þare is
one ymage of oure ladi in grete reuerence, and he tuke a ringe of golde 20
and putt vpone þe ymage finger and left it þare, and saide opinli,
'Ladi, þou wote þat I haue euir loued þe, and þerefore mi saule I
comende to þe.' þan resaiued he his sacramentes and died full
deuoteli. And þan saide oure ladi to þe spouse, 'Treweli, whiles he
leued he loued me of all his herte, and in all his werkes and domes he 25
dred mi son. And I haue present his saule to þe compani of aungels
and saintes, for God accept[ed] his gude will als mekill als if he had
died vpon þe Sarazines for þe faithe.'

Capitulum xciiii. How byfor one euell | Popes dede þe   f. 266ʳᵃ
bellis of Saint Petir kirke brent.   30

It fell a litill before one of þe Popes dethe þat wonderfulli þe bellis
of Saint Petir kirke in Rome brent. And Criste aperid to þe spouse and
saide, 'þis is a grete token, for he leued noȝt als he suld. He þat suld
haue cried to þe pepill, "Com, and ȝe sall finde hele of ȝoure saules",
he cried, "Com, and see me in mi pompe and mi pride, more þan 35

16 againe] againe to, *Lat.* contra   27 accepted] accept

Salomon was. Com and vndo ʒoure purses, and ʒe sall find dampnacion of ʒoure saules." þus he criede in dede and ensampill, and
þerefor þe dome of him commes nere, for he hase shent Petirs floke.
Neuirþelesse ʒit, while þe life is in him, and he will turne him, I will
5 gladli resaiue him.'

Capitulum xcv. Of one euell man þat had seuene
feendes within him.

It fell þat þare was a grete man in þe world, and was seke. And þe
spouse praied for him. þan bad Criste þat hir confessoure suld wende
10 to him to shriue him, for he was noʒt shriuen of longe time bifore. Bot
f. 266ʳᵇ þe seke man wald noʒt be shriuen, | bot saide þat he was ofte time
shriuen. þe second dai þe confessoure come againe, and had þe same
answere. þe þird dai com þe confessoure againe and saide, 'Criste,
Goddes son of heuen and lord of þe fende, sendis þe worde þat þou
15 hase within þe seuen fendis. One sittis in þi herte and haldes it so
bunden þat þou may hafe no confession. þe second sittes in þi eyn to
let þe of þi gosteli sight; þe þird in þi mouthe, to let þe of gude speche;
þe firth in þi neþir partis, for þou loued vnclennes; þe fift in þi hende
and þi fete, þat ledis þe to wirke þe euell, and rob men of þaire gudes;
20 þe sext in þi endir partis, for þou gafe þe to gluttonnes and
dronkennes; þe seuent euen within þi saule, where God suld sitt. And
þarefore aske forgeuenes, and þou mai haue it.'
þan answerde þe seke man againe with teris, and saide, 'How mai
þou hight me forgiuenes þat am gilti in þus mani sinnes?' þan saide þe
25 confessoure, 'I hight þe þat if þou will be shriuen, with sorow of þi
herte þat þu hase greued God, þat þou sall be saufe.' þan saide he
f. 266ᵛᵃ againe with teris, 'I dissposed me noʒt | to hele of mi saule, for I haue
made homage to þe fende, and I ame sexti ʒere olde. And I was neuir
shriuen ne howsellede, bot I feined me erandes when oþir ware how-
30 selled. Bot now I will shriue me.' And he shrafe him þat dai foure sithe
with teres, and on þe dai folowing he was howsilled, and þe sext dai he
died. And þan said Criste to þe spouse, 'þis man sall be saufe for his
contricion and his shrifte. Bot þou mai aske me howe þat he þat was so
lange euell come to contricion. And to þis I answere, þat was for mi
35 merci, þat abides a mannes turninge to þe laste point, and þe praier
of mi modir. Neuirþelesse, when it com in his minde or herd speke of

34 þat] twice, first subpuncted

þe sorowe þat sho had in mi passion, he had grete compassion of hir in his hert, and þat is a wai to helpe to safe him to blise, eftir þe time þat he had bene clensid.'

Capitulum xcvi. Criste likens ane euell abbas.

Criste saide, 'þat abbas is one of þe fatt kye þat gone in þe filth, and 5
with hir taile files oþir aboute hir. So dose sho | with euell ensampill to   f. 266ᵛᵇ
hir sustirs. And þat proues wele–hir curiowste of cloþinge [als]o–þat
sho is noȝt Saint Benet doghtir. For hir rewele sais þat sho suld be
clede in store cloth and pore, and sho hase þe beste and þe fareste and
sotelleste þat sho can gete. Hir reule sais þat sho suld ete and drinke 10
and [haue] nedefull metes mesurabili and with drede, and haue
noþinge propir. Bot sho etes to hir luste, and is fat as one cowe, and
folowes hir awen will. One abbais suld geue gude ensampill to oþir
and be folowere of Saint Benet, bot sho haldis þat name for pride and
vanite, and takes no heede þat sho moste geue me a rekeninge of þe 15
saules of hir sisters. And þerfore wit wele þat, bot scho amend hire and
hire sisters, þat þe crawes of hell sall ete hir as a fat cowe, for scho
walde `not fle up to heuen'.'

Capitulum xcvii. Howe þe fende of coueitise sterid
nonnes to haue gret possessions of landes and rentes.   20

It was shewed to þe spouse þat in one abbai amange nunnes [þare
stode an Ethiope als a nonne. þan it] was saide to þe spouse, þat he
was þe fende of couetise, 'þat steris þame to gedir grete possessions
ande riches, | þat þai mai leue more delicatli, and vndir þe couloure of   f. 267ʳᵃ
greter almos to wende awai fro pouert, and þus to forfet þe rewle and 25
lose þe saules. And þerfor, bot þai beware of þis wolfe of coueitise, and
hold þame paide of þat þat þai haue, and will to hafe no more, þe
gude hole shepe sall be filed and worowed and loste, for it is more
plesinge vnto me þat þai kepe þame in þe gude pouert þat þai are
professid to þan besi þame for worldeli gudes, and haue vaineglori of 30
þaire almos dedis.'

---

1 þe] þe spouse   2-3 þat he had] *twice, first subpuncted*   7 proues] proues
hir, hir *subpuncted*   also] do   11 haue¹] *om.*   16 þat bot] *trsp.*
21-2 þare . . . it] *om., pres. haplography; cf. Lat.* videbatur ethiops . . . inter velatas moniales
existere   27 þat þat] þat *three times, second subpuncted*   28 filed] filled

Capitulum xcviii. How Criste hase two armes, and with
one vmbilappis heuen, and with oneoþir þe erth.

Criste apperid to þe spouse when sho was dredefull of withsainge of
hir wordes, and saide to hir, 'I haue two armes, and with þe one I
5 vmbilappe þe heuene and all þat is þerein. With þe oþir I vmbilape þe
erthe and þe see. þe firste I sprede ouir þame þat are chosen to me in
heuen, and I wirship þam in erth. With þe oþir I suffir mercifulli
f. 267rb mennes malice and refreines þame, þat þai do | noȝt so grete harme as
þai walde. And þerefor, drede þe noȝt, for þere mai none lete mi
10 wordes, bot þai sall here þame þat me likes to here þame. And wit wele
þat mi wordes are as oile. And þarefore þai most be preste of envious
men, and þai sall softe þe hertes of gude men, so þat mi wirshipe sall
be encressed.'

Capitulum 99. Criste likens himselfe to a lorde whos
15   `childer´ þe enemis thralles.

Criste saide þat he was like a lorde, and his enemi has comen and
cherist his childir, and broght þame in thraldome, þat þai toke no
heede of þaire fadir no þaire eritage. And þarefore he bad þe spouse
þat sho suld write þe wordes þat sho herde and send þame to þe
20 panems, if þai wald ken þaire vnkindenes and his gudenes, for he wald
shew to þame his rightwisnes and his charite.

Capitulum c. Grete commendacion of perdon.

One ladi þat had bene longe time seke in Rome saide, als it were in
f. 267va scorn, herringe þe spouse, 'þe [f]ame is þat [h]ere | in Roome is abso-
25 lucion fro trespas and paine, scilicet a pena `et´ culpa.' And in þe morning
next eftir, þe spouse herde one voice sai to hir, 'Doghtir, þis womman
is dere to me, both for sho hase leued wele, and sho hase techid wele
hir doghtirs. Sai to hir þat þe indulgens of Rome are more þane þai are
saide, ore soundes in þameselfe, for þai þat commis with a perfite
30 herte to þe indulgensis, he sall noȝt oneli haue forg[eu]enes of sinnes,
bot he sall haue also þe blis þat euir is lastinge. And all if a man might
noght leue so mani ȝeres, for man hase done so mani sinnes þat

---

3-4 of hir] *twice, second subpuncted*   11 þat mi] þat mi þat, *second* þat *subpuncted*
15 childer] child   24 fame] name, *Lat.* fama   here] ȝere   25 fro] for
26 þe spouse] *twice, first subpuncted*   30 forgeuenes] forgenes   32 for] bot for

ponishing withouten ende are answereinge to þame, and a mane mai
noȝt fullfill þame in þis life, þarefore bi þe indulgens are mani
releised, and mani þat were greuous turned to lighter, and þose þat
hase þe indulgens in full charite, and wendin oute of þe werlde, þai are
deliuerd noȝt oneli of þe trespas bot also of þe paine. And þerefore bid   5
ȝone woman haue paciens in hir sekenes and stabilnes in þe faithe,
and I sall do to hir þat is for | hir saule hele.'

Capitulum ci. How Saint Nicholas apperid to þe
spouse and told whi he springes oile.

It fell þat þe spouse visit Saint Nicholas towmbe and þoght of þe   10
oile, and saw in hir spirit one persone enoynted with oile, of nobill
smell, þat saide to hir, 'I ame Nicholas þat apperis to þe in likenes þat
I was in mi saule in þe time of mi liueinge. For right as one þinge þat is
enointed with oile is softe and bowand, so was I meke and pliand to þe
will of God. And wit þou wele þat, right as þe rose bringes furthe his   15
gude sauoure, and þe grape his swetenes, so gaue God to mi bodi one
speciall grace of springinge of oile, for noȝt oneli he wirshipes þame
þat loued him in heuen, bot also in erth, to oþir to take ensampill bi in
foloweinge of his grace.'

Capitulum cii. Howe Saint Anne apperid to þe spouse.   20

Saint Anne, modir of oure ladi, apperid to þe spouse when sho had
getin relikes of hir in Rome, and saide to hir | þus: 'I ame Anne, ladi of
all weddid folke þat were byfor þe lawe. Doghtir, wirshepe God of þis
manere: "Blissed be þou, Jesu Criste, þe son of God þat chesid þe one
modir of þe weddinge of Joachim and Anne. And þerefor, for þe   25
praiers of Anne, haue merci of all þame þat are in wedeloke or þinkes
to be weddid, þat þai mai bringe furth froite to þe wirshipe of Gode."
And kepe wele þe relikes þat þou hase of me.'

Capitulum ciii. þe spouse pleines hir þat sho visitid
noȝt holi places in Rome, to whome þe modir saide.   30

The spouse pleined hir þat sho ȝode noȝt to visit þe holi places in

7 do] do hir, hir *subpuncted*   10 and] *twice, first subpuncted*   11 of] of þe oile
of   13 liueinge] liueninge   16 sauoure] sauouore   20 spouse] spouse
and tolde whi he springes oile, *erron. rep. l. 9*   26 all] *twice, first subpuncted*

Rome, where þere are so grete indulgens bi þe blode of saintes and þe medis of Criste. þan saide þe modir, 'Go þan. Bot, for þat, leue noght þi leryng in gramere, and þine obeinge to þi gosteli fadir.'

Capitulum ciiii. Howe a man praied þe spouse to aske
of God how he might best plese Gode.

þare come a man to þe spouse and praid hir þat sho wald aske of God in what state þat | he might plese God. And Criste saide to þe spouse, 'þis man hase not ȝete commen to þe watir of Jordane. And it is wretin of Heli þat when he was passed þe watir of Jordane and commen into deserte, þan he herde þe preuatese of God. þis watir of Iordane is þe werlde, for þe godes of it now liftis a man vp in prosperite, and now castis him downe in aduersite, als þe watir flowes and ebbis. And þarefore, he þat wald kun knawe heuenli þinges moste passe þe affeccion of þis worlde. Bot þis man is noȝt passid þe lufe of þe worlde, ne hase noȝt left his awen will, and þarefore he mai noȝt ȝete here þe priuatese of God.'

Capitulum cv. Criste bad þe spouse wirshipe þe bodi of
Saint Andrewe, and whi he loues him.

Criste saide to þe spouse þat sho suld wende to wirshipe þe bodi of Saint Andrewe þe apostill, for it was þe tempill of God, and þere is depose for gude men and helpe for sinfull. 'And þai þat come þidir with gude deuocion are noȝt oneli discharged of sin, bot þai are holeli comforthe[t]. For he shamed noȝt to take mi crosse, þare|fore I shame noȝt to here þame, and take þame þat he praies fore, for his will is mi will. And when þ[ou] haue bene at him, come againe to Napils to mi birth.' þan saide þe spouse, 'Lord, þe time is shorte, and eld and sekenes drawes nere, and þare is litill to spende.' þan saide Criste, 'I ame maker of kinde and reformere þareof. I ame helper in nede, and defender and rewarder, and I make þame þat loues me to do wele to mi frendes, þat þai mai be holpin thurght þaire praiere.'

Capitulum cvi. How þe spouse wirshipes Saint Steuen,
and how Saint Steuen spake to hir.

þe spouse praied at þe graue of Saint Steuen and saide þus: 'Blissed

1 Rome] Rorome   23 comforthet] comforthe   25 þou] þai

be þou, Saint Steuen, euen in mede with Saint Laurans. For right als
he prechid to þe panems, so did þou to þe Jewes. And right als he
suffird gladli þe fire, so suffird þou stones. Amange martirs þou arte
þe firste.' þan saide Steuen, 'Fro mi 30uthe I had one lufe to God, for
mi fadir and mi modir ware besi to þe heele of mi saule. And when 5
Criste | bigan to preche, I herd him gladli, and, son eftir þe asscension,   f. 268ᵛᵇ
I drewe me to þe apostils and serued þame full trewli. And I reproued
þe Jewes þat blasphemid Criste, and I was glad þat I might speke
againe þame. Bot þe firste þinge þat helpid me to blis was mi gude
wille. þe second was þe praiere of þe apostills. þe þird was þe passion 10
and þe lufe of Criste. And þarefor I haue now, firste, sight of þe visage
and þe blis of God; þe second, þat I haue what þat I will; þe þirde is
þat mi blis sall be withouten ende. And for þou hase ioi of mi blis,
þarefore mi praiere sall helpe þe to com to blis.'

Capitulum c`viii´. How, if a man haue one sin with   15
mani vertuse, it is `as´ a venom with gude metis.

þe modir saide þat, 'Haue a man neuir so mani vertuse, and he haue
likinge in one sinne, it profites him no3t, no more þan gude mete
sauers a man and þare be poison þerein. And þarefore sai to mi freend
þat if he will plese mi son and me, traiste no3t in his awen ver|tu, and   f. 269ʳᵃ
withdrawe his tonge fro mekill speche and scorn, and kepe [him] fro 21
light maners. He suld bere floures in his mouth to cheris þame þat are
no3t saueri to gude fruite. And if he finde ani bittir þinge amange þe
floures, þe floures will no3t be sett bi, and þe frute is no3t desirede.
And sai to him þat it is more plesinge to God þat a man leue in þe 25
world, and trauaile with his handes, þan leue in religion or in deserte
withouten charite.'

In þe name of God, fadir and son and holi goste, here endes þe sext
buke of heuenli reuelacions, graciousel[i] shewed by þe fre gudenes of
God vnto glorious Bride, princes of Nerrici in þe realme of Sweþire. 30

---

3 suffird¹] ssuffird   15 cviii] ciii *and superior mark*   20 and me] *subpuncted,*
cf. Lat. et michi   21 fro¹] for   him] þe   29 graciouseli] graciousl, *and*
superior mark

f. 269ʳᵇ In þe name of one God þat ordeynde seuen sacramentes, and
remembra[n]s of þe seuen giftes of þe holi goste, here biginnes þe
seuent buke of heuenli reuelacions, throw þe endles gudenes of þe
sam Gode, for helpe and speciall remedie againe þe seuen hede
5 sinnes, graciousli shewed to gloriouse Bride, Princes of Nerice in þe
realme of Sweyne.

Capitulum primum. How þe spouse þoght in Rome of
þe birth of Criste, and how þe modir spake to hir.

It fell in Rome in one time þat þe spouse þoght of þe birth of Criste
10 and of his blissed modir; and þare fell so warme a lufe in hir hert þat
sho saide, 'Mi ladi qwene, mi hert hase so grete ioy in þat þat God
chesed þe to be his modir, and put þe to so grete wirshipe, þat I hade
leuer be in hell, lastand þe world, þan þou suld lose þe lest point of þi
f. 269ᵛᵃ blis, or þat þou suld want þi heuenli wirshipe.' | And so sho was
15 rauished fro hirselfe and hir wittes, for swetenes of loue þat had made
hir dronken. þan saide þe modir to hir, 'For þou loues me so wele,
þou sall com to Bedlem, and þare sall I shew þe þe maner þat I bare
mi son Iesu.'

Capitulum 2m. A reuelacion þat Saint Bride hade in
20 Rome of þe swerde of sorowe þat Simeon spake of.

It fell in þe Purificacion dai in Rome þat þe spouse sawe in heuen
all þinge ordeined to one grete feste; and sho sawe a wonder faire
tempill, and þere was Simeon redi. And þare come þe modir, and bare
hir son in hir arme to offir him, and aboute hir a grete compani of
25 aungells and saintes. And one aungell went bifor hir þat bare one
lange blodi swerde, þat bitokened þe swerde of sorowe, and persid þe
modirs herte, þat Simeon made propheci of. And Simeon toke þe
child in his armes with grete mirth and gladnes. þan saide one to þe
spouse, 'Se what wirshipe is done to oure ladi þis dai for þe sorowe þat
30 sho suffird in þe dethe of hir son oure lorde.' |

2 remembrans] remembras

F. 269ra   Book VII ch. 22: St Bridget's vision of the birth of Christ

Capitulum iii. Howe Saint Fraunces bad þe spouse to   f. 269ᵛᵇ
mete and drinke with him.

In þe feste of Saint Fraunces, in his kirke in Rome, he apperid to
þe spouse and saide to hir, 'Come to mi chambir to ete and drinke
with me.' And sho ordeined hir to Assise, and when sho had bene 5
þare fife dais, and þoght to turne againe to Rome, sho went into þe
kirke and commend[ed] hir and hirs to Saint Fraunces. And he
apperid to hir and saide, 'þou art welcom. I bad þe com to mi
chambir. Mi chambir is lawelenes and obeinge þat I helde euir, so
mekill þat I was noȝt withouten one soueraine, for I had with me 10
euirmore one preste þat I obeide vnto, and loke þat þou do so. Mi
mete was besines to withdrawe folke fro vanite of þe worlde, and
þarewith was I fede full likandeli. Mi drinke was likinge þat I had in
deuocion of þame þat were turned bi me (and þat þai ware besi to
turne oþir) to be pore and forsake þe world. þerefor, doghtir, com 15
þou to þis chambir, and ete of þis mete and drinke of þis drinke, and
þou sall be filled ende|lesli with God.'   f. 270ʳᵃ

Capitulum iiii. Criste commendes sekinge of saintes
bodis, and telles how he is displesid for weddinge
againe þe statutes of holi kirke. 20

Criste apperid to one persone þat in hir praiere had onis so grete
likinge in hir herte, and ioi, þat hir þoght þe bodi might noȝt laste.
And þan saide Criste 'þat þis ioi þat þou felis in þi saule is mi tresoure
þat I giue to mi frendes. Bot I haue in erth oneoþir tresour, and þat is
þe bodis of þe saintes þat loued me and are here in erthe: and I shewe 25
miraklis in þam, and þaire bodis are canonised bi þe Popes of Rome.
And I sall rewarde þame þat visites þaire places þat þai are wirshiped
in eftir þaire wille and þaire trauaile. And in þis place are þe relikes of
Sainte Thomas mine apostill. And I will þat it be prechid þat, right as
þe bodis of Petir and Paule are in Rome, so are þe relikes of Sainte 30
Thomas here in þis cite þat is called Ortona in Napiles. For, all if þe
lordes of Napiles big kirkes and gife almus to plese `me´, neuirþelesse,
þare is one þinge þat I am misplesed with, and | þat is þat þai wed   f. 270ʳᵇ
againe þe ordinance of holi kirke and þe statutes of holi fadirs. And all if
þat shall stonnde þat þe Pope dispensis with, neuirþeles þe will of þame 35
þat had þe leue was noȝt gude, and þerefore it moste be discussid.'

7 commended] commend   17 filled] filled with

Capitulum v. How a kinge biggid one house, an of all
þat longes þareto: *ideo vide et cetera*.

`þer´ was one kinge, and biggid one house, and put þerin his awen
doghtir, and assigned a keper, and saide þus to him: 'Do all þi besines
5 to kepe mi doghtir, for sho hase dede enemis. Be wele ware þat none
mine thurght þe grounde, no clim ouir þe wale, nor breke þe walles,
ne com in bi þe ʒates.' Bi þis house is vndirstonnde þe bodi, þat þe
kinge of heuen made of erthe. Bi þe doghtir is vndirestonde man saule,
þat is putt into þe bodi. Bi þe keper is vndirstonde reson, þat suld
10 kepe þe saule. Bi þe gronde is vndirstonde gude will, þat suld be
stabilli set on God to fulfill his will, for withouten it mai no gude werke
be biggid.

f. 270ᵛᵃ   Bot þis gronde are þai aboute for to mine þat commen | to one ʒonge
man and sai to him, 'Sir, I rede þou be a weddid man and bringe furth
15 froite into þe werld and haue þi likinge'; and also þai þat saine, 'If þou
will be a clerke giue þe to þe seuen sciens, þat þou be cald a maistir
and gete þe grete auawnsementes in holi kirke, and so mai þou haue
worshipe and grete riches.' Bot reson sall answere againe, and sai þat
þou will kepe þe clene to þe serues of God, and þat þou will noʒt lere
20 for to get þe worldeli wirshipe no riches, bot þou will lere to þe
wirshipe of God, to enforme þame þat are simpill of coninge, and for
to defende þe faithe. And lat reson þus defende þe gude will.

þe seconde is þe hight of þe wallis, þat is, charite (for it is þe hieste
vertu of all.) And þarefore, reson sai to þe feend þat þou will soner
25 suffir þe dethe or þou will greue God; and what þat þou can do to
helpe of þine euine cristen, þat þu will do it, lettinge for no dissese þat
mai falle to þi bodi.

þe þird is to kepe wele þis wallis. By þam are vndirstanden foure
þinges. þe firste is to haue a feruent will to see God in his blis. þe |
f. 270ᵛᵇ   second is to will here þe aungels singe and loue God. þe þirde is to
31 desire to com to þame, þat þou mai loue God with þame. þe ferde is to
haue comforde of aungels and holi saules. And, right as he þat is in one
house is closed in foure wallis, right so if þou be closid in þere foure,
þat a[rn]e þer foure–to se God in his blis, to here þe aungels wirshipe
35 him, to will wirshipe him with þam, and desire to be with þam–þan art
þou siker fro þine enemis.

Bot ʒete most þe keper beware, for þat enemi will com bi two wais–

3 þer] here   17 gete þe] *twice, second subpuncted*   34 arne] ame
37 þe] þe be, be *subpuncted*

þe one, bi þine heringe of wanton sonnges and worldli minstralsi and
fabills: þe oþir wai is sight of worldli þinges. And þarefor sall þe kepar,
þat is reson, nowþir suffir luste of þe fleshe, ne coueitise of worldli
þinges, breke þes foure walles, no let þi minde to be occupied
in þame.   5

Bi þe ferde, þat are þe ȝates, are vndirstonden þose þinges þat
nedeli fallen to a mannes bodi, als for to ete and drinke, wake and
slepe, sometime to be merri and some|time heuy. þarefore moste f. 271ʳᵃ
reson be wele ware in eteinge and drinkinge—ware fro excesse, and
also of vndiscrete abstinens, also fro to mani mesis and grete waste in 10
daintes. Also be wele ware þat þe slepe be noght to longe, ne to litill,
and also þat þe wakinges be in honest dedis and in Goddes seruis, and
þat he be noȝt idill bot wele occupied. And euir, in etinge and
drinkinge, slepinge and wakinge, haue þe drede of God in minde, and
if ani turbill com, or dissese, fle angir and drede þe greuance of God, 15
and al[s]o, when ani mirth commes into þi hert, prai þat God so mesur
it þat he be noȝt greuid.

Capitulum vi. How Criste apperid to Bride in Rome,
    and bad hir dispose hir to Jerusalem.

Criste apperid to Saint Bride in Rome, and bad hir ordeine hir to 20
Jerusalem to visit þe sepulcre and oþir holi places, and þat sho suld
wende when he warned hir.

Capitulum vii. How þe modir bad speke to a frere, in
    mani gude maters, of forgifnes of sinnes, and praiers. |

þe modir saide to þe spouse, 'Sai to þat frere mi frende þat sothe it f. 271ʳᵇ
is, if a persone had trespassed againe God in all þe sinnes, and he with 26
verrai contricion and will to amend him wald aske merci, withouten
ani doute God ware redi as a gudeli fadir, with ioi and gladnes, to take
him to merci. And þerefore sai þat frere, on mi bihalfe, þat for his gude
wille, and mi praiere, all þe sinnes þat euir he dide are forgifen him; 30
and sai him also þat, for mi praiere, þe charete þat he hase to God sall
be encressed ai to his liues ende. And sai also þat it is plesinge to mi
son þat he dwell still in Rome, and preche and counseill folke to þe

3 þat] and þat, and *subpuncted*   7 to a mannes] *twice, second subpuncted*
8 some-] *Quire catchphrase,* time heuy, *below*   9 eteinge] etetinge   16 also]
alo   20 ordeine] ordeinde

gude, and enioine to þam helefull penance eftir þaire shrifte, bot it so
be þat his prelate for som nedefull þinge send him oute of þe towne.

'And bid him þat he stir with gude wordes and sharpe his breþir to
þe loue of Gode, and to kepe þaire rewle and amend þame; and lat
5 him wit þat his messis and his praiers and his redinges are plesinge to
God. And sai him þat, right als he kepis him fro excesse of mete and

f. 271ᵛᵃ drinke | and slepe, so kepe him fro vndiscrete abstinens þat he faile
noȝt in Goddes seruise. And sai him þat he haue cleþinge þat is nedefull
bot none waste, þat nowþir pride ne coueitise be in him, bot mekenes
10 eftir þe rewele of Saint Fraunces: for þe porer þat his cleþinge is, þe
richer sall be his mede. And bid him be obediand to his prelate in all
þinges þat are noȝt againe þe wirshipe of God þat he mai do.

'Sai also to him þat he sall answere þame þat sais þat þe Pope is
noȝt verra Pope. And bid him sai þat þe Pope [þat] is none eritike (be
15 he neuir so sinfull on oþir sides) is verrai Pope in bindinge and
lawesinge men saules by þe powere þat was graunted to Petir of God.
For mani Popes þat were bifore Jon þe two and twenti are in helle:
neuerþeles, þaire rightwis domes þat þai gaue standes and are
aproued bifor God. Also, all þai þat haue taken þe ordir of preste, and
20 þai be none eritikes, þai saker verai Goddes bodi on þe auter, all if þai
be in oþir sinnes.'

Capitulum viii. þe modir bad telle þe frere hir frende
þat it was noȝt lawfull to him to witt wheþir þe saule of

f. 271ᵛᵇ Pope Jon | xxii were in heuen or in helle.

25 The modir bad þe spouse sai to þe frere hir frende þat 'it is not lefull
to him to wit weþir þe saule of John þe two and twenti be in heuen or
in hell, no it is nowþir lefull to þe to wit of þe sinnes þat he was blamed
of before þe dome. And sai him þat þe decretals þat he made of þe
propirte of Criste are noȝt againe þe faithe, and þai contene no herisi.
30 For I bere witnes þat he had one þinge propir–þat was þe cot þat I
made with mi handis, for þar was [no]ne þat weldid it bot he, wit-
nesinge þe prophete, þat saide, "On mi cote þai keste lote." Lo, he
saide, "Of mine", and noght "Of oure." And witt þou wele þat when
þat euir I cled him in þat cote, mine eyn were full of terris and mi hert
35 full of bittir sorow, for I wist þat time o[f] his passion suld com and he
suld be spoiled of þat cote, and be done naked on þe crosse, for on it

14 þat²] om.   23-4 of Pope] of Pope of   29 are noȝt] twice, first subpuncted
31 none] men   35 of²] or

þai kest lote, and in all his life had none þat cote bot he, for it was his awen.'

Capitulum ix. Criste bad þe spouse go to Jerusalem. |

Criste bad þe spouse þat sho suld wende to Jerusalem, and þat sho f. 272ʳᵃ
suld noȝt lete for eld, for he was maker of kinde, and he mai gif hele als 5
him liste, and he suld strengþe hir and hirs and puruai for þame and
bringe againe to Rome.

[Capitulum x.] It was bedin to þe spouse in one reuelacion þat þare
was one archebishope þat saide, and he were Pope, he suld gife leue to
clerkes to wed þame wifes, for he trowed þat it ware les euell. 'Bot sai 10
þou to þe archebishop þat þe circumcision was gifen to Abraham
lange or þe lawe was gifen to Moises. First þai leued folke eftir þaire
reson and sithen eftir þe lawe. Right so, first was it lefull to prestis to
leue in matrimone, and som of þaim plesid mi son and scorned his
bodi. Bot eftirwarde it was set in þe Popes hert þat rewled holi kirke 15
þat time, bi þe inspiracion of þe holi goste, þat þai þat suld trete þat
bodi þat is so clene suld be clene withouten lusti dalians of woman:
and þarefor þa prestis þat are filed with wem|men are noȝt worthi to f. 272ʳᵇ
towche þat worþi bodi and clene, nor it is noȝt lefull to þe Pope to
dispens with prestis to be weddid. For if Saint Gregore had giuen lefe 20
þareto (als he did noȝt), he suld noȝt haue bene saued bot he had
reuokid it befor his dede.'

Capitulum xi. Crist telles how he [gaue] fredome of will
both to aungels and to men.

Criste saide, 'I gaue aungels and man fredome to folow me and do 25
mi will, and þe aungels þat turned þame fro me are feendis. And man
folowd þe strengþe of þe fende and forfet mi commandmentes. Bot I
deliuerd man fro þe fendis thraldome with þe blode of mi herte. And it
is ordinede þat gife man will folowe mi will he sall haue þe blis þat euir
is lastinge: and if he folow þe feende he sall haue paine.' 30

Capitulum 12. Criste spake to þe spouse of a bishope,
tellinge what he suld do if he wald com vnto blis.

---

1 in] in his, his *subpuncted*　　　　8 Capitulum x] *om., blank space before* It *for Chapter*
title　　　10 þat it] i *of* it *over* þa *of second* þat, þa *ruled through*　　　23 gaue] *om.*

Criste bad þe spouse þat sho suld sai to one bishop þat if he wald be called to blis at þe grete dome þat he sall noȝt folowe þe condicions of
f. 272ᵛᵃ þaim þat were rewlers in holi kirke, | for þere ware no men þat had so fer forgetin his wordes als þai had, for þaire pride and þaire coueitise
5 and þaire lusti lifeinge: 'and so haue þai giuen euell ensampill to oþir, and þerefor me moste do exercise of my rightwisnes agans þam and put þame oute of þe boke of life, and put þam to be with Lucifer withouten ende, bot it so be þat þai amende þame or þai dye and turne þame to me with all þaire hert.

10   'Sai þarefore to þat bishope þus: "Sir, somtime oute of a foule blake chimne commis a faire lowe and profitabill to mani faire werkes. And, neuirþeles, men praises noȝt þe blakenes of þe chimne, bot þai prais þe werkeman." ' ('Right so', saide þe spouse, 'if ani gude be done bi me, God is worthi to be praised and noȝt I.')

15   ' "And þarefore I sai ȝou þat ȝe sall beware þat ȝe promote none to holi ordirs bot þaim þat are abill in lifinge and in conninge bi þe dome of gude men, and make all ȝour suffragans to do so. Also luke þat all ȝoure curatis of ȝour diosis be onis in þe ȝere bifore ȝou, þat ȝe mai comon togedir how þat þai rewele þare awen saules and also þe saules
f. 272ᵛᵇ of þaire soiettes, | and teche þame how þai suld liue and rewle þaire
21 parishin. And luke þat ȝe chasti wele þe prestis þat haldis concubins, for þai are abhominabill in þe sight of Gode als warne þe dwellers of Sodome, all if þai mai noȝt paire þe mese in þe selfe. (Neuirþeles, þe kis of pes is als euell to God as is þe kise of Judas.)

25   ' "Also I rede þat ȝoure mene be esi, and noght to mani for pride. And be besi þat þe clerkis be honeste and noght proudeli araide, and be besi to teche þame and haue no pride in ȝoure clerkes ne ȝoure oþir mene, and hald no vicious man in ȝoure compani þat will noȝt sone amend him. Also I rede þat ȝe haue noȝt togidir passinge thre paire of
30 arai, and for bede and burde haue sufficient arai and no superfluite. And haue siluir vessell for ȝour awen burde, and þe remenand gife for þe lufe of God, for þe pride of siluir vesell þat is vsed nowodais is full abhominabill in þe sight of God, þat made himselfe so pore for man.
f. 273ʳᵃ Also beware of mani metis and dellites, no be noȝt besi of grete arai of
35 hors and harnes, for as oft as a prelate with pride wendis vp on a grete hors, þan þe feende wendis vp into þaire neke, and smites þame in þaire brestes when þai smite þe hors with þaire spurres for pride or vaine glori.

22 als] also   27 and haue no pride in ȝoure] *twice*, va-cat *to* haue no pride in ȝoure and

' "Also I rede ȝou make ȝour comissaris to swere þat þai sall do right and none wrange; and if þai do ani wrange loke þat ȝe do amende it eftir. And if ȝe do þus, traiste wele þat ȝe sall kepe ȝoure consciens clere. Also, for þe saules þat ȝe wald wit of, do singe euirilkea dai on twelue monethes two messes for þame, and fede ilke dai two pore men, 5 and euirilke weke gife one floraine of monee. Also sai to ȝoure parishe prestis þat þai chasti þaire parisheinges, and þai þat will not be amendid bi him, amende ȝe þame, in þat þat in ȝou is, and if þai will [noȝt] be amendid bi ȝoue, leue þame to þe dome of God, þat sall rewarde ȝou for ȝour gude wille: bot ȝet leue noȝt for bodeli drede." ' 10

Capitulum xiii. Criste spekes to þe spouse of Charlles
hir son, what he did for him in his time of his dede. |

þe modir saide to þe spouse, 'When Charles þi son deed, I was nere f. 273ʳᵇ
him and helpid so þat þe lufe of Gode was noȝt lettid in him for ani
fleshli or worldeli lufe. And I helpid him þat in þe departenge of [þe] 15
saule and þe bodi þat he suffird noȝt so hard paine þat suld make him
to fall in ani misbeleue or elles forgete God. Also, I helpid him þat þe
feendes hade no pouer þan to touche his saule. Bot what dome þat he
had eftir, I sall shewe þe when me liste.'

Capitulum xiiii. þe modir shewed to þe spouse in   20
bodeli likenes what was done with þe soule of hir son.

þe modir shewed eftir to þe spouse in bodeli liknes what was done
with þe saule of hir son. Scho sawe in hir sprete one faire felde, and
þerin sho sawe Iesu sittinge in one trone, als it were one kinge
crouned, and in euirilkea side aboute him grete compani of aungels 25
and saintes, and þe modir of merci stondinge nere and listeninge þe
dome. And þere stode bifor þe domesman one saule, tremellinge for
drede, and naked als one childe þat | is newe born, and als it were f. 273ᵛᵃ
blinde (bot he knewe wele in his consciens what was saide in þe
dome). One þe right hand of þe saule þare stode one aungell, and on 30
þe left hand one fende, bot noþir of þame neght þe saule.
þan criede þe feende and saide to þe domesman, 'Almighti, I pleine
on þi modir and oure all ladi, þat sho hase done me wronge of þis
saule: for sho wald noȝt lat me com nere it, and to me it fell to haue

9 noȝt] om., Lat. noluerint (possibly misread as uoluerint)   15 þe²] mi
17 ani] ami, third minim subpuncted   27 þe] þe saule, saule subpuncted

present it.' þan saide þe modir, 'þou feende, þis saule fell noȝt to þe
bot to me, and þerefor I present it to þe domesman. For while þis
saule was in þe bodi it loued me so wele þat þare was no warldli
likinge þat might lett þe gladnes þat he had in his hert of þat þat I was
5 modir to God; and for God did þat grace to me, he loued God of all his
hert. For þis loue þat he had to mi son and to me, I gat grace of mi son
þat noþir þou ne non oþir fende suld com ne[re] his saule at his
passinge.' þan saide þe fende, 'I haue wretin his synnes, for, when he
com to ȝeres of discrecion and vndirstode sin, he assentid to worldli
f. 273ᵛᵇ pride and fleshli likinge.' þan answerde þe aungell and | saide, 'Als
11 sonn as his modir sawe þat he was enclined to sin, sho stirred him to
werkes of merci, and praied God full hertli þat he suld haue merci on
him and lat him neuir be loste. And so, bi praier of his modir, he fell to
þe drede of Gode, þat als oft as he trespassed he rose againe bi shrifte.'
15 þan saide þe feende, 'I will reherse his sinnes.' And he luked eftir
his bille and it was awai. And þan cried þe feende, 'Alas! I can nowþir
finde þe sinnes [no] haue minde of þe time þat he sinned in.' þan
saide þe aungell, 'þat hase made þe praiers of his modir, and hir teris,
and hir grete morninges for þis sinne, for þai gat him contricion of his
20 sinne, and grace to shriue him of þame: and þerfore þai are oute of þi
minde.'
þane saide þe fende, 'Ȝit haue I mani þinges þat he suld be mine
fore: for he was slawe in Goddes seruise, and lefte þe gude þat he suld
haue done.' þan luked þe fende and all was awai, and he cried, 'Alas!'–
25 all was lorn. þan saide þe aungell, 'þat hase þe terres of his modir
made.'
f. 274ʳᵃ þan saide þe fende, 'Ȝet I haue his | veniall sinnes.' þan saide þe
aungell, 'He gat leue and he went oute of his cuntre to pilgramage, and
haues fulfilled þame, and left his frendis and put him to grete trauails.
30 And so he gat indulgens and pardon in visitinge of holi places, and he
was besi to make amendes to God for his sin. And þat he gat thrught
praiere of his modir, þat trauaild and praied full mekill for him.'
þan saide þe fende, 'þare is one þinge ȝit, and þat is þat he gat with
wronge gude.' þan saide þe aungell, 'For þat hase his modir made
35 assethe with almosdede: and also, he dide seke thrugheoute þe cite to
make amendis to all þat he had harmed. And of þat þat is vndone, his
aires sall make asethe.'
þan saide þe feende, 'Ȝit moste him be chastide, for he did not so

7 nere] ne   17 no] I   25-8 þat hase þe . . . saide þe aungell] *twice* (*second*,
teres, fennde)

mekill gude as he might haue done in his liue.' þan saide þe aungell,
'It is wretin, þat "To him þat askes it sall be geuen, and to him þat
knokkis, it sall be oppinde": | and his modir more þan thirtti ȝere hase f. 274ʳᵇ
asked and praide for him with mani one tere þat God suld geue him
grace to serue him trewli. And þis knight had so birninge a loue to God 5
þat him list noȝt life bot to be Goddes seruand and to plese him, and
þis gaue God him: and þis gat him fulfillinge of all þat him wantid to
com with to heuen. And for þat grete will þat he hade, to haue gone in
pilgramage to Jerusalem, and for he was in grete will to haue holpin to
haue broght þe holi land into cristen mens handis, so þat þe sepulcre 10
suld haue bene in wirshipe–for þis it is fulfilled all þat he wantid of
vertu, at þe helpinge of þe modir of merci, to bringe him to blis. And
þarefor þou, fende, hase no right in him.' þan saide þe feende, 'Werid
be þe olde wife þat [wepid] so mani teres.'

And þan saide þe domesman, Criste himselfe, 'Go heens þou 15
feende!' And þan he saide to þe knight, 'Com to me, mi derlinge.' þan
saide þe spouse, 'Blissed be God.' And þe aungell saide to hir, 'þis
reuelacion is | noght oneli for þe, bot þat Cristes freendes mai wit how f. 274ᵛᵃ
mikill þat he loues þame, and what he will do for teris and praiers of
his frendes. And wit wele þat þi son had noght had þat grace had he 20
noȝt set him timeli to loue God.'

      Capitulum xv. Crist telles how clene þai are þat
      commis into his tempill.

Criste saide to þe spouse, 'When ȝe com into mi tempill þat is
halowed with mi blode, ȝe are als clene of all ȝour sinne als if ȝe ware 25
now lift oute of þe fonte stone, and for ȝoure trauaile and ȝour
deuocion, som saules of ȝour frendes þat ware in purgatori are
deleuerd and went to blis. For all þat commen with gude deuocion
vnto þis place Jerusalem, with will to amend þame and noght to turn
againe to sinne, all þaire sinnes are forgifen þame, and þai sall hafe 30
grace of wele doinge.'

      Capitulum xvi. How Criste shewed to þe spouse in
      monte of Calueri þe maner of his deinge and his
      passion. 34

Criste shewed in þe monte of Caluerri | to þe spouse, wepinge and f. 274ᵛᵇ

14 wepid] *om.*

heui, þe maner of his dyinge on þe crosse. He bad hir take hede to one
hole þat was kut of þe stone in þe hille, for in it was festned þe fote of
þe crosse, in time of his passion, fast, þat it suld noȝt fall. þan were
þare festind two burdes about þe crosse, as þai were gresis, while þai
5 com to þe place where þe fete suld stand, þat þai þat suld do him on
þe crosse might wende vpe and stand more eseli. þan went þai vpon
þe gresis and drew Iesu vp with þaim with mekill scorn and shame,
and he folowd þaim as one lambe þat sulde be slaine. And when he
com on þe highest burde, wilfulli he spred oute his arme and opind his
10 right hand, and þai smote him thrugh to þe cros, in þat parti where þe
bone was moste sade. þan þai drewe þe left arme with one corde as
sadli as þai couthe, and festened of þe sam manere to þe crosse. þan
þai drewe done þe bodi bi þe fete with all þaire might and laide þe one
f. 275ᵛᵃ fote ouir þe oþir, and þan festned þame | downe with two nailes, and
15 þai drowe his bodi so sore þat all þe vains and þe sinnows fore als þai
had brosten. þai put on þe crowne of þorne vpon his heued, and set it
so faste þareto þat þe blode of his heued filled his eyn full, and his eris
and his berd were all rede of blode. And þan þai þat did him on þe
crosse tuke awai þe burdes, and þan hange he vpon þe crosse.

20   And þan loked þe spouse beside, and sho sawe his sorowfull modir
liinge at þe erthe, tremelinge as sho suld die, and Jon and hir sistirs
comforth hir þat were fast bi. ('Bot þan bigan in me a newe sorowe of
þat sorowfull modir, so þat me þoght þat one grete swerde went
throwe me of bittirnes.') And when þat sorowefull modir, allmoste
25 dede, luked vpon hir son, þe swerde of sorowe wan throw hir. And
when hir son sawe hir and his oþir frendes make sorowe and wepe so
sore, with one wepinge voice he bitaght his modir to Jon, þat men
might wele knaw bi his voice þat his hert was full of sorowe.

f. 275ʳᵇ   þan his ein, þat were so clere, se|med all dede, and his mouthe was
30 opin and full of blode, and his visage all pale, sprenkled with blode.
His bodi was blo and wan withouten blode. His fleshe was so tendir
þat at þe leste towchinge of þe scourges þe blode ran oute and it left all
blo. He shrenked vpon þe cros for bittirnes of his paine. And somtime
þe sorowe of his woundes went to his hert. And so his deth went throw
35 all þe partes of his bodi.

    þan cried he to þe fadir with one hie voice and on wepinge, 'A fadir,
whi hase þou forsaken me?' His lippis were pale and his tonge was
blodi; his wombe was clongen so hard to his bake þat it semed þat he
had no bowels within him. And þan cried he eft againe with on lowde

5 þat¹] *twice, first subpuncted*   25 dede] dede and

voice, 'O fadir, into þi handes I betake mi spirit': and þan he held vp
his heed a litill and bowed downe againe, and ȝelde þe goste.

And when his modir saw þis, sho tremelid for sorowe, and wald
haue fallen downe to þe erthe, had noȝt þe oþir wimmen halden hir
vpe. And þan with weght of his bodi, his handes somwhat satild fro þe 5
nailes, and | þan þe nailes þat were in þe fete bare vp all þe bodi. His
handes and his fingirs and his bake bone were so stife þat þai might
noght wele bowe.

þan þase wikked turmentoures cried on his modir with scorn. þan
com one als it hade bene one wode man, and smote him in at þe right 10
side so desp[e]touseli þat it went throw his breste allmoste to þe oþir
side; and when he drewe oute þe spere, þare com oute grete gote of
blode eftir, and þe iren of þe spere and somwhat of þe shaft was all
blodi. And when þe modir sawe þat, she swowned.

And when þis was done, and þe pupill was withdrawen, þare com of 15
his freendis and tuke him downe of þe crosse, and his modir tuke him
in hir armes and sat downe with him, and laide him on hir knee, all
torent and wounded. And with teres of hir een, and otheres, sho weshe
his woundes and wipede þame with a linen cloth, and sho closed his
een and kist þame and lappid him in a clene sendall. And with sorow- 20
full hertes þai laide him in þe graue.

Capitulum xvii. Criste telles howe lordes of þe world |
takes litill hede to þat at sho had sene.

Criste saide to þe spouse, 'Lordes of þe worlde takes full litill heede
to þat at þou hase sene now and of þis place, bot all vnto worldli likinges. 25
And bot þai, and prelates also, turn þaire hertes to me and þinke on mi
passion, þai sall be dampned with þame þat partid mi cloþis.'

Capitulum xviii. þe modir tald howe in Mont Syon are
two maner of folke.

þe modir saide to þe spouse, 'In þis place of Mont Syon are two 30
maner of folke. Som loues God with all þaire herte, and som wald
haue God, bot þai haue more likinge in þe world þan in God: and it
were bettir to þaim to dwell in þe place þat is ordened to pilgrimes þan
þere': et cetera.

11 despetouseli] desptouseli   16 modir] *twice, first subpuncted*   28 xviii. þe
modir tald] *twice (first, viii)*   Syon] *marg.*, Sion

Capitulum xix. þe fi[rs]t counsell þat was bedin þe
spouse geue to þe Kinge of Cipir.

þe first counsell þat was bedin to þe spouse gife to þe Kinge of
Cipir was þat ilke man suld shriue him clene, and all his, of þaire
f. 276ʳᵃ sinne, and with drede and loue resaiue | Goddes bodi. 'þe second
6 counsaile, þat ȝe be knit togidir in loue, so þat ȝe be one hert to þe
wirshipe of God, gude gouernans of þe kingdom and rest to ȝoure
soietts. þe þird is, þat at þe reuerens of Gode and of his passion, þat ȝe
forgeue all þame þat were of counsell, fauoure or doers of þe dede of
10 Kinge Petir, and resaiue þame to charite.

'The ferthe is þat siþen God has ordened ȝou to be gouernours of
þis kingedome, þat ȝe do ȝoure prelates of hali kirke and of religione
þat þai amend þameselfe and þaire soietts, and turn to gosteli lifinge,
as þair hali predecessours dide bifore time, and þat þai mai win þe
15 frenshep of God, and prai him to reforme all hali kirke.

'þe fift is, þat ȝe counsell and stir ȝour cheuailri þat þai shriue þame
and amend þame of þaire leuinge, and submit þame fulli to þe kirke of
Rome, and þat þai a[cor]d fulli with þame þat haue greued þame or
þat þai haue greued, and resaiue Goddes bodi with drede and charite:
20 and þat þai leue trewli in þaire statis, whedir it be in matrimone or
f. 276ʳᵇ elles | in wedowheede or elles in maidenhede: and þat þai geue gude
ensampill in worde and werke to all oþir men. And wit þai wele þat þai
þat will noȝt do þus, þai sall be shent both in bodi and saule.

'þe sext is, þat ȝe speke to þe prelates, þat þai charge all þe curetes
25 þat if þare be in þaire parishe ani man or womman þat leuis in opin
sinne, þat will noȝt amende þame for þaire biddinges, þat þai sai to
oþir prelates, and if þe prelates mai noȝt nor dar noght chasti þame,
put ȝe hand to to maintene þe prelates in chastiinge and amendinge of
þame þat are rebell in contempt of holi kirke.'

30 þaire counsels ware sente to þe Kinge of Cipir and þe Prince of
Antioche how þat þai suld get grace of God.

Capitulum xx. Of a wounder fare place þat was shewed
to þe spouse in hir contemplacione.

It was shewed to þe spouse in hir contemplacion one wounder faire

---

1 first] fift   10 Petir] Petir ȝoure, ȝoure *subpuncted*   13 þai amend] *twice*
(*second*, amende), *second subpuncted*   18 acord] and, *Lat.* reconcilient
30 sente to þe] *twice* (*second*, sent), to þe sent *subpuncted*

palas, and Iesus Criste sittinge in his trone als one kinge. And he saide
þat he loued mankinde als mekill now as þat time þat he died on þe
crosse. For, if it were possibill, 3ete wald he | dye for mannes saule. Bot
he mai noght dye: 'And þerefor þare is no saule þat gose to helle,
sethin þat I died, þat euer mai come oute þareofe, fro it [be] dampned
to hell, bot it sall be ai in paine, for it wald not leue sinne for þe loue of
me; and bi encheson of þat offens and greuance þat are to me moste
rightwisenes be shewed, and þere [awe] none to be domesman bot
miselfe. þarefore, mi charite þat I shewed to mankinde pleines to mi
rightwisnes, þat mi rightwisnes buse deme eftir mi will. And þarefore
now I pleine vpon þe euell lifers of þe kingedome of Cipir als on one
man. Take heed, þou, þe folke of Cipir. I loue þe as þe fadir loues his
oneli son þat he wald wirshipe. I sende þe plente to þe sustinaunce of
þi bodi. I sende þe þe hete of mi spirit, and light to vndirstande and
knawe cristen faithe þat þou bond þe to. I set þe in a place where þou
might be a trewe seruand amange mi frendes, þat for þi bodeli
trauailes þou suld win to mi blis, þat is euir full and endeles. I kepe þe
as | þe apill of mi ee, as lange as þou kepis mi commandementes and þe
ordinans of holi kirke, and was obeiand þerto.

'þan com of þe kingdome of Cipir to me saules withouten nowmbir:
bot now þou art turned and do[s]e þine awen will, and þou dredes
no3t for me to do þine awen wille, þat ame þi domesman and þi maker,
and boght þe with full bittir dede. þou has spit me oute of þi mouthe
als one stinkeinge þinge, and þou hase closed þe fende in þi chambir
of þi hert; and þou hase no shame to sinne in mi presens, more þan it
were one vnresonabill best.

'þerfor mi rightwise dome is to holde þe fro heuen, þat þou com
noght amange mi frendes, bot for to put þe euirlastingeli in helle
amange mine enemis. And wit þou wele þat oute of mi mouthe com
neuir bot trewthe. And þerfore wit þou þat none þat is disposed als
þou arte now, and will no3t amend him, shall go oþir wai þan Lucifer
3ode for his pride, and Judas, þat solde me for his coueitis, and
Zambry, þat Phinees slewe for his licheri. þarefore | I tell þe, þe pupill
of Cipir, þat if þou will no3t amende þe, I sall distroi þi kinde oute of
þe kingdome of Cipir, and I sall neuir spare riche ne pore, and þat in
short time, als þou had neuir bene. And I sall sett on new folke þarein.

'Neuirþeles, what he be þat wille amende him and turne him to me,
I will gladli mete him, and bere him on mi shulders, als þe gude hirde,

f. 276ᵛᵃ

5

10

f. 276ᵛᵇ

20

25

30

f. 277ʳᵃ

35

---

3 he] twice   5 be] *om.*   8 awe] *om.*   13 sustinaunce] sustiinaunce
14 hete] he hete, he *subpuncted*   21 dose] done

to mi floke. Mi shulders are mi passion þat is offird in mi bodi, þat he
sall be saued bi þat will turne to me. Mi floke are þe saintes in heuen.
þis warneinge is made to þe folke of Cipir, for þare are ȝet som gode
þat louen me.

5 'Bot wit þou wele þat þare is bot one cristen mens faithe, and oneli
one cheue heede kirke (þat is, Rome), and oneli one generall vicare of
Criste here in erthe, Pope of Rome, whome to all cristen folke awe
obediens and meke subiection. Bot þai, for þere pride and þaire
coueitise and luste of fleshe, will noght obei þareto. And þarefore are
10 þai, and sall be, in tribulacion of enemis, and þaire empire sall noȝt
f. 277ʳᵇ fare wele, | vnto þe time þat þai obei fulli to þe kirke of Rome and þe
Pope þareof, and eftir þaire dede þai shall finde no merci. Neuirþeles,
yf þare be ani þat wald faine ken þe trewe faithe and submit þam to þe
Pope of Rome, and þai ware enformed, with þat shall be done merci in
15 ponisheinge eftir þaire dede. And þarefore, bid þame of Rome submitt
þame fulli to þe Pope and þe kirke of Rome.'

Capitulum xxi. A reuelacion of Sainte Fraunces and his
ordir.

Criste saide to þe spouse, 'þare was a man was called Fraunces, þat
20 turned him all fro þe worldli pride and coueitise and luste of fleshe
and all oþir vices, and had one grete will of mendinge of his life, and
saide þus: "þare is noȝt in þe worlde bot I wald gladli leue it for þe
loue and þe wirshipe of mi lorde Iesu Criste, and to þis will I besi me
to bringe all oþir to in þat þat I mai." þis rewle þat Fraunces biganne
25 was noȝt of mennes makinge, nor of mannes wit, bot it was of mi awen
f. 277ᵛᵃ makinge, eftir mine awen will. Euirilke worde þat | is wretin in it was
inspirit by mine spirit, and so ware þe oþir rewles þat mi frendes
bigane and kepit þameseluen, and broght oþir to þe kepinge of þame.

'Fraunces freres, þat are cald menoures, longe time kepid þis reule
30 right wele gosteli and deuoteli eftir mi will; and þat hade þe fende
grete invie at. And at þe laste, when he had lange time besid him to
dissese þir freres, he fand one clerke þat þoght þus: "I wald gladli be
in swilke a state whare I might haue worshepe of þe worlde and rest of
mi bodi, and where I suld wante noþinge and I might gedir mone. I
35 will entir þe ordir of Fraunces, and I sall feine me full meke and lawli

3 warneinge] warneninge   5 Bot wit þou wele] twice (first, well), first subpuncted
8 þai] þai of grete, of grete subpuncted   13 þe²] þe faithe, faithe subpuncted
23 I] I bringe me, bringe me ruled through   29 þis] twice, first subpuncted

and obedient." And þus he entird þe ordir of Fraunces; and þe feende
for his falshede entird into him. And þan þoght þe fende þus: "Right
als bi Fraunces were mani drawen to leue þe worlde and com to blis,
so sall þis frere aduersari, and þat sall be his name, drawe mani fra
mekenes to pride, fro wilfull pouert to coueitise, fro obediens to do 5
þaire awen will and bodeli likinge": | so þat he was aduersari to f. 277ᵛᵇ
Fraunces rewele.

'þan þoght he þus: "When oþir fastis I sall ete preuali, and when
oþir haldes þaire silens I sall get me compani and make meri þat oþir
sall noȝt wit, for in sight of oþir I sall be meke to be holden holi. Also, 10
bi þe rewle I mai noȝt handill siluer no golde, ne haue it. þarefore I
sall gete me som speciall frende þat mai kepe preuali mi golde and mi
siluer to me, to haue when me liste. Also I will go to þe scole and lere,
þat I mai hafe wirshipe in þe worlde and in mine ordir, and þat I mai
haue hors and siluer vessell and precious cloþis and faire arrai. And if 15
ani aske me whi I do so, I sall answere and sai þat I do it for wirship of
mine ordir: and ȝet will I be besi if I mai gete to be a bishope, and þan
ware I wele at ese, for þan ware I at mine awen fredome and miȝt haue
likinge of mi bodi."

'Here þou what þe fende hase done in Fraunces ordir. For þere are 20
mani þat folowes frer aduersari, and þai are mengid with Fraunces
freres. Neuer|þeles, eftir þaire dede I sall departe þame, and I sall f. 278ʳᵃ
deme Fraunces freres to be with him in blis, and þe oþir to paine, bot
þai amend þame mekeli befor þaire dede. And wit þose freres wele þat
oþir religious þat are forbedin bi þe rewele to haue propir againe þe 25
rewele, all if þai wald gife me som þareof, þaire giftes are abhominabill
to me and worthi no þanke, for it is more plesinge to me þat þai hald
þe pouert þat þai are profeste to bi þaire rewelis þan þai made me
present of all þe gold and þe siluer þat is in þe worlde. And wit þou
wele þat þou suld noȝt haue sene no herde þis, had it noȝt bene for þat 30
frere menowre þat loued me and praied me so hertli þat he might here
some profitabill counsels to his saule.'

Capitulum xxii. þe spouse telles howe sho sawe in
Bedlem þe fairest ladi with child þat euir sho sawe.

The spouse saide þus: 'When I was in Bedlem I sawe one maiden with 35
child, þe fairest þat euir I saw, clede in one white mantill, and | one smale f. 278ʳᵇ

6 bodeli] boldeli   16-17 wirshipe of mine] *twice* (*first,* mi) mi wirshipe *sub-*
puncted   30 haue] haue bene, bene *subpuncted*

kirtill: and with hir one semeli olde man, and with þame on ox and ane asse. And he bonde þe ox and þe asse at þe stalle, and he went and lighted to þat maiden one candill, and festind vpon þe walle. And þan went he furthe, for sho was nere time of deliueringe. þan laide sho fro
5 hir hir mantill, and tuke of þe kirchefe of hir hede, and stode in hir kirtill allone, and hir heere hange done aboute hir shuldirs faire als golde. And sho tuke two clene clowtes of linen and two of cloth þat sho broght with hir, to lappe þe childe in when he ware born. And sho laide þame done bi hir, to time were.

10 'And when sho had made all redi, sho knelide downe with grete reuerens and praied, and sett hir bake againe þe cribe, and turned hir visage to þe este and helde vp hir handes and hir een vp into þe heuen, and sho was raised in contemplacion with so grete a swetenes þat hard it is to tell. And þan saw I in hir wombe a þinge stire; and sodanli sho
15 bare hir son. And þare com so grete a light and brightnes þat it passed
f. 278ᵛᵃ þe brightenes of þe son, and þe | lightnes of þe candill þat Joseph sett on þe wall might noȝt be sene. And it was so sodan, þat beringe of þe child, þat I might noȝt persaiue þe passinge furthe of þe childe. Neuirþelesse I sawe þat blisfull childe liinge naked on þe erthe, and
20 he had þe fairest skin þat euir I sawe, withouten spot. Also I sawe þe secondine, þat is þe rim þat þe child was born in, liand all white. þan herde I sange of aungells wounder swete and likinge.

'And when þe maiden felide þat sho had born hir childe, sho bowed doune hir heed and held vp hir handes and wirshipe[d] þe childe, and
25 saide to him: "Welcom mi God, mi lord, and mi son!"

'And þe child, wepand and tremeland for colde and hardnes of þe pament, streked him to seke refresheinge. þan his modir tuke him in hir armes, and streined him to hir breste, and with hir cheke and hire breste scho warmed him with grete ioy and lykynge. þan sat sho
30 doune on þe erthe, and laide þe childe on hir kne, and tuke him and laide him, firste, in on linen clothe, and sithen in one wolle, and
f. 278ᵛᵇ band his bodi, | his armes and his legges with one band; and þan sho band two linen litill cloþis, þat sho broght with hir, aboute his heued.

35 'And þan com Joseph in and fell done on his knees and wirshiped him, and he wepid for ioi. And þe modir was nowþir chaungid in howe, ne sho had no seknes no febilnes of hir strengþe, and hir wombe was als smale as it was before sho had consaiued. And þan rose sho vp,

13 contemplacion] comtemplacion   21 in] in þe   24 wirshiped] wirshipe
28 breste] breste sho war, sho war *subpuncted*   32 bodi] *twice, second subpuncted*

and Joseph helped hir to lai þe child in þe crib, and knelid doune þai
bothe and wirshiped him.'

Capitulum xxiii. þe modir remembris to þe spouse how
sho had hight `to´ shew hir Bedleeme.

þe modir aperid in þe same place to þe spouse and saide: 'Doghtir, 5
it is lange sithen þat I hight þe in Rome þat I suld shewe to þe in
Bedleeme þe maner of mi beringe of mi son, all if I shewed þe somwhat in Napils. þus I did als I haue now shewed vnto þe, for when I
was allone, knelinge on mi knees in þe stabill, I was deliuerd with
grete gladshipe and withouten helpe of ertheli | creature.' f. 279ra

Capitulum xxiiii. It was shewed to þe spouse how þre 11
shepherdes wirshipe þe child.

It was shewed to þe spouse in þe same place, howe þat þe
shepherdes come to wirshipe þe childe. And þai asked wheþir it was
man or woman. And þe modir shewed to þaim þat it was a man. And 15
þai fell downe and wirshipe him with grete reuerens and ioi, and þan
þai turned againe.

Capitulum xxv. þe modir tellis hir sones chere when
the kinges come.
20
þe modir saide to þe spouse þat when þe kinges come to þe stabill to wirshipe hir son, þan þe childes chere was mikill gladder þan
it was before. And sho had a grete likinge and kepid in hir hert these
wordes.

Capitulum xxvi. Howe Criste sittes on his fadir right 25
hande and here[s] men speke.

þe modir saide, 'Right als mi son was meke when þat he was laide in
þe cribbe bitwene þe bestis and spake noght, all if he knewe all þinge
in his godhede, right so he sittis nowe on his fadir right | hand and f. 279rb
heris mennes spekinge with charite, and spekis to som with gude 30
inspiracion, and with som als it were mouthe bi mouthe, als him liste.

10 ertheli] *Quire catchphrase*, Capitulum xxiiiim, *below*   13 shewed] *twice, second*
subpuncted   26 heres] here

Also I, þe modir, þat ame lift vp aboue all pure creatures in mi bodi, I
ame als meke now as when I was weddid with Joseph.

'Bot wit þou wele þat, or þe time þat Joseph weddid me, he wiste
wele bi inspiringe of þe hali gaste þat I had awowed chaste (bot God
5 walde oþirwais dispose of me), and þerefore his entent was to serue
me and haue me to his ladi. And when he sawe mi wombe grete, he
supposid none euell, bot he had minde how þe prophetes had saide
bifore how þat Goddes son suld be born of one maiden; and, for he
þoght him to simpill to be in mi compani, he wald haue left me, had
10 noȝt þe aungell bidin him abide.

'He and I kepid vs no more þan was nedefull to oure leueinge. þe
remeland we gaue for þe wirshipe of Gode. Bot all if I was ordende to
be in wirshipe aboue all oþir creature and all men oþir þan mi son,
f. 279ᵛᵃ neuirþeles ȝet serued I Joseph, and ordeinde for him þat was | nedefull
15 to him, and mi son was laweli and soiett to vs bothe. And for þis
mekenes ame I ȝet with mekenes redi to present mens praier to
mi son.'

Capitulum xxvii. Apparicion made bi þe modir to þe
spouse in þe vale of Josophat.

20 The modir aperid to þe spouse in þe vale of Josophat at hir graue,
all bright shininge, and saide to hir, 'Doghtir, fro þe time þat mi son
stied vp to heuen I leued in erthe xv ȝere, and als mikill more as is fro
þe assencion to þe time þat I died. And I lai fiften dais in þis graue,
and þan was I taken vp with gret wirshipe. And þe cloþis þat I was
25 berid in, I lefte þame in þis graue, and I was clede as mi son and mi
lorde was clede. Also, witt þou wele þat þare is no mans bodi in
heuene bot þe blissed bodi of mi son and mine. Wende now ȝoure wai
and kepe ȝou besili, sithen ȝe haue visit þis place where mi son and I
leued.'

30 Capitulum xxviii. Criste apperid to þe spouse and bad
hir noȝt lett to speke þat sho suld here.

f. 279ᵛᵇ Crist apperid to þe spouse in hir praier and | bad hir þat scho suld
sai þat þat sho suld here and lett noght for drede of man, no tell it not
for ani worldeli wirshipe: 'for þis reuelacion is noȝt for þi sake, bot for
35 mi frendis þat are in Napils, þat longe time haue prayede me for mi

1 modir þat] *twice*, þat modir *subpuncted*   14 was] *twice*

enemis in þat cite. And þarefore sai þis wordis. I sai þat I ame lorde of
aungells and feendis; and þe feend trespassed againe me on þre
maners–þat is to sai, with pride, invie, and lufe of his awen will. He
was so proude þat he desired to be aboue me; he was so envious þat he
rught noȝt what he had done, so þat he might haue slaine me; he loued 5
so wele his awen will þat he roght right noght of mi will, and þere he
fell to þe depenes of hell and is made one fende. And þan I gaue to
man certaine commandmentes þat he suld kepe for to com to blisse
and withstande þe fenndes malice. And I com miselfe into þe werld,
and teched þaim þe wai of blis, and with mi blode opind to þame 10
heuen. Bot mine enemis dispises mi commandmentes. þai kast | me f. 280ʳᵃ
awai oute of þair hertes als I were venom. þai haue als grete horroure
of me as I ware stinkinge mesell. And þai bringe in þe fende into þaire
saules, and done his will. Bot for þaire pride þai sall haue euirlastinge
sham; for þaire coueitise þai sall be filled with venom, so þat noȝt sall 15
be voide in þame; and for þair lecheri þai sall brin and neuir se mi
visage, and [be] reft þaire awen will.

'Bot wit þou þat right as dedeli sinnes are heui, so veniall sin, if a
man haue likinge þarein with will to continew it, it will bicom a dedeli
sinne. And þare are two þat are vsed in Napils: for þe likinge in þame 20
and will to laste in þame þai are dedeli. þe firste is þat folke depainte
þaire visage with diuers colours, als þai do to ymages, to seme fairer
þan oþir. þe second is shape of þaire cleþinge for pride, and plesinge
of oþir, and stiringe to lichori, and þat als wele in wemmen als in men.
And þerfor wit þou wele þat als ofte as þai dight þaire visage, so oft þai 25
lose one pointe of grete grace of þe holi goste, and þai drawe | þe fende f. 280ʳᵇ
more nere þame, and als oft as þai arai þaire bodis with swilke arai þai
losse one pointe of þe gude arai of þe saule, and þe fendes pouer
encresses vpon þame.

'Bot I sai to ȝou, mine enemis, þat paintes so ȝoure visage, how þat 30
it was paint with blode, and mine een liddis ware couered with blode.
Mi mouthe, mi erres, mine berde and all mi bodi was colowrde with
blode, and vndir þe blode it was full blo. I sai also to ȝou þat cleþis ȝou
also of þat manere, "Whi take ȝe no heede howe þat I stode naked, bun
to þe piler, scourged and bett? Mi bodi was filled full of woundes, and 35
cled in blode." For þis ȝe forget. And ȝet when I knok at þe ȝates of
ȝoure hertes `[w]ith´ mi grace to stir ȝou to contricion, ȝe put me awai

14 euirlastinge] euirlastinge paine, paine *subpuncted*   17 be] *om.*
20 þame] þame þai are dedeli, *exc.* þame, *subpuncted*   22 do to] *trsp.*   31 and
mine een] *twice, second subpuncted*   37 with] ? loiht

and excusis ȝoure sinne, and will noȝt leue þame, bot haue a likinge to
laste in þame. þarefore ȝe putt me awai, and takin þe fende to ȝou. Bot
ȝet mi merci is so grete þat þare is none of mine enemis þat will aske
with meke hert merci bot he sall haue it.

f. 280ᵛᵃ   'Bot þre þinges bose him do. Firste, haue sorowe | and contricion in
6   all þaire hert þat þai haue greued me þat boght þame so dere. þe
seconde is þat þai moste be clene shreuin, and take þaire penaunce
and make assethe eftir þe counsaile of þaire confessoure. þe þirde is
þat when þai haue fulfilled þis with gude deuocion and perfite charite,
10 to be howseled and haue will to laste in gude liuinge and neuir to turn
againe to sinne. And whoso amendes him on þis manere, I sall resaiue
him to grace, and I sall be with him and he with me. Bot to þame þat
will noȝt amend þame sall be done mi rightwisnes, and I sall ponishe
þame with dede þat is endeles.'

15   Capitulum xxix. þe modir liknes hirselfe to a gardenere
          þat festnes his ȝonge trees.

The modir aperid to þe spouse and saide to hir, 'I am als one gude
gardenere þat festnes his ȝonge trees to som stalworth þinge, þat þe
winde breke þame noȝt don. Right so do I when I se þe fandinges of þe
f. 280ᵛᵇ fennde com nere to mennes hertes. I prai to mi son to sende som | of
21 his grace into þair hertes to kepe þame stabill and stedfaste in gude
leuinge, þat þai fall noȝt with blastes of his fandinges. And þai þat will
take his grace at mi praier mai be sikir ynoghe fro þe fende, and þai
sall bringe furth gude froite and plesinge to God. Bot þai þat dispises
25 þe grace, þa[i] are blowen in vanite at þe fendis liste, and fallen downe
atte laste into þe depnes of hell.
'Bot in þe cite of Napills ar mani preui sinnes þat I will noȝt shewe
to þe. Bot þare are two opin sinnes þat, bot þai amend þame, þai sall
be ponished for þame full sore. þe firste is, þe men of Napils, þai bi
30 paynems to be þaire thralles, and fro þai haue boght þame, þai will
noȝt be aboute to conuerte þame and baptise þaim. And sometime,
when som of þame are baptized, þe maisters will noȝt lerne þame ne
informe þame in þe cristen mannes bileue, ne how þai shuld haue
þame in resaiuinge of þe sacramentes; and so þai can noȝt haue
35 contricion and shrift as

25 þai] þat

[Loss of remaining leaves of the quire, containing end
of VII. 29 and, probably, rest of Book VII: missing
material supplied from Ju]

to be restorid to grace. Also, sum holdis woman seruantis with soche f. 244ᵛ
shame as þei were doggis, sumtyme putting them to þe bordel hous to
get mony of onclennes. And some holdis them in ther housis as
comoun wemen for themself and for odir, and þat is abomynabil and
odious to God and to me, and to all the celestial court. And sum of þe ₅
lordis greuys the seid seruantis insomech with contumelious wordis
þat sum of the seruantis fallis in desperacioun and in wil to sle
themself, the wheche synnes and necgligens displesis God mech; for
he louys them in þat he made them. They þat beyes soch paynemys to
þat intent to make them cristend and in wil to informe them in liff or in ₁₀
deth, so þat the seid seruantis goo not to þe heredauns, and the lordis
þat dos so, shal be acceptabil to God, and þei that do þe contrary shal
be ponyshid greuously of God.

  'The secund kende of synne is þat many men and women has with
them summe wiches and diuinys and charmeris. Sumtyme thei aske of ₁₅
them to do charmys and incantaciouns þat thei may conceyue and
childe and þat summe may haue the loue of women, and some to
knowe thingis to come, and some to haue helþe of þer diuers seke-
nessis. Al þo þat holdis soche or þus doos, or they that askys of them
helpis or counselys or remedyes of sekenes ar acursid ageins | God, f. 245ʳ
and as longe as thei perseuer in soche state and purpoos, neuyr infu- ₂₁
sion nen grace of þe holy gost schal descende nen entre into þer hertis.
Neuertheles, and thei wil be penitent and amende, purposing to do no
moore, þei shal haue grace and mercy of myn sone.' This herd and
seen, this vision vanyshid. ₂₅

11 heredauns] herendiauns